The LAWS *of*
GOVERNMENT

The LAWS *of* GOVERNMENT

THE LEGAL FOUNDATIONS *of* CANADIAN DEMOCRACY

Craig Forcese & Aaron Freeman

The Laws of Government: The Legal Foundations of Canadian Democracy
© Craig Forcese and Aaron Freeman, 2005

Published in 2005 by

Irwin Law
347 Bay Street
Suite 501
Toronto, Ontario
M5H 2R7

www.irwinlaw.com

ISBN: 1-55221-105-3

Library and Archives Canada Cataloguing in Publication

Forcese, Craig
    The laws of government : the legal foundations of Canadian democracy / Craig Forcese & Aaron Freeman.

Includes bibliographical references and index.

ISBN 1-55221-105-3

1. Public law—Canada. I. Freeman, Aaron, 1969– II. Title.

KE4120.F67 2005   342.71   C2005-902853-X
KF4482.F67 2005

The publisher acknowledges the financial support of the Government of Canada through the Book Publishing Industry Development Program (BPIDP) for its publishing activities.

Printed and bound in Canada.

1 2 3 4 5   09 08 07 06 05

Summary Table of Contents

Preface and Acknowledgments xvii

Chapter 1: **Introduction** 1

Chapter 2: **Constitutional Basis for Canadian Democracy: An Overview** 9

Chapter 3: **Voting, Elections and the Selection of Members of Parliament** 75

Chapter 4: **The Selection, Tenure and Dismissal of Unelected Officials** 165

Chapter 5: **Parliament, Democracy and the Legislative Process** 297

Chapter 6: **Parliament, Cabinet, Democracy and Responsible Government** 352

Chapter 7: **Democracy, Ethics and Governance in the Public Interest** 410

Chapter 8: **Lobbying, Democracy and Governance in the Public Interest** 458

Chapter 9: **Information and the Currency of Democracy** 481

Chapter 10: **Democratic Governance in Times of Emergency** 576

Chapter 11: **Democratic Accountability in a Globalized Confederation** 601

Chapter 12: **Concluding Thoughts on the Law of Canadian Democracy** 616

Appendix 1: **The Public Administration of Canada** 621

Appendix 2: **Statistical Trends in Law-Making** 637

Glossary 645

Table of Cases 653

Index 667

About the Authors 689

Detailed Table of Contents

Preface and Acknowledgments   *xvii*

Chapter 1
Introduction   *1*

A. Government by the People   *1*

B. Democracy and Limited Government   *3*

C. Democracy and Accountability   *3*

D. About This Book: Accountability and Law   *5*

Chapter 2
**Constitutional Basis for Canadian Democracy:
An Overview**   *9*

A. Democracy in Canada's Written Constitution   *10*

B. Democracy in Canada's Unwritten Constitution   *12*

    1. Overview   *12*
    2. The "Democracy Principle"   *13*
    3. Implications of the Unwritten Democracy Principle   *16*
       a) The Legal Impact   *16*

b) The Troubling Provenance   *18*

C. Parliamentary Supremacy and the Separation of Powers   *20*

    1. Separation of Powers Between the Executive and Parliament   *21*
        a) Parliament's Jurisdictional Supremacy   *22*
        b) Parliament's Institutional Supremacy   *31*
    2. Separation of Powers Between the Judiciary and Parliament   *37*
        a) Jurisdictional Separation of Powers   *38*
        b) Institutional Separation of Powers   *62*

D. Conclusion   *74*

Chapter 3

Voting, Elections and the Selection of Members of Parliament   *75*

A. Voting and Electoral Rights   *76*

    1. Constitutional Voting Rights   *76*
        a) Effective Representation and the Right to Participate in Elections   *77*
        b) Effective Representation and the Right to a Roughly Equal Impact on Electoral Outcomes   *79*
    2. Statutory Voting Rights   *80*
        a) The Right to Vote in the *Elections Act*   *80*
        b) Protection of the Right to Vote   *81*
        c) The Right to Representation and Electoral Boundary Readjustment   *83*

B. The Key Actors in Elections   *86*

    1. Electoral Officials   *86*
        a) The Chief Electoral Officer   *86*
        b) Returning Officers   *87*
    2. Parties and Candidates   *89*
        a) Parties   *89*
        b) Electoral District Associations   *94*
        c) Party Leaders   *94*
        d) Nomination Contestants and Candidates   *95*

C. How Elections Are Run   *97*

    1. How Elections Are Triggered   *97*
        a) General Elections   *97*

b) By-elections   *97*

2. Electoral Financing   *100*
   a) Competing Values   *100*
   b) Expenses   *103*
   c) Donation Limits   *106*
   d) Public Subsidies   *114*
   e) Electoral Finance Disclosure   *116*

3. Election Advertising   *118*
   a) Advertising Rules Generally   *118*
   b) Third-Party Spending Limits   *124*
   c) Government Advertising   *131*

4. Voter's List   *132*

D. After the Vote   *132*

   i. Reporting on Election Results   *133*
   2. Judicial Recounts and Contested Elections   *134*
      a) Recounts   *134*
      b) Contested Elections   *134*
   3. Enforcement and Penalties   *135*

E. Emerging Issues in Canada's Election Law and Policy   *136*

   i. Voter Participation   *136*
   2. Fixed Election Dates   *139*
   3. Leaders' Debates   *140*
   4. Proportional Representation   *141*
      a) Canada's Current First-Past-the-Post System   *141*
      b) Proportional Representation   *143*
   5. Toward a More Diverse Parliament   *151*
   6. Recall   *154*
   7. Referendums   *156*
      a) Overview   *156*
      b) Pros and Cons of Referendums   *158*
      c) Legal Issues   *159*
      d) Referendum Mechanics   *161*

F. Conclusion   *162*

Chapter 4
The Selection, Tenure and Dismissal of Unelected Officials   *165*

A. Legislative Branch Unelected Officials *168*

    1. Monarch and Governor General *168*
        a) Appointment *169*
        b) Tenure and Dismissal *173*
        c) Reform *175*
    2. The Senate *178*
        a) Appointment *178*
        b) Tenure and Dismissal *185*
        c) Senate Reform *190*
    3. Employees of Parliament and Parliamentarian Political Staff *199*

B. Executive Branch Unelected Officials *200*

    1. Members of the Ministry and Cabinet *200*
        a) Defining the Ministry and Cabinet *201*
        b) Prime Minister *203*
        c) Ministers and Ministers of State *212*
    2. Ministerial Political Staff *215*
    3. Professional Public Service *216*
        a) Appointment *216*
        b) Dismissal *222*
        c) Conclusion *233*
    4. Nonjudicial Governor-in-Council Appointees *233*
        a) Appointment *234*
        b) Tenure and Dismissal *238*
        c) Reform *241*
    5. Officers of Parliament *246*
        a) Appointment *247*
        b) Dismissal *248*
        c) Financial and Administrative Independence *254*
        d) Conclusion *256*

C. Judicial Branch *257*

    1. Appointment *258*
        a) Non–Supreme Court Federal Appointments *260*
        b) Supreme Court Appointments *269*
    2. Financial and Administrative Independence *290*
    3. Removing Judges: Security of Tenure and Judicial Independence *291*
        a) Canadian Judicial Council *291*
        b) Address of Parliament *292*

D. Conclusion *294*

Chapter 5

Parliament, Democracy and the Legislative Process   *297*

A. The Parliamentary Legislative Enterprise   *298*

    I. Overview of the Parliament of Canada   *298*
        a) Summoning, Prorogation and Dissolution of Parliament   *298*
        b) The Sources of Parliamentary Procedure   *303*
        c) Key Parliamentary Actors   *304*
        d) Rules of Debate and Decision-Making in the Commons   *319*
    2. Parliament's Legislative Function   *325*
        a) Parliament's Legislative Jurisdiction   *325*
        b) Enacting Parliamentary Legislation   *327*

B. Executive Law-Making   *337*

    I. Types of Executive Laws   *338*
        a) Definition of a Statutory Instrument   *338*
        b) Definition of a Regulation   *339*
    2. Executive Branch Regulation-Making   *340*
        a) Process   *340*
        b) Parliamentary Role   *342*
    3. Nonregulatory Orders-in-Council   *343*
        a) Less Transparent Procedure   *344*
        b) No Parliamentary Revocation Powers   *344*
    4. Executive Law-Making Jurisdiction and the Role of the Courts   *345*
        a) Ensuring That Delegated Legislation Is Authorized by Parliamentary Grant or Some Other Source   *345*
        b) Due Process and Delegated Legislation   *347*

C. Conclusion   *349*

Chapter 6

Parliament, Cabinet, Democracy and Responsible Government   *352*

A. Cabinet's Role in Executive Governance   *353*

    I. Cabinet Procedure and Structure   *353*
        a) Cabinet Purpose and Organization   *353*
        b) Cabinet Solidarity and Confidence   *354*
    2. Structure of Executive Government   *355*

a) Structural Hierarchy 355
b) Cabinet Control over Structure 357
3. Executive Branch Accountability Mechanisms 359
a) Institutional Control: The Role of the Central Agencies 360
b) Public and Departmental Inquiries 361
4. Conclusion 369

B. Responsibility to Parliament 370

1. The Collective Responsibility of Cabinet 370
a) Resignation of the Government 370
b) Cabinet's Responsibility to Parliament for Overall Government Policy 373
c) The Government's Responsibility on Financial Matters 376
2. The Individual Responsibility of Ministers 384
a) Legal and Political Culpability for Wrongdoing by Department Officials 385
b) Ministerial Responsibility to Inform Parliament 392
3. Officers of Parliament 404
a) Parliamentary Reporting Function 405
b) Office of the Auditor General 406

C. Conclusion 409

Chapter 7

Democracy, Ethics and Governance in the Public Interest *410*

A. Core Principles of Canadian Ethics Rules 411

1. Regulating the Private Interest 411
2. Ethics and the Allure of Public Service 412

B. Legal Standards 413

1. *Criminal Code* Provisions 413
2. *Parliament of Canada Act* Provisions 415
3. Civil Law Standards 416

C. Ethical Codes of Conduct for the Ministry and Parliamentarians 417

1. Ethics Commissioner and Senate Ethics Officer 417
a) General Functions 417
b) Independence 418
c) The Ethics Commissioner's Bifurcated Responsibilities 419

2. MP Code   *421*
   a) General Principles   *421*
   b) Specific Provisions   *422*
3. Public Office Holders Code   *426*
   a) Principles   *427*
   b) Compliance Measures   *428*
4. When the Public Office Holders Code and the MP Code Apply   *437*
   a) Application of MP Code   *438*
   b) Application of Public Office Holders Code   *439*
5. Standard of Judicial Review for Ethics Matters: MPs, Senators and Public Office Holders   *442*
   a) Judicial Review of Ethics Commissioner Decisions   *442*
   b) Legal Status of the Codes   *444*
6. Professional Responsibility Obligations   *449*

D. Public Servants Code   *450*

   1. Values and General Principles   *450*
   2. Disclosure   *452*
   3. Specific Duties in the Course of Employment   *452*
   4. Post-employment   *454*
   5. Enforcement and Oversight   *455*

E. Ethics Rules for Judges   *456*

F. Conclusion   *457*

Chapter 8

Lobbying, Democracy and Governance in the Public Interest   *458*

A. Lobbying: An Overview   *459*

B. The Lobbying Industry   *460*

C. The Law of Lobbyist Regulation   *461*

   1. The *Lobbyists Registration Act*   *462*
      a) Application   *462*
      b) Registration   *465*
      c) Exceptions to Registration   *470*
      d) Lawyers as Lobbyists   *470*
   2. The Lobbyists' Code of Conduct   *471*
      a) Overview   *471*

b) Legal Status and Oversight of the Lobbyists' Code   472

3. Important Regulatory Issues Not Addressed in the *LRA*   475

a) Contingency Fees   475

b) Multitasking Lobbyists   477

D. Conclusion: An Alternative to Lobbying?   478

Chapter 9

Information and the Currency of Democracy   481

A. Information Disclosure   482

1. Information Disclosure and Democracy   482

2. International Context   484

a) Access to Information as an International Right   484

b) International "Best Practices" for Information Access   486

3. Canada's Federal "Open Government" Information Laws   487

a) *Access to Information Act*   487

b) *Privacy Act*   512

c) Judicial Review of Exemption Decisions under the *Access* and *Privacy Acts*   518

B. Protecting Privacy   525

1. Privacy and Democracy   525

2. International Standards   527

3. Federal Privacy Laws   528

a) Constitutional Protections   528

b) *Privacy Act*   529

c) *Personal Information Protection and Electronic Documents Act*   532

C. The National Security Challenge to Access and to Privacy   540

1. Legitimate National Security Constraints on Access to Information   540

a) Openness and National Security   541

b) The *Johannesburg Principles on National Security and Information Access*   541

2. Canadian Government Secrecy Laws   543

a) *Security of Information Act*   544

b) National Security Exemptions Under the *Access* and *Privacy Acts* and the *PIPEDA*   552

c) *Canada Evidence Act* and the National Security Exclusions Under the *Access* and *Privacy Acts*   555

d) Extraneous National Security-Related Restrictions on Privacy   *560*

D. Conclusion   *573*

Chapter 10

Democratic Governance in Times of Emergency   *576*

A. Emergency Powers and International Law   *579*

B. Emergency Powers and the Constitution   *580*

    1.   *Canadian Bill of Rights*   *580*
    2.   *Charter of Rights and Freedoms*   *581*
        a)   Section 33   *581*
        b)   Section 1   *582*
        c)   Section 4(2)   *582*

C. Emergency Powers in Statutory Law   *584*

    1.   *Emergencies Act*   *585*
        a)   Content   *585*
        b)   Parliamentary Oversight   *586*
        c)   Judicial Review of Orders and Regulations under the *Emergencies Act*   *592*
    2.   *National Defence Act*   *596*
    3.   *Emergency Preparedness Act*   *598*
    4.   *Public Safety Act*   *599*

D. Conclusion   *599*

Chapter 11

Democratic Accountability in a Globalized Confederation   *601*

A. The Internationalization of Public Policy   *601*

    1.   The Democratic Deficit and Intergovernmental Organizations   *602*
    2.   The Democratic Deficit and the Separation of Powers   *603*
    3.   Responses   *607*

B. Other Levels of Government Within Canada   *609*

    1.   Law and Democracy at the Provincial and Municipal Level   *609*
    2.   Law and Democracy in Canada's First Nations   *610*
    3.   The Challenges of Diffuse Government   *613*

C. Conclusion   615

Chapter 12
Concluding Thoughts on the Law of Canadian Democracy   616

A. The Democratic Selection of Officials   616

B. The Accountability of Unelected Officials   617

    1. Selection, Dismissal and Ethics   617
    2. Parliamentary Oversight   618
    3. Transparency   618

C. How Much Law Is Enough?   619

Appendix 1
The Public Administration of Canada   621

Appendix 2
Statistical Trends in Law-Making   637

Glossary   645

Table of Cases   653

Index   667

About the Authors   689

p

Preface and Acknowledgments

This is a book about the legal foundation of Canadian democracy — the law of politics as it exists at the federal level. It is designed as a detailed legal resource for all who participate in Canada's democratic process, as lawyers, judges, politicians, academics, journalists or simply as voters. More than that, it is a book that critiques policy. If we think the emperor is without clothes, we've pointed a finger.

Boiled down to the essence, these policy critiques reflect rather conventional democratic liberalism tinged with an element of popular sovereignty. Our perspective includes: a strong suspicion of executive-dominated governance; a belief in the need for transparency and accountability in the exercise of power; a healthy regard for a "limited" government constrained by human and civil rights and for the legitimate and vital role of an independent judiciary in guaranteeing these principles; and finally, a core faith that, given a chance to be taken seriously, most people will make mostly right decisions most of the time. These are the views that pervade our thinking on the technical legal issues that are the basis of Canadian democracy.

Our approach reflects our accumulated experience: for well over a decade, one or both of us has taught these laws, lobbied or litigated regarding them, and voted for, against, or because of them. This book is as much a product of our experiences as citizens as it is of our roles as academics and public policy writers.

This book is also the product of much research, some of it obscure. It would not have been possible without the assistance of Lise Rivet, a second-year LL.B. student at the University of Ottawa's Faculty of Law and a tenacious researcher and careful critic. It has also benefited enormously from the thoughtful commentary of many people with practical wisdom and insight into the workings of federal democracy: Thomas Balint, the Hon. Ed Broadbent, John Chenier, Penny Collenette, Dan Dupuis, Salim Fakirani, Martha Jackman, Stephen Knowles, the Hon. Gar Knutson, Karen Kraft Sloan, Philippa Lawson, Heather MacIvor and Ed Ratushny. Thanks go also to Jeffrey Miller, Pamela Erlichman and others at Irwin for their support of this project and their diligent editorial work.

In writing this book, we stand on the shoulders of the many scholars who have come before us, both in academia and in the judiciary. Their work is acknowledged throughout, as are the important public policy critiques made by individuals such as Duff Conacher of Democracy Watch. We have also benefited from open government — the presence in the public domain of massive quantities of government literature and documentation accessible electronically. We thank the many anonymous public servants responsible for writing this material and then disseminating it to the country.

A book on the law of politics, unlike most legal works, depends on the day-to-day dispatches of the press corps. Like no one else, these people document the working of Canadian democracy and are the vital elements of its success. In particular, we would like to thank the staff of The Hill Times, Canada's parliamentary newspaper, for providing us with valuable research assistance.

This project benefited from the tremendous patience and support of our families and friends. Thanks go to Erin Simpson and Sandra Cotton, who were unwavering in this regard. During the course of writing this work, one of us welcomed a daughter into the world. Thanks are owed to Madeleine Forcese, and redoubled thanks to her mother, Sandra Cotton, for their support, patience and infectious enthusiasm for life during the long hours of research and writing. This book on democracy is dedicated to Madeleine and others of her generation — people for whom the persistence of a robustly democratic Canada is a promise to be kept.

We hope we have done justice to these many individuals and resources. We stress that any mistakes made here are our own. The opinions expressed are also, obviously, ones we hold and are not necessarily shared by those who have contributed their expertise to our product.

Finally, research for this book was completed in December 2004, and references in the text to "at the time of this writing" refer to this date. We have, however, done our best to update the material during final production of the book to reflect important developments up until the end of February 2005.

Craig Forcese & Aaron Freeman
Ottawa, March 2005

Introduction

Two key principles inform "liberal" democracy — the kind of democracy we enjoy in Canada. First, government should be by the citizenry, at least indirectly. Second, government by that citizenry cannot become a tyranny of the majority, or as Oscar Wilde put it, the "bludgeoning of the people by the people for the people."[1] Each assertion requires greater explanation.

A. GOVERNMENT BY THE PEOPLE

As defined by the *Oxford English Dictionary*, democracy is "that form of government in which the sovereign power resides in the people as a whole, and is exercised either directly by them ... or by officers elected by them." In practice, government by the people is conducted via universal suffrage; that is, the election of representatives by the entire electorate, a body defined by shared citizenship and minimum-age requirements. The selection of representatives through the electoral process is largely a leap of faith that having more people involved in governance — or at least the selection of governments — is better than having fewer. Democracy is predicated, in the words of E.B. White, on a "recurrent suspicion that more than half of the people are right more than half of the time."[2]

---

1 "The Soul of Man Under Socialism," *Fortnightly Review* (Feb. 1891).
2 "World Government and Peace," *The New Yorker* (3 July 1944).

Given such a modest batting average, it is perhaps possible to imagine a better style of government. Plato, in his *Republic*, argued for a benign, but exclusive, government by the elite. Plato's government by the rational few is always immensely attractive, particularly to the rational few. A cadre of enlightened individuals seems well-equipped to tap that capacity for reason and justice innate to the human form. However, it is the antithesis — humanity's inclination to injustice — that makes democracy necessary.[3] Winston Churchill famously told the United Kingdom House of Commons in 1947: "Many forms of Government have been tried, and will be tried in this world of sin and woe. No one pretends that democracy is perfect or all-wise. Indeed, it has been said that democracy is the worst form of Government except all those other forms that have been tried from time to time."[4]

As Churchill's remarks imply, no other system of government but a democracy ensures that the excesses of a few are held in check by the levelling wisdom (and the individual and collective self-interest) of the many. Democracy apparently cures what ails every other system.

First, a representative democracy headed by an elected leadership solves the succession problem in government. Unlike a monarchy or aristocracy, it does not depend for good governance on competence being inherited. Unlike one-party dictatorship or a plutocracy or any other sort of oligarchy, however sophisticated, it is not so brittle that it depends on ability being present in a single class, caste or narrow cadre of party favourites. Unlike a revolutionary regime, it does not depend on the coincidence in a single person of wisdom and martial or authoritarian power. In a democracy, the gene pool of potential leaders runs deep.

Second, democracy is a purgative for rotten government. Where elected leaders prove corrupt or imprudent, a democracy can "throw the bums out." There is no such quick fix for a monarchy, oligarchy or dictatorship. There, tossing out the scoundrels usually has a literal dimension, sometimes involving guillotines, pistoleros or war. Even a meritocracy — where the best rise to govern the state as philosopher-kings through some Platonic system of education — may founder without a clear and stable means of replacing these people when their sheen goes dull.

---

3   See Reinhold Niebuhr, *The Children of Light and the Children of Darkness* (New York: Scribner, 1960).

4   Robert Rhodes James, ed., *Winston S. Churchill: His Complete Speeches, 1897–1963* (New York: Chelsea House Publishers, 1974) at 7566, citing a speech made in the House of Commons on 11 Nov. 1947.

Thus, government by the people may not be the best government we can envisage. It is, however, probably the best we can manage. If it in fact carries the seeds of tyranny — the rule of the mob — perhaps that may be forestalled by the second attribute of liberal democracy: limited government.

B. DEMOCRACY AND LIMITED GOVERNMENT

Majority rule does not always come up with the right policies, and sometimes the majority will make serious errors. A democracy must therefore have some cure for — and safeguards against — the mistakes of the majority. In a liberal democracy, the answer comes in the form of a shared code specifying that the democratic will of the majority stops where the rights of the individual and the minority begin.

It may be that the potent power of the state, left unchecked, could in many circumstances be marshalled to better serve the interests of the majority, or even the individual or minority themselves. A liberal democracy accepts, however, that the consequences of error where certain core rights of that individual or minority are in play may simply be too grave to gamble on success. It agrees, therefore, to a policy of at least partial abstinence in relation to violations of civil and political rights. More grudgingly (and more rarely), it intervenes to protect certain economic and social rights, even when inconsistent with the dictates of the majority.

Liberal democracy is, therefore, a system that accepts only provisionally the wisdom of the majority and protects against its natural fallibility by carving out spaces where even the democratic state shall not go. In that respect, a liberal democracy is like a child learning to ride a bicycle: it wobbles along under majority rule in a somewhat erratic, but mostly straight, line. All the while, it is propped up by a set of training wheels — government-limiting rights — that keep it from careening dangerously to one side or the other. Rights, in other words, are not inconsistent with government by the people. They are its guarantor.

C. DEMOCRACY AND ACCOUNTABILITY

It is one thing to agree that liberal democracy is the rule of the majority tempered by the fundamental rights of the individual. It is quite another to design a system that meets both of those objectives. The actual mechanics of the democratic project vary enormously from state to state. We do not intend in this book to canvass the differences between parliamentary and republican systems or the many variations in between and within these categories. Let us propose, however, that in their mechanical construction, all contemporary democracies likely have rules creating two tiers of democratic "accountability." We follow Canada's Auditor General in defining accountability as "the obligation to render an account of, and accept responsibility for, one's actions, both the results obtained and the means used."[5]

In a modern representative democracy, the expectation is that the elected representatives of the people will exercise the authority of the state. Every representative democracy must, therefore, have rules on elections, governing the selection and dismissal of these representatives. These rules ensure that representatives remain accountable to the people.

In a modern democracy, however, there is by necessity a second tier of accountability. Not all — or even most — of the people governing in contemporary democracies are elected. The modern, administrative state depends on a massive bureaucratic apparatus, staffed mostly by unelected officials. If these officials, exercising many of the powers of the state, are not selected and dismissed by the people, democracy is imperilled, absent some other mechanism of accountability. The classic response in the liberal democratic tradition is to shape rules ensuring that those who are not selected by the people are somehow accountable to those who are. Elected officials, in other words, have primacy over their unelected counterparts.

Together, these rules create the two levels of democratic accountability — direct election and then the pre-eminence of the elected over the appointed — and ensure that majorities shape, however indirectly, governance.

Checking the excesses of this majoritarian impulse requires a separate, third set of accountability mechanisms less receptive to democratic desires. Elected officials, and the unelected bureaucracy they direct, are creatures and servants of the majority. They are ill-equipped to prevail in the face of that majority's opposition. Thus, if there are to be rights that the democratically elected and commanded government cannot trump, those rights must be protected by institutions other than those controlled by the majority itself. In practice, these bodies are courts protected by a concept resistant to raw democratic accountability: judicial independence.

In at least the Anglo-Canadian and American liberal democratic tradition, the net result of these systems of accountability are three branches of government — the legislature, mostly or entirely elected; the executive, governed by directly elected chiefs or somehow subordinated to the elected

---

5   Auditor General of Canada, *Matters of Special Importance — 2004* (Nov. 2004).

legislature; and the judiciary, at least partially protected from the manoeu-vrings of the other two "political" branches and charged with defending fundamental rights and liberties.

D. ABOUT THIS BOOK: ACCOUNTABILITY AND LAW

This institutional structure permitting democratic accountability obviously depends on rules. These three branches of government, their interrelation-ship and the accountability associated with them, are very much creatures of the law. Legal principles, therefore, lie at the heart of liberal democracy.

In practice, the most fundamental of these laws is constitutional law. In Canadian democracy, constitutional law establishes the institutional context for democratic governance, anticipating the three, classic branches of government. It lays the framework for the (at least partially) democratic selection of representatives to the legislature and the accountability of unelected executive branch officials to these representatives. It circum-scribes the powers of these two political branches in order to better pre-serve fundamental rights and freedoms and authorizes the judicial branch to protect these norms. As will be discussed in chapter 2, it does so through a complex series of written texts, unwritten principles and formalized habits. Indeed, the precise legal source of some of the most fundamental practices of Canadian democracy — not least responsible government — are barely anticipated by formal constitutional instruments, instead arising out of customary practice subsequently given the stamp of constitutional "convention."

The Constitution, however, is merely a superstructure upon which the edifice of Canadian democracy is constructed. The detail work of democra-cy stems from a series of other laws and quasi-legal concepts. Therefore, following chapter 2 on the Constitution, we divide the remainder of the book into two broad parts.

Chapters 3 and 4 explore how those who conduct federal governance in Canada are selected and dismissed. Chapter 3 examines the election of Members of Parliament and focuses on the role of the *Canada Elections Act* and its various provisions and proscriptions. Here we discuss both the fun-damental values that imbue electoral law, as well as the nuts and bolts of running an election.

The *Canada Elections Act* governs the selection of MPs sitting in the House of Commons. It is silent, however, on the selection and tenure in office of many other thousands of individuals who collectively conduct Canadian governance.

In chapter 4, we examine the selection of Canada's many unelected officials, organized by branch of government. In our discussion of the legislative branch, we examine laws and practices governing the selection and dismissal of the Governor General, senators and those who staff Parliament's internal bureaucracy.

Under the heading "the executive," we look at means by which the ministry — comprising the prime minister, ministers and ministers of state — is determined and dismissed. We then turn our attention to the public service, examining the appointment, tenure and removal of civil servants. Subsequently, we focus on these same processes in relation to another class of government officials: nonjudicial, Governor-in-Council appointees. Finally, we consider the selection and discharge of officers of Parliament, a group of individuals who fit very uncomfortably under the "executive" label.

Turning to the judicial branch, we focus on the selection, tenure and dismissal of lower-court superior court judges. We then do the same for Supreme Court judges; this area has garnered much public attention recently.

In the second part of the book, we focus on the rules obliging this panoply of officials to govern in a democratically accountable manner. Chapter 5 examines the principal activity associated in the public mind with government: law-making. There, we flesh out in greater detail the institutional structure of Parliament, describing its key players, and examine the "parliamentary law" governing the process of parliamentary decision and law-making. We also consider the important law-making powers of the executive branch, focusing closely on the legal principles governing this process.

In chapters 6 through 9, we examine issues central to preserving democratic governance in Canada. In chapter 6, we pick up on themes implied in much of our discussion on the selection and dismissal of unelected officials by discussing the concept of "responsible government" — the principle that the ministry (and through it, the broader executive government) is accountable to Parliament, and more particularly to the House of Commons. Here, we highlight the means by which Cabinet exercises control over the public administration of Canada and then look at legal and pseudo-legal mechanisms of collective and individual ministerial responsibility to Parliament, defining these concepts broadly to incorporate everything from Question Period in the Commons to the role of the Auditor General of Canada.

In chapter 7 we shift gears, moving from the processes of accountability to specific, substantive standards of good behaviour imposed on public officials. Here, we examine laws and policies relating to government ethics — rules that require power to be exercised in the public rather than private interest.

In chapter 8, we turn to a related issue: the regulation of lobbying. In this chapter we review the extent to which Canadian law attempts to preserve governance in the public interest by mitigating the influence of special-interest lobbyists on government decision-making.

In chapter 9, we look at transparency in government — mechanisms to insure that what government does is readily ascertainable by not only parliamentarians, but also the general public. We focus on the *Access to Information Act*. We also look at a related information issue, one vital to the concept of limited government: strictures on how much the government may know about the public. Here, we examine the role of privacy law in democratic governance. Finally, we consider an issue very much in the public eye: the extent to which the national security imperatives of our democratic state affect information access and privacy.

Chapter 10 is the first of two brief chapters dealing with extraneous issues in Canadian democracy. In it, we examine how Canada's laws preserve Canadian democracy — and doctrines of democratic accountability — in times of emergency, a matter of more than theoretical concern in the post-9/11 and post-SARS world.

Chapter 11 focuses on emerging issues for federal democratic accountability: the internationalization of much governance, on the one hand, and the consequences for accountability of diffusion of some power away from the national government to intergovernmental initiatives, non-governmental bodies and, in the case of Canada's aboriginal peoples, increasingly to First Nations governments.

Finally, in chapter 12 we set out our brief conclusions concerning the legal foundations of Canadian democracy.

The laws of Canadian democracy recounted in this book may seem, at times, esoteric. These laws have very real implications, however, for all Canadians. This is most true when principles of democratic accountability are disregarded. For example, when proper oversight, accountability and transparency provisions governing public spending are circumvented, taxpayers' dollars are spent less efficiently. For businesses, when lobbyists have undue influence over public officials, conducting business with the government becomes an expensive and uncertain game. For voters, when the electoral system does not adequately reflect democratic principles, or if the influence of wealthy special interests is not restricted during an election, they may justifiably feel that their vote is "wasted." For citizens, a lack of checks and balances in government can prove disastrous for governance in the public interest, including in such vital areas as health care, job creation, consumer protection, environmental protection and the like. For all these reasons, the legal foundations of Canadian democracy provide more than just the mechanics of government. They both determine and reflect the sort of civilization we create.

Constitutional Basis for Canadian Democracy: An Overview

The Constitution is the starting point in a discussion of the legal foundations of Canadian democracy. The Constitution establishes the basic framework of political governance in Canada and sets the parameters within
which that governance must operate. Napoleon Bonaparte once said that a
constitution "should be short and obscure."[1] The Canadian Constitution
meets Napoleon halfway: it is not short, but it certainly is obscure. By the
express terms of the *Constitution Act, 1982*, the Constitution "includes"
three categories of instruments: first, the *Canada Act, 1982*, which contains
the *Constitution Act, 1982* (which in turn includes the *Canadian Charter of
Rights and Freedoms*); second, thirty imperial or Canadian statutes and
orders (such as the *Constitution Act, 1867*) set out by schedule to the *Constitution Act, 1982*; and third, amendments to any of these instruments (of
which there are presently eight).[2]

If that were the end of the story, a full understanding of Canadian constitutional law would require some cutting and pasting but would other-

---

1   Napoleon Bonaparte (1769–1821) at Conference of Swiss Deputies, 29 Jan. 1803.
2   See Peter Hogg, *Constitutional Law of Canada*, looseleaf ed. (Toronto: Carswell, 2003)
    at 1-7. See also s. 52 of the *Constitution Act, 1982* defining the Constitution of Canada
    as including "(a) the *Canada Act, 1982*, including this Act; (b) the Acts and orders
    referred to in the schedule; and (c) any amendment to any Act or order referred to in
    paragraph (a) or (b)."

wise be reasonably straightforward, and this book would be brief. However, much of what we recognize as democracy is not entrenched in these documents. Instead, it flows from other sources, the constitutional status of which has been readily affirmed by political practice and in the jurisprudence of the Supreme Court of Canada.

This chapter considers, first, the extent to which democracy is constitutionally entrenched in Canada's written Constitution. Second, we look at democracy as an unwritten constitutional "principle" supported by unwritten constitutional "conventions." In the course of this discussion, we introduce, discuss and sometimes critique some of the weightiest issues in Canadian democracy: parliamentary supremacy, responsible government, the rule of law, and the separation of powers among the legislative, executive and judicial branches of government.

A. DEMOCRACY IN CANADA'S WRITTEN CONSTITUTION

A discussion of democracy and Canada's Constitution begins with the *Constitution Act, 1867* (hereafter referred to as the 1867 Act). Known as the *British North America Act*[3] until 1982, the 1867 Act is the statute of the United Kingdom Imperial Parliament creating a federal union of British North American colonies. As such, it is an instrument concerned largely with partitioning jurisdiction between the federal government and the provinces,[4] a "division of powers" that preoccupies Canadian democracy to this day.

However, the 1867 Act also defines Canada's key political institutions. Thus, the "Executive Government" is vested in the Queen,[5] with many of the Queen's powers to be exercised by the Governor General, pursuant to the 1867 Act itself[6] or by reason of the 1947 Letters Patent issued by George VI.[7] By express reference in the 1867 Act, the Governor General's respon-

---

3   1867, 30-31 Vict., c. 3 (U.K.).
4   *Constitution Act, 1867*, ss. 91 and 92.
5   *Ibid.*, s. 9.
6   *Ibid.*, s. 10.
7   C. Gaz. 1947.I.3104, vol. 81, available also at
     www.solon.org/Constitutions/Canada/English/LettersPatent.html. The Letters Patent
     empower the Governor General "to exercise all powers and authorities lawfully
     belonging to Us in respect of Canada" (at para. II), including the Crown's royal pre-
     rogative powers discussed later in the chapter. See also the discussion in *Black v.
     Canada (Prime Minister)* (2001), 54 O.R. (3d) 215 at para. 31 (C.A.). There are two pow-
     ers not delegated by the Letters Patent: the power to appoint or dismiss the Governor
     General and, arguably, the power to appoint additional senators, expanding the senate
     pursuant to s. 26 of the 1867 Act. See Hogg, *Constitutional Law* at 9-5.

sibilities include the appointment of a "Queen's Privy Council for Canada,"[8] a body to "aid and advise in the Government of Canada."[9] The Governor General is also empowered to endorse (or not) a bill of Parliament, by giving or refusing the royal assent.[10] Alternatively, the Governor General may reserve this assent for the Queen "in Council," which then has the discretion to accord that approval.[11]

Meanwhile, the "Parliament of Canada" consists "of the Queen, an Upper House styled the senate, and the House of Commons."[12] The Act anticipates the *appointment* of senators by the Governor General and the popular *election* of members of the House of Commons,[13] thus creating only a partly democratic legislative branch.

These "pseudo-democratic" 1867 Act provisions are enhanced by the *Constitution Act, 1982* (1982 Act), via the *Canadian Charter of Rights and Freedoms* (*Charter*).[14] Section 3 of the *Charter*, discussed at length in chapter 3, provides that "[e]very citizen of Canada has the right to vote in an election of members of the House of Commons or of a legislative assembly and to be qualified for membership therein." Moreover, there is little risk in Canada of a "long Parliament." The 1867 Act limits the duration of a Commons to five years,[15] as does the *Charter*.[16] The *Charter* also provides that "[t]here shall be a sitting of Parliament and of each legislature at least once every twelve months."[17]

Both the 1867 and 1982 Acts are silent, however, on what, if any, roles parliamentarians play in executive governance. They do not expressly anticipate a "Cabinet" comprising ministers who are also parliamentarians. They fail to acknowledge even the existence of ministers as the legal heads of government departments. In other words, no mention is made of "responsible government" — the notion that the executive branch should be rendered accountable to an elected legislature by requiring that those who run the executive also sit in Parliament. Indeed, the 1867 Act suggests

---

8   *Constitution Act, 1867*, s. 11.
9   *Ibid.*
10 *Ibid.*, s. 55.
11 *Ibid.*, ss. 55 and 57.
12 *Ibid.*, s. 17.
13 *Ibid.*, ss. 24 and 37.
14 Enacted as Schedule B to the *Canada Act, 1982*, (U.K.) 1982, c. 11.
15 *Constitution Act, 1867*, s. 50.
16 *Canadian Charter of Rights and Freedoms* (*Charter*), subs. 4(1). As discussed in more detail in ch. 10, this five-year limitation may be suspended "in time of real or apprehended war, invasion or insurrection." Subs. 4(2).
17 *Charter*, s. 5.

that the Houses of Parliament are a subordinate branch of government: as noted, the Queen (acting "in Council") has the power to disallow any statute passed by the Canadian Parliament.[18]

In sum total, the *Constitution Act, 1867* on paper anticipates a form of government not greatly dissimilar to that of the United Kingdom under the absolutist, seventeenth-century Stuart monarchs. For its part, the *Charter* — although it articulates a broad right to vote that is alien to the seventeenth century — does little to change this fact. Nevertheless, Canadians are in practice governed by a federal Cabinet accountable to a (perhaps only theoretically) supreme Parliament, and not from Buckingham Palace or Rideau Hall. Constitutionally, this responsible and democratic government stems from the seemingly innocuous preamble to the *Constitution Act, 1867* and the "unwritten" principles and conventions of the Constitution.

B. DEMOCRACY IN CANADA'S UNWRITTEN CONSTITUTION

1. Overview

A key passage in the preamble to the *Constitution Act, 1867* specifies that Canada is to have a "Constitution similar in Principle to that of the United Kingdom." Preambles, as the Supreme Court has noted, do not have "enacting force."[19] They are not a source of "positive" law, or binding legal obligations.[20] But not all preambles are equal. The preamble to the 1867 Act serves, in the Supreme Court's words, as "the grand entrance hall to the castle of the Constitution."[21] It expresses "the political theory which the [1867] Act embodies."[22] Specifically,

> [i]t recognizes and affirms the basic principles which are the very source of the substantive provisions of the *Constitution Act, 1867.* ... As such, the preamble is not only a key to construing the express provisions of the *Constitution Act, 1867*, but also invites the use of those organizing principles to fill out gaps in the express terms of the constitutional scheme. It is the

---

18 *Constitution Act, 1867*, s. 56.

19 *Reference re Resolution to Amend the Constitution*, [1981] 1 S.C.R. 753 at 805; *Re Remuneration of Judges*, [1997] 3 S.C.R. 3 at paras. 94–95.

20 *Ibid.* at para. 95 (noting also that under "normal circumstances, preambles can be used to identify the purpose of a statute, and also as an aid to construing ambiguous statutory language").

21 *Ibid.* at para. 109.

22 *Ibid.* at para. 95, citing *Switzman v. Elbling*, [1957] S.C.R. 285 at 306.

means by which the underlying logic of the Act can be given the force of law.[23]

The preamble serves, in this way, as the pre-eminent source of unwritten constitutional doctrines. It renders the Canadian Constitution more than a mere medley of sometimes-obscure, statutory documents. Instead, the Constitution draws also on its United Kingdom patrimony and includes elements of the common law constitutional tradition of that nation. Thus, the preamble expresses "the manifest intention ... that Canada retain the fundamental constitutional tenets upon which British parliamentary democracy rested."[24]

Reflecting this continuity of constitutional principles between Canada and the United Kingdom,[25] the preamble incorporates by reference certain vital concepts into Canada's Constitution.[26] Not least among these precepts are the rule of law,[27] parliamentary supremacy,[28] responsible government,[29] parliamentary privilege,[30] judicial independence[31] and freedom of speech.[32] In terms of their constitutional effects, these concepts, discussed below, range from judicially enforceable obligations of governments to politically policed constitutional "conventions." They all lie, however, at the heart of Canadian democracy.

2. The "Democracy Principle"

Indeed, even more than that, Canada's unwritten constitution apparently entrenches a constitutional principle of democracy itself. For the Supreme Court, in the landmark 1998 *Quebec Secession Reference*, the "democracy

---

23   *Ibid.* at para. 95.

24   *New Brunswick Broadcasting Co. v. Nova Scotia*, [1993] 1 S.C.R. 319 at 377.

25   *Reference Re Secession of Quebec*, [1998] 2 S.C.R. 217 at para. 44 [*Quebec Secession Reference*].

26   *Ibid.*

27   *Manitoba Language Reference*, [1985] 1 S.C.R. 721 at 750 (rule of law is implicitly incorporated into the Canadian Constitution by the preamble).

28   See Part C later in this chapter.

29   See Part C later in this chapter.

30   *New Brunswick Broadcasting*, [1993] 1 S.C.R. 319 at 377 ("It seems indisputable that the inherent privileges of Canada's legislative bodies ... fall within the group of principles constitutionalized by virtue of this preamble").

31   *Re Remuneration of Judges*, [1997] 3 S.C.R. 3 at para. 83 (judicial independence "whose origins can be traced to the *Act of Settlement* of 1701, is recognized and affirmed by the preamble to the *Constitution Act, 1867*").

32   *Fraser v. Public Service Staff Relations Board*, [1985] 2 S.C.R. 455 at 462 (freedom of speech is a "principle of our common law constitution, inherited from the United Kingdom by virtue of the preamble").

principle" is situated at the very core of Canada's constitutional fabric, serving as a "sort of baseline against which the framers of our Constitution, and subsequently, our elected representatives under it, have always operated."[33] Indeed, so fundamental is the democratic principle that there was hardly any mention of it in the text of the original Constitution: "To have done so might have appeared redundant, even silly, to the framers. ... The representative and democratic nature of our political institutions was simply assumed."[34]

The Supreme Court, in the *Quebec Secession Reference*, filled this silence left by the framers.[35] In the Supreme Court's words "[d]emocracy is commonly understood as being a political system of majority rule." It is "fundamentally connected to substantive goals, most importantly, the promotion of self-government." It is a system by which "a sovereign people exercises its right to self-government through the democratic process." Institutionally, "democracy means that each of the provincial legislatures and the federal Parliament is elected by popular franchise." In individual terms, it means "the right to vote in elections to the House of Commons and the provincial legislatures, and to be candidates in those elections."

But the democratic principle must be reconciled with other unwritten principles considered part of the Canadian Constitution. Because of one of these other principles — federalism — "there may be different and equally legitimate majorities in different provinces and territories and at the federal level." These majorities are each "an expression of democratic opinion."[36] Moreover, multiple democratic majorities necessitate flexibility and compromise:

> No one has a monopoly on truth, and our system is predicated on the faith that in the marketplace of ideas, the best solutions to public problems will rise to the top. Inevitably, there will be dissenting voices. A democratic system of government is committed to considering those dissenting voices, and seeking to acknowledge and address those voices in the laws by which all in the community must live.[37]

Indeed, other constitutional principles ensure that even the largest of majorities may not run roughshod over dissent. The Canadian Constitu-

---

33   *Quebec Secession Reference*, [1998] 2 S.C.R. 217 at para. 62.
34   *Ibid.*
35   The quotations that follow are drawn from *ibid.* at 252–62, except as otherwise noted.
36   *Ibid.* at para. 66.
37   *Ibid.* at para. 68.

tion is not "all sail and no anchor,"[38] as historian Thomas Macaulay described its U.S. counterpart. In the Supreme Court's view, "democracy in any real sense of the word cannot exist without the rule of law," another unwritten principle lying at the heart of the Canadian Constitution. "To be accorded legitimacy, democratic institutions must rest, ultimately, on a legal foundation." Thus, "they must allow for the participation of, and accountability to, the people, through public institutions created under the Constitution."[39] Accountability, in a state governed by the rule of law means that the government, as much as the people, are regulated by — and subject to — the law. In this fashion, the rule of law "vouchsafes to the citizens and residents of the country a stable, predictable and ordered society in which to conduct their affairs. It provides a shield for individuals from arbitrary state action."[40]

But more than that, the rule of law may act as a brake on the excesses of the democratic will. The law imposes its own, inherent limits of probity: "Our law's claim to legitimacy also rests on an appeal to moral values, many of which are imbedded in our constitutional structure."[41] In this respect the Court echoes de Tocqueville's observation that "[t]he best laws cannot make a constitution work in spite of morals; morals can turn the worst laws to advantage."[42]

In the Supreme Court's view, "[i]t would be a grave mistake to equate legitimacy with the 'sovereign will' or majority rule alone, to the exclusion of other constitutional values."[43] Instead, as the Court notes elsewhere in its reasoning, democracy includes other ideals, including "respect for the inherent dignity of the human person, commitment to social justice and equality, accommodation of a wide variety of beliefs, respect for cultural and group identity, and faith in social and political institutions which enhance the participation of individuals and groups in society."[44]

"Constitutionalism" — a close cousin of the rule of law — entrenches many of these values beyond the easy reach of simple majorities. In so doing it constitutes "an added safeguard for fundamental human rights

---

38   Letter to Henry Stephens Randall, 23 May 1857, available at www.bartleby.com/66/96/ 37096.html.

39   *Quebec Secession Reference*, [1998] 2 S.C.R. 217 at para. 67.

40   *Ibid.* at para. 70.

41   *Ibid.* at para. 67.

42   Alexis de Tocqueville, "Concerning the Superiority of Morals to Laws," vol. 2, aph. 5, in *Democracy in America* (New York: Colonial Press, 1899).

43   *Quebec Secession Reference*, [1998] 2 S.C.R. 217 at para. 67.

44   *Ibid.* at para. 64, citing *R. v. Oakes*, [1986] 1 S.C.R. 103 at 136.

and individual freedoms which might otherwise be susceptible to government interference." After all, while democratic governments are "generally solicitous of those rights, there are occasions when the majority will be tempted to ignore fundamental rights in order to accomplish collective goals more easily or effectively." Likewise, "a constitution may seek to ensure that vulnerable minority groups are endowed with the institutions and rights necessary to maintain and promote their identities against the assimilative pressures of the majority."[45] True liberal democracy, therefore depends as much on Macaulay's anchors as his sails.

3.   Implications of the Unwritten Democracy Principle

This picture of Canadian democracy painted by the Supreme Court, while attractive in content, is somewhat problematic in effect and origin.

a)   The Legal Impact

First, it is no easy task assessing exactly how much of the Supreme Court's insightful exegesis is substantive constitutional law, as opposed to philosophical backdrop. In the *Quebec Secession Reference*, the Court underscored that recognition of unwritten principles is not "an invitation to dispense with the written text." The written constitution has primacy. Nevertheless, the unwritten principles may "constitute substantive limitations upon government action. These principles may give rise to very abstract and general obligations, or they may be more specific and precise in nature. The principles are not merely descriptive, but are also invested with a powerful normative force, and are binding upon both courts and governments."[46] For this reason, the courts may have regard to these principles "in the process of Constitutional adjudication."[47]

In the *Quebec Secession Reference* itself, the Court balanced these unwritten principles of democracy, federalism, rule of law, and another concept — respect for individuals and minorities — to lay out constitutional ground rules for any breakup of the Canadian federation. Thus, the democratic principle would be triggered by a clear majority vote in Quebec on a "clear question in favour of secession." However, "[t]he democratic vote, by however strong a majority, would have no legal effect on its own and could not push aside the principles of federalism and the rule of law, the

---

45   *Ibid.* at para. 74.
46   *Ibid.* at para. 54.
47   *Ibid.*

rights of individuals and minorities, or the operation of democracy in the other provinces or in Canada as a whole." Instead, secession would have to be negotiated. These negotiations "would need to address the interests of the other provinces, the federal government, Quebec and indeed the rights of all Canadians both within and outside Quebec, and specifically the rights of minorities."[48]

Yet, having thus laid out the rules of the game, the Court suggested it would not police in detail their application. All these obligations are binding under the Constitution of Canada. However, "it will be for the political actors to determine what constitutes 'a clear majority on a clear question' in the circumstances under which a future referendum vote may be taken." Likewise, in the subsequent negotiations, "[t]he reconciliation of the various legitimate constitutional interests is necessarily committed to the political rather than the judicial realm precisely because that reconciliation can only be achieved through the give and take of political negotiations. To the extent issues addressed in the course of negotiations are political, the courts, appreciating their proper role in the constitutional scheme, would have no supervisory role."[49]

This approach suggests two things: first, that the unwritten principles of the Constitution, as articulated by the Court, are binding on the political branches of government; and second, that there is an outer limit on the extent to which these unwritten principles — including the democracy principle — can be enforced by the court. In this respect, the unwritten democratic principle resembles another species of unwritten constitutional norm discussed later — constitutional conventions.

Exactly where the limit lies in terms of enforcing the unwritten democracy principle is a matter that will be decided on a case-by-case basis. To date, lower courts have declined to employ the democracy principle aggressively to curb actions by the political branches of government. Indeed, one court has even pointed to the democratic principle in declining to impose judicially crafted remedies on the political branches for other constitutional breaches.[50] Other courts have refused to see democratic principles *per se* as constituting a source of affirmative law empowering courts to declare,

---

48　*Ibid.* at para. 151.

49　*Ibid.* at para. 153.

50　*Halpern v. Canada*, (2002), 60 O.R. (3d) 321 at 368 ("The principle of democracy underlies the Constitution and the *Charter*, and is one of the important factors guiding the exercise of a court's remedial discretion. It encourages remedies that allow the democratic process of consultation and dialogue to occur"), aff'd, but not on the issue of remedy, (2003), 65 O.R. (3d) 161 (C.A.).

for instance, that a senator elected under Alberta's senatorial election law must be appointed to the Upper Chamber.[51] The Supreme Court has itself recently voiced a note of caution: the unwritten principles of the Constitution "must be balanced against the principle of Parliamentary sovereignty."[52] To all appearances, the Supreme Court's professed reluctance to step deeply into the political arena on the authority of the common law constitution is an acknowledgment of the bull in the constitutional china shop: unwritten constitutional law means judge-made law.

b) The Troubling Provenance

Judge-made law is commonplace in our system. It is, after all, the exclusive basis for the common law extant in nine of Canada's provinces — the centuries-old, evolving body of precedential jurisprudence that governs most legal relations in the Anglo-Saxon tradition. This common law can work very well. Yet, for all its virtues, when raised to constitutional principle, it presents clear perils in a democratic polity.

First, unwritten norms compound the obscurity noted (perhaps for cynical reasons) by Napoleon. As the Supreme Court itself has observed, "[t]here are many important reasons for the preference for a written constitution over an unwritten one, not the least of which is the promotion of legal certainty."[53] Measured against this criterion, the Supreme Court's unwritten principles fare badly. As Professor Peter Hogg has noted, unwritten constitutional principles "are vague enough to arguably accommodate virtually any grievance about government policy."[54]

Second, to this question of uncertainty is added the problem of democratic legitimacy. Written constitutions are the product of drafting processes, whether in constitutional conferences and congresses or via legislative proceedings, usually undertaken by elected representatives. While the practices of the political branches may inform their content, unwritten constitutions are the product of courts, insulated from democratic accountability by the vital concept of judicial independence. As the Supreme Court acknowledges, an unwritten constitution raises concerns about the "legitimacy of constitutional judicial review."[55]

---

51   *Brown v. Alberta* (1999), 177 D.L.R. (4th) 349 (Alta. C.A.); *Samson v. Canada (Attorney General)*, (1998) 165 D.L.R. (4th) 342 (F.C.T.D.).
52   *Babcock v. Canada*, [2002] 3 S.C.R. 3 at para. 55.
53   *Re Remuneration of Judges*, [1997] 3 S.C.R. 3 at para. 93.
54   Hogg, *Constitutional Law* at 15-47.
55   *Re Remuneration of Judges*, [1997] 3 S.C.R. 3 at para. 93.

We can find no better way of expressing this point than to cite at length Justice La Forest, dissenting in *Re Remuneration of Judges*:

> [The written Constitution] (in Canada, a series of documents) expresses the desire of the people to limit the power of legislatures in certain specified ways. ... Judicial review, therefore, is politically legitimate only insofar as it involves the interpretation of an authoritative constitutional instrument. ... [T]he court's role is to divine the intent or purpose of the text as it has been expressed by the people through the mechanism of the democratic process. Of course, many (but not all) constitutional provisions are cast in broad and abstract language. Courts have the often arduous task of explicating the effect of this language in a myriad of factual circumstances, many of which may not have been contemplated by the framers of the Constitution. While there are inevitable disputes about the manner in which courts should perform this duty, for example by according more or less deference to legislative decisions, there is general agreement that the task itself is legitimate. ... This legitimacy is imperiled, however, when courts attempt to limit the power of legislatures without recourse to express textual authority.[56]

Canada is a somewhat awkward hybrid system: it now operates under a regime of constitutional supremacy, circumscribing the powers of the political branches, while possessed of a Constitution in part comprising judge-made law. A common law constitution works well in a system like the United Kingdom, where it may be changed by Parliament. It is less palatable in a system where judge-made constitutional law is supreme. Such law is alterable only through subsequent iterations, illuminations and clarifications by the Supreme Court, or by express (and very difficult) amendment to the written constitution itself.

Entire books have been written by eminent scholars on the subject of constitutional judicial review, and the proper balance of powers between the political and judicial branches.[57] We too grapple with this problem from time to time in this book. Suffice it to say here that, in our view, common

---

56   *Ibid.* at 180–81.

57   See, e.g., K. Roach, *The Supreme Court on Trial: Judicial Activism or Democratic Dialogue* (Toronto: Irwin Law, 2001); C.P. Manfredi, *Judicial Power and the Charter: Canada and the Paradox of Liberal Constitutionalism* (Toronto: McClelland & Stewart, 1992); F.L. Morton and R. Knopff, *The Charter Revolution and the Court Party* (Peterborough, ON: Broadview Press, 2000); A. Petter, "The Politics of the *Charter*" (1986), 8 Sup. Ct. L. Rev. 473. See also Hogg, *Constitutional Law* at 15-46; J. Leclair, "Canada's Unfathomable Unwritten Constitutional Principles" (2002) 27 Queen's L.J. 389.

law constitutionalism is to be expected, and largely welcomed, at least
where courts breathe meaning into the succinct phrases of the written constitution to meet unexpected circumstances. On the other hand, like La
Forest J., we believe it is more troubling — even undemocratic — if vast
constitutional treatises are extracted from ambivalent provisions that bear
no clear relationship to the detailed principles gleaned from them. In this
sort of circumstance, Canadian democracy is particularly dependent on the
wisdom of nine women and men sitting as the Supreme Court of Canada,
appointed at the discretion of the prime minister and insulated by judicial
independence.

On the other hand, we acknowledge that the specific unwritten constitutional norms derived by the Supreme Court to date are not the idiosyn-
cratic inferences of a few judicial minds. They are widely accepted
prerequisites to a functioning democracy. Like democracy itself, these concepts demand constitutionalization. The Supreme Court has filled a silence
where perhaps the framers of the Constitution (and their political succes-
sors) should have spoken. We turn now to several specific, unwritten democratic principles.

C. PARLIAMENTARY SUPREMACY AND THE SEPARATION OF POWERS

The separation of powers and the related concept of parliamentary
supremacy or sovereignty are fundamental to Canadian democratic governance. The Supreme Court readily acknowledges that the Constitution
does not expressly provide for the separation of powers. Yet, it has repeatedly pointed to — and been preoccupied by — the "functional separation
among the executive, legislative and judicial branches of governance."[58]
Viewed this way, the separation of powers is an unwritten principle of the
Constitution.[59]

---

58   *Doucet-Boudreau v. Nova Scotia (Minister of Education)*, [2003] 3 S.C.R. 3 at para. 33.
59   See *Babcock*, [2002] 3 S.C.R. 3 at para. 54, seemingly accepting a characterization of
the separation of powers as an unwritten principle; *Wells v. Newfoundland*, [1999] 3
S.C.R. 199 at para. 42 ("The doctrine of separation of powers is an essential feature of
our constitution"); *Harvey v. New Brunswick*, [1996] 2 S.C.R. 876 at para. 68, *per*
L'Heureux-Dubé and McLachlin JJ., concurring (the 1867 Act "preamble also incorporates the notion of the separation of powers, inherent in British parliamentary democracy, which precludes the courts from trenching on the internal affairs of the other
branches of government").

At least in theory, "[o]ur democratic government consists of several branches: the Crown, as represented by the Governor General and the provincial counterparts of that office; the legislative body; the executive; and the courts."[60] The Crown and the executive are often lumped together, producing three branches: the executive, the legislature and the judiciary. As we will see, however, important constitutional conventions regulate the relative powers of the Crown and Cabinet within the executive branch.

Each branch has its own function: "[i]n broad terms, the role of the judiciary is ... to interpret and apply the law; the role of the legislature is to decide upon and enunciate policy; the role of the executive is to administer and implement that policy."[61] As will become clear, this theoretical division of labour is a generalization, often tempered with exceptions. Nevertheless, the Supreme Court requires that each branch be cognizant of the mandate of the others: "It is fundamental to the working of government as a whole that all these parts play their proper role. It is equally fundamental that no one of them overstep its bounds, that each show proper deference for the legitimate sphere of activity of the other."[62] We will now look at parliamentary supremacy and the separation of powers on a branch-by-branch basis.

1. Separation of Powers Between the Executive and Parliament

The separation between the executive branch — the "government" — and Parliament is the oldest, most-settled, but (as discussed in chapters 5 and 6), in practice most-disregarded relationship. In practice, the same people who control the executive branch usually control the legislative branch — namely, the Cabinet and particularly the prime minister. Recognizing this fact, the Supreme Court has noted that there is "a considerable degree of integration between the Legislature and the Government. ... [I]t is the Government which, through its majority, does in practice control the operations of the elected branch of the Legislature on a day to day basis."[63] For this reason, the separation between the two branches is not rigid and, in adjudicating such matters, the "Court should not be blind to the reality of Canadian governance that, except in certain rare cases, the executive frequently and *de facto* controls the legislature."[64]

---

60 *New Brunswick Broadcasting Co.*, [1993] 1 S.C.R. 319 at 389.
61 *Fraser*, [1985] 2 S.C.R. 455 at 469–70.
62 *New Brunswick Broadcasting Co.*, [1993] 1 S.C.R. 319 at 389.
63 *Attorney General of Quebec v. Blaikie*, [1981] 1 S.C.R. 312 at 320.
64 *Wells*, [1999] 3 S.C.R. 199 at 221.

Nevertheless, the executive branch is legally *subordinate* to Parliament. The constitutional law of the United Kingdom (incorporated "in principle" into the Canadian Constitution by the 1867 Act preamble) has been a history of struggle between Parliament and the Crown. The culmination of this conflict made Parliament supreme over the monarch; the *Bill of Rights, 1689* established (or, in the eyes of parliamentarians at the time, affirmed) that the Crown had no authority to suspend parliamentary laws or raise money without parliamentary authorization. Meanwhile, the courts were to have no power to impeach or question "the freedom of speech and debates or proceedings in Parliament." The resulting supremacy — or sovereignty — of Parliament is also part of Canadian constitutional law, either because of direct incorporation of the *Bill of Rights, 1689*,[65] or as a more inchoate, unwritten principle.[66] This supremacy has two implications for the separation of powers between the legislative and executive branches: one jurisdictional and the other institutional. By jurisdictional we mean the powers of the branches in relation to one another. By institutional we mean the rules and conventions that govern how the branches exercise these powers.

a) Parliament's Jurisdictional Supremacy

Parliamentary supremacy means that Parliament is the source of all power. As the Second Earl of Pembroke once famously quipped about the United Kingdom legislature in 1648, "a parliament can do any thing but make a man a woman, and a woman a man." Technology may have rendered this precise observation anachronistic, but the point remains: traditionally, Parliament has the power "to make or unmake any law whatever."[67]

This parliamentary supremacy is tempered in Canada, of course, by other constraints in the Constitution. These restrictions create limited gov-

---

65   See *Reference re Resolution to Amend the Constitution*, [1981] 1 S.C.R. 753 at 785 (describing "art. 9 of the *Bill of Rights* of 1689, undoubtedly in force as part of the law of Canada, which provides that 'Proceedings in Parliament ought not to be impeached or questioned in any Court or Place out of Parliament'."). But see *New Brunswick Broadcasting Co.*, [1993] 1 S.C.R. 319 at 374 ("the wording of the preamble should not be understood to refer to a specific article of the English *Bill of Rights*. This is not to say that that principles underlying art. 9 of the English *Bill of Rights* of 1689 do not form part of our law and inform our understanding of the appropriate relationship between the courts and legislative bodies in Canada.").

66   See *Babcock*, [2002] 3 S.C.R. 3 at para. 55, noting that the unwritten principles of the Constitution must be balanced against parliamentary sovereignty, suggesting the latter too is part of the Constitution; see *Singh v. Canada (Attorney General)*, [2000] 3 F.C. 185 at para. 12 (F.C.A.), labelling parliamentary sovereignty a constitutional principle.

67   Albert Venn Dicey, *Introduction to the Study of the Law of the Constitution*, 10th ed. (London: Macmillan, 1964) at 39.

ernment, circumscribing the jurisdiction of both Parliament and the executive branch. Limited government stems from the division of powers between the federal and provincial governments, constitutionally protected rights and freedoms, and certain rare, constitutionalized aspects of the separation of powers. These matters are discussed in greater detail in section C.2 below.

Absent these limitations, Parliament is free to do as it wishes. As the Supreme Court noted recently, so long as it does not fundamentally alter or interfere with the constitutionalized relationship between the courts and the other branches of government, "[i]t is well within the power of the legislature to enact laws, even laws which some would consider draconian."[68]

Parliamentary supremacy used in this fashion (the plenary powers of Parliament) has two consequences. First, it means that every Parliament is equally supreme. No Parliament can unalterably bind another; for instance, by purporting to dictate the course of action of a future Parliament.[69]

Second, parliamentary supremacy, interacting with the separation of powers, means that "there is a *hierarchical* relationship between the executive and the legislature, whereby the executive must execute and implement the policies which have been enacted by the legislature in statutory form."[70] For these reasons, official actions undertaken by the executive branch usually must flow from "statutory authority clearly granted and properly exercised."[71]

We use the word "usually" because in practice the executive has very few self-standing, autonomous powers. Certain powers are reserved for the executive in the *Constitution Act, 1867* — technically in the person of the Queen or the Governor General, practically in the person of the prime minister or in the committee of ministers known as "Cabinet." These powers are inviolable, without constitutional amendment. As well, Cabinet and the prime minister exercise other powers by unwritten constitutional "convention," discussed below. Other than these very limited powers, parliamentary supremacy means the executive is beholden to Parliament for its legal authority, either directly through parliamentary delegation of power or indirectly through parliamentary tolerance of the executive's historic "royal prerogative." We discuss each of these sources of power in turn.

---

68 *Babcock*, [2002] 3 S.C.R. 3 at para. 57.

69 *Reference Re Canada Assistance Plan*, [1991] 2 S.C.R. 525 at 563 ("It is clear that parliamentary sovereignty prevents a legislative body from binding itself as to the substance of its future legislation.").

70 *Re Remuneration of Judges*, [1997] 3 S.C.R. 3 at para. 139 [emphasis added].

71 *Babcock*, [2002] 3 S.C.R. 3 at para. 20.

The Exercise of Delegated Power by the Executive

Delegation of power by Parliament is the most important source of executive branch power. For example, Parliament does not directly police borders, levy antidumping duties, adjudicate human rights complaints, collect taxes or do any of the millions of other things that we associate with "government." It does, however, authorize the executive to do these things, through Acts of Parliament.

Administrative Law and Parliamentary Supremacy

The fact that most government powers are parliamentary grants has important legal implications. As the Supreme Court notes, "[i]n a system of responsible government, once legislatures have made political decisions and embodied those decisions in law, it is the constitutional duty of the executive to implement those choices."[72] Moreover, because the executive's jurisdiction over these matters extends only as far as mandated by Parliament, it must be careful not to overstep that authorization.

If the executive branch were to act without regard to its empowering parliamentary statutes, it would behave inconsistently with parliamentary supremacy and the rule of law, two unwritten principles of the Constitution. Recall that the rule of law requires that government officials exercise their powers in accordance with the law of land. As Justice Rand observed in the famous *Roncarelli v. Duplessis* case, for statutory duties imposed by legislatures to be supplanted "by action dictated by and according to the arbitrary likes, dislikes and irrelevant purposes of public officers acting beyond their duty, would signalize the beginning of disintegration of the rule of law as a fundamental postulate of our constitutional structure."[73]

Policing the bounds of the delegated power and ensuring that the executive remains onside is usually the job of the courts, and is the subject matter of an area of public law known as administrative law. There are numerous excellent treatises on administrative law, including one prepared by Professor Mullan for the Essentials of Canadian Law series.[74] We too focus on important aspects of administrative law repeatedly in this book.

Constitutional Law and Parliamentary Supremacy

A point needs to be made regarding the constitutional limitations on delegation by Parliament to the executive. In Canada, there are few such constitutional prohibitions. Even the division of powers between the federal

---

72   *Re Remuneration of Judges*, [1997] 3 S.C.R. 3 at 91.

73   [1959] S.C.R. 121 at 142.

74   David Mullan, *Administrative Law* (Toronto: Irwin Law, 2001).

and provincial levels is no barrier. For instance, Parliament may delegate powers to the executive branch of the provinces.[75]

Nor are there "functional" bars on delegation. Parliament regularly delegates to government officials substantial "discretionary" powers: the authority to make decisions constrained by few or no criteria prescribed by Parliament. Moreover, Parliament is even free to delegate to the executive branch "legislative" authority: the power to make law in the form of regulations and orders. Chapter 5 discusses this delegated legislative power.

Caution is warranted, however, in concluding that there are no constitutional limits on the amount and sort of powers that Parliament may delegate to the executive. Certainly, those powers reserved strictly to the legislature in the written Constitution may not be delegated. For instance, section 53 of the 1867 Act prohibits any body "other than the directly elected legislature, from imposing a tax on its own accord."[76] Full delegation of such a power to the executive would violate this constitutional bar on "no taxation without representation."[77]

A second restraint requires that Parliament's delegation not be so comprehensive and sweeping that it effectively assigns all of Parliament's responsibilities to the executive.[78] There is a third constitutional issue in delegation: given the existence of separation of powers in which each branch of government has responsibilities, should Parliament have the power to delegate to the executive responsibilities typically associated with the *judiciary*? It is clear that the jurisdictional separation of powers between the judiciary and the executive is not strict, and that Parliament may accord

---

75 See *P.E.I. Potato Marketing Board v. H.B. Willis Inc.*, [1952] 2 S.C.R. 392.

76 *Eurig Estate (Re)*, [1998] 2 S.C.R. 565 at para. 30.

77 That said, where Parliament authorizes a tax and then delegates the power to impose it, including the setting of rates, the Constitution is not offended. *Ontario English Catholic Teachers' Assn. v. Ontario (Attorney General)*, [2001] 1 S.C.R. 470 at para. 73 (if "the legislature expressly and clearly authorizes the imposition of a tax by a delegated body or individual, then the requirements of the principle of 'no taxation without representation' will be met. In such a situation, the delegated authority is not being used to impose a completely new tax, but only to impose a tax that has been approved by the legislature.").

78 See *Re Gray*, [1918] 57 S.C.R. 150 at 157 holding that the broad delegation of powers under the *War Measures Act, 1914* was *intra vires* Parliament, but also noting "Parliament cannot, indeed, abdicate its functions, but within reasonable limits at any rate it can delegate its powers to the executive government. Such powers must necessarily be subject to determination at any time by Parliament, and needless to say the acts of the executive, under its delegated authority, must fall within the ambit of the legislative pronouncement by which its authority is measured"; see *British Columbia Native Women's Society v. Canada*, [2000] 1 F.C. 304 at para. 23 (T.D.) noting that the federal Parliament must not abdicate its legislative functions or efface itself.

the executive substantial *judicial* powers.[79] There are, however, important limits on this reallocation of judicial powers. In this last respect, despite its rather innocuous language, the Supreme Court has attributed significant constitutional weight to section 96 of the 1867 Act. Section 96 reads: "[t]he Governor General shall appoint the Judges of the Superior, District, and County Courts in each Province, except those of the Courts of Probate in Nova Scotia and New Brunswick."

This is the provision, in other words, that places the power to appoint provincial "superior court" judges in the hands of the federal government. These superior — or "section 96" — courts are the most potent judicial institutions in the land, exercising the better part of the judicial jurisdiction inherited from the Royal Courts of the United Kingdom. The appointment aspect of section 96 is discussed in chapter 4.

The point to be made here is this: the Supreme Court regards the language in section 96 of the 1867 Act as conveying much more than an appointment power for superior courts. Among other things, it protects the superior courts from legislative curbs on their traditional functions. Thus, section 96 is "a means of protecting the 'core' jurisdiction of the superior courts so as to provide for some uniformity throughout the country in the judicial system. ... The jurisdiction which forms this core cannot be removed from the superior courts by either level of government, without amending the Constitution."[80]

Exactly what the Supreme Court views as a "core" jurisdiction of the superior courts depends on a complex test, focused at least in part on whether the power in question was exercised by the superior courts at the time of Confederation.[81] Suffice it to say that much of the Supreme Court jurisprudence on this issue has had a provincial/federal division of powers dimension. It has focused on whether Parliament or the provincial legislatures could empower provincial courts — courts whose judges are appointed by the provinces — to perform duties traditionally performed by section 96 superior courts. Section 96, in other words, has preserved the traditional powers of the federally appointed superior court judges from encroachment by provincially appointed provincial court judges or administrative tribunals.[82]

---

79   *Quebec Secession Reference*, [1998] 2 S.C.R. 217 at para. 15 ("Parliament and the provincial legislatures may properly confer other legal functions on the courts, and may confer certain judicial functions on bodies that are not courts.").

80   *MacMillan Bloedel Ltd. v. Simpson*, [1995] 4 S.C.R. 725 at para. 15.

81   See *Re Residential Tenancies Act*, [1981] 1 S.C.R. 714.

82   See, e.g., *MacMillan Bloedel Ltd.*, [1995] 4 S.C.R. 725 at para 11. See also *Cooper v. Human Rights Commission (Canada)* , [1996] 3 S.C.R. 854, 872, *per* Lamer C.J., con-

However, there is at least one area in which the protection of this core superior court jurisdiction extends also to efforts by legislative bodies to strip powers from the superior courts and delegate them exclusively to the executive branch. Thus, it now appears settled that, by reason of section 96, the legislative branch cannot purport to remove fully from the superior courts the power to judicially review the actions of (at least the provincial) executive branch. Specifically, section 96 superior courts retain a constitutional power to perform their administrative law function and ensure that these government officials operate within the parameters of their jurisdiction.[83] This issue is discussed more fully in section C.2 below.

It is less clear whether there are other core superior court powers that may not be delegated to the executive (federal or provincial). At one juncture, there was debate as to whether Parliament could delegate to executive tribunals the authority to employ the *Charter*, and render Acts of Parliament inoperative. In *Cooper v. Human Rights Commission*, Chief Justice Lamer, writing for himself, argued that the "constitutional status of the judiciary, flowing as it does from the separation of powers, requires that certain functions be exclusively exercised by judicial bodies."[84]

Specifically, the judiciary "must have exclusive jurisdiction over challenges to the validity of legislation under the Constitution of Canada, and particularly the *Charter*. The reason is that only courts have the requisite independence to be entrusted with the constitutional scrutiny of legislation when that scrutiny leads a court to declare invalid an enactment of the legislature."[85] Further, to allow parts of the executive branch — such as human rights commissions — to decide the constitutionality of an Act of Parliament inverts the classic hierarchical relationship between the legislative and executive branches: "Instead of being subject to the laws of the legislature, the executive can defeat the laws of the legislature. On each occasion

---

curring in the result and noting that "some commentators had suggested that s. 96 was concerned as much with the division of powers as with safeguarding the role of the courts, because it was intended to prevent the provinces from undermining a unitary judicial system."

83 See *Crevier v. Attorney General of Quebec*, [1981] 2 S.C.R. 220 where the Court employed section 96 to strike down a provincial law which allocated the power to make final decisions on questions of whether certain government officials were acting within their jurisdiction exclusively to an administrative appeal tribunal, not a superior court; see also *Cooper*, [1996] 3 S.C.R. 854 at para. 11, *per* Lamer C.J., concurring in the result, citing *Crevier* and concluding that "s. 96 has also been relied on to constitutionalize judicial review of administrative decisionmakers."

84 *Ibid.* at para. 13.

85 *Ibid.*

that this occurs, a tribunal has disrupted the proper constitutional relationship between it and the legislature."[86]

Justice Lamer's critique has not prevailed at the Supreme Court. After
all, as Justice McLachlin, dissenting in *Cooper*, argued, "[t]he *Charter* is not
some holy grail which only judicial initiates of the superior courts may
touch. The *Charter* belongs to the people. All law and law-makers that
touch the people must conform to it. Tribunals and commissions charged
with deciding legal issues are no exception."[87] This, in effect, is the
Supreme Court's current position.[88]

Ultimately, we believe that this is the most sensible view. So long as Parliament has chosen to extend to tribunals the jurisdiction to apply law — in
other words, so long as they have done so by statute — the constitutional prerequisites are satisfied. The fact that the administrative bodies applying this
law (and the *Charter* itself) lack protections associated with judicial independence (discussed later in this chapter) is an indifferent detail. So long as
there is a court with judicial independence available to judicially review
Charter decisions made by the administrative tribunal, the abusive potential
stemming from the nonindependence of that tribunal is minimized.

This reasoning suggests that the zone of core competencies that may
not be delegated to the executive branch should be quite small. So long as
the judicial review authority of the courts is preserved, it seems irrelevant
whether the executive branch is empowered to do something once undertaken in the first instance by a superior court.

The Exercise of Prerogative Powers by the Executive

A second source of executive power, beyond that delegated by Parliament, is
the residue of discretionary or arbitrary authority possessed by the Crown.[89]
Known as the royal prerogative, this power is described, rather obtusely, as
"the pre-eminence the Sovereign enjoys over and above all other persons. It
comprehends all the special dignities, liberties, privileges, powers and roy-

---

86 *Ibid.* at para. 25.

87 *Ibid.* at para. 70.

88 *Nova Scotia (Worker's Compensation Board) v. Martin*, [2003] 2 S.C.R. 504 at para. 3
    ("Administrative tribunals which have jurisdiction — whether explicit or implied — to
    decide questions of law arising under a legislative provision are presumed to have
    concomitant jurisdiction to decide the constitutional validity of that provision. This
    presumption may only be rebutted by showing that the legislature clearly intended to
    exclude *Charter* issues from the tribunal's authority over questions of law.").

89 See *Krieger v. Law Society of Alberta*, [2002] 3 S.C.R. 372 at para. 31; *Reference re Effect of
    Exercise of Royal Prerogative of Mercy Upon Deportation Proceedings*, [1933] S.C.R. 269 at
    272–73.

alties allowed by common law to the Crown of England, and all parts of the Commonwealth."[90] More succinctly, the royal prerogative means "the powers and privileges accorded by the common law to the Crown."[91]

If left to run amok, the royal prerogative risks causing serious damage to the concept of parliamentary supremacy, the separation of powers and responsible government. A robust royal prerogative invulnerable to parliamentary intervention would leave powers in the hands of the executive immune to legislation, and thus to parliamentary supremacy. Moreover, royal prerogative powers with legislation-like authority would put the executive branch in the business of legislating without reference to a parliamentary bestowal of power, raising concerns about the separation of powers. Finally, a prerogative exercised by the monarch him- or herself runs counter to the democratic legitimacy and responsible government created by an executive branch accountable, and subordinate, to Parliament. In practice, however, these concerns have not been justified.

The responsible government concern has been remedied in much the same way the absence of express mention of responsible government in the *Constitution Act, 1867* has been resolved: by constitutional conventions, discussed more fully later in this chapter. First, the monarch and his or her agent, the Governor General, do not necessarily exercise the royal prerogative personally.[92] The prime minister and ministers, as privy councillors and thus part of the "Crown," are permitted to exercise some of these powers.

Second, even where the Governor General exercises the royal prerogative, he or she generally does so on the advice of the prime minister or Cabinet. The Governor General may retain discretion to refuse to follow this advice, but "in Canada that discretion has been exercised only in the most exceptional circumstances."[93] In these ways, responsible government is preserved.

In response to the other concerns voiced above, the royal prerogative is not a catch-all for whatever it is that the executive branch wishes to do, and for which it lacks delegated power. In keeping with parliamentary supremacy, the royal prerogative is easily supplanted by Parliament.

Some courts have implied substantial staying power for the royal prerogative, concluding that it "cannot be limited except by clear and express

---

90   *Ontario v. Mar-Dive Corp.* (1996), 141 D.L.R. (4th) 577 at 588 (Ont. Gen. Div.).

91   *Ross River Dena Council Band v. Canada*, [2002] 2 S.C.R. 816 at para. 54, citing Hogg, *Constitutional Law* at 1-14.

92   *Black*, (2001) 54 O.R. (3d) 215 at para. 32 (C.A.).

93   *Ibid.*

statutory language."[94] Other courts have implied a less stringent test. As one lower court has observed, "[w]here Parliament, or in the case of a province the legislature, has provided a regime of law to govern the affairs of citizens, the original prerogative of the Crown is excluded."[95] In these circumstances, "[t]he Crown may no longer act under the prerogative, but must act under and subject to the conditions imposed by the statute."[96] This threshold for abrogation was a live issue in the recent Supreme Court case of *Ross River Dena Council Band v. Canada*, where a majority apparently resolved this debate: an Act of Parliament may curtail a prerogative power, both explicitly and by necessary implication.[97]

Further, a purported exercise of the royal prerogative is subject to review by the courts to determine its existence.[98] The prerogative is, for all practical purposes, a branch of judge-made common law "because decisions of courts determine both its existence and its extent."[99] In practice, courts have held that "legislation has severely curtailed the scope of the Crown prerogative."[100] As the Privy Council Office — effectively, the prime minister's governmental department — has noted, "[t]he history of parliamentary government has been a process of narrowing the exercise of the prerogative authority by subjecting it increasingly to the pre-eminence of the statutory authority, substituting the authority of the Crown in Parliament for the authority of the Crown alone."[101]

This limitation of royal prerogative powers minimizes much of the concern that might be sparked by the executive branch *de facto* legislating in a fashion unanticipated by an Act of Parliament. Indeed, the Supreme Court would appear to have expressly ruled out that possibility: "There is no principle in this country, as there is not in Great Britain, that the Crown may legislate by proclamation or order in council to bind citizens where it so acts without the support of a statute of the Legislature."[102]

---

94 *Mar-Dive Corp*, (1996), 141 D.L.R. (4th) 577 at 588.

95 *Scarborough (City) v. Ontario (Attorney-General)* (1997), 144 D.L.R. (4th) 130 at 135 (Ont. Gen. Div.).

96 *Black*, (2001) 54 O.R. (3d) 215 at para. 27.

97 *Ross River Dena Council Band*, [2002] 2 S.C.R. 816 at para. 54.

98 *Scarborough (City)* (1997), 144 D.L.R. (4th) 130 at 134 (holding it would be inimical to principles of responsible government "if the court assumed that a residual royal prerogative prevails to validate any executive action for which legislative authorization is absent").

99 *Black*, (2001) 54 O.R. (3d) 215 at para. 26.

100 *Ibid.* at para. 27.

101 Privy Council Office, *Responsibility in the Constitution* (1993).

102 *Reference re Anti-Inflation Act*, [1976] 2 S.C.R. 373 at 433.

Detailing the precise scope of prerogative powers as they exist at present is difficult. As Professor Robert MacGregor Dawson observed in his authoritative work on Canadian government, "the prerogative, finding its origin in the misty past and interpreted by the courts only as the occasion has arisen, is uncertain."[103] The clearest residual prerogative is in the area of foreign affairs. There, the executive has authority to make treaties and pursue Canada's foreign policy, a matter discussed in chapter 11. There are also prerogative powers to grant mercy to those convicted of crimes, to bestow honours and to issue passports.[104] Other classic prerogatives — such as the appointment of prime ministers and ministers — are more properly regarded in contemporary Canadian law as constitutional conventions.

b) Parliament's Institutional Supremacy

Separation of Powers Between the Crown and Cabinet
At the institutional level, parliamentary supremacy gives rise to what one might call a separation of powers *within* the executive branch, between the Crown and a prime minister and Cabinet accountable to the legislative branch. As the House of Lords — the final court of appeal in the United Kingdom — has observed, "Parliamentary supremacy over the Crown as Monarch stems from the fact that the Monarch must accept the advice of a prime minister who is supported by a majority of Parliament. Parliamentary supremacy over the Crown as executive stems from the fact that Parliament maintains in office the prime minister who appoints the ministers in charge of the executive."[105]

Thus, in Canada, "Canadian constitutional law does not grant Governors General and Lieutenant Governors the powers of absolute monarchs. Instead, it recognizes that these monarchical powers are now vested in the legislature."[106] Put another way, "[d]ecisions once made by a monarch in the name of the Crown are now made by the executive branch of government under the authority of the legislature."[107] Parliamentary supremacy in this mix is justified by the fact that, as one Canadian lower court put it, Parliament "represents the will of the people."[108]

---

103 Norman Ward, *Dawson's The Government of Canada*, 6th ed. (Toronto: University of Toronto Press, 1987) at 178.
104 See Hogg, *Constitutional Law* at 1-16 and 19-21.
105 *In Re M. (A.P.)*, 154 N.R. 358 at para. 2, *per* Lord Templeton (H.L.).
106 *P. (N.I.) v. B. (R.)* (2000), 193 D.L.R. (4th) 752 at para. 24 (B.C.S.C.).
107 *Ibid.* at para. 25
108 *Ibid.* at para. 24.

The Concept of Responsible Government and Constitutional Conventions
Viewed this way, parliamentary supremacy morphs into "responsible government" — the means by which the executive is held structurally accountable to the legislature. In Canada, it is more common to view responsible
government as a self-standing unwritten principle of the Constitution, supported by a series of constitutional "conventions."

Constitutional conventions are a perplexing component of the Constitution. Unlike other unwritten attributes of the Constitution, these conventions are "not based on judicial precedents but on precedents established
by the institutions of government themselves."[109] As such, any remedy for
their breach must flow from a source other than the courts.[110] The courts
may not, in other words, enforce conventions.[111]

Even so, constitutional conventions "ensure that the legal framework
of the constitution will be operated in accordance with generally accepted
principles."[112] These generally accepted principles relate, as the Supreme
Court puts it, "to the principles of responsible government,"[113] and stem at
least in part from the preamble to the 1867 Act.[114]

In practice, these responsible government conventions have several
attributes. For at least some members of the Supreme Court, constitutional conventions include a "general rule that the Governor General will act
only according to the advice of the prime minister," that "after a general
election the Governor General will call upon the leader of the party with the
greatest number of seats to form a government" and a requirement that "a
government losing the confidence of the House of Commons must itself
resign, or obtain a dissolution."[115] Impartiality in the civil service is also
regarded as a component of responsible government.[116]

---

109   *Reference Re Resolution to Amend the Constitution*, [1981] 1 S.C.R. 753 at 880.
110   *Ibid.*
111   Hogg, *Constitutional Law* at 1-18.
112   *Reference Re Objection by Quebec to a Resolution to Amend the Constitution*, [1982] 2
        S.C.R. 793 at 803.
113   *Ontario Catholic Teachers Association v. Ontario (Attorney-General)*, [2001] 1 S.C.R. 470
        at para. 63.
114   See *Re Resolution to Amend the Constitution*, [1981] 1 S.C.R. 753 at 805 ("Federal union
        'with a Constitution similar in Principle to that of the United Kingdom' may well
        embrace responsible government and some common law aspects of the United King-
        dom's unitary constitutionalism, such as the rule of law and Crown prerogatives and
        immunities").
115   *Ibid.* at 857–58, *per* Dickson, Estey and McIntyre JJ., dissenting in part. See also
        Figueroa v. Canada (Attorney General), [2003] 1 S.C.R. 912 at para 141 *per* Gonthier,
        LeBel and Deschamps JJ., concurring in the result ("The Constitution gives the Gover-
        nor General the formal power of selecting the prime minister and Cabinet, but by

These elements of responsible government also receive regular recognition in treatises on the Constitution, and in the practices of Canada's political branches of government. The chief conventions of responsible government are outlined in Table 2.1.

Table 2.1   *Constitutional Conventions of Responsible Government*

Power	Constitutional Convention
Queen	
Power of disallowance of statutes of the Canadian Parliament pursuant to section 56 of the 1867 Act	This power of disallowance, reserved to the Queen in Council (which can be read as the British Cabinet), can no longer be exercised.[117]
Appointment of Governor General	The Queen follows the prime minister's recommendations.[118] The prime minister's recommendations are his or her special or "personal" prerogative that does not need to be exercised in association with Cabinet colleagues.[119] Note, however, that the Imperial Conference of 1930 anticipated the appointment of the Governor General on the advice of "His Majesty's Ministers in the Dominion concerned."[120] Nor is the appointment of the Governor General included in the 1935 Privy Council minute detailing the prime minister's powers.[121]

convention she invariably appoints the leader of the party that has won the majority of seats in Parliament (assuming that there is one) as prime minister, and follows his recommendations in appointing the other ministers.").

116 *OPSEU v. Ontario (Attorney General)*, [1987] 2 S.C.R. 2 at 27; *Osborne v. Canada*, [1991] 2 S.C.R. 69 at 86, *per* Sopinka, Cory and McLachlin JJ., concurring.

117 See Hogg, *Constitutional Law of Canada* at 9-17, pointing to the 1930 Imperial Conference establishing that "the powers of reservation and disallowance must never be exercised." This passage was cited with approval in *Hogan v. Newfoundland (Attorney General)*, 156 D.L.R. (4th) 139 at para. 30 (Nfld. S.C.), aff'd 163 D.L.R. (4th) 672 (Nfld. C.A.). But see *Reference Re Power of Disallowance and Power of Reservation*, [1938] 2 D.L.R. 8 (S.C.C.) (holding that the equivalent power of disallowance of *provincial* legislation, possessed by the Governor General in Council by s. 90 of the *B.N.A. Act, 1867*, persisted, despite the Imperial Conference). For a more contemporary discussion of the implications of this and related powers, see *Ontario Hydro v. Ontario (Labour Relations Board)*, [1993] 3 S.C.R. 327 at 371–72, *per* La Forest, L'Heureux-Dubé and Gonthier JJ., concurring.

118 Ward, *Dawson's The Government of Canada* at 180 ("The prime minister of Canada recommends the appointment to the queen, and the later acts on the advice so given.").

119 Hogg, *Constitutional Law* at 9-9, n26.

120 Imperial Conference 1930, Summary of Proceedings, HMSO, Cmd. 3717 (1930).

121 Privy Council minute, P.C. 3374 (25 Oct. 1935).

Power	Constitutional Convention
Queen	
Appointment of additional senators expanding the size of the senate under section 26 of the 1867 Act	In practice, the Queen (acting personally or through the Governor General) follows the advice of Cabinet, but there may be no legal (as opposed to constitutional conventional) obligation that this advice be followed.[122]
Governor General	
Selection of the prime minister	The power has been described as a personal prerogative of the Governor General, as he or she exercises discretion in an effort to appoint a prime minister who can form a government enjoying the support of the Commons.[123] In practice, the Governor General appoints the leader of the party winning the "majority of seats in Parliament (assuming that there is one)" as prime minister.[124] This convention has also been (more correctly) stated as: the Governor General will call upon the leader of the party with the *greatest* number of seats to form a government,[125] and serve as prime minister. This is the way the convention works in practice, because of party discipline. In theory, however, there may be more nuance to the convention. So long as the leader of party commands the confidence of the House, the Governor General should be able to appoint him or her prime minister, regardless of the relative party distribution of seats.[126]
Dismissal of the prime minister	The Governor General's powers of dismissal is probably restricted to circumstances in which the prime minister's government loses the confidence of the House of Commons,[127] in which case the government must itself resign, or obtain a dissolution.[128]

---

122 See *Re Constitutional Question Act (British Columbia)* (1991) 78 D.L.R. (4th) 245 (B.C.C.A.).

123 Hogg, *Constitutional Law* at 9-7. See also *Angus v. Canada* (1990), 72 D.L.R. (4th) 672 at 683 (F.C.A.). (The Governor General "retains reserve or personal powers, such as the choice of a prime minister.").

124 *Figueroa*, [2003] 1 S.C.R. 912 at para. 141 *per* Gonthier, LeBel and Deschamps JJ., concurring in the result.

125 *Re Resolution to Amend the Constitution*, [1981] 1 S.C.R. 753 at 857 *per* Dickson, Estey and McIntyre JJ., dissenting.

126 See discussion by Professor C.E.S. Frank, Commons Standing Committee on Government Operations and Estimates, *Evidence*, 37th Parl., 3d Sess. (25 March 2004).

127 See Hogg, *Constitutional Law* at 9-25.

128 *Re Resolution to Amend the Constitution*, [1981] 1 S.C.R. 753, 857–58 *per* Dickson, Estey and McIntyre JJ., dissenting.

Power	Constitutional Convention
Governor General	
Selection of Cabinet ministers	The Governor General follows the prime minister's recommendations.[129] The prime minister's recommendations are his or her personal prerogative that does not need to be exercised in association with Cabinet colleagues.[130]
Royal assent of bills	Assent must be given once a bill has been passed by the Houses of Parliament.[131]
Dissolution of Parliament and summoning Parliament into session	The Governor General follows the prime minister's recommendations. Again, this is a special prerogative power of the prime minister.[132] Whether the Governor General retains certain special "reserve" powers enabling him or her to disregard this advice is a matter discussed in chapters 4 and 5.
Appointment of senators under section 24 of the 1867 Act	The Governor General follows the advice of the prime minister,[133] though some authorities suggest the advice flows from the Cabinet.[134] Some observers argue that Governor General may refuse to make senate and other appointments recommended by a government defeated in an election, thus preserving the rights of the incoming prime minister.[135]
Appointment of judges under section 96 of the 1867 Act	The Governor General follows the advice of Cabinet, though chief justices are appointed on the advice of the prime minister.[136]
Reserve power to exercise the Governor General's power *without* or *against* the advice of the prime minister or Cabinet	There are instances (discussed from time to time in this book) where the Governor General might act properly in rejecting advice from Cabinet or the prime minister, or act independently of these persons. Two important examples already alluded to are in selecting or dismissing the prime minister and in granting a requested dissolution. Exactly where these reserve powers

129 *Figueroa*, [2003] 1 S.C.R. 912 at 984, *per* Gonthier, LeBel and Deschamps JJ., concurring in the result.

130 Hogg, *Constitutional Law* at 9-9. Privy Council minute, P.C. 3374 (25 Oct. 1935).

131 *Hogan v. Newfoundland (Attorney General)*, 156 D.L.R. (4th) 139 at para. 29 (Nfld. S.C.), aff'd 163 D.L.R. (4th) 672 (Nfld. C.A.).

132 Hogg, *Constitutional Law* at 9-9.

133 *Ibid.* at 9-26.2 and n74. See also Privy Council minute, P.C. 3374 (25 Oct. 1935) describing the appointment of senators as a special prerogative of the prime minister.

134 See *Samson v. Canada (Attorney General)*, (1998) 165 D.L.R. (4th) 342 at para. 6 (F.C.T.D.) ("[i]n practice, the Governor General exercises his power of appointment on the advice and recommendation of the Governor-in-Council").

135 See discussion in Andrew Heard, *Canadian Constitutional Conventions* (Toronto: Oxford University Press, 1991) at 38.

Power	Constitutional Convention
Governor General	
	may be exercised is a matter of some ambiguity. Professor Dawson urged that the Governor General's reserve powers should only be exercised where Cabinet is acting in a way that would "perpetuate for some time a state of affairs which was plainly intolerable and a violation of the spirit and intent of the constitution." Moreover, "there should be no reasonable doubt of the essential wisdom and justice of the governor's intervention."[137]
Prime Minister and the Ministry	
Membership in Cabinet or the post of prime minister	The prime minister and other ministers are expected to be Members of Parliament, though ministers may hold office pending election to the Commons or pending (or during) appointment to the senate.[138]
Persistence of the ministry	The ministry endures for the life or tenure of the prime minister. It persists even after an election is called, to preserve continuity of government. If the government party loses the election (i.e., does not have the seats to command the confidence of Parliament), the prime minister will resign, and the ministry terminates.[139] However, even if the incumbent prime minister's party has fewer seats in the Commons after the election than another party, that prime minister is not automatically dismissed without an opportunity first to cobble together the votes sufficient to hold the confidence of the Commons.[140]
Powers associated with the "Privy Council," the "Governor General in Council" or the "Governor-in-Council"	Cabinet effectively exercises any powers attributed to these bodies.[141]

136   Hogg, *Constitutional Law* at 9-26.2 and n74; Privy Council minute, P.C. 3374 (25 Oct. 1935). Note that the Supreme Court, created under section 101 of the 1867 Act, has a similar appointment process: judges are appointed by the Governor-in-Council. See discussion in ch. 4.

137   Ward, *Dawson's The Government of Canada* at 190–91. For another discussion of the reserve power, see David Smith, *The Invisible Crown* (Toronto: University of Toronto Press, 1995) at 31 *et seq.*; Eugene Forsey, *The Royal Power of Dissolution of Parliament in the British Commonwealth* (Toronto: University of Toronto Press, 1968).

138   Hogg, *Constitutional Law* at 9-7.

139   *Ibid.* at 9-7 to 9-8.

140   The classic example is Mackenzie King's 1925 government, which held only 101 seats to the Conservative 116 members, and survived only in coalition with the Progressives. See Ward, *Dawson's The Government of Canada* at 199–200.

141   Hogg, *Constitutional Law* at 9-9.

As a final note, it is commonplace for the powers of the Governor General to be exercised by a "deputy" Governor General, the Chief Justice of the Supreme Court or, in his or her absence, another senior judge of the Supreme Court. Delegation is authorized both by the 1867 Act[142] and the 1947 Letters Patent, authorizing the Governor General to exercise the monarch's constitutional powers.[143]

For this reason, royal assent may sometimes be accorded a bill of Parliament by a Supreme Court justice. This phenomenon raises the uncomfortable prospect of Supreme Court justices, acting in their deputized capacity, authorizing legislation that they — and courts lower in the judicial hierarchy — may later scrutinize on constitutional grounds. Preoccupied by the separation of powers implications of this practice, the Federal Court of Appeal concluded recently that the deputization of Supreme Court justices was legal, but undesirable.[144] It is to this issue of separation of powers between the courts and the other branches that we turn next.

2.   Separation of Powers Between the Judiciary and Parliament

As well as regulating executive/legislature interactions, parliamentary supremacy also means that within the zone in which Parliament remains sovereign, Parliament dictates the marching orders that must be followed by the courts. As the Supreme Court explains, in the "residual area reserved for the principle of parliamentary sovereignty in Canadian constitutional law, it is Parliament and the legislatures, not the courts, that have ultimate constitutional authority to draw the boundaries."[145]

This comment raises the thorny issue of the separation of powers between the courts and Parliament. There is a trip switch in Canadian constitutional law — a point at which parliamentary supremacy gives way to "constitutional" supremacy. On one side, Parliament is supreme and the courts must simply interpret and carry out Parliament's dictates expressed in Acts of Parliament. On the other side, Parliament strays beyond its constitutional jurisdiction and must be subordinated to the Constitution. On this uncomfortable side, courts do two things: first, they are the arbiters of where that switch is, by interpreting the Constitution and, sometimes, dis-

---

142   *Constitution Act, 1867*, s. 14.
143   C. Gaz. (1947) I.3104, vol. 81, Part VII and VIII.
144   *Tunda v. Canada*, 2001 FCA 151.
145   *Canada (Auditor General) v. Canada (Minister of Energy, Mines and Resources)*, [1989] 2 S.C.R. 49 at 91.

cerning even binding unwritten constitutional principles by which Parliament must abide; and, second, they decide whether a given statute of Parliament trips the switch. Once it is triggered, Canadian democracy becomes a system of *de facto* judicial supremacy. For these reasons, the separation of powers between the judicial and the legislative branch is critically important to Canadian democracy — and is often the source of heated debate.

As with the separation of powers between the executive and Parliament, the relationship between the courts and Parliament has both jurisdictional and institutional dimensions. Again, by jurisdictional we mean the relative powers of the branches in relation to one another. By institutional, we mean rules governing how exactly these branches go about exercising these powers in relation to one another.

a)   Jurisdictional Separation of Powers

The courts are charged with interpreting and applying the law. As noted above, some of that "law" in the common law provinces flows from a long legacy of judge-made jurisprudence. This is most often the case in the classic "private" law area — torts, contracts and property — the law of civil obligations.

However, even in the "public law" areas — basically, such things as criminal law and the law relating to the powers of the state — courts are often obliged to discern the meaning of legislative language, and to apply that language to circumstances not contemplated by legislators. In this area, too, judges are therefore obliged to craft a sort of common law jurisprudence, enabling them to interpret sometimes ambiguous statutory — including written constitutional — provisions consistently in highly variable circumstances. Judges judge, in other words.

This potent judicial role is an inevitable component of even the most robust of democracies, such as Canada. Statutes and constitutions can never create a fully comprehensive code of behaviour, anticipating every eventuality. Thus, even in areas governed by Acts of Parliament or the written Constitution, there must always be some level of judicial discretion to craft standards for applying these laws to the messy facts of reality. Judicial creativity, in other words, is inherently part of the separation of powers, not a challenge to it.

For the purposes of this book, the judicial role in the separation of powers arises in two forms of "judicial review": judicial review of the executive and legislature on constitutional grounds and administrative law review of the executive. Each interacts in a complex way with the separation of powers, parliamentary supremacy and constitutional supremacy.

Constitutional Judicial Review: Courts and Parliament

Overview

Judicial review of the political branches of government — and Parliament in particular — on constitutional grounds is very much in the public eye. In the 2004 federal election, for example, comments by Conservative MP Randy White on what he viewed as the usurpation of Parliament's powers by *Charter*-wielding courts became a cause célèbre in the last days of the campaign.[146] What may have cost the Conservatives support (at least in Ontario) was not so much White's view of the separation of powers between the judicial and legislative branches. Instead, it was the particular court "interpretations" to which White objected: "I think our courtrooms are much misguided and miss the conservative social reality of our times."[147]

As White's comments suggest, in Canada, as in the United States, the judicial branch is front-row-centre in the clash of cultural and social norms labelled "family values." More generally, since the advent of the *Canadian Charter of Rights and Freedoms* in 1982, the courts have played a not-quite-new, but certainly more vigorous, role in second-guessing the majoritarian impulses of the legislative branch when it comes to individual and minority rights.

On the whole, the *Charter* — and the courts' interpretation of it — has been largely popular.[148] But because courts now regularly strike down (and reinterpret by "reading into") parliamentary statutes, they have sparked a wave of academic critiques and political polemics that query or outright denounce their performance.

Limited Government

Before addressing these concerns, we will clarify the role of the courts in constitutional judicial review. Constitutional judicial review comes in three flavours: first, there is review of legislation to determine whether it is consistent with the division of powers between the federal and provincial levels of government (federalism judicial review); second, there is review of legislation to ensure consistency with the *Charter* (*Charter* judicial review); and, last, as we have seen, there is review of legislation to measure compliance with unwritten constitutional principles (nontextual judicial review).

---

146 As reported by *CBC News*, "Tory's Interview on *Charter* Creates Storm," 27 June 2004.
147 As reported in Campbell Clark, Brian Laghi and Steven Chase, "Leaders' Last Push for Power," *Globe and Mail*, 26 June 2004.
148 See Institute for Research on Public Policy (IRPP), "Public Opinion and the Courts" by Joseph Fletcher and Paul Howe, Choices 6, no. 3 (May 2000).

Together, these constitutional provisions constrain the scope of parliamentary supremacy, creating "limited" government. We have already discussed unwritten principles. It is worth looking briefly at the content of the written Constitution's government-limiting provisions.

First, the division of powers between the federal and provincial governments is a matter governed by the *Constitution Act, 1867*. The 1867 Act includes a list of powers to be exercised by the provincial governments and a list of powers to be exercised at the federal level. These powers are summarized in Table 2.2. Discerning the precise meaning of the often antiquated language used in the 1867 Act has been a matter for litigation since Confederation and is a topic well covered in other works.[149]

Table 2.2   Constitutional Division of Powers

Exclusive Powers	
Federal Powers (s. 91 of the 1867 Act)	**Provincial Powers (ss. 92, 92A and 93 of the 1867 Act)**
Chapeau: Laws for the Peace, Order, and good Government of Canada, in relation to all Matters not coming within the Classes of Subjects by this Act assigned exclusively to the Legislatures of the Provinces. 1A. The Public Debt and Property. 2. The Regulation of Trade and Commerce. 2A. Unemployment insurance. 3. The raising of Money by any Mode or System of Taxation. 4. The borrowing of Money on the Public Credit. 5. Postal Service. 6. The Census and Statistics. 7. Militia, Military and Naval Service, and Defence. 8. The fixing of and providing for the Salaries and Allowances of Civil and other Officers of the Government of Canada. 9. Beacons, Buoys, Lighthouses, and Sable Island. 10. Navigation and Shipping.	2. Direct Taxation within the Province in order to the raising of a Revenue for Provincial Purposes. 3. The borrowing of Money on the sole Credit of the Province. 4. The Establishment and Tenure of Provincial Offices and the Appointment and Payment of Provincial Officers. 5. The Management and Sale of the Public Lands belonging to the Province and of the Timber and Wood thereon. 6. The Establishment, Maintenance, and Management of Public and Reformatory Prisons in and for the Province. 7. The Establishment, Maintenance, and Management of Hospitals, Asylums, Charities, and Eleemosynary Institutions in and for the Province, other than Marine Hospitals. 8. Municipal Institutions in the Province. 9. Shop, Saloon, Tavern, Auctioneer, and other Licences in order to the raising of a Revenue for Provincial, Local, or Municipal Purposes.

---

149 See, in particular, Hogg, *Constitutional Law* and Patrick Monahan, *Constitutional Law*, 2d ed. (Toronto: Irwin Law, 2002). For a casebook compilation of key cases, see J.E. Magnet, *Constitutional Law of Canada*, 8th ed. (Edmonton: Juriliber, 2001).

Exclusive Powers	
Federal Powers (s. 91 of the 1867 Act)	**Provincial Powers (ss. 92, 92A and 93 of the 1867 Act)**
11. Quarantine and the Establishment and Maintenance of Marine Hospitals. 12. Sea Coast and Inland Fisheries. 13. Ferries between a Province and any British or Foreign Country or between Two Provinces. 14. Currency and Coinage. 15. Banking, Incorporation of Banks, and the Issue of Paper Money. 16. Savings Banks. 17. Weights and Measures. 18. Bills of Exchange and Promissory Notes. 19. Interest. 20. Legal Tender. 21. Bankruptcy and Insolvency. 22. Patents of Invention and Discovery. 23. Copyrights. 24. Indians, and Lands reserved for the Indians. 25. Naturalization and Aliens. 26. Marriage and Divorce. 27. The Criminal Law, except the Constitution of Courts of Criminal Jurisdiction, but including the Procedure in Criminal Matters. 28. The Establishment, Maintenance, and Management of Penitentiaries. 29. Such Classes of Subjects as are expressly excepted in the Enumeration of the Classes of Subjects by this Act assigned exclusively to the Legislatures of the Provinces.	10. Local Works and Undertakings other than such as are of the following Classes: (a) Lines of Steam or other Ships, Railways, Canals, Telegraphs, and other Works and Undertakings connecting the Province with any other or others of the Provinces, or extending beyond the Limits of the Province; (b) Lines of Steam Ships between the Province and any British or Foreign Country; (c) Such Works as, although wholly situate within the Province, are before or after their Execution declared by the Parliament of Canada to be for the general Advantage of Canada or for the Advantage of Two or more of the Provinces. 11. The Incorporation of Companies with Provincial Objects. 12. The Solemnization of Marriage in the Province. 13. Property and Civil Rights in the Province. 14. The Administration of Justice in the Province, including the Constitution, Maintenance, and Organization of Provincial Courts, both of Civil and of Criminal Jurisdiction, and including Procedure in Civil Matters in those Courts. 15. The Imposition of Punishment by Fine, Penalty, or Imprisonment for enforcing any Law of the Province made in relation to any Matter coming within any of the Classes of Subjects enumerated in this Section. 16. Generally all Matters of a merely local or private Nature in the Province. s. 92A Certain rights over non-renewable natural resources, forestry resources and electrical energy. s. 93 Laws in relation to education.
Shared Federal and Provincial Powers	
s. 95 Provinces may make laws in relation to agriculture in the Province, and to immigration into the Province. However, the Parliament of Canada may make laws in relation to agriculture in all or any of the Provinces, and to immigration into all or any of the Provinces. Any provincial law on these matters will have effect only if not repugnant to any Act of the Parliament of Canada.	

Second, the other, key source of government-limiting constitutional principles is the *Canadian Charter of Rights and Freedoms,* introduced via the *Constitution Act, 1982.* We summarize these *Charter* rights in Table 2.3. We note that sections 7 and 11(d) receive particularly detailed treatment from time to time in this and other chapters that follow, as do the democratic rights in sections 3 through 5.

Table 2.3   Charter of Rights and Freedoms

Subject		
Fundamental freedoms	Section 2	Everyone has the following fundamental freedoms: *a*) freedom of conscience and religion; *b*) freedom of thought, belief, opinion and expression, including freedom of the press and other media of communication; *c*) freedom of peaceful assembly; and *d*) freedom of association.
Democratic rights	Section 3	Citizens have the right to vote in an election of members of the House of Commons or of a legislative assembly and to be qualified for membership therein.
	Section 4	House of Commons and legislative assemblies must continue for no more than five years from the date fixed for the return of the writs of a general election of its members, subject to being extended in time of real or apprehended war, invasion or insurrection.
	Section 5	Parliament and of each legislature must sit at least once every twelve months.
Mobility rights	Section 6	Citizens of Canada have the right to enter, remain in and leave Canada and citizens and permanent residents have the right to move to and take up residence in any province, and to pursue the gaining of a livelihood in any province, subject to certain exceptions.
Legal rights	Section 7	Everyone has the right to life, liberty and security of the person and the right not to be deprived thereof except in accordance with the principles of fundamental justice.
	Section 8	Everyone has the right to be secure against unreasonable search or seizure.
	Section 9	Everyone has the right not to be arbitrarily detained or imprisoned.
	Section 10	Everyone has the right on arrest or detention *a*) to be informed promptly of the reasons therefore; *b*) to retain and instruct counsel without delay and to be informed of that right; and *c*) to have the validity of the detention determined by way of *habeas corpus* and to be released if the detention is not lawful.
	Section 11	Any person charged with an offence has the right *a*) to be informed without unreasonable delay of the specific offence;

Subject		
		b) to be tried within a reasonable time; *c*) not to be compelled to be a witness in proceedings against that person in respect of the offence; *d*) to be presumed innocent until proven guilty according to law in a fair and public hearing by an independent and impartial tribunal; *e*) not to be denied reasonable bail without just cause; *f*) except in the case of an offence under military law tried before a military tribunal, to the benefit of trial by jury where the maximum punishment for the offence is imprisonment for five years or a more severe punishment; *g*) not to be found guilty on account of any act or omission unless, at the time of the act or omission, it constituted an offence under Canadian or international law or was criminal according to the general principles of law recognized by the community of nations; *h*) if finally acquitted of the offence, not to be tried for it again and, if finally found guilty and punished for the offence, not to be tried or punished for it again; and *i*) if found guilty of the offence and if the punishment for the offence has been varied between the time of commission and the time of sentencing, to the benefit of the lesser punishment.
	Section 12	Everyone has the right not to be subjected to any cruel and unusual treatment or punishment.
	Section 13	A witness who testifies in any proceedings has the right not to have any incriminating evidence so given used to incriminate that witness in any other proceedings, except in a prosecution for perjury or for the giving of contradictory evidence.
	Section 14	A party or witness in any proceedings has the right to the assistance of an interpreter.
Equality rights	Section 15	Every individual is equal before and under the law and has the right to the equal protection and equal benefit of the law without discrimination and, in particular, without discrimination based on race, national or ethnic origin, colour, religion, sex, age or mental or physical disability. Affirmative action programs are not precluded by this right.
Language rights	Subsections 16–22	Rights giving equal status to French and English in Parliament, the government of Canada, the courts established by Parliament and in the equivalent institutions in New Brunswick.
Minority language educational rights	Section 23	Setting out the scope of the right to be educated in French or English.

The Judicial Function in Limited Government

Federalism review and, to a certain extent, nontextual judicial review pre-date the 1982 constitutional amendments. Courts repeatedly concluded that the *British North America Act* (as the 1867 Act was then known) had primacy over any Act of Parliament or the legislatures. In modern law, that preeminence is made emphatic in section 52 of the *Constitution Act, 1982*: the Constitution "is the supreme law of Canada, and any law that is incon-sistent with the provisions of the Constitution is, to the extent of the incon-sistency, of no force or effect."

The precise role of courts in policing laws to ensure compliance with the Constitution is clearest in the *Charter*. Section 24(1) of that instrument provides that "[a]nyone whose rights or freedoms, as guaranteed by this *Charter*, have been infringed or denied may apply to a court of competent jurisdiction to obtain such remedy as the court considers appropriate and just in the circumstances."

The Supreme Court has read sections 52 and 24 as implying that "courts in their trustee or arbiter role must perforce scrutinize the work of the legislature and executive not in the name of the courts, but in the inter-ests of the new social contract that was democratically chosen" in 1982.[150] Indeed, "the overriding effect of the *Constitution Act, 1982*, s. 52(1), is to give the Court not only the power, but also the duty, to regard the inconsistent statute, to the extent of the inconsistency, as being no longer 'of force or effect.'"[151]

Courts have interpreted this language of no "force or effect" in section 52 as opening the door to a number of remedies: "Depending upon the cir-cumstances, a court may simply strike down [legislation], it may strike down and temporarily suspend the declaration of invalidity, or it may resort to the techniques of reading down or reading in."[152] "Reading in" — where the Court incorporates new language into a statute that it believes may not be constitutionally omitted — has proven the most contentious application of section 52. In enunciating a reading in approach, the Court indicated that its purpose "is to be as faithful as possible within the requirements of the Constitution to the scheme enacted by the Legislature."[153] More recent-ly, in *Vriend v. Alberta*, the Court has set a firmer line.

In *Vriend*, the Court relied on the *Charter* to read in a protection against discrimination on the basis of sexual orientation into Alberta human rights

---

150   *Vriend v. Alberta*, [1998] 1 S.C.R. 493 at 564.

151   *R. v. Big M Drug Mart*, [1985] 1 S.C.R. 295 at 353.

152   *Schachter v. Canada*, [1992] 2 S.C.R. 679 at 695.

153   *Ibid.* at 700.

law. It did so in circumstances where the exclusion of sexual orientation protections in the law was "a conscious and deliberate legislative choice." Nevertheless, the Court called this enactment "undemocratic," holding that a "democracy requires that legislators take into account the interests of majorities and minorities alike, all of whom will be affected by the decisions they make. ... Where the interests of a minority have been denied consideration, especially where that group has historically been the target of prejudice and discrimination ... judicial intervention is warranted to correct a democratic process that has acted improperly."[154]

"Dialogue" Between the Courts and Parliament

In *Vriend*, the Court also explicitly endorsed a theory of judicial and legislative branch relations in which each side engages in a constitutional "dialogue":

> In reviewing legislative enactments and executive decisions to ensure constitutional validity, the courts speak to the legislative and executive branches. As has been pointed out, most of the legislation held not to pass constitutional muster has been followed by new legislation designed to accomplish similar objectives. ... By doing this, the legislature responds to the courts; hence the dialogue among the branches.[155]

The result is greater accountability because the work of each branch is reviewed by the other. This dialogue and enhanced accountability "have the effect of enhancing the democratic process, not denying it."[156]

The concept of dialogue has apparently tempered the Court's approach in at least one case where Parliament modified and reenacted a law initially found unconstitutional.[157] But dialogue does not mean that *Charter* remedies are exhausted once Parliament steps to the plate a second time: "Parliament must ensure that whatever law it passes, at whatever stage of the process, conforms to the Constitution. The healthy and important promotion of a dialogue between the legislature and the courts should not be debased to a rule of 'if at first you don't succeed, try, try again.'"[158]

---

154 *Vriend*, [1998] 1 S.C.R. 493 at 577–78.
155 *Ibid.* at 565.
156 *Ibid.* at 566.
157 See *R. v. Mills*, [1999] 3 S.C.R. 668 at para. 58, holding that "[i]f constitutional democracy is meant to ensure that due regard is given to the voices of those vulnerable to being overlooked by the majority, then this court has an obligation to consider respectfully Parliament's attempt to respond to such voices" and extending deference to Parliament's newest effort to enact the law in question.
158 *Sauvé v. Canada (Chief Electoral Officer)*, [2002] 3 S.C.R. 519 at para. 17.

Implications

Finding the soft spot in the relationship between the legislative and judicial branches on constitutional judicial review is a difficult task. What is remarkable, however, is the extent to which this issue has been politicized and the degree to which the Court has repeatedly felt the need to articulate expressly its view on the proper separation of powers. In their more thoughtful forms, criticisms of constitutional judicial review boil down to two complaints: first, that under the banner of constitutional supremacy, courts have usurped power that is properly the domain of Parliament. Put another way, wielding the Constitution — and particularly the *Charter* — the courts have unduly shrunk the zone of parliamentary supremacy.

Some critics object to this development on principle, preoccupied with the erosion of power of the one truly democratic branch of government. As one then-Reform Party Member of Parliament urged the Commons in 1998:

> federal legislation should not be amended or redrafted by judicial rulings. ... That is a centrally important subject which ought to seize all members of this place. ... This essentially is a debate not between parliamentary supremacy and judicial review, but between parliamentary supremacy or judicial supremacy. ... Ultimately in any system of government where checks and balances are divided and authority is separated between different branches of government, one must be supreme. ... The answer which the tradition of parliament and our common law has provided to us over the last several hundred years is that parliament is supreme. This is the highest court of the land. The buck stops here with respect to the law that is made for all Canadians.[159]

Other criticisms concerning Parliament's shrunken powers are sparked by the substantive approach to particular rights taken by the

---

159   Mr. Jason Kenney (Calgary Southeast, Ref.), *Hansard*, no. 117, 36th Parl., 1st Sess. (8 June 1998); see also Mr. Rick Casson (Lethbridge, Ref.), *ibid.* ("Regardless of personal beliefs, one way or another, the essence of this argument is founded in democracy. Either someone respects the tradition of parliamentary supremacy or they do not. If the Liberal government wants to rewrite laws in order to include same sex spouses, that is for the legislature and not for the judiciary to decide. This could not be more clear"); Senator Cools, *Debates of the Senate*, 35th Parl., 2d Sess., vol. 135 (16 April 1997) ("Judicial activism is the tendency by judges to use the courts to advance their political ideas and actions, usually relying on *Charter* and legislative protection of minority rights issues, by actively reading up, reading in, and striking down legislation. This judicial activism seeking constitutional domination and supremacy over Parliament is subverting parliamentary sovereignty and responsible government. It subverts the constitutional concept of consent of the governed and proposes government by the unelected judiciary.").

courts. Effectively, these complaints are of a system of government of the people, by the judges, for a minority of the people. Controversially, this minority tends to include criminals.[160] Adding a partisan air to the debate, it also includes other people doing things social conservatives in Canada's right-leaning political parties tend not to like, like marrying people of the same sex.[161]

A second, broad series of criticisms bemoan the propensity of Parliament itself to duck its responsibilities, leaving difficult questions of social policy to be adjudicated by the courts, not debated by the people's elected representatives. Of course, to the extent this second criticism is true, it inevitably compounds the first complaint: the courts do what Parliament should be doing.

The Usurping Court

On the whole, the first complaint — the courts stealing parliamentary sovereignty — is a paper tiger.

First, as the Court itself has pointed out,[162] the Canadian Constitution — at least in its *Charter* guise — preserves a huge swath of parliamentary sovereignty.[163] In *Vriend*, the Supreme Court noted that "parliamentary safe-

---

160 See, e.g., Mr. Bill Blaikie (Winnipeg–Transcona, NDP), *Hansard*, no. 172, 36th Parl., 1st Sess. (2 Feb. 1999) expressing "outrage" at a court decision on child pornography, urging a reaction by Parliament, and noting that "parliamentary supremacy ... is what the notwithstanding clause is all about and one of the reasons why I voted for the *Charter* at that time."

161 For complaints about the role of judges in "overstepping their jurisdiction" on same-sex marriage and criminal law issues, see, e.g., Mr. Jim Pankiw (Saskatoon–Humboldt, Ref.), *Hansard*, no. 117, 36th Parl., 1st Sess. (8 June 1998) ("in the 35th Parliament Motion no. M-264 proposing the legal recognition of same-sex spouses was defeated in this House by a vote of 52 to 124, almost a three to one margin. The will of Parliament on this issue is clear. Why then are the courts writing it in when Parliament has clearly already said no? The courts are overstepping their boundaries. They are overstepping their jurisdiction."); Mr. Vic Toews (Provencher, Conservative Party), *Hansard*, no. 016, 36th Parl., 3d Sess. (23 Feb. 2004) ("this Liberal government has allowed judges to become the most powerful force in setting social policy in Canada. Whether it is by allowing convicted murders to vote or by changing fundamental institutions like marriage, this government has substituted the supremacy of an elected Parliament with unelected judges."). See also Conservative Party of Canada, *The Issues* ("The Conservative Party will fight to give a greater voice to Parliament. We will ensure that issues like marriage are decided by Parliament, not the courts.").

162 *Vriend*, [1998] 1 S.C.R. 493 at 578.

163 See also Peter Hogg and Allison Thornton, "The Charter Dialogue between Courts and Legislatures," in Paul Howe and Peter Russell, eds., *Judicial Power and Canadian Democracy* (Kingston, ON: McGill-Queen's University Press, 2001) discussing how various aspects of the *Charter* leave the door open to a "dialogue" between courts and

guards" remain, despite the Court's "reading in" approach: "Governments are free to modify the amended legislation by passing exceptions and defences which they feel can be justified under s. 1 of the *Charter*. ... Moreover, the legislators can always turn to s. 33 of the *Charter*, the override provision, which in my view is the ultimate 'parliamentary safeguard.'"[164]

Section 1 of the *Charter* provides that the rights contained within it are guaranteed, but then subject "to such reasonable limits prescribed by law as can be demonstrably justified in a free and democratic society." Drawing from this language, the Court has articulated a complex justification test that may excuse a violation of a substantive *Charter* right, should its conditions be met.[165] In other words, rights in the Canadian Constitution are not absolute.

In any event, most of the rights in the *Charter* may be overridden by the exercise of democratic will. Section 33 — the "notwithstanding" provision — allows Parliament to "expressly declare in an Act of Parliament ... that the Act or a provision thereof shall operate notwithstanding" most *Charter* rights. Section 33 does not require a "super-majority." It may be invoked through the regular enactment process. It is, in other words, abundantly available to any Parliament, as opposition Members of the Commons have repeatedly noted.[166] Thus, section 33 preserves a large measure of parliamentary supremacy.

Yet, it has been used only a handful of times,[167] and never by the federal Parliament. There appears to be something deeply discomforting to legislatures about the prospect of announcing to the Canadian people, and the world at large, that rights will be ignored. Political inhibition, in other

---

legislatures. See also Janet Hiebert, *Charter Conflicts: What is Parliament's Role?* (Kingston, ON: McGill-Queen's University Press, 2002) discussing shared *Charter* responsibility between the courts and legislatures.

164 *Vriend*, [1998] 1 S.C.R. 493 at 578.

165 See, e.g., *R. v. Oakes*, [1986] 1 S.C.R. 103 and its progeny.

166 See Mr. Jason Kenney (Calgary Southeast, Ref.), *Hansard*, no. 117, 36th Parl., 1st Sess. (8 June 1998). ("This Parliament should maintain, as it has for hundreds of years, the ultimate power to re-enact legislation which it believes is consistent with our constitutional framework. ... That is why the framers of the 1982 *Constitution Act* included section 33, the notwithstanding clause, as the ultimate guarantor of parliamentary supremacy and we ought not be afraid to use it at the appropriate time.")

167 See discussion in Library of Parliament, *The Notwithstanding Clause of the Charter*, BP194-E (1997) discussing use by Quebec and Saskatchewan. But see also Tsvi Kahana, "The Notwithstanding Mechanism and Public Discussion: Lessons from the Ignored Practice of Section 33 of the *Charter*," (2001) 44 *Canadian Public Administration* 255, noting that the clause has in fact been used in sixteen pieces of legislation or bills in four Canadian jurisdictions.

words, is the most important constraint on parliamentary recourse to section 33. Indeed, section 33 was always intended as a last-ditch measure. In describing this override provision to Parliament in 1981, then-Minister of Justice Jean Chrétien called it a "safety valve which is unlikely ever to be used except in noncontroversial situations" and that it would be "politically very difficult for a government to introduce without very good reason a measure which applies notwithstanding the *Charter*."[168]

If section 33 is rarely used, that alone answers the objection to the "nondemocratic" nature of constitutional judicial review. If the political branch cannot muster up the courage to override a decision of the courts — and if parties that promise to do so are not elected — then perhaps court judgments do not offend the democratic will after all.[169]

It follows that where section 1 and section 33 do not apply, or legislatures chose not to rely upon them in *Charter* matters, it is an anachronism to argue that Canada possesses a system of parliamentary sovereignty. Instead, even outside the division of powers area, it now possesses a system of constitutional supremacy and of limited government, one that was devised by the political branches of government in 1982.[170] It seems disingenuous for a different generation of parliamentarians to label undemocratic the system put in place by their equally elected predecessors.

In any event, we also agree with the Supreme Court's conclusions in the *Quebec Secession Reference* that democracy means more than majoritar-

---

168 House of Commons, *Debates*, vol. 12, 32d Parl., 1st Sess. (20 Nov. 1981) at 13042–43.

169 As already noted, some pundits attribute the Conservative Party's unexpected erosion of electoral support in the last days of the 2004 federal election to anti-*Charter* comments such as those of Randy White noted earlier. See, e.g., John Ibbitson, "Tory Leader Should Study Tony Blair," *Globe and Mail*, 30 June 2004 ("The [socially conservative] blatherings of Randy White, Cheryl Gallant and Scott Reid cost Stephen Harper seats, especially in Ontario."); *Canadian Press*, "Harper to Stick Around Despite Loss," 8 July 2004 ("Randy White's musings about overriding the *Charter of Rights* to outlaw same-sex marriage sparked a storm in the final week of the campaign."); CTV Television, Inc. CTV News, 7 July 2004 ("Critics blame inflammatory comments from Harper's own MPs for derailing the campaign, like Randy White who suggested overriding Supreme Court decisions to outlaw gay marriage."); Robert Benzie, "Tories Pin Blame on Fear, Rogue Candidates," *Toronto Star*, 30 June 2004, quoting the Conservative Party's Ontario co-chair, John Baird: "... the Randy Whites and Cheryl Gallants put the fear of God in many voters."

170 Hon. Irwin Cotler (Minister of Justice and Attorney General of Canada, Lib.), *Hansard*, no. 016, 37th Parl., 3d Sess. (23 Feb. 2004) ("I want to advise the member opposite that we do not speak any longer about parliamentary supremacy. We have moved from being a parliamentary democracy to being a constitutional democracy, and that is the law of the land.").

ian rule.[171] It also means protection of certain individual and minority rights. The source of conflicts between Crown and Parliament ultimately culminating in parliamentary supremacy in the United Kingdom are revealing. Those disagreements were sparked, in large measure, by Parliament's disgust with the Crown's failure to repress vigorously religious minorities.[172] To that extent, the parliamentary supremacy celebrated by critics of judicial activism is actually a product of intolerance. As Senator Taylor mused in 2001, a "minority group is bound to be frightened about Parliament holding supremacy, especially if they are in a panic to trample on minority rights."[173]

Second, some critiques of "judicial activism" under the *Charter* seem to view *Charter* jurisprudence as an open-ended policy-making enterprise.[174] The result, say these critics, is that the Supreme Court "now functions more like a *de facto* third chamber of the legislature than a court."[175]

Certainly, the text of the *Charter* is often terse and the *Charter* remains a young instrument. For both of these reasons, courts regularly confront difficult and original *Charter* issues never before contemplated. The result is decisions that appear cut from whole cloth. It is also true, as we have said before, that courts in the common law tradition are law-makers.

They are, however, bound by practices and traditions that make them quite different than legislatures. Over time the Canadian Supreme Court has devised, and will continue to refine, an important body of precedent. Precedent is not an insignificant detail in the Canadian court system; it does influence outcomes in future cases, constrain judicial discretion and limit the mutability of *Charter* concepts. We do not wish to overstate the case: precedent can be distinguished or even overturned. Nevertheless, it does funnel courts in their "policy-making" enterprise. In these circumstances, the precise dictates of the *Charter*, as measured by the Court, should become more predictable with time. It is misleading, therefore, to see the *Charter* as an invitation for whimsical judges to impose their vision *du jour* on the political branches of government.

---

171 See also discussion in Lorraine Weinrib, "Canada's Constitutional Revolution: From Legislative to Constitutional State," (1999) 33 Isr. L.R. 13.

172 See discussion in, e.g., Ann Lyon, *Constitutional History of the United Kingdom* (2003) at 238 *et seq.*, describing Parliament's reactions to Charles II's tolerance of Catholicism.

173 The Standing Senate Committee on Energy, the Environment and Natural Resources, *Evidence* (10 Dec. 2001).

174 See, e.g., Morton and Knopff, *The Charter Revolution* at 33 ("[t]he *Charter* does not so much guarantee rights as give judges the power to make policy by choosing among competing interpretations of broadly worded provisions").

175 *Ibid.* at 58.

Where we would side with the critics in their objection to the usurping court is in relation to the Supreme Court's ready willingness to unearth unwritten constitutional principles. For reasons set out above, we find this tendency troubling. Further, we are strongly sympathetic to those who complain about the current judicial appointments process. An approach to appointments developed for a system of parliamentary supremacy is entirely inadequate for a system of constitutional supremacy. We return to this matter in chapter 4.

The Cowardly Political Branch

The second, and ultimately more persuasive, argument relating to constitutional judicial review is the propensity of the political branches of governments to leave matters to the court that should be decided by the legislature itself. This tendency is reflected through both actions and omissions.

With respect to omissions, the political branches appear often to have simply abandoned the field, leaving politically unpalatable decision-making to the judiciary. As Professor Harry Arthurs writes in a luminous critique of Canada's constitutionalism:

> important national issues often fail to appear on the parliamentary agen-
> da, or if they do, Parliament seems unwilling or unable to produce any-
> thing like a national consensus; and if a consensus does somehow
> emerge, it is seldom translated into effective public policies or backed up
> by adequate public resources. This has caused frustration especially
> among groups that feel — and often are — excluded or marginalized.
> When these groups are unable to influence public policies through con-
> ventional social and political mobilization, constitutional litigation seems
> the only possible alternative.[176]

In other words, the political branches are not doing their job, and citizens view the courts as more likely to meet their aspirations.

Some critics, examining this phenomenon, see courts as the problem. They envisage the so-called dialogue between courts and legislatures as a monologue because judicial opinions give political credence to one policy position on an issue, lending the advantages of political inertia to that group. After courts have spoken, polarized political institutions find it easier to abdicate responsibility than to step to the plate again.[177] These objec-

---

176 Harry Arthurs, "Constitutional Courage," (2004) 49 McGill L.J. 1 at 12.
177 F.L. Morton, "Dialogue or Monologue," in Howe and Russell, *Judicial Power and Cana-
     dian Democracy.*

tions typically set the stage for a strong condemnation of *Charter*-era judicial review.

For our part, we agree fully that courts should be cognizant of their proper role and not reach beyond their anointed tasks. It is wrong, however, to lay the blame for a feeble political branch at the feet of the courts. In fact, the very actions of the political branches compound the problem of omission and abdication, not least excessive use of "references" to the courts. For instance, section 53 of the *Supreme Court Act*[178] allows the Governor-in-Council — the Governor General acting on the advice of the federal Cabinet — to refer to the Supreme Court for "hearing and consideration important questions of law or fact concerning," among other things, "the interpretation of the *Constitution Acts*," the "constitutionality or interpretation of any federal or provincial legislation" or "the powers of the Parliament of Canada, or of the legislatures of the provinces, or of the respective governments thereof, whether or not the particular power in question has been or is proposed to be exercised."

The Supreme Court has held that this reference procedure is constitutional, "even though the rendering of advisory opinions is quite clearly done outside the framework of adversarial litigation, and such opinions are traditionally obtained by the executive from the law officers of the Crown."[179] In fact, the federal executive has often relied on the reference procedure to refer constitutional matters to the Court, including in cases involving difficult political issues.[180]

Yet, in our view, recourse to reference jurisdiction in these matters invites the courts to step in exactly where elected parliamentarians should be expected to weigh important political, legal and policy considerations. In other words, courts are asked to take a predominant role in crafting constitutionally proper approaches to public policy issues. In the constitutional "dialogue" discussed earlier in this chapter, the court is asked to speak first, and to issue sometimes detailed marching orders to legislatures.

Here, complaints concerning the erosion of parliamentary supremacy have traction.[181] In many instances, these references create the wrong optic

---

178 R.S.C., 1985, c. S-26.

179 *Quebec Secession Reference*, [1998] 2 S.C.R. 217 at 233.

180 For example, *Quebec Secession Reference*, [1998] 2 S.C.R. 217, *Reference re Resolution to Amend the Constitution*, [1981] 1 S.C.R. 753, and *In the Matter of a Reference by the Governor in Council concerning the Proposal for an Act respecting certain aspects of legal capacity for marriage for civil purposes, as set out in Order in Council P.C. 2003-1055*, 2004 SCC 79.

181 See, e.g., Senator Grafstein, *Debates of the Senate*, vol. 138, 36th Parl., 2d Sess. (6 April 2000) ("I do not believe in advisories. They are fundamentally in conflict with parliamentary supremacy. We take our duties here; we legislate here. It is not fair for us to

as to how our democracy should work, and which branches of government should be asked to take a first stab at policy. Enhancing the suspect nature of references is the fact that, under section 53 of the *Supreme Court Act*, it is the federal Cabinet — not Parliament — that refers the matter to the Court. This further muddles the separation of powers: under section 53, the executive branch is empowered to usurp Parliament's (often unrealized) policy-contemplation function and hand it to the Court.

We do not claim here that there is no room for references. References, in our view, are legitimate if there is no other practicable way to place important and intractable questions of constitutional law before the Court. We might place the *Quebec Secession Reference* in this category: it was a case establishing the constitutional parameters of momentous political events that, were they to happen, could quickly spin out of control absent a shared understanding of the constitutional ground rules.

However, other issues that the Court pronounces upon in references could well have been ultimately adjudicated through the adversarial process. This is most acutely the case in the recent (and controversial) reference to the Supreme Court concerning the definition of marriage.[182] In these circumstances, even the weak concept of separation of powers in our system, coupled with Parliament's residual supremacy, should mean that Parliament takes the first shot at crafting constitutionally compliant law. This may not be the most efficient procedure. It is, however, the most democratically appropriate.

To this we would add: referrals to the Supreme Court sometimes smack of partisan politics, where governments of the day duck controversial issues either to delay having to deal with them, or anticipating a deci-

---

criticize the courts, as we have done, and then turn an issue over to the courts. That is why I do not believe in advisories. We take our responsibilities here and let the courts, in their independence, take their responsibilities.").

182 Order-in-Council P.C. 2003-1055, dated 16 July 2003. This case raised equality right issues. Notably, the government finances private litigation on equality rights, reducing the prospect that poor financing will preclude effective litigation of these matters. See Court Challenges Program of Canada, www.ccppcj.ca/. In its decision, the Supreme Court declined to answer at least one of the questions referred to it — on whether the proposed federal legislation was compliant with the *Charter*. In so doing, it noted "[t]here is no precedent for answering a reference question which mirrors issues already disposed of in lower courts where an appeal was available but not pursued." *Certain aspects of legal capacity for marriage for civil purposes*, 2004 SCC 79 at para. 68. This move was perceived as a clever response to the government's attempt to obtain political cover from the Court for its potentially divisive same-sex legislation. Kirk Markin, "Deft Court Crafts Elegant Opinion," *Globe and Mail*, 10 Dec. 2004, A7.

sion that they can then claim ties their hand. In either instance, the government portrays itself as at the mercy of the judicial process, and diverts political attention from its failure of nerve.

All told, either through its inaction and its actions, Parliament and the executive have themselves politicized the judicial process. We agree that Canadian democracy is the poorer for it. But it is politicians, and not the courts, who are to blame.

Administrative Judicial Review: Courts and the Executive

Overview

Courts have a relationship with the executive that is quite different from their relationship with Parliament. Certainly, the executive is subject to the same constitutional "limited" government provisions as is Parliament. However, the courts also have a supplemental role in judicially reviewing the executive.

As has already been suggested, courts review actions taken by the executive branch to ensure that they comply either with the grant of power delegated by Parliament, or with another source of authority, usually the royal prerogative. Acting in this capacity, courts *defend* parliamentary supremacy, and the hierarchical relationship between the legislative and executive branches. They also preserve the rule of law: members of the executive branch must "justify their actions by pointing to specific legislative authority in the same way that any citizen would have to be prepared to show that his or her acts were lawful."[183]

Though ultimately justified for these constitutional reasons, this form of judicial review does not typically engage constitutional issues. It is conducted, in other words, on the parliamentary supremacy side of the trip switch: the courts are Parliament's foot soldiers in holding the executive to account. They ensure that the executive does not stray beyond its mandate, and engage in a "jurisdictional" error.

Parliament is thus generally free to dictate to the courts exactly how this judicial review of executive action should be conducted, by whom, on what grounds, and how aggressively. And in fact, Parliament often does limit the circumstances in which courts may review decisions made by the executive agencies and tribunals to which it delegates power by introducing into the relevant statutes so-called "privative clauses."

---

183 *National Corn Growers Association v. Canada*, [1990] 2 S.C.R. 1324 at 1333 *per* Dickson, Lamer and Wilson JJ.

Constitutional Basis for Judicial Review on Jurisdictional Grounds

We need to underscore, however, that a legislature is only *generally* free to introduce these court-excluding, privative clauses. Parliamentary supremacy in administrative law gives way to constitutional supremacy on at least one matter: the question of whether courts can be barred by a legislature from conducting any sort of administrative judicial review at all. As noted above, where the issue is "may the legislative branch bar review by a provincial superior court of whether the provincial executive remains within its jurisdiction," the answer is "no," by reason of section 96 of the 1867 Act.[184]

Judicial review for jurisdictional error by the executive is, in other words, constitutionalized, at least where superior courts are asked to review provincial executives. Parliamentary supremacy does not extend so far as to permit the elimination of a superior court function in policing the separation of powers between the executive and the legislative branches, and maintaining parliamentary supremacy itself.

In our view, this is a sensible prohibition, if difficult to discern from the text of section 96 itself. If a legislature were, with one breath, to delegate powers to the executive branch, and in another, preclude review by courts ensuring that the executive does not stray beyond this legislative grant, no effective means of holding the executive branch to its place in the separation of powers would exist. The rule of law, in such circumstances, would be dependent on the legislature itself policing every little detail of the executive's actions, an enormous undertaking likely well beyond the capacity of its membership. It is difficult to imagine, for instance, a legislature deciding whether a given public official complied fully in every case with the full complement of complex rules governing licensing of some regulated activity.

It is possible to imagine the legislature creating a separate administrative tribunal to handle such matters, as it often has. However, absent mechanisms to ensure the independence of these tribunals from the rest of the executive, the legislature would be leaving the proverbial henhouse protected by guard dogs accountable to foxes. The inevitable question would be: who reviews the actions of these tribunals (i.e., the guard dogs)? As we have already suggested above, we believe it logical — and probably necessary — to reserve ultimate review jurisdiction over the executive in the hands of courts already sheltered by judicial independence, a concept discussed below.

---

184 See section C.1.a) above.

That said, this section 96 jurisprudence raises at least two issues, one a narrow question of law and the other a mixed legal and policy question: first, does the section 96 limitation apply also to judicial review of *federal* administrative action; second, if review for jurisdictional error is preserved for constitutional reasons, what is a "jurisdictional error"?

Section 96 of the *Constitution Act* and Federal Judicial Review

Turning to the first question, the existence of a constitutionalized judicial review power of courts in relation to the *federal* executive is remarkably unclear.

As a point of principle, the same justifications for preserving judicial review of provincial executives extend to the federal executive: except for those narrow powers assigned it in the 1867 Act, the federal executive branch is subordinate to Parliament, and the courts should be able to ensure that the executive does not stray beyond its jurisdiction. The Supreme Court has itself concluded that in relation to "the maintenance of the rule of law through the protection of the judicial role," section 96 "restricts not only the legislative competence of provincial legislatures, but of Parliament as well."[185] Institutionally, however, the relationship between the courts and the federal executive is different than the relationship between the courts and the provincial executives.

At the provincial level, the superior courts — staffed by federal appointees pursuant to section 96 — are the default judicial review courts. At the federal level, however, the *Federal Courts Act* assigns most administrative judicial review functions to the Federal Courts of Canada.[186] Notably, the Federal Courts are not section 96 courts. They are courts created by Parliament under section 101 of the 1867 Act. Section 101 empowers Parliament to create a "General Court of Appeal for Canada" — the Supreme Court of Canada — and "any additional Courts for the better Administration of the Laws of Canada" — in practice the Tax Court of Canada and the Federal Courts of Canada.

These provisions raise an important question: is the authority of the section 101 Federal Courts of Canada to review the federal executive constitutionalized, at least in relation to jurisdictional errors? After all, these Federal Courts are not section 96 courts, and thus do not benefit from the

---

185 *Re Remuneration of Judges*, [1997] 3 S.C.R. 3 at para. 88.

186 Note that the Federal Courts enjoy concurrent jurisdiction with the provincial superior courts where "applicants are seeking to challenge the constitutionality of legislation or where the applicants are seeking *Charter* remedies." *Gao v. Canada (Minister of Citizenship and Immigration)*, [2000] O.J. No. 2784 at para. 23 (S.C.J.). See also *Reza v. Canada*, [1994] 2 S.C.R. 394.

section 96 origin for constitutionalized judicial review. The answer to this question is "maybe."

The Federal Courts themselves have cited the Supreme Court's section 96 jurisprudence in concluding that judicial review of the federal executive is always available for jurisdictional error.[187] Strangely, however, there is no crystal clear jurisprudence holding that a privative clause purporting to deny the Federal Courts judicial review authority over jurisdictional errors would be constitutionally infirm.[188] Indeed, recent Supreme Court jurisprudence underscores that the Federal Courts have no "inherent jurisdiction," and thus their powers are limited to those given to them by statute.[189] From this it follows that were Parliament to take the judicial review power away, the Federal Court's supervisory administrative law role would evaporate.

In so acting, however, Parliament could not insulate the executive from court review of *any kind*. Provincial superior courts would likely fill the vacuum. These provincial superior courts likely preserve a residual constitutional authority to review the federal executive for jurisdictional errors.[190]

187　See *Canada (House of Commons) v. Vaid*, [2003] 1 F.C. 602 at 638 (C.A.), on appeal to the Supreme Court of Canada at the time of this writing; *Canada (Privacy Commissioner) v. Canada (Labour Relations Board)*, [1996] 3 F.C. 609 at para. 77 (T.D.) ("The supervisory authority of superior courts over administrative tribunals in the case of an alleged want or excess of jurisdiction has been held to have its source in the constitution"). But see *Global Television v. CEP*, 2004 FCA 78 at para. 14 (where the court suggested that the Federal Court's judicial review powers "rests on express statutory language, rather than, as in the case of provincial boards, on the common law of judicial review and the judicial interpretation of preclusive clauses, backed by the constitutional guarantee of a right to the judicial review of the proceedings of administrative agencies for excess or lack of jurisdiction").

188　But see *Canadian Imperial Bank of Commerce v. Rifou*, [1986] 3 F.C. 486 at 493 (C.A.), *per* Urie and Mahoney JJ.'s separate concurring reasons (suggesting that there is a core of judicial powers that the federal Parliament may not constitutionally transfer to administrative bodies, and that "the availability of judicial review is a *sine qua non*").

189　*Canada (Human Rights Commission) v. Canadian Liberty Net*, [1998] 1 S.C.R. 626 at 653 ("even when squarely within the realm of valid federal law, the Federal Court of Canada is not presumed to have jurisdiction in the absence of an express federal enactment").

190　See, e.g., *ibid.* at 658 ("the doctrine of inherent jurisdiction operates to ensure that, having once analysed the various statutory grants of jurisdiction, there will always be a court which has the power to vindicate a legal right independent of any statutory grant. The court which benefits from the inherent jurisdiction is the court of general jurisdiction, namely, the provincial superior court."); *Black* (2001), 54 O.R. (3d) 215 at para. 76 ("if Parliament has left a 'gap' in its grant of statutory jurisdiction to the Federal Court, the institutional and constitutional position of provincial superior courts warrants granting them this residual jurisdiction over federal matters").

Jurisdictional Error

The second issue raised by this constitutional (and in the case of federal administrative law, presumed constitutional) judicial review power is "what exactly do the courts mean by 'jurisdictional error'"? Put another way, if Parliament can deny courts a judicial review function in relation to the executive branch for everything but a jurisdictional error, what exactly constitutes such an error? At first blush, whether the executive acts without jurisdiction or not seems a simple question. If a statute authorizes a minister to regulate deer, and that minister issues licences for lobster, his or her jurisdiction is obviously exceeded. On the other hand, where the delegating statute is more ambiguous, and the breadth of the minister's authority less certain, it may be more difficult to discern the precise zone of that minister's jurisdiction.

The Pragmatic and Functional Test

Grappling with this conundrum is not something we can do in detail in this book. Suffice it to say, however, that the Supreme Court has traced a perplexing and confusing line on this question, and presently applies what it terms a "pragmatic and functional test" designed (at least in its original iteration) to distinguish between jurisdictional and non-jurisdictional errors committed by the executive.[191]

Not surprisingly, this test was originally sparked by the advent of sweeping legislative privative clauses purporting to rob the courts of their reviewing powers. It has now taken on a slightly different hue, one prompted by the Supreme Court's rethinking of its role in policing the separation of powers between the executive and the legislative branches, even in the absence of privative clauses. Specifically, in the course of performing its role in preserving the hierarchy of the *legislative* and executive branches, the Supreme Court's approach has been affected by its views on the proper separation of powers between the *judicial* and executive branches.

In this respect, for all the complaints about judicial overreaching in constitutional judicial review, the Supreme Court has carved out a largely deferential role for the courts in the area of administrative judicial review. At least nominally, the Supreme Court's pragmatic and functional test is designed to

---

191 See, e.g., *U.E.S., Local 298 v. Bibeault*, [1988] 2 S.C.R. 1048 at 1088, setting out the purpose and content of the pragmatic and functional test; *Canadian Broadcasting Corp. v. Canada*, [1995] 1 S.C.R. 157 at para. 30, discussing the role of the pragmatic and functional test in "distinguishing jurisdictional questions from questions of law within a tribunal's jurisdiction."

extract from an assortment of variables Parliament's "intent" as to where the jurisdictional limits of the power delegated to the executive lies.[192]

In no small measure, the perceived expertise of the executive agency in the area at issue, relative to that of the courts, determines the outcome of this legislative intent analysis.[193] Thus, the Court's approach to administrative judicial review has involved "a growing recognition on the part of courts that they may simply not be as well equipped as administrative tribunals or agencies to deal with issues that Parliament has chosen to regulate through bodies exercising delegated power."[194] Specialized administrative bodies — and particularly the many specialized tribunals established by statute — may know their business better than do the generalist courts.

The Spectrum of Standards of Review

This approach makes sense, in theory. The practice has been more difficult. For instance, should the court conclude that that the agency is highly expert in the subject matter of the lawsuit, it will often accord a highly deferential "standard of review" in assessing the legitimacy of the agency's decisions. It may conclude that it should intervene only where the decision is "patently unreasonable." A patently unreasonable decision is, in the Court's longstanding view, a clear jurisdictional error.[195] It includes a decision the court views as "clearly irrational."[196] In this category also fall otherwise proper powers exercised by a government official in bad faith, for improper purposes or on the basis of irrelevant considerations.[197] In each instance, the Court has effectively determined that Parliament could not have intended that the power delegated by it to the executive be exercised in this way, at least absent express statutory language to this effect.

---

192 *Pezim v. British Columbia (Superintendent of Brokers)*, [1994] 2 S.C.R. 557 at 589–90 (the test for the standard of review is designed to discern the legislative intent regarding the scope of the agency's jurisdiction).

193 *Canada (Director of Investigation and Research) v. Southam Inc.*, [1997] 1 S.C.R. 748 at para. 50, describing expertise as the "most important of the factors that a court must consider in settling on a standard of review."

194 *National Corn Growers*, [1990] 2 S.C.R. 1324 at 1336.

195 *Bibeault*, [1988] 2 S.C.R. 1048 at 1086.

196 *Canada (Attorney General) v. Public Service Alliance of Canada*, [1993] 1 S.C.R. 941 at 963–64, *per* Cory J.

197 See, e.g., *Suresh v. Canada (Minister of Citizenship and Immigration)*, [2002] 1 S.C.R. 3 at para. 29, labelling as patently unreasonable a discretionary decision "made arbitrarily or in bad faith," unsupported on the evidence, or where the minister failed to consider the appropriate factors.

A less expert agency is likely to attract less deference from the courts, who will then set a much lower threshold for jurisdictional error. Thus, in some instances, the courts will intervene with a nonexpert body to correct a "jurisdictional" error simply where the court views the decision as incorrect.

Finally, lying somewhere in between "patently unreasonable" and "correctness" is a third standard of review: unreasonableness *simpliciter*, or "clearly" unreasonable. This intermediate standard of review is usually reserved for executive decisions in circumstances where the variables the court considers as part of its pragmatic and functional test point in different directions, some counselling high levels of deference, others suggesting low levels of deference.

Procedural Fairness

Meanwhile, irrespective of any pragmatic and functional test, the courts will intervene in response to violations of something called "common law procedural fairness" — basically a due process standard imposed by the courts on executive branch decision-making.[198] Here, the courts have essentially concluded that Parliament could not possibly have intended that power delegated by it to the executive would be exercised without reference to basic standards of due process,[199] although this supposition may be reversed by clear statutory language.

The precise content of this procedural fairness depends enormously on the context. However, it inevitably requires some form of notice of a pending decision to a person owed the fairness, and an opportunity for that person to comment. It also requires that the official making the decision be sufficiently unbiased.

This is a reasonable bit of common law law-making, if somewhat dependent on the legal fiction of an absent-minded Parliament.[200] Even in the area of procedural fairness, however, the courts have sometimes pulled their punch: where a court concludes that the power being exercised by the

---

198 *Moreau-Berube v. New Brunswick (Judicial Council)*, [2002] 1 S.C.R. 249 at para. 74, (procedural fairness requires "no assessment of the appropriate standard of judicial review. Evaluating whether procedural fairness, or the duty of fairness, has been adhered to by a tribunal requires an assessment of the procedures and safeguards required in a particular situation").

199 See, e.g., *Xwave Solutions Inc. v. Canada (Public Works & Government Services)*, 2003 FCA 301 at para. 12 ("Parliament is presumed not to authorize agencies to breach the duty of fairness.").

200 See Martha Jackman, "Rights and Participation: The Use of the *Charter* to Supervise the Regulatory Process," (1990) 4 C.J.A.L.P 23 for a discussion of these sorts of procedural protections and democratic governance.

executive is, in fact, a form of delegated *legislative* power — say, a power to make regulations — procedural fairness need not be observed. After all, as discussed in chapter 5, the courts may not review the process followed Parliament itself on the basis of due process standards.[201] As we note in chapter 5, this approach is deeply unsatisfactory, not least because of ambiguity as to what exactly constitutes a delegated "legislative" power.

Implications

As is no doubt clear from even this cursory discussion, judicial review of the executive branch has become perplexingly complex, to the point that even justices of the Supreme Court have expressed dismay.[202] This complexity stems from the Supreme Court's valiant effort to be measured in its oversight role, and acknowledge the limitations of the judicial branch.

In practice, however, the sheer opacity of the Court's administrative judicial review jurisprudence has rendered the circumstances in which courts will intervene to police jurisdictional errors by the executive impossible to predict in advance, and difficult to explain clearly afterwards.

Like many others, we are not persuaded by the angels-on-pinheads quality of some of the legal distinctions and tests employed by the Supreme Court in this area of the law. More than that, we do not see how a system based on the rule of law is preserved where, even absent express authorization from Parliament, courts conclude that at least some agencies may act in a fashion just short of patently unreasonable (i.e., clearly irrational), and still be immune to judicial review. Many lawyers, no doubt, have tried valiantly to explain to dumbfounded clients that they lost their judicial review case because the government acted, yes, unreasonably, but not clearly irrationally. Certainly, the credibility of a democratic governance system is not enhanced by such holdings.

In our view, in this area, the courts have become too mired in contemplating the separation of powers between executive and *judiciary*. If the ultimate objective of administrative judicial review is to preserve the separation of powers between the executive and *Parliament*, parliamentary supremacy and the rule of law, then the courts should simply get on with these jobs. If, in the course of performing this function, questions arise about the proper separation of powers between the judicial and executive branches — the question of deference — then this is a matter for Parliament to regulate.

---

201 See, e.g., *Wells*, [1999] 3 S.C.R. 199 at para. 59.

202 See, e.g., *Toronto (City) v. C.U.P.E., Local 79*, [2003] 3 S.C.R. 77, *per* LeBel and Deschamps JJ., critiquing the Court's standard of review jurisprudence.

Courts will, for constitutional reasons, continue to review for jurisdictional errors. Parliament should now indicate exactly where these jurisdictional lines lie through legislative provisions much clearer than ineffective privative clauses or the "intent" discerned through an unpersuasive "pragmatic and functional" test. Outlining specific standards of review to be employed in reviewing specified powers by specific executive agencies cannot anticipate every instance in which jurisdictional questions may arise. But inserting such provisions in the statutes delegating power to executive bodies would be a start, one properly consistent with parliamentary supremacy. If people are to be left without a judicial remedy where executive agencies render simply unreasonable or incorrect decisions, it should be politicians accountable to an electorate that send out these marching orders.

b) Institutional Separation of Powers

Having outlined the jurisdictional separation between the courts and the political branches, we note that there is also an "institutional" dimension to this separation. Specifically, the judicial and parliamentary branches have carved out zones where each may not meddle with the other. The judiciary is protected by judicial independence, rendering them arm's-length from the other branches of government. Parliament, for its part, retains certain core parliamentary privileges, effectively preserving it from courts' intrusions. Both of these immunity-like concepts stem (at least in part) from the unwritten constitution and in particular the preamble to the 1867 Act.

Judicial Independence

Significance

One does not need to search the Supreme Court's jurisprudence for long to find many pithy statements about "judicial independence." Judicial independence, says the Supreme Court, is the "lifeblood of constitutionalism in democratic societies."[203] It is "essential to the achievement and proper functioning of a free, just and democratic society based on the principles of constitutionalism and the rule of law."[204]

Judicial independence requires "objective conditions that ensure the judiciary's freedom to act without interference from any other entity."[205] It ensures that "judges, as the arbiters of disputes, are at complete liberty to decide individual cases on their merits without interference."[206] By insulat-

---

203 *Beauregard v. Canada*, [1986] 2 S.C.R. 56 at 70.
204 *Mackin v. New Brunswick (Minister of Finance)*, [2002] 1 S.C.R. 405 at para. 34.
205 *Ell v. Alberta*, [2003] 1 S.C.R. 857 at para. 18.
206 *Ibid.* at para. 21.

ing judges from retaliation for their decisions, it guarantees that "the power of the state is exercised in accordance with the rule of law and the provisions of our Constitution. In this capacity, courts act as a shield against unwarranted deprivations by the state of the rights and freedoms of individuals."[207]

Judicial independence also preserves the separation of powers between the three branches of our democracy by "depoliticizing" the relationship between the judiciary and the other two branches: "the legislature and executive cannot, and cannot appear to, exert political pressure on the judiciary, and conversely ... members of the judiciary should exercise reserve in speaking out publicly on issues of general public policy that are or have the potential to come before the courts, that are the subject of political debate, and which do not relate to the proper administration of justice."[208]

Constitutional Basis

Judicial independence is a richly constitutional principle, accorded "explicit constitutional reference" in sections 96 to 100 of the *Constitution Act, 1867* and section 11(d) of the *Canadian Charter of Rights and Freedoms.*[209] Thus, in the Supreme Court's words, "s. 99 guarantees the security of tenure of superior court judges; s. 100 guarantees the financial security of judges of the superior, district, and county courts; and s. 96 has come to guarantee the core jurisdiction of superior, district, and county courts against legislative encroachment, which I also take to be a guarantee of judicial independence."[210]

For its part, section 11(d) of the *Charter* provides that any person charged with an offence has the right "to be presumed innocent until proven guilty according to law in a fair and public hearing by an independent and impartial tribunal." These textual provisions have, however, a limited scope. Thus, sections 96 through 100 of the 1867 Act are restricted to superior courts and section 11(d) of the *Charter* is confined to courts adjudicating the guilt of those charged with (usually) criminal offences.[211]

Nevertheless, judicial independence applies more broadly than simply to these courts. At some level, judicial independence is one of the principles of "fundamental justice" promised by section 7 of the *Charter.*[212] More crit-

---

207 *Ibid.* at para. 22.
208 *Re Remuneration of Judges,* [1997] 3 S.C.R. 3 at para. 140.
209 *Ell,* [2003] 1 S.C.R. 857 at para. 18.
210 *Re Remuneration of Judges,* [1997] 3 S.C.R. 3 at para. 84.
211 *Ell,* [2003] 1 S.C.R. 857 at para. 18; *Re Remuneration of Judges,* [1997] 3 S.C.R. 3.
212 *Re Application under s. 83.28 of the Criminal Code,* 2004 SCC 42 at para. 81.

ically in the Supreme Court's jurisprudence, the written Constitution does not "comprise an exhaustive and definitive code for the protection of judicial independence."[213] Judicial independence is "one of the original principles of the English Constitution,"[214] dating to the *Act of Settlement* of 1701.[215] Mostly an effort to secure the British Crown for Protestantism, this Act provides that judges are to hold office *quamdiu se bene gesserint* — during good behaviour — removable only upon the address of both Houses of Parliament. Meanwhile, their salaries are to be "ascertained and established."

Drawing on this U.K. legacy, the preamble to the 1867 Act — promising a constitution in principle similar to that of the United Kingdom — incorporates judicial independence into the Canadian Constitution as "one of the pillars upon which our constitutional democracy rests."[216] Because of this unwritten constitutional norm, judicial independence has "grown into a principle that now extends to all courts, not just the superior courts of this country."[217]

Assessing Judicial Independence

For the Supreme Court, "[t]he general test for the presence or absence of independence consists in asking whether a reasonable person who is fully informed of all the circumstances would consider that a particular court enjoyed the necessary independent status."[218] Thus, independence includes both a requirement of actual independence, and also conditions sufficient to give rise to a reasonable perception of independence on the part of a reasonable and well-informed person.[219] As the Court puts it, "[c]onfidence in our system of justice requires a healthy perception of judicial independence to be maintained amongst the citizenry. Without the perception of independence, the judiciary is unable to 'claim any legitimacy or command the respect and acceptance that are essential to it.'"[220]

Elements of Judicial Independence

In practice, judicial independence has two dimensions. First, the "individual" impartiality of judges must be preserved: "The integrity of judicial

---

213 *Re Remuneration of Judges*, [1997] 3 S.C.R. 3 at para. 85.
214 *Re Application under s. 83.28*, 2004 SCC 42 at para. 80, citing W.R. Lederman, "The Independence of the Judiciary," in A. Linden, ed., *The Canadian Judiciary* (Toronto: Osgoode Hall Law School, 1976) at 2.
215 12 & 13 Will. 3, c. 2. See discussion in *Ell*, [2003] 1 S.C.R. 857 at para. 19.
216 *Ell*, [2003] 1 S.C.R. 857 at para. 19.
217 *Re Remuneration of Judges*, [1997] 3 S.C.R. 3 at para. 106.
218 *Mackin*, [2002] 1 S.C.R. 405 at para. 38.
219 *Ibid.*
220 *Ell*, [2003] 1 S.C.R. 857 at para. 23, citing *Mackin*, [2002] 1 S.C.R. 405 at para. 38.

decision making depends on an adjudicative process that is untainted by outside pressures. This gives rise to the individual dimension of judicial independence, that is, the need to ensure that a particular judge is free to decide upon a case without influence from others."[221] Thus, "no outsider — be it government, pressure group, individual or even another judge — should interfere in fact, or attempt to interfere, with the way in which a judge conducts his or her case and makes his or her decision."[222] Further, "[t]he judge must not fear that after issuance of his or her decision, he or she may be called upon to justify it to another branch of government."[223]

Second, the "institutional" independence of the judicial branch from the legislative and executive branches must be guaranteed, a reflection of the deep commitment "to the separation of powers between and amongst the legislative, executive, and judicial organs of government."[224] Absent this protection, courts could not be expected to play their vital role adjudicating disputes between the federal and provincial governments, safeguarding the constitutional distribution of powers and ensuring "that the power of the state is exercised in accordance with the rule of law and the provisions of our Constitution."[225]

In practice, both of these forms of independence depend on three guarantees: financial security, security of tenure and administrative independence. Financial security relates to the pay judges receive for performing their job. It protects against an "unscrupulous government" that "could utilize its authority to set judges' salaries as a vehicle to influence the course and outcome of adjudication."[226]

Security of tenure goes to how judges may be dismissed. It insulates judges from the fear that their job may depend on a given outcome in a case before them.

Administrative independence centres on the means by which judges hearing a given matter are determined. It precludes governments selecting judges viewed as most likely to favour its case.

Table 2.4 outlines the individual and institutional independence requirements the Supreme Court has identified for each of these three guarantees.

---

221 *Ell, ibid.* at para. 21.
222 *Beauregard v. Canada*, [1986] 2 S.C.R. 56 at 69.
223 *MacKeigan v. Hickman*, [1989] 2 S.C.R. 796 at 830.
224 *Re Remuneration of Judges*, [1997] 3 S.C.R. 3 at para. 125.
225 *Ell*, [2003] 1 S.C.R. 857 at para. 22.
226 *Re Remuneration of Judges*, [1997] 3 S.C.R. 3 at para. 145.

Table 2.4   Constitutional Judicial Independence Requirements

	Individual Dimension	Institutional Dimension
Security of tenure	Judges may not be dismissed by the executive before the age of retirement except for misconduct or disability, following a judicial inquiry. Thus, a judge may only be removed from office for a reason relating to his or her capacity to perform his or her judicial duties. Arbitrary removal is prohibited.[227]	Before a judge may be removed for cause, "there must be a judicial inquiry to establish that such cause exists, at which the judge affected must be afforded an opportunity to be heard."[228] Superior court judges are removable only by a joint address of the House of Commons and the senate, *per* section 99 of the *Constitution Act, 1867.*[229]
Financial security	Judges' salaries must be provided for by law and the other branches may not arbitrarily encroach upon this right in a manner affecting the independence of the courts.[230]	Judges' salaries may generally be reduced, increased or frozen. However, in making these decisions the government must resort to a salary commission that is independent, effective and objective, and that will make recommendations on judicial wages.[231] If government decides to ignore these recommendations, the decision must be justified, if necessary, in a court of law on the basis of a simple rationality test.[232] Negotiation — "in the sense of trade-offs — concerning the salaries of the judges between a member or representative of the judiciary, on the one hand, and a member or representative of the executive or legislative branch, on the other hand, is prohibited. Such negotiations are fundamentally inconsistent with the independence of the judiciary."[233] Finally, "reductions in the salaries of judges must not result in lowering these below the minimum required by the office of judge. Public trust in the independence of the judiciary would be weakened if the salaries paid to judges were so low that they led people to think that the judges were vulnerable to political or other pressures through financial manipulation."[234]

227 *Mackin*, [2002] 1 S.C.R. 405 at paras. 42 and 43.
228 *Re Therrien*, [2001] 2 S.C.R. 3 at para 39.
229 *Ell*, [2003] 1 S.C.R. 857 at para. 31.
230 *Mackin*, [2002] 1 S.C.R. 405 at para. 50.
231 *Ibid.* at para. 57.
232 *Ibid.* at para. 57.
233 *Ibid.* at para. 58.
234 *Ibid.* at para. 59.

	Individual Dimension	Institutional Dimension
Administrative independence	N/A[235]	Courts themselves have control over the administrative decisions "that bear directly and immediately on the exercise of the judicial function," such as "assignment of judges, sittings of the court, and court lists — as well as the related matters of allocation of court rooms and direction of the administrative staff engaged in carrying out these functions."[236]

Parliamentary Privilege

Significance

Just as judicial independence inhibits the capacity of the executive and legislature to meddle with the judiciary, the doctrine of parliamentary privilege carves out a zone in which legislatures are immune from court (or Crown) intervention. These privileges are, in the words of the Supreme Court, "necessary to ensure that legislatures can perform their functions, free from interference by the Crown and the courts. Given that legislatures are representative and deliberative institutions, those privileges ultimately serve to protect the democratic nature of those bodies."[237]

Meaning of Parliamentary Privilege

"Privilege" in this context means "the legal exemption from some duty, burden, attendance or liability to which others are subject."[238] Privilege has been defined comprehensively in several learned treatises, frequently relied upon by the courts. Thus, Joseph Maingot's *Parliamentary Privilege in Canada*, defines it as:

> the necessary immunity that the law provides for Members of Parliament, and for Members of the legislatures of each of the ten provinces and two territories, in order for these legislators to do their legislative work. It is also the necessary immunity that the law provides for anyone while taking part in a proceeding in Parliament or in a legislature. In addition, it is the right, power, and authority of each House of Parliament and of each legislative assembly to perform their constitutional functions. Finally, it is

---

235 *Re Remuneration of Judges*, [1997] 3 S.C.R. 3 at para. 120.

236 *Ibid.* at para. 117.

237 *Ibid.* at para. 101.

238 *New Brunswick Broadcasting Co.*, [1993] 1 S.C.R. 319 at 378, *per* L'Heureux-Dubé, Gonthier, McLachlin and Iacobucci JJ.

the authority and power of each House of Parliament and of each legislative assembly to enforce that immunity and to protect its integrity.[239]

Content of Parliamentary Privilege

The question of exactly who gets to decide the existence and scope of privilege — Parliament or the courts — is an emerging controversy. Parliamentarians apparently see Parliament as playing the key role in assessing the scope and existence of a privilege. Thus, in response to court cases narrowing the immunity of Parliamentarians from summonses to attend court proceedings, the Commons Standing Committee on Procedure and House Affairs urged in 2004 "it is for Parliament to review or modify its privileges, not the courts."[240]

Courts demur. They have urged a judicial primacy in at least assessing the existence of a privilege, though not its application. Thus, courts have regularly applied a "necessity" test in discerning the existence of a privilege in a given context. A privilege exists where a matter falls within the "necessary sphere of matters without which the dignity and efficiency of the House cannot be upheld."[241] Where the subject matter of a lawsuit falls within this "necessary sphere," the courts have no role in adjudicating its application. As a consequence, "[t]he courts may determine if the privilege claimed is necessary to the capacity of the legislature to function, but have no power to review the rightness or wrongness of a particular decision made pursuant to the privilege."[242]

Courts have not yet adjudicated the full range of these privileges employing this necessity test. There is, however, judicial or expert authority for the chief privileges, as set out in Table 2.5.[243]

239 Joseph Maingot, *Parliamentary Privilege in Canada*, 2d ed. (Ottawa and Montreal: House of Commons and McGill-Queen's University Press, 1997) at 12. See also *Erskine May's Treatise on the Law, Privileges, Proceedings and Usage of Parliament*, 21st ed. (London: Butterworths, 1989) at 69 and 82; Canada, House of Commons, *Beauchesne's Rules and Forms of the House of Commons of Canada*, 6th ed. (Toronto: Carswell, 1989) at 11.

240 Standing Committee on Procedure and House Affairs, *Report 8, Question of privilege relating to Members' being compelled to attend court* (8 March 2004).

241 *New Brunswick Broadcasting Co.*, [1993] 1 S.C.R. 319 at 383, *per* L'Heureux-Dubé, Gonthier, McLachlin and Iacobucci JJ.

242 *Ibid.* at 384.

243 For an exhaustive review of parliamentary privileges, see Maingot, *Parliamentary Privilege in Canada*. See also Canada, House of Commons, *Beauchesne's Rules and Forms* at ch. 2.

Table 2.5   Key Parliamentary Privileges

Privilege	Content
The parliamentary power to control and discipline membership	Parliament itself may expel members to enforce discipline within the House, and remove those whose behaviour has made them unfit to remain as members.[244] Parliamentary privilege extends to officers of Parliament, such as an ethics commissioner, gathering information which may assist the legislature in dealing with its own members,[245] though not necessarily to everything this commissioner does.[246] Where Parliament has delegated the power to adjudicate membership (e.g., controverted election results) to the courts, it has surrendered its privilege in this area.[247]
The parliamentary jurisdiction over the parliamentary precincts, facilities and personnel	Parliament has authority to allow (or deny) access to the parliamentary facilities, including by the media[248] and other "strangers."[249] Impeding access by Parliamentarians to these buildings may constitute a violation of this privilege.[250] Parliament has authority to control its administrative staff, but parliamentary privilege with respect to staff management "does not preclude a review of the necessity to possess and exercise the privilege where there is an allegation of racial or ethnic discrimination" in violation of the *Charter* or human rights law.[251]
Privileges accorded to parliamentarians enabling them to perform their functions	Parliamentarians possess freedom of speech, freedom from arrest in civil process, and exemption from jury service. This freedom of speech means that a parliamentarian cannot be held liable for what is said in Parliament, at least on the floor of the House.[252] Parliamentarians also enjoy immunity from being summoned as witnesses during sessions of Parliament, and

244 *Harvey*, [1996] 2 S.C.R. 876 at para. 76, *per* L'Heureux-Dubé and McLachlin JJ., concurring in the result.
245 *Tafler v. British Columbia (Commissioner of Conflict of Interest)*, (1995) 31 Admin. L.R. (2d) 6 (B.C.S.C.) at para. 53, aff'd (1998), 11 Admin. L.R. (3d) 228 (B.C.C.A.); *Morin v. Northwest Territories (Conflict of Interest Commissioner)* (1999), 14 Admin. L.R. (3d) 284 (N.W.T.S.C.).
246 *Groenewegen v. Northwest Territories (Legislative Assembly)* (1998), 12 Admin. L.R. (3d) 280 (N.W.T.S.C.) holding that parliamentary privilege does not mean that the commissioner has the power to engage publicly funded counsel for anyone but herself.
247 *Friesen v. Hammell* (1999), 57 B.C.L.R. (3d) 276 (B.C.C.A.).
248 *New Brunswick Broadcasting Co.*, [1993] 1 S.C.R. 319.
249 *Zündel v. Liberal Party of Canada* (1999), 181 D.L.R. (4th) 463 (Ont. C.A.).
250 *Ontario (Speaker of the Legislative Assembly) v. Casselman*, [1996] O.J. No. 5343 (Gen. Div.).
251 *House of Commons v. Vaid*, [2003] 1 F.C. 602 (C.A.), leave to appeal allowed, [2003] 2 S.C.R. vii.
252 *Re Ouellet* (1976), 67 D.L.R. (3d) 73 at 86 (Que. S.C.) agreeing that "communications by a Member to another person outside the walls of the House are not covered by the privilege," aff'd 72 D.L.R. (3d) 95 (Que. C.A.).

Privilege	Content
	perhaps for as long as forty days before and forty days after a session.[253] However, Parliamentarians do not enjoy immunity from civil or criminal liability by virtue of their status as parliamentarians,[254] although it would seem that they may not be arrested for civil matters[255] or more generally, while on the floor of the sitting House.[256]
Control of parliamentary proceedings	Parliament has the power to administer that part of the statute law relating to its internal procedure,[257] as well as to determine the content of such things as Standing Orders on Procedure.[258]
	Parliament has the power to determine the location in which a Budget speech will be given.[259]
	The publishers of parliamentary debates are protected from libel lawsuits.[260] Further, Parliament has "the right to control the publication of its debates and proceedings and those of its committees by prohibiting their publication."[261]
	Parliament has the right to institute inquiries and call for witnesses (persons, papers and records), and has the power to punish for contempt.[262] This power includes the right to send for persons in custody.[263]

253   *Telezone Inc. v. Canada (Attorney General)* (2004), 235 D.L.R. (4th) 719 at 726, 730 and 732 (Ont. C.A.). But see *Samson Indian Nation and Band v. Canada* (2003), 238 F.T.R. 68 at para. 45 (F.C.T.D.) where the court limited the immunity to fourteen days before and fourteen days after a session and *Ainsworth Lumber Co. v. Canada (Attorney General)* (2003), 226 D.L.R. (4th) 93 at para. 45 (B.C.C.A.), disagreeing that immunity extends to periods before or after sessions. This last case provoked a rebuke from the Commons Standing Committee on Procedure and House Affairs in its *Report 8, Question of privilege relating to Members' being compelled to attend court* (8 March 2004).

254   See discussion in *Seniuk v. Saskatchewan (Minister of Justice)* (1996), 143 Sask. R. 268 (Q.B.).

255   Maingot, *Parliamentary Privilege in Canada* at 155.

256   Canada, House of Commons, *Beauchesne's Rules* at 24.

257   *Carter v. Alberta* (2002), 222 D.L.R. (4th) 40 at 48 (Alta. C.A.), citing Maingot, *Parliamentary Privilege in Canada* at 183–87.

258   *Ontario (Speaker of the Legislative Assembly) v. Ontario Human Rights Commission,* (2001) 54 O.R. (3d) 595 at 610 (C.A.).

259   *Martin v. Ontario,* [2004] O.J. No. 2247 (S.C.J.)

260   *Harvey,* [1996] 2 S.C.R. 876 at para. 79, per L'Heureux-Dubé and McLachlin JJ., concurring in the result.

261   *Carter* (2002), 222 D.L.R. (4th) 40 at para. 18, citing Maingot, *Parliamentary Privilege in Canada* at 183–87.

262   *Telezone Inc.,* 235 D.L.R. (4th) 719 at para. 19; *Canada (Attorney General) v. Prince Edward Island (Legislative Assembly)* (2003), 46 Admin. L.R. (3d) 171 (P.E.I.S.C.).

263   *Carter* (2002), 222 D.L.R. (4th) 40 at para. 19, citing Maingot, *Parliamentary Privilege in Canada* at 183–87.

Constitutional Basis

Parliamentary privilege is considered part of parliamentary supremacy.[264] More than that, the concept of parliamentary privilege is an independent constitutional precept, incorporated into Canada's Constitution by the preamble of the 1867 Act.[265]

An alternative source of privilege is found in section 4 of the *Parliament of Canada Act*.[266] This provision grants to the senate and the Commons, and their members,

> (*a*) such and the like privileges, immunities and powers as, at the time of the passing of the *Constitution Act, 1867*, were held, enjoyed and exercised by the Commons House of Parliament of the United Kingdom and by the members thereof, insofar as is consistent with that Act; and

> (*b*) such privileges, immunities and powers as are defined by Act of the Parliament of Canada, not exceeding those, at the time of the passing of the Act, held, enjoyed and exercised by the Commons House of Parliament of the United Kingdom and by the members thereof.

Section 4 is authorized by section 18 of the 1867 Act, which empowers Parliament, to define "by Act of the Parliament of Canada" privileges and immunities not to exceed the scope of those "held, enjoyed, and exercised by the Commons House of Parliament of the United Kingdom of Great Britain and Ireland, and by the members thereof" in 1867. Thus, courts examining privileges in the context of section 4 of the *Parliament of Canada Act* often query whether the claimed privilege existed at the time of Confederation.[267]

The preamble to the 1867 Act and the *Parliament of Canada Act* should probably be regarded as alternative sources of parliamentary privilege at the federal level.[268] Indeed, the *Parliament of Canada Act* is likely redundant. Courts have found identical parliamentary privileges to exist at both the fed-

---

264 See *Canada (Auditor General) v. Canada (Minister of Energy, Mines & Resources)*, [1989] 2 S.C.R. 49 at 88, citing Lord Simon in *Pickin v. British Railways Board*, [1974] A.C. 765 (H.L.).

265 *New Brunswick Broadcasting Co.*, [1993] 1 S.C.R. 319 at 377, *per* L'Heureux-Dubé, Gonthier, McLachlin and Iacobucci JJ.

266 R.S.C. 1985, c. P-1. See, e.g., *Samson Indian Nation and Band* (2003), 238 F.T.R. 68 (F.C.T.D.).

267 See, e.g., *Ainsworth Lumber Co.* (2003), 226 D.L.R. (4th) 93 at para. 43 (B.C.C.A.).

268 See *Vaid*, [2003] 1 F.C. 602, 615 (C.A.) *per* Letourneau. J.A., apparently treating the constitutional and statutory sources as alternative sources, leave to appeal allowed, [2003] 2 S.C.R. vii.

eral and provincial level, notwithstanding the applicability of section 18 of the 1867 Act and the *Parliament of Canada Act* to the federal Parliament only.

Implications

The constitutional nature of parliamentary privilege raises two issues. First, difficulties arise where this unwritten norm conflicts with other constitutional principles. For instance, in *New Brunswick Broadcasting Corporation v. Nova Scotia*, at issue was whether a bar by the Nova Scotia legislature on television cameras in the legislative assembly violated the freedom of the press provision in section 2(b) of the *Charter*. A majority of the Supreme Court concluded that the *Charter* did not apply, as the Nova Scotia House of Assembly was exercising its constitutional parliamentary privileges. In arriving at this position, a plurality of the Court noted that "one part of the Constitution cannot be abrogated or diminished by another part of the Constitution."[269] It then held that "if the privilege to expel strangers from the legislative assembly is constitutional, it cannot be abrogated by the *Charter*, even if the *Charter* otherwise applies to the body making the ruling."[270]

The Court's protestation to the contrary notwithstanding, the effect of this reasoning is to prioritize constitutional provisions, something that is inevitable where constitutional principles conflict.[271] Here, however, the *Charter* — part of the written Constitution — is subordinated to parliamentary privilege — unwritten constitutional provisions. In *Harvey v. New Brunswick*, Justice McLachlin, concurring in the result, apparently recognized that her language in *New Brunswick Broadcasting* came perilously close to creating a troubling constitutional hierarchy. In *Harvey*, she wrote: "Both parliamentary privilege and the *Charter* constitute essential parts of the Constitution of Canada. Neither prevails over the other. ... Where apparent conflicts between different constitutional principles arise, the proper approach is not to resolve the conflict by subordinating one principle to the other, but rather to attempt to reconcile them."[272] In practice, this process of reconciliation depends on interpreting the *Charter* — in the *Harvey* case, section 3 — in a "purposive" way, "consistent with Parliamentary privi-

---

269 *New Brunswick Broadcasting*, [1993] 1 S.C.R. 319 at 373, *per* L'Heureux-Dubé, Gonthier, McLachlin and Iacobucci JJ.

270 *Ibid.*

271 See, e.g., *Reference re Bill 30, An Act to amend the Education Act (Ont.)*, [1987] 1 S.C.R. 1148.

272 [1996] 2 S.C.R. 876 at para. 69, *per* L'Heureux-Dubé and McLachlin JJ., concurring in the result.

lege."[273] This is another way of saying that the *Charter* extends only so far as parliamentary privilege does not exist.

The net result of both *New Brunswick Broadcasting* and McLachlin J.'s *Harvey* reasoning is the same: parliamentary privilege is a special limitation on *Charter* rights in circumstances where the legislative branch's core legislative functions are being challenged on *Charter* grounds. The practical implications of this approach remain unclear. For instance, by virtue of privilege, is Parliament a zone where members are free to violate the rights of Canadians who work for the legislature itself by, for example, engaging in racial discrimination? The Federal Court of Appeal's decision in *House of Commons v. Vaid*[274] suggests, sensibly, that it is not. At the time of this writing, it remained to be seen whether the Supreme Court would uphold this approach on appeal.

A second issue worth flagging is the implication of privilege for the legislative process. Specifically, is the current process by which a bill becomes a statute mandatory, or would changes to that process be constitutionally insulated by parliamentary privilege? We discuss the bill process in chapter 5. Here we ask: is Parliament free to dispense with traditional three readings, referrals to committees, and debates in both Houses, instead simply meeting the minimal voting and royal assent requirements for the promulgation of a law included in the *Constitution Act, 1867*?

The answer to this question is likely "yes." In the British parliamentary tradition, it is for "Parliament to lay down the procedures which are to be followed before a Bill can become an Act."[275] While the Supreme Court has implied that "three readings in the Senate and House of Commons" is a "procedure due any citizen of Canada" by "[l]ong-standing parliamentary tradition,"[276] nothing constitutionalizes the procedure. If Parliament were, therefore, to dispense with current requirements that allow proposed legislation to be debated and vetted, it likely would be free to do so.[277]

---

273 *Ibid.* at para. 70.

274 [2003] 1 F.C. 602 (C.A.), leave to appeal to S.C.C. granted, [2003] 2 S.C.R. vii.

275 Lord Morris of Borth-y-Gest in *Pickin v. British Rys. Board*, [1974] A.C. 765 (H.L.) at 790, cited with approval in *Martin*, [2004] O.J. No. 2247 at para. 21.

276 *Authorson v. Canada (Attorney General)*, [2003] 2 S.C.R. 40 at para. 37.

277 See *Wells*, [1999] 3 S.C.R. 199 at para. 59 ("legislative decision making is not subject to any known duty of fairness. Legislatures are subject to constitutional requirements for valid law-making, but within their constitutional boundaries, they can do as they see fit"); *P.H.L.F. Family Holdings Ltd. v. Canada*, [1994] T.C.J. No. 445 (invocation of closure of debate on a bill a matter of privilege).

D. CONCLUSION

Canada's Constitution is a bit of a muddle. "Given our constitutional obsessions of the past quarter century" writes Professor Arthurs, "we ought by now to be able to answer the simple question: what is the constitution of Canada? But we cannot, in fact, draw an accurate map of our constitution."[278] As Arthurs argues, and this chapter suggests, we do not always have a terribly clear idea of what the Constitution is, what it means or what it does. This is most acutely the case in relation to the "unwritten" principles, discerned from time-to-time by the courts. It is even the case, however, with our written Constitution. As this chapter suggests, not every provision can be read at face value. The Queen is not as potent as a simple reading of the *Constitution Act, 1867* would suggest.

Democracy in Canada is, in fact, poorly represented in the written constitutional texts as a whole. Where democracy has been given a constitutional imprint, it has been through the articulation of a somewhat bizarre menagerie of unwritten constitutional instruments, such as "principles" and "conventions." In many ways, therefore, democracy in this country exists despite — not because of — most of the formal, written provisions of the Constitution.

The Supreme Court has reinterpreted these written provisions, and discerned an unwritten constitutional backstop to our democracy, as well as very specific democracy-enhancing principles such as parliamentary supremacy, the separation of powers, parliamentary privilege, judicial independence, the rule of law, and the protection of minorities. In so doing, the Court has responded to impulses that make democracy a source of constitutional law, and not its product. At some level, the constitutional legal foundation of Canadian democracy is democracy itself. And, as we shall see in the chapters that follow, this democracy is supported by a whole corpus of other, nonconstitutional legal principles.

---

278 Harry Arthurs, "Constitutional Courage," (2004) 49 McGill L.J. 1 at 5.

Voting, Elections and the Selection of Members of Parliament

As discussed in chapter 1, at the heart of democratic accountability is the principle that those with power are either themselves elected or at least accountable to others who are. For this reason, no other issue is as central to a functioning democracy as the question of how citizens choose their elected representatives. As the Supreme Court has held, "each citizen must have a genuine opportunity to take part in the governance of the country through participation in the selection of elected representatives. ... Absent such a right, ours would not be a true democracy."[1]

This chapter will outline some of the key elements of how elections to the House of Commons are regulated. It begins with a discussion of voting and electoral rights, as enshrined in the *Charter* and our democratic traditions, and expressed in statutory law, most notably the *Canada Elections Act*.[2] The chapter then describes how elections are triggered and who may seek office as a candidate or party. This section is followed by a nuts-and-bolts analysis of how elections are run and of the major players in administering elections. We focus in particular on the question of how elections are financed, examining public subsidies provided to parties and candidates, and limits on election expenses, contributions and third-party spending.

---

1   *Figueroa v. Canada (Attorney General)*, [2003] 1 S.C.R. 912 at para. 30.
2   *Canada Elections Act*, R.S.C. 2000, c. 9 (*Elections Act*).

The chapter concludes with a discussion of emerging issues in electoral regulation, including the leaders' debates, fixed election dates, proportional representation, and the challenge of encouraging a more diverse Commons. Finally, we look at two related issues straddling elections and democratic governance: recall and referendums.

A. VOTING AND ELECTORAL RIGHTS

As noted by Professor Tremblay, the right to vote is a manifestation of two values — freedom and equality: "Freedom, because not only must each person be able to exercise freely the right to vote and choose representatives, but choosing them through universal suffrage is a guarantee that democratic freedoms will be protected. Equality, because everyone has the right to vote for representatives and everyone has intrinsically equal value in this process that leads to democratic legitimacy."[3] Canadian law recognizes both of these principles in the Constitution and in Acts of Parliament.

1. Constitutional Voting Rights

In 1982, a citizen's right to vote was codified as constitutional law in section 3 of the *Canadian Charter of Rights and Freedoms*. Section 3 reads: "Every citizen of Canada has the right to vote in an election of members of the House of Commons or of a legislative assembly and to be qualified for membership therein." For the Supreme Court of Canada, especially because section 3 is not subject to the section 33 "notwithstanding" provision, the right to vote lies "at the heart of our constitutional democracy."[4] The central focus of section 3, the Court has held, "is the right of each citizen to participate in the electoral process." This right "to participate in the political life of the country is one that is of fundamental importance in a free and democratic society." Thus, interpretations of section 3 should embrace "a content commensurate with the importance of individual participation in the selection of elected representatives in a free and democratic state."[5]

---

3   M. Tremblay (introductory report for the third preparatory meeting on electoral issues, April 2000, leading up to the Symposium on Democratic Practices, Rights and Freedoms in La Francophonie, Bamako, Mali, Nov. 2000), cited in "The Right to Vote: The Heart of Democracy," *Electoral Insight* (Jan. 2001).

4   *Thomson Newspapers Co. v. Canada (Attorney General)*, [1998] 1 S.C.R. 877 at para. 79.

5   *Figueroa*, [2003] 1 S.C.R. 912 at para. 26.

To date, the Supreme Court of Canada has discussed section 3 in the context of pre-election blackouts of opinion polls,[6] electoral boundaries,[7] the disqualification of inmates from voting,[8] voting in referendums,[9] a fifty-candidate threshold for official party standing under Canadian election law[10] and third-party advertising restrictions.[11] In these cases (discussed later in this chapter), the Court has repeatedly urged that the purpose of section 3 incorporates the "right to 'effective representation.'"[12] Summarizing the Court's approach to section 3 in 1993, Madam Justice L'Heureux-Dubé suggested that "[t]he purpose of s. 3 of the *Charter* is, then, to grant every citizen of this country the right to play a *meaningful* role in the selection of elected representatives."[13]

a) Effective Representation and the Right to Participate in Elections

Logically, this right to play a *meaningful* role in candidate selection extends to ensuring a fair process for both voters and those running for office, and it reflects an egalitarian model of democracy.[14] As the Supreme Court observed in *Harper v. Canada*, the egalitarian model is premised "on the notion that individuals should have an equal opportunity to participate in the electoral process."[15]

In keeping with this emphasis on political participation, voting is not merely a device for determining the identity of democratic representatives. Section 3 guarantees more "than the bare right to place a ballot in a box."[16] Rather, it is also a form of expression. In the words of Justice McLachlin in *Reference re Provincial Electoral Boundaries (Sask.)*: "Ours is a representative democracy. Each citizen is entitled to be represented in government. Representation comprehends the idea of having a voice in the deliberations of

---

6   *Thomson*, [1998] 1 S.C.R. 877.

7   *Reference re Provincial Electoral Boundaries (Sask.)*, [1991] 2 S.C.R. 158.

8   *Sauvé v. Canada (Chief Electoral Officer)*, [1993] 2 S.C.R. 438; *Sauvé v. Canada (Chief Electoral Officer)*, [2002] 3 S.C.R. 519.

9   *Haig v. Canada*, [1993] 2 S.C.R. 995.

10   *Figueroa*, [2003] 1 S.C.R. 912.

11   *Harper v. Canada (Attorney General)*, 2004 SCC 33.

12   See *Haig*, [1993] 2 S.C.R. 995; *Harvey v. New Brunswick (Attorney General)*, [1996] 2 S.C.R. 876; *Thomson*, [1998] 1 S.C.R. 877; and *Figueroa*, [2003] 1 S.C.R. 912.

13   *Haig*, [1993] 2 S.C.R. 995 at para. 63 [emphasis added]; see also see *Figueroa, ibid.*

14   Colin Feasby, "*Libman v. A.G. Quebec* and the Administration of the Process of Democracy under the *Charter*: The Emerging Egalitarian Model," (1999) 44 McGill L.J. 5.

15   *Harper*, 2004 SCC 33 at para. 62.

16   *Dixon v. British Columbia (Attorney General)*, [1989] 4 W.W.R. 393 at 403, cited with approval by *Figueroa*, [2003] 1 S.C.R. 912 at para. 19.

government as well as the idea of the right to bring one's grievances and concerns to the attention of one's government representative."[17] For this reason, the process of voting is not only the means but an end in its own right. As the Court put it in *Figueroa v. Canada (Attorney General)*:

> participation in the electoral process has an intrinsic value independent of its impact upon the actual outcome of elections. ... The right to run for office provides each citizen with the opportunity to present certain ideas and opinions to the electorate as a viable policy option; the right to vote provides each citizen with the opportunity to express support for the ideas and opinions that a particular candidate endorses. In each instance, the democratic rights entrenched in s. 3 ensure that each citizen has an opportunity to express an opinion about the formation of social policy and the functioning of public institutions through participation in the electoral process.[18]

Further, as the Court put it in *Harper*:

> The right to meaningful participation includes a citizen's right to exercise his or her vote in an informed manner. For a voter to be well-informed, the citizen must be able to weigh the relative strengths and weaknesses of each candidate and political party. The citizen must also be able to consider opposing aspects of issues associated with certain candidates and political parties where they exist. In short, the voter has a right to be "reasonably informed of all the possible choices."[19]

That said, a right to be informed is not, "a right to unlimited information or to unlimited participation." If it were, "those having access to the most resources [would] monopolize the election discourse, [and] their opponents [would] be deprived of a reasonable opportunity to speak and be heard." The result would be a diminishment of "the voter's ability to be adequately informed of all views."[20] For these reasons, both governments and the courts have safeguarded the right to an informed vote by, for example, limiting the influence of wealthy interests during elections. We discuss this issue in detail later, in the sections on electoral financing and third-party advertising.

---

17   [1991] 2 S.C.R. 158 at para. 49 (Electoral Reference Case) [emphasis in original].
18   [2003] 1 S.C.R. 912 at para. 29.
19   *Harper*, 2004 SCC 33 at para. 71, citing *Libman v. Quebec (Attorney General)*, [1997] 3 S.C.R. 569 at 47.
20   *Harper, ibid.*, at para. 72.

b)   Effective Representation and the Right to a Roughly Equal Impact on Electoral Outcomes

The "effective representation" promised in section 3 should not, in every instance, be confused with a right to absolute equality in the weight each vote is accorded in selecting that representation. Thus, for McLachlin J., writing in a case dealing with the apportionment of electoral district (or "riding") boundaries, "effective representation" did not necessarily connote "absolute voter parity." Instead, "deviations from absolute voter parity may be justified on the grounds of practical impossibility or the provision of more effective representation."[21] In the result, not all electoral districts have the same populations, and votes in some electoral districts, especially those in rural electoral districts or small provinces, may be "worth more" than votes in others.

There is, however, an outer limit in the dilution of voter parity where the section 3 right will be offended: "Only those deviations [from voter parity] should be admitted which can be justified on the ground that they contribute to better government of the populace as a whole, giving due weight to regional issues within the populace and geographic factors within the territory governed."[22] It follows that any change to the electoral system that would alter the "weight" of citizens' votes based on considerations not squarely encompassed by a question of "better government" would run afoul of section 3.[23]

These pronouncements from the Supreme Court, taken together, suggest that the section 3 right to vote includes a right to effective representation, which in turn guarantees an opportunity to participate in elections and to make an informed vote in the selection of representatives.[24] Adherence to the latter right is measured, not necessarily in terms of absolute voter equality, but with an eye to guarding against deviations from voter parity that do not contribute to the better governance of the populace as a whole.

---

21   *Reference re Provincial Electoral Boundaries (Sask.)*, [1991] 2 S.C.R. 158 at para. 55.

22   *Ibid.*, citing with approval *Dixon v. British Columbia (Attorney General)*, [1989] 4 W.W.R. 393 at 414 (B.C.S.C.).

23   For a rare example of electoral boundaries that were so unequal as to precipitate a successful challenge under section 3 (at the territorial level), see *Friends of Democracy v. Northwest Territories (Attorney General)* (1999), 171 D.L.R. (4th) 551 (N.W.T. S.C.).

24   The right to an informed vote may also be protected at times by the free expression right in s. 2(b) of the *Charter*. See *Thomson*, [1998] 1 S.C.R. 877, holding that a poll blackout during the election period was a violation of free expression. At times, however, the informed vote right and free expression have clashed, as discussed in greater detail in the section on election financing and advertising.

2. Statutory Voting Rights

a) The Right to Vote in the *Elections Act*

In the current *Elections Act*, the right to vote is codified very simply: subject to certain exceptions, "every person who is a Canadian citizen and is eighteen years of age or older on polling day is qualified as an elector."[25] Every elector is then "entitled to have his or her name included in the list of electors for the polling division in which he or she is ordinarily resident and to vote at the polling station for that polling division."[26]

Canadian law does permit some limits on the voting franchise. Historically, elector restrictions were tied to gender and wealth. In the early years following Confederation, the vote was restricted to men who possessed a sufficient amount of property. The franchise was extended to women federally in 1918, and the property restriction was gradually eliminated by 1920.[27]

Modern voting restrictions are modest. As noted above, Canada does retain a minimum age requirement — eighteen years of age on polling day.[28] The vote is also denied the chief electoral officer and the assistant chief electoral officer.[29] The Act appears to make no provision for voting by citizens living outside of Canada continuously for more than five consecutive years.[30] Finally, the Act once contained a provision prohibiting anyone in a correctional institution from voting.[31] This latter prohibition was struck down by the Supreme Court in 2002 as contrary to section 3 of the *Charter*.[32]

Indeed, it is difficult to see any of these voting limitations as consistent with section 3. Section 3 extends the vote to every citizen, without exception. If challenged, therefore, the current *Canada Election Act* voting prohibitions would only be upheld if defensible as reasonable limitations in a free and democratic society, in keeping with section 1 of the *Charter*. This

---

25   *Elections Act*, s. 3.

26   *Ibid.*, s. 6.

27   Elections Canada, *A History of the Vote in Canada* (1997).

28   *Elections Act*, s. 3.

29   *Ibid.*, s. 4.

30   *Ibid.*, s. 11 and Part 11 (making arrangements for voting by persons overseas for less than five years who intend to return to Canada as a resident); Elections Canada, *Voting by Canadians Residing Outside of Canada* (making same point).

31   *Elections Act*, former s. 51(e), current s. 4.

32   *Sauvé v. Canada (Chief Electoral Officer)*, [2002] 3 S.C.R. 519, holding unconstitutional a provision barring voting by prisoners serving two or more years. See also an earlier case holding unconstitutional a more sweeping, absolute ban on prisoner voting: *Sauvé v. Canada (Attorney General)*, [1993] 2 S.C.R. 438.

is exactly the approach taken by the lower courts in challenges to electoral minimum age requirements. In *Fitzgerald v. Alberta*, the Alberta courts concluded recently that while any limitation on the right of a citizen to vote under section 3 must be justified under section 1, such a justification was found in the need to limit voting to those with sufficient maturity and experience. The age eighteen was regarded as a reasonable demarcation point for such qualities.[33]

b) Protection of the Right to Vote

The right to vote has received careful legal protection in Canada for generations, even in pre-*Charter* cases. As noted by an Ontario court in the 1876 case *Re Lincoln Election*: "The Court is anxious to allow the person who claims it the right to exercise the franchise, in every case in which there has been a reasonable compliance with the statute which gives him the right he seeks to avail himself of. No merely formal or immaterial matter should be allowed to interfere with the voter exercising the franchise."[34] And as Crease J. observed in the 1884 case *Cawley v. Branchflower*: "The law is very jealous of the franchise, and will not take it away from a voter if the Act has been reasonably complied with. ... It looks to realities, not technicalities or mere formalities, unless where forms are by law, especially criminal law, essential, or affect the subject-matter under dispute."[35]

In modern law, the integrity of the right to vote is protected through defensive measures — such as prohibitions on interfering with people marking their ballots or attempting to deter them from voting[36] — and also by creating positive duties on the government and on private citizens and entities to encourage voting. The most important "defensive" measure is the secret ballot. The Act emphatically requires that the vote be secret.[37] The voting procedure enables electors to complete their ballot in private and then submit this document without fear that, at that time, their voting preference will be noted by others.[38]

---

33 *Fitzgerald (Next friend of) v. Alberta* (2002), 104 C.R.R. (2d) 170, aff'd, (2004), 27 Alta. L.R. (4th) 205 (C.A.), leave to appeal to S.C.C. refused (2005), [2004] S.C.C.A. 349 (in a challenge to Alberta's election laws). See also *Reid v. Canada* (1994), 73 F.T.R. 290 (F.C.T.D.) coming to a similar conclusion with respect to the *Elections Act*.

34 *Re Lincoln Election* (1876), 2 O.A.R. 316 at 323, cited by Cory J., dissenting, in *Haig*, [1993] 2 S.C.R. 995 at para. 107.

35 *Cawley v. Branchflower* (1884), 1 B.C.R. (Pt. II) 35 (S.C.) at 37, cited by Cory J., dissenting, in *Haig*, [1993] 2 S.C.R. 995 at para. 106.

36 *Elections Act*, ss. 166(1)(c), 281 and 282.

37 *Ibid.*, ss. 163 and 164(1).

38 *Ibid.*, ss. 150 *et seq.* and 281.

To enhance the integrity of the ballot casting process, election advertising is prohibited on election day, a matter discussed in detail later in this chapter. Further, there are specific and strict provisions governing partisan activities at polling stations. For instance, no one may wear or display campaign paraphernalia,[39] or promote or oppose a candidate or party using a loudspeaker within hearing distance of the station.[40] Indeed, electors are even prohibited from disclosing publicly at a polling station their voting intentions.[41]

Among the "positive" measures designed to enhance participation, employers must ensure employees have sufficient time off from work in order to vote,[42] and there are special provisions for the mentally and physically impaired to facilitate voting.[43] Voting is made convenient by advance polls that must be established on the tenth, ninth and seventh days before polling day.[44]

Voters may also vote by "special ballot," a system of secrecy-protected envelopes that are usually mailed in before polling day.[45] This system is often used by those who are out of the country, by those incarcerated in correctional facilities, or persons with disabilities who may have difficulty reaching the polling station on any of the polling or advance polling days.

Members of the Canadian Forces may choose to have their vote count in the electoral district they are posted in, where they lived prior to being posted with the Forces, or where they would be living were they not posted with the Forces.[46]

Finally, the right to vote encompasses a right not to vote for any of the listed candidates. Voters may "spoil" their ballot. Distinguishing between intentionally spoiled ballots and ineptly completed ballots is difficult. A ballot that is improperly filled out, to the point where the voter's choice cannot be determined, is simply counted as a "rejected" ballot under the Act.[47] Indeed, rejected ballots include ballots "marked with a name other than the

---

39 *Ibid.*, s. 166.
40 *Ibid.*, s. 165.
41 *Ibid.*, subs. 164(2).
42 *Ibid.*, ss. 132–34. If the employee does not have three consecutive hours off work during polling hours, the employer must provide paid time for the employee to vote.
43 *Ibid.*, ss. 154–57, 159.
44 *Ibid.*, s. 171.
45 *Ibid.*, s. 227.
46 *Ibid.*, subs. 194(4).
47 *Ibid.* s. 279.

name of a candidate," preventing electors from "writing in" candidates not represented on the party tickets.[48]

In recent elections, the number of rejected ballots has been on the order of 1 percent, but because the Act's concept of rejected ballots is broad enough to encompass both intentionally and unintentionally spoiled ballots, rejected ballots cannot automatically be viewed as an indicator of voter dissatisfaction. The low percentage of rejected (including intentionally spoiled) ballots may reflect a lack of awareness that the option to spoil consciously one's ballot exists. It may also be that voters are demonstrating dissatisfaction, not by spoiling ballots, but simply by failing to show up at the polls.

c) The Right to Representation and Electoral Boundary Readjustment

The right to vote obviously encompasses a right to vote for someone; namely, a representative. Section 40 of the *Constitution Act, 1867* anticipates the division of the country into "electoral districts" from which Members are elected. This provision is prefaced by the phrase "until the Parliament of Canada otherwise provides," permitting Parliament to readjust these districts from time to time without constitutional amendment.

These readjustments are governed by two other constitutional provisions, both related to provincial representation. First, section 51A (also discussed in chapter 4) guarantees minimum numbers of MPs from each province equal to no fewer than the province has representatives in the senate. This senate floor rule is of importance mainly to smaller, Maritime Provinces.[49]

Second, section 52 of the *Constitution Act, 1867* empowers Parliament to increase the number of MPs, "provided the proportionate Representation of the Provinces prescribed by this Act is not thereby disturbed." Section 51[50] provides the formula for this, requiring that each province's total number of seats in the House be proportionate to its overall population. (It should be noted that this provision does not preclude electoral district size variations within each province, such that some electoral districts have greater populations than others.)

---

48 *Ibid.* See also *Canada Election Act*, s. 76, specifying that any votes for persons not registered as a candidate are void.

49 See discussion in *Campbell v. Canada (Attorney General)* (1988), 49 D.L.R. (4th) 321 at 326, Lambert J.A., dissenting, showing the effect of the senate floor rule applying to New Brunswick and P.E.I.

50 As amended by the *Representation Act, 1985*, S.C. 1986, c. 8, named the *Constitution Act (Representation), 1985*.

There is, however, a "grandfather" clause in section 51 that in practice impairs absolute provincial representation by population:[51] in no circumstance can the number MPs calculated through the population formula fall below the number coming from each province as of the coming into force of the provision, in 1986. For several provinces, this provision has resulted in a higher number of MPs than the raw proportionate representation calculation would have produced.[52]

As a result of this system, electoral boundaries are readjusted, and at times, some electoral districts are merged, or new ones created. Population growth also commonly results in seats being added in the Commons. For example, following the 2001 readjustment, the number of seats went from 301 to 308.

These readjustments are often controversial, as they may result in two existing MPs from the same party having to contest the party's nomination for the district. Leading up to the 2004 election, there were several high-profile cases where MPs, including one former minister,[53] ended up losing their seats in such disputes.

The adjustment of districts was once the purview of MPs themselves, a system encouraging the "gerrymandering" of electoral district boundaries for partisan advantage.[54] Currently, electoral boundaries are now readjusted according to the 1964 *Electoral Boundaries Readjustment Act*.[55] The Act establishes separate, three-member independent boundary commissions for each province, created by the Governor-in-Council (GIC). The chief justice of the province names a judge to chair the commission,[56] and the two other members are named by the Speaker of the House of Commons.[57]

Under the Act, each commission prepares a report recommending readjustments, aiming to maintain the population size of each electoral district "as close as reasonably possible" to the average for electoral districts in the province, and taking into consideration:

---

51 See discussion in *Campbell* (1988), 49 D.L.R. (4th) 321 at 333 (B.C.C.A.).

52 *Ibid.* at 326, Lambert J.A., dissenting, showing the grandfather provision affecting representation from Quebec, Nova Scotia, Manitoba, Saskatchewan.

53 Sheila Copps lost her nomination race against another Liberal incumbent, Tony Valeri. Copps ran against Paul Martin in the party's preceding leadership campaign, and complained that party operatives had lined up against her in the nomination battle.

54 J. Courtney, *Elections* (Vancouver: UBC Press, 2004) at 47–50.

55 *Electoral Boundaries Readjustment Act*, R.S.C. 1985, c-E3.

56 *Ibid.*, subs. 5(1).

57 *Ibid.*, subs. 6(1).

i) the community of interest or community of identity in or the historical pattern of an electoral district in the province, and

ii) a manageable geographic size for districts in sparsely populated, rural or northern regions of the province.

Deviations from equality in the population size of electoral districts should not be greater or lesser than 25 percent of the provincial average.[58] As noted above, the Supreme Court of Canada has essentially endorsed such variation. It has not interpreted section 3 of the *Charter* as demanding absolute parity in district population size, so long as deviations "contribute to better government of the populace as a whole, giving due weight to regional issues within the populace and geographic factors within the territory governed."[59]

"Interested persons," including MPs, may make representations to the commission on redistricting.[60] The commission then compiles a report with suggested changes to electoral boundaries. The report is submitted to Parliament and is referred to a standing committee,[61] usually the Procedure and House Affairs Committee. Objections may be filed by MPs with the committee, considered, and reported back to the Speaker, who in turn refers these concerns to the chief electoral officer for reconsideration by the commission.[62] The commission, which must then respond to the objection within thirty days, maintains the authority to decide whether to amend the report in response to the objection.[63]

The commission's final decision is subject to judicial review. For instance, in a recent case, the Federal Court held that the commission erred (as measured on a patently unreasonable standard) where in realigning the boundaries of an electoral district, "it did not consider whether it was desirable to allow a variance provided for in the Act in order to preserve a community of interest in an electoral district."[64] This decision prompted a parliamentary bill in December 2004[65] changing the electoral district boundaries in question and introduced to "ensure full compliance with the Federal Court's ruling."[66]

---

58 *Ibid.*, s. 15.

59 *Reference re Provincial Electoral Boundaries (Sask.)*, [1991] 2 S.C.R. 158 at para. 55.

60 *Electoral Boundaries Readjustment Act*, s. 19.

61 *Ibid.*, subs. 21(1).

62 *Ibid.*, s. 22.

63 *Ibid.*, subs. 23(1).

64 *Raîche v. Canada (Attorney General)*, 2004 FC 679 at para. 69.

65 Bill C-36, 38th Parl., 1st Sess., 53 Elizabeth II, 2004.

66 Government of Canada, *News Release: Minister Bélanger introduces legislation to implement the recommendations of the Miramichi and Acadie-Bathurst Electoral Boundaries Commission* (Dec. 10, 2004).

B. THE KEY ACTORS IN ELECTIONS

We shift our focus to the mechanics by which a candidate elicits votes from electors, in the hope of becoming a representative for an electoral district. To this end, this section describes the key players in an election (other than voters themselves), namely, the chief electoral officer, political parties and candidates for the House of Commons, for party leadership and for party nominations.

1. Electoral Officials

a) The Chief Electoral Officer

The *Elections Act* grapples with the potential conflict between the legislative branch's oversight role and the need for fairness and impartiality in the process of electing legislative representatives. The early years of Confederation exposed the pitfalls of a politicized electoral process. According to Professor Massicotte:

> Elections in Canada were quite corrupt throughout the 19th century and beyond. The 1917 general election was arguably the worst since the 1841 campaign in the United Canadas. The rules had been altered shortly before Parliament was dissolved. The electoral register was subjected to what might be described today as a kind of ethnic cleansing, as immigrants from countries with which Canada was at war were disfranchised if they had been naturalized for less than 15 years. Women were enfranchised selectively, as only those with a relative in the military were given the right to vote at an election focused on conscription for military service overseas. Women who had already been enfranchised in a few provinces were excluded if they had no such relatives. There were allegations of tampering with the soldier vote. As Norman Ward put it, "the wartime franchise of 1917 could hardly fail to return a majority in Parliament for the party which enacted it."[67]

To oversee an overhauled and professionalized elections process, Parliament created the post of chief electoral officer (CEO) in 1920. As discussed in chapter 4, the CEO is an officer of Parliament who is appointed by and reports to the House of Commons rather than the Governor-in-Council. Although the CEO post has the rank of deputy head of a department, it maintains legislative protections against political interference. For

---

67 L. Massicotte, "The Chief Electoral Officer of Canada," (2003) 26 Canadian Parliamentary Review no. 3.

instance, the CEO's salary is set at the same level as a Federal Court judge (as specified in the *Judges Act*). The CEO may serve until age sixty-five, and may otherwise be removed only for cause by the Governor General on address of the senate and House of Commons.[68] As already noted, a unique feature of the office is that neither the CEO nor his or her assistant may vote, further emphasizing the neutrality of the post.

The CEO oversees most election administration,[69] and heads a staff comprising "an officer known as the Assistant Chief Electoral Officer, appointed by the Governor in Council, and any other officers, clerks and employees that may be required, who shall be appointed in accordance with the *Public Service Employment Act*."[70] The CEO may also retain such other staff as is required to implement his or her obligations on a casual basis.[71] Collectively, these people comprise the "Elections Canada" organization.[72]

In practice, the CEO also assists in the interpretation of the *Elections Act*, a law whose provisions must be implemented by thousands of Canadians, from candidate and party agents to polling station staff. To assist these people, the CEO prepares forms, booklets and Internet materials interpreting the legal provisions that affect their work.

The CEO also reports to the Speaker of the Commons following general elections and by-elections.[73] After a general election, the CEO is also obliged to "make a report to the Speaker of the House of Commons that sets out any amendments that, in his or her opinion, are desirable for the better administration of" the *Elections Act*.[74] This matter is then referred by the Speaker to the Commons.[75]

b) Returning Officers

A returning officer is appointed by the GIC for each electoral district. Working under the direction of the CEO, the returning officer is responsible for administration of the election at the electoral district level,[76] includ-

---

68 *Elections Act*, ss. 13–15.

69 *Ibid.*, s. 16.

70 *Ibid.*, s. 19.

71 *Ibid.*, s. 20.

72 Elections Canada describes itself as "an independent body established by Parliament" whose primary task is to be "prepared at all times to conduct an election." Elections Canada, *Backgrounder: The Role and Structure of Elections Canada* (2003). In fact, Elections Canada is not *per se* a creature of Parliament, existing instead as the manifestation of the CEO's hiring powers under the *Elections Act*.

73 *Elections Act*, ss. 533 and 534.

74 *Ibid.*, s. 535.

75 *Ibid.*, s. 536.

76 *Ibid.*, s. 24.

ing the hiring of staff such as deputy returning officers, registration officers and poll clerks to operate polling stations.

Although the returning officer has some security of tenure under the
Act,[77] appointment of the officer by the GIC raises the spectre of political
favouritism, sparking much criticism, particularly from the CEO,[78] as well
as members of the NDP, Bloc and the Conservative Party and its predecessors, the Reform and Canadian Alliance parties.[79]

The critics argue — rightfully, in our view — that elections must be
administered in an impartial and independent fashion. Partisanship on the
part of returning officers could undermine the integrity of the electoral
process. For instance, the powers of the returning officer include deciding
on the location of polling stations.[80] In modern elections, parties generally
know where in an electoral district they have the most support. Situating
polling stations in more accessible locations in areas where a party is
strong, or less accessible locations in areas where a party is weak, is just
one of many partisan considerations that an impartial returning officer
should be expected to reject.

In these circumstances, a more independent process for appointing
these officers is clearly warranted. The current CEO Jean Pierre Kingsley
has urged the appointment of returning officers on the basis of merit after
a competitive process.[81] Following the 2004 election, he repeated concerns
with the current appointment process for returning officers:

77   Ibid., subs. 24(7).

78   Chief Electoral Officer, Report of the Chief Electoral Officer of Canada on the 38th General
     Election Held on June 28, 2004 (Oct. 2004) at 2.

79   See, e.g., Mr. Ted White (North Vancouver, Ref.), Hansard, no. 57 (25 Feb. 2000) ("All
     301 returning officers are appointed by the Prime Minister of Canada. They are Liber-
     al patronage appointments to what should be non-partisan positions throughout Elec-
     tions Canada. It is a disgrace.") At the time of writing, Bloc and NDP members were
     working on private members' bills to remove the GIC-appointment power, while Con-
     servative House Leader John Reynolds was pushing for committee recommendations
     to do the same: "Cabinet-Appointed Election Officers International Embarrassment,
     Says Kingsley," The Hill Times, 1 Nov. 2004, 1 and 24.

80   Elections Act, s. 120.

81   Mr. Jean-Pierre Kingsley (Chief Electoral Officer of Canada, Office of the Chief Elec-
     toral Officer of Canada), Standing Committee on Procedure and House Affairs, Evi-
     dence (28 Oct. 1999) ("In my reports, I recommended that returning officers be
     appointed by the Chief Electoral Officer in a competitive process based on merit. It is
     important that returning officers be well prepared to deal with technological chal-
     lenges, the complexity of the law and the shorter election period, and that they be per-
     ceived by all stakeholders and candidates as neutral.").

it remains difficult to provide service of uniform quality across the country when the returning officers appointed for this purpose by the Governor in Council are not selected on the basis of merit and still less, it seems, on any test of their ability to carry out their duties. The work of the Chief Electoral Officer becomes all the more challenging when some returning officers do not feel obliged to respect his authority because they owe their appointment to another body.[82]

We join others in concluding that the integrity of Canada's electoral system would be enhanced by the appointment of local agents strictly by the CEO, an individual who is him- or herself endowed with substantial independence.

2. Parties and Candidates

a) Parties

Although parties are the central actors in the Canadian electoral and political system, there is no mention of them in the Constitution and they were not recognized even in the *Elections Act* until 1970. The current Act defines a political party as "an organization one of whose fundamental purposes is to participate in public affairs by endorsing one or more of its members as candidates and supporting their election."[83]

In order to enjoy benefits, such as receiving public financing, issuing tax receipts for contributions, appearing on the ballot next to the names of candidates affiliated with it, and receiving an allocation of broadcast advertising time, a political party must register with the CEO.[84] Parties may be subsequently deregistered if they fail to file various documents, field sufficient candidates or meet several other administrative requirements.[85]

Until recently, the *Elections Act* required a registered party to run candidates in at least fifty electoral districts.[86] This rule was struck down by the Supreme Court in 2003 in *Figueroa v. Canada*.[87] In that case, the Court underscored the importance of parties in an electoral democracy: "political parties enhance the meaningfulness of individual participation in the electoral process for reasons that transcend their capacity (or lack thereof) to

---

82   Chief Electoral Officer, *Report of the Chief Electoral Officer of Canada on the 38th General Election Held on June 28, 2004* at 2.

83   *Elections Act*, s. 2.

84   *Ibid.*, ss. 366 *et seq.*

85   *Ibid.*, ss. 385 *et seq.*

86   *Ibid.*, s. 370, prior to amendment by S.C. 2004, c. 24, s. 5.

87   *Figueroa*, [2003] 1 S.C.R. 912.

participate in the governance of the country subsequent to an election. Irrespective of their capacity to influence the outcome of an election, political parties act as both a vehicle and outlet for the meaningful participation of individual citizens in the electoral process."[88]

The Court held that the fifty-candidate threshold in relation to three benefits under the Act — the rights to issue tax receipts for donations received outside the election period, to retain unspent election funds, and to list party affiliations on ballots — violated section 3 of the *Charter* and was not justified under section 1 as demonstrably justified in a free and democratic society.

The Court suspended its judgment for twelve months, allowing Parliament to formulate an alternative rule. However, Parliament did not pass legislation to deal with this issue until just before the June 2004 election.[89] The result of the rushed, last-minute process was a provision allowing registration of a party so long as it runs a candidate in a *single* electoral district, in addition to meeting some other administrative requirements such as having at least 250 electors as members.[90] The 2004 law included a "sunset clause," added as an amendment by the parliamentary committee examining the bill. The clause states that the new party rule will cease to have effect two years after the coming into force, in practice in 2006.[91] This provision will allow Parliament to take a more measured look at this issue.

In particular, it is at best unclear whether *Figueroa* requires a threshold as low as a single candidate for *all* purposes in election law. The Court of Appeal in that case suggested that twelve candidates — the same required to maintain party status in the House of Commons — might be an appropriate threshold for registration. At the Supreme Court, a concurring judgment by Justice LeBel and two other justices foresaw the possibility of a threshold higher than a single candidate, noting that "a requirement of nominating *at least one* candidate, *and perhaps more*, in order to qualify for registration as a party would not raise any serious constitutional concerns."[92] The three justices were also more sympathetic than the majority to the risks of groups abusing the party system, observing that "many of the benefits of registration are virtually meaningless outside the context of electoral competition — although some, such as tax credits to contributors,

88   *Ibid.* at para. 39.
89   S.C. 2004, c. 24.
90   *Elections Act*, ss. 366, 370, 380.1 and 385.
91   S.C. 2004, c. 24, s. 26.
92   *Figueroa*, [2003] 1 S.C.R. 912 at para. 149 [emphasis added].

could be attractive to groups that do not seriously intend to compete in elections. Making them available to such groups as well as genuine parties could undermine the purposes of the registration scheme."[93] However, the six-judge majority was more rigid on this issue, stating that "[i]t may well be that the government will be able to advance other objectives that justify a 12-candidate threshold. But suffice it to say, the objectives advanced do not justify a threshold requirement of any sort, let alone a 50-candidate threshold."[94]

This language does not close the door on a threshold above one candidate, but does suggest strongly that the Court would be suspicious of such a move. Still, a one-candidate threshold in response to the Supreme Court's language may be overkill, and the potential for abuse of the generous benefits of party status may be enormous.

This is especially the case for the tax credit provisions. We discuss problems with the tax credit subsidy later in the chapter. Here, we simply note that the credit is vulnerable to abuse in cases where supporters contribute to a party (or candidate) that then pays these supporters stipends to compensate for a portion of what they contributed. Subsequently, the tax credit covers the balance of the donation, meaning the supporter breaks even on his or her donation. But the party comes out ahead. For example, a supporter might contribute $400, receiving $300 back as a tax credit. If the party pays the supporter a $100 stipend, the latter breaks even and the party is $300 ahead, albeit at the taxpayer's expense. Multiplied by several supporters, the potential revenues of this scheme for parties — especially smaller parties — may be significant. As a related problem, parties may also direct tax-receipted contributions to causes unrelated to election campaigns.

In refusing to uphold the fifty-candidate requirement for parties under the old provision, the Supreme Court was unpersuaded that an abuse of the tax credit system for donations to political parties was a valid complaint, if only because the original rules allowed any candidate — whether from a registered political party or otherwise — to issue tax credits for donations *during* (as opposed to between) an election period.[95] But a one-candidate rule makes it (indisputably) easier for interest groups to form themselves into political parties to take advantage of other benefits offered under the *Elections Act*. This problem is most acute where groups wish to circumvent the

---

93   *Ibid.* at para. 148.
94   *Ibid.* at para. 92 [emphasis added].
95   *Ibid.* at para. 76.

controversial third-party advertising spending restrictions. We discuss party, candidate and third-party electoral spending caps below. Here, we simply observe that the combined candidate and party spending cap allowed by the *Elections Act* could well exceed the equivalent limit imposed on third-party spending, even if a "party" were to run only one or two candidates. The result would be an end run around the third-party advertising restrictions where a special interest group forms a "flag of convenience" party.

"Flag of convenience" parties would, of course, be a clear affront to the objectives of the Act, but the Act's provisions are arguably inadequate to guard against them. For example, party status may be policed by the CEO (or a court) attentive to the definition of "political party" in the Act, a definition supplemented with a requirement that the party certify that it meets this definition.[96] But this definition — "an organization one of whose fundamental purposes is to participate in public affairs by endorsing one or more of its members as candidates and supporting their election" — is broad enough to capture an advocacy group with an active involvement in public affairs seriously implicated in an election, something third-party advertisers may be intent on being anyway.

Likewise, the 2003 amendments to the Act preclude money being fundraised for a party by a person or entity making "a representation to the contributor or potential contributor that part or all of the contribution would be transferred to a person or entity, other than [among other things] the registered party."[97] This provision has been touted as defending "against a political party falsely created as a front to feed money elsewhere."[98] However, the provision does not appear to guard against monies generated by the political party being diverted to other uses, so long as it does not fundraise explicitly on this basis.

The effects of a circumvention of third-party spending limits might be mitigated somewhat by financial contributions limits, also discussed later in this chapter. Specifically, once an entity becomes a political party, it is restricted in the sorts of donations it might receive, not least from corporations who might be bankrolling third-party entities. Still, nothing in the Act appears to regulate how an entity acquires assets *prior* to being registered as a political party. A "flag of convenience" political party, therefore, could participate in an election campaign with a substantial war chest accumulat-

---

96   *Elections Act*, para. 366(2)(j); s. 384.1 (no leader of a party shall provide the Chief Electoral Officer with information under section 366 that they know is false or misleading).

97   *Elections Act*, s. 405.21.

98   Library of Parliament, *Bill C-3: An Act to amend the Elections Act and the Income Tax Act*, LS-461E (Feb 2004).

ed prior to registration as a political party. (Again, this would be dependant on the entity conforming to the "party" definition in the Act, for example by endorsing candidates and supporting their election.)

In *Figueroa*, the Court appeared to be alive to the concerns its approach to a party registration threshold raises:

> this decision does not stand for the proposition that the differential treatment of political parties will always constitute a violation of s. 3. Nor does it stand for the proposition that an infringement of s. 3 arising from the differential treatment of political parties could never be justified. Consequently, although the disposition of this case will have an impact on sections of the *Elections Act* that provide access to free broadcast time, the right to purchase reserved broadcast time, and the right to partial reimbursement of election expenses upon receiving a certain percentage of the vote, *I express no opinion as to the constitutionality of legislation that restricts access to those benefits.* It is possible that it would be necessary to consider factors that have not been addressed in this appeal in order to determine the constitutionality of restricting access to those benefits.[99]

The assertion gives resonance to one of the CEO's proposal to Parliamentarians studying Bill C-3 in 2004:

> the act itself would simply be amended to grant eligible parties that run between 1 and 49 candidates the three benefits stipulated by the Supreme Court, the rights to issue income tax receipts, to have their name on the ballot, and to receive a candidate surplus — strictly those three. Under these revised rules, eligible parties would be subject to the same reporting requirements as registered parties. However, they would not gain access to other benefits, including reimbursements and annual allowances, even if they meet the relevant vote thresholds.[100]

While cognizant of the constraints imposed by *Figueroa*, we would suggest that CEO's approach is the right idea, but aimed at the wrong benefits. First, for a party to receive a reimbursement or annual allowance, it must win a significant proportion of the popular vote. Given the logic of these provisions themselves, it is difficult to argue that a party that reaches such a threshold is not a "genuine" party. While the court in *Figueroa* did not pronounce on these subsidies, it is likely that its reasoning would (and should,

---

99 *Figueroa*, [2003] 1 S.C.R. 912 at para. 91 [emphasis added].
100 Mr. Jean-Pierre Kingsley (Chief Electoral Officer of Canada, Office of the Chief Electoral Officer), Standing Committee on Procedure and House Affairs, *Evidence*, 37th Parl., 3d Sess. (9 March 2004).

in our view) apply to these provisions. More importantly, restricting these benefits would not address the problem of "flag-of-convenience" parties. A group wishing to transform itself into a party solely for the purpose of taking advantage of the Act's provisions would primarily be interested in conveying their message rather than winning actual votes. As a result, they would be most interested in the tax credit measures and perhaps the free broadcast time and the ability to circumvent third-party spending limits.

To minimize the potential for such abuse, we support the principle of the CEO's recommendation, but would apply it differently. First, parties failing to meet a certain threshold of candidates should not be allowed to incur advertising expenses in excess of the third-party spending limits. Such parties should also not be entitled to other benefits such as the free and paid broadcast allocations, but would be entitled to benefits that are contingent on winning a percentage of the popular vote (for example, expense reimbursement and annual allowances), provided the requisite voting thresholds are achieved.

b)   Electoral District Associations

Among the administrative requirements a party must fulfill,[101] it must register its electoral district associations if they are to participate financially in an election.[102] Electoral district associations are the local unit of the party, and provide support to candidate campaigns. They also may accept campaign donations and receive and transfer funds from candidates and parties. Before electoral finance reforms introduced in 2004, electoral district associations had no registration requirements, and disclosure was limited.

Often, electoral district associations are grassroots entities that are highly dependent on voluntary contributions of time and money. As a result, the *Elections Act* aims to ease administrative burdens on these entities. For example, the Act provides that electoral district associations may be reimbursed for their auditing expenses.[103]

c)   Party Leaders

The centralized nature of Canadian politics means that party leaders enjoy tremendous clout within the party, and not only in the governing party. Leaders have authority to accept or reject candidates nominated at the electoral district level, and exercise additional control over MPs through party discipline, as discussed in chapter 5.

---

101   See *Elections Act*, ss. 366, 368, 371, 372 and 373.
102   *Ibid.*, s. 403.01. This registration is done by the district associations themselves, which must include a statement signed by the party leader: *Elections Act*, s. 403.02.
103   *Ibid.*, s. 403.39.

As discussed also in chapter 4, party leaders are elected by the party membership, rather than voters at large, at a leadership convention. Historically, leadership races have remained outside the regime for regulating elections, the prevailing view in political circles being that parties are private entities and should be free to regulate themselves.[104] This position has been whittled away in recent years, a recognition of the power that party conventions have in anointing party leaders wielding significant power in Canadian politics. (Consider that the 2003 Liberal leadership convention resulted in the appointment of a new prime minister, without voters at large having any say.)

Yet, with the exception of new political fundraising rules applying contribution limits and disclosure obligations (discussed further in the section on electoral contributions later in this chapter), most of the rules for leadership conventions are still developed by the parties themselves.

Some observers point to common allegations of irregularities during these campaigns, and advocate that the process be "professionalized" by bringing in Elections Canada to oversee leadership races, as well as nomination races, discussed below.[105] One of the most famous claims of leadership race shenanigans was the reported busing in of "instant voters" from Montreal's Old Brewery Mission to support Brian Mulroney's 1983 Progressive Conservative leadership bid.[106] However, reports of voter irregularities are commonplace in many leadership and nomination races of various parties.[107]

d)   Nomination Contestants and Candidates

Any qualified elector is eligible to be a candidate in an election, with some exceptions such as sitting members of a provincial or territorial legislature,[108] a "sheriff, clerk of the peace or county Crown Attorney in any of the provinces," "a judge appointed by the Governor in Council, other than a cit-

---

104   But see *Cureatz v. Progressive Conservative Party of Canada*, [1997] O.J. No. 2309 (Gen. Div.) where the court exercised modest judicial review authority over a political party. See also *Cameron v. Boyle*, [1994] O.J. No. 782 (Gen. Div.) applying procedural fairness concepts to a dispute concerning the meeting procedure of the Natural Law Party.

105   See J. Manley, "Let's Tame Riding Politics," *Globe and Mail*, 3 February 2005.

106   R. Bull, "National General News," *Canadian Press*, 14 March 1986.

107   In the Liberal nomination battle between Sheila Copps and Tony Valeri leading up to the 2004 federal election, there were allegations of irregularities from both sides, including hundreds of eligible party members being left off the voters list, open ballot boxes, and preferential partisan treatment of voters: A. Panetta, "National General News," *Canadian Press*, 10 March 2004.

108   *Elections Act*, subs. 65(c). Also see *Parliament of Canada Act*, R.S.C. c. P-1, s. 22.

izenship judge appointed under the *Citizenship Act*," and election officers.[109] The *Parliament of Canada Act* also specifies that a candidate running for Parliament may only run in one electoral district at any one time,[110] although the person need not live in the electoral district in which he or she is running.

A candidate may be endorsed by a party or may run as an independent (unaffiliated) candidate.[111] His or her nomination papers must be filed with the local returning officer in the electoral district in which he or she is running. These papers must include the signatures of at least 100 residents of that electoral district. Only fifty signatures are required in certain electoral districts with small populations.[112] A $1,000 deposit is also required,[113] which is refunded provided the candidate adheres to election reporting requirements[114] outlined later in this chapter.

Where the candidate is running on behalf of a party, the nomination papers must include "the name of the political party that has endorsed the prospective candidate."[115] Further, when filed, the nomination papers must be accompanied with "an instrument in writing, signed by the leader of the political party" or by a designated representative of the party, "that states that the prospective candidate is endorsed by the party."[116]

This instrument from the party leader is usually obtained by winning a nomination contest in the electoral district, although from time to time a leader may "parachute" a candidate into an electoral district, denying the local association the opportunity to elect its own candidate (a practice some consider undemocratic). As noted above, parties each have their own rules governing nomination races, but new *Election Act* provisions place limits on donations and spending in nomination campaigns.

For the purposes of electoral finance rules, a person becomes a candidate from the moment he or she accepts a contribution or incurs an election expense.[117] A candidate must appoint an official agent, who authorizes the incurring of expenses and receipt of campaign contributions, and an auditor, who must verify the candidate's finances.[118]

---

109 *Ibid.*, s. 65.
110 *Parliament of Canada Act*, s. 21.
111 *Elections Act*, s. 66.
112 *Ibid.*, paras. 66(1)(e) and (f).
113 *Ibid.*, para. 67(4)(a).
114 *Ibid.*, s. 468.
115 *Ibid.*, para. 66(1)(a).
116 *Ibid.*, subs. 67(4).
117 *Ibid.*, ss. 82 and 365.
118 *Ibid.*, ss. 82–88.

Candidates or their appointed representatives have a right to be present at polling stations, to have access to voter lists, and to observe the counting of ballots.[119] If a candidate is employed in any area of federal constitutional jurisdiction (for example, banking, transport, radio and television broadcasting), he or she is entitled to paid or unpaid leave to seek nomination and election.[120] The rules for public servants who wish to contest an election are discussed in chapter 4.

C. HOW ELECTIONS ARE RUN

1. How Elections Are Triggered

a) General Elections

In chapter 5, we discuss at length constitutional law and conventions concerning the duration of a Parliament. Here, we focus on the statutory basis for elections.

Under the *Canada Elections Act*, a general election is triggered by a proclamation from the Governor-in-Council directing the CEO to issue a legal order, or "writ," to each returning officer. This proclamation sets out the date of the writ, as well as a voting day which must be at least thirty-six days following the date of the writ.[121] The writ date, in other words, is the first day of an official campaign that must be at least thirty-six days long. The polling day itself must occur on a Monday (or a Tuesday if the Monday of the week of the election is an official holiday).[122]

b) By-elections

An "election" under the *Elections Act* also includes a "by-election," held after a Commons seat becomes vacant. The Act deals with by-elections in very general terms: a by-election is defined in the Act as an election other than a general election.[123] The Act provides that the "Governor in Council shall make an order in order for a by-election to be held."[124] These basic provisions must be read, however, in conjunction with the *Parliament of Canada Act*, which places modest constraints on the Governor-in-Council's *Election Act* discretion to time a by-election.

---

119 *Ibid.*, ss. 136, 139 and 140.
120 *Ibid.*, s. 80.
121 *Ibid.*, s. 57.
122 *Ibid.*, subss. 57(3) and (4).
123 *Ibid.*, s. 2.
124 *Ibid.*, s. 57.

The *Parliament of Canada Act* anticipates a Commons seat becoming "vacant" for several reasons. These provisions can be divided (generally) into those that expressly require the Speaker to issue a "warrant" to the Chief Electoral Officer for a by-election writ, and those that do not.

The Act specifically requires the Speaker to issue such a warrant in response to an MP's resignation,[125] death, contestation of his or her office under the *Elections Act*, or acceptance by an MP of another "office."[126] On this last issue, as noted in chapter 7, except for certain exemptions for members of the military and Ministry,[127] an MP may not accept or hold any paid office in the Government of Canada, or serve as a "sheriff, registrar of deeds, clerk of the peace or county crown attorney in any of the provinces."[128]

Vacancies that do not oblige a Speaker's warrant under the Act include some instances in which a vacancy is prompted by the Act's conflict of interest rules, discussed in greater detail in chapter 7. For instance, with some exceptions, an MP who engages in a banned contract by providing goods or services to the Government of Canada for which public money is paid thereby vacates his or her seat.[129]

A vacancy may also be created by the expulsion of an MP by the Commons itself pursuant to its parliamentary privileges. The power to expel is not firmly defined and has been used rarely; since Confederation, only four times. In the words of parliamentary expert Joseph Maingot, the House of Commons power to expel: "is not confined to offences committed by a member as member or during a session of Parliament, but extends to all cases where the offence is such as, in the judgment of the House, to render the Member unfit for Parliamentary duties."[130]

In practice, the offence prompting an expulsion would likely be a serious one. In Maingot's words, "it is unlikely that the House of Commons would take any action unless the offence was one that it felt involved serious moral turpitude rendering the person unfit to be a Member of the House."[131] The resulting vacancy of the expelled MP's seat does not automatically trigger a Speaker's warrant under the *Parliament of Canada Act*.

---

125 *Parliament of Canada Act*, s. 25.
126 *Ibid.*, ss. 28 and 29.
127 *Ibid.*, subss. 33(1) and (2).
128 *Ibid.*, s. 32.
129 *Ibid.*, ss. 34 and 35.
130 Joseph Maingot, *Parliamentary Privilege in Canada*, 2d ed. (Ottawa and Montreal: House of Commons and McGill-Queen's University Press, 1997), 211.
131 *Ibid.*, 212.

It is, however, unclear what significance should be read into the Act's silence in relation to a Speaker's warrant in response to these two (rare) sorts of vacancies. It may be that in practice, the Speaker would choose to issue such a warrant even in these instances, exercising a parliamentary privilege.

Where the Speaker does issue a warrant to the CEO, this act has implications for the timing of a by-election. The *Parliament of Canada Act* provides that a by-election writ must be issued between eleven and 180 days "after the receipt by the Chief Electoral Officer" of the warrant, unless Parliament is dissolved for a general election in the interim or unless the vacancy occurs within six months of the maximum duration of a Parliament (that is, four and a half years into a Parliament).[132] The Speaker's warrant, in other words, prevents the GIC from delaying indefinitely a by-election by failing to order the CEO to issue a by-election writ under the *Elections Act.*

An even more stringent time limit arises where a vacancy flows from the acceptance by an MP of a seat in a provincial legislature. Here, "a writ shall issue *forthwith* for the election of a member to fill the vacancy."[133]

These time frame requirements are, however, not as potent as they may seem. When the required writ is issued, nothing in either the *Elections Act* or the *Parliament of Canada Act* bars the Governor-in-Council from instructing the CEO to fix an attenuated *polling* date. As noted above, the *Elections Act* simply provides that, in ordering the CEO to issue an election writ, the Governor-in-Council is to "fix the date for voting at the election, which date must be at least thirty-six days after the issue of the writ." Put another way, a Commons vacancy may endure 180 days after a Speaker notifies the CEO of the vacancy, and then when the required writ is issued, an indefinite additional period of at least thirty-six days.

The prospect of a prolonged vacancy is more than theoretical, as recent history in the Ottawa Centre electoral district suggests. Incumbent MP Mac Harb resigned his Commons seat, taking a senate post on 9 September 2003.[134] The CEO received the warrant from the Speaker concerning the vacancy that same day.[135] The GIC ordered the CEO to issue a by-election writ on 7 March 2004, fully 180 days later.[136] In that order, 29 November

---

132 *Parliament of Canada Act*, s. 31.

133 *Ibid.*, s. 23 [emphasis added].

134 C. Gaz. 2003 I, vol. 137, issue 39 at Government Notices (27 Sept. 2003).

135 Elections Canada, *Chief Electoral Officer of Canada Receives Notice of Vacancy in House of Commons for Ottawa Centre*, press release, 12 Sept. 2003.

136 Order-in-Council, PC 2004-0161 (2004-03-07).

2004 was fixed as the election date, a point 456 days after Mr. Harb's senate appointment. Ultimately, the 28 June 2004 general election intervened. However, the net effect was to leave the residents of Ottawa Centre without Commons representation for almost ten months. Given these sorts of experiences, a refinement to the law ensuring that electoral districts not go unrepresented for long or even indefinite periods seems prudent.

2. Electoral Financing

As noted above, fairness is a central theme in Canada's electoral law. It is with a view to this objective that limits are placed on how much those running for office can raise and spend on their campaigns, and public subsidies are provided to help prevent financial restraints from being a barrier to running for office. These limits also reduce the dependence of those running for office on moneyed interests, who often have a tremendous stake in government decision-making.[137]

a) Competing Values

When it comes to this and related areas of electoral law, however, there are countervailing values to the fairness objective. The *Charter*'s freedom of expression and freedom of association provisions have been used to challenge measures such as bans on releasing election results before the polls close in certain parts of the country, bans on releasing public surveys of voter preferences, and limits on third-party spending.

The debate represents a clash of values between an egalitarian conception of democracy contained in section 3 of the *Charter*, and a libertarian view reflected in the free expression guarantee in section 2(b) that, especially in an electoral context, seeks to ensure that the broadest array of views are expressed.

Under the egalitarian model, the ability of the wealthy to dominate the electoral process to the detriment of those with less economic power is constrained through limits on spending. By contrast, under the libertarian model, an unregulated freedom of speech within the "market of ideas"

---

137 For example, an October 2002 study by one of the authors showed that seventeen out of the top twenty-five federal government contractors was a significant donor to the Liberal Party, while only 1 to 2 percent of Canadian corporations donate to any political party. The study showed that contractors were 6.5 times more likely to donate to the Liberal Party than to all opposition parties combined. At the riding level, top twenty-five contractors donated to Liberal candidates verses all other candidates at a ratio of thirty-to-one: A. Freeman, "Lobbying and Donations by the Top 25 Federal Government Contractors," *Democracy Watch*, 31 Oct. 2002.

ensures that no party or individual can restrict the speech of another, and as a result, the voter receives maximum exposure to all political views in order to inform his or her voting preference. In the libertarian model, free speech trumps virtually all other rights. From an egalitarian perspective, the effect is to allow the privileged to express themselves disproportionately, since limitless persuasive speech is subject only to the ability to pay for media exposure or other campaign costs.[138]

South of the border, U.S. election law's principal focus has been libertarian, with some constraints imposed to forestall corruption in government. While lawmakers in the early days of U.S. electoral finance regulation did attempt to impose spending limits on those running for office, these limits were struck down by the U.S. Supreme Court in 1976, which held that freedom of speech is the primary constitutional value to be considered in evaluating money in politics legislation. In the precedent-setting case, *Buckley v. Valeo*, the U.S. Supreme Court held that "the concept that government may restrict the speech of some elements of our society in order to enhance the relative voice of others is wholly foreign to the First amendment."[139] In coming to this conclusion, the U.S. Court recognized the need to prevent actual or apparent corruption in politics. For this reason, the Court upheld limits on political contributions and disclosure obligations. However, it accepted that money is necessary to communicate political views in a modern society and rejected the government's interest in providing an equal playing field. It therefore struck down restrictions on campaign expenditures.[140]

Buckley and subsequent U.S. court decisions suggest strongly that the egalitarian model has had little traction historically in the United States, a source of constant frustration for those seeking reform to campaign finance laws in that country. For example, former New York mayoral candidate Mark Green narrowly lost his 2001 campaign to billionaire Michael Bloomberg. While Green raised and spent an impressive U.S.$16.2 million, Bloomberg self-financed his own campaign, to the tune of U.S.$73.9

---

138 For a broader discussion of the egalitarian-libertarian debate, see Colin Feasby, "*Libman v. Quebec (A.G.) and the Administration of the Process of Democracy Under the Charter*," cited in *Harper*, 2004 SCC 33 at para. 62.

139 *Buckley. v. Valeo*, 424 U.S. 1 at 48 (U.S.S.C. 1976).

140 In practice, there remain spending limits for presidential candidates, but these only apply on a "voluntary" basis. Presidential candidates may agree to adhere to these limits in exchange for public subsidies that match, one for one, each dollar they raise from private sources. Many candidates, however, forego these subsidies in order to spend in excess of the limits.

million. Most attributed Bloomberg's win to the enormous sums he spent in the campaign, and for many, it highlighted the need to rein in the costs of running for office. Commenting on the need for legal reform, Green argued,

> Of course, free speech is a "compelling interest" in our constitutional galaxy; but that doesn't mean it's legal to publish child pornography, to shout "fire" in a crowded theater, to electioneer within 100 feet of a polling place, or to give a speech through a 100-decibel sound system and drown out other speakers in a residential community. Are dollars like decibels? Should special interests be free to make 100-decibel contributions that threaten to monopolize the public conversation? ... If elephants are free to dance among the chickens, isn't it clear who's going to get crushed?[141]

Noting *Buckley*'s distinction between limits on contributions and expenditures, Green wrote: "[I]f spending money is a precondition for expression, as *Buckley* says, isn't it just as necessary for a campaign to have received contributions before it can make campaign expenditures? By *Buckley*'s own suggestion, both are to some degree antecedents of expression, and ought to be treated similarly."[142]

Three decades after *Buckley*, there are signals that even U.S. courts are retreating from their raw libertarian approach. In a December 2003 judgment, *McConnell v. FEC*,[143] the U.S. Supreme Court upheld the *Bipartisan Campaign Reform Act*. This law established both a ban on unregulated "soft money" political contributions and disclosure requirements for third-party "electioneering communication."[144]

Meanwhile, Canada and other countries[145] have interpreted their freedom of speech constitutional provisions far less absolutely than has the United States, placing greater emphasis on the need for electoral fairness,

---

141   Mark Green, *Selling Out: How Big Corporate Money Buys Elections, Rams Through Legislation, and Betrays Our Democracy* (New York: Harper Collins, 2002) at 13.

142   *Ibid.*, 60.

143   *McConnell v. Federal Election Commission*, 540 U.S. 93 (2003).

144   The U.S. provisions are somewhat narrower in scope than the Canadian law. "Electioneering communication" is restricted to "broadcast, cable or satellite communication" whereas the Canadian law includes nearly all forms of advertising. Electioneering communication also requires a clearer link to the candidate than the Canadian provisions, which cover ads dealing with issues that are "particularly associated" with a candidate; *Elections Act*, para. 350(2)(d).

145   In *Bowman v. United Kingdom* (1998), 26 E.H.R.R. 1, for example, the European Court of Human Rights found that spending limits on third parties in elections are necessary to ensure electoral fairness.

as discussed in the section on election advertising later in this chapter. Canada has adopted, in other words, an egalitarian philosophy, one that permits more aggressive efforts to limit the influence of wealth in Canadian elections.

The primary tools used for this purpose, since 1974, have been party and candidate spending limits. Far more recently, other electoral actors, including nomination contestants and third-party actors, have been subjected to their own spending limits, and contributions have also been restricted. In part to compensate for some of these limits, parties and candidates also now enjoy quite generous public subsidies to help finance their campaigns.

b) Expenses

Canadian electoral finance provisions rely on an "agency" principle. Each candidate — including leadership, nomination and electoral candidates — as well as each party and party electoral district association, appoint an official agent who is solely responsible for receiving donations and approving expenses.[146]

In terms of these expenses, the *Elections Act* defines a candidate's or party's "election expenses" as including both "costs incurred" as well as "non-monetary contributions received, by a registered party or candidate."[147] Thus, contributions of in-kind goods and services are generally included in the tabulation of election expenses. The definition limits expenses to those "used to directly promote or oppose a registered party, its leader or a candidate during an election period."[148] Expenses include:

- the production of advertising or promotional material and its distribution, broadcast or publication in any media or by any other means;
- the payment of remuneration and expenses to or on behalf of a person for their services as an official agent, registered agent or in any other capacity;
- securing a meeting space or the supply of light refreshments at meetings;
- any product or service provided by a government, a Crown corporation or any other public agency; and
- the conduct of election surveys or other surveys or research during an election period.[149]

---

146 See, e.g., *Elections Act*, s. 416 (relating to parties).
147 *Ibid.*, subs. 407(1).
148 *Ibid.*
149 *Ibid.*, subs. 407(3).

The law generally exempts from the definition of election expenses "[e]xpenses for a fund-raising activity and expenses to directly promote the nomination of a person as a candidate or as leader of a registered party."[150] Thus, while candidate nomination contests are governed by separate expense limit rules, party leadership convention expenses remain unregulated.

"Personal expenses" are exempted from the definition of election expenses, but must still be disclosed to the CEO. The CEO may establish maximum limits for these expenses. Personal expenses are costs reasonably incurred in relation to a campaign and include items such as:

- travel and living expenses;
- childcare expenses;
- expenses relating to the provision of care for a person with a physical or mental incapacity for whom the candidate normally provides such care; and
- in the case of a candidate who has a disability, additional personal expenses that are related to the disability.[151]

Expense Limits for Political Actors

From 1974 until the 2003 passage of Bill C-24, which limited campaign donations in the fashion discussed later, the primary tool used to regulate federal electoral finance was expense limits. These expense limits remain a central element of Canada's electoral finance regime.

For each party in each election, the calculation of their spending limits depends on the number of electoral districts in which the party is running candidates multiplied by $0.70 per elector in those districts, as adjusted by an inflation index.[152] In 2004, for a party running candidates in all 308 electoral districts, this amount was approximately $17.5 million.

Candidates also face expense limits based on the number of electors in their electoral districts, with an adjustment factor allowing a higher limit in electoral districts that are less densely populated.[153] This formula reflects the added expenses associated with travelling longer distances to reach electors in these districts. The average candidate expense limit in 2004 was approximately $78,500.

Candidates for a party nomination race face limits of 20 percent of the spending limit that would apply in their electoral district in a general election.[154] On average, the nomination race limit is about $15,700.

---

150   *Ibid.*, subs. 407(2).
151   *Ibid.*, s. 409.
152   *Ibid.*, subs. 422(1).
153   *Ibid.*, ss. 440 and 441.
154   *Ibid.*, s. 478.14.

For their part, electoral district associations may not incur election expenses, as only a candidate or party may do so. This prohibition extends to advertising expenses.[155]

Key Areas for Reform

Spending Levels

Historically, expense limits have kept the cost of running for office in Canada affordable, and prevented many of the excesses of the U.S. system. As noted earlier, for a party running a full slate of candidates, the national expense limit was approximately $17.5 million in 2004. Typically, only the governing party has been able to afford to spend the maximum. This situation will likely change with the new public financing provisions. Parties will reap more from these public financing mechanisms than they previously did from corporate, union, and high-end individual donations. As a consequence, they can be expected to spend more in general elections and transfer more to candidates.

These current expense limits may not, however, reflect how much parties ought to be able to spend. Especially at the party (versus candidate) level, there is ample room to bring expense limits down. Reining in the costs of party spending is essential both from the standpoint of electoral fairness — keeping the cost of running for office low to ensure it remains accessible to all parties and candidates — and taxpayer fairness, given that taxpayers now foot the bill for roughly 80 percent of party revenues.

While parties may resist further limitations on their spending, one way to ease the pain would be to increase the free broadcast provisions and lower the expense limit by the value of the broadcast time being provided. Broadcast advertising is the number-one expense for all parties, so all parties would benefit.

While candidates collectively spend more than their parties do individually, candidate limits are quite low. It is therefore not advisable, in our view, to lower the candidate expense limit in the near future.

Leadership Contests

Perhaps the most serious remaining loophole in the expenses regime relates to party leadership races. While parties, candidates, electoral district associations and even nomination race contestants all face the strict expense limits noted above, those running to be the leaders of their parties do not. This bizarre omission may reflect the fact that an unofficial leadership race was taking place in the governing Liberal Party at the time that the spending limits

---

155   *Ibid.*, s. 403.04.

issue was last revisited during the 2003 *Elections Act* overhaul. Whatever its reason, the absence of spending rules in leadership contests seems incongruous given the power that party leaders have. As noted above, even the prime minister is sometimes "elected" first by the party in a leadership race — a campaign that faces no legal limits on how much can be spent to win the leadership. As a result, someone running to be a fourth-row opposition backbencher may face a more stringent limit on his or her public electoral campaign than will someone running in a party contest to inherit the party leadership from a resigning incumbent prime minister, the most powerful office in the country.

c)   Donation Limits

Overview

Under the 2003 overhaul of election financing rules, political donations — called "contributions" in the *Elections Act* — are also regulated. The Act defines contributions as including monetary or nonmonetary contributions.[156] Notably, contributions include "money that is used for a candidate's, leadership contestant's or nomination contestant's campaign out of the candidate's or contestant's own funds."[157] A nonmonetary contribution, meanwhile, means "the commercial value of a service, other than volunteer labour, or of property or of the use of property or money to the extent that they are provided without charge or at less than their commercial value."[158]

The Act restricts contributions in two ways. First, the Act limits the size of contributions, capping the limit for each person to $5,000 to each party per year,[159] adjusted for inflation.[160] This ceiling includes contributions to all of the party's candidates, electoral district associations and nomination contestants. A person may make additional $5,000 contributions to each independent candidate running in an election, and to contestants in a party's leadership race.[161] The cap does not apply to a contribution made by way of "an unconditional, non-discretionary testamentary disposition" (that is, a will),[162] and candidates may donate up to a total of $10,000 to their own campaigns.[163]

---

156 *Ibid.*, s. 2.

157 *Ibid.*, s. 404.2.

158 *Ibid.*, s. 2.

159 *Ibid.*, subs. 405(1).

160 *Ibid.*, s. 405.1.

161 *Ibid.*, subs. 405(1).

162 *Ibid.*, subs. 405(2).

163 *Ibid.*, subs. 405(4) states that contributions from a candidate (leadership race, nomination race or general election) that do not exceed $5,000 are not taken into account in the calculation of "contribution" under the Act. The candidate could then spend an additional $5,000 as a contribution to him- or herself.

Second, the Act limits who may make donations. Generally only citizens or permanent residents may make contributions.[164] More recently, amendments to the Act discussed at length below restrict corporate and union contributions, although they do not grapple with trust fund donations.

The Act also includes important disclosure features, outlined below. These disclosure requirements may mean that contributions are regulated even beyond the election period. If, for example, a candidate receives a donation after the election, perhaps to pay off a campaign debt, he or she must file an updated report with Elections Canada regarding the donation.[165]

Corporate and Union Contributions

As of January 2004, corporations and unions are barred from making contributions to parties or leadership candidates, although they may make contributions to individual candidates running in an election, candidates for a party nomination race, or registered electoral district associations.[166] The total amount a corporation, union or other organization may donate to these recipients generally must not exceed $1,000 in a calendar year,[167] adjusted for inflation.[168] A corporate donor making such a donation must carry out business in Canada, and a union donor must hold bargaining rights for employees in Canada. Government-owned corporations, or those that receive more than half of their funding from government, are not eligible to make contributions.

Unincorporated associations are subject to provisions similar to those for corporations and unions, although additional disclosure obligations apply. For example, the name and address of any individuals whose contribution forms part of the organization's contribution must be disclosed.[169] The law has forced the larger parties to broaden their base, moving away from high-end and corporate donors and toward a more "grassroots" approach.[170]

---

164 *Ibid.*, s. 404(1).

165 *Ibid.*, ss. 451 and 455.

166 *Ibid.*, s. 404.1.

167 *Ibid.* If there is a second election called for an electoral district, a corporation, union or organization may make an additional $1,000 total in donations to a party's candidates and associations: *Elections Act*, s. 404.1(1.1).

168 *Ibid.*, s. 405.1.

169 *Ibid.*, s. 405.3.

170 For example, Liberal Party vice-chairman Daryl Friedhandler told the *Ottawa Citizen*, "I see the whole new financing regime as something that is absolutely going to drive things more towards the grassroots. We will definitely be broadening the target." The party is considering lowering membership fees and expanding it into smaller communities and regions: A. Dawson, "Cash-Strapped Grits Eye Grassroots," *Ottawa Citizen*, 15 Nov. 2004, A5.

Background

The new law's constraints on corporate and union donations are not the first time Parliament has delved into this area. In 1908, Parliament passed a ban on contributions from corporations,[171] which was extended to "unincorporated associations" such as unions in 1920.[172] The ban was not enforced. Indeed, noting the capacity of businesspeople to circumvent the law by giving as individuals and the absence of any enforcement or penalties, the 1966 Committee on Election Expenses (the Barbeau Commission) called the measure a "legal platitude."[173]

In 1930, Parliament repealed the ban at the urging of J.S. Woodsworth and William Irvine of the CCF, the predecessor to the NDP.[174] Ironically, the year after the repeal, the Beauharnois scandal erupted. Revelations emerged that some $700,000 to $800,000 had been provided by the Beauharnois company to the prior Liberal government "and that an extremely valuable government contract had been given to the corporation."[175] Yet, while these events constituted what the Barbeau Commission considered "one of the worst scandals in Canadian history,"[176] the electoral reforming spirit had dissipated. Only with the striking of the Barbeau Commission in 1964 did Parliament really turn its attention to electoral reform once more, this time sparked not by scandal but by the parties' own concerns about spiralling costs of campaigning and the discomforting dependence of political parties on a handful of donors.[177]

Notably, up until 1974, it was estimated that less than 500 donors — mostly companies — had been providing the Liberals and Conservatives with virtually all of their funding.[178] For example, in 1953, the Liberal party received 50 percent of its donations from companies and another 40 percent from "businessmen linked to particular firms."[179]

---

171   *An Act to amend the Dominion Elections Act*, S.C. 1908, c. 26, s. 36.
172   *The Dominion Elections Act*, S.C. 1920, c. 46, s. 10.
173   Committee on Election Expenses, *Report* (1966) at 20.
174   W.T. Stanbury, *Money in Politics: Financing Federal Parties and Candidates in Canada*, vol. 1, Research Studies, Royal Commission on Electoral Reform and Party Financing (Toronto: Dundurn Press, 1991) at 29. These individuals may have been motivated by the prospect of union contributions to the CCF.
175   Committee on Election Expenses, *Report* at 22.
176   *Ibid.*
177   K.D. Ewing, *Money, Politics and Law* (Oxford: Clarendon Press, 1992) at 12.
178   Stanbury, *Money in Politics* at 291.
179   Ewing, *Money, Politics and Law* at 6.

Substantial changes to elections law recommended by the Barbeau Commission in 1966 and then by the Chappell Committee in 1971[180] led ultimately to the enactment of the *Elections Act* in 1974.[181] Yet, while the Act introduced a number of essential reforms concerning expenditures, public funding and disclosure, it did not seek to control the source of donations by regulating corporate or union giving.

The Barbeau Commission had contemplated recommending limits by source of donations, but concluded that a combination of modest public funding and disclosure would reduce "reliance on special interests."[182] This position was echoed by the 1978 Royal Commission on Corporate Concentration. It reasoned that suspicions of undue corporate influence could be defeated via extensive disclosure,[183] a position shared by the 1991 Royal Commission on Electoral Reform and Party Financing (the Lortie Commission). The latter Commission — established in part in response to immense corporate involvement in the Free Trade election of 1988 — concluded that corporate donations were less important than they had been in the past and that, at any rate, "Canadian organizations with a stake in the political future of the country should not be prevented from supporting parties and candidates who share policies and values, provided the public has full opportunity to be informed about these financial activities."[184]

As late as 1999, the Liberal Government House Leader Don Boudria echoed this reasoning, arguing against a ban on corporate donations by urging that "[c]ompanies and individuals have almost identical rights according to the law. What a company can legally do in terms of contributions, an individual can also do. They are not treated differently by the law."[185]

There are, however, good reasons to limit donations from these entities. As noted by Cross, "The democratic interest in citizen participation in the electoral process lies solely with voters. Corporations, trade unions, foreign entities and other organizations or associations have no such protected interest. There is no compelling democratic or legal reason why these groups should be permitted to participate as independent expenditors."[186]

---

180 *Minutes of Proceedings and Evidence of the Special Committee on Election Expenses*, 28th Parl., 3d Sess. (1 June 1971).

181 Now *Canada Elections Act*, RSC 1985, c. 14 (1st supp.) as amended.

182 Committee on Election Expenses, *Report* at 34–35.

183 Royal Commission on Corporate Concentration, *Report* (1978) at 343.

184 Royal Commission on Electoral Reform and Party Financing, *Reforming Electoral Democracy* (1991) at 450.

185 Standing Committee on Procedure and House Affairs, *Evidence* (26 Oct. 1999).

186 See W. Cross, "Regulating Independent Expenditures in Federal Elections," (1994) 20 *Canadian Public Policy* 253 at 258.

Corporations are not voters. Nor is a corporation a book club or community centre where people gather to debate ideas. A company is a profit-generating institution, one that by virtue of its special legal status is able to attract substantial shareholder capital. At the same time, the political preferences of the directing minds of these corporations — its directors and executives — cannot be presumed to reflect the political positions of their numerous human stockholders-cum-voters.

Thus, corporate donations are not at all reflective of a party's appeal in the *voter* marketplace of ideas. Instead, they reflect the attractiveness of that party's platform to an elite cadre of company managers able to exploit their control over a substantial pool of shareholder assets. In fact, in the United States, the U.S. Supreme Court has rejected First Amendment constitutional challenges to bans on corporate electoral donations on the grounds that the state has a compelling reason "to protect the individuals who have paid money into a corporation or union for purposes other than the support of candidates from having that money used to support political candidates to whom they may be opposed."[187]

Corporate donations, in other words, disproportionately favour the vision of a small sub-set of Canadians and electoral laws permitting corporate donations give citizens controlling corporate capital an unequal opportunity to play a meaningful role in the selection of elected representatives. Similar objections can be directed at union donations.

This reasoning has clearly proved persuasive in some provinces. Quebec (in 1977) and Manitoba (in 2000) passed laws banning contributions from corporations and other organizations to provincial political parties, and applying a $3,000 limit on all other contributions from individuals. These laws served as precedent for federal legislation passed in 2003.

Like the provincial laws, the federal bill initially proposed an outright ban on corporate and union donations. The watering down of the final law to allow for candidate and association donations up to $1,000 was likely a sop to party insiders, and to some backbench Liberal MPs, who were worried that if corporate and union donations were to end, they would find it more difficult to raise sufficient funds to run their campaigns.[188]

---

187   *Federal Election Commission v. National Right to Work Committee*, 459 U.S. 197 at 208 (1982). Indeed, it should be regarded as an open issue as to whether corporate donations to political actors are consistent with the fiduciary obligations a director owes the company.

188   Opposition to the corporate ban from within the Liberal Party included several backbench MPs and party officials such as party President Stephen LeDrew, and stemmed in part from concern that the party would not be able to raise sufficient revenues

Splitting Donations

While the $1,000 candidate contribution compromise may have helped pave the way for the law's passage, it will likely create headaches for Elections Canada officials and donors alike. As noted by one Liberal member of the committee reviewing the bill, elections officials will be "using dollars to chase nickels" to try to determine whether corporations with multiple subsidiaries, franchises, or unincorporated associations have been adhering to the limit.[189]

No doubt to avoid exactly this problem, the $1,000 contribution limit to candidates applies to "any other corporation controlled, directly or indirectly in any manner whatever, by the corporation; and ... any other corporation that is controlled by the same person or group of persons that controls the corporation, directly or indirectly in any manner whatever."[190] Application of this provision clearly hinges on "control." A corporation controlling, directly or indirectly, a string of subsidiaries will be capped at $1,000, irrespective of the number of those subsidiaries. The situation is different in the case of separately owned enterprises. A franchise that is separately owned by a local franchisee might not be considered "controlled" by the head office corporation, and might be allowed to make a separate contribution in addition to any made by this head office enterprise.

It remains to be seen whether these control safeguards will prove effective. Following the 2004 election, there was some evidence that corporate donors were using various methods, including splitting their donations among multiple corporations, to bump overall donations above $1,000.[191]

Downstream Donations

Another troubling aspect to the $1,000 contribution rule relates to the mutability of such donations. While corporate and union donations to *parties* are banned, these donations may still find their way to party coffers through candidates and electoral district associations, who may transfer funds to their parties.[192] While there is an anti-avoidance provision pro-

---

without corporate donations: see Standing Committee on Procedure and House Affairs, *Hansard* (13 May 2003); and S. LeDrew, letter to the editor, "Don't Ban Corporate Political Donations," *National Post*, 4 Dec. 2002, A19.

189 A. Freeman, "Here's the Bottom Line on PM's Campaign and Elections Finance Bill," *The Hill Times*, 9 June 2003.

190 *Elections Act*, subs. 404.1(2).

191 In one instance, a re-elected Liberal MP, after returning a corporate donation of $5,000 because it was above the $1,000 limit, received donations of $1,000 each from the company owner, his brother, and several companies controlled by the two: A. Freeman, "Election Was a Lesson in Fundraising Loopholes," *The Hill Times*, 5 July 2004.

192 *Elections Act*, subs. 404.2(2).

hibiting corporate and union donations from being included in such a transfer,[193] in most cases it will be difficult if not impossible to disaggregate corporate and union contributions from the pool of contributions received by candidates. Candidates, in other words, provide a ready means to launder corporate and union donations.

On the whole, we believe that an outright ban on corporate and union donations to candidates as well as parties is a more sensible approach to this campaign finance reform issue, borrowing from the example of Quebec and Manitoba. Unfortunately, by early 2005, there were few prospects for such a ban. In fact, Liberal MPs were considering raising the $1,000 limit during the post-2004 election review of the *Elections Act*, in response to concerns about revenue shortfalls at the electoral district level.

MP concern about their campaign revenue shortfall is, in our view, valid. However, the blame should be placed on their own parties, which require candidates and their electoral district associations to hand over a portion of fundraising revenues to the national party coffers. The Liberal Party, for example, requires candidates to transfer roughly half of their expense reimbursement. Parties, which enjoy the lion's share of public subsidies, should be helping finance the grassroots, rather than the other way around.

Displaced Donations

A common objection to bans (or even limits) on corporate donations relates to indirect contributions. Some observers fear that companies and unions circumvent the restrictions in Quebec by donating through employees or members, or by giving contributions in-kind.[194] To pre-empt this sort of circumvention, the new federal law bars "indirect contributions": "No person or entity shall make a contribution to a registered party, a registered association, a candidate or a leadership contestant or a nomination contestant that comes from money, property or the services of another person or entity that was provided to that person or entity for that purpose."[195] This provision compounds a more general prohibition on avoidance of the contribution limit rules: no person or entity shall "circumvent, or attempt to circumvent" the contribution limits.[196]

---

193 *Ibid.*, subs. 404.2(4).
194 See W. Cross, "Regulating Independent Expenditures" at 258; R.T. Gabor, "Election Laws an NDP Trojan Horse," *Winnipeg Free Press*, 15 July 2000; and House of Commons Standing Committee on Procedure and House Affairs, *Evidence*, 37th Parl., 2d Sess. (30 April 2003).
195 *Elections Act*, s. 405.3.
196 *Ibid.*, s. 405.2

By early 2005, it was too soon to determine whether donation diversions would prove an important issue, and whether the anticircumvention rules would work. Some solace may be taken, however, in the fact that since 1977, when the Quebec law was passed, empirical evidence that this abuse occurs on any significant scale is remarkably scarce. Nor is there any empirical evidence that such circumvention has taken place in Manitoba since 2000. One would expect, if such abuse were indeed rampant, that at least some companies or unions would be caught breaking the rules.

A final concern raised by the new limits on corporate and union contributions is that these restrictions may lead these entities to direct more money to third-party election spending, discussed below.

Trust Funds

One of the key electoral finance issues not dealt with in the *Elections Act* is money contributed to trust funds controlled by MPs or parties. If money moves from these accounts into a campaign fund, the contribution limits (and disclosure obligations discussed later in this chapter) would apply. But there is an infinite number of things that a trust fund could pay for that might allow them to avoid these requirements.

The most obvious examples are funds that would boost an MP's retirement benefits. Canada has a long history of such funds that dates back to Laurier,[197] although most of these funds likely remain hidden from the public. If the proceeds from the fund are accrued after the MP leaves office, they would not be covered by the *Elections Act* provisions. Similarly, funds could also pay for community events between elections that boost the MP's profile without being caught by any legal limits or disclosure obligations.

During deliberations over the 2003 *Election Act* amendments, some, including the CEO, suggested that because the law already regulated transfers from these funds to election campaigns,[198] trust funds should best be dealt with by ethics rules for MPs, discussed in chapter 7. However, there are two problems with this approach. First, it is unclear whether the new MP Ethics Code deals effectively with this issue. Whether it does likely hinges on whether a donation to a trust fund would be considered a "gift," but this term is left undefined in the MP Code. Second, the MP Code

---

197 W.T. Stanbury, *Money in Politics* at 375–77.

198 Under the law at present, Elections Canada treats trust fund contributions as contributions by the individual or entity behind the trust fund, and applies the contribution rules applicable to that source (i.e., a ceiling of $1,000 to candidates of contributions by corporations or unions). See Elections Canada, *Making Contributions through Trusts* (Jan. 2004).

applies to neither trust funds controlled by political parties, nor to electoral candidates, other than incumbent MPs. As a result, failing to ban trust funds provides a large loophole for many key electoral players.

In our view, trust funds should be banned by law, with existing funds grandfathered.

d) Public Subsidies

The fairness objective of electoral legislation envisions as few barriers as possible to running for public office, including financial impediments. To this end, and because running an election campaign can be an expensive endeavour, the government provides financial subsidies to candidates and parties. Often, but not always, these subsidies are tied to some measure of the popular support that the party or candidate enjoys. They were enhanced starting in 2004, at least in part as a *quid pro quo* for the limitations on corporate and union donations and the individual donation ceiling.

Expense Reimbursement

Both parties and candidates benefit from a partial reimbursement of their election expenses. For a registered party, to qualify for the reimbursement, it must have won the support of at least 2 percent of votes cast in the election, or 5 percent of votes cast in the electoral districts in which the party ran candidates. If they achieve either threshold, they are eligible to be reimbursed for one-half of their election expenses.[199]

For candidates, the threshold for reimbursement is 10 percent of the votes cast in their electoral district. Candidates who achieve this threshold are eligible for a reimbursement of 60 percent of their election and personal expenses.[200] In 2004, roughly half of the candidates who ran in the general election were eligible for reimbursement, with most of these from the larger parties.[201]

Quarterly Allowance

If a party receives at least 2 percent of valid votes cast in the election, or 5 percent of votes cast in the electoral districts in which the party ran candidates, it also qualifies for an annual subsidy of $1.75 multiplied by the number of votes the party received in the previous election, as adjusted for inflation from 2004.[202] This money, distributed quarterly to the parties,

---

199 *Elections Act*, s. 435.
200 *Ibid.*, ss. 464 and 465.
201 Chief Electoral Officer, *Report of the Chief Electoral Officer of Canada on the 38th General Election Held on June 28, 2004* at 66.
202 *Elections Act*, s. 435.01.

constitutes the largest public subsidy. Based on the results of the 2004 election, for example, parties will receive $24.1 million per year from the quarterly allowance.[203]

This allowance is, in our view, flawed for two reasons. First, it is excessively generous with taxpayers' money. Combined with the expense reimbursement for parties discussed above, the new subsidies more than replaced the revenues lost by the Act's new restrictions on contributions.[204] Second, the allowance framework does little to alleviate the real problem stemming from recent restrictions on contributions discussed above: The new subsidies are primarily directed at parties, leaving candidates and electoral district associations with a revenue shortfall from the loss of corporate contributions, and further concentrating resources with parties and their leadership.

Tax Credit

Taxpayers indirectly subsidize private contributions made to parties and candidates. A generous tax credit is provided for political contributions to parties and candidates, at the following levels: 75 percent up to the first $400 contributed; 50 percent of the amount above $400, up to $750; and 33.3 percent of the amount above $750, up to $1,275. At the level of a $1,275 contribution, the tax credit is worth $650 to the contributor at tax time. There is no additional credit for amounts donated above $1,275.[205]

The idea behind the tax credit is to encourage contributions, particularly smaller contributions, from a large number of sources. In this way, it is meant to encourage the parties to broaden the base of their support. Its effect, however, is likely only minimal in this regard. Research reports prepared for the Lortie Commission found that only 43 to 65 percent of individuals making a political contribution actually claimed the credit. For corporate donors, only 20 percent of firms claim the credit.[206] It appears contributors generally do not make their donation with a view to tax planning.

---

203 This figure derived from Elections Canada, "Quarterly Allowances to the Registered Political Parties" (15 Oct. 2004).

204 For the year 2002, the Liberal Party raised $5.5 million from corporate/union and high end (i.e., more than the new $5,000 limit) donations. In higher years, usually those in which an election or leadership race takes place, this figure generally doubles. Had the quarterly allowance been in place in 2002, the Liberals would have reaped more than $9 million. The allowance would be considerably higher if voter turnout rates rebound from current historical lows.

205 *Income Tax Act*, R.S.C. 1985, c. 1 (5th Supp.), subs. 127(3).

206 Stanbury, *Money in Politics* at 227.

The present system may be vulnerable to abuse. As noted above, parties could encourage those working on election campaigns to make contributions, a portion of which is, in effect, routed back to the contributor in the form of a salary with the balance being returned to the contributor as a tax credit. Thus, the net payment for the contributor may be zero, but the party is enriched at the expense of the federal fisc.

Other dubious uses of the tax credit are also possible. For example, in the early days of the Reform Party, it devised the following scheme, as described by Professor Stanbury:

> A Calgary member called "Anne" arranged to purchase a life insurance policy with the Reform Party named as the beneficiary. The ownership of the policy was then transferred to the party. "Anne" then made a donation to the Reform Canada Fund to cover the annual premium for which she received a receipt for the tax credit for political contributions. In subsequent years, "Anne's" donations to cover the annual premium will be eligible for the tax credit. The party is also able to borrow against the cash value of the policy.[207]

Various ministers and members of other parties roundly criticized the arrangement. The minister of national revenue at first said it was illegal, but later admitted that while he thought it was unethical, it was not technically illegal.[208]

In another example, the Green Party in 1993 issued receipts to those who made party donations to help pay fines imposed on Clayoquot Sound protesters. While tax experts decried the use of the tax credit in this manner, it was not declared illegal by Elections Canada.[209]

e) Electoral Finance Disclosure

Parties,[210] candidates for party nominations[211] and the party leadership,[212] electoral district associations[213] and — in general elections – candidates[214] must report to Elections Canada all contributions of more than $200, iden-

---

207 *Ibid.*, 206.

208 *Ibid.*

209 W.T. Stanbury, "Getting and Spending: The Effect of Federal Regulations on Financing Political Parties and Candidates in Canada," in H.G. Thorburn, ed., *Party Politics in Canada* (Scarborough, ON: Prentice-Hall Canada, 1996) at 86–87.

210 *Elections Act*, s. 424.

211 *Ibid.*, s. 478.23.

212 *Ibid.*, s. 435.3.

213 *Ibid.*, s. 403.35.

214 *Ibid.*, s. 451.

tifying the contributor along with date and amount of each contribution. For numbered company contributors, the name of a director must also be disclosed.[215]

Receipts must be kept for all donations. A *de minimus* threshold of $25 is permitted for anonymous donations received at an event held for a candidate (leadership, nomination or electoral), a party or an association, so long as a description of the event, the date and the total amount collected is disclosed.[216]

All donations and expenses must be professionally audited, except in the case of electoral district associations, leadership candidates who spend on campaign expenses (or receive in donations) less than $5,000,[217] and nomination contestants spending (or receiving) less than $10,000.[218] In these last three cases, audits need not be conducted by certified accountants.

Parties with significant enough public support to receive an annual subsidy must file certain financial reports on a quarterly basis.[219] For all parties, financial information is presently included in annual financial transactions reports that must be audited[220] and submitted to the CEO six months following the end of the year. The report must also include a statement of the party's revenues, expenses, assets, liabilities, surpluses and deficits. Transfers to or from candidates (leadership, nomination, or electoral) or electoral district associations must also be disclosed.[221] In addition, the *Elections Act* requires reporting of the terms of loans made to parties.[222] (There is no separate provision on disclosure of loan terms for candidates, although because loans are included in the definition of "contribution," the amount and source of the loan are required to be reported.)[223]

Within six months after the end of an election, parties must also submit an audited election expenses return detailing all election expenses (paid or unpaid) and nonmonetary contributions used by the party.[224]

Similar reporting obligations are imposed on other electoral actors. For candidates, the electoral campaign report detailing this information must

---

215 *Ibid.*, paras. 403.35(2)(d), 451(2)(h.1) and 478.23(2)(g).
216 *Ibid.*, subs. 404.4(1).
217 *Ibid.*, subs. 435.33(1).
218 *Ibid.*, s. 478.25.
219 *Ibid.*, s. 424.1.
220 *Ibid.*, s. 426.
221 *Ibid.*, s. 424.
222 *Ibid.*, para. 424(2)(j).
223 *Ibid.*, subs. 451(3).
224 *Ibid.*, s. 429.

be filed within four months of polling day.[225] For nomination race candidates, the deadline is within four months of the nomination vote.[226] And electoral district associations must file within five months after the end of the year.[227] Party leadership candidate reports are due six months after the leadership campaign is over.[228] A leadership candidate must also file reports disclosing contributions and expenses four weeks before the leadership vote, and for each of the three weeks subsequent.[229]

3. Election Advertising

We turn now to another key issue in elections, one with important financial implications for parties. "Election advertising" is a defined term in the Act, and means "the transmission to the public by any means during an election period of an advertising message that promotes or opposes a registered party or the election of a candidate, including one that takes a position on an issue with which a registered party or candidate is associated."[230] While those running for office, as well as third parties, may conduct election advertising, the definition excludes groups communicating with their members, employees or shareholders (through newsletters, for example), publications of books that would be have been published regardless of the election call, "transmission to the public of an editorial, a debate, a speech, an interview, a column, a letter, a commentary or news," and generally, transmissions made over the Internet.[231]

a)   Advertising Rules Generally

For all major political parties, advertising is now the largest single expense in a national election campaign, although for individual candidates, advertising generally makes up only a small proportion of the campaign budget owing to tighter expense limits and the difficulty in raising funds at the local level.

---

225 *Ibid.*, s. 451.
226 *Ibid.*, subs. 478.23(6).
227 *Ibid.*, s. 403.35.
228 *Ibid.*, s. 435.3.
229 *Ibid.*, s. 435.31.
230 *Ibid.*, s. 319.
231 *Ibid.*, s. 319. Subsection (d) exempts "the transmission by an individual, on a non-commercial basis on what is commonly known as the Internet, of his or her personal political views." However, this exemption does not extend to advertising over the Internet. According to the chief electoral officer, "examples of advertising messages include unsolicited e-mail sent out by a third party, or banner ads placed on other Web sites by the third party": *Report of the Chief Electoral Officer of Canada on the 37th General Election Held on November 27, 2000* (21 March 2001).

The *Elections Act* regulates advertising in three ways. First, it facilitates some advertising by requiring television and radio networks to set aside broadcast time for parties. Second, it imposes transparency requirements. Last, it imposes some limitations on advertising.

Facilitating Advertising

Signage

The *Elections Act* facilitates election communication in several ways. For example, it limits efforts by landlords or condominium corporations to restrict the display of election advertising posters in a tenant's or owner's property, although "reasonable conditions relating to the size or type of election advertising posters" may be set, and such advertising may be prohibited in common spaces within the property.[232]

Likewise, courts have held that reasonable limits may be imposed on signage in public places. While a complete ban on signage on public property has been held to be unconstitutional,[233] municipalities do not violate freedom of expression by limiting election advertising on road right-of-ways.[234] Whether municipalities can go further and regulate election signs on private property is more doubtful. In fact, Ottawa passed such a by-law in 2004, purporting to bar election signs on private property more than sixty days prior to an election.[235] The measure is almost certainly a violation of section 2(b) free expression rights in the *Charter*, and it is difficult to see how such a sweeping measure is necessary in a free and democratic society, the justification under section 1.

Broadcasting Time

Even more importantly, the *Elections Act* includes provisions on access to electronic broadcast time. In order to ensure that each registered party has fair access to radio and television media outlets, broadcasters are required to set aside six-and-a-half hours of broadcast time, to be made available for purchase by registered parties during prime time.[236] Parties cannot be overcharged for advertising by media outlets; they must be offered the lowest rate the outlet charges other advertisers for the equivalent advertising time or space.[237]

---

232 *Elections Act*, s. 322.
233 *Ramsden v. Peterborough (City)*, [1993] 2 S.C.R. 1084.
234 *Beaumier v. Brampton (City)*, [1998] O.J. No. 1303 (S.C.J.), aff'd, [1999] O.J. No. 4407 (C.A.).
235 City of Ottawa, Temporary Signs on Private Property, By-Law No. 2004-239.
236 *Elections Act*, s. 335.
237 *Ibid.*, s. 348.

Broadcast time is allocated among the parties according to a formula that generally takes into equal consideration the percentage of seats the party has in the House of Commons and the percentage of the popular vote received in the previous election. Relative to each of these two variables, the number of candidates run by a party in the previous general election, as a percentage of the total number of candidates running for all parties, is given a half-weight consideration in the formula.[238]

Despite the obvious unfairness of this formula to new parties (which would likely receive a "zero" for most if not all of the variables), a court challenge to the system with reference to the free expression guarantees in section 2 of the *Charter* by the then-nascent Reform Party failed.[239] The Alberta Court of Appeal concluded that the allocation formula did not directly or indirectly limit or restrict speech or expression. Moreover, even if it did restrict expression, the Court held that the formula would be saved under section 1. A key factor in the court's reasoning on this issue was the existence of a Broadcasting Arbitrator, usually appointed by the Chief Electoral Officer after consultation with the parties.[240] The Arbitrator oversees the allocation, and has the discretion to alter the formula if he or she deems it to be unfair to a particular party, or to be in the public interest to do so.[241]

In addition to the broadcast time allocations, major network broadcasters must also provide free broadcast time to parties: a minimum of two minutes to each registered party that makes a request, and otherwise allocated according to the paid broadcast allocation formula described above.[242] For CBC television, the total allocation worked out to 214 minutes in 2004.[243] Free broadcast time does not need to be during prime time, and is not counted in tabulating a party's election expenses.[244]

---

238 *Ibid.*, s. 338.

239 *Reform Party of Canada v. Canada (Attorney General)*, [1995] A.J. No. 212 (C.A.).

240 If all parties represented in the House of Commons cannot agree on an arbitrator, the chief electoral officer appoints him or her after consultation with the parties. *Elections Act*, s. 332.

241 *Elections Act*, subs. 338(5).

242 *Ibid.*, s. 345.

243 Chief Electoral Officer, *Report of the Chief Electoral Officer of Canada on the 38th General Election Held on June 28, 2004* at 75. Strangely, due to a corporate reorganization, CTV was no longer considered a "network" subject to the free-time requirements under the *Elections Act* by 2004, with the result that CBC was the only English-language television network providing free broadcast time. In our view, it is worth re-examining how the Act defines "network" to ensure greater application of the provisions.

244 *Elections Act*, subs. 345(3).

While the broadcast provisions may be seen as an infringement on the rights of broadcasters, especially private broadcasters, it should be kept in mind that the airwaves are public assets that are merely licensed to these companies. As users of a public asset, it is reasonable to require that broadcasters set aside a portion of what is licensed to them in order to facilitate fairness in the democratic process.

Transparency Requirements

To ensure transparency in the way advertising is employed by political actors, the *Elections Act* requires a candidate or party to indicate that any election advertising paid for by a campaign is authorized by the candidate or party's official agent.[245] Further, the first person to transmit opinion survey results is also required to disclose information concerning the sponsor of the survey and details on its sample size, date and margin of error, amongst other things.[246]

Advertising Restrictions

The Act contains several constraints on election advertising.

Polling Day

A key restriction relates to advertising on polling day: subject to a few exceptions,[247] "[n]o person shall knowingly transmit election advertising to the public in an electoral district on polling day before the close of all of the polling stations in the electoral district."[248] "Persons" in this context include political parties and third parties.[249] This election-day advertising ban is relatively clear. However, there are allegations in most recent elections that this rule is broken.[250] It seems that in the dying days of a campaign, some candidates — often those who are seen as trailing behind a front-runner —

---

245 *Ibid.*, s. 320.

246 *Ibid.*, s. 326.

247 *Ibid.*, ss. 323–24. Exceptions include information posted on the Internet before polling day, as well as signs and pamphlets.

248 *Ibid.*, s. 323.

249 *Ibid.*

250 For example, during the June 2004 election, in the Ottawa Centre race between NDP Ed Broadbent and Liberal Richard Mahoney, Mahoney's campaign called homes in the riding on election day, leaving an automated message propagating a false rumour that Broadbent would be willing to give up his seat if Layton lost his own election and needed somewhere to run. "The people of Ottawa Centre can elect someone who's committed for the long term, Richard Mahoney, and prevent Stephen Harper from becoming prime minister," the message urged: A. Freeman, "Election Was a Lesson in Fundraising Loopholes," *The Hill Times*, 5 July 2004.

are willing to risk breaking the rules, given that complaints and investigations will not be resolved until well after the polls close.

Opinion Surveys

While not advertising *per se*, polls clearly affect the fortunes of those running for office. In addition, while media outlets generally forbid journalists from working for political parties or candidates, the same restriction does not apply to pollsters. For these reasons, the *Elections Act* bans the transmission of a new election survey on election day before the polls close.[251] This election day restriction replaces an older provision that barred release of surveys in the last three days of the election period. The Supreme Court held the latter law unconstitutional in 1998 as an undue restriction on freedom of expression.[252]

The polling blackout was recommended by the Lortie Commission, whose somewhat paternalistic concerns stemmed largely from the potential for polls to mislead voters:

> Although the industry in general has become highly professional since public polling was introduced in Canada in 1941, the incidence of technically deficient and poorly reported polls is still substantial. In recent elections, there have been instances of misleading polls, some because of technical errors and others because of partisan misrepresentation. There have even been allegations of fraudulent polls, where the data were said to have been fabricated to counter a poll showing the opposition in the lead. Such "bogus" polls and the more common misrepresented poll have been released to the media in many democracies. ... It is the willingness of the media to report such polls that makes them significant and troublesome.[253]

The polling blackout was one of the few recommendations enacted by legislators in the decade following the release of the commission's final report.

Some argue that releasing polls before the outcome of the election can create a "bandwagon effect," in which voters rally behind the front-runner, or, as Kay phrases it, "voters desert ... a sinking ship and mov[e] ... toward a vessel with better prospects."[254] Kay's study of each election from 1945 to

---

251 *Elections Act*, s. 328.
252 *Thomson Co.*, [1998] 1 S.C.R. 877.
253 Royal Commission on Electoral Reform and Party Financing, *Reforming Electoral Democracy* at 457.
254 B. Kay, "Polls and the Bandwagon Effect on the Electoral Process?" (1996) 19 Canadian Parliamentary Review no. 4.

1993 was ambivalent on the existence of such a phenomenon: it found an "absence of any prevailing general bandwagon effect, [but] little basis to suggest that the thesis can be categorically dismissed in all circumstances." Of course, even if there were a bandwagon affect, a broader question of policy remains: should people be denied an opportunity to vote strategically, in response to recent best guesses on the popularity of a given party? For our part, we are not persuaded that releasing opinion surveys would be so prejudicial to the election process to justify the constraint on free expression.

Foreign Advertisers

The *Elections Act* emphatically bans campaign advertising from outside Canada,[255] and prohibits nonresidents who are not citizens or permanent residents from attempting to influence Canadians' voting preferences.[256] The circumstances in which these sections could be enforced are limited. Certainly, if a person within Canada — and thus amenable to enforcement action within Canada — violated these provisions, they could be applied. But if the person is located beyond Canada's borders, enforcement would require extradition, a recourse that would be legally complex and politically awkward.[257]

The little-known ban on foreign involvement in Canadian elections garnered some media attention during the 2004 election. On a June 2004 visit to Toronto to promote a recent film, U.S. director and activist Michael Moore urged Canadians to reject the Conservative Party in the upcoming election. A Conservative activist indicated that he would complain to Elections Canada that Moore was in violation of the Act.[258] It was not known by early 2005 whether the Commissioner of Canada Elections would pursue a (probably fruitless) case against Moore.

---

255 *Elections Act*, s. 330.

256 *Ibid.*, s. 331.

257 Whether an extradition application would be successful or not would depend, of course, on the facts, not least the existence of an extradition treaty between Canada and the other state. Among the hurdles, even if such a treaty existed, is the "double-criminality" requirement in many extradition treaties: the requirement that the wrong for which extradition is required be an offence under the law of both states. See discussion in John Currie, *Public International Law* (Toronto: Irwin Law, 2001) at 296. In the case of the United States (from which a campaign ad is most likely to originate), there are provisions prohibiting election advertising by foreign nationals: 2 U.S.C § 441e. However, the Canadian offence does not apparently fall within the schedule of extraditable offences in the Canada-U.S. extradition treaty. Moreover, that agreement precludes extradition where "the offense in respect of which extradition is requested is of a political character."

258 *CBC News*, "Michael Moore Broke Election Law, Alleges Young Tory," 14 July 2004.

b)   Third-Party Spending Limits

Overview

Canadian electoral law also includes special rules for "third-party spending" on election advertising — that is, election advertising spending by
groups other than a party, candidate or electoral association.[259] These
restrictions supplement the total ban on election advertising by *any* political entity on polling day.[260]

In 2000, following a successful court challenge to an earlier, more
sweeping restriction on third-party spending,[261] the federal government
amended the *Elections Act* to restrict third-party election advertising expenses. "Election advertising expenses" are defined broadly to include "the production of an election advertising message; and ... the acquisition of the
means of transmission to the public of an election advertising message."[262]
As noted above, "election advertising" means "the transmission to the public by any means *during an election period* of an advertising message that promotes or opposes a registered party or the election of a candidate, including
one that takes a position on an issue with which a registered party or candidate is associated."[263] Thus, the law regulates only election advertising campaigns that take place during the (typically) five-week election period.

Under the Act, advertising expenses of an individual third party during
a general election are capped at $150,000. Not more than $3,000 of this
$150,000 is to be incurred to promote or oppose the election of one or
more candidates in a given electoral district. Efforts to promote or oppose
a particular candidate are evidenced by such things as naming them or por-
traying their likeness or "taking a position on an issue with which [the candidate is] particularly associated."[264]

With regard to election advertising that targets more than one candidate, according to Elections Canada,

> If the election advertising promotes or opposes a number of specific can-
> didates in a number of ridings, then the limit is $3,000 multiplied by the
> number of ridings to a total limit of $150,000.

---

259   *Elections Act*, s. 349 *et seq.*

260   *Ibid.*, s. 323.

261   *Somerville v. Canada (Attorney General)*, [1996] 8 W.W.R. 199 (Alta. C.A.) holding that
       then-provisions of the *Elections Act* limiting third-party advertising expenses to a maxi-
       mum of $1,000 individual, were contrary to freedom of expression under the *Charter*.

262   *Elections Act*, s. 349.

263   *Ibid.*, s. 319 [emphasis added].

264   *Ibid.*, s. 350.

For example, if a newspaper advertisement identified and promoted or opposed six candidates who were running for election in six different ridings, the limit would be $3,000 multiplied by 6, or $18,000.

Election advertising that identifies the leader of a registered political party is subject to the $150,000 limit, unless the advertising is intended to promote or oppose the election of the leader in his or her own electoral district. If the election advertising is specifically targeted at the electoral district where the leader is a candidate, then the limit is $3,000.[265]

The Act also limits spending in by-elections: third-party spending in the electoral district is limited to $3,000.[266] These limits are all indexed to inflation, starting in 2000,[267] and individuals may not combine their limits to permit pooling of financial resources. Third parties are also prohibited from splitting themselves into multiple third-party organizations for the purposes of circumventing the limits.[268]

There are also important transparency provisions. Third parties must identify themselves in any ads.[269] If the advertising expense is greater than $500, the third party must publicly register with the chief electoral officer,[270] and disclose the identity and amounts contributed (over $200) of those who funded the advertising campaign during the period beginning six months before the writ and ending on election day.[271] If the third party is unable to disaggregate advertising expenses from other revenues it receives, it must disclose the identity of all contributors who gave more than $200 from six months leading up to the start of the writ period through to election day.[272]

Constitutional Issues

A twenty-year history of controversial constitutional challenges to third-party advertising spending laws in Canada was largely settled by the Supreme Court in 2004 in *Harper v. Canada*.[273] Stephen Harper brought the case in 2000, while head of the National Citizens Coalition (NCC) and

---

265 Elections Canada, "Questions and Answers about Third Party Election Advertising" (20 Sept. 2004).

266 *Elections Act*, s. 350.

267 *Ibid.*, s. 350.

268 *Ibid.*, s. 351.

269 *Ibid.*, s. 352.

270 *Ibid.*, ss. 353 and 356.

271 *Ibid.*, subs. 359(4).

272 *Ibid.*, s. 359(4) and (7).

273 *Harper*, 2004 SCC 33.

before re-entering politics to become, eventually, the leader of the Conservative Party. The NCC argued in *Harper* that third-party advertising spending restrictions are a constraint on free expression. As such, these limits were portrayed as a dangerous incursion by the state curtailing the ability of citizens to communicate on political issues at a scale that is meaningful, given modern communication technologies and the various political interests that compete using these technologies during an election. As noted by the dissenting Supreme Court judges in *Harper*, "In the democracy of ancient Athens, all citizens were able to meet and discuss the issues of the day in person. In our modern democracy, we cannot speak personally with each of our co-citizens. We can convey our message only through methods of mass communication."[274] The dissent observed that political speech "is the single most important and protected type of expression,"[275] and that because the *Elections Act* third-party spending restriction was too low to allow for significant national advertising campaigns, it amounted to "a virtual ban on citizen communication through effective advertising."[276]

The NCC challenge was, however, ultimately rejected by a majority of the Supreme Court, motivated by considerations justifying restraints on speech; specifically, concern that third-party spending skews election outcomes, in effect by making contributions to some parties but not others.

This concern is borne out by experience. Third-party spending was a major factor in the 1988 federal election. At issue in that election was the Canada-U.S. Free Trade Agreement. The Progressive Conservative Party favoured the deal, while the two other parties, the Liberals and the New Democratic Party, were opposed. Third parties weighed in through television, radio and print ads. While ads ran on both sides of the issue, it is estimated that business interests spent roughly $13 million on advertising in favour of the deal, while opponents of the deal spent approximately $1 million.[277] Given the Conservatives were the only party that favoured the trade deal, many concluded the pro-free trade ads were *de facto* contributions to the party.

The controversy over third-party election spending led to the creation of the Lortie Commission on electoral reform and party financing. The Commission in 1991 outlined the various ways that unlimited third-party

---

274   *Ibid.* at para. 20, McLachlin and Major JJ.
275   *Ibid.* at para. 11.
276   *Ibid.* at para. 35.
277   D.C. MacDonald, "1988 Election Expenditures: A Canadian-American Comparison" in *Canadian Legislatures* (Toronto: Global Press, 1992) 16 at 21.

spending can undermine electoral fairness. As summarized by the Supreme Court in *Harper*,

> First, it can lead to the dominance of the political discourse by the wealthy. Second, it may allow candidates and political parties to circumvent their own spending limits through the creation of third parties. Third, unlimited third party spending can have an unfair effect on the outcome of an election. Fourth, it can erode the confidence of the Canadian electorate who perceive the electoral process as being dominated by the wealthy.[278]

These same considerations drove a majority of the Court to accept that, while third-party limits were an infringement of freedom of expression, they were justified in a free and democratic society under section 1. Among other things, the majority observed:

> Section 350 [restricting third-party spending] has several salutary effects. It enhances equality in the political discourse. By ensuring that affluent groups or individuals do not dominate the political discourse, s. 350 promotes the political expression of those who are less affluent or less capable of obtaining access to significant financial resources and ensures that candidates and political parties who are subject to spending limits are not overwhelmed by third party advertising. Section 350 also protects the integrity of the candidate and political party spending limits by ensuring that these limits are not circumvented through the creation of phoney third parties. Finally, s. 350 promotes fairness and accessibility in the electoral system and consequently increases Canadians' confidence in it.[279]

In *Harper*, the Court obviously confronted a difficult balancing task, and its outcome has not pleased everyone. It should be noted, however, the reach of the third-party spending limits upheld by the Court is not as sweeping as some critics seem to believe. As discussed earlier, the definition of "election advertising" excludes groups communicating with their members, employees or shareholders (through newsletters, for example), publications of books that would be have been published regardless of the election call, "transmission to the public of an editorial, a debate, a speech, an interview, a column, a letter, a commentary or news," and non-commercial transmissions made over the Internet.[280] Amounts spent on these activities are therefore exempted from the third-party rules. As a result, the

---

278 *Harper*, 2004 SCC 33 at para. 79 [references omitted].
279 *Ibid.* at para. 120.
280 *Elections Act*, s. 319.

third-party advertising limits apply neither to the most common forms of electoral expression by individuals and organizations (press releases, speeches, mobilization of memberships, etc.), nor to noncommercial use of the most quickly emerging medium of electoral expression, the Internet.

Unresolved Questions: Issue Advertising

While the *Harper* case established a firm justification for third-party spending limits in Canada, there may be further (and much more difficult) legal challenges in the near future in the area of "issue advertising."

The Problem of Definition

When an ad contains what U.S. courts[281] have referred to as "magic words" such as "Vote for Candidate X" or "Don't vote for Candidate Y," it is obvious that the ad is intended to influence the election outcome. But what if an ad focuses solely on an issue, without mentioning a candidate or party?

The *Elections Act* definition of "election advertising" would appear to capture both "magic word" and issue communication. As noted above, the definition includes advertising that "promotes or opposes a registered party or the election of a candidate, *including one that takes a position on an issue with which a registered party or candidate is associated.*"[282] Meanwhile, no more than $3,000 of the $150,000 third-party spending limit may used to "promote or oppose the election of one or more candidates in a given electoral district, including by ... *taking a position on an issue with which they are particularly associated.*"[283]

Given these rules, where third parties are using what U.S. writers call "sham issue advertising"[284] as a way of circumventing spending limits and indirectly supporting a candidate or party, Canadian law would apply spending limits. However, a key question will always be "how strong does the association have to be for the issue to be associated or particularly associated, as the case may be, with those running for office, thus triggering the Act's requirements?"

---

281 The most recent U.S. Supreme Court case on this issue is *McConnell,* 540 U.S. 93. (2003).

282 *Elections Act,* s. 319 [emphasis added].

283 *Ibid.,* subs. 350(2) [emphasis added]. The added term "particularly" is applied only to advertising that relates to candidates, suggesting a slightly higher threshold for such ads to be considered subject to the restrictions. It is unclear, however, how the law will differentiate between an issue that is "associated" and one that is "particularly associated" with a candidate.

284 See R.L. Hasen, "The Surprisingly Complex Case for Disclosure of Contributions and Expenditures Funding Sham Issue Advocacy," (2000) 48 UCLA L. Rev. 265.

In *Harper*, the Supreme Court majority did not squarely address this issue, but did conclude that the definition of election advertising, "although broad in scope, is not unconstitutionally vague. ... [I]t is possible to discern whether an issue is associated with a candidate or political party from their platform. Where an issue arises in the course of the electoral campaign, the response taken by the candidate or political party may be found in media releases."[285]

The Supreme Court's comment anticipates only evident cases, where political positions on issues are clear-cut. For instance, in the lead-up to the 2004 election period, the Christian values organization Focus on the Family ran a national series of ads featuring images of "traditional," two-parent (one male, one female) families, with the captions "We Believe in Mom and Dad" and "We Believe in Marriage." The ad was a thinly veiled advocacy campaign opposing the legalization of same-sex marriage, and was clearly timed to influence the election.

Because the ad campaign was halted before the election — in fact on the day the *Harper* ruling was released — it did not fall under the third-party limit provisions. However, had the ads continued into the election period, they would likely have been subject to the spending cap. Since same-sex marriage was frequently raised as an issue in the election, any sensible reader would conclude that the ad was intended to promote or oppose a candidate or party.

Such a case would have been reasonably clear-cut. But there will undoubtedly be instances where it is far less clear whether issue advertising is intended to support or oppose a candidate or party. Here, the application of spending limits will prove difficult, and potentially troubling. As noted by Professor Feasby, "If freedom of expression, particularly political expression, is highly prized, then it is impossible to justify the extension of third party expenditure limits to communications that are imperfectly aligned with the message of a candidate or political party, or that only indirectly prejudice the campaign of a candidate or political party."[286]

The Problem of Timing

Beyond deciding when an issue is sufficiently associated with a party or candidate, there are additional, chronological difficulties with the concept of issue advertising. Not least is the question of *when* an issue has to be associated with a party or candidate.

---

285 *Harper*, 2004 SCC 33 at paras. 89–90.
286 C. Feasby, "Issue Advocacy and Third Parties in the United Kingdom and Canada" (2003) 48 McGill L.J. 11 at 22.

Party positions on issues change with time, sometimes radically. The Liberal Party, in 1988, was opposed to free trade. Since then, the Party has become a vigorous proponent of trade liberalization. Obviously, a third-party issue advertising campaign favouring or opposing trade liberalization would have a different impact on Liberal fortunes now than in 1988.

It seems to us that, as party and candidate positions change over time, the only plausible time frame for deciding whether an issue is "associated" with a party or candidate is the election period itself. Even if a candidate or party has been historically associated with an issue, it is the election campaign when citizens are most attentive to political discourse. For many of the same reasons that ads outside the election period itself are not covered by third-party spending provisions, issue associations extracted from positions taken outside the election period should not be considered in the analysis of whether an issue is associated with a party or candidate.

There is also a practical reason for taking this approach: if the measure of issue association extends beyond the election period, third-party advertisers not fully cognizant of the shifting positions of parties and candidates over time would constantly risk running afoul of the issue advertising regulation. Forcing the sponsor of an ad to be familiar with every issue with which candidates and parties have ever been associated would be an unreasonable and unrealistic burden for the sponsor to bear.

For the same reason, the Act's third-party election advertising rules should not apply to issue ads that are run *during* an election period, but *before* a candidate or party has actually taken a position on the advertised issue. This approach is consistent with the logic and justification of third-party limits, and how the courts have balanced concerns over freedom of expression. Citizens who feel their views are not represented by the parties and candidates running for office should not face spending limits when trying to raise their issue before the public during an election. Only once that issue actually has been addressed by a party or candidate — in a platform, on a website, or in statements to the media, for example — and a position has been taken by that party or candidate, should the issue be considered part of the partisan election discourse.

Thus, the same ad, run throughout an election campaign, could start out being outside the third-party provisions, but midway through the campaign, if a party or candidate adopted a position aligned or opposed to the position of the ad, end up as an official third-party election expense. In such a case, only ads run *after* the issue has been adopted by a candidate or party should be considered third-party advertising expenses, subject to the spending cap.

There is one caveat to this view: under the law, production costs of the ad are also considered to be part of the expense.[287] As a result, the production costs of ads run *after* a party or candidate takes a position on an issue should be included in the third-party expense even if these production costs were incurred before the party or candidate adopted the issue.

c)   Government Advertising

A final advertising issue involves government spending on messages during the election period. Incumbent political parties often boost government advertising in the lead-up to an election as a way of improving their image with voters. As noted by Paltiel, parties in power "are not averse" to "using bill-boards, circulars, and envelope stuffers fostering one or another government program as a means of blowing their own horn during election campaigns."[288] As a result, some jurisdictions, such as Manitoba[289] and Saskatchewan,[290] place restrictions on government advertising during elections, to diminish this often-exploited incumbency advantage. Sub-section 277(2) of the Saskatchewan *Elections Act* states "During a general election, no Government department shall publish in any manner any information with respect to the activities of the department." Sub-section (5) provides exemptions for

(a)   information that, because of an emergency, is required to be published in the public interest; or

(b)   advertising by a Crown corporation that was contracted prior to the issue of a writ and is related to the Crown corporation's competitive business interests.

The federal *Elections Act* does prohibit "election advertising" (that is, partisan messages) to be transmitted by the federal government during the election period.[291] In addition, a federal treasury board policy incorporates the key elements of Manitoba and Saskatchewan laws. It reads: "Institutions must suspend their advertising during general elections of the Government of Canada. Advertising is only permitted when: an institution is required by statute or regulation to issue a public notice for legal purposes; an institution must inform the public of a danger to health, safety or the

---

287   *Elections Act*, s. 319.
288   K.Z. Paltiel, "Canadian Election Expense Legislation, 1963–1985: A Critical Appraisal or Was the Effort Worth It?" in H.E. Alexander, ed., *Comparative Political Finance in the 1980s* (Cambridge: Cambridge University Press, 1987) 51 at 68.
289   *Elections Finances Act*, C.C.S.M., c. E32, s. 56.
290   *Elections Act*, R.S.S. 1996 c. E-6.01, s. 277.
291   *Elections Act*, s. 321.

environment; or an institution must post an employment or staffing notice."[292]

In our view, enshrining this policy in law is a sensible measure given the importance of preventing government resources from being used for partisan purposes.

4. Voter's List

A final requirement prior to polling day is the identification of voters. Maintaining the list of electors is a major undertaking when one considers that 20 percent of elector information changes each year.[293] Unlike the United States, where electors must proactively register in each election, the CEO keeps a permanent register of electors.[294] Electors may update the information themselves, or may expressly authorize a federal body or agency to convey updated information to the CEO.[295] This express consent is most commonly granted via a check-off box on federal tax forms, although other government information sources, such as change-of-address data provided by Canada Post, are also used to improve the list's accuracy.

The permanent list replaced a door-to-door canvas previously used in Canada. Advocates of returning to this method argue that many electors are left off the permanent list, especially those who move to another electoral district between elections. However, proponents of the new system argue it is more reliable and cost-effective than the door-to-door method, and that reliability is increasing. Elections Canada estimates that 95 percent of electors are now on the list, with 83 percent at the correct address.[296]

Even if an elector is not on the register, he or she may vote by providing proof of identity and residence, or by taking an oath.[297]

D. AFTER THE VOTE

We turn now to events occurring after the writ period has ended.

---

292 Treasury Board Secretariat, "Communications Policy of the Government of Canada" (29 Nov. 2004) at s. 23.
293 "National Register of Elections," backgrounder (Ottawa: Elections Canada, 2002).
294 *Canada Election Act*, s. 44.
295 *Ibid.*, s. 46.
296 Chief Electoral Officer, *Report of the Chief Electoral Officer on the 38th General Election Held on June 28, 2004* (Ottawa: Chief Electoral Officer, 2004) at 4.
297 *Canada Election Act*, s. 161.

1. Reporting on Election Results

The *Elections Act* sets out the times that polling stations will remain open in each part of the country.[298] These times are somewhat staggered to account for time zone changes, but there is still a period of time in which the polls remain open in western parts of the country while they have closed in the east. For example, polls remain open in the Pacific Time zone (British Columbia and the Yukon) two and a half hours after they have closed in the Atlantic. Many suggest this is unfair, as it may discourage those in the west from voting after the polls are closed and results from the east have been reported, perhaps giving a strong indication of which party has won the election.

Parliament attempted to deal with this dilemma by banning the reporting of election results from another part of the country in an area in which polling stations remain open.[299] However, in *R. v. Bryan*,[300] the B.C. Supreme Court held that the ban violated the *Charter*'s freedom of expression protections in section 2. The accused had posted election results from the Atlantic Provinces on his website. In deciding whether the violation of Mr. Bryan's free expression rights could be saved by section 1 of the *Charter*, the court held that there was no evidence showing that that ban actually addressed a legitimate concern about voter behaviour. It did not, in other words, meet a "pressing and substantial objective" that would allow it to be deemed "a reasonable limit prescribed by law and demonstrably justified in a free and democratic society" under section 1 of the *Charter*. An appeal of the case to the B.C. Court of Appeal is pending, but in the 2004 federal election, the CEO announced the provision would not be enforced in the meantime.[301]

The trial court's view is, in our view, a sensible one. As noted in the case, even if all results from Atlantic Canada were to be reported before the western polls close, these Atlantic results would not show which party had won the election.[302] Logically, it is only when the overall winner can be discerned that the western vote could be influenced in the way feared. This scenario emerges only when the Ontario and Quebec results are available. However, these results are not available until the polls in these two provinces themselves close, something that occurs only thirty minutes prior to the close of

---

298 *Ibid.*, s. 128.
299 *Ibid.*, s. 329.
300 *R. v. Bryan* (2003), 233 D.L.R. (4th) 745 (B.C.S.C.), leave to appeal granted, (2004), 236 D.L.R. (4th) 340 (B.C.C.A).
301 Elections Canada, *Chief Electoral Officer Announces Policy on Application of British Columbia Supreme Court Decision,* press release, 10 June 2004.
302 *Bryan* (2003), 233 D.L.R. (4th) 745 at paras. 30 and 32.

the B.C. polls. In other words, the staggered polling hours across the country already effectively accomplish the objectives of ensuring ignorance of the election's outcome while western Canadians are casting their ballot.

While some argue that the broadcast of even a partial result can create a "bandwagon" effect,[303] it is questionable whether this effect exists in any substantial form. Even if it does, we raise the same concern posed in relation to the polling day opinion survey blackouts discussed above: it is not necessarily fair to deny voters information that will assist them to vote strategically.

In any event, the information ban is anachronistic. As *Bryan* suggests, with modern broadcasting techniques — like the Internet and cable and satellite television — it is unlikely that a publication ban will now ever be effective in preventing polling results from reaching western voters.

2. Judicial Recounts and Contested Elections

a) Recounts

If the margin of victory for a candidate is less than 1/1000 of the votes cast, the returning officer in that electoral district must request that a provincial superior court judge supervise a recount of the ballots.[304] In other circumstances, an elector, including a candidate, may apply to a judge for a recount, which the judge must grant if it appears from the evidence of a credible witness that errors have been made in the original counting of the ballots.[305] In both scenarios, the application must be made within four days of validation of the vote, and, if granted or required, the recount must take place within four days of the application.[306]

In the highly unlikely event of a tie, a by-election must be called to determine a winner.[307]

b) Contested Elections

The *Elections Act* empowers "any elector who was eligible to vote in an electoral district, and any candidate in an electoral district" to apply to a provincial superior court or the Federal Court in order to "contest the election in that electoral district on the grounds that ... the elected candidate was not eligible to be a candidate" for the ineligibility reasons discussed at the beginning of this chapter or if "there were irregularities, fraud or corrupt or ille-

---

303 *Ibid.* at para. 31.
304 *Elections Act*, s. 300.
305 *Ibid.*, s. 301.
306 *Ibid.*, subss. 300(3) and 301(4).
307 *Ibid.*, s. 318; *Parliament of Canada Act*, s. 29.

gal practices that affected the result of the election."[308] An election may be contested in this manner within thirty days of the results being announced or "the day on which the applicant first knew or should have known of the occurrence of the alleged irregularity, fraud, corrupt practice or illegal practice."[309] If the court concludes that the candidate was not eligible, it must declare the election null and void. Where it holds that there were improper practices, it may annul the election.[310] Any appeal must be brought directly to the Supreme Court of Canada, on "any question of law or fact."[311]

As noted above, where the outcome of an election is successfully contested, the Commons seat is considered vacant under the *Parliament of Canada Act*, precipitating a by-election.

3. Enforcement and Penalties

The Commissioner of Canada Elections enforces all provisions of the *Elections Act*. The commissioner is an independent official appointed by the CEO,[312] and is charged with receiving and investigating complaints about infringements of the Act. Investigation is at the commissioner's discretion, although the CEO may direct that the commissioner investigate a particular case under certain sections of the Act.[313]

The most common complaints to the commissioner are in the following areas:

- failure to indicate the authority for election advertising;
- electors voting more than once;
- conducting election advertising on election day;
- failure of third parties to register with respect to election advertising;
- prevention or impairment of election advertising; and
- failure to provide nomination contest reports within the prescribed time limits.[314]

The commissioner is solely responsible for authorizing the laying of a charge, and must decide whether to proceed under summary conviction or

---

308 *Ibid.*, s. 524.
309 *Ibid.*, s. 527.
310 *Ibid.*, s. 531.
311 *Ibid.*, s. 532.
312 *Ibid.*, s. 509. Certain provisions relating to "Peace and good order" are enforced by the RCMP.
313 These are *Elections Act*, ss. 486(3)(a) and (d), 488, 489(3)(g), 493 and 499(1): *ibid.* at s. 510.
314 Chief Electoral Officer, *Report of the Chief Electoral Officer of Canada on the 38th General Election Held on June 28, 2004* at 90.

indictment, a decision reflecting the seriousness of the charge.[315] Upon conviction, the Act authorizes a judge to impose a range of penalties, which may include performing community service, performing the obligation that gave rise to the offence (for example, filing a missing report), and compensating for damages. Where a political party commits an offence, penalties may include deregistration of the party or its registered associations, and liquidation of its assets. For a third party guilty of exceeding third-party spending limits, penalties include a fine of up to five times the election advertising expenses exceeded. Jail terms are also among the penalties for spending limit violations and certain other offences, although this penalty has rarely, if ever, been applied in the history of the Act.

For certain illegal practices, such as taking a false oath or corrupt practices such as offering a bribe, additional penalties include losing the right to be candidate in a future election,[316] to sit as a member in the House of Commons, and to hold any GIC appointment. These penalties may apply for five years in the case of an illegal act, and seven years in the case of a corrupt practice.

Injunctions may also be sought under the Act in cases where there are reasonable grounds to conclude that an alleged offence may influence the election outcome if it is allowed to continue. In deciding whether to grant the injunction, a court will weigh three variables: the nature and seriousness of the breach; the need to ensure electoral fairness; and the public interest.[317]

E. EMERGING ISSUES IN CANADA'S ELECTION LAW AND POLICY

In this final section on the selection of Canada's elected representatives, we canvass several emerging issues in election law and policy.

1. Voter Participation

The health of a democracy is dependent on public participation in elections. However, Canadian voter participation is quite low by international standards, and like many industrialized countries, this rate has declined

---

315 The range of offences appear in *Elections Act*, ss. 480–99.

316 This sort of penalty has been held by the Supreme Court of Canada to be constitutionally valid in provincial elections law. Despite being an infringement of s. 3, the penalty was found to be justified under s. 1: *Harvey v. New Brunswick (Attorney General)*, [1996] 2 S.C.R. 876.

317 *Elections Act*, s. 516.

dramatically in recent decades. Consider that in 1988, 75 percent of registered voters cast a ballot, consistent with the post–World War II average. This figure slipped to 69.6 percent in 1993, 67 percent in 1997, 61.2 percent in 2000 and 60.9 percent in 2004.[318] These figures are roughly 10 percentage points below the average of 15 other Anglo-American, Nordic and Western European democracies that do not impose compulsory voting requirements.[319]

These numbers mask even more troubling trends. First, they reflect only those on the official list of electors. As noted by Johnston, because of deficiencies in this list, the 2000 official figure of 62 percent is actually 55 percent, only slightly higher than the (notoriously low) U.S. rate.[320]

Second, the numbers mask a serious decline in voting among young people. Among voters between the ages of 18 and 24, only 25 percent typically cast a ballot (although in the 2004 election, this figure jumped to 38.7 percent).[321] Less educated and poorer Canadians are also less likely to vote.[322] And countrywide, aboriginal people have a lower voter turnout rate.[323]

While the decline in voter participation is rooted in many complex causes,[324] including negative perceptions of politicians and government and a declining interest in politics,[325] a comprehensive study of nonvoters also revealed "a widespread feeling that political participation is meaningless." Within this category, nonvoters cited "the lack of choice in elections, that voting would not change anything. 'It's always the same thing over and over,' said some. Others referred to the situation of 'single party dominance,' which made it seem that there was no realistic hope of an alternative government."[326]

---

318 Elections Canada, "Thirty-eighth General Election 2004, Official Voting Results, Table 4: Voter turnout for the 2004, 2000, 1997 and 1993 General Elections."

319 E. Gidengil, A. Blais, N. Nevitte and R. Nadeau, *Citizens* (Vancouver: UBC Press, 2004) at 107.

320 R. Johnston, "A Conservative Case for Electoral Reform" (2001) 22 Policy Options at 7. Young people are disproportionately affected by this. As noted by the CEO, 75 percent of those aged eighteen to twenty-four appeared on the permanent voter's list, compared to 95 percent of the population at large: Chief Electoral Officer, *Report of the Chief Electoral Officer of Canada on the 38th General Election Held on June 28, 2004* at 5.

321 *Ibid.* at 84. The rise may be attributable, in part, to extensive efforts by Elections Canada to encourage young people to register and cast a ballot: *ibid.* at 15–16.

322 Gidengil *et al., Citizens* at 142.

323 D. Guérin, "Aboriginal Participation in Federal Elections: Trends and Implications" (Nov. 2003) *Electoral Insight*.

324 Gidengil *et al., Citizens* at 103–42.

325 J. Pammet and L. LeDuc, "Explaining the Turnout Decline in Canadian Federal Elections: A New Survey of Non-voters" (Elections Canada, March 2003).

326 *Ibid.*

Certainly, education and ensuring access to voting mechanisms — including the voter registration list — are important elements to increasing voter participation rates, but there is also ample room for legal reform.[327]

For one thing, many of the legal reforms listed in other chapters of this book, such as improvements to parliamentary governance, ethics codes, whistleblower protection and access to information laws would undoubtedly go a long way in reducing voter skepticism of governments and politicians, one of the key factors producing low voter turnout rates. Also, many advocates of reforming our winner-take-all, first-past-the-post voting system argue that a proportional representation system would enhance voter participation. As described by Courtney:

> Electors who supported an unsuccessful candidate in a [first-past-the-post] constituency may sense after the election that because they backed a loser they are somehow "unrepresented." Magnified many times, that representational frustration on the part of large numbers of voters in a region could contribute to cynicism about or loss of interest in the political system generally. In turn this could contribute to lessened participation in political affairs and to lower voter turnout.[328]

Indeed, studies show that, when other variables are factored out, proportional representation systems generate voter turnout rates that are significantly higher than first-past-the-post (FPP) systems.[329] We discuss FPP and proportional representation later.

According to analysts Blais, Dobrzynska and Massicotte, an even greater factor in voter participation rates is whether there is a legal requirement for citizens to vote. At least eighteen countries[330] have made voting a legal obligation, including Australia, which has had such a law for more

---

327 *Ibid.* Also see Courtney, *Elections,* above note 54.
328 J. Courtney, "Plurality-Majority Elected Systems: A Review" (presented to the Advisory Committee of Registered Political Parties, Elections Canada, 23 April 1999) at 6.
329 Blais and Carty's 1990 study showed PR countries have voter turnout rates that are 8 percent higher than FPP countries: A. Blais and R.K. Carty, "Does Proportional Representation Foster Voter Turnout" (1990) European Journal of Political Research 18 at 179. A more recent study by Blais, Dobrzynska and Massicotte showed this figure to be 5 to 6 percent: A. Blais, A. Dobrzynska and L. Massicotte, "Why Is Turnout Higher in Some Countries than in Others?" (Elections Canada, 2003).
330 The eighteen countries were Cape Verde, Sao Tome, Costa Rica, Panama, *Argentina, *Bolivia, *Brazil, *Chile, *Ecuador, *Uruguay, Venezuela, *Cyprus, *Philippines, *Belgium, *Australia, *Luxembourg, Italy and Portugal. Those with asterisks have penalties for failing to vote: *ibid.*

than eighty years. In such countries, voter participation rates are 13 percent higher than in countries that do not have such measures, provided there are penalties for failing to vote. And when the Netherlands dropped its compulsory voting law in the 1970s, voter participation fell by approximately 10 percent.[331]

Compulsory voting has both pros and cons. On the con side, an increased quantity of votes motivated by compulsory voting rules does not necessarily translate into adequate voting quality. When people are forced to vote, they may simply vote for the first name on the ballot, or spoil their ballot, out of frustration of being forced to do something they do not wish to do. On the pro side, it may also be that legal penalties for failing to vote communicate to electors that voting is considered by society to be a serious duty. The higher rates flowing from the rules may reflect, not a response to coercion, but an internalization of this civic value. Voters may become, in other words, more serious about their civic duty.

For our part, we are agnostic on whether voting should be made compulsory in Canada. It does, however, seem an idea ripe for debate in a country experiencing a serious decline in democratic participation.

2. Fixed Election Dates

As discussed in chapter 5, the timing of an election is almost always the prerogative of the prime minister. This power has several negative effects on the democratic process.

First, as the 2004 election period suggested, much of the business of government stays on hold when the possibility of an election looms. The longer the period of uncertainty, the fewer the things accomplished. Like any well-run organization, having a fixed deadline to achieve a task — a fixed election date — would better focus the mind of any government.

Second, fixed elections would remove an unfair advantage held by the governing party. Opposition parties are forced to spend scarce resources planning for every contingency while the governing party can focus its efforts on the only date that matters. Incumbents can also use their power to set the election date to manage the fallout of events having the potential to turn the electorate against them. While this may succeed in improving the party's election results, allowing the governing party to manipulate the system in this fashion does little to enhance voter enthusiasm for the election process.

---

331   *Ibid.*

Finally, fixing an election date would make campaign spending and fundraising more transparent and accountable. In the weeks or months during which an election call is anticipated, parties and candidates spend considerable sums on campaign advertising. These are obviously election-related expenses, but most of the money spent does not end up listed in expense disclosure forms, as it is spent outside the five-week election campaign. Other pre-election expenses are also for the most part not counted in campaign expense limits, despite the fact that these expenses are obviously incurred to get people elected.

This loophole exists because it would be difficult to regulate party and candidate expenses before the election period if one doesn't know when that election period is going to begin. By having a fixed election date, Elections Canada could reasonably require parties and candidates to disclose all of their campaign expenses over a longer period, say six months.

Those who oppose fixed election dates argue that it undermines responsible government. As discussed in chapter 5, a key plank of responsible government is the capacity of the Commons to vote no confidence in a government and precipitate its resignation or an election call. Elections, in a system of responsible government, may therefore be unpredictable. However, exceptions to the fixed date could easily be made for those (rare) instances in which the Commons votes no confidence in a government. If the fixed date is based on a four-year term, for example, the clock could begin ticking again once the new election takes place following the successful no-confidence motion.

Provincial practice demonstrates that there is no fundamental inconsistency between fixed elections and parliamentary democracy. British Columbia has recently implemented a fixed election date mechanism.[332] The Ontario government has introduced similar legislation.[333]

3. Leaders' Debates

In every federal election of the past twenty years, televised leaders' debates have played an integral role. Although their influence is often overestimated, debates offer an unparalleled opportunity for party leaders to communicate their message to voters.[334] The leaders' debates are often the most important single event that influences voter behaviour in an election.

---

332 *Constitution Act*, R.S.B.C. 1996, c. 66, s. 23.

333 *Bill 86, Election Statute Law Amendment Act, 2004*, Hon. Mr. Bryant (Attorney General). First Reading June 1, 2004. Second Reading debated June 9, 14, 23; October 26.

334 W. Cross, *Political Parties* (Vancouver: UBC Press, 2004) at 136.

For these reasons, having a spot in the leadership debate is important for any aspiring party. Inclusion of smaller parties has, however, proved controversial. In the 2004 election, the Green Party was polling as high as 6 percent in national polls. Yet the major television networks excluded it from the televised leaders' debates. No stated reasons were given for the decision, although many speculated that the justification was based on the party's lack of representation in the House of Commons. This criterion creates, however, a chicken-and-egg scenario: it is difficult for a party to have its MPs elected without significant television exposure, and it difficult to obtain television exposure if the party is excluded from the debates.

While courts have declined to intervene on constitutional grounds to ensure representation by smaller parties in the leaders' debates,[335] several commentators[336] argue that, given the importance of the leaders' debates to the democratic process, it is disingenuous for the networks to argue that these events are simply private affairs in which the public should have no say. In our view, it would be appropriate at least to require those hosting televised debates to disclose the criteria by which parties are invited to participate.

4. Proportional Representation

In recent years, there has been significant debate at both the provincial and federal levels in Canada about reforming our electoral system. This section examines the pros and cons of the current regime for electing representatives, as well as some of the alternatives that exist elsewhere.

a) Canada's Current First-Past-the-Post System

Canada's electoral voting regime is a single-member plurality, or first-past-the-post (FPP) system. Candidates run in each electoral district and the winner for each district is the candidate with the highest number of votes. Most often in recent elections, candidates do not win a majority of votes. Rather, a plurality is sufficient. As a result, nationally, the party in power only occasionally wins with a majority of the popular vote. In the 1997 election, for example:

---

335 Lower courts have held that although CBC is a government institution, when covering the leaders' debates it is not acting in a government function and is therefore not bound by the *Charter: National Party of Canada v. Canadian Broadcasting Corp. (CBC)*, [1993] A.J. No. 677 (Q.B.); and *Natural Law Party of Canada v. Canadian Broadcasting Corp. (CBC)*, [1994] 1 F.C. 580 (T.D.).

336 See A. Coyne, "It's a Debate, Not a Boxing Match," *National Post*, 12 June 2004. Also see CBC broadcast from *As It Happens*, 27 June 2004.

- the Liberals received the lowest popular vote (38.36 percent) since Confederation for a party forming a majority government;
- taking into account the voter turnout (66.7 percent), the lowest number of eligible voters since Confederation (25.57 percent) actually cast a ballot for the party forming the majority government; and
- the Liberals did not receive a majority of the popular vote in any province or territory.

As noted by Professor MacIvor, "the majority of voters in the majority of ridings 'wasted' their votes. Their preferences were not translated into parliamentary seats and had effectively no effect on the outcome of the election."[337]

In the provinces, the results of FPP voting can be even more skewed. In the 1996 British Columbia election, the NDP won the most seats despite having fewer votes than the rival Liberal Party. In 2001, the Liberals turned the tables with a vengeance, taking 97 percent of the seats, despite winning only 57 percent of the vote. In 1987, the New Brunswick Liberals won 60 percent of the popular vote, but took every seat in the legislature.

As these figures suggest, there are many weaknesses of the FPP system. Some of those noted in a 2004 Law Commission of Canada report[338] include:

> The first-past-the-post system is overly generous to the party that wins a plurality of the vote in a general election, rewarding it with a legislative majority that is disproportionate to its share of the vote. ...
>
> It allows the governing party, with its artificially swollen legislative majority, to dominate the political agenda almost completely for a period of four or five years, thereby contributing to the weakening of Parliament. ...
>
> It promotes parties formed along regional lines, thus exacerbating Canada's regional divisions, and conversely penalizes parties with diffuse national support. Many argue that, under the first-past-the-post system, parties are encouraged to focus their efforts on regions of the country where they are most likely to win a plurality of the votes. At the same time, parties with diffuse national support but no regional stronghold might have difficulty winning in enough ridings to gain representation in the House of Commons.

---

337 H. MacIvor, "A Brief Introduction to Electoral Reform," in H. Milner, ed., *Making Every Vote Count: Reassessing Canada's Electoral System* (Peterborough, ON: Broadview Press, 1999), 23.

338 B. Schwartz and D. Rettie, *Valuing Canadians: The Options for Voting System Reform in Canada* (Ottawa: Law Commission of Canada, 2002), summarized in *Voting Counts: Electoral Reform in Canada* (Ottawa: Law Commission of Canada, 2004) at 1.3.

...

Due to the regional nature of the first-past-the-post system, the ruling party's success is often attributable to winning a large percentage of seats in particular regions of the country. Many observers express concern about the fact that the ruling party may have few or no caucus members from certain parts of the country.

This system disregards a large number of votes: unless a voter supports the winning candidate in a given riding, there is no connection between the voter's choice and the eventual makeup of the House of Commons. Many critics suggest that this aspect of the electoral system discourages people from voting since it leaves them with the impression that their vote does not matter.

It prevents diversity within the House of Commons. As a result of regional concentration, disproportionate votes to seats, and an under-representation of women and minority candidates, legislatures within this system lack a diversity of voices in political decision-making processes.

The Commission concluded:

A growing number of Canadians believe that the strengths of the first-past-the-post system may come at too great a cost — that it's "too much of a good thing" — by allowing governments with "artificial" majorities to misrepresent the views of the Canadian public. In short, they argue that the drawbacks of our electoral system may outweigh its advantages. ... For many, adding an element of proportionality to the electoral system — one which more accurately translates percentage of votes won into seats in the legislature or House of Commons — would help in addressing the many drawbacks of this system.[339]

b) Proportional Representation

Discontent with Canada's FPP approach has sparked substantial recent discussion of proportional representation (PR). Instead of electing one winner-take-all representative per region, PR systems allot the number of seats per party according to the proportion of the popular vote received by that party.

Many jurisdictions have adopted this approach. Our FPP system was inherited from Great Britain. Yet, regional governments in Britain, Scotland and Wales have done away with FPP in favour of proportional representation models of various forms, as have New Zealand, Japan and Italy. Australia's senate is also elected through PR, with each of the country's six states given an equal number of representatives.

---

339 *Ibid.*

In Canada, it is possible that a working provincial PR model could be in place within the next decade. By 2004, legislatures in Prince Edward Island, New Brunswick, Ontario, Quebec and British Columbia had all recently launched major democratic reform processes of various types, and each were considering the adoption of PR models.

In British Columbia, the province initiated an electoral reform initiative that is, itself, an innovative experiment in democratic participation. In November 2003, 160 citizens were selected at random to form the BC Citizens' Assembly. The assembly examined alternatives to the current FPP voting system and recommended in late 2004 that the province switch to a form of PR known as Single Transferable Voting (STV). The new model will be put to a vote during the 2005 provincial election, and if approved, may be in place by the 2009 election. (As already noted, British Columbia has fixed election dates.)

The assembly received testimony from a wide range of experts, but the final decision on the recommended model rested with the citizens who comprised the assembly. This is a major shift from the standard policy-making procedure of bureaucrats drafting policy that is approved of by elected officials, and for this reason, the process has been closely watched by democratic reform advocates. In November 2004, Ontario proposed that a similarly constituted citizen's assembly be struck in that province to come up with an alternative voting system model that could be in place as early as 2007.[340] Until recently, the NDP was pushing for a similar consultative process to take place federally, and the federal Liberal minority government included a promise to examine alternatives to the current FPP system in the October 2004 Speech from the Throne.

Fractious Parliaments

Certainly not everyone favours PR. Opponents of proportional representation argue that it promotes "single-issue extremism" and that it makes the voting system more complicated for the average citizen.[341] Many also point to the simplicity and stability of FPP, a system that tends to produce majority governments able to take decisive action.

Some of these criticisms of PR are illusory. For example, opponents are right to point out that PR systems give increased clout to "special interests"

---

340 Dalton McGuinty, Premier of Ontario, "Ontarians to Have a Say on Electoral Reform," press release, 18 Nov. 2004.

341 See comments by Don Boudria, MP, in "Round Table on Proportional Representation," (1997) 20 Canadian Parliamentary Review no. 1. Also see J. Courtney, "Plurality-Majority Elected Systems: A Review," above note 328 at 5.

and minorities, but this clout is dependant on these groups' actual support among the electorate; in other words, democracy. If the goal is to minimize the likelihood of, say, hate-espousing groups gaining a foothold in Parliament, threshold measures may be put in place to ensure that groups must have a certain basement floor level of popular support before they are entitled to any representation.

PR does encourage some balkanization in politics. In the FPP system, coalitions are encouraged *within* parties.[342] Under PR, coalitions are encouraged between parties. However, this is not to say that PR is inherently destabilizing. Critics often point to the examples of Israel, Italy and pre–World War II Germany to illustrate how PR systems can result in shaky governments. Yet, it is clear from a more comprehensive scan of international electoral systems that "it is simply inaccurate to blame the electoral system for the political turmoil in those regimes."[343] There are many examples of PR systems that maintain Parliaments longer in duration, on average, than Canada's current system, including Austria, the Netherlands, Switzerland and Sweden. In addition, given that in an FPP system, small swings in the electorate can result in wholesale changes of government, one may legitimately question whether such a system is, in fact, as stable as its proponents claim.

To this last point we would underscore an observation may by the Law Reform Commission, cited above: Because it emphasizes geographic support above all else, Canada's FPP system skews the political spectrum in favour of regionalism and discourages an issue focus that might have a better unifying effect on the country. Under the FPP system, "50 percent minus one" support for a party in one part of the country may go totally unrepresented, while the party may be disproportionately represented in a "50 percent plus one" region. While one may argue such a situation may "even out in the end," it may still present a false but enduring impression on the national psyche of a country divided. Other detrimental effects in this regard might include the lack of representation by the "50 percent

---

342 As noted by Courtney, "For the better part of Canadian history, coalitions have been built within Canadian parties rather than between, reflecting an incentive contained in the [FPP] system for centrist, mainstream parties dedicated to minimizing inter-regional and inter-linguistic conflicts. It cannot be assumed that the same incentives for parties to broker social cleavages would be present in other electoral systems": J. Courtney, "Plurality-Majority Elected Systems: A Review," above note 328 at 2.

343 H. MacIvor, "Proportional and Semi-Proportional Electoral Systems: Their Potential Effects on Canadian Politics" (presented to the Advisory Committee of Registered Political Parties, Elections Canada, Ottawa, Ontario, 23 April 1999) at 14.

minus one" region in the governing party's caucus and in Cabinet, further reinforcing the divided image.

The stability argument is, therefore, a two-edged sword for both PR and FPP models. No doubt in part for this reason, most advocates of PR for Canada do not favour a full system of proportional voting. Rather, a model blending the current FPP system with some PR representation is generally seen as the best way to balance the need for stability and geographic representation with the desire to have a government that is more representative of the general public's views.

Germany possesses such a model. There, citizens cast a two-part ballot. The first is to elect their constituency representative, as in Canada's FPP regime. The second is to vote for a party. For each party, the number of seats won through the proportional vote is subtracted from the number of seats won through the constituency vote. This resulting number represents how many seats the party can name from its list, to sit as nonconstituency representatives. The result is a legislature comprised of both constituency-based and PR-based members, with overall numbers adjusted to reflect the proportional vote. (If the number of constituency seats won by a party exceeds the number of seats won through the proportional vote, rather than see its seat count revised downward, the party is allowed to keep the surplus and the additional seats are added to the total number of seats, resulting a larger than normal legislature.) To qualify for the election of any representatives from the party list via the second, PR vote, a party must achieve at least 5 percent of the popular vote or elect three constituency representatives.

This type of system, known as mixed-member proportional (MMP), increases the representation for parties unduly penalized by the geographically based FPP system. Admittedly, the German system's approach to surplus seats might prove unworkable in Canada, possibly producing surplus MPs on a provincial basis disrupting the provincial proportionality requirements of the *Constitution Act, 1867*.[344] An alternative, simpler model would involve setting aside a quota of seats filled through a proportional system, while the remaining seats would be elected through the current single-member FPP system. This system would be less proportional that Germany's system, since a party's overall seat count would not be determined proportionally. It would, however, be easier to graft on to Canada's current electoral regime.

---

344 Law Reform Commission, *Voting Counts: Electoral Reform for Canada*.

Prime Ministerial Power

Some scholars urge that an MMP system could make the Commons a more capable body. MacIvor, citing Franks, argues that, "Under [FPP] small swings in the national vote can lead to huge gains or losses in seats by a particular party. The result is a high turnover in the Canadian House of Commons. The Commons is weakened by the inexperience of most of its members, who lack policy expertise and a working knowledge of the rules. Therefore a more stable membership would make the Commons a more powerful legislative body."[345]

On the other hand, it is possible that a PR (or even MMP) system could render Parliament even more accommodating of prime ministers than at present, and therefore a less effective legislative body. In PR systems, parties often rank their candidates for office, appointing the number warranted by the percentage of the popular vote in the election. Most incumbent candidates are assured re-election, except in cases where support for the party drops significantly. As a result, unless voters have the option of choosing candidates on the party list (which adds a level of complexity to the ballot), elected representatives owe their allegiance primarily to their party (and its leader) rather than the electorate or constituency.

This phenomenon would present an especially serious pitfall in the Canadian context, with its already high concentration of power in the hands of the party leadership. Specifically, as discussed in chapters to come, a key feature of the current system is the influence wielded by the governing party's leader — the prime minister — over ministers and parliamentary secretaries, who together can make up half of the governing party's caucus. In addition to these MPs, many others in the party may toe the party line in the hopes of advancing to these positions, or to win or maintain seats on committees or other appointments. It is this sword-of-Damocles influence over governing party MPs that, more than any other factor, already allows the prime minister to maintain significant power over the legislative branch.

Under a PR or an MMP system, this same party leader would control the naming of new MPs elected through proportional voting. These MPs may be selected for their party (or personal) loyalties, and without a grass-roots constituency base, may feel overwhelming pressure to maintain their allegiance to the party's leader. These MPs will undoubtedly join the ranks of prime ministerial loyalists in caucus, increasing the latter's grip over the governing party and ultimately Parliament.

---

345 MacIvor, "Proportional and Semi-Proportional Electoral Systems" at 8.

As most independent commentators appear to be, we are convinced that some measure of proportionality should be grafted on to the Canadian parliamentary system, if only in a reformed senate, a matter we discuss briefly in chapter 4. There may also be room for a blended MMP form for the House of Commons. However, if such a model is adopted for the House, it should be done in tandem with other measures that do not further enhance the power of party leaders and the executive. For instance, party members (rather than the leadership) could be given a role in determining the party list of candidates.

Legal Issues with an MMP System

Two legal questions are raised by this discussion of representation reform. First, is there any legal objection to the present FPP system? Second, is there any bar precluding reform of the FPP system?

In terms of legal objections to the FPP approach, some critics of the current system suggest that a move toward a PR system is mandated by Canada's constitutional law. Specifically, they have suggested that the current FPP system undermines the voting and equality rights under the *Charter*.[346]

For our part, we would be surprised if Canada's courts were to intervene on constitutional grounds on the FPP issue. The Supreme Court of Canada's language in *Figuerora v. Canada* suggests that section 3 of the *Charter*, at least, holds no promise for proportional representation: "that s. 3 should be understood with reference to the right of each citizen to play a meaningful role in the electoral process, *rather than the election of a particular form of government, is found in the fact that the rights of s. 3 are participatory in nature.* Section 3 does not advert to *the composition of Parliament subsequent to an election*, but only to the right of each citizen to a certain level of participation in the electoral process."[347]

On the question of whether anything in law *inhibits* a reform of the FPP system, in fact, nothing in the Constitution requires a first-past-the-post approach. As discussed above, section 40 of the *Constitution Act, 1867* does anticipate the division of the country into "electoral districts" from which Members are elected. However, this provision is prefaced by the

---

346 See arguments in *Russow & The Green Party of Canada v. Canada (Attorney General)* (1 May 2001), Doc. 01-CV-210088 (Ont. S.C.J.). Also see T. Knight, "Unconstitutional Democracy? A *Charter* Challenge to Canada's Electoral System" (1999) 57 U.T. Fac. L. Rev. 1; and H. MacIvor, "Proportional and Semi-Proportional Electoral Systems" at 10, 16–17.

347 *Figueroa*, [2003] 1 S.C.R. 912 at para. 26 [emphasis added].

phrase "until the Parliament of Canada otherwise provides." This caveat has allowed Parliament to readjust these districts from time to time, without triggering the traditional constitutional amendment formula. On a plain reading, it would also allow Parliament to dispense with electoral districts entirely, or reduce their number in an MMP system to open up room for PR representatives.

Beyond section 40, the *Constitution Act, 1867* contains only two other requirements governing the composition of the Commons, all related to provincial representation: section 51A guaranteeing minimum numbers MPs from each province equal to no fewer than the province has representatives in the senate; and section 52 of the *Constitution Act, 1867* empowering Parliament to increase the number of MPs, "provided the proportionate Representation of the Provinces prescribed by this Act is not thereby disturbed." As noted above, the "proportionate Representation of the Provinces prescribed by this Act" is found in section 51 of the *Constitution Act, 1867*.[348]

In a reformed MMP system (that is, one that did not allow German-style surplus representation), these two constitutional requirements could easily be met. The section 51A minimums could be achieved through the FPP element of the mixed model, or by specifying that the requisite number of PR-determined representatives will be selected from each province. Likewise, allocating the PR-determined representatives on a provincial basis would also satisfy the section 51 and 52 representation requirements.

In sum, adoption of an MMP system for electing MPs in Canada need not precipitate a constitutional amendment. Nonetheless, in a mixed system, careful consideration would have to be given to how many seats would be elected through FPP and how many through PR. If the number of FPP seats in the House were significantly reduced, this would necessitate the merging of many electoral districts. In addition to the intense squabbling that electoral boundary readjustments always attract, it is possible that some constituencies that are already geographically vast with dispersed populations would have to become even larger.

One alternative might be a slight shaving of FPP seats while adding only a modest number of new seats to be filled through PR. For example, reducing the FPP seats by 25 and adding 50 seats to be filled on a PR basis would produce a 333-seat Commons. Of course, since only 15 percent of the

---

348 As amended by the *Representation Act, 1985*, S.C. 1986, c. 8, named the *Constitution Act (Representation), 1985*.

seats would be filled through PR, such a compromise would have a limited impact on correcting any distortions associated with the FPP system.

Other Electoral Models
Canada may also wish to consider other forms of voting that achieve many
of the democratic objectives of MMP. There is a vast and growing literature
on these alternatives, and it is beyond the scope of this book to canvas them
in full. However, some models workable in a Canadian context are worth
specific mention.

Single Transferable Vote
Australia's senate employs a "single transferable vote" (STV) system in
which voters rank the various candidates on the ballot in multimember constituencies. At the counting of the first-choice votes, once a candidate
receives a winning threshold of votes, the remaining voters who ranked his
or her as their first choice will have their votes transferred to their second
choice until another candidate reaches the winning threshold. This latter
step may be repeated until the required number of candidates is elected. The
BC Citizens Assembly, discussed above, has recommended this system.

While more complicated than FPP, the STV system is significantly
more democratic, as it reflects not only a voter's choice of one candidate
over another, but the voter's depth of support for each candidate. It is perhaps the system in which the fewest votes possible are "wasted."

Although STV retains a geographic basis for electing members, the
model is somewhat impractical for Canada's federal government, as it
requires multiple candidates to be elected from any one electoral district.
As noted by MacIvor, unless the number of MPs was increased accordingly, this would require making existing electoral districts significantly larger, an especially difficult endeavour in the north and in other sparsely
populated areas.[349]

Alternative Vote
A single-candidate variant on the STV system is the "instant run-off" or
"alternative vote" (AV) system. Although not a proportionally based system,
the AV system, used in the Australian House of Representatives, is simpler
and perhaps more applicable to Canada. It is also touted as a reform in the
United States.

Like the STV system, under an AV approach, candidates are ranked by
voters. But here, if no single candidate wins 50 percent of the first choices,
the candidate with the least number of votes is excluded and the prefer-

---

349 H. MacIvor, "Proportional and Semi-Proportional Electoral Systems," 17.

ences recalculated until a majority candidate emerges. Alberta and Manitoba experimented with STV and AV systems in the 1920, only to return to FPP systems thirty years later.[350]

Run-Off

In the "two-vote" or "run-off" system of voting, rather than list preferences on the ballot, voters mark an "X" next to their preferred candidate (as is done in the current FPP system), but unless a candidate receives a majority, there is a subsequent run-off election to determine the winner. Candidates that receive below a certain threshold on the first ballot are eliminated from competition in the second ballot. Such a system is used in France, and a form of it is generally used in Canadian party leadership conventions. It has similar advantages to the STV system, although determining a winner may result in multiple votes, involving higher cost and potential for voter fatigue.

One feature of the two-vote system, as noted by Courtney, is that it

> encourages the creation of coalitions (either personal or party) among candidates between the two rounds of voting. This can be seen in a favourable light in that it encourages a measure of inter-party or inter-candidate bargaining and trade-offs. These can be healthy in socially and ethnically diverse communities, can encourage a measure of openness to public scrutiny of inter-elite bargaining and can help to accommodate inter-regional tensions or rivalries.[351]

Under the two-vote system, there can be a delay of days or even weeks to determine a winner, although delays may become greatly reduced in the coming years as vote-counting technology improves. A more pressing weakness, however, is that the distorted results of FPP are not necessarily improved by a two-vote system, nor is the record of female or minority parliamentary representation any better as it would likely be under a PR system.[352] We turn to this diversity issue next.

5. Toward a More Diverse Parliament

A key question is whether the present electoral system produces governments that are broadly *representative* of the electorate. When one looks at

---

350 J. Courtney, *Commissioned Ridings: Designing Canada's Electoral Districts* (Montreal: McGill-Queen's University Press, 2001) at 36–44.

351 J. Courtney, "Plurality-Majority Elected Systems: A Review," above note 328 at 13.

352 *Ibid.* at 14.

the composition of our Parliament, the answer is clearly "no," at least when measured with reference to women and visible minorities. Following the 2004 election, eighteen visible minorities were elected federally — or 6 percent of the House of Commons — compared to 14 percent in the general population.

With regard to parliamentary representation of women, as of August 2004, Canada ranked thirty-third in a 183-nation survey conducted by the Inter-Parliamentary Union, with 21 percent female representation in the House of Commons, and 32 percent in the senate.[353] The ranking places Canada sixteenth out of thirty industrialized countries.

Canadian female parliamentary representation has steadily increased in recent decades. From a single member of Parliament in 1968, ten were elected in 1979, thirty-nine in 1988, and sixty in 1997. Since that time, however, the increase in representation for women has slowed.

For women who are members of visible minority groups, the lack of representation in Parliament creates a "double minority status."[354] Following the 2004 election, there were just six visible minority women in the House of Commons (2 percent of MPs).

Some countries have taken legislative measures to address diversity issues. In Sweden, for example, each gender is guaranteed a minimum of 40 percent and a maximum of 60 percent of seats in Parliament. In New Zealand, four seats in the country's legislature are set aside for its Indigenous Maori population.

However, these quotas would be difficult to implement in a first-past-the-post system such as Canada's, and it appears there is little appetite in Canada for such a system. A Canadian Advisory Council on the Status of Women publication entitled, "Missing Persons: Women in Canadian Federal Politics," states: "There are no magic solutions to the problem of low female representation: if women want to get elected they have to learn the rules of the game and be prepared for a great deal of hard work and a good measure of personal sacrifice, as many have done in the past and as, it is hoped many more will do in the future."[355]

Although the wage gap, stereotypes and other factors that inhibit women and minorities in the workforce more generally are undoubtedly at

353   Inter-Parliamentary Union, "Women in National Parliaments" (Aug. 2004).
354   J.H. Black, "Minority Women in the 35th Parliament: A New Dimension of Social Diversity," (1997) 20 Canadian Parliamentary Review no. 1.
355   Cited in E. Bakopanos (address to the Third Canadian Parliamentary Seminar for the Commonwealth Parliamentary Association, Ottawa, 29 Nov. 2003).

play in electoral politics, one of the most serious obstacles for women and minorities is nomination races, where those with higher disposable incomes and better connections to influential sectors — disproportionately white men — have an enormous advantage. As MP Eleni Bakopanos put it: "In politics, as in the corporate world or academia, the barriers that women face are systemic and structural. The bottom line for women's entry into politics is economic equality. It takes money to make a nomination bid — and most women simply do not have access to the networks that provide financing for candidates."[356]

Reforming the first-past-the-post system may be the place to start looking for answers to the representation imbalance. Even without a quota mechanism, a proportional system of voting would likely result in better representation for women and minorities. An international comparison of women's representation provides support for this assertion. Every one of the fifteen industrialized countries that fared better than Canada in the Inter-Parliamentary Union survey cited above use either full or blended PR systems, although it should be noted that cultural factors and policy measures may also have a strong influence on representation in at least some of these countries.

In Canada, because major parties have a strong interest in maintaining an appeal to a broad cross-section of society, if some MPs were chosen from party lists rather than through the local politics of nomination contests, it is likely that parties would make a serious effort to ensure gender and socio-economic balance on these lists. A PR system would especially benefit First Nations, and other ethnic, linguistic and minority groups whose vote is geographically dispersed across the country,[357] and thus of little effect in any one FPP riding contest. The appointed senate's record on diversity — generally better than that of the elected Commons — provides some evidence in support of the diversity advantages of party-appointed candidate selections.

In addition to electoral system reform, other measures not enshrined in law or government policy may also help achieve diversity objectives. In the United States, EMILY's List was founded in 1985 to help finance the campaigns of pro-choice Democratic Party women candidates. EMILY, which stands for "Early Money Is Like Yeast," is the largest financial resource for minority-women candidates seeking U.S. federal office, directing $5.7 million toward such campaigns, including every one of the four-

---

356 *Ibid.*

357 H. MacIvor, "Proportional and Semi-Proportional Electoral Systems," at 13–14.

teen Democratic African-American and six Latina woman who have served in the House of Representatives since the fund's inception.[358]

In Canada, the Liberal Party maintains the Judy LaMarsh Fund, which directs money to women candidates in that party. In the 2004 election, the fund supported only new women candidates, donating a modest $2,500 to each campaign. These sorts of nonlegislative efforts certainly have an important place in encouraging underrepresented groups to run for election, but to date have proved insufficient.

6. Recall

Once an MP is elected, their seat will only be vacated in the limited circumstances discussed at the beginning of this chapter. Not all systems are as kind to elected representatives. One mechanism currently used in fourteen U.S. states but only one Canadian province — British Columbia[359] — is the "recall," a means for citizens to remove their representatives midterm.

A brief experiment with recall was introduced by former Alberta Premier William Aberhart in 1935, but ended in embarrassment when the premier himself was recalled by his own riding. The government repealed the law in 1937, declaring the recall null and void.[360]

McCormick describes the two recall models generally in use:

> The first model, the most common one, has a three-stage process. First, there is a petition that must be signed by a specific percentage of the electorate. Second, there is a vote on the question of recall, where the citizens of the constituency are asked whether or not they want to recall the representative. Third, if that second vote was positive, you would then have a by-election to fill the vacancy that resulted. This three-stage process is the most common method used in the United States. ...
>
> The second model is a two-stage process. It has the petition trigger the actual by-election directly with no intervening vote. If you get enough signatures the seat is vacant and a by-election must take place. This second model is used by a minority of the US states that have this provision in place.[361]

358 EMILY's List website at http://69.20.85.216/newsroom/presskit/women-candidates.html.

359 *Recall and Initiative Act*, R.S.B.C. 1996, c. 398.

360 A. Adamson, "We Were Here Before: The Referendum in Canadian Experience" (March 1980) *Policy Options* at 53.

361 P. McCormick, "The Recall of Elected Members" (1994), 17 Canadian Parliamentary Review no. 2.

The threshold level, or number of signatures required on the petition that triggers the by-election, is the key factor in how easy or difficult it will be for citizens to remove the elected official from office. For the first model, the threshold will likely be lower than for the second. In the United States, the threshold under this three-step model is usually 15 percent.[362] British Colombia follows the two-step model. Its law requires a threshold of 40 percent of electors from the member of the Legislature's electoral district.[363]

Under recall legislation, there is usually a time limit for gathering signatures. In the United States, time limits often range between 60 and 270 days.[364] In British Columbia, the time period is 60 days.[365] Further, in British Columbia, the petition can only be made after the member has been in office for eighteen months.

Recall is controversial. At the federal level, the Reform Party and its successor, the Canadian Alliance, advocated in favour of federal referendum and recall legislation. However, the party, and the new Conservative Party created by a merger of the Alliance and the Progressive Conservatives in 2004, have not forcefully advanced the policy following a spoof referendum promoted by the CBC satire show "This Hour Has 22 Minutes." Leading up to the 2000 election, the show asked Canadians to sign an Internet petition asking Alliance leader Stockwell Day to change his first name to "Doris." More than one million people logged on to sign the petition. Day declined to change his name, replying to the petition stating, "Que sera sera."

Recall advocates urge that even if the mechanism is rarely used — and used successfully even less often — it can encourage elected officials to be more attuned with their electorate. The mere threat of a recall campaign may prompt an official to spend more time communicating with constituents and justifying his or her views. "Recall is often a demand for an explanation," notes McCormick.[366]

On the other hand, one of the concerns raised by recall is the fear that it may be abused by rival parties and candidates, and that MPs will see their time and resources spent fighting recalls rather than governing. Taken to its logical extreme, one could devise a system with the use of modern technology in which voters can register their displeasure at any time through a computerized registry. When support for a particular MP drops below 50 percent among those who elected him or her, the MP could be summarily

---

362 *Ibid.*
363 *Recall and Initiative Act*, para. 23(1)(b).
364 McCormick, "The Recall of Elected Members."
365 *Recall and Initiative Act*, para. 23(1)(a).
366 McCormick, "The Recall of Elected Members."

removed from office. Such a system would of course make governance impossible, since the whims of the electorate must be balanced with the need for officials to govern effectively.

This objection may go, however, to process rather than substance. As with any referendum procedure, by setting a higher threshold level and stricter time limit for gathering signatures, the concern over frivolous recall campaigns may be abated. In our view, it is worth a conversation as to whether recall should be employed at the federal level, reserved for cases in which a large percentage of the electorate — like B.C.'s 40-percent threshold — is willing to mobilize, via a regulated petition and referendum process.

7. Referendums

A final issue addressed in this chapter is how a voting system can be employed, not simply as a means of selecting representatives, but as a form of direct democratic governance by the electorate.

a) Overview

A referendum has been defined as "a method of referring a question or set of questions to the people directly as opposed to allowing them to be set-tled by the people's representatives in the legislature."[367] Generally phrased as a "yes" or "no" question, whichever answer receives the most votes is binding on the government. The process is based on the notion of "direct democracy." Rather than representative democracy, which transfers author-ity from citizens to representatives, direct democracy places decision-mak-ing authority directly with the people.

As a democratic device, referendums date back at least to the ancient Greeks. Today, they are provided for in the constitutions of many nations, including Australia, Denmark, France, Ireland, Italy, Spain, and Switzer-land. In addition, many other jurisdictions provide for referendums by statute.

In Switzerland, a nation that celebrates itself as a "direct democracy," referendums date back to the thirteenth century. The Swiss structure of government considers citizens, rather than Parliament, to be supreme. As a result, neither government nor the courts can overrule a referendum, even in cases dealing with human rights or equality rights.[368]

---

367 D. Robertson, *A Dictionary of Modern Politics* (London: Europa Publications, 1985) at 285.

368 J. Steiner, "Reflections on Referendums," in *The Referendum Device*, ed. Austin Ran-ney (Washington: Conference for the American Institute for Public Policy Research and the Hansard Society for Parliamentary Governments, 1981) at 6.

In some cantons (the equivalent of Canadian provinces), all cantonal legislation, excluding financial bills, must be approved of by referendum. All amendments to the Swiss constitution must also be approved by the country's citizens in a referendum. In addition to a national majority, the initiative must succeed in a majority of cantons. This helps prevents larger urban cantons from imposing their will on smaller rural ones.[369]

Switzerland suggests that binding referendums are consistent with democratic governance. More ominously, government by referendums may be a reason that Switzerland was one of the last industrialized countries where women gained the right to vote, a reform not made until 1971.[370]

Switzerland is not alone in favouring referendums. Both provincially and internationally, there are also jurisdictions that *require* referendums on a variety subject matters. As Girling notes, these include:

- approval for changes to the constitution, as in Australia, Ireland, British Columbia and Alberta;
- prior approval of the raising of public money by way of issuing bonds, as in many local and state U.S. jurisdictions;
- prior approval to the introduction of certain types of bills, as under the *Alberta Taxpayer Protection Act* in relation to the levying of provincial sales taxes and in Manitoba in relation to increases in certain taxes;
- prior approval before a law already enacted may come into force (in effect ratification of a law), as in certain U.S. jurisdictions;
- in response to a citizens' petition to enact law (often called an initiative), as in British Columbia and Saskatchewan;
- in response to a citizens' petition to amend a law already enacted by way of initiative, as in California where, because a positive vote in an initiative actually creates substantive law, that law may only be amended by further initiatives; and
- in response to a citizens' petition to recall or remove from office an elected representative before the end of his or her term, as in British Columbia and Kansas.[371]

"Ballot initiatives" — in which a referendum can be triggered if a given percentage of the electorate sign a petition agreeing to place the question

369 D. Pond, "Direct Democracy: The Wave of the Future?" (1991) 15 Canadian Parliamentary Review no. 1.

370 J. Steiner, "Reflections on Referendums," at 6.

371 J. Girling, "Will Referendums Make Government More Accountable" (1998) 21 Canadian Parliamentary Review no. 4.

on a ballot — exist in at least twenty-four U.S. states.[372] Ballot initiative legislation generally requires that a threshold of electors indicate their support for holding the referendum, usually by way of a petition. For example, the Saskatchewan *Referendum and Plebiscite Act* includes a threshold of 15 percent of the electorate in order to trigger a referendum.[373] In British Columbia, the equivalent level is 10 percent, but it must be achieved from every electoral district in the province.[374] Achieving this threshold requires a major effort in every part of the province, including sparsely populated areas where it may be more difficult to reach voters.

b)   Pros and Cons of Referendums

Critics argue that referendums often oversimplify complex policy issues and inhibit the development of compromises that may take a broader range of interests into account. Some argue that voters lack the expertise to make informed decisions on many issues, while others note that referendums may be cynically employed by politicians as a way of avoiding the consequences of making hard decisions.

Still others argue that referendums undermine the very foundations of representative democracy: we elect representatives for their ability to govern, but also to allow these representatives to dedicate themselves full-time to study the many nuanced issues and processes associated with governance.

In our view, these critiques are valid, but limited to extreme circumstances where referendums displace representative democracy. Used judiciously, referendums could be a valuable way of augmenting representative democracy, of rendering representatives accountable and of engaging the electorate in public policy.

Those who see referendums as an accountability mechanism argue that it is a purer form of democracy than elections. First, rather than electing a representative who will then decide on various issues with which the voter may or may not agree, a referendum allows voters to decide directly these issues, and, in the case of initiative referendums, actually to formulate the question — and potentially the law project — to be put to voters. In this way, referendums may encourage voters to become engaged in the democratic process, promoting individual responsibility and reducing apathy among the electorate. Of course, whether this will prove true empirically is a difficult question. Switzerland, the country that employs the widest

---

372   Council of State Governments, *The Book of the States*, vol. 34 (Lexington, KY: 1998).
373   *Referendum and Plebiscite Act*, S.S. 1990–1991, c. R-8.01, s. 7.
374   *Recall and Initiative Act*, R.S.B.C. 1996, c. 398, para. 7(1)(b).

use of referendums, has a voter turnout that is actually lower than most industrialized countries.[375]

Second, referendums may divorce broader questions about the qualities of a government from a given public policy issue. "Throwing the bums out" may not be the most efficient way of influencing government decision-making on individual and very particular public policy issues.

Third, referendums may reduce the role of lobbyists and special interest groups that can sway officials on these particular issues, beneath the public's radar screen. This benefit is significantly dependent on having limits on donations and spending applied in referendum campaigns as much as elections, a matter discussed later.

Last, and perhaps most importantly, the classic justification for representative democracy, as opposed to direct democracy, is the cumbersome nature of governing a large population. With modern communication techniques permitting broad and regular communication with citizens and the introduction of less cumbersome voting techniques, such as electronic voting, there is no longer any technical hurdle standing in the way of more direct democracy.

c) Legal Issues

Although observers commonly use the term "referendum" to describe all of the processes outlined above, many would be more appropriately termed "plebiscites," a much older term that dates back to fourth-century B.C. Rome.[376] A plebiscite is not legally binding on elected officials, although because it is thought to reflect the direct will of the electorate, it carries significant moral weight.

At the federal level in Canada, there has never been a true, binding referendum, but there have been three non-binding plebiscites: in 1899, on prohibition (the culmination of a series of referendums on the issue at the local and provincial levels);[377] in 1942, on conscription; and in 1992, on the Charlottetown constitutional accord. Each province and territory, except for the Yukon, has also held plebiscites.[378]

---

375 M. Dunsmuir, "Referendums: The Canadian Experience in an International Context" (Library of Parliament, Jan. 1992), BP-271E. Although the United States also employs referendums, this is done only at the state and municipal level. Comparing voter turnout rates at this level of government to federal levels in other countries would be highly misleading.

376 D. Pond, "Direct Democracy: The Wave of the Future?"

377 P. Boyer, *Direct Democracy in Canada: The History and Future of Referendums* (Toronto: Dundurn Press, 1992) at 17–18.

378 T. Mowrey, "Referendums in Canada: A Comparative Overview" (Jan. 2001) *Electoral Insight*.

The federal statute permitting these events is the *Referendum Act*. However, its name aside, it is clear from its terms that this statute governs only plebiscites. The Act states a "referendum" may be held "Where the Governor in Council considers that it is in the public interest to obtain by means of a referendum the opinion of electors on any question relating to the Constitution of Canada."[379] It is clear from this wording that the purpose of the "referendum" is "to obtain ... the opinion of electors." The vote's outcome does not bind the government.

The B.C. legislation goes further. The B.C. *Referendum Act* includes triggering language similar to that in the federal counterpart: "If the Lieutenant Governor in Council considers that an expression of public opinion is desirable on any matter of public interest or concern, the Lieutenant Governor in Council may, by regulation, order that a referendum be conducted."[380] However, the B.C. law provides that "[i]f more than 50% of the validly cast ballots vote the same way on a question stated, that result is binding on the government that initiated the referendum."[381]

To meet this obligation, the government must "as soon as practicable, take steps, within the competence of the government, that the government considers necessary or advisable to implement the results of the referendum including ... changing programs or policies, or introducing new programs or policies, that are administered by or through the executive government" or "introducing legislation in the Legislative Assembly during its first session after the results of such a referendum are known."[382] The Saskatchewan *Referendum and Plebiscite Act* has similar provisions.[383]

British Columbia also has a "ballot initiative" law, the *Recall and Initiative Act*, permitting a registered voter to "apply to the chief electoral officer for the issuance of a petition to have a legislative proposal introduced into the Legislative Assembly" covering "any matter within the jurisdiction of the Legislature."[384] If supported with a petition bearing the required number of signatures, the proposal is referred to a committee of the Legislature, which may propose its adoption or refer the matter back to the province's chief electoral officer for the holding of an initiative vote. If this vote garners the level of support named in the Act, the government is obliged to introduce the proposed bill into the Legislature.[385]

---

379 *Referendum Act*, S.C. 1992, c. 30, s. 3.
380 *Referendum Act*, R.S.B.C. 1996, c. 400, s. 1.
381 *Ibid.*, s. 4.
382 *Ibid.*, s. 5.
383 *Referendum and Plebiscite Act*, S.S.1990–1991, c. R-8.01, ss. 3–6.
384 *Recall and Initiative Act*, R.S.B.C. 1996, c. 398 at ss. 2 and 3.
385 *Ibid.*, s. 16.

The Saskatchewan *Referendum and Plebiscite Act* and the B.C. *Referendum Act* and the *Recall and Initiative Act* compel, therefore, executive action upon a successful vote. They do not, however, appear to oblige the Legislature to pass a bill introduced by the government in response to a successful vote (as many U.S. states are required to do). If they did, they might be unconstitutional. In *Re The Initiative and Referendum Act*, the Judicial Committee of the Privy Council — then Canada's highest court of appeal — concluded that a Manitoba law empowering electors to initiate legislation that would come into force should the requisite votes in favour be obtained violated what is now the *Constitution Act, 1867*.[386] By purporting to create legislation upon a vote of the electorate, the statute sidestepped the power of the Lieutenant Governor to extend (or not) Royal Assent to the bill. Further, in *obiter dicta*, the law lords suggested that the Act constituted an impermissible delegation of the law-making function accorded the legislature by the *Constitution Act, 1867*.

It is questionable that this dated decision should be taken as the last word on the issue. Parliament or a provincial legislature could amend their orders of internal legislative procedure — the Standing Orders — to indicate that a bill initiated and approved via a referendum process is to be treated as if it had passed three readings of, in the case of Parliament, the Commons and senate. Here, Parliament has delegated nothing to the electorate as it is still technically making the law, although employing a different procedure to vet the law project. As we note in chapter 5, there is no constitutional requirement that the internal process followed in parliamentary law-making follow the actual, conventional three-readings procedure. Internal rules of procedure are a matter of parliamentary privilege, unassailable in the courts.

If these same rules of procedure then provided that the bill would be presented to the Governor General for royal assent, that official's constitutional role in law-making would not be undermined. Since by convention, the royal assent will not be refused, the net affect of this system would be to allow binding initiative referendums without running afoul of the constitutional concerns raised by the Privy Council.

d) Referendum Mechanics

Where referendums or plebiscites are held, campaigning should be regulated in a fashion analogous to election campaigns. For example, just as there are federal rules on campaign donations and expenditures during elections, similar limits and reporting requirements are justified for refer-

---

386 (1919), 48 D.L.R. 18 (J.C.P.C.).

endum campaigns to prevent the process from being a mere tool for wealthy interests to manipulate the democratic process. In U.S. states with referendum legislation in place, there are generally no limits on either spending or contributions. As a result, a burgeoning signature collection industry has emerged in these states, and it is routine for ballot proponents to spend millions of dollars on companies that undertake this activity. Not surprisingly given this pattern, research has shown that referendums are often used by wealthy interests to promote causes that are far from the "grassroots."[387] In Canada, the federal *Referendum Act* limits campaign spending,[388] but does not regulate the quantity of contributions (although it does limit their source).[389]

In the case of ballot initiatives, government should also define the duration of the campaign period, including the period allowed for gathering signatures. This is the case in most jurisdictions that have these initiatives, including B.C.

Third-party expenditures — that is, spending by entities other than the two official sides — should also be limited, although given that most referendums are primarily about issues rather than individuals or political parties, differentiating general issue advertising from advertising aimed at influencing the issue being decided in the referendum will be especially difficult. The federal *Referendum Act* contains a third-party-spending limit of $5,000,[390] and the Supreme Court has stated that a limit of $1,000 is constitutionally acceptable.[391]

F. CONCLUSION

The first step in a democracy is designing an electoral system that most closely reflects the opinions of the electorate, measured on a one-person, one-vote basis. Stating this principle is one thing. As this chapter suggests, designing such a system is far more complicated, especially where there are other, sometimes competing values that inform election law. Professor

---

387 S. Bowler, T. Donovan and C. Tolbert, *Citizens as Legislators: Direct Democracy in the United States* (Columbus, OH: Ohio State University, 1998); L. Sabato, H. Ernst and B. Larson, *Dangerous Democracy: The Battle over Ballot Initiatives in America* (Latham, MD: Rowman and Littlefield, 2001); and D. Smith, *Tax Crusaders and the Politics of Direct Democracy* (New York: Routledge, 1999).

388 *Referendum Act*, R.S.C. 1992, c. 30 at subs. 15(2).

389 *Ibid.*, s. 14.

390 *Ibid.*, subs. 15(1).

391 *Libman*, [1997] 3 S.C.R. 569.

André Blais suggests a set of criteria for assessing the democratic integrity of electoral systems. These are:

1. Does the system produce ... governments readily accountable to voters?
2. Does it produce ... governments broadly *representative* of the electorate?
3. Is there an absence of *systemic bias* against certain groups or interests?
4. Does *each vote count equally?*
5. Does the electoral system produce ... governments that are *both relatively effective and accommodating?*
6. Does the electoral system produce *relatively strong parties and relatively strong local representatives?*
7. Is the vote *simple enough and yet a relatively precise reflection of citizens' preferences?*[392]

Canada, like most modern democracies, has undoubtedly come a long way in balancing these objectives in its electoral system. Expanding the right to vote, protecting citizens' right to "effective representation," and recognizing and limiting the influence that wealthy interests can have are all examples of how Canadian law has evolved to reinforce each of these goals at some level.

Still, we have a ways to go. In this chapter, we have identified holes in the fabric of Canadian election law — such as the limited regulation of party leadership contests. Arguably, inadequate regulation in this area measures up poorly against Blais' first, accountability criterion. More systemically, many would argue that Blais' first four criteria are compromised by a first-past-the-post system, one that allows parties that win fewer than 50 percent of the votes to control almost all the power of the federal government. It is true that the FPP system conforms well with the sixth and seventh criteria. But other electoral systems can meet these two criteria, without overlooking other important democratic values.

As the expectations that Canadians have of their government evolve, and as we learn more about the deficiencies in our current system and the innovative solutions available, there is both enormous need and potential for Canada to modernize and further democratize its electoral system. In so doing, we will hone the first prong of democratic accountability, the selection of elected representatives.

---

392 A. Blais, "Criteria for Assessing Electoral Systems" (presented to the Advisory Committee of Registered Political Parties, Elections Canada, 23 April 1999) at 2–9.

Elected representatives comprise, however, only a small portion of the federal public administration. The issue to which we turn our attention next is how Canada fills the posts of the many unelected officials who comprise most of the federal government.

The Selection, Tenure and Dismissal of Unelected Officials

For many Canadians, a federal election in which citizens designate their Members of Parliament is the central event in Canadian democracy. However, the Government of Canada comprises many thousands of other people who are not elected. Democracy in Canada depends, therefore, on mechanisms designed to hold these unelected officials politically accountable. This accountability stems from the "primacy" of elected representatives over unelected officials. This primacy — ultimately the hard core of responsible government — comes in several forms:

- First, primacy may exist in the institutional, or "command and control," authority elected representatives exercise over their unelected counterparts, and the related notion that these elected officials are "responsible" for the activities of their unelected counterparts.
- Second, primacy may flow from the role of Cabinet or individual ministers in appointing and selecting these unelected officials. Here, democratic accountability is preserved by the monopoly of elected officials on hiring and firing their unelected counterparts.

In Canada's modern democracy, these two forms of primacy are sometimes disregarded, reflecting the emergence of values other than raw accountability to elected representatives. After all, accountability to politicians is a double-edged sword. On the one hand, it extends to unelected officials the umbrella of democratic legitimacy. On the other hand, allowing politicians to police unelected officials infuses the accountability imperative with partisan politics. Partisanship in the selection of unelected officials raises two key issues:

- First, Canadian law recognizes that in some circumstances partisanship (especially when coupled with a strong command and control primacy) irremediably corrupts the functions of unelected officials. Judicial independence, for instance, is a clear rejection of political primacy in the courts of law and, increasingly, in quasi-judicial administrative tribunals.
- Second, partisanship in appointments and dismissals produces that great bugbear of Canadian governance: political "patronage" or favouritism. There are two ways to look at patronage. The most popular way — usually championed by parties when in opposition — is to view patronage as official corruption; an illegitimate sharing of public spoils. On the other hand, patronage may also be viewed as the inevitable, and perhaps desirable, product of democratic transitions of power between parties. Should we not expect that the parties we have elected — presumably for their different views on public policy — will staff government with officials sympathetic to that public policy vision?

Certainly, political favouritism is an accepted way of doing business in the United States, where overtly political appointments are made very deep into the public service. U.S. political parties try to score points against one another by sometimes contesting individual candidates, but no mainstream critic appears to view these politicized appointments as illegitimate *per se*.

Still, there is something troubling to the modern mind about government authority being handed on a platter to unelected party faithful. It may be that a candidate's *curriculum vitae* is a relatively minor factor taken into consideration by the electorate during elections. Indeed, as the Supreme Court has observed, in elections, "[m]any individuals are unaware of the personal identity or background of the candidate for whom they wish to vote."[1]

Nevertheless, when those same elected officials are tasked with either selecting — or designing a system for selecting — their unelected counterparts, we expect that credentials will prevail over other considerations in determining the outcome of that process. We are far more inclined, in other words, toward the competence-based "merit" principle when it

---

1   *Figueroa v. Canada (Attorney General)*, [2003] 1 S.C.R. 912 at para. 56.

comes to selecting unelected officials. In an era that places emphasis on aptitude, and not political pedigree, appointments influenced by partisan leanings appear to do violence to this principle of meritocracy.

Moreover, the U.S. comparison itself casts a suspect light on Canadian procedure: the United States differs from Canada in that executive appointments must be preceded by confirmation by the senate, at least for those officers exercising significant authority under the laws of the United States.[2] No such requirement exists in Canada. The Constitution is either silent on appointments or, as with some judges, gives the executive exclusive constitutional power to appoint unelected officials. As a strict constitutional matter, the opposition parties in Parliament are given no opportunity to participate in this process. Thus, absent any other legal intervention, the only check on truly egregious governing party patronage practices would be political and media exposure and condemnation.

As John Turner learned in the 1984 election, popular outrage over patronage appointments can be potent. Political checks on patronage, however, tend to deepen contempt, not just for the governing party, but also for the political process and public institutions. Therefore, patronage scandals — although one of the true constants in Canadian politics — are not a sound basis on which to build a viable, accountable, democratic state. There is room for law.

One legal solution to patronage is to impose a clear competence-based merit principle in appointments and dismissals, removing politics from the process entirely. This approach obviously minimizes the prospects of patronage. On the other hand, it also arguably reduces the potency of the primacy concept: civil servants, for instance, are insulated from their political masters, giving them an autonomy not shared by their politically appointed counterparts. Political patronage may not be commonplace in the professionalized, semi-autonomous civil service. But a professionalized bureaucracy potentially also opens the door to *Yes Minister*'s Sir Humphrey Appleby: officials serving their own interests with only token deference to the will of their elected masters.

A second solution — usually associated with unelected officials over which the government lacks full command and control primacy — is to limit the government's dismissal powers while throwing open the appoint-

---

2   Article II of the U.S. Constitution empowers the president, with the advice and consent of two-thirds of the senate to appoint and commission "officers" of the United States. It pertains to persons exercising "significant authority" by reason of the laws of the United States.

ments process. In some instances, we have introduced new political checks on egregious political favouritism by obliging the executive branch to test its selections against the recommendations of professional bodies and/or parliamentarians. In order to make such a process work, a number of questions must be addressed: How are the professional bodies selected? What role do they play? How do we ensure that a parliamentary process does not result in a political circus? Is it administratively possible to review the large number of appointments at stake?

In this chapter we take up these issues, examining the full range of unelected officials, divided by branch of government — legislative, executive and judicial. We focus on rules and practices governing the selection, tenure and dismissal of these persons. In each instance, we highlight the extent to which legal checks and balances exist and are consistent with the concept of democratic accountability outlined in our introductory chapter.

A. LEGISLATIVE BRANCH UNELECTED OFFICIALS

We turn first to the legislative branch of government. Under this heading, we examine the appointment, tenure and dismissal of the monarch, the Governor General, senators and the parliamentary civil service.

1. Monarch and Governor General

The monarch and the Governor General are difficult officials to classify. By the specific terms of the *Constitution Act, 1867*, the executive government of Canada is vested in the monarch.[3] In this book, we have chosen, however, to place the Queen — and her representative, the Governor General — under the category of legislative branch. In doing so, we respond to another aspect of the 1867 Act, one defining the Queen as part of the Parliament of Canada.[4]

As is made clear elsewhere in this book, the Queen and the Governor General have a largely nominal governance role, at least in times of majority government. With a few important exceptions, the monarch and her representative respond to the advice of Cabinet (or at least the prime minister) in exercising their power.

These officials do, however, play a key role in representing the Canadian state. Thus, in their most public roles, the Queen and her Governor General act as Canada's titular head of state, an important symbolic and

---

3   *Constitution Act, 1867*, s. 9.
4   *Ibid.*, s. 17.

ceremonial function. In that head of state role, the Governor General represents Canada at home and abroad. Thus, he or she receives foreign dignitaries and heads of state at Rideau Hall and is the Commander-in-Chief of Canada's Armed Forces. In this latter capacity, the Governor General "encourages excellence and dedication in military personnel, visits Canadian Forces bases in all regions of the country, often welcomes troops on their return from overseas missions and performs other ceremonial duties."[5]

Domestically, the Governor General "strives to promote national identity and Canadian unity and to enhance awareness of Canada's cultural wealth and diversity" and "takes part in community activities, visits hospitals and schools, joins in the festivities at fairs and festivals, gives speeches and supports a wide range of organizations." He or she also "awards honours to pay tribute to remarkable individuals in all fields of human activity."[6]

a) Appointment

In contrast to many republican systems, the Canadian head of state is not elected. His or her identity depends, in the case of the monarch, on birth, and in the case of the Governor General, on appointment.

The Monarch

The Canadian constitutional monarch is determined in the United Kingdom according to rules of heredity and antiquated laws of succession, most notably the famous *Act of Settlement* of 1701. Among other things, the latter statute bars Catholics from assuming the Crown, and even precludes the monarch from marrying a Roman Catholic. Further, the monarch must be in communion with the Church of England. Whether these prohibitions will fall prey to more contemporary conceptions of religious tolerance, incorporated into the law of the United Kingdom by virtue of the European Convention on Human Rights, remains to be seen.[7]

More immediately, this same *Act of Settlement* has been challenged unsuccessfully in Canadian courts as a violation of the *Canadian Charter of Rights and Freedoms*. In *O'Donohue v. The Queen*,[8] retired Toronto City

---

5   Commons Standing Committee on Government Operations and Estimates, *Second Report: The Governor General of Canada: Role, Duties and Funding for Activities*, 37th Parl., 3d Sess. (2 April 2004).

6   *Ibid.*

7   See Clare Dyer, "A Challenge to the Crown: Now Is the Time for Change," *The Guardian*, 6 Dec. 2000; Clare Dyer, "Catholic Bar to Throne 'Must Be Ended,'" *The Guardian*, 12 March 2001.

8   (2003), 109 C.R.R. (2d) 1 (Ont. S.C.J.).

Councillor Tony O'Donohue sought a declaration that provisions concerning the royal succession in the *Act of Settlement* were of no force or effect. Mr. O'Donohue urged that these sections discriminated against Roman Catholics in violation of the equality provisions of the *Charter*.

In a fascinating constitutional exegesis, the Ontario Superior Court rejected Mr. O'Donohue's application. In its key holding, the court concluded that the *Act of Settlement* was part of Canadian constitutional law. Pointing to the preamble in the *Constitution Act, 1867*,[9] it reasoned that "the rules of succession for the monarchy must be shared and be in symmetry with those of the United Kingdom and other Commonwealth countries." This requirement restricted the capacity of a Canadian court to declare provisions of the succession law illegitimate. If it were to do so, "Canada could break symmetry with Great Britain, and could conceivably recognize a different monarch than does Great Britain. ... This would clearly be contrary to settled intention, as demonstrated by our written Constitution, and would see the courts changing rather than protecting our fundamental constitutional structure."[10]

This conclusion was bolstered by the court's interpretation of the imperial *Statute of Westminster*,[11] a key instrument precluding the application of United Kingdom legislation to the Dominions without their consent. In its preamble, this 1931 law indicates "any alteration in the law touching the Succession to the Throne or the Royal Style and Titles shall hereafter require the assent as well as of the Parliaments of all the Dominions as of the Parliament of the United Kingdom." Since the *Statute of Westminster* is listed as part of the Constitution of Canada in the *Constitution Act, 1982*,[12] the court concluded that this bar on unilateral Canadian amendment of the succession rules was constitutionalized. Any changes to the succession rules required, therefore, a constitutional change made pursuant to the amendment formula in the *Constitution Act, 1982*.[13]

Because of the *Act of Settlement*'s constitutional status, the court found Mr. O'Donohue's *Charter* claim unavailing: the "*Charter* cannot be used to amend or trump another part of our constitution."[14] From *O'Donohue* it follows that, without a constitutional amendment, laws other than those of

---

9   As discussed in ch. 2, the key phrase in the preamble is the reference to Canada possessing "a Constitution similar in Principle to that of the United Kingdom."
10   *O'Donohue* (2003), 109 C.R.R. (2d) 1 at paras. 27 and 29.
11   1931 (U.K.), 22 and 23 Geo. 5, c. 4.
12   See *Constitution Act, 1982*, s. 52 and the schedule.
13   *O'Donohue*, (2003), 109 C.R.R. (2d) 1 at para. 33.
14   *Ibid.* at para. 15.

Canada — namely those existing presently in the United Kingdom — will determine Canada's next monarch.

The Governor General

In contrast, the identity of the monarch's Canadian representative — the Governor General — is now determined closer to home. Until the early twentieth century, the Governors General of the then-Dominions of the British Empire were selected by the monarch on the advice of the United Kingdom colonial secretary, and with the approval of the British prime minister. By 1890, there was an understanding — sometimes ignored — that the colonial government would be consulted prior to the appointment.[15]

In 1926, the members of the British Empire concluded that the traditional function of the Governor General as proxy of the imperial government was obsolete.[16] Subsequently, members of the empire convening at the 1930 imperial conference outlined how appointments to the post of Governor General were to be conducted:

1. The parties interested in the appointment of a Governor-General of a Dominion are His Majesty the King, whose representative he is, and the Dominion concerned.
2. The constitutional practice that His Majesty acts on the advice of responsible Ministers applies also in this instance.
3. The Ministers who tender and are responsible for such advice are His Majesty's Ministers in the Dominion concerned.
4. The Ministers concerned tender their formal advice after informal consultation with His Majesty.
    ...
6. The manner in which the instrument containing the Governor-General's appointment should reflect the principles set forth above is a matter in regard to which His Majesty is advised by His Ministers in the Dominion concerned.[17]

---

15   Norman Ward, *Dawson's The Government of Canada*, 6th ed. (Toronto: University of Toronto Press, 1987) at 179–80.

16   Imperial Conference 1926, Inter-Imperial Relations Committee, *Report, Proceedings And Memoranda*, E (I.R./26) Series ("In our opinion it is an essential consequence of the equality of status existing among the members of the British Commonwealth of Nations that the Governor-General of a Dominion is the representative of the Crown, holding in all essential respects the same position in relation to the administration of public affairs in the Dominion as is held by His Majesty the King in Great Britain, and that he is not the representative or agent of His Majesty's Government in Great Britain or of any Department of that Government.").

17   Imperial Conference 1930, Summary of Proceedings, HMSO, Cmd. 3717 (1930).

These principles establish, first, that the monarch appoints the Governor General. Second, this appointment is made in consultation with the Canadian, rather than the United Kingdom, Cabinet.

As it turns out, the current Canadian constitutional convention is slightly different: in appointing the Governor General, the Queen follows the Canadian prime minister's recommendations, not the Cabinet's.[18] Thus, while she is customarily consulted in advance,[19] the Queen takes her direction from what is known as an "Instrument of Advice," essentially a personal letter from the prime minister.[20]

The prime minister's authority to recommend a Governor General is said to be part of his or her "personal prerogative," a power that does not need to be exercised in association with Cabinet colleagues.[21] However, actually documenting the source of this power is difficult. It is not noted in the 1935 Privy Council minutes reportedly detailing the prime minister's personal prerogatives.[22] Further, past practice shows that some prime ministers have discussed Governor General appointments with, and sought approval from, Cabinet colleagues.[23]

There are no legal criteria constraining the prime minister's choice for Governor General. Convention probably dictates that only Canadians may now be appointed, and Canadian practice strongly favours alternating

---

18   Ward, *Dawson's The Government of Canada* at 180 ("The prime minister of Canada recommends the appointment to the queen, and the later acts on the advice so given."); Andrew Heard, *Canadian Constitutional Conventions* (Toronto: Oxford University Press, 1991) at 16 ("A firmly established convention dictates that the initiative for selecting a new Governor General lies with the prime minister personally.").

19   Ward, *Dawson's The Government of Canada* at 180 ("it seems to be customary to ascertain Her Majesty's wishes in the matter by previous consultation, inasmuch as the governor general is the sovereign's representative").

20   These documents are not published in the *Canada Gazette* and are available to the public in the National Archives only for the period prior to 1953. Library of Parliament, *Deputy Prime Minister of Canada, 1977 to Date* (July 2004).

21   Peter Hogg, *Constitutional Law of Canada*, looseleaf ed. (Toronto: Carswell, 2003) at 9-9. See, e.g., Cabinet document entitled "Appointment of the Governor General," RG2, Privy Council Office, Series A-5-a, vol. 6323, 1967/04/04 (prime minister informing Cabinet of his recommendation to the Queen concerning the appointment of Roland Michener as Governor General, and Cabinet "noting" this recommendation).

22   Privy Council minute, P.C. 3374 (25 Oct. 1935).

23   See, e.g., Cabinet document entitled "Office of Governor General; relinquishment by Lord Alexander; appointment of successor," RG2, Privy Council Office, Series A-5-a, vol. 2649, reel T-2368, 1952/01/09 (Prime Minister St. Laurent consulting with his colleagues concerning the appointment of a Canadian, Vincent Massey, as the next Governor General and receiving their approval).

anglophone and francophone representatives.[24] At base, however, the prime minister's selection is a political decision.

In the beginning, the first Canadian Governors General were former diplomats[25] or at least diplomat/politicians.[26] Subsequently, between 1979 and 1999, Canada's four Governors General were former politicians.[27] In three instances, these former Members of Parliament were from the party in power at the time of the appointment. Commentators condemned this practice as debasing the Governor General's position from diplomatic symbol to political patronage plum.[28] Prime Minister Chrétien's appointment of the apparently nonpartisan Adrienne Clarkson to the post in 1999 was greeted as an enlightened and refreshing change.[29]

b) Tenure and Dismissal

No limit on the Governor General's tenure is specified in the *Constitution Act, 1867*. The proclamation by which the Queen appointed the current Governor General speaks of the appointment being "during Our Pleasure," suggesting a potentially indefinite term of office.[30] However, Professor Dawson writes: "[t]he term may be simply, if somewhat ambiguously, stated as being officially recognized as six years, customarily treated as five years, while on occasion it has been seven years."[31] Professor Dawson's conclusions are generally borne out by past practice. The average tenure of Canada's twenty-five Governors General, from Viscount Monck in 1867 to Romeo LeBlanc in 1999, was just over five years. Five Governors General served approximately six years and another three held office for approximately seven years.

Nevertheless, the longest-serving Governor General to date, the Right Honourable George Vanier, served several months shy of eight years, a tenure that likely would have persisted had he not died. Originally appoint-

---

24 Heard, *Canadian Constitutional Conventions*, 17.

25 Governors General Massey, Vanier and Léger.

26 Governor General Michener.

27 Governors General Schreyer, Sauvé, Hnatyshyn and LeBlanc.

28 See, e.g., Editorial, "Next in Rideau Hall," *Ottawa Citizen*, 4 Sept. 1999, B5.

29 See, e.g., Editorial, "A Strong Nationalist for Governor-General," *Toronto Star*, 9 Sept. 1999, 1; Richard Foot, "Challenge for Clarkson Is to Win Hearts of Canadians: Public Cynical: Recent PMs have Treated Job as Patronage Posting," *National Post*, 9 Sept. 1999, A6.

30 See, e.g., Proclamation, C. Gaz. I, extra vol. 133, no. 3 (7 Oct. 1999) appointing Adrienne Clarkson Governor General.

31 Ward, *Dawson's The Government of Canada* at 181; Heard, *Canadian Constitutional Conventions* at 16 ("The traditional period of tenure for Governors General is now generally limited to five years, although they serve 'at pleasure'.").

ed on August 1, 1959, Vanier's tenure was formally extended for a year in July 1964.[32] In this respect, Vanier's experience is consistent with more recent practice with Adrienne Clarkson. Ms. Clarkson's five-year term was extended for an additional year. It is questionable, however, whether periodic renewals of this sort are legally necessary, given the "during Our Pleasure" language in the original appointing instrument. Nor does there appear to be a formal, legal outer limit in terms of how long a given individual may hold the Governor General's office.[33] Indeed, upon the expiry of Vanier's first extended term in July 1965, the prime minister recommended to the Queen that Vanier's term of office be extended *indefinitely*.[34]

The reference to tenure "during Our Pleasure" also suggests that the Queen may dismiss the Governor General. Such a power has never been exercised. However, it is generally presumed that, if she were to do so, the Queen would act on the advice of the Canadian Cabinet, or at least the prime minister.[35] Professor Dawson suggests that, as a result, the Governor General is potentially placed "at the mercy" of Cabinet, "a subordination that makes assertions of independent opinions unlikely and any strong line of conduct impossible, and is apt to undermine the governor's influence and reputation for impartiality."[36]

In most instances, this lack of independence would not be controversial. There are circumstances, however, where a Governor General may be called on to exercise his or her so-called reserve powers, and refuse to act on the advice of the Cabinet or prime minister. These rarest of circumstances are discussed in chapter 5, and include instances where a prime minister refuses to resign his or her government (or at least seek a dissolution of Parliament) on losing the confidence of the Commons.

If a Governor General may be removed at the behest of the prime minister, it seems improbable that he or she could exercise effectively the necessary reserve power to dismiss the prime minister's government. For this

---

32   See Cabinet document entitled "Extension of term of office of Governor General," RG2, Privy Council Office, Series A-5-a, vol. 6265 (21 July 1964).

33   Robert Marleau and Camille Montpetit, *House of Commons Procedure and Practice* (Ottawa: House of Commons, 2000) at 18, n89.

34   Cabinet document entitled "Extension of term of Governor General," RG2, Privy Council Office, Series A-5-a, vol. 6271 (14 July 1965).

35   Ward, *Dawson's The Government of Canada* at 181 ("The governor general may now be removed by the queen acting on advice tendered by the Canadian cabinet"); Heard, *Canadian Constitutional Conventions* at 40, noting the view of many scholars that Commonwealth precedent suggests that the Queen would act on the advice of the prime minister, but arguing that the Queen should act in response to the entire Cabinet.

36   Ward, *Dawson's The Government of Canada* at 182.

reason, Professor Andrew Heard argues persuasively that the "Queen might be justified in refusing advice to remove a Governor General if the dismissal were an attempt to overturn a decision taken with all constitutional propriety by the governor."[37] Noted parliamentary scholar Senator Eugene Forsey went even further in 1985, proposing a security of tenure for Governors General that would bar their dismissal without consent from the Houses of Parliament.[38]

c) Reform

Canada's status as a constitutional monarchy has not generated the same sort of controversy that has arisen in Australia from that country's similar standing. Certainly, the occasional Cabinet minister muses about a move to a republican system,[39] but there is no potent political movement directed to this end.[40]

In fact, there are benefits in Canada's status as a constitutional monarchy, even when reviewed from the perspective of democratic accountability. In his or her most common role, the Governor General performs the important ceremonial duties of a head of state, with all the pomp and circumstance. In this respect, the Governor General is similar to a republican president. However, unlike such a president, the Canadian head of state has no true political power. In the Canadian system, the head of government — the prime minister — calls the shots.

Professor C.E.S. Frank has argued that there is real value in vesting the functions of head of state and head of government in two different persons, and peeling away from the government leader the ceremonial status reserved for heads of state.[41] For one thing, the prime minister can concentrate on government, and not the ceremony a titular head of state must oversee.

Further, a head of government who is also a head of state tends to receive a large measure of deference. It is hard to imagine a U.S. president, for instance, undergoing the hurly-burly of a Commons Question Period. A head of government imbued with the magical aura of a head of state

---

37   Heard, *Canadian Constitutional Conventions* at 43.

38   Eugene A. Forsey and G.C. Eglington, *The Question of Confidence in Responsible Government* (Ottawa: Special Committee on the Reform of the House of Commons, 1985), 184.

39   See Joanne Laucius, "Parliament Should Elect Governor-General: Manley: Deputy PM wants Canada to Cut Ties with Crown," *National Post*, 29 Oct. 2002, A9.

40   Juliet O'Neill, "A Republic, You Say? Not Just Yet: Why a Militant Minority Wants to Dump the Queen," *Victoria Times-Colonist*, 7 Oct. 2002, A11.

41   Professor C.E.S. Frank, Commons Standing Committee on Government Operations and Estimates, *Evidence*, 37th Parl., 3d Sess. (25 March 2004).

might actually prove less accessible and less accountable than our current prime minister.

The fact that Canada's head of state is not elected directly by the public does not strike us as a resounding flaw in the Canadian democratic polity. Indeed, appointment rather than election may well enhance the Governor General's role. On the whole, the best Governors General are those who conduct their largely ceremonial duties more like diplomats than partisan politicians. Electing a politician as head of state might create new and fractious constitutional quandaries. A Governor General with a true democratic constituency might feel empowered to test the often inchoate constitutional conventions limiting his or her role. Thus, any reform of the Governor General's appointment process would require a much clearer rendition of his or her constitutional role and the terms and tenure of the office, a task requiring careful constitutional law-making.

All this prompts our bottom-line conclusion: converting Canada from a constitutional monarchy with an anointed but largely titular head of state to a republic with an elected but (presumably) equally titular head of state seems an exhausting enterprise, one with no discernable impact on the quality of democratic governance. The political energy consumed in such an enterprise would be best directed to reforming offices with real power, not least the senate.

In relation to the Governor General, the single preoccupation should be ensuring that prime ministers select candidates who exemplify shared civic values and present an able and admirable public face for Canada. Here, there is room for modest process reform. Recently, controversy in 2004 over Governor General Clarkson's spending habits prompted some real parliamentary consideration of Parliament's relationship with the Governor General. Among other things, the Commons Standing Committee on Government Operations and Estimates recommended in 2004 that Parliament "conduct a review and initiate a debate on the mandate, constitutional role, responsibilities, and future evolution of the Office of the Governor General of Canada (the Head of State) in which all Canadians be included." It also called on Parliament to "conduct a review of the process for selecting and appointing the Governor General (Head of State) of Canada."[42]

In testimony before the committee, Professor Franks proposed that the Governor General be selected in a fashion analogous to that employed for

---

42   Commons Standing Committee on Government Operations and Estimates, *Second Report: The Governor General of Canada: Role, Duties and Funding for Activities*, 37th Parl., 3d Sess. (2 April 2004).

the Indian president: election by the two federal houses and the regional legislatures.[43] Canada's constitutional fabric may preclude the direct importation of the Indian model without constitutional amendment. In Canada, these legislative bodies could not directly appoint the Governor General — as noted, that power rests with the Queen. However, the Queen in turn is obliged by constitutional convention to act on the advice of the prime minister. Nothing precludes prime ministers from conveying advice consistent with the will of elected representatives, opening the door to participation in Governor General selection by Members of Parliament.

We agree that a greater role for federal legislators in the selection of the Governor General might prove an excellent development. After all, parliamentary governance itself would depend on a judicious exercise of a Governor General's reserve powers should a prime minister disregard constitutional conventions and ignore a no confidence vote in the Commons. Legislators might reasonably be concerned with the calibre of the individual who might be called upon to exercise judgment in these rarest (indeed, unprecedented) circumstances. Participation by elected representatives in the selection process might enhance the democratic legitimacy of the Governor General while minimizing the likelihood of a dubious prime ministerial choice.

To avoid politicizing the office of head of state, however, we believe that elected representatives would have to put aside partisan impulses and agree on a candidate with sufficiently prestigious qualifications to merit appointment to the Governor General's post. To this end, the present *Governor General's Act*[44] — essentially a law establishing the Governor General's salary and benefits — might be usefully amended to specify the qualities that Canada envisages in its head of state. Once established, these standards could guide the prime minister and parliamentarians in their debate and selections. Selection and appointment of persons not meeting these standards would likely generate public criticism of Parliament and the government, potentially deterring suspect appointments.

With those changes accomplished, Canada's elected representatives could turn their attention to a more pressing reform issue: the senate.

---

43 Professor C.E.S. Frank, Commons Standing Committee on Government Operations and Estimates, *Evidence*, 37th Parl., 3d Sess. (25 March 2004).

44 R.S.C. 1985, c. G-9.

2. The Senate

Canada's democratic system has its roots in the Victorian era, and nowhere is this more evident than in the composition of its senate. The *Constitution Act, 1867*, creating Canada's legislative branch, reflects the Victorian period's suspicion with true democracy by crafting a parliamentary house of "sober second thought" immune to the whims of electoral politics. Canada is therefore unusual among modern democracies in possessing two roughly co-equal legislative houses, one elected and one not.

We use the phrase "roughly co-equal" intentionally. As is discussed in chapter 6, money bills may not originate in the senate. The *Constitution Act, 1982* further subordinates the senate by rendering a senate failure to endorse Commons-approved constitutional amendments legally inconsequential, after the expiry of 180 days.[45] Further, although senators may be — and not irregularly have been — ministers, responsible government in Canadian democracy hinges on the Commons, not the senate.

The senate, however, is more than the legislative equivalent of an appendix. It has substantial legislative powers. Parliamentary procedure requires that, before a bill becomes law, it pass through both the Commons and the senate, receiving the requisite three readings in each House. Indeed, the *Constitution Act, 1867* itself provides that bills only become law when they pass through "Houses of the Parliament"; that is, both the Commons and the senate.[46]

For this reason, an appointed senate is a true departure from the notion reflected in the Commons and in each provincial legislature: that, in Canada, we elect those with true legislative power. Before reviewing the many issues and proposals designed to correct this problem, we discuss how senators are appointed to, and dismissed from, the senate at present.

a)   Appointment

Regional Distribution

Representation by Division
The *Constitution Act, 1867* has a lot to say about the senate. First, as any student of Canadian history knows, the senate was not conceived as a sinecure for old friends of the prime minister or senior cultural icons. It was a

---

45   *Constitution Act, 1982*, subs. 47(1).
46   *Constitution Act, 1867*, s. 55. See also s. 91, authorizing the Queen to make federal laws "by and with the Advice and Consent of the Senate and House of Commons."

House intended to incorporate provincial interests into the very fabric of the federal legislative branch. Political reformer George Brown, explaining his support for Confederation in 1865, said, "[t]he very essence of our compact is that the union shall be federal and not legislative. Our Lower Canada friends have agreed to give us representation by population in the Lower House, on the express condition that they shall have equality in the Upper House. On no other condition could we have advanced a step."[47]

Sir John A. Macdonald made the regional justification for the senate even plainer:

> In order to protect local interests and to prevent sectional jealousies, it was found requisite that the [then-]three great divisions into which British North America is separated, should be represented in the Upper House on the principle of equality. ... To the Upper House is to be confided the protection of sectional interests: therefore is it that the three great divisions are there equally represented for the purpose of defending such interests against the combinations of majorities in the Assembly.[48]

Reviewing this legislative history, the Supreme Court has held that the "primary purpose of the creation of the Senate, as a part of the federal legislative process, was, therefore, to afford protection to the various sectional interests in Canada in relation to the enactment of federal legislation."[49]

For this very reason, section 22 of the *Constitution Act, 1867* partitions Canada into four "divisions," entitled to equal representation in the senate. These divisions are: Ontario, Quebec, the Maritime Provinces and the Western Provinces. Each province within these last two divisions, and the two territories, are to be represented by a specified number of senators.[50] Pursuant to the *Constitution Act, 1999 (Nunavut),*[51] one senator represents Nunavut. The resulting senate representation by province, as contrasted to proportion of the population, is set out in Table 4.1.

---

47 Reported in Ward, *Dawson's The Government of Canada* at 152–53.

48 *Parliamentary Debates on the Subject of the Confederation of the British North American Provinces* (Quebec: Hunter Rose, 1865) at 35 and 39.

49 *Re Authority of Parliament in Relation to the Upper House,* [1980] 1 S.C.R. 54 at 67.

50 *Constitution Act, 1867,* s. 22, reflecting amendments made to the original *British North America Act* via the *Constitution Act, 1915,* 5-6 Geo. V, c. 45 (U.K.), the *Newfoundland Act,* 12-13 Geo. VI, c. 22 (U.K.), and the *Constitution Act (No. 2), 1975,* S.C. 1974-75-76, c. 53.

51 S.C. 1998, c. 15, Part 2, s. 43.

Table 4.1 Senate Representation by Province

Division under the 1867 Act	Province	Number of Senators Mandated by Law	Proportion of the Senate (%)	Proportion of the Canadian Population, 2003 (%)[52]	Difference (%)
N/A	Newfoundland	6	5.71	1.6	4.11
Maritime Division	Nova Scotia	10	9.52	3.0	6.52
	Prince Edward Island	4	3.81	0.4	3.41
	New Brunswick	10	9.52	2.4	7.12
Quebec Division	Quebec	24	22.86	23.7	−0.84
Ontario Division	Ontario	24	22.86	38.7	−15.84
Western Division	Manitoba	6	5.71	3.7	2.01
	Saskatchewan	6	5.71	3.1	2.61
	Alberta	6	5.71	10.0	−4.29
	British Columbia	6	5.71	13.1	−7.39
N/A	Nunavut	1	0.95	0.1	0.85
	Northwest Territories	1	0.95	0.1	0.85
	Yukon Territory	1	0.95	0.1	0.85
Total		105	100	100	N/A

As these statistics suggest, the fast-growing provinces of Ontario, Alberta and British Columbia are significantly underrepresented in the Upper Chamber as compared to the country's other regions. The senate, in other words, does not treat each province equally, as does the equivalent United States institution. Nor is it a body that reflects contemporary demographics. Instead, it calcifies historical, regional population distributions, especially in the overrepresentation it guarantees the Atlantic Provinces.

Senate Expansion

A total of 105 senate seats are generated by the 1867 Act's pattern of representation by division.[53] At the same time, the Act does allow a senate of up to 113 members.[54] Thus, up to eight new senators may be added to the

---

52   Generated from Statistics Canada, *Population by Sex and Age Group* (2003).
53   *Constitution Act, 1867*, ss. 21 and 22.
54   *Ibid.*, s. 28.

Upper Chamber by the Queen on the recommendation of the Governor General, pursuant to section 26. At first blush, assigning these eight seats to underrepresented provinces seems a likely "quick fix" to the demographic imbalance in the 105-member senate. This possibility founders, however, on other language found in section 26. Specifically, any increases in senate numbers must be made proportionally, based on the pre-existing four divisions.[55]

Section 26 must also be read in association with section 27. Section 27 bars the Governor General from appointing any additional, individual senators (under the regular process discussed later in this chapter) until the number of senators in each division returns to its regular (pre-section 26) level. In other words, the effect of the section 26 expansion dissipates as senators retire or die. The Governor General cannot keep "topping up" the expanded senate, except by re-applying section 26 itself. For this reason, section 26 expansions are temporary,[56] as well as proportional. Finally, it is probably the case that section 26 may only be used in the event of a legislative "deadlock" between the Commons and the senate,[57] and not as a means of addressing disparities in representation.

Section 26 has been employed once: in 1990, by the Queen at the behest of the Mulroney government.[58] Controversially, the expansion of the senate by eight senators — two from each division — was designed to ensure passage in the senate of several pieces of legislation, including the

---

55 *Ibid.*, s. 26 ("If at any Time on the Recommendation of the Governor General the Queen thinks fit to direct that Four or Eight Members be added to the Senate, the Governor General may by Summons to Four or Eight qualified Persons [as the Case may be], representing equally the Four Divisions of Canada, add to the Senate accordingly").

56 *Singh v. Canada* (1991), 3 O.R. (3d) 429 at 439 (C.A.).

57 Library of Parliament, *The Senate: Appointments under Section 26 of the Constitution Act, 1867* (1990), completing an exhaustive review of the legislative history of section 26 and concluding that "it seems clear that the original intent of section 26 was to provide a 'deadlock' mechanism in the event of an irreconcilable clash of wills between the two Chambers." See also Senate, *Journals* (19 March 1877) at 130, recording the senate's own opinion as "any addition to the Senate under the provisions of the 26th clause of the *British North America Act* which is not absolutely necessary for the purpose of bringing this House into accord with the House of Commons, in the event of an actual collision of a serious and permanent character, would be an infringement of the constitutional independence of the Senate, and lead to a depreciation of its utility as a constituent part of the Legislature."

58 Letters Patent, PC 1990-2061, directing that eight members be added to the senate in order that the Governor General may by summons to eight qualified persons, representing equally the Four Divisions of Canada, add to the senate accordingly; C. Gaz. 1990.I.3569.

introduction of the goods and services tax.[59] It was subsequently tested in a series of lawsuits, launched in the courts of three of Canada's divisions.

Two of these cases hinged largely on the interaction between section 26 and another provision of the 1867 Act, section 51A. The latter provision reads: "Notwithstanding anything in this Act a province shall always be entitled to a number of members in the House of Commons not less than the number of senators representing such province."

Notably, the 1990 senate expansion assigned an eleventh senator to New Brunswick, producing a senate with more New Brunswick senators than New Brunswick had seats in the Commons. For this reason, the senate expansion raised questions about the applicability of section 51A.

In the Ontario case,[60] the Ontario Court of Appeal held that section 51A was a "Senate floor rule ... intended to ensure that, with changes in population, a province's representation in the House of Commons does not fall below its representation in the Senate." However, that floor rule applied strictly to the regular 105-member senate created by section 22: a province could have no fewer Commons seats that it had regular senators allocated to it by section 22. Section 51A did not apply to the temporary expansion by divisions authorized by section 26. The 1990 expansion was, therefore, not improper, despite the temporary presence in Parliament of one more senator than MP from New Brunswick.

While not an indisputable reading of the 1867 Act, this is a reasonable conclusion. Any other approach would require Commons seats to be added and then evaporate as the section 26 senate expansion was introduced and then abated with time through the operation of section 27. Indeed, the Ontario Court of Appeal's conclusions were echoed by its New Brunswick equivalent in the Maritime case.[61] There, the New Brunswick Court of Appeal held: "Section 51A was enacted to guarantee that Prince Edward Island would always have a minimum of four seats in the House of Commons. It was worded so as to extend the same guarantee to any other province whose population might decline or grow so slowly that its Common's representation would, on a population basis, fall below its normal senate representation." It was not "intended to thwart the implementation of s. 26."[62]

---

59   See PC 1990-2061 indicating that the increase in senate numbers is required to further the government's legislative project, including Bill C-62, the GST.

60   *Singh* (1991), 3 O.R. (3d) 429 at 439.

61   *Weir v. Canada* (1991), 84 D.L.R. (4th) 39 (N.B.C.A.).

62   *Ibid.* at 45.

Perhaps more importantly for our present purposes, both the Ontario Court of Appeal and its British Columbia counterpart in the third, Western division case,[63] concluded that section 26 remained good constitutional law. Thus, the British Columbia Court of Appeal declined to declare that section 26 had been rendered inoperative by the evolution of constitutional governance in Canada. Instead, it held that the Queen — acting personally or through the Governor General — retained a legal right to appoint senators, on the recommendation of the Cabinet. Notably, the court also held that she is not, as a matter of law (as opposed to constitutional convention), obliged to follow this recommendation.[64] For its part, the Ontario Court of Appeal agreed that section 26 remained in force, and also rejected a series of conditions plaintiffs wished imposed on its exercise.

In sum, the senate's distorted regional makeup is mandated by the 1867 Act, and is not vulnerable to a simple correction through the addition of new senators from underrepresented areas. That sort of re-jigging would require a constitutional amendment, a matter discussed later in the section on senate reform.

Selection of Individual Senators

The 1867 Act establishes a number of baseline qualifications for membership in the senate. Thus, a senator must be at least thirty years of age and a Canadian national. He or she must be a resident of the province for which the senator is appointed, and must own in that province real property with a net value in excess of $4,000. Further, the sum of the senator's net worth measured in terms of personal and real property must be no less than $4,000.[65] Since the famous 1929 "persons" case, the senator may be a man or a woman.[66]

Senators are appointed, not elected. The Governor General is empowered by the 1867 Act to "summon qualified Persons to the Senate."[67] In exercising this power, the Governor General follows the advice of the prime minister,[68]

---

63   *Reference re Appointment of Senators Pursuant to the Constitution Act, 1867, s. 26* (1991), 78 D.L.R. (4th) 245.
64   *Ibid.* at 264.
65   *Constitution Act, 1867*, s. 23.
66   *Edwards v. Canada (Attorney General)* (1929), 1 D.L.R. 98 (Judicial Committee of the Privy Council) holding that women are eligible to be summoned to and become members of the senate of Canada.
67   *Constitution Act, 1867*, s. 24.
68   Hogg, *Constitutional Law of Canada* at 9.26.2 n74. See also Privy Council minute, P.C. 3374 (25 Oct. 1935) describing the appointment of senators as a special prerogative of the prime minister.

though at least one lower court has suggested that the requisite advice flows from the Cabinet.[69] It may be, however, that the Governor General may refuse to make senate and other appointments recommended by a government defeated in an election, thus preserving the rights of the incoming prime minister.[70]

The Federal Court has characterized the Governor General's appointment power as "purely political in nature" and as "purely discretionary." Courts have little or no role in policing appointment decisions. Thus, a "Court cannot impose procedural or other limitations on the Governor General's express power of appointment to the senate, or otherwise fetter the exercise of his [or her] discretion."[71]

Despite these rules, several provincial governments have been aggressive (and largely unsuccessful) in asserting control over appointments. Two provincial legislatures have enacted "senatorial selection laws," and at the time of this writing, the legislatures of two other provinces were reviewing a similar measure, contained in private member's bills.[72] These laws and bills provide for the direct election of senatorial candidates. Once selected by election, the provincial government is to submit the nominee's names to the federal government, identifying these individuals as persons who may be summoned to the senate for the purpose of filling vacancies relating to the province in question.

The effect of these measures has been modest. Alberta has had three elections, in 1989, 1999 and 2004. Stan Waters was elected in 1989, and in fact was appointed to the senate in 1990 by Prime Minister Mulroney, then in the midst of efforts to elicit provincial support for the *Meech Lake Accord*. However, Prime Minister Chrétien declined to appoint the two so-called senators-in-waiting elected in 1999 — Bert Brown and Ted Morton.

In response, Mr. Brown sued in the Alberta courts seeking a declaration that the senatorial appointment provisions of the 1867 Act were contrary to democratic principles, as set out by the Supreme Court in the *Quebec Secession Reference* and discussed in chapter 2. He urged that con-

---

69   See *Samson v. Canada (Attorney General)* (1998), 165 D.L.R. (4th) 342 at para. 6 ("[i]n practice, the Governor General exercises his power of appointment on the advice and recommendation of the Governor-in-Council").

70   See discussion in Heard, *Canadian Constitutional Conventions* at 38.

71   *Samson* (1998), 165 D.L.R. (4th) 342 at paras. 5–6.

72   See, e.g., Alberta, *Senatorial Selection Act*, R.S.A. 2000, c. S-5; British Columbia, *Senatorial Selection Act*, R.S.B.C. 1979, c. 70 (since lapsed); Ontario, Bill 72, *Senatorial Selection Act*, 2004 (Private Member's Bill) (First Reading: 29 April 2004); Nova Scotia, Bill 112, *Senatorial Selection Act* (Private Member's Bill) (First Reading: 1 Oct. 2004).

formity with those principles required senators to be appointed pursuant to the Alberta *Senatorial Selection Act*.[73] His application was dismissed. The Alberta Court of Appeal concluded that whether the standard appointment process was "democratic" or not was simply not a legal issue.

In a second case, brought in the Federal Court, the then-Reform Party sought an interlocutory injunction to restrain the Governor General from appointing a senator from Alberta, unless that person has been elected pursuant to the provisions of the *Senatorial Selection Act*.[74] As in Brown's case, the court rejected the applicant's reliance on the unwritten constitutional principles invoked by the *Quebec Secession Reference*. In the court's view, "nothing in that case supports the proposition that a court may ignore the express and unequivocal provisions of the *Constitution Act, 1867*."[75] It also disagreed that the appointment of Mr. Waters in 1990 created a constitutional "convention" requiring the appointment of elected nominees. A senate appointment, in the court's words, is "simply a political decision made by the Government of the day at that particular time in our nation's history."[76]

By December 2004, three Alberta "senators-in-waiting" were elected in the 2004 Alberta provincial elections. In March 2005, Prime Minister Martin filled the three Alberta vacancies in the senate with other, non-elected candidates.

b) Tenure and Dismissal

The 1867 Act includes rules on the tenure of persons appointed to the senate. An appointee remains a senator until age seventy-five, although the 1867 Act allows resignations.[77] However, that person's senate seat may be considered "vacant" for any number of other reasons. Events creating vacancies in the senate are set out in Table 4.2.

Table 4.2   Events Leading to Vacancies in the Senate

Legal Source	Vacancy of a Senate Seat
Constitution Act, 1867, section 29	Death of current senator
	Current senator reaches 75 years of age
Constitution Act, 1867, section 30	Current senator retires
Constitution Act, 1867, section 31	Senator fails to attend two consecutive sessions of Parliament

---

73   *Brown v. Alberta* (1999), 177 D.L.R. (4th) 349 (Alta. C.A.).
74   *Samson* (1998), 165 D.L.R. (4th) 342.
75   *Ibid.* at para. 7.
76   *Ibid.* at para. 8.
77   *Constitution Act, 1867*, ss. 29–30.

Legal Source	Vacancy of a Senate Seat
Constitution Act, 1867, section 31	Senator takes an oath or declaration of allegiance to a foreign power, or becomes a subject or citizen, or entitled to the rights or privileges of a subject or citizen, of a foreign power
	Senator is adjudged bankrupt or insolvent, or applies for the benefit of any law relating to insolvent debtors, or becomes a public defaulter
	Senator is attainted of treason or convicted of a felony or of any "infamous" crime
	Senator ceases to be qualified as such in respect of his or her property holdings or residence (though, with respect to residence, residency in Ottawa in order to perform his or her duties does not taint the senator's qualifications)

Under the 1867 Act, disputes concerning the qualifications of senators — and any question as to whether a seat has been vacated — are heard and determined by the senate.[78] However, the senate has never expelled a senator, a reticence to police itself that sparked controversy in three recent cases.

The Thompson Case

Perhaps most notoriously, the senate suspended Senator Andrew Thompson in February 1998, reportedly stripping him of his $64,000-a-year salary, his $10,000-a-year tax-free allowance, his telephone privileges, his travel allowance and his right to sit in the senate.[79] Senator Thompson, who subsequently resigned,[80] had reportedly attended 47 of 1,088 senate sittings over fifteen years.[81]

Senator Thompson's suspension — rather than dismissal — reflected uncertainty as to whether the senate could expel him outright.[82] A suspen-

---

78   *Ibid.*, s. 33.
79   William Walker, "Truant Senator Suspended: Thompson Stripped of Salary, Perks but Can Still Draw Pension," *Toronto Star*, 20 Feb. 1998.
80   *Canadian Press*, "Truant Senator Gives Up Seat but Keeps Hefty Pension," 24 March 1998.
81   Graham Parley and Jack Aubry, "Thompson First to Be Suspended by Senate," *Hamilton Spectator*, 20 Feb. 1998.
82   See Senator Grafstein, *Debates of the Senate (Hansard)*, 36th Parl., 1st Sess., vol. 137, issue 37 (11 Feb. 1998) ("I am not sure from reading this statute, namely the *British North America Act, 1867*, whether we have the power to expel when the statute says that we can only vacate under certain preconditions. Are we taking the Constitution into our hands? I think the Constitution is above us. This chamber has to do its work under the Constitution.").

sion, while unprecedented, could be crafted under the *Parliament of Canada Act*.[83] However, the legal authority for an outright expulsion was less clear. The senator apparently was in attendance in the senate on at least one occasion each session, thus remaining onside the absenteeism rule in section 31 of the 1867 Act.[84] Meanwhile, legal opinions elicited by the senate were split on the question of whether the vacancy criteria in section 31 of the 1867 Act constituted an exclusive basis for removing a senator.

One view, expressed by the constitutional lawyer Neil Finkelstein, was that the senate could not expel a senator unless one of the criteria in section 31 was met.[85] For his part, parliamentary privilege authority Joseph Maingot urged that the senate possessed an independent parliamentary privilege to "regulate its internal affairs free from interference, including determining whether a person is unfit for membership."[86] Confronted with this dilemma, the senate opted for the more cautious suspension, rather than expulsion, of Thompson.[87]

In fact, both of these legal experts were probably right, in their own way. The differing views on the senate powers to "expel" may be more a question of semantics than substance. A robust suspension over a long period of time clearly constitutes a *de facto* expulsion, one that lies within the senate's traditional parliamentary privileges. For reasons outlined in chapter 2, the exercise of these privileges likely could be challenged in only the most rudimentary way in the courts. Courts would ask whether the

---

83 R.S.C. 1985, c. P-1. Specifically, s. 59 provides: "The Senate or the House of Commons may make regulations, by rule or by order, rendering more stringent on its own members the provisions of this Act that relate to the attendance of members or to the deductions to be made from sessional allowances." This provision was interpreted as allowing the senate to eliminate Senator Thompson's sessional allowance. The power to outright suspend the senator (and remove his expense allowance) flowed from s. 4 of the *Parliament of Canada Act*, extending to the senate the powers and privileges held, enjoyed and exercised by the Commons House of Parliament of the United Kingdom in 1867, *per* s. 18 of the *Constitution Act, 1867*. See testimony of Neil Finkelstein, Proceedings of the Standing Senate Committee on Privileges, Standing Rules and Orders, Issue 6 — Evidence (18 Feb. 1998).

84 Senator Murray, *Debates of the Senate (Hansard)*, 36th Parl., 1st Sess., vol. 137, issue 41 (19 Feb. 1998).

85 Proceedings of the Standing Senate Committee on Privileges, Standing Rules and Orders, *Issue 6 — Evidence* (18 Feb. 1998).

86 *Ibid., Issue 5 — Evidence* (10 Feb. 1998).

87 See Senator Carstairs, *Debates of the Senate (Hansard)*, 36th Parl., 1st Sess., vol. 137, issue 41 (19 Feb. 1998).

privilege existed, but if it did, they would not probe its use.[88] To that extent, Mr. Maingot's approach was perfectly sound.

However, as Mr. Finkelstein noted, the senate probably could not convert this sort of expulsion into a vacancy triggering the Governor General's appointment power, absent one of the reasons set out in section 31 of the 1867 Act. Put another way, the senate likely can, *de facto*, expel one of its members — stripping him or her of everything but the title "senator"[89] — through the exercise of its privilege. It cannot, however, empower the Governor General to appoint a replacement for the expelled senator if the criteria in the 1867 Act — most notably section 31 — are not satisfied.

The Cogger and Berntson Cases

The issue of expulsions was revisited again soon after the Thompson case. In September 2000, Senator Michel Cogger resigned his seat, following his 1998 conviction for influence peddling.[90] He was later discharged of the offence by the Quebec Court of Appeal, which held that the stigma suffered by Mr. Cogger outweighed the gravity of his offence.[91]

Subsequently, in February 2001, Senator Eric Berntson resigned his senate seat following his conviction (and subsequent failed appeals) for fraud involving public funds while Saskatchewan deputy premier.[92]

In both instances, the grounds for expelling these men from the senate prior to their resignations were much clearer than in the Thompson case: both had been convicted of crimes, potentially triggering application of the section 31 vacancy rules. In this regard, section 31 compels a vacancy where a senator is convicted of a felony or of any infamous crime. These terms — "felony" and "infamous crime" — are not defined in the 1867 Act and both

---

88   Mr. Finkelstein also reached this conclusion before the Senate Committee on Privileges, Standing Rules and Orders. See Proceedings of the Standing Senate Committee on Privileges, Standing Rules and Orders, *Issue 6 — Evidence* (18 Feb. 1998).

89   Mr. Finkelstein told the Senate Committee on Privileges, Standing Rules and Orders that the senate could not strip Senator Thompson of his accumulated pension, as this would constitute a fine and a fine was not authorized by the senate's parliamentary privileges. See Proceedings of the Standing Senate Committee on Privileges, Standing Rules and Orders, *Issue 6 — Evidence* (18 Feb. 1998). Mr. Maingot agreed that the senate did not possess a power to fine as part of its privileges, and that any fine could only be levied pursuant to a legislated power. Proceedings of the Standing Senate Committee on Privileges, Standing Rules and Orders, *Issue 5 — Evidence* (10 Feb. 1998).

90   *Canadian Press*, "Quebec Tory Senator Michel Cogger Quits Upper Chamber," 7 Sept. 2000.

91   *R. v. Cogger*, [2001] J.Q. no 2262 (C.A.).

92   *Canadian Press*, "Berntson Resigns After Supreme Court Upholds His Conviction for Fraud," 26 Feb. 2001; See *R. v. Berntson*, [2001] 1 S.C.R. 365.

are antiquated. Indeed, the concept of felony is "legally anachronistic in terms of Canadian law," and is no longer employed in the Canadian *Criminal Code.*[93] In a legal opinion on similar language in the *Constitution Act* of British Columbia[94] (as it was in 1989) Professor McWhinney concluded that the terms "felony" and "infamous crime" denote "only criminal offences of extreme gravity" or "of a particularly heinous character."[95] In fact, this interpretation may understate the true scope of the terms. Arguably, the expression "infamous crime" in English common law also included crimes speaking to the trustworthiness of the accused, such as fraud and perjury.[96]

From this discussion, it seems clear that convictions entered for influence peddling and fraud — especially as related to public functions — infringe section 31, either as crimes of extreme gravity or as crimes relating to trustworthiness.

Nevertheless, the senate resisted calls for the expulsion of the two senators, reportedly arguing that it would not act until all appeals had been exhausted.[97] On the whole, this seems a sensible approach, especially given the outcome in the Cogger case. It remains unclear, however, why the senate did not follow the Thompson precedent and suspend — partially or fully — Senators Berntson and Cogger pending the conclusion of their appeals. Suspensions — with or without pay — are commonplace where public officials face charges, let alone convictions. In such circumstances, the continued presence of the individual in question threatens the public

---

93 Edward McWhinney, "Forfeiture of Office on Conviction of an 'Infamous Crime,'" (1989) 12 Canadian Parliamentary Review no. 1. See also *Bar and Bench Daily News Digest*, 2 March 1999 ("the term felony was eliminated from the Criminal Code more than 100 years ago").

94 *Constitution Act*, R.S.B.C. 1979, c. 62, s. 54. This section does not appear in the current version of the statute. *Constitution Act*, R.S.B.C. 1996, c. 66.

95 McWhinney, "Forfeiture."

96 See Gordon Mackintosh, "The Right of Legislatures to Expel Members: A Manitoba Case Study," (1981) 4 Canadian Parliamentary Review no. 4, discussing s. 54 of the B.C. *Constitution Act*, as it then was, and observing "it must be recognized that there is great latitude for interpretation of what constitutes an 'infamous crime.' *Black's Law Dictionary* (5th ed.) states that the term, 'was applied at common law to certain crimes ... upon the theory that a person would not commit so heinous a crime unless he was so depraved as to be unworthy of credit. These crimes are treason, felony, and the *crimen falsi.*'"

97 See William Walker, "Segal Says Cogger Should Be Ousted if Conviction Upheld," *Toronto Star*, 16 July 1998; Davis Sheremata and Rachel Evans, "Senator Defends Rights of Convicted Colleagues," *Edmonton Sun*, 18 March 1999; Tom Hanson, "Convicted Senators Under Fire," *Toronto Star*, 18 March 1999.

reputation of the public institution. There is no reason why senators —
charged with an important law-making role — should be held to a less
demanding standard. Indeed, convictions for crimes connoting dishonesty
and unethical conduct provide stronger justification for suspension — and
arguably cast the senate in greater disrepute — than did Senator Thompson's absenteeism. We return to the question of senate ethics in chapter 7.

c) Senate Reform

We turn now to the thorny issue of senate reform. We make plain our position, right at the outset: in our view, an unelected Upper House whose
members have virtual lifetime tenure does real violence to the concept of
democratic accountability described in the introduction to this book.
Democracy requires that those who exercise the powers of the state be
either directly elected or at least accountable to those who are. Senators are
neither, prompting regular calls for senate change.

One senate observer commented recently, "[D]iscussion of Senate
reform has been a near-constant feature of the Canadian political landscape
over the past forty years."[98] In the thirty years prior to 2003, there had been
at least twenty-eight government and political party proposals on senate
reform.[99] These proposals range from outright abolition through to minor
tinkering with the appointments process and everything in between,
including an elected Upper House.[100] Several of the most significant recent
reform proposals are summarized in Table 4.3. Needless to say, all these
senate reform initiatives have failed, sometimes spectacularly.

Since the early 1990s, senate reform has remained a preoccupation on
the Opposition benches of the Commons and in certain provincial capitals.
Further, most Canadians remain strongly discontented with the senate,
favouring its reform or abolition in almost equal measure.[101] Nevertheless,
reform of Canada's anachronistic Upper House has virtually fallen off the
radar screen for the federal government. For some in the political class,

---

98 Jack Stillborn, "Forty Years of Not Reforming the Senate," in Serge Joyal, ed., *Protecting Canadian Democracy: The Senate You Never Knew* (Kingston, ON: McGill-Queen's
University, 2003) at 31.

99 Serge Joyal, "Introduction," in Joyal, *Protecting Canadian Democracy* at xix.

100 For summaries of these proposals see Stillborn, "Forty Years of Not Reforming the
Senate"; Library of Parliament, *Senate Reform Proposals in Comparative Perspective* (BP-
316E, Nov. 1992).

101 See "Unloved, Unwanted," *The Vancouver Province*, 12 May 1998, A20. ("More than
80 per cent of Canadians say the Senate should be reformed or abolished, according
to a new Angus Reid poll. Reform is favored by 43 percent of the 1,500 questioned,
abolition by 41 percent. Only 11 percent think it should be kept as it is.").

Table 4.3   Recent Senate Reform Proposals[102]

Proponent	Selection of Senators				Distribution of Seats
	Appointment Process	Electoral Process	Constituencies	Timing and Terms	
Molgate-Cosgrove Report (1984)	N/a	Single-member constituencies, to counter the party focus likely to flow if senators were elected by proportional representation	Single-member senate constituencies, established with reference to geographic, community, linguistic and cultural factors	Triennial elections, renewing one-third of the senate's membership and held on fixed dates	Senate seats adjusted to reflect population distributions between provinces
Alberta Select Committee (1985)	N/a	First-past-the-post (plurality) voting in multiple-member and province-wide constituencies	Province-wide constituencies	Elections held at same time as those for provincial legislatures	Each province to have an equal number of senators
Macdonald Commission (1985)	N/a	Proportional representation	Six-member constituencies	Elections held simultaneously with the Commons	Senate seats adjusted to reflect population distributions between provinces
Beaudoin-Dobbie Report (1992)	N/a	Proportional representation including a slate of candidates nominated by parties, but also open to independent candidates and with an eye to gender and diversity representation	Multi-member constituencies electing at least four senators	Fixed elections separate from those of either the Commons or the provincial legislatures	Senate seats adjusted to reflect population distributions between provinces
Charlottetown Proposal (1992)	Provinces could opt for a system of selection of senators by provincial legislatures	Provinces could choose a system of direct election by the people of the province	Not specified	Elections to the senate to be held at same time as those to the Commons	Each province to have an equal number of senators

102 Information tabulated from Stillborn, "Forty Years of Not Reforming the Senate."

this complacency likely reflects political exhaustion after decades of dashed reform efforts and momentous constitutional brouhahas like the *Charlotte-town Accord*.

On the other hand, there are those who defend the present order, or at least the role of the senate in it. Thus, Senator Serge Joyal, in his edited collection of (sometimes) *apologia* for the senate urged:

> [a]bolishing or diminishing the Upper Chamber would have a profound and nefarious impact on the equilibrium of our constitutional polity and the effectiveness of its institutions. ... The Senate is perhaps the last remaining obstacle to the total domination of Parliament by the executive government. Its demise would signal the atrophy of parliamentary federalism in Canada and the birth of a less Canadian system of government.[103]

These assertions may exaggerate somewhat the role of the senate in preserving parliamentary supremacy. Nevertheless, Senator Joyal's book argues forcefully in favour of a bicameral legislature, and also asserts that the senate as it exists at present is ill understood and its contribution to Canadian governance underappreciated. No less an authority than Professor C.E.S. Franks urges that "the senate is far from ineffectual and ... many senators work very hard at their duties. ... The real senate is a far better and more effective legislative body than its critics would have Canadians believe."[104]

These views require acknowledgment. If the senate is not all rotten and has a role to play in parliamentary governance, this is certainly a response to those who favour abolition of the second chamber. It is not, however, an adequate answer to those who query whether the senate can truly ever be effective when composed of individuals hand-picked by the prime minister, not elected by the citizenry.

Two points buttress this conclusion. First, that some or even most senators have performed their functions earnestly and competently is an indifferent fact if one believes that legislation in this country is something to be debated and determined by elected representatives. There have, in history, been absolute monarchs who governed with competency. Still, our society prefers democracy. Democracy is a value choice, not something to be dismissed because unelected forms of government can, at times, get the job done.

---

103 Serge Joyal, "The Federal Principle," in Joyal, *Protecting Canadian Democracy* at 307.
104 C.E.S. Franks, "Modern Times," in Joyal, *Protecting Canadian Democracy* at 185.

Second, there is a more practical reason for converting the senate into an elected body: because Canadians have, in fact, opted for a democratic system of governance, an unelected senate is gravely hamstrung in its abilities to perform its legitimate functions. Professor Ronald Watts, in his firm defence of bicameralism in federal systems, notes that the Canadian senate's role in "representing regional interests" has been impaired by "its perceived lack of legitimacy as a regionally representative body due to its method of appointment and composition."[105]

To this observation we would add: the current, unelected senate's effectiveness also suffers from the partisan appointment process employed by sitting prime ministers. Like prime ministers before him, Jean Chrétien appointed senators mostly from his own party. At present, members of the Liberal Party overwhelmingly populate the senate.[106] As a result, even if senators may indeed be hardworking, there is little opportunity for the meaningful debate of government policy that might occur in a chamber with an effective counterbalance to the governing party.[107]

For these reasons, it is our view that the real choice is not between the *status quo* and reform, but between different sorts of reform.

The Dangers of Incrementalism

Sensitive to the perception that the senate is a vast pasturage for patronage appointments, the Martin government's approach to the senate quandary by early 2005 was best described as benign neglect: a reluctance to appoint senators, ensuring that many seats remained unfilled.[108] While attrition may sidestep calling attention to the senate selection process, it is not a sustainable reform strategy. Thinning and ultimately extinguishing the ranks of senators may not, as a constitutional matter, be used to abolish the

---

105 Ronald Watts, "Federal Parliamentary Systems," in Joyal, *Protecting Canadian Democracy* at 101.

106 As of April 2005, sixty-four senators, roughly two-thirds of those sitting in the Upper Chamber, were Liberals. Of the remaining thirty-four, twenty-three were Conservatives, five were Progressive Conservatives, one was NDP, and five were Independent. There were seven vacancies. Based on current senate statistics, the senate is almost certain to remain majority Liberal for at least another decade.

107 Opposition senators have themselves expressed this view. See Jack Aubry, "Empty Senate Seats Save Martin $2.6M, but Anger Opposition," *Ottawa Citizen*, 7 Dec. 2004, A3.

108 "Senate Primed for Reform," *Calgary Herald*, 8 Sept. 2004, A18, reporting that vacant senate seats are expected to reach fifteen by fall 2004; Jack Aubry, "Martin's Fence-Sitting on Senate Vacancies Has Saved $1.75M," *Ottawa Citizen*, 7 Sept. 2004, A5. While Martin appointed five senators, seven vacancies remained.

senate. The *Constitution Act, 1867* compels the filling of senate vacancies.[109] Further, as noted earlier, with no senate, there could be no constitutional Acts of Parliament.

A modest alternative to the present appointments system is to broaden the group of people doing the choosing of senators. Thus, press reports in mid-2004 suggested that the government might select senators from a list presented by each province.[110] Presumably, some of those provinces would submit names determined under provincial senate election laws, such as that which exists in Alberta.

This change in the appointment process, while superficially an improvement over the present system, would create its own problems. Appointment from a list presented by the provinces is still just that, appointment. Only if provinces themselves determine names with reference to a broad electoral process does this appointment system render selection more democratic. Even then, being elected once does not produce a true system of democratic accountability. Existing constitutional provisions securing the tenure of senators would mean that, once appointed, even the democratically elected senator would be insulated from an electorate, sometimes for decades.

Meanwhile, these new senators — be they directly elected or simply anointed by their provinces — would likely view themselves as the legitimate tribunes of the people or provinces, as the case may be. Bolstered by their one-time democratic endorsement, the new senators might feel empowered to flex muscles left unflexed by today's more diffident Upper Chamber, producing difficult deadlocks between the two Houses of Parliament. Senator Lowell Murray has put his finger on this problem, writing, "[t]he elected senators would have no reason to exercise the restraint that has guided the present Senate in the exercise of our legislative veto [that is, the power to decline to pass bills] and other powers."[111] These puffed-up, once-only elected senators could continue operating in this fashion, as Commons and governments came and went, until their seventy-fifth birthday.

Put another way, it is likely not a good idea to mix one-time election (and the democratic legitimacy it brings) with virtual life tenure (and the

---

109 *Constitution Act, 1867*, s. 32 ("When a Vacancy happens in the Senate by Resignation, Death, or otherwise, the Governor General *shall* by Summons to a fit and qualified Person fill the Vacancy) [emphasis added].

110 Jack Aubry, "The New Liberal Agenda," *Ottawa Citizen*, 28 April 2004, A1.

111 Lowell Murray, "Which Criticisms Are Founded?" in Joyal, *Protecting Canadian Democracy* at 145.

political insulation it brings), especially in a bicameral Parliament comprising two, mostly co-equal Houses. Indeed, the bifurcation of democratic legitimacy likely to flow from senate elections was one reason Canada's leaders at the time of Confederation preferred an appointed senate to an elected chamber. George Brown put it this way in 1865:

> It has been said that members of the Upper House ought not to be appointed by the Crown, but should continue to be elected by the people at large. On that question my views have been often expressed. I have always been opposed to a second elective chamber and I am so still, from the conviction that the two elective Houses are inconsistent with the right working of the British parliamentary system. ... [W]hen the elective element becomes supreme, who will venture to affirm that the Council would not claim that power over money bills which this House claims as of right belonging to itself? Could they not justly say that they represent the people as well as we do, and that the control of the purse strings ought, therefore, to belong to them as much as to us. It is said they have not the power. But what is to prevent them from enforcing it?[112]

Constitutional Reform

Given this problem, it seems to us that senate reform is not a quick fix to be undertaken by tinkering within the confines of the present constitutional straitjacket. Instead, it is one that will need to be undertaken boldly, by amending the *Constitution Act, 1867* itself. Per the applicable amending formula, any such change would require approval by the federal Parliament and at least two-thirds of the provinces with at least 50 percent of the population.[113] This would be a difficult undertaking. It is also, in our view, necessary, in order to render the senate a truly democratic institution.

We do not in this book presume to present a manifesto on what a reformed senate would look like. However, we believe that at the very least constitutional senate reform should be guided by several precepts, as follows.

Independence Issues

First, the senate should enjoy independence relative to the Commons and the government. This is a classic (if often nominal) quality of the senate. As the Supreme Court of Canada has observed, "[i]n creating the Senate in the manner provided in the [1867] Act, it is clear that the intention was to make

---

112 *Parliamentary Debates on the Subject of the Confederation of the British North American Provinces* (Quebec: Hunter Rose, 1865) at 88–89.

113 *Constitution Act, 1982,* ss. 38 and 42.

the Senate a thoroughly independent body which could canvass dispassion-ately the measures of the House of Commons."[114] Enhancing senate inde-pendence could counter, in our view, the unfortunate tendency of the Commons simply to act as the legislative arm of executive government, a matter discussed at length in later chapters.

As a few examples of independence-enhancing reforms, the senate should have a Speaker elected by senators themselves in a fashion analo-gous to that employed by the Commons for its own Speaker, a matter dis-cussed in chapter 5. At present the appointment of a senate Speaker is something done by the Governor General, and in practice by the prime minister.[115] Also, sections 26 and 27 of the *Constitution Act, 1867* allowing the Governor General to expand temporarily the size of the senate should be repealed. Stacking the senate to accommodate the government obvious-ly undermines that body's independence.

Democracy Issues

Second, senate reform should be driven by a democratic imperative. By the standards set in this book, democratic accountability means that those who exercise the powers of the state must be either directly elected or at least accountable to those who are. Since the second, indirect form of accounta-bility — accountability through other elected officials — would gravely undermine the senate's independence, the only way we can envisage a sen-ate that is both democratically legitimate and independent is through direct election by the people.

Exactly how senators would be elected is an issue we leave to another work. If the Commons persists in a first-past-the-post, constituency sys-tem, however, it seems sensible to us that the senate be elected on some sort of proportional representation basis. This approach would avoid the conundrum of representatives in two Houses, each claiming a similar con-stituency legitimacy. It would also partially correct the distortions in elec-toral representation created by the first-past-the-post system in the Commons, discussed in chapter 3, perhaps preserving the senate's better record on diversity.

---

114 *Re Authority of Parliament in relation to the Upper House,* [1980] 1 S.C.R. 54 at 77, addressing the question of whether, prior to the *Constitution Act, 1982,* the Parliament of Canada could unilaterally amend the 1867 Act provisions governing the senate and concluding that it could not.

115 See Privy Council minute, P.C. 3374 (1935) listing recommendations on appointment of the Speaker of the senate as one of the prime minister's personal prerogatives.

Regional Representation Issues

Third, the express purpose of the senate is to foster regional equality in the federal Parliament. This is an important but, in our view, antiquated purpose. The provinces are much more potent entities in the twenty-first century than the framers of the Constitution ever anticipated in the nineteenth century. Much of the delivery of modern government services — such as health and education — is now squarely within provincial jurisdiction to an extent unknown in 1867. Meanwhile, in the early twentieth century, the jurisprudence of the U.K. Judicial Committee of the Privy Council endowed the provinces with sweeping powers under the *Constitution Act, 1867.*[116]

Federal authority has been reclaimed in part by the Supreme Court since it became Canada's final court of appeal in the 1940s, strengthening the federal Parliament. At the same time, however, other once potent federal powers have fallen in abeyance. Thus, the federal power to disallow provincial legislation has fallen into disuse, to the point that commentators now suggest that no room for its exercise persists.[117]

From this, it is fair to conclude that the provinces are powerful all by themselves, much more so than in 1867. Given this evolution of the Canadian federation, it is anachronistic to view the senate as a vital instrument defending these provincial interests. The provincial governments are well-equipped to do that themselves. For this reason, provincial representation issues should not be the key preoccupation in any senate reform. Indeed, overcoming the regional tensions that divide Canada might be best accomplished by a fixed-size senate elected by national vote, on the proportional representation basis mooted above.

Primacy Issues

Fourth, as already noted, we are concerned with the implications of democratic legitimacy being bestowed on a co-equal House of Parliament and the prospect for deadlock that might present. Such deadlocks have occurred from time to time in Australia, where both houses in the Parliament are elected.

---

116 See Hogg, *Constitutional Law of Canada* at 5-17 and 18, noting that in cases between 1880 and 1928, the Privy Council "gave a narrow interpretation to the principal federal powers ... and a wide interpretation to the principal provincial power" and noting that "the distribution of powers in the Constitution of Canada is much less favourable to the federal power than would be suggested merely by comparing the text with that of the American or Australian Constitutions."

117 *Ibid.* at 5-19, discussing *Constitution Act, 1867*, s. 90. See also *Re Resolution to Amend The Constitution, Supreme Court of Canada*, [1981] 1 S.C.R. 753 at 802, noting that "disallowance[s] of provincial legislation, although in law still open, have, to all intents and purposes, fallen into disuse."

One solution to this problem is to follow the Australian pattern of dissolving Parliament when deadlocks occur and going to the country.[118] Another, perhaps less drastic solution is to limit the power of the Upper House to veto Commons measures. Indeed, this is the regular prescription of many senate reform proposals, many of which call for only a senate "suspensive veto": the power to block Commons bills for only a limited period of time.[119] Indeed, even now on constitutional matters, the senate has only such a limited veto.[120] The 180-day period established for constitutional matters in the *Constitution Act, 1982* seems a reasonable time period for all legislation: long enough to make it costly for the Commons and government to run roughshod over the senate; not so long as to paralyze Parliament.

Sober Second Thought Issues

Last, we agree with commentators who urge that, as it exists at present, the senate's key qualities include a longer-term perspective, fostered by greater continuity in the membership of the senate relative to the Commons. One means of preserving this feature in an elected senate would be to stagger senator terms, dividing the senate into classes. For instance, if the senate were partitioned into two classes, on dissolution of the Commons and a new election, one-half of the senate would be contested. In this fashion, the entire senate, and each member of that chamber, would pass through an electoral cycle at least once every ten years.

Further, we also agree that the senate's members also sometimes possess significant professional and life experience.[122] Senate reform should retain these features, to the extent compatible with democratic accountability. Thus, the outdated property qualifications for senate membership in section 23 should be abolished. However, the notion that the senate should be a chamber composed of experienced individuals might be preserved

---

118 See s. 57 of the Australian Constitution, which reads, in part, "[i]f the House of Representatives passes any proposed law, and the Senate rejects or fails to pass it, or passes it with amendments to which the House of Representatives will not agree, and if after an interval of three months the House of Representatives, in the same or the next session, again passes the proposed law with or without any amendments which have been made, suggested, or agreed to by the Senate, and the Senate rejects or fails to pass it, or passes it with amendments to which the House of Representatives will not agree, the Governor-General may dissolve the Senate and the House of Representatives simultaneously."

119 See discussion in Stillborn, "Forty Years of Not Reforming the Senate."

120 *Constitution Act, 1982*, s. 47, limiting the senate's capacity to hold up constitutional reform to 180 days.

121 See discussion in Gil Rémillard and Andrew Turner, "Senate Reform: Back to Basics," in Joyal, *Protecting Canadian Democracy* at 112.

through the retention of a minimum age requirement and, perhaps, the introduction of minimum education or experience prerequisites. With senate reform accomplished, the most serious democratic accountability issue would be resolved in the legislative branch.

3. Employees of Parliament and Parliamentarian Political Staff

Before leaving the legislative branch, we should briefly note that Parliament has its own internal "unelected" civil service of parliamentary staff. Persons working for the House of Commons are employed by that body's Board of Internal Economy,[122] a committee chaired by the Speaker and comprising two ministers, the leader of the Opposition and representatives from other official parties.[123] The senate and the Library of Parliament are also separate employers.[124]

The Governor-in-Council appoints certain senior parliamentary personnel. These persons include the clerks of the senate and Commons[125] — essentially the chief executive officers of each house — and the parliamentary librarian.[126] Other persons may be appointed by resolution of the relevant house.[127] Individual parliamentarians may also be employers, retaining their own office and constituency staff using funds determined by rules of their respective chambers.[128]

Employment-related discipline and dismissal of parliamentary employees is usually governed by the *Parliamentary Employee and Staff Relations Act*, which creates a grievance system for employment disputes roughly similar to that existing for public servants, discussed later in section B of this chapter.[129] Setting out the precise mechanics of this process

---

122 House of Commons, *Fact Sheet: Board of Internal Economy*. See also *Parliamentary Employment and Staff Relations Act*, R.S.C. 1985, c. 33 (2d Supp.), s. 3, empowering the senate and Commons to designate a committee to serve as employer for the purposes of that statute.

123 *Parliament of Canada Act*, s. 50.

124 *Parliamentary Employment and Staff Relations Act*, s. 3. *Parliament of Canada Act*, s. 19.3, naming the Standing Senate Committee on Internal Economy, Budgets and Administration as charged with financial and administrative matters relating, *inter alia*, to senate staff.

125 *Public Service Employment Act (PSEA)*, S.C. 2003, c. 22, s. 130 (not in force as of 2004). See also the law still in force in 2004, R.S.C. 1985, c. P-33, s. 40.

126 *Parliament of Canada Act*, s. 5.

127 For instance, the senate law clerk and parliamentary counsel is appointed by resolution of the senate. See *Senate of Canada Annual Report 2002–2003*, 6. Senate Administration.

128 See, e.g., *Commons Members Office and Travel Expenses 2002–2003*.

129 *Parliamentary Employment and Staff Relations Act*, s. 62 *et seq*.

falls beyond the scope of this book. One pressing issue worth raising, however, is the extent to which parliamentary privilege gives Parliament a free hand to terminate employees as it wills, for even discriminatory reasons. In a case on appeal to the Supreme Court by December 2004, the Federal Court of Appeal concluded Parliament has authority to control its administrative staff. However, parliamentary privilege with respect to staff management "does not preclude a review of the necessity to possess and exercise the privilege where there is an allegation of racial or ethnic discrimination" in violation of the *Charter* or human rights law.[130]

B. EXECUTIVE BRANCH UNELECTED OFFICIALS

We turn now to unelected officials in the executive branch. Under this heading, we deal with the ministry, ministerial staff, the public service, Governor-in-Council appointees and a group of officials inhabiting a nether zone between the executive and legislative branches, officers of Parliament.

1. Members of the Ministry and Cabinet

We begin with a word of explanation as to why we deal with the ministry here, in a section on appointed representatives. The answer is straightforward: although the prime minister and his or her ministers are usually Members of Parliament, they do not become ministers simply by being elected parliamentarians. A parliamentarian is appointed to a ministerial post by the Governor General at the behest of the prime minister. As Senator Eurgene Forsey observed, "[G]overnments are not *elected* but are *appointed* and Ministers serve, not for a term, but until they die, resign or are dismissed. Ministers are just what the word means, servants, the Queen's confidential, political servants upon whom devolves the good government of Her subjects."[131]

Even more importantly, a person may on occasion be a minister without being an elected parliamentarian at all. Such occurrences are rare and fleeting. If they were to endure, such appointments would de-link the minister from the elected House of Commons, raising serious questions for responsible government in Canada. Thus, by constitutional convention, the prime minister and other ministers are expected to be Members of Parliament.[132]

130 *House of Commons v. Vaid*, [2003] 1 F.C. 602 (C.A.), leave to appeal allowed, [2003] 2 S.C.R. vii.
131 Forsey and Eglington, *The Question of Confidence* at 19 [emphasis in original].
132 See Heard, *Canadian Constitutional Conventions* at 49.

There is, however, a caveat: ministers may hold office pending election to the Commons or while a senator.[133] As a result, the appointment of unelected persons does occur. Since Confederation, some eighty-one ministers have served in the Cabinet prior to seeking election in the Commons.[134] Indeed, John Turner was appointed prime minister before being re-elected to the Commons.[135] Further, unelected senators have often been ministers since Confederation.[136] Indeed, in five cases, ministers were named, and then appointed to the senate, not elected to the Commons.[137] Meanwhile, the government leader in the senate also generally sits at the Cabinet table.

In sum, the formal appointment role of the Governor General and the absence of an airtight requirement that ministers be elected in any capacity mean that ministers are truly appointed officials.

a) Defining the Ministry and Cabinet

Ministers and the prime minister together comprise the ministry,[139] a category sometimes also referred to colloquially as the government. The terms "ministry" and "Cabinet" are usually used interchangeably. Technically, however, Cabinet is the collective decision-making body of the ministry, and need always be co-extensive with that ministry. A minister is not automatically a Cabinet member. The question of who obtains a seat at the Cabinet table is a political matter for the prime minister to decide.[140]

---

133 Hogg, *Constitutional Law of Canada* at 9-7.

134 Library of Parliament, *Ministers Named from Outside Parliament*. Notable recent examples include Brian Tobin (2000), Stéphane Dion (1996), and Pierre Pettigrew (1996).

135 Turner was appointed prime minister on 30 June 1984. He was elected to Vancouver Quadra on 4 Sept. 1984. See Library of Parliament, *Prime Ministers of Canada* [online].

136 Since Confederation, seventy-five senators have been ministers, mostly without portfolio, but sometimes in important departments. See Library of Parliament, *Senators in Cabinet — 1867 to Present*. Recent examples include Senator Lowell Murrey, who served as minister of state (federal-provincial relations) and acting minister of communications in the Mulroney government; Joyce Fairbairn, minister with special responsibility for literacy in the Chrétien government; Hazen Argue, minister of state (Canadian Wheat Board) in the Trudeau government; Horace Olsen, minister of state for economic development in the Trudeau government; Raymond Perault, minister of state (fitness and amateur sport) in the Trudeau government; Martial Asselin, minister of state for the Canadian International Development Agency in the Clark government; Robert De Cotret, minister of industry, trade and commerce and minister of state for economic development in the Clark government; and Jacques Flynn, minister of justice in the Clark government.

137 Library of Parliament, *Ministers Named from Outside Parliament*.

138 See Privy Council Office, *The Canada Ministry (in Order of Precedence)*.

139 See discussion in Marleau and Montpetit, *House of Commons Procedure and Practice* at 28.

Cabinet is a mysterious creature whose existence is not anticipated in law. In terms of Acts of Parliament, various departmental and other statutes anticipate the existence of "ministers." They do not, however, compel the existence of a community of ministers known as Cabinet. For its part, the federal *Interpretation Act* defines the title Governor-in-Council — a term we have used repeatedly in the book — as "the Governor General of Canada acting by and with the advice of, or by and with the advice and consent of, or in conjunction with the Queen's Privy Council for Canada."[140]

As discussed in chapter 2, this "Queen's Privy Council for Canada" is created by the *Constitution Act, 1867*. Its task is to "aid and advise in the Government of Canada."[141] However, in modern Canada, the Privy Council is not the same thing as Cabinet. First, the Governor General swears in privy councillors for life. Cabinet ministers serve in their Cabinet capacity for a much shorter tenure.

Second, the Privy Council's membership is very different from that of Cabinet. Until 1891, all privy councillors were current or former ministers. After that date, the Governor General began swearing in other, "distinguished" Canadians.[142] At present, the Privy Council is a sizable body, with many scores of members.[143] For this reason, all Cabinet ministers are privy councillors, but not all (or even a majority) of privy councillors are sitting Cabinet ministers.

The lack of statutory or written constitutional recognition does not, however, render Cabinet illegitimate. As discussed further in chapters 2 and 6, Cabinet governance — the heart of responsible government — is regulated by custom and constitutional convention. For instance, by constitutional convention, only those privy councillors who are also presently in Cabinet are entitled to exercise the powers of the Privy Council.[144]

Likewise, the selection and dismissal of these Cabinet members, and indeed all ministers, is a practice infused with convention, not law. As Professor Dawson observes, "one may search the law books in vain for answers" to such questions as how does a Cabinet minister obtain office?

140   *Interpretation Act*, s. 35.

141   *Ibid.*

142   Governor General of Canada, *Fact Sheet: The Swearing-In of Privy Councillors.* For instance, "[i]n 1967, on the occasion of Canada's centennial, and in 1982, on the occasion of the patriation of the Constitution, the provincial premiers then in office were summoned and sworn in the Privy Council at a ceremony on Parliament Hill in the presence of The Queen."

143   See Privy Council Office, *Members of the Queen's Privy Council for Canada — Current Alphabetical List.*

144   Heard, *Canadian Constitutional Conventions* at 18.

When should a Cabinet resign? How is a prime minister chosen?[145] In this section, we address these questions.

b) Prime Minister

Appointment

The prime minister is the so-called first among equals, or *primus inter pares*, in the ministry and Cabinet system. By convention, the Governor General appoints the prime minister. Indeed, this power has been described as a personal prerogative of the Governor General: here, the Governor General exercises discretion in an effort to appoint a prime minister who can form a government enjoying the support of the Commons.[146]

Commanding the Confidence of the House

Determining a prime minister with the support of the Commons is usually a straightforward undertaking. As some Supreme Court of Canada judges have put it, the Governor General typically appoints the leader of the party winning the "majority of seats in Parliament (assuming that there is one)" as prime minister.[147] Certainly, this is the way the convention works with majority governments. Party discipline generally means that the majority party in the Commons commands that chamber's confidence. However, the convention also accommodates minority governments. A better statement of the convention is, therefore, that the Governor General will usually call upon the leader of the party with the *greatest* number of seats to form a government,[148] and serve as prime minister.

Even this rendition may not, however, capture the full nuance of the convention. The Governor General might also exercise his or her appointment power where two minority parties form a coalition able to command a majority of votes in the Commons, and anoint a leader to serve as prime

---

145 Ward, *Dawson's The Government of Canada* at 195.

146 Hogg, *Constitutional Law of Canada* at 9-7. See also *Angus v. Canada*, 72 D.L.R. (4th) 672 at 683 (F.C.A.), holding the Governor General "retains reserve or personal powers, such as the choice of a prime minister." See also *Quebec (Attorney General) v. Blaikie*, [1981] 1 S.C.R. 312 at 320, discussing the provincial lieutenant governor and observing that this official "appoints members of the Executive Council and ministers … and these, according to constitutional principles of a customary nature referred to in the preamble of the *B.N.A. Act* [1867 Act] … must be or become members of the Legislature and are expected, individually and collectively, to enjoy the confidence of its elected branch."

147 *Figueroa*, [2003] 1 S.C.R. 912 at para. 141, *per* Gonthier, LeBel and Deschamps JJ., concurring in the result.

148 *Re Resolution To Amend The Constitution*, [1981] 1 S.C.R. 753 at 857, *per* Dickson, Estey and McIntyre JJ., dissenting.

minister. In effect, this was the situation in 1925, when Mackenzie King served as prime minister with 101 Liberal seats against the Conservative's 116 members.[149] King held the confidence of the Commons only through a coalition with the remaining 28 members of the House.[150] From this, it follows that so long as the leader of a party commands the confidence of the Commons, the Governor General should be able to appoint him or her prime minister, regardless of the relative party distribution of seats.[151]

While the 1925 scenario is the unique example in Canadian history of a premiership held by a leader without the largest party in the Commons, the possibility of a replay lurks in every close election. Indeed, it was a favourite topic for pundits in 2004, when pre-election polls showed the Liberals and Conservatives neck-in-neck. Because of the ambiguities in existing constitutional conventions, a 1925 scenario would place the Governor General in a difficult predicament.

Unusually for the largely ceremonial office, it might oblige the Governor General to exercise his or her own judgment in determining how best to proceed with the selection of a prime minister capable of commanding the requisite Commons support.[152] This is particularly true given disagreements in the academic literature on the appropriate course of action for a Governor General confronting a fractured Commons with a roughly even distribution of members between parties. One thing that does appear certain: like King in 1925, an incumbent prime minister should be given the first opportunity to form a government with majority support in the House.[153]

However, assuming that effort fails, the procedure to be followed by the Governor General is most uncertain. Some authorities recommend that the Governor General should simply call on party leaders to attempt to form a government, starting with the leader of the single largest party. Others counsel a more active role, in which the Governor General mediates between the assorted party leaders in an effort to hash out an agreement.[154]

---

149 See Statistics Canada (Jean-Louis Roy), *Historical Statistics of Canada, Section Y: Politics and Government*, chart Y199-210.

150 Robert Bothwell, Ian Drummond, and John English, *Canada 1900–1945* (Toronto: University of Toronto Press, 1987) at 205.

151 See discussion by Professor C.E.S. Frank, Commons Standing Committee on Government Operations and Estimates, *Evidence*, 37th Parl., 3d Sess. (25 March 2004).

152 Heard, *Canadian Constitutional Conventions* at 20; Marleau and Montpetit, *House of Commons Procedure and Practice* at 22.

153 See discussion in Ward, *Dawson's The Government of Canada* at 200; Heard, *Canadian Constitutional Conventions* ("All the constitutional authorities are agreed that a government has the right to remain in office to meet the legislature when an election results in no majority position for any party").

154 *Ibid.* at 22.

The Role of Political Parties and Replacement Prime Ministers

Because the Governor General looks to the leader of a political party in selecting a prime minister,[155] Canadians electing a political party to a dominant role in the House also *de facto* anoint that party's leader as the head of government, in control of the executive branch. The electorate, however, has no direct say in how a given party selects this leader. The party itself determines its leadership, according to its own internal rules.[156] Thus, as has often been the case, the Governor General may replace a retiring prime minister with a new party leader who did not head the party at the time of the last election, and thus was never vetted by the electorate in his or her leadership role.[157]

In practice, all Canada's political parties have systems in which grassroots party members — not party parliamentarians — determine the outcome of leadership races, an approach very different from that employed in other parliamentary systems.[158] This membership-centric approach raises two issues.

First, the grassroots method of leadership selection provokes massive membership drives by the candidates during leadership contests. In some instances, tightly contested leadership campaigns prompt allegations of fraud in the compilation of party membership lists.[159] In these circumstances, law should closely regulate leadership campaigns. Only belatedly, however, is law creeping into these party-run leadership campaigns. Some campaign finance laws now apply to the leadership process, as discussed in chapter 3. A selection process impaired by serious procedural flaws

---

155 *Ibid.* ("Canadian and British practice appears to preclude the appointment of someone other than a party leader as first minister, which sometimes happens in European countries").

156 See, e.g., *Constitution of the Liberal Party of Canada*, s. 17.

157 Recent examples include Paul Martin (2003), Kim Campbell (1993), and John Turner (1984).

158 See Heard, *Canadian Constitutional Conventions* at 25. See also discussion in David McFadden, "Choosing the Party Leader: Is There a Better Way?" (1986) 9 Canadian Parliamentary Review no. 2; Christopher Moore, "Backbenchers Fight Back," *National Post*, 13 Feb. 2001, A16. For instance, Canada's political parties generally do not permit the party's Parliamentarians to give their leader a Margaret Thatcher–style "heave." *Ibid.* See also, e.g., the *Constitution of the Liberal Party of Canada*, s. 17 apparently restricting the calling of a leadership convention to instances where the current leader has died or resigned.

159 See, e.g., Tim Harper, "Alliance Race Turns Nasty in Final Days," *Toronto Star*, 17 June 2000, A1; David Gamble, "Alliance Turmoil: Long Apologizes for Recruitment Tactics in Gaspé," *The Gazette*, 22 June 2000, A1; Peter Shawn Taylor, "The Best and 'Wurst' Ways of Choosing a Party Leader," *National Post*, 26 June 2000, A6.

might hypothetically also attract scrutiny by the courts, pursuant to common law procedural fairness considerations.[160]

Second, the grassroots approach to leadership campaigns potentially interfaces uncomfortably with constitutional convention, at least where leadership of the governing party is at stake. It is the Governor General, after all, who ultimately appoints a prime minister, not the party. Some commentators take the view that where a new prime minister is to be appointed during the tenure of a Parliament, "the only discretion that a governor [general] might properly exercise today is in the appointment of an interim prime minister, and even then it would have to be in circumstances where the party could not reach a decision after a prime minister had died or resigned suddenly."[161]

This may, however, understate the Governor General's role. A party should be able to determine a prime minister via a leadership contest only if the Governor General is persuaded that the person presented will command the confidence of the Commons. Typically, being selected by the party means that the leader also enjoys the support of that party's Members of Parliament; in other words, that the confidence of a party and the *party's members* in the House are co-extensive.

This seems a safe assumption, given the centrality of party loyalties in the Commons. There are, however, exceptions. As Stockwell Day discovered during his stint as the head of the Alliance Party, a party leader elected by the membership may soon find his or her caucus support evaporate.[162] Given this possibility, constitutional convention must mean that the Governor General retains a limited discretion in appointing a replacement prime minister during the life of a Parliament, one tied to whether that person can maintain the confidence of the Commons. Theoretically, a new leader disputed by a party's Members of Parliament (either sitting in a majority or in coalition with opposition members) could be blocked from the Prime Minister's Office. Members of Parliament, in other words, retain a technical primacy over selections engineered by a party and its membership.

---

160 See, e.g., *Cameron v. Boyle*, [1994] O.J. No. 782 (Gen. Div.) applying procedural fairness concepts to a dispute concerning the meeting procedure of the Natural Law Party. Courts are generally reluctant to extend administrative law procedural fairness to private voluntary associations, unless "a property or civil right turns on the question of membership." *Lakeside Colony of Hutterian Brethren v. Hofer*, [1992] 3 S.C.R. 165 at 174.

161 Heard, *Canadian Constitutional Conventions* at 25.

162 See, e.g., James Travers and Tonda MacCharles, "Day of Reckoning: Alliance Leader Will Hear Demands from Caucus for Him to Step Down," *Toronto Star*, 17 July 2001, A1.

Dismissal

Collective Dismissal of the Government by the Governor General

Once the Governor General appoints the leader of the political party as prime minister, his or her ability to dismiss that individual is limited to circumstances in which the prime minister's government loses the confidence of the House of Commons.[163] At that juncture, the government — more technically, the ministry — must itself resign and an effort must be made to cobble together a new ministry with the confidence of the House. Or alternatively, the prime minister must obtain dissolution of Parliament, prompting new elections.[164] As Professor Dawson puts it, "either the cabinet must be changed so that the Commons can obtain an executive to give it the leadership it will accept, or the Commons must itself be changed to provide the cabinet with the support it must have if it is to remain in office."[165]

In effect, these conventions mean that the Commons has the power to fire the prime minister, by firing his or her government. Indeed, responsible government is built on this ultimate accountability of the prime minister to Parliament. Exactly how the "confidence of the Commons" is measured is a matter in flux. We discuss this issue more fully in chapter 6. For our purposes here, the Commons demonstrates no confidence in the government in the form of a successful "no confidence" vote.

Typically, the fate of the prime minister and his or her government is not determined during a Parliament, but is instead tied to the outcome of a general election. A ministry persists even after an election is called, to preserve continuity of government. If the government party "loses" the election by electing too few members to command the confidence of the House, the prime minister will resign, and his or her ministry will terminate.[166] Technically, the losing government is not required to resign until confronted with a successful no confidence vote in the House. There is, however, a "well-established body of precedents" encouraging immediate resignation upon the "loss" of an election.[167]

The one exception to this rule favouring immediate resignation appears to be in closely divided Parliaments, where it is unclear which

---

163 See Hogg, *Constitutional Law of Canada* at 9-25.
164 *Re Resolution To Amend The Constitution*, [1981] 1 S.C.R. 753, 857–58, *per* Dickson, Estey and McIntyre JJ., dissenting.
165 Ward, *Dawson's The Government of Canada* at 199.
166 Hogg, *Constitutional Law of Canada* at 9-7 to 9-8.
167 Ward, *Dawson's The Government of Canada* at 199.

party will command the Commons' confidence. In those circumstances, incumbent governments may delay their resignation in an effort to cobble together Commons support. Indeed, to dissolve a fractured Parliament and return to the polls before Parliament had a chance to meet would violate constitutional convention. As Senator Eugene Forsey urged in his authoritative 1985 review of responsible government a "new House of Commons has an indefeasible right to meet, and to see whether it can transact business."[168] The classic example is the 1925 election, in which the incumbent King Liberal government remained in office and negotiated the support of Progressive members, despite the fact that the Conservatives were the single largest (though not majority) party in the House.[169]

A prime minister who refuses to resign his or her government (or seek dissolution) when the confidence of the Commons is lost faces a legitimate intervention and dismissal by the Governor General.[170] Thus, the Supreme Court has recognized that a failure by the government to resign after a lost election (read as shorthand for a loss of confidence from the House) would do violence to the democratic order and oblige the personal intervention of the Governor General:

> if after a general election where the opposition obtained the majority at the polls the government refused to resign and clung to office, it would thereby commit a fundamental breach of convention, one so serious indeed that it could be regarded as tantamount to a *coup d'etat*. The remedy in this case would lie with the Governor General ... who would be justified in dismissing the ministry and in calling on the opposition to form the government.[171]

Other than in circumstances where the confidence of the Commons is lost, there is no clear basis for arguing that the Governor General may dismiss a prime minister and his or her government, even for reprehensible acts. At the provincial level, lieutenant-governors — the provincial equivalent of the Governor General — did dismiss premiers and their governments on ethical grounds in 1891 and 1903. In 1891, the lieutenant-governor dismissed the Mercier government in Quebec following Royal Commission findings concluding that fraudulent payments had been made to the government's supporters with the knowledge of Cabinet. Likewise, in 1903,

---

168   Forsey and Eglington, *The Question of Confidence* at 157.

169   *Ibid.* at 200.

170   See Derek Lee, *The Power of Parliamentary Houses to Send for Persons, Papers and Records* (1999) at 215.

171   *Reference re Resolution to Amend the Constitution*, [1981] 1 S.C.R. 753 at 882.

the lieutenant governor dismissed the British Columbia government after an investigation into government corruption revealed corrupt interactions between two ministers and the railways.[172]

These two cases are likely exceptional, however, and at least some academic commentary suggests that they do not reflect an existing power of dismissal by Governors General for corrupt administration of government.[173] Professor Dawson argues, however, in his writings that a Governor General should be able to dismiss a prime minister shown beyond doubt to have accepted a bribe, should that official refuse both to resign and to recall a prorogued Parliament to deal with the manner.[174] At base, this act would preserve responsible government, by denying the prime minister an opportunity to sideline Parliament.

If that is the objective, however, we believe that the better course of action for the Governor General would be to ignore the prime minister's advice, and exercise independently the Governor General's power to call Parliament to session. In any event, since the advent *Canadian Charter of Rights and Freedoms* in 1982, Parliament must sit at least once every twelve months, putting a clear time limit on any prime minister's autocratic inclinations.[175]

Other Means of Dismissal

As this discussion suggests, dismissing the prime minister of Canada during the tenure of a Parliament essentially requires that the Commons fire his or her government, and then be prepared to go to the polls. There is some nuance here. As hinted above and discussed in chapter 6, there are instances where the Commons may defeat a government in the expectation that the Governor General will refuse a requested dissolution and turn to the leader of another party to cobble together a government. These are, however, the rarest of circumstances, confined probably to instances where opposition parties form coalitions securing the majority of the Commons.

A no-confidence vote is, therefore, a rather blunt instrument for politicians seeking to express discontent with an individual prime minister, but not with his or her government. Governing party politicians might temper their opposition to an unpopular leader for fear that a no-confidence vote would precipitate an election, one that would place their own jobs on the

---

172 Heard, *Canadian Constitutional Conventions* at 28.
173 *Ibid.* at 29.
174 Ward, *Dawson's The Government of Canada* at 189.
175 *Charter*, s. 5.

line.[176] In these circumstances, two interesting and entirely hypothetical questions present themselves.

Parliamentary Impeachment

First, does the Commons possess the power to "impeach" the prime minister (or any other minister) and secure his or her dismissal, without voting no confidence in his or her government and compelling the resignation of the entire ministry and possibly the dissolution of Parliament as a whole? The answer is almost certainly "no," although it is possible to imagine indirect means of arriving at that outcome.

It is true that the United Kingdom Parliament, for instance, retains a theoretical power to impeach all persons for any crimes whatsoever.[177] This power has not been employed, however, since 1806, and is not viewed as an existing means of removing the prime minister.[178] In Canada, Parliament also possesses a penal power: the right to punish for contempt of Parliament. This authority is discussed further in chapter 6. Likewise, the Commons may discipline and potentially expel its Members of Parliament, a practice discussed in chapter 3.

The prime minister would not be immune to these parliamentary privileges. However, committal for contempt and expulsion from the Commons would not, in its own right, strip the prime minister of his or her executive office. These parliamentary powers are not, therefore, tantamount to a U.S.-style impeachment procedure. At best, a determined Parliament might expel the prime minister and then hope that the convention that the prime minister be a Member of Parliament will (eventually) provoke his or her resignation. However, the prime minister's more probable response would be to treat the censure as a confidence measure and ask the Governor General for a dissolution of Parliament and new elections.

From this discussion it follows that Parliament has no real ability to engineer directly the dismissal of a prime minister other than through a vote of no confidence in the government, precipitating either an outright resignation or a parliamentary dissolution followed by an election in which the incumbent government is defeated. From this it seems clear that the prime minister's parliamentary caucus would have to be labouring under a

---

176 Jean Chrétien was accused of using the threat of declaring unpopular measures non-confidence votes as a means of keeping backbench Liberal members in-line. See Tim Naumetz, "PM Uses Fear to Cow Caucus, Rebel MP Says," *Ottawa Citizen*, 6 March 2003, A5.
177 See U.K. House of Commons Library, *Impeachment* (2003).
178 *Ibid.*

death wish before it would support such aggressive action against even an unpopular first minister.

The absence of a real parliamentary dismissal power has not gone unnoticed. Strong differences of opinion with the Chrétien Liberals on national unity policies prompted then-Reform Party leader Preston Manning to advocate the introduction of a species of prime ministerial impeachment procedure in 1995. At that time, the Reform Party submitted a letter to the Commons committee on procedure and House affairs reading:

> On behalf of the undersigned members of the House, we hereby request the following: That the committee recommend a procedure whereby Parliament may petition the Governor General for the removal of a prime minister who fails to uphold the Constitution of Canada or fails to protect the Canadian interest in any dealings with a provincial government committed to secession.
>
> This request is prompted by the actions of the present prime minister who, without a mandate from the people or the provinces, and on dubious legal grounds, has presented a bill to the House of Commons granting a veto over the Constitution of Canada to the separatist Government of Quebec.[179]

Nothing came of this initiative, of course.

Dismissal by the Party

The second question is whether the Governor General may dismiss a prime minister from office where that official's own party drums him or her from the party leadership. Certainly, Jean Chrétien's "long goodbye" as the head of the Liberal Party suggests that even governing party leaders may outlive their welcome.

At some level, it makes sense that ejection from the party leadership should prompt the Governor General to fire the prime minister. At first blush, dismissal of a prime minister rejected by his or her party would be symmetrical with the practice of appointing new leaders to the prime ministership upon their advancement to the governing party's leader's office.

However, from the perspective of constitutional convention, this approach would be troublesome. As already noted, constitutional convention ties the prime minister's tenure to his or her ability to command the confidence of the House, not the party. Certainly, rejection by the prime minister's party may correlate with a similar absence of support from the

---

179 Sheldon Alberts, "Manning Ridicules PM," *Calgary Herald,* 14 Dec. 1995, A1.

Commons caucus. On the other hand, commanding the confidence of the House and enjoying the support of the party may be very different things. It is conceivable that a party's constitution might allow a leader to be dismissed even against the wishes of its sitting parliamentarians. In those circumstances, the elected party MPs might refuse to support any no confidence motion.

To remove the prime minister from his or her office in this situation would supplant Parliament's role in guaranteeing responsible government, replacing it with decisions made by an unelected party membership. Constitutional convention should demand, therefore, that a sitting prime minister not be *obliged* to step down, even if stripped of his or her party leadership, unless Parliament itself votes a motion of no confidence in the government.

c) Ministers and Ministers of State

We turn now to the appointment and tenure of ministers other than the prime minister. The terms used to categorize the different species of minister who comprise the ministry are variable and confusing. The most important (and common) minister is one who heads up a government department. Most statutes creating government departments expressly anticipate such ministers, charged with responsibility for the department.

There are, however, other officials who also form part of the ministry. The *Ministries and Ministers of State Act*, for instance, envisages two sorts of minister: first, there are "Ministers of State" presiding over what the Act calls a "Ministry of State."[180] As discussed in chapter 6, ministries of state are a very narrow class of government agency. There are, therefore, few (if any) of these ministers in a typical Canadian government.

Second, the *Ministries and Ministers of State Act* also anticipates ministers of state who may be assigned to assist ministers who have departmental responsibilities.[181] In other words, the Act creates a junior or assistant minister. At one point, these officials were called secretaries of state.[182] The Martin government has now abandoned that practice, returning to the ministers of state terminology.[183] To simplify matters in this book, we use

---

180 *Ministries and Ministers of State Act*, R.S.C. 1985 c. M-8, s. 7.

181 *Ministries and Ministers of State Act*, ss. 11–12.

182 Orders-in-Council naming these officials usually specified that the individual was "a Minister of State to be known as Secretary of State." See, e.g., the following Orders-in-Council: P.C. 2003-0954 (2003-06-17); P.C. 2003-0554 (2003-04-11); P.C. 2002-0885 (2002-05-26).

183 See, e.g., Orders-in-Council P.C. 2004-0839, 840, 841, 843 and 844 (2004-07-20).

the term "ministers" as a generic term capturing both regular ministers and ministers of state unless otherwise noted.

Appointment

The Governor General appoints all the various ministers who constitute the ministry. However, by constitutional convention, the Governor General follows the prime minister's recommendations in appointing these ministers,[184] responding to a prime ministerial "Instrument of Advice." Recommendations concerning the composition of the ministry are the prime minister's personal prerogative, one that does not need to be exercised in association with Cabinet colleagues[185] or anyone else. As noted previously, most ministers are also Members of Parliament at the time of appointment, though this is not always the case. Ministers who are not parliamentarians are expected to obtain a parliamentary position with only modest delay, either in the Commons or the senate. Beyond this emphasis on (usually elected) parliamentarians, the prime minister's selection of individuals to constitute his or her ministry and ultimately Cabinet has been a matter of politics and not law.

Some of these political considerations have, however, produced firm practices. Thus, a parliamentarian from each province — with the occasional exception of Prince Edward Island — can be expected to be at the Cabinet table, if available.[186] Indeed, some scholars have viewed this custom as having developed into constitutional convention.[187] Adequate francophone and anglophone representation in Cabinet is also viewed as a vital consideration.[188] Finally, gender and ethnic representation increasingly constitute a political variable factored into a prime ministers' Cabinet construction.

Dismissal

A ministry endures as a collective entity for the life or tenure of the prime minister. As noted in the preceding section, a government falls if it loses a vote of no confidence, obliging the resignation of the prime minister (and by extension that of his or her ministry) or a dissolution of Parliament.

---

184 *Figueroa*, [2003] 1 S.C.R. 912 at para. 141, *per* Gonthier, LeBel and Deschamps JJ., concurring in the result.
185 Hogg, *Constitutional Law of Canada* at 9-9. Privy Council minute, P.C. 3374 (25 Oct. 1935).
186 Heard, *Canadian Constitutional Conventions* at 49–50.
187 Ward, *Dawson's The Government of Canada* at 204.
188 Heard, *Canadian Constitutional Conventions* at 49–50.

Individual ministers, for their part, have no security of tenure. For ministers of state assisting departmental ministers, removal from this support role has a quasi-statutory basis. The *Ministries and Minister of State Act* empowers the Governor-in-Council to make these assignments.[189] The Privy Council Office has apparently interpreted this Act as also permitting the Governor General to remove these assisting ministers from their assignment, on the advice of the prime minister.[190] The *Ministries and Ministers of State Act* also contains language specifying that those ministers of state presiding over ministries of state hold office "during pleasure."[191] As discussed later in this chapter, "during pleasure" is language signifying that the appointment — and its tenure — is discretionary.

These *Ministries and Minister of State Act* provisions aptly capture the approach taken to dismissals of all other ministers. Specifically, by strong convention, the tenure of ministers during the duration of a government is the prime minister's personal prerogative. The prime minister is free to (and often does) dismiss his or her ministers, either from the ministry as a whole or from a given ministerial portfolio.[192] Thus, in practice, the Governor General dismisses ministers of all stripes, at the sole discretion of the prime minister.[193]

As discussed later in relation to Governor-in-Council appointees, it is true that common law principles sometimes constrain the manner and circumstances by which even discretionary appointments may be terminated. These include a requirement that the appointee be given some modicum of notice of his or her removal, and a modest opportunity to comment. Nevertheless, these common law principles clearly do not apply to the prime minister in determining the membership of his ministry. Famously, ministers often have no notice and no opportunity to comment prior to a change in the ministry.

While ministers may be shuffled out of their positions, ministers in practice appear not to be outright "fired" by the prime minister between ministry reorganizations. Instead, they tender their resignation, no doubt often at the urging of the prime minister. Since the Second World War,

---

189 *Ministries and Ministers of State Act*, s. 11.

190 See, e.g., Order-in-Council, P.C. 2004-0837 (2004-07-20), terminating the assignment of nine ministers of state by "Her Excellency the Governor General in Council, on the recommendation of the Prime Minister, pursuant to section 11 of the *Ministries and Ministers of State Act*."

191 *Ministries and Ministers of State Act*, s. 7.

192 Privy Council Office, *Governing Responsibly: A Guide for Ministers and Ministers of State* (2003).

193 Heard, *Canadian Constitutional Conventions* at 26.

some twenty-one ministers have resigned in response to revelations of ethical infractions. Seven have resigned following disagreements concerning government policy.[194]

The issue of whether Parliament should also have a role in dismissing ministers is a matter we discuss in chapter 6, in the context of ministerial responsibility.

2. Ministerial Political Staff

As ministers are (ultimately) both parliamentarians and the political leadership of the executive branch, they have a strong interest in retaining assistants and advisors able to assist them in the political dimensions of their role. Under current Treasury Board rules, ministers are entitled to a minimum of seven political staff positions.[195] Actual numbers of persons on staff will vary, and may exceed seven so long as staff salaries do not cumulatively exceed the minister's staff budget.[196] These people are appointed under the *Public Service Employment Act* — the law governing the public service discussed in the next section.[197] However, they are exempted from that statute's regular public service rules, most notably merit-based hiring.[198] As a consequence, ministers have broad hiring discretion and need not follow set hiring criteria.

Subject to being hired by another minister or in the same minister's new portfolio, ministerial staff cease employment within thirty days of the minister leaving office.[199] As such, their tenure is highly uncertain, a key reason for the generous severance payments to which these individuals have traditionally been entitled.[200] These ministerial officials also have pref-

---

194 Numbers compiled from a review of Library of Parliament, *Ministerial Resignations*.

195 These positions are chief of staff; senior policy advisor; director of communications; director of parliamentary affairs; policy advisor; senior special assistant; special assistant for communications, parliamentary affairs, and regional offices. Ministers of state are entitled to a minimum of four positions (which, again, can be exceeded depending on salary levels): chief of staff; senior special assistant; special assistant; and support staff. See Treasury Board of Canada, *Guidelines for Minister's Offices*.

196 *Ibid.*

197 *PSEA*, S.C. 2003, c. 22, s. 128 (not in force as of 2004; unless otherwise noted, references to the *PSEA* in these notes is to the 2003 Act. See also the law still in force in 2004, R.S.C. 1985, c. P-33, s. 39).

198 Treasury Board of Canada, *Guidelines for Minister's Offices*, part 3.2.

199 *PSEA*, s. 128. See also R.S.C. 1985, c. P-33, s. 39.

200 Tim Naumetz, "Chrétien Aides Well Rewarded," *National Post*, 2 Aug. 2004, A1, reporting: "Forty political aides to Jean Chrétien received a total of $2-million in severance pay and allowances when he stepped aside as prime minister last December, fed-

erential rights to positions in the public service, a category of the executive branch to which we now turn.

3. Professional Public Service

In terms of sheer numbers, the professional public service is the most important institution of the executive branch of government. Indeed, the public service comprises the better part of what is popularly known as the "Government of Canada."

By December 2004, the laws governing this public service were in a state of flux,[201] reflecting the newest package of civil service reforms promised in the 2001 Speech from the Throne.[202] In this work on the legal foundations of Canadian democracy, we do not examine the many important public administration and human resources issues associated with this public service "modernization" project. Instead we examine the legal relationship between the public service and the political branches of government, specifically as it relates to the appointment and tenure of civil servants. To this end, we focus our discussion on the key statutes that had been enacted by the end of 2004, but had not yet been brought into force. We anticipate that these laws will be in place by the time (or soon after) our readers review this book.

a) Appointment

Originally, appointment to the public service was a power exercised by the monarch — and ultimately Cabinet — pursuant to the royal prerogative. Acts of Parliament governing the civil service mostly superseded this practice in Canada.[203]

---

eral records show. The sendoff amounted to an average payment of $50,000 a person. By way of comparison, a senior rank-and-file employee in the federal public service could expect a severance payment of about $40,000 after 30 years service if he or she retired early at age 55." See Treasury Board of Canada, *Guidelines for Minister's Offices*.

201 The discussion in this section reflects the law as it exists under the *Public Service Modernization Act*, S.C. 2003, c. 22. Not all this statute is in force at the time of this writing. When it does come into force, probably sometime in 2005, it will replace the existing *Public Service Staff Relations Act* with the *Public Service Labour Relations Act* and bring online a new *Public Service Employment Act*, S.C. 2003, c. 22, replacing its predecessor of the same name, R.S.C. 1985, c. P-33.

202 In the Speech from the Throne, the Liberal government promised "the reforms necessary [to] ensure that the public service is innovative, dynamic and reflective of the diversity of the country [and] able to attract and develop the talent needed to serve Canadians in the 21st century."

203 *Thomson v. Canada (Deputy Minister of Agriculture)*, [1992] 1 S.C.R. 385 at 395.

The new, 2003 *Public Service Employment Act* (*PSEA*) specifies, in its preamble, that "Canada will continue to benefit from a public service that is based on merit and non-partisanship and in which these values are independently safeguarded." It thus places Canada in the camp of those countries that have sought to de-politicize government administration.

The "public service" is carefully defined in this statute to include assorted departments, organizations and agencies, as listed in schedules to the *Financial Administration Act*.[204] The vast web of entities that together make up the public administration of Canada, along with an indication as to whether these bodies are governed by the *PSEA*, is set out in Appendix 1 at the end of this book.

To meet its merit-oriented objectives, the *PSEA* continues the Public Service Commission, an agency created by its predecessor statute. Consisting of a president and two or more part-time commissioners, this commission enjoys fairly robust security of tenure. The Governor-in-Council appoints the president and commissioners. However, the president's appointment must be approved by resolution of the senate and House of Commons. Commissioners — including, presumably, the president — serve during good behaviour for a term of seven years, but may be removed by the Governor-in-Council at any time on address of the senate and House of Commons.[205] The implications of similar parliamentary address and good-behaviour provisions are discussed in detail in the section on officers of Parliament, later in this chapter. For our purposes here, it suffices to say that commissioners enjoy substantial protection against arbitrary dismissals by government, enhancing the commission's independence.

The commission is tasked with several functions. Most notably, it has "the exclusive authority to make appointments, to or from within the public service, of persons for whose appointment there is no authority in or under any other Act of Parliament."[206] Put another way, where a statute does not assign appointing authority to another entity — most notably, the Governor-in-Council — the appointment must be made by the commission.

Critically, the commission's appointments must generally be made "on the basis of merit and must be free from political influence."[207] "Merit" means that the commission "is satisfied that the person to be appointed meets the essential qualifications for the work to be performed," and "has

---

204 R.S.C. 1985, c. F-11.
205 *PSEA*, s. 4.
206 *Ibid.*, s. 9 and s. 11.
207 *Ibid.*, s. 30.

regard to" any additional qualifications that might be an asset for the employer, and the employer's current or future needs or operational requirements.[209] The "deputy head" of the hiring organization — typically the deputy minister — may establish these essential qualifications.[209] Additional qualifications standards may be developed by Treasury Board relating to "education, knowledge, experience, occupational certification, language or other qualifications, that the employer considers necessary or desirable having regard to the nature of the work to be performed and the present and future needs of the public service."[210]

Unlike its predecessor, the new *PSEA* does not give preference in appointments to current employees of the public service, although it does distinguish between "internal" and "external" appointment processes. Internal appointments are only open to persons presently in the public service.[211]

Also unlike its predecessor, the new statute does not mandate selection via a formal competition. Indeed, the new Act opens the door to filling positions without first advertising them,[212] a practice discouraged by the competitive process employed under the old statute. For these reasons, some critics have complained that the new "merit" definition and approach are problematic. In its review of the legislation, law firm Nelligan O'Brien Payne concluded:

> [t]his new definition of merit places tremendous power in the hands of Deputy Heads (or their delegates) to choose which person they want to appoint. Instead of appointing the best or most qualified candidate, Deputy Heads will simply appoint a candidate of their choosing so long as they meet the essential qualifications for the job. ... The new *PSEA* states that the public service is not out to hire the best candidate, but one that is basically qualified. ... The new system may also be seen to be unfair to employees who are the most qualified for an appointment but, for whatever reason, are passed over in favour of a less qualified candidate who meets the minimum requirements of the job.[213]

---

208 *Ibid.*
209 *Ibid.*
210 *Ibid.*, s. 31.
211 *Ibid.*, s. 2. The Act continues a tradition of giving veterans a leg up over other non-veterans in external competitions. This preference does not trump the priority rules discussed below. *PSEA*, s. 39.
212 See *PSEA*, s. 33 ("In making an appointment, the Commission may use an advertised or non-advertised appointment process.").
213 Christopher Rootham, Nelligan O'Brien Payne LLP, *The Public Service Modernization Act* at 11.

Generally, an unsuccessful candidate in an internal appointment process may appeal an appointment made by the commission to a specialized quasi-judicial body, the Public Service Staffing Tribunal, on the ground of "abuse of authority."[214] The Act defines this term as including "bad faith and personal favouritism."[215]

Case law under the old *PSEA* may also be of interpretive value in understanding "abuse of authority."[216] Indeed, relying on these decisions, the Library of Parliament's analysis of the new law equates abuse of authority with the conventional administrative law concept, abuse of discretion. For instance, authority is abused where the deputy head acts with "an improper purpose in mind, which subsumes acting for an unauthorized purpose, in bad faith, or on irrelevant considerations."[217] Federal Court jurisprudence under the old *PSEA* also equates "abuse of authority" with efforts by managers to circumvent "checks and safeguards" associated with the merit principle.[218]

Tribunal proceedings constitute at least a theoretical barrier to non-meritorious appointments, including various forms of bureaucratic, political and personal nepotism. There are, however, important and explicit modifications to the regular merit rule specified by the *PSEA*.[219] Several raise few issues for this book. For instance, deputy heads may appoint "surplus" employees slated for layoff ahead of all other persons, if the Public Service Commission is persuaded that the employee meets the essential qualifications of the job and the appointment is in the interest of the public service. Similarly, persons on leaves of absence have a staffing priority on their return, as do persons actually laid off from the public service.

---

214 *PSEA*, s. 77. The Act gives no such right to persons hired via an external appointment process.

215 *PSEA*, s. 2.

216 In that statute, abuse of authority served as a ground for challenging deployment of public servants between positions in the civil service. See R.S.C. 1985, c. P-33, s. 34.3.

217 Library of Parliament, *Bill C-25: The Public Service Modernization Act*, 13 March 2004, citing *Tucci v. Attorney General of Canada* (1997), 126 F.T.R. 147 at para. 8 (T.D.) defining abuse of authority in a case concerning a complaint against the deployment of a public servant in keeping with standard administrative law abuse of discretion concepts, as they then were.

218 *Laidlaw v. Canada (Attorney General)* (1999), 166 F.T.R. 217 at para. 28 (T.D.) "since the authority to make deployments is not subject to the checks which apply to other staffing arrangements within the public service (for example, the application of the merit principle) ..., the use of deployment to circumvent those checks and safeguards is an abuse of authority."

219 *PSEA*, s. 38.

A more controversial deviation from the regular merit rule relates to high-level political staff. These staff have primacy in public service appointments above all other persons and all priority groups, except surplus employees and employees on leaves of absence. Political staff come in two categories. First, "[p]riority for appointment over all other persons shall be given to a person employed in the office of a minister, or in the office of a person holding the recognized position of Leader of the Opposition in the Senate or Leader of the Opposition in the House of Commons, for a period of one year after the person ceases to be so employed," at least so long as the commission has concluded in the past via an external appointment process that the person possesses "the essential qualifications for an appointment to the public service."[220]

Second, "[p]riority for appointment, to a position at a level at least equivalent to that of executive assistant to a deputy head, shall be given over all other persons to a person who for at least three years has been employed as the executive assistant, special assistant or private secretary in" these same political offices.[221] The *PSEA* includes no caveat that these second sorts of individual have been found by the commission suitable for the public service. That being said, the commission must agree that all priority groups — including political staff — meet the essential qualifications for the public service position at issue.[222]

Priority groups receive a second benefit: an appeal to the Public Service Staffing Tribunal may not be brought where the successful candidate was selected by virtue of one of the several priority rules discussed above.[223] As a result, the appointment of former ministerial staff is not subject to review by the tribunal. Even if it was, a successful appeal would not mean that the complaining individual would obtain a job: while the tribunal may order the commission not to proceed with an impugned appointment or to revoke that appointment, it may not order the commission to hire a person or repeat the hiring process.[224]

In sum, high-level political staff receive a privileged *entrée* into the public service predicated, not on a simple merit-based competition, but on past employment as a staff member; a past employment that itself stems from a partisan selection process. It is true that the Act requires these candidates to meet the essential qualifications for the job. But because these political

---

220 *Ibid.*, s. 41.
221 *Ibid.*, s. 41.
222 *Ibid.*, s. 41.
223 *Ibid.*, ss. 77 and 87.
224 *Ibid.*, ss. 81 and 82.

staff are given priority over most other equally (or more) qualified applicants and their appointments may not be challenged before the Tribunal for abuse of authority, the Act creates a form of structural political favouritism: political staff will likely be partisans of their party.

In its assessment of the new law, the Public Service Commission itself was wary of political priorities, noting: "[b]ecause the priority is a right acquired by the individual, the PSC can find itself faced with making an appointment that could be perceived as impairing the political impartiality of the public service. This could be the case, for example, where such a priority candidate is being considered for a strategic position in the same department where he or she was engaged by the former Minister."[225]

Accordingly, the commission asked parliamentarians that it be given "the discretion not to proceed with the appointment of a member of a Minister's staff to a specific position where it considers that this appointment could be perceived as impairing the political impartiality of the public service."[226] No such language appears, however, in the final Act, an unfortunate oversight in our view.

Still, other provisions in the new statute potentially reduce the peril of a truly politicized job placement process. In this regard, the commission itself may review appointments made to the public service, and has substantial powers to revoke these hirings.[227] Not least, "[i]f it has reason to believe that an appointment or proposed appointment was not free from political influence, the Commission may investigate the appointment process and, if it is satisfied that the appointment or proposed appointment was not free from political influence, the Commission may ... revoke the appointment or not make the appointment, as the case may be; and ... take any corrective action that it considers appropriate."[228]

Notably, an employee hired via an internal appointment process whose appointment has been revoked by the commission generally has a right to appeal to the Public Service Staffing Tribunal on the grounds that the rev-

---

225 Public Service Commission of Canada, *Submission to the Standing Committee on National Finance of the Senate of Canada Studying Bill C-25*, 18 June 2003. The equivalent recommendation made to the Commons is worded slightly differently: "Notwithstanding the priority given to the appointment of staff of Ministers, the PSC should have discretion not to proceed with a specific appointment where it considers that the appointment could be perceived as impairing the political impartiality of the Public Service." Public Service Commission of Canada, Submission to the Standing Committee on Government Operations and Estimates Studying Bill C-25, 19 March 2003.

226 *Ibid.*

227 *PSEA*, s. 66 et seq.

228 *Ibid.*, s. 68.

ocation was unreasonable.[229] This appeal right does not, however, extend to commission revocations motivated by a finding of political influence in the hiring process.[230] In other words, on this issue, the commission's conclusions are final, though obviously subject to conventional administrative law judicial review.

It is not immediately clear how these political influences and the priority staffing provisions in the *PSEA* should be read together. As the Public Service Commission obviously fears, prioritizing political staff in the hiring process incorporates a *prima facie* political dimension into the public service appointment process. Thus, the (new) political influence section must be intended to guard against something other than preferences in the selection of ministerial-level staffers. One logical interpretation is that the political influence provision bars informal preferences provided by deputy heads to non-ministerial level political staff. Another possibility is that the new political influence rules preclude deputy heads from *creating* (as opposed to simply staffing) positions to accommodate ministerial-level political staff.

b)   Dismissal

The tenure and dismissal of a public servant are subject to a number of considerations, not least whether the employment is for a term or an "indeterminate" period of time and whether the employee is a member of a public service union and thus a beneficiary of a collective agreement. In this book, we do not examine fully the complicated labour and employment law issues raised by public servant dismissals. Instead, we flag here some of the protections that preclude public servants dismissals motivated by political considerations: dismissal for partisan political activity and dismissal for public criticism of government conduct or policies.

Dismissal for Overt Political Activity

Public servants are expected to be apolitical. Indeed, it is a constitutional convention — "central to the principle of responsible government" — that civil servants are politically neutral.[231] For some time, therefore, special statutory rules have precluded public servants from undertaking partisan activities, and impose discipline up to dismissal where these laws are ignored.

---

229   *Ibid.*, s. 74.
230   *Ibid.*, s. 77 ("The Tribunal may not consider an allegation ... that an appointment or proposed appointment was not free from political influence."); s. 74 (not listing Commission decisions concerning political influence in the hiring process among the appeals that may be brought).
231   *Osborne v. Canada (Treasury Board)*, [1991] 2 S.C.R. 69 at para. 31, *per* Sopinka J.

At the same time, public servants need not all be politically inert. Clearly, public servants, like other Canadians, have a *Charter*-protected right to vote.[232] Further, they have rights to other forms of political participation. Thus, in *Osborne v. Canada (Treasury Board)*,[233] at issue was the constitutional propriety of certain provisions of the then-*Public Sector Employment Act* relating to public service politicking. These sections purported to prohibit public servants from "engaging in work" for or against a candidate or a political party. As interpreted by the Supreme Court, the "impugned legislation bans all partisan-related work by all public servants, without distinction either as to the type of work, or as to their relative role, level or importance in the hierarchy of the public servant."[234] In other words, the prohibition was sweeping.

Not surprisingly, the Supreme Court concluded that this proscription violated the freedom of expression guarantees in section 2 of the *Charter*. Moreover, because of its broad scope, it was not saved by section 1 of the *Charter*. In the words of the majority of the Court: "[t]he restrictions on freedom of expression in this case are over-inclusive and go beyond what is necessary to achieve the objective of an impartial and loyal civil service."[235]

The new *PSEA* responds to *Osborne* by distinguishing between types of public servants and, for most of them, allowing some political involvement. The Act defines "political activity" broadly, as "carrying on any activity in support of, within or in opposition to a political party; ... carrying on any activity in support of or in opposition to a candidate before or during an election period; or ... seeking nomination as or being a candidate in an election before or during the election period."[236] It then specifies the sorts of political activity in which public servants may engage.

The strictest rules are reserved for the senior government mandarins. Deputy heads — typically, deputy ministers — must "not engage in any political activity other than voting in an election."[237] Unlike the old law, this new provision appears to preclude even political donations or attendance at political meetings by deputy heads.[238]

In comparison, the Act opens the door to reasonable political involvement by more junior officials. Thus, other public servants are entitled to

232 *Charter*, s. 3.
233 *Osborne*, [1991] 2 S.C.R. 69.
234 *Ibid.* at para. 64.
235 *Ibid.* at para. 65.
236 *PSEA*, s. 111.
237 *Ibid.*, s. 117.
238 See R.S.C., 1985, c. P-33, subs. 33(2).

participate in a political activity "so long as it does not impair, or is not per-ceived as impairing, the employee's ability to perform his or her duties in a politically impartial manner."[239] This test requires a much more nuanced assessment than existed under the law challenged in *Osborne*.

The role of policing public-servant politicking is assigned to the Public Service Commission. For one thing, a public servant contemplating run-ning for federal, provincial or territorial office must apply to the Public Ser-vice Commission for permission and a leave of absence. That permission and leave will be granted by the commission only if it is satisfied that the employee's ability to perform his or her duties in "a politically impartial manner" will not be "impaired or perceived to be impaired."[240]

In addition, the commission will respond to, and investigate, com-plaints concerning contravention of the public-servant political-activity pro-visions. In the case of deputy heads, the commission may report its findings to the Governor-in-Council, which may then dismiss "during pleasure" appointees.[241] In the case of other public servants, the commis-sion itself may discipline — and terminate — the employee for violation of the political activity rules.[242]

Some public service watchers have criticized these new rules as too permissive of civil service politicking. In 2003, legendary former clerk of the Privy Council Gordon Robertson reportedly called the new law a "seri-ous mistake" and "completely in conflict with the basic principle of neutral-ity, which has been the basic principle of the public service."[243] Mr. Robertson's comments, however, reflect a no longer legally tenable posi-tion. In *Osborne*, the Supreme Court clearly tempered the basic principle of public service neutrality. Admittedly, difficult issues will arise under the new law, as they did under existing practices when a federal official in the Heritage Department was fired for accepting the presidency of a Quebec sovereignty group.[244] However, in the present legal context, the new rules strike a reasonable balance between the rights of public servants to have a

---

239   *PSEA*, s. 113. On the recommendation of the commission, the Governor-in-Council may make regulations specifying political activities that are deemed to impair the political impartiality of an employee.

240   *Ibid.*, s. 114. Similar, but slightly different, rules apply in relation to municipal elections.

241   *Ibid.*, s. 119.

242   *Ibid.*, s. 118.

243   Bill Curry, "Letting Public Servants Become Politically Active a 'Mistake': Former Advi-sor to PMs," *National Post*, 5 March 2003, A7.

244   Vito Pilieci, "Canadian Heritage Fires Bureaucrat Who Heads Quebec Sovereignty Group," *Ottawa Citizen*, 30 April 2004, A2.

voice in the political process, and the need to preserve the neutrality of the civil service.

Dismissal for Disclosure of Wrongdoing

Until amendments to the *Financial Administration Act* found in the *Public Service Modernization Act* come into force, public servants may be dismissed or otherwise penalized for misconduct pursuant to policies established by the Treasury Board,[245] a committee of Cabinet. Disciplinary action against public servants under these policies must be "for cause."[246] When the *Financial Administration Act* changes are brought into force, deputy heads will make disciplinary and termination policy, although such actions must still only be taken for cause.[247] The Public Service Labour Relations Board will hear appeals and subsequent adjudications of grievances in respect to discipline in the new system.[248]

From this discussion, it is clear that public servant termination generally hinges on the concept of cause. Public servants are therefore insulated from arbitrary dismissals. Precisely what constitutes legitimate cause obviously varies on a case-by-case basis. Here, we focus only on the circumstances in which a public servant may be penalized for publicly opposing government policy or disclosing government misdeeds.

Disclosure of Wrongdoing at Common Law

As a starting point, public servants owe a duty of loyalty to the government. This duty obliges the employee to treat his or her "employer with good faith and fidelity and to not deliberately do something which may harm his [or her] employer's business."[249] A public servant, the Federal Court has held, "is required to exercise a degree of restraint in his or her actions relating to criticism of Government policy, in order to ensure that the public service is perceived as impartial and effective in fulfilling its duties."[250] Indeed, public servants are obliged to swear an oath upon taking up their position: "I

---

245 See *Financial Administration Act*, R.S.C. 1985, c. F-10, paras. 11(2)(f) and (g); Treasury Board, *Treasury Board Guidelines for Discipline* (07/2002).
246 *Financial Administration Act*, subs. 11(4). At the time of this writing, and subject to any relevant collective agreements, Treasury Board guidelines specify that "disciplinary termination" may only be made "after a series of acts of misconduct when a 'culminating incident' has been reached or for a single act of serious misconduct." Discipline is to be administered only after a "fair and objective investigation." Treasury Board, *Treasury Board Guidelines for Discipline*.
247 *Public Service Modernization Act*, s. 8.
248 *Public Service Labour Relations Act*, S.C. 2003, c. 22, s. 2 at s. 209.
249 *Haydon v. Canada (Treasury Board)*, 2004 FC 749 at para. 43.
250 *Ibid.*

will faithfully and honestly fulfill the duties that devolve on me by reason of my employment in the public service of Canada and that I will not, without due authority, disclose or make known any matter that comes to my knowledge by reason of such employment."[251]

However, this duty of loyalty is not absolute. In *Fraser v. Canada*, at issue were certain rather vehement public statements made by a public servant concerning implementation of the metric system, amongst other things. This public servant was ultimately dismissed, prompting a lawsuit that reached the Supreme Court of Canada. That Court concluded that while a public servant "must not engage ... in sustained and highly visible attacks on major Government policies,"[252] this restriction was not absolute. A public servant may speak out without impairing his or her duty of loyalty if the government "engaged in illegal acts, or if its policies jeopardized the life, health or safety of the public servant or others, or if the public servant's criticism had no impact on his or her ability to perform effectively the duties of a public servant or on the public perception of that ability."[253]

Fraser was not decided on *Charter* grounds. Since 1982, freedom of speech has been guaranteed by section 2 of the *Charter*, subject to a section 1 limitation. These developments add constitutional muscle to the *Fraser* exceptions. Thus, in *Haydon v. Canada*,[254] two Health Canada drug evaluators — Doctors Haydon and Chopra — raised serious health concerns relating to bovine growth hormones, then being considered for approval in Canada. Concluding that their alarm had not been addressed properly internally, the drug evaluators went public, appearing in the media. Amongst other things, they complained that Health Canada was not listening to their worries, and indeed was responding to political rather than health imperatives in its drug approval process. Both employees were reprimanded and grieved the reprimand in a complaint that ended up in Federal Court. At issue was the constitutional validity of the duty of loyalty used by the government to justify the penalties imposed on the scientists.

In holding for the public servants, the Federal Court concluded that the free speech rights of the scientists were impaired by this duty of loyalty. This constraint on free speech was saved by section 1 of the *Charter*, but only to the extent "necessary to achieve the objective of an impartial and effective public service."[255] To meet this requirement, the court concluded

---

251 *PSEA*, s. 54.
252 *Fraser v. Canada (Public Service Staff Relations Board)*, [1985] 2 S.C.R. 455 at para. 41.
253 *Ibid.* at para. 41. See also *Haydon*, 2004 FC 749 at para. 45.
254 *Haydon v. Canada*, [2001] 2 F.C. 82 (F.C.T.D.).
255 *Ibid.* at para. 86.

that the duty of loyalty must include the important exceptions set out in *Fraser*. On the facts of the case, the Federal Court held that "public statements made by the Applicants expose[d] their frustration, however, they disclose[d] a legitimate public concern with respect to the efficacy of the drug approval process within the Bureau of Veterinary Drugs."[256] Health Canada, in the court's view, had failed to apply properly the *Fraser* considerations in levelling discipline on the two scientists.

Read together, *Fraser* and *Haydon* create a constitutionalized common law whistleblower defence for public servants. Indeed, Dr. Chopra relied on this defence successfully in a second case to grieve discipline imposed on him by virtue of statements he made in a public forum concerning racism at Health Canada.[257]

The defence is not, however, open-ended, as Dr. Haydon discovered in her second run-in with Health Canada. This recent case concerned Dr. Haydon's views on trade measures imposed on Brazilian beef by Canada in the wake of a mad cow scare. Dr. Haydon reportedly told the *Globe and Mail* in 2001 that the trade measures were motivated by political considerations, and not public health. She was disciplined by Health Canada, prompting a grievance that again ended up before the Federal Court.

Like its predecessor, the court agreed that "a balance must be struck between the employee's freedom of expression and the Government's desire to maintain an impartial and effective public service."[258] It held that assessing whether the duty of loyalty has been breached requires consideration of several variables. These are:

> the working level of the employee within the Government hierarchy; the nature and content of the expression; the visibility of the expression; the sensitivity of the issue discussed; the truth of the statement made; the steps taken by the employee to determine the facts before speaking; the efforts made by the employee to raise his or her concerns with the employer; the extent to which the employer's reputation was damaged; and the impact on the employer's ability to conduct business.[259]

---

256 *Ibid.* at para. 120.

257 *Re Treasury Board (Health Canada) and Chopra* (2001), 96 L.A.C. (4th) 367 at para. 78 (Public Service Staff Relations Board) ("Like other individuals living in Canada, public servants are entitled to hold opinions and to express them publicly within certain limits. They have the right to express themselves publicly on issues such as, for instance, employment equity, equality before the law and the right to protection of the law without discrimination based on race, national or ethnic origin and colour.").

258 *Haydon*, [2004] F.C. 749 at para. 45.

259 *Ibid.* at para. 49.

After reviewing these variables, the court concluded that Dr. Haydon's suspension was warranted. In the court's view, Dr. Haydon's reported statements did not "involve public interest issues of the same order as in" her prior case. Moreover, they did not "address pressing issues such as jeopardy to public health and safety (or Government illegality)." Dr. Haydon, the court ruled, "did not check her facts or address her concerns internally before she spoke to the *Globe and Mail*." Finally, "[i]t also appears that her statements were not accurate."[260] For all these reasons, Dr. Haydon was not protected by the *Fraser* exception to the duty of loyalty.[261]

These cases establish that public servants are entitled to oppose publicly government policies as a matter of mixed common law/constitutional law. They may only do so, however, in narrow circumstances involving pressing circumstances, and only when it is reasonable to go public, given the inadequacy of internal procedures. If these requirements, and the others listed above, are not met, an employee's public opposition to the government may be a legitimate cause for discipline, including termination.

The power of the employer eventually to circumvent these whistleblower protections should not be underestimated. In 2004, Health Canada fired Doctors Chopra and Haydon, and a third scientist for "insubordination."[262] The scientists, all of whom had complained of Health Canada's approach to the bovine growth hormone, condemned the move as delayed retaliation, prompting a denial from the prime minister himself.[263] Whether a labour tribunal will be persuaded that these firings were motivated by an attenuated grudge on the part of Health Canada — and thus violate the common law whistleblowing standard — remains to be seen.

Whistleblowing Law and Policy

While the common law establishes basic protections for public servant whistleblowers, it provides little precise guidance to public servants con-

---

260 *Ibid.* at para. 69.

261 At the time of this writing, this decision was being appealed to the Federal Court of Appeal. See also *Stenhouse v. Canada (Attorney General)*, 2004 FC 375 at para. 39, involving the release of confidential documents by a subsequently disciplined RCMP officer in which the court held that "[w]hile the freedom of public servants and, in the present case, members of the RCMP, to speak out is protected in common law and by the *Charter*, the 'whistle-blowing' defence must be used responsibly. It is not a licence for disgruntled employees to breach their common law duty of loyalty or their oath of secrecy. ... The documents [at issue] do not disclose either an illegal act by the RCMP or a practice or policy which endangers the life, health or safety of the public."

262 Bill Curry, "Whistleblowing Not the Reason for Firings," *Ottawa Citizen*, 16 Aug. 2004, A3.

263 Bill Curry, "Scientists Demand Reasons for Firings," *Ottawa Citizen*, 19 Aug. 2004, A5.

templating disclosure of government wrongdoing and perhaps insufficient protection against retaliation. Legislation is required to remedy this uncertainty.

While protection of sorts is extended by statute to some specialized government officials,[264] there was no general federal whistleblower statute by December 2004. The Martin government promised to correct this omission and in fact introduced the first-ever government whistleblower bill in the House of Commons in March 2004. This legislation — roundly condemned as inadequate — died on the order paper when Parliament was dissolved for the 2004 election. A new, and amended, law project was introduced into the thirty-eighth Parliament in October 2004 and remained in committee in the Commons by the time this book went to press in February 2005.

The original bill was introduced not long after the sponsorship scandal, and was touted by the government as part of the Martin team's "broader commitment to ensure transparency, accountability, financial responsibility and ethical conduct."[265] It followed several years of internal government mulling over the issue. Specifically, in 1996, the Task Force on Public Service Values and Ethics recommended, in its "Tait Report," the development of a public service code that included a disclosure rule allowing employees to raise concerns about actions viewed as "potentially illegal, unethical or inconsistent with the public service values."[266]

Subsequently, in 2001, Treasury Board introduced a whistleblower policy — the Internal Disclosure Policy.[267] This policy remained in force at the time of this writing. In keeping with the common law standard, the Policy emphasizes that "[p]ublic servants owe a duty of loyalty to their employer." At the same time, "when an employee has reasonable grounds to believe that another person has committed a wrongdoing in the workplace, he/she should be able to disclose this information through clearly defined processes with confidence that he/she will be treated fairly and protected from reprisal."

The policy obliges deputy heads to task a senior officer with receiving information about alleged workplace wrongdoing. Wrongdoing is defined

---

264 See, e.g., *Security of Information Act*, R.S.C 1985, c. O-5, s. 15, as it pertains to members of the security and intelligence community.

265 Office of the Prime Minister, *News Release: Disclosure protection legislation introduced*, 22 March 2004.

266 *Strong Foundation: Report of the Task Force on Public Service Values and Ethics* (1996) at 44.

267 Treasury Board of Canada, *Policy on the Internal Disclosure of Information Concerning Wrongdoing in the Workplace* (07/04).

as: a violation of any law or regulation; a breach of the *Values and Ethics Code for the Public Service* (discussed in chapter 7); misuse of public funds or assets; gross mismanagement; or a substantial and specific danger to the life, health and safety of Canadians or the environment.

The policy also creates the position of public service integrity officer, a government-wide official to whom employees may turn if they feel their concerns have not been addressed adequately through the departmental process. The officer — acting as a "neutral entity" — has a number of responsibilities. One of his or her tasks is to "protect from reprisal employees who disclose information concerning wrongdoing in good faith." In this regard, the policy indicates that employees and managers may be subject to discipline if they "retaliate against another employee who has made a disclosure in accordance with this policy or against an employee who was called as a witness." At the same time, whistleblowers may also be disciplined if they "choose to disclose in a manner that does not conform to this policy and its procedural requirements."

The Public Service Integrity Office (PSIO) began operations in 2002. As Table 4.4 suggests, in its first year, the office received essentially no substantiated complaints of wrongdoing.[268]

Table 4.4   Public Service Integrity Office, 2002

Case/Resolution[269]	Number
Number of cases received	105
Number of cases received within mandate	87
Files closed after preliminary review	20
Files referred to a more appropriate recourse authority	47
Remaining files in which no wrongdoing was found	8
Remaining files found to be outside the office's jurisdiction	7
Cases remaining under investigation on March 31, 2003	5

In its annual report and accompanying summary, the PSIO arrived at a series of damning conclusions about its role and effectiveness. In its view,

[t]he past year and more has demonstrated that in its present form and context, and with its current mandate and tools, the PSIO does not have suffi-

---

268 See Public Service Integrity Office, *2002–2003 Annual Report to Parliament*. In one case, the office did make a finding that an employee had been disciplined in retaliation for disclosure.

269 Public Service Integrity Office, *Highlights from the 2002–2003 Annual Report to Parliament*.

cient support and confidence of the public sector employees for whom it was established. ... Despite considerable efforts to show that this Office is functionally independent in the investigation and disposition of cases, and despite a degree of success in the cases it has taken on, skepticism persists. The skepticism is not unreasonable and can be expected to persist.

As a consequence, the office recommended the introduction of a legislative framework governing its operations, one that would provide greater structural independence to the PSIO:

> Such legislation should remove this Office or successor agency from the ambit of the Treasury Board, the employer of at least the "core" public servants. This Office or a successor agency would thereby also be removed from the human resource, employment and management context. ... The head of this Office or successor agency should be appointed or approved by Parliament. The Office or agency should report to Parliament. Also, while its operations and expenditures should be overseen by a designated Parliamentary committee, it should remain at arm's-length regarding the investigation and disposition of cases.

The PSIO also recommended that its successor be endowed with substantial new powers:

> Rather than simply make recommendations, this Office or successor agency should be able to make orders or enforceable recommendations. Such recommendations would be enforced by the agency or by another related and legally designated stage in the process. ... This Office or successor agency should be able to receive and investigate allegations of wrongdoing in the public sector regardless of the source of the allegation. It should be able to extend protection from reprisal accordingly. Such sources could include private citizens, advocacy groups or Public Service unions.

Public service employees — more broadly defined to also include employees of Crown corporations — should have "direct access to this Office or successor agency without first being required to exhaust departmental mechanisms."

The Auditor General reviewed the office's conclusions in her 2003 report and recommended that the government "give serious consideration to the PSIO report recommendations, including that the PSIO should be based on legislation rather than policy."[270]

---

270 "Accountability and Ethics in Government," 2003 *Report of the Auditor General of Canada*, c. 2 at 2.71.

Subsequently, Treasury Board formed a working group on whistleblowing and parliamentarians took up the issue in the Commons Standing Committee on Operations and Estimates. Both the Working Group[271] and the Standing Committee[272] recommended that disclosure policies and protection against retaliation be codified in legislation.

The result was Bill C-25, the *Public Servants Disclosure Protection Act*, introduced at the end of the thirty-seventh Parliament. Had it been enacted, the bill would have created a legislated "Public Service Integrity Commissioner" and codified disclosure rules. Nevertheless, the public service integrity officer at the time of this writing — Mr. Edward Keyserlingk — was scathing in his assessment of the bill, calling it "disappointingly and surprisingly deficient."[272] After Bill C-25 died on the order paper, the government reintroduced the law in the thirty-eighth Parliament as Bill C-11.

The new bill revised its predecessor. Nevertheless, the PSIO described the proposed law as a:

> second-best compromise, a compilation of approaches and elements from other jurisdictions where they have already proven to be inadequate. It will remain an initiative that will not inspire sufficient confidence in those it is designed for but may produce quite the opposite. Left as it is, it will tend to engender perceptions of conflict of interest and will make it difficult at best to convince public servants that the process will be impartial, uncomplicated, expeditious and protective.[274]

Mr. Keyserlingk was particularly concerned that the office to which whistleblower complaints would be directed under the bill — the Public Service Commission — would not be sufficiently independent of the executive branch of government. A better approach, in his view, would the creation of a new officer of Parliament post. As this book went to press in February 2005, it remained to be seen whether Parliament would respond to this or other recommendations strengthening the law.

---

271   *Report of the Working Group on the Disclosure of Wrongdoing* (January 2004).

272   Standing Committee on Government Operations and Estimates, *13th Report: Study of the Disclosure of Wrongdoing (Whistleblowing)* (Nov. 2003).

273   Edward W. Keyserlingk, Public Service Integrity Officer, *Submission to the House Standing Committee on Government Operations and Estimates on Bill C-25, the Public Servants Disclosure Protection Act* (April 2004).

274   Public Service Integrity Officer, *Appearance of the Public Service Integrity Officer before the House Standing Committee on Government Operations and Estimates on Bill C-11, The Public Servants Disclosure Protection Act* (30 Nov. 2004).

c) Conclusion

In sum total, appointment and dismissal decisions in relation to the public service are reasonably insulated from the political branches of government. A bureaucratic commission makes appointments, not the political branches, and selections are typically made with reference to the merit principle, not political considerations. Canadian law makes certain questionable exceptions to this rule for high-level political staff. However, while problematic in its own right, the number of people able to take advantage of this lacuna is vanishingly small in relative terms. The political staff priority rule is not, therefore, a true Trojan horse for politicizing the public service.

Dismissals for political reasons, meanwhile, are greatly constrained, first, by recognition that some political activity by public servants is compatible with their functions. Public servants preferring an opposition party or candidate need not, in other words, fear for their jobs. Second, the law governing the federal public service requires that discipline — including terminations — meted out to public servants must be for "cause." Supreme and Federal Court jurisprudence, Treasury Board policies and potentially new federal legislation recognize that public opposition to government policies by public servants does not necessarily constitute this cause. Drawing the line between the duty of loyalty and the public servant's free expression right — and the broader public interest — in whistleblowing will remain a difficult issue.

Nevertheless, the current legal standards discussed in this section are refined enough to support an overall conclusion: the government's political branches are simply not in a position to graft their political ideologies onto the public service through the appointments and dismissal process.

4. Nonjudicial Governor-in-Council Appointees

The Governor-in-Council (GIC) — the Governor General acting on the advice of Cabinet — appoints approximately 500 full-time and 1,900 part-time nonjudicial officials to approximately 170 federal agencies, boards, commissions and Crown corporations.[275] These positions include deputy ministers, heads of agencies, members of quasi-judicial tribunals, and CEOs and directors of Crown corporations. The responsibilities of these appointees obviously vary, ranging "from making quasi-judicial decisions and socio-economic develop-

---

275 Public Policy Forum, *Governor-in-Council Appointments: Best Practices and Recommendations for Reform* (Feb. 2004) at 5 and 9.

ment recommendations to the management of large, diversified corporations."[276] Cabinet also appoints approximately 100 heads of foreign missions at the Ambassador or High Commissioner levels.[277]

Whereas diplomatic appointments are made pursuant to royal prerogative powers, most GIC appointments are authorized by statute. As a consequence, the precise type, terms and tenure of these appointments vary. Here, we simply undertake a high-level overview of the GIC appointment process and relevant law. We also note at the outset that some GIC appointees will be drawn from the ranks of the public service. The comments we make in this section pertain to their appointment to, tenure in and dismissal from GIC appointed–positions, not their employment in the public service more generally.

a) Appointment

Overview

The appointment process is governed by policy, not regimented by law in a fashion analogous to the public service. In theory (though apparently not always in practice), GIC appointments to a statutory body are made on the advice of the responsible minister for the statute in question.[278] In most instances, there is no formal requirement that this minister or Cabinet as a whole undertake consultations prior to making appointments. Several entities may be involved, however, in the selection process.

It may be, for instance, that the head of the agency or Crown corporation to which the candidate will be appointed will advise the minister on the organization's needs, and the skill set that an appointee should possess. In devising recommendations on appointments, the minister will also work with (and indeed sometimes play a less important role than) the Office of the Director of Appointments in the Prime Minister's Office.

This director of appointments provides "political advice to the Prime Minister on appointments" and is tasked with ensuring "that appointments take into account Canada's diversity and meet the needs of the organization

---

276 Privy Council Office, *A Guide Book for Heads of Agency* (1999).

277 *Ibid.*

278 The discussion that follows summarizes the Public Policy Forum, *Governor-in-Council Appointments*, and Privy Council Office, *A Guide Book for Heads of Agency*, review of the appointment process. Note, however, that the actual appointment process sometimes deviates from this policy. Indeed, appointments are sometimes made via so-called "walkabouts" where a handful of Ministers approve an appointment on an urgent basis. For another resource, see the excellent summary of the process found in Penny Collenette, "So you want an Order-in-Council Appointment?" 1 *Administrative Agency Practice* No. 5 at 103 (November 1995).

to which they are being made."[279] Jean Chrétien's director of appointments reportedly told journalists in 2000 that "the first principle of hiring is merit" but "we have always believed that previous service to Canada as a member of a political party — or as an MP — should not disqualify one from being appointed."[280] Finally, it is understood — though not officially documented — that regional ministers play a role in conveying their regional priorities.

As a matter of "government practice" most full-time, fixed-term positions are advertised in the *Canada Gazette*, with the "Director of Appointments in the Prime Minister's Office and the responsible Minister consult[ing] as to whether there is a need to advertise in the *Canada Gazette* to fill a vacancy."[281] The minister, the relevant agency and the director prepare the notice of vacancy, the job description, and the selection criteria. On receipt of applications, applicants' qualifications and experience are "evaluated against the requirements of the position."[282]

Privy Council and ministerial department officials handle legal and technical aspects of the hiring process, including the drafting of the appointing order-in-council. Subsequently, the Office of the Ethics Commissioner contacts "all full-time appointees" to "ensure compliance" with the *Conflict of Interest and Post-Employment Code for Public Office Holders*. Part-time appointees, although not bound by the code, are asked to comply with "the spirit and principles of the Code."[283] This code, and ethics generally, are discussed in greater detail in chapter 7.

Once the appointment is made, the appointing order-in-council is tabled in the Commons. The Standing Orders of the House empower Commons standing committees to review all nonjudicial appointments. The committee seized of the matter may call the appointee as a witness. It may then examine his or her qualifications: "[t]he committee, if it should call an appointee or nominee to appear ... shall examine the qualifications and competence of the appointee or nominee to perform the duties of the post to which he or she has been appointed or nominated."[284] This is not, however, a confirmation process. Appointments may only be reviewed after they have been made, and standing committees may not override GIC appointments.[285] In practice, Parliament has used this reviewing power

---

279 Privy Council Office, *Guide Book*.
280 Jack Aubry, "Chrétien's 'Game of Friends,'" *Ottawa Citizen*, 21 Oct. 2000.
281 Privy Council Office, *Guide Book*.
282 *Ibid.*
283 *Ibid.*
284 House of Commons, *Standing Orders*, Order 111.
285 Privy Council Office, *Guide Book*.

infrequently, although the minority thirty-eighth Parliament was paying more attention to this matter by December 2004.

Political Favouritism

As the discussion above suggests, Cabinet possesses substantial discretion in making GIC appointments. Some appointments likely reflect no political favouritism. The elevation of public servants to GIC-appointed positions generally falls into this category. At the same time, other GIC appointments — particularly those to government corporations, commissions, boards and tribunals — are often viewed as classic patronage positions. An *Ottawa Citizen* study of appointments made in July 2000 concluded that half of those selected had governing party ties.[286] Certain bodies with GIC-appointed members may have an even higher proportion of individuals with governing party ties. To test this assertion, we reviewed the membership of one relatively prominent federal board, the National Capital Commission (NCC), as it stood in early 2004.

Thirteen "members," a vice-chairperson and a chairperson govern the NCC.[287] These "members" are appointed by the "minister," defined as the prime minister or another minister appointed by the Governor-in-Council. In practice, the appointing minister is the minister of Canadian heritage,[288] and appointments are made by order-in-council.[289] The Governor-in-Council, meanwhile, appoints the vice-chairperson and the chairperson.[290]

---

286 Aubry, "Chrétien's 'Game of Friends'"; Jack Aubry, "Eighty Appointments: About the Citizen's Investigation," *Ottawa Citizen*, 21 Oct. 2000, B2. These appointments were to nonregular public service positions, typically federal boards or commissions and some judicial appointments. More recent press reports also point to patronage in GIC appointments. See, e.g., Robert Fife, "Chrétien Cabinet Approves 50 Patronage Jobs," *National Post*, 17 Sept. 2003, A7. See also a similar October 2000 report, Jack Aubry, "Liberals Dole Out Patronage Bucks: Survey Shows Politics Rife in Appointments," *Calgary Herald*, 26 Oct. 2000, A5.

287 *National Capital Act*, R.S.C. 1985, c. N-4, s. 3.

288 Section 2 of the *National Capital Act* defines "minister" as "the Prime Minister of Canada or such other member of the Queen's Privy Council for Canada as is designated by the Governor in Council as the Minister for the purposes of this Act." Under *Order Designating the Minister of Communications as Minister for Purposes of the Act*, SI/93-230, the minister of communications is designated the minister for the purposes of the *National Capital Act*. Pursuant to s. 15 of the *Department of Canadian Heritage Act*, S.C. 1995, c. 11, the minister of Canadian heritage inherits the powers possessed, *inter alia*, by the minister of communications that fall within the scope of the subject matter assigned the minister of Canadian heritage by the *Department of Canadian Heritage Act*.

289 See NCC discussion on website at www.nationalcapitalcommission.gc.ca/corporate/aboutthencc/board_directors/index_e.asp (as of 08/04).

290 *National Capital Act*, s. 3.

Press reports suggest that the NCC is at least partially staffed on a patron-age basis.[291] We attempted to test this assertion empirically by researching the background of the fifteen individuals on the commission, relying on publicly available newspaper databases and the Elections Canada political donation database. We then classified these persons into four categories: "probable supporters" of the Liberal Party; "possible supporters" of the Liberal Party; or "probable" or "possible" supporters of opposition parties.

Probable supporters were those who are identified in the press as affil-iated with the party in a fashion that allows reasonable certainty that the person noted in the press and the person on the NCC board were one and the same (for example, geographic or biographical similarities). Alterna-tively, probable supporters had given money to a political party since 1993 in a fashion that allowed reasonable certainty that the donor and the NCC board member were one and the same (for example, the donation was made by a partnership of which the NCC board member was a partner or the name was matched in the database down to the middle initial or name).

In comparison, possible supporters were those persons whose names were both common and were reported in the Elections Canada database with-out middle initials. In those circumstances, we had a much lower confi-dence that the appointee and the donor were one and the same.

In one case, a person with a commission member's name gave money to two different political parties. Rather than double-count this person as a supporter of both the Liberal and an opposition party, we removed that commissioner from our list, treating her as politically neutral. Table 4.5 sets out our results.

Table 4.5   National Capital Commission Patronage Appointments, 2004

	Number	% (of 15)
"Probable supporter" of the Liberal Party of Canada	7	47
"Possible supporter" of the Liberal Party of Canada	5	33
"Possible supporter" of an opposition party	0	0
"Probable supporter" of an opposition party	0	0
Total	12	80

We acknowledge readily that this study is based on an imperfect methodology, given the lack of absolute certainty that the commissioner

291 Jane Taber, "Watson to Copps: Rein in the NCC: Mayor Goes to Top in Bitter Dispute with Federal Body," *Ottawa Citizen*, 28 Feb. 2000, A1.

and the donor (or person identified in the news reports) are one and the same. However, absent access to party membership lists and the full *curriculum vitae* of appointees, it is the best that may be done to measure political affiliation. These results suggest that between 47 and 80 percent of commissioners of the NCC are supporters of the governing party. This correlation is enough to suggest, in our minds, that political considerations affect NCC appointments.

We return to the issue of political favouritism in our discussion on GIC-appointment reform later.

b) Tenure and Dismissal

Generally, there are two sorts of Governor-in-Council appointments: those who hold tenure "during pleasure" and those in office on "good behaviour." Without any indication to the contrary in the governing statute or order-in-council, GIC appointments are "during pleasure." In the words of the *Interpretation Act,* "[e]very public officer appointed by or under the authority of an enactment or otherwise is deemed to have been appointed to hold office during pleasure only, unless it is otherwise expressed in the enactment, commission or instrument of appointment."[292]

Good-Behaviour Appointees

Good-behaviour appointees have a relatively robust tenure: the Governor-in-Council may remove them only "for cause."[293] In assessing whether a public officeholder "meets the standard of good behaviour necessary to remain in office," the Governor-in-Council "must examine the conduct of that individual to assess whether it is consistent with the measure of integrity the Governor-in-Council deems necessary to maintain public confidence in federal institutions and the federal appointment process."[294] In practice, this means an appointee may not be removed from office capriciously, in response to a decision made by him or her in the course of his or her duties.[295]

Moreover, the removal decision must meet the requirements of procedural fairness. Thus the official must be given sufficient notice of the pending decision and an opportunity to be heard. Procedural fairness in these

292 *Interpretation Act*, R.S.C. 1985, c. I-21, s. 23.
293 Privy Council Office, *Terms and Conditions of Employment for Full-Time Governor in Council Appointees* (2002).
294 *Wedge v. Canada (Attorney General)* (1997), 4 Admin. L.R. (3d) 153 at para. 30 (F.C.T.D.).
295 *Bell Canada v. Canadian Telephone Employees Association*, [2001] 3 F.C. 481 at para. 44 (C.A.), aff'd [2003] 1 S.C.R. 884.

circumstances does not, however, mean a full-blown trial. Thus, it does not require a full hearing, with examination and cross-examination of witnesses, and full disclosure of documents.[296]

More formal proceedings concerning dismissals of good-behaviour officers are anticipated by the *Judges Act*. Under this statute, the minister of justice may ask the Canadian Judicial Council — a body discussed in greater detail later in this chapter — to examine whether a good-behaviour appointee should be dismissed by reason of infirmity, misconduct, failing in the due execution of office, or having been placed, by his or her conduct or otherwise, in a position incompatible with the due execution of that office.[297] The Governor-in-Council, however, need not pursue this process prior to making a good-behaviour dismissal.[298]

During-Pleasure Appointees

By comparison, appointees holding office "during pleasure ... may be replaced or removed at the discretion of the Governor-in-Council."[299] Thus, the expression "during pleasure" has traditionally connoted an absolute ability to dismiss, even without cause. The federal *Interpretation Act* specifies that "[w]ords authorizing the appointment of a public officer to hold office during pleasure include, in the discretion of the authority in whom the power of appointment is vested, the power to (*a*) terminate the appointment or remove or suspend the public officer; (*b*) re-appoint or reinstate the public officer; and (*c*) appoint another person in the stead of, or to act in the stead of, the public officer."[300]

Yet, the Governor-in-Council's power of dismissal is much less absolute than might be expected from this language. First, courts will require the government to observe at least minimal procedural fairness in dismissing even during-pleasure officeholders, allowing them notice of the pending decision on dismissal and an opportunity to comment.[301]

Second, a second element of procedural fairness is the concept of an unbiased decision-maker. Notably, some GIC appointees are members of

---

296 *Weatherill v. Canada (Attorney General)*, [1999] 4 F.C. 107 at paras. 87–88 (T.D.).

297 R.S.C., 1985, c. J-1, ss. 65 and 69.

298 *Weatherill*, [1999] 4 F.C. 107 at paras. 81–83.

299 Privy Council Office, *Terms and Conditions of Employment*.

300 *Interpretation Act*, s. 24.

301 See, e.g., *Knight v. Indian Head School Division No. 19*, [1990] 1 S.C.R. 653 at para. 34, holding that "the characterization of the respondent's employment as an office held at pleasure is not incompatible with the imposition of a duty to act fairly," allowing the officer notice of the reasons for the government's dissatisfaction and affording him or her an opportunity to be heard.

"quasi-judicial" tribunals required to adjudicate disputes brought before them. Like courts themselves, quasi-judicial decision-makers generally attract very strict impartiality requirements. Over time, these common law obligations have slowly morphed. Courts now demand that some quasi-judicial bodies be sufficiently independent of the government. Thus, administrative law is now replete with a perplexing case law analyzing whether and when these bodies must be protected by judicial independence-like security of tenure.

The Supreme Court held recently that, as a general rule, administrative tribunals need not enjoy these potent tenure protections. Thus, it has expressly allowed during-pleasure appointments to quasi-judicial bodies where the legislature has so authorized. The Court has, however, carved out an exception where constitutional issues are engaged.[302] In this respect, section 7 of the *Charter* bars deprivation of life, liberty or security of the person in the absence of fundamental justice. Likewise, the *Canadian Bill of Rights* — a 1960 statute of Parliament that purports to trump all inconsistent federal laws — guarantees that no law may "deprive a person of the right to a fair hearing in accordance with the principles of fundamental justice for the determination of his rights and obligations."[303] The Supreme Court has recognized that where a body exercises power of a sort triggering these provisions, a high measure of security of tenure may be required of that organization.[304] Read together, this case law greatly constrains the capacity of the GIC to make truly during-pleasure dimissals, at least from those administrative bodies exercising powers that attract the application of the *Charter* or the *Canadian Bill of Rights*.

Third, the GIC sometimes appoints during-pleasure appointees for a fixed term. The inclusion of this set term may constrain the ability of the Governor-in-Council to dismiss these persons at its discretion. In a relatively recent Ontario Court of Appeal decision, *Hewat v. Ontario*,[305] the appellants were vice-chairs of the Ontario Labour Relations Board appointed by

---

302 See *Ocean Port Hotel Ltd. v. British Columbia (Liquor Control and Licensing Branch)*, [2001] 2 S.C.R. 781 at 783 ("While tribunals may sometimes attract *Charter* requirements of independence, as a general rule they do not" and holding that judicial independence-like concerns with "during pleasure" appointments had no place where the legislature specifically authorized such appointments and the *Charter* did not apply).

303 S.C. 1960, c. 44, subs. 2(e).

304 Thus, in *Bell Canada v. Communications, Energy and Paperworkers Union of Canada*, [2003] 1 S.C.R. 884, the Court agreed that the Canadian Human Rights Tribunal must be protected by security of tenure guarantees by virtue of the *Canadian Bill of Rights*.

305 (1998), 37 O.R. (3d) 161 (C.A.).

order-in-council for fixed terms of three years. The new Harris government revoked these appointments, without cause, by its own order-in-council prior to the expiry of the fixed terms. At issue before the Court of Appeal was whether the fact that these positions were "at pleasure" permitted this revocation. Holding that it did not, the Court concluded that "the open discretion, or the power to act at pleasure, was subordinated or exhausted by the inclusion of a fixed term in the original appointment."[306]

Hewat concerned the dismissal of quasi-judicial tribunal members. In rendering its decision, the Court of Appeal was clearly preoccupied with the impact of the Harris government's decision on the independence of the tribunal. It is uncertain, therefore, whether that court's reasoning will have relevance in other, nonquasi-judicial tribunal contexts. This very matter may, however, be adjudicated in the near future. Several of the high-profile GIC appointees dismissed by the Martin government in 2004 were during-pleasure but fixed term appointees. These persons include Mr. Jean Pelletier, former chair of VIA Rail,[307] and Mr. Marc LeFrançois, former President of VIA Rail.[308] At the time of this writing, these individuals were suing the federal government for wrongful dismissal, among other things.[309] It remained to be seen how the Quebec courts would handle these lawsuits.

c) Reform

As this discussion shows, GIC appointees are selected in a largely informal manner by a political body — Cabinet — prepared to contemplate political

---

306 *Ibid.* at 166.

307 See, e.g., P.C. 2001-1294 ("Appointment of Jean Pelletier, of Quebec, Quebec, as chairman of the board of directors of VIA Rail Canada Inc., to hold office during pleasure for a term of five years, effective September 1, 2001."). Mr. Pelletier was appointed pursuant to the *Financial Administration Act* that provides, in s. 105, "Each officer-director of a parent Crown corporation shall be appointed by the Governor in Council to hold office during pleasure for such term as the Governor in Council considers appropriate." He was also dismissed pursuant to this section, though it is silent on a dismissal power other than the reference to "during pleasure." See P.C. 2004-0158. His dismissal was attributed to a "loss of confidence" by the GIC.

308 See P.C. 2001-1293 ("Appointment of Marc LeFrançois, of Montreal, Quebec, as the President and Chief Executive Officer of VIA Rail Canada Inc., to hold office during pleasure for a term of three years, effective September 1, 2001") See also P.C. 2004-0160, terminating the appointment by reason of a "loss of confidence" in Mr. LeFrançois, stemming from "Chapter 3 of the November 2003 Report of the Auditor General, and in particular the transactions involving VIA Rail Canada Inc. described in that Report." The November 2003 report concerned Government of Canada sponsorship irregularities in Quebec.

309 "Former VIA Rail president files wrongful dismissal lawsuit," *Ottawa Citizen*, 7 April 2004, A3

considerations in making appointments. Patronage and political favouritism, in other words, is permitted by the GIC appointment system.

There is no basis to conclude that patronage always produces inept GIC appointees. We agree that meritorious candidates should not be excluded because of a governing party affiliation. However, patronage has in practice often subordinated the merit principle to political imperatives, leading to dubious selections. In 2004, the President of the Public Service Commission complained of the quality of appointees to federal agencies, commissions and boards, noting that appointees sometimes lacked the experience and background to "understand what is required of them."[310] In 2001, Auditor General Denis Desautels condemned government appointments to the boards of Crown corporations. He concluded that these appointees "reflect Canada's diversity but lack other key skills and capabilities that are needed to function effectively and to carry out their important responsibilities under the *Financial Administration Act* for the affairs of the corporation."[311] Patronage in GIC appointments may also have a corrosive effect, not only on public perceptions of the government as a whole, but also on the public service. Foreign Service officers, for instance, are reportedly deeply demoralized by patronage appointments to foreign ambassadorships.[312]

Suspect patronage appointments are particularly problematic when directed at the many federal bodies adjudicating the rights and obligations of individuals. As the government has (belatedly) acknowledged with its reforms of the Immigration and Refugee Board discussed later, nonmeritorious appointments to these entities imperil the interests of parties who appear before them. Further, through the evolution of constitutional and administrative law principles and under the express terms of many of the statutes that govern them, many of these tribunals now enjoy substantial independence from the rest of government. In these circumstances, the ultimate protection against a prior unworthy appointment — the capacity of the Governor-in-Council to dismiss the official — is constrained.

Reform of the GIC appointments process has been on the radar screen for some time. The Liberal Party's 1993 electoral platform — the "Red Book" — promised a review of boards, commissions and tribunals and pledged that competency would play a key role in appointments. In its first term, the Chrétien government did eliminate 665 GIC-appointed posi-

---

310   Kathryn May, "Patronage Puts Wrong People in Cushy Jobs," *Ottawa Citizen*, 20 Oct. 2004, A3.

311   Auditor General of Canada, *Report to the House of Commons for December 2000*, ch. 18.

312   Jack Aubry, "Patronage Postings Irritate Diplomats," *Ottawa Citizen*, 6 April 2004, A1.

tions. This move was celebrated in the media as a blow against patronage.[313] However, formal changes to the appointment process have been slow in coming.

In February 2004, the Martin government pledged a parliamentary role in at least some GIC appointments, as part of its democratic reform initiative: "The government believes that appointments to certain key positions, including heads of Crown Corporations and agencies, should be subject to prior parliamentary review. At the same time, it is essential that the appointment process does not deter qualified candidates from public office by partisan excesses during parliamentary review."[314]

Parliamentary committees were asked by the government to report on the positions lying within their mandate on which they wished to be consulted. Parliamentarians took up the matter in March 2004, at a meeting hosted by the Commons Standing Committee on Procedure and House Affairs.[315] In an open-ended, roundtable discussion, parliamentarians expressed positions both for and against parliamentary review of GIC appointments. Some worried that the number of reviews would be overwhelming, given the quantity of GIC appointees, and that parliamentarians would be ill equipped to evaluate the credentials of nominees. Others questioned a process that might involve a partisan inquisition of candidates. Still others urged that Parliament needed to participate, in order to reduce the instance of patronage. Several MPs suggested — very sensibly in our view — that the number of GIC appointees be reduced, and that more of these positions be filled pursuant to the regular public service procedure, controlled by the Public Service Commission. Parliamentarians were particularly concerned that electoral returning officers are GIC appointees, despite calls by the Chief Electoral Officer for a professionalization of this function and the appointment of persons on the basis of merit.

Exactly how this appointments issue will evolve in the thirty-eighth Parliament remained to be seen by December 2004. At the end of the thirty-seventh Parliament, there were, however, two high-profile consequences of reform discussions: changes to the Immigration and Refugee Board (IRB) member and the Crown corporation director selection processes.

---

313 Editorial, "Less Patronizing," *Ottawa Citizen*, 23 Dec. 1994, A10.

314 Privy Council Office, *Ethics, Responsibility, Accountability: An Action Plan for Democratic Reform* (4 Feb. 2004).

315 See Standing Committee on Procedure and House Affairs, *Evidence*, 37th Parl., 3d Sess. (10 March 2004); see also Standing Committee on Procedure and House Affairs, *Report 21: Democratic Reform* (26 April 2004).

The IRB — the administrative body charged with adjudicating refugee claims — has been a notorious sinecure for party favourites.[316] Under the new process, as announced by the minister of citizenship and immigration in March 2004:

- Candidates will be screened against strengthened merit-based criteria.
- Candidates' applications will be screened by an advisory panel of lawyers, academics, members of organizations that assist newcomers to Canada and human resources experts. Selected candidates will be interviewed by a selection board, chaired by the IRB chairperson and made up of experts with an in-depth understanding of the IRB and its decision-making processes.
- The final selection of appointees by the Minister will be based on the recommendations of the IRB chairperson.[317]

Also in March 2004, Treasury Board President Reg Alcock announced reforms in the appointment of Chief Executive Officers, directors and chairs of Crown corporations. The promised changes were as follows:

- A permanent nominating committee would be formed for each Crown corporation, establishing appropriate criteria for candidate selection.
- A professional recruitment firm would be engaged to assist these nominating committees in the search for meritorious candidates and public advertisements would be posted in newspapers and in the *Canada Gazette*.
- The nominating committee would make recommendations to the Board of Directors, which would them provide a short list of candidates to the minister responsible for the corporation. Based on this list, the minister would make a recommendation for appointment.

---

316 See Alexander Norris, "Liberals Load Tribunal: Refugee Claimants Face Flawed System, Critics Say," *The Montreal Gazette*, 28 April 2001, A1; Elizabeth Thompson, "Sgro Vows to Clean Up Refugee Board," *National Post*, 17 March 2004, A6. Further, the IRB was rocked in 2004 by a corruption scandal involving a (GIC-appointed) IRB adjudicator. See Kevin Dougherty, "Refugee Board Judge Among 11 Charged with Soliciting Bribes," *Montreal Gazette*, 19 March 2004, A1. The individual in question reportedly had Liberal ties. This scandal no doubt contributed to the reform initiative. Andrew McIntosh, "IRB Overhaul Put on Fast Track," *Montreal Gazette*, 16 Dec. 2003, A13; Bruce Campion-Smith, "Bribe Scandal Rocks Immigration Board: Liberal Appointee at Centre of Probe," *Toronto Star*, 19 March 2004, A1. See also James Bissett, "Scrap the Refugee Board," *National Post*, 30 March 2004, A14.

317 Immigration and Citizenship Canada, "Minister Sgro Announces Reform of the Appointment Process For Immigration And Refugee Board Members," press release, 16 March 2004.

- The appropriate parliamentary committee would then review the candidate recommended by the minister.[318]

Related measures were proposed in a February 2005 Treasury Board follow-up report.[320]

By early 2005, the effectiveness of these reforms remained to be determined. Notably, however, the Martin government circumvented the new Crown corporation procedure in 2004 in naming the new CEO of Canada Post without the requisite advertisement or pre-appointment parliamentary review.[321] The Commons Standing Committee on Government Operations and Estimates responded with a report critical of the government and calling for further reforms to the Crown corporation appointment process.[321]

All told, three quick fixes to GIC appointments appear to be in order. First, the IRB-appointment reforms prioritizing merit and involving third-party vetting of candidates announced by the government in 2004 should be extended to appointments to all federal boards, commissions and tribunals. This, in effect, is what the Public Policy Forum recommended in its authoritative review of GIC appointments: "To reduce concerns about politicization of the appointment process and to increase transparency and accountability, the government should establish an independent advisory committee that will act as a central clearinghouse for appointment recommendations to the prime minister and the responsible ministers."[322] As a related and equally sensible requirement, "[c]urrent boards should be tasked to produce profiles that specify the skills and competencies required to fulfill their mandates. These board profiles should include the skills and competencies of the current board, those required to complement the existing board and those needed in the future."[323]

Second, more GIC appointments — not least those in the diplomatic service and those of electoral returning officers — should be converted into public service positions, governed by the *Public Service Employment Act.*

---

318 Treasury Board, "President of the Treasury Board Announces New Appointment Process for Top Executives of Crown Corporations," press release, 15 March 2004.

319 Treasury Board, *Review of the Governance Framework for Canada's Crown Corporations — Meeting the Expectations of Canadians* (2005) at 30–32.

320 Gloria Galloway, "Liberals Bent Rules to Appoint Mail CEO," *Globe and Mail*, 2 Oct. 2004, A1.

321 Standing Committee on Government Operations and Estimates, *Report 3 - Examination of the appointment process for top executives, including members of the Board, of Crown Corporations, Agencies and Foundations* (presented in the House, 20 Dec. 2004).

322 Public Policy Forum, *Governor-in-Council Appointments* at 43.

323 *Ibid.*

Third, Parliament should take up the Martin government's offer to review at least some GIC candidates prior to appointment. Since parliamentary resources are limited, priority should be given to senior-level appointees — directors and officers of Crown corporations, for instance — and members of quasi-judicial tribunals. These are the officials in a position to wreak real havoc if inept, either on the taxpayer or on those having their rights and obligations adjudicated.

5. Officers of Parliament

An officer of Parliament is a peculiar sort of official, one who straddles the executive and legislative branches of government. The Commons Standing Committee on Government Operations and Estimates recently described officers of Parliament as "creations of Parliament, established to provide Parliament with information, advice and other services needed in holding governments accountable. Officers of Parliament make specific contributions through their investigative and auditing functions and frequently perform an ombudsman function relating to their areas of responsibility."[324]

By December 2004, there were six functioning federal "agents" or "officers" of Parliament: the chief electoral officer, the Auditor General, the ethics commissioner, the information commissioner, the privacy commissioner, and the official languages commissioner. A seventh officer, the senate ethics officer, was anticipated in the statute book as of 2004, but came into existence only as this book went to press in early 2005.[325]

While their tasks vary enormously, these officers share one quality: their offices are structured to be independent of the executive branch. As the Commons committee notes, "reporting and removal procedures, the guarantee of financial independence, fixed terms of appointment, and the Officer's general control over the operations of the office," safeguard this independence.[326]

The focus on independence greatly restricts the capacity of Cabinet to select and dismiss officers at its discretion, making officers more like public servants than GIC appointees. Yet, in contrast with public servants, these constraints on Cabinet's appointment and dismissal powers are not designed to deter political favouritism in the *selection* of officials. Instead, they are part of a package of measures intended to preclude political favouritism by the officer in the performance of his or her *functions*.

---

324 Commons Standing Committee on Government Operations and Estimates, Matters Relating to the Office of the Privacy Commissioner (June 2003) at 2.

325 See chapters 6-8 for a further discussion of some of these officers of Parliament.

326 Commons Standing Committee on Government Operations and Estimates, Matters Relating to the Office of the Privacy Commissioner (June 2003) at 2–3.

The Selection, Tenure and Dismissal of Unelected Officials **247**

In this section we deal with each of these issues, focusing on appointments and dismissals. We also highlight the financial and administrative independence of officers.

a) Appointment

Although the precise process of appointment and dismissal varies, in all instances Parliament participates in either appointing or dismissing the officer. In some instances, it plays a role in both processes. Table 4.6 sets out the appointment, tenure and dismissal process for each officer of Parliament.

Table 4.6   Appointment, Tenure and Dismissal Processes for Officers of Parliament

Officer	Appointment Process	Tenure	Dismissal Process
Auditor General[327]	• Appointed by the Governor-in-Council	• Holds office during good behaviour for a term of office of ten years • May not be reappointed	• May be removed by the Governor-in-Council on address to Parliament • May only hold office until age 65
Chief Electoral Officer[328]	• Appointed by resolution of the House of Commons	• Holds office during good behaviour	• May be removed for cause by the Governor General on address of the senate and House of Commons • May only hold office until age 65
Ethics Commissioner[329]	• Appointed by the Governor-in-Council after consultation with the leader of every recognized party in the House of Commons and after approval of the appointment by resolution of that House	• Holds office during good behaviour for a term of seven years • May be reappointed for one or more terms of up to seven years each	• May be removed for cause by the Governor-in-Council on address of the House of Commons
Senate Ethics Officer[330]	• Appointed by the Governor-in-Council after consultation with the leader of every recognized party in the senate and after approval of the appointment by resolution of that House	• Holds office during good behaviour for a term of five years • May be reappointed for one or more terms of up to five years each	• May be removed for cause by the Governor-in-Council on address of the senate

327 *Auditor General Act*, R.S. 1985, c. A-17, s. 3.
328 *Canada Elections Act*, S.C. 2000, c. 9, s. 13.
329 *Parliament of Canada Act*, ss. 72.01 and 72.02.
330 *Ibid.*, ss. 20.1 and 20.2 (provisions not in force by late 2004).

Officer	Appointment Process	Tenure	Dismissal Process
Information Commissioner[331]	• Appointed by the Governor-in-Council after approval of the appointment by resolution of the senate and House of Commons	• Holds office during good behaviour for a term of seven years • May be reappointed for a further term not exceeding seven years	• May be removed by the Governor-in-Council at any time on address of the senate and House of Commons
Privacy Commissioner[332]	• Appointed by the Governor-in-Council after approval of the appointment by resolution of the senate and House of Commons	• Holds office during good behaviour for a term of seven years • May be reappointed for a further term not exceeding seven years	• May be removed by the Governor-in-Council at any time on address of the senate and House of Commons
Official Languages Commissioner[333]	• Appointed by the Governor-in-Council after approval of the appointment by resolution of the senate and House of Commons	• Holds office during good behaviour for a term of seven years • May be re-appointed for a further term not exceeding seven years	• May be removed by the Governor-in-Council at any time on address of the senate and House of Commons

As this table suggests, with the notable exception of the Auditor General, all officers are endorsed by Parliament prior to their appointment. This feature distinguishes officers from both public servants and regular GIC appointees.

b) Dismissal

Subsequently, officers of Parliament hold office "during good behaviour," a concept discussed in great detail in the preceding section on GIC appointments. As noted there, good behaviour means that the appointee may not be dismissed without cause — that is, for bad behaviour. However, officers differ from these good-behaviour GIC appointees. Each officer is also protected by a requirement that they be removed "on address" of one or both Houses of Parliament. The phrase "on address of Parliament" is not defined in the relevant statutes, but is understood as "a resolution express-

331 *Access to Information Act*, R.S.C. 1985, c. 1, s. 54.

332 *Privacy Act*, R.S.C. 1985, c. P-21, s. 53.

333 *Official Languages Act*, R.S.C. 1985, c. 31 (4th Supp.), s. 49.

ing the wish or request of Parliament,"[334] presumably in the form of an affirmative vote for dismissal by the relevant houses of Parliament. Given these provisions, it is usually presumed that unilateral dismissal of an officer by the executive branch is impermissible.[335]

The Meaning of the Address of Parliament Requirement

Nevertheless, the legal issues raised by officer dismissals are more confounding than this presumption suggests. Reading the good-behaviour requirement together with the prohibition on dismissal without a vote in Parliament raises a difficult question of interpretation. Do these requirements constitute a single removal process, or are they instead two alternatives? Put another way, may an officer of Parliament be removed *either* for cause by the government *or* by the relevant houses of Parliament for any reason at all? Or alternatively, may removal be engineered only for cause through the procedure of an address by the houses of Parliament?

The answer to these questions for at least some officers seems to be found in a close reading of the relevant statutes themselves. Thus, the *Canada Elections Act*, governing the chief electoral officer, specifies that this officer "may be removed for cause by the Governor General on address of the senate and House of Commons." Likewise, the *Parliament of Canada Act*, governing the Senate Ethics Officer and the Ethics Commissioner, provides that these officers may be "removed for cause by the Governor in Council on address of" the senate or House of Commons, as the case may be. In our view, a plain reading of these passages precludes removal by the Governor General absent, first, cause and, second, an address of Parliament. Parliament may not act independently to remove an officer without cause.

Other statutes are more ambiguous, invoking the good-behaviour standard without linking it so firmly to the parliamentary address process. Thus, under the *Auditor General Act*, the Auditor General is to "hold office during good behaviour for a term of ten years, but the Auditor General may be removed by the Governor in Council on address of the senate and House of Commons." The statutes governing the privacy, information and official language commissioners are equally indefinite: these officers hold office "during good behaviour for a term of seven years, but may be removed by the Governor in Council at any time on address of the senate and House of Commons."

---

334 *Roberts v. Northwest Territories (Commissioner)* (2002), 45 Admin. L.R. (3d) 45 at para. 81 (N.W.T.S.C.).

335 Commons Standing Committee on Government Operations and Estimates, *Matters Relating to the Office of the Privacy Commissioner* (June 2003) at 2–3.

This language mimics section 99 of the *Constitution Act, 1867*, governing dismissal of superior court judges. As discussed later, section 99 reads, in part, that superior judges "shall hold office during good behaviour, but shall be removable by the Governor General on Address of the Senate and House of Commons."

Notably, jurists have queried the meaning of section 99, asking exactly the same question we have raised in relation to officers. In the words of Professor Hogg:

> The question is whether s. 99 provides for one mode of removal or two. It could be read as meaning that a judge may be removed only by joint parliamentary address and then only for bad behaviour. But the section could also be read as meaning that a judge may be removed for bad behaviour by the government without the need for a joint parliamentary address, and may in addition be removed for any reason whatsoever (not necessarily involving bad behaviour) by a joint parliamentary address. On principle, the former interpretation is preferable, because it is more apt to secure the independence of the judiciary, which is the purpose of the provision.[336]

In fact, an inquiry committee of the Canadian Judicial Council tackled this issue in 1994, while considering the removal of a judge. That committee concluded that, by reason of judicial independence, superior court judges could not be removed under section 99 without a joint address of Parliament. This position has now been echoed in more recent Supreme Court jurisprudence discussed in the section that follows on dismissal of judges. However, the inquiry committee also concluded that Parliament was not confined to bad behaviour as the ground for dismissing judges in this joint address.[337] While the committee declined to spell out the implications of its conclusion, its reasoning suggested that Parliament could engineer a removal even without cause. Subsequently, when the committee's interpretation was judicially reviewed in *Gratton v. Canada (Judicial Council)*, the Federal Court flatly rejected this view.[338]

Yet, while this court decision appears to resolve the address issue in relation to judges, it is not clear whether the holding would — or even should — be extended to officers. In *Gratton*, the court was preoccupied with judicial independence — the independence of courts from both the

---

336 Hogg, *Constitutional Law of Canada* at 7-9.

337 Canadian Judicial Council, *Decision of the Gratton Inquiry Committee re Constitutional Questions with respect to the jurisdiction of the Canadian Judicial Council and the Inquiry Committee* (Feb. 1994) at 31.

338 *Gratton v. Canadian Judicial Council*, [1994] 2 F.C. 769 at 791–92 (T.D).

executive and legislative branches. These principles of judicial independence, held the court, negate the capacity of Parliament to dismiss judges for anything other than bad behaviour.

Whether similar principles should constrain Parliament in dismissing officers of Parliament is less clear. Officers of Parliament are just that — officers of Parliament. They are essentially an executive branch "arm" of Parliament, charged with holding the remainder of the executive accountable to legislators. As such, there is clearly a need to insulate them from manipulation by Cabinet, through restrictions on removal and in other ways. However, it makes much less sense to shield this vital agent of Parliament from Parliament itself, at least at a theoretical level. From one perspective, therefore, it seems eminently reasonable that if Parliament has lost confidence in its agent, few restrictions should stand in the way of dismissals.

In our view, this interpretation is belayed by at least two considerations. First, account must be had of the reality of separation of powers in the parliamentary system. Cabinet controls the executive branch and, through party discipline in a majority government, Parliament. In these circumstances, it makes little sense to insulate officers from Cabinet, but not from arbitrary dismissals by the (typically) Cabinet-dominated Parliament.

Second, it may be that, as with judges, "cause" is actually a constitutional prerequisite for any affirmative address by Parliament. Certainly, officers are not judges, and thus are not entitled to judicial independence by virtue of the preamble to the *Constitution Act, 1867*. Yet, each of these officers has potent investigatory powers. They may, therefore, occasionally adjudicate individual rights in a fashion attracting independence requirements imposed by the *Charter*, including judicial independence-like security of tenure guarantees.

In fact, the independence of an officer of Parliament as measured against *Charter* standards was tested in *Rowat v. Information Commissioner of Canada*.[339] Under the *Access to Information Act*, the information commissioner has the power to "summon and enforce the appearance of persons before the Information Commissioner and compel them to give oral or written evidence" or to produce documents.[340] At issue was whether this potent provision — and the accompanying power to punish for contempt where it is violated — were unconstitutional by virtue of the commissioner's alleged lack of independence. Examining the indicia of independence — security of tenure and financial and administrative independence — the

---

339 *Rowat v. Information Commissioner of Canada* (2000), 77 C.R.R. (2d) 79 (F.C.T.D.).
340 *Access to Information Act*, s. 36.

Federal Court concluded that the commissioner was sufficiently independent to meet the strict requirements of section 11(d) of the *Charter*; namely, the requirement that penal matters be heard by an "independent and impartial tribunal."[341] In so concluding, it observed that only removal for cause satisfies independence requirements.[342] It follows that a parliamentary address procedure allowing officers with strong investigatory powers to be removed without cause might well prove unconstitutional.

Recent Controversies

In fact, this debate about how officers of Parliament may be removed has an angels-on-pinheads quality. It is difficult to imagine efforts to remove an officer by Parliament not motivated by allegations of improper behaviour. Indeed, no officer has ever been removed for any reason.[343]

Privacy Commissioner George Radwanski might have earned that dubious distinction had he not resigned in 2003 over controversy concerning his handling of the privacy portfolio.[344] However, the Radwanski scandal may say more about Parliament's failure to scrutinize carefully officer appointments and activities than it does about any shortcomings in the dismissal process.

In the senate, the motion approving Mr. Radwanski's appointment as a privacy commissioner received forty-nine affirmative votes to seven nays, with four abstentions.[345] In the Commons, the motion attracted 174 votes in favour as against seventy-four opposed.[346] The Liberal government and the official opposition supported his appointment. Other opposition mem-

---

341 *Rowat* (2000), 77 C.R.R. (2d) 79.

342 *Ibid.* at para. 27.

343 See Louise Elliot, "Radwanski Fails to Appear Late Thursday as Commons Committee Broadens Probe," *Canadian Press*, 13 June 2003, noting that if then-Privacy Commissioner Radwanski had been removed, "it would be a first; no officer of Parliament has ever been removed in Canadian history."

344 Commons Standing Committee on Government Operations and Estimates, *Matters Relating to the Office of the Privacy Commissioner* at 17–18 ("We believed that the Privacy Commissioner deliberately misled the Committee on several recent occasions. As a result, we had lost confidence in the Privacy Commissioner, in particular because we were unable to believe, unconditionally, that information he may have provided to Parliament, had he continued in his position, would have been accurate, complete and intact, with no exceptions. We therefore would have recommended: That the House of Commons adopt a motion for an Address to her Excellency requesting the removal of Mr. Radwanski from the position of Privacy Commissioner, and that a message be sent to the Senate of Canada informing Senators of the decision of the House and requesting that the Senate unite with the House in that Address").

345 Senate of Canada, *Journals*, 36th Parl., 2d Sess., Issue 81 (17 Oct. 2000).

346 House of Commons, *Journals*, no. 126 (4 Oct. 2000).

bers, however, were less sanguine, expressing concern about the process by which the appointment was made. Querying Mr. Radwanski's ties to the Liberal Party, these members questioned a process in which Parliament was asked to "rubber-stamp" a government-selected nominee, without vetting fully alternatives:

> I am sure that there are Canadians who would have been great nominees. Parliament could have had some role in short listing them and suggesting to the government that it select from half a dozen people. This would have been a much more meaningful process and would have helped, in the public's mind, to reduce the cynicism about parliament being a rubber stamp for things that are decided elsewhere. Let us not kid ourselves. This was clearly decided elsewhere.[347]

Whether a more careful review by Parliament would have forestalled the subsequent crisis at the privacy commissioner's office is impossible to answer. Nevertheless, the controversy has prompted the Commons Standing Committee on Government Operations and Estimates to recommend to the Commons a study of officers of Parliament appointments.[348] In its words, "[t]he appointment processes that currently apply to privacy commissioners and other officers of Parliament may be deficient. The imbalance, in practice, between the respective roles of the Governor in Council and Parliament in such appointments warrants examination." As a consequence, the committee recommended a comprehensive review of officers, including:

- the process by which Officers of Parliament are appointed;
- the independence and authorities required by Officers of Parliament and related practical proposals;
- applicable salary and benefits, and how these should be determined;
- the annual estimates process in respect of the Offices of Officers of Parliament, and other elements in their accountability to Parliament; and
- appropriate provisions for their removal.[349]

At the time of this writing, no such review had commenced, although in early 2005, the Standing Committee on Access to Information, Privacy and Ethics began studying the financing of officer operations.

---

347 Mr. Bill Blaikie (Winnipeg–Transcona, NDP), *Hansard*, no. 124, 36th Parl., 2d Sess. (28 Sept. 2000).

348 Commons Standing Committee on Government Operations and Estimates, *Matters Relating to the Office of the Privacy Commissioner* at 18–19.

349 *Ibid.*

c) Financial and Administrative Independence

Security of tenure is only one component of officer independence. Officers are also protected by varying degrees of financial and administrative independence. As Table 4.7 suggests, in every instance except those of the new Ethics Commissioner and the senate ethics officer, the officer's salary is tied to that of judges of either the Federal or Supreme Courts. Since, as discussed later, these judicial salaries are protected by potent judicial independence guarantees, the linking of officer to judicial wages creates substantial financial independence for officers.

Administrative independence — officer control over their offices and their budgets — is less commonplace. As Table 4.7 suggests, the Auditor General has the clearest statutory administrative independence. Thus, the Auditor General has substantial management authority over his or her office, not least in setting the terms of employment of staff. However, the financing of this office and the appropriations sought from Parliament are reportedly dependent on negotiations with the government, a matter of some contention in late 2004. The Auditor General has repeatedly called for funding to be determined by an independent body, not via negotiations with the Treasury Board.[350]

Other officers have also argued that their operations are impaired by the control exercised by Treasury Board over their financing. In his 2003–2004 annual report, for instance, the information commissioner complained that the current financing process has created "a real problem of inadequate funding and the result is a weakened ability to do the job Parliament has asked the Information Commissioner to do."[351]

Table 4.7   *Financial and Administrative Independence for Officers of Parliament*

Officer	Financial Independence	Administrative Independence
Auditor General[352]	The Auditor General shall be paid a salary equal to the salary of a puisne judge (i.e., a judge other than the Chief Justice) of the Supreme Court of Canada.	The Auditor General supplies annual estimates of the sums that will be required to be provided by Parliament for the payment of the salaries, allowances and expenses of his or her office during the fiscal year. He or she possesses substantial management powers, including the authority to:

---

350   Kathryn May, "Auditor General's Budget Slashed by $11.5M," *Ottawa Citizen*, 19 Nov. 2004, A1.

351   Access Commissioner, *Annual Report 2003–2004* at 76.

352   *Auditor General Act*, ss. 4, 15, 16 and 19.

Officer	Financial Independence	Administrative Independence
		• hire such officers and employees as are necessary to enable the Auditor General to perform his or her duties, in accordance with the *Public Service Employment Act*; • exercise and perform, in such manner and subject to such terms and conditions as the Public Service Commission directs, most of the powers, duties and functions of the Public Service Commission under the *Public Service Employment Act*; and • determine the terms and conditions of employment and the responsibility for employer and employee relations.
Chief Electoral Officer[353]	The chief electoral officer is paid a salary equal to the salary of a judge of the Federal Court, other than the Chief Justice of that Court.	The chief electoral officer has the rank and all the powers of a deputy head of a department. His or her employees are appointed in accordance with the *Public Service Employment Act*.
Ethics Commissioner[354]	The ethics commissioner is paid the remuneration set by the Governor-in-Council.	The ethics commissioner has the rank of a deputy head of a department of the Government of Canada and has the control and management of the office of the ethics commissioner, including the power to: • enter into contracts, memoranda of understanding or other arrangements; and • employ any officers and employees and engage the services of any agents, advisers and consultants that the commissioner considers necessary for the proper conduct of the work of the office of the ethics commissioner. Prior to each fiscal year, the ethics commissioner provides an estimate of the sums that will be required to pay the charges and expenses of the office of the commissioner during the fiscal year to the Speaker of the House of Commons, who then transmits this estimate to the president of the Treasury Board.
Senate Ethics Officer[355]	The senate ethics officer is paid the remuneration set by the Governor-in-Council.	The senate ethics officer has the rank of a deputy head of a department of the Government of Canada and has the control and

353   *Canada Elections Act*, ss. 15 and 19.
354   *Parliament of Canada Act*, ss. 72.03 and 72.04.
355   *Ibid.*, ss. 20.3 and 20.4 (not in force by late 2004).

Officer	Financial Independence	Administrative Independence
		management of the office of the senate ethics office, including the power to: • enter into contracts, memoranda of understanding or other arrangements; and, • employ any officers and employees and engage the services of any agents, advisers and consultants that the senate ethics officer considers necessary for the proper conduct of the work of the office of the senate ethics officer. Prior to each fiscal year, the senate ethics officer provides an estimate of the sums that will be required to pay the charges and expenses of the office of the senate ethics officer during the fiscal year to the Speaker of the senate, who then transmits this estimate to the president of the Treasury Board to be laid before the House of Commons.
Information Commissioner[356]	The information commissioner is paid a salary equal to the salary of a judge of the Federal Court, other than the Chief Justice of that Court.	The information commissioner ranks and has all the powers of a deputy head of a department. His or her employees are appointed in accordance with the *Public Service Employment Act*.
Privacy Commissioner[357]	Same as information commissioner.	
Official Languages Commissioner[358]	The official languages commissioner is paid a salary equal to the salary of a judge of the Federal Court, other than the Chief Justice of that Court.	The official languages commissioner ranks and has all the powers of a deputy head of a department. Such officers and employees as are necessary for the proper conduct of the work of the office of the commissioner shall be appointed in the "manner authorized by law."

d)   Conclusion

In sum, officers of Parliament are a branch of executive government over whom Cabinet has shared control of dismissals and, in most cases, appointments with the legislative branch. Whether in practice this distribution of authority provides Parliament with a meaningful role in the selection of officers is less certain. Certainly, some parliamentarians have

---

356 *Access to Information Act*, ss. 55 and 58.
357 *Privacy Act*, ss. 54 and 58.
358 *Official Languages Act*, ss. 50 and 51.

questioned a process in which parliamentarians are simply asked to confirm an executive nominee, rather than vet a roster of candidates. These issues will likely be revisited in future Parliaments.

In the meantime, other measures, including financial and heightened administrative independence, may ultimately be more important in preserving the capacity of officers to operate at arm's length of the executive.

C. JUDICIAL BRANCH

The federal government appoints 1,029 judges,[359] falling into two classes: those selected for the "provincial superior" or "Section 96" courts; and, those selected for courts established under section 101 of the *Constitution Act, 1867.*

Section 96 courts are the key judicial bodies in each of the provinces and indeed the most important courts in the land. Created pursuant to section 96 of the *Constitution Act, 1867,* these courts have "inherent," general jurisdiction over "all civil and criminal, provincial, federal, and constitutional matters."[360] This notion of inherent jurisdiction "arises from the presumption that if there is a justiciable right, then there must be a court competent to vindicate the right."[361] Thus, section 96 courts are the place where every right can presumptively be adjudicated, subject only to a narrowing of that jurisdiction where legislatures have assigned powers to other bodies. The constitutional standard for — and constraints on — this reallocation of section 96 court authority are discussed in chapter 2.

Section 96 courts are also distinguished by the extent to which they institutionally straddle the division of powers between the provinces and the federal government: judges are appointed by the federal government under section 96 itself, but the structure of these courts is a construct of the provinces by reason of section 92(14) of the 1867 Act.[362]

For their part, section 101 courts include the Supreme Court of Canada, the Federal Court of Canada and the Tax Court of Canada. As with section 96 courts, the federal government appoints judges of these section 101 bodies. However, unlike section 96 courts, these are judicial institutions

---

359 Office of the Commissioner for Federal Judicial Affairs, *Performance Report for the Period Ending March 31, 2003.*

360 *Canada (Human Rights Commission) v. Canadian Liberty Net,* [1998] 1 S.C.R. 626 at 653.

361 *Ibid.* at 656.

362 Section 92(14) of the *Constitution Act, 1867* provides for provincial jurisdiction over "The Administration of Justice in the Province."

established by the federal Parliament. Further, they do not possess inherent jurisdiction, exercising only such authority as is accorded to them by the Acts of Parliament that create them.

Judicial tenure and the process of judicial dismissal for both of these sorts of courts are strongly constitutional issues, reflecting both written and unwritten constitutional principles of judicial independence. The constitutional origin and content of judicial independence is addressed in chapter 2. Here, we focus on its practical application, examining the judicial appointment process and the concrete manifestation of the three prerequisites of judicial independence: administrative and financial independence and security of tenure.

1. Appointment

While the provinces create the courts in which they sit, the Governor General appoints section 96 judges under the express terms of the 1867 Act.[363] This apparent incongruity — courts created by the provinces and judges appointed by the federal government — reflects efforts by the framers of the 1867 Act to maintain federal control over a key source of patronage. Fear was expressed during the deliberations leading to Confederation that provincial appointments would produce a bench "filled with obscure and incompetent men who would excite the contempt, instead of commanding the respect of those practicing before them."[364] By contrast, federal appointments would not be so short-sighted: "by leaving these appointments to the Central Government, we are satisfied that the selection will be made from men of the highest order of qualifications, that the external and local pressure will not be so great, and the Government will be in a position to act more freely."[365]

The actual federal appointment process stems from a mix of law, policy and convention. By constitutional convention, the Governor General follows the advice of Cabinet in making section 96 appointments, although chief justices are appointed on the advice of the prime minister.[366] For their part, the

---

363 *Constitution Act, 1867*, s. 96.

364 Correspondence of Lieut. Governor Gordon to Edward Cardwell, 26 Sept. 1864, cited in Martin Friedland, *A Place Apart: Judicial Independence and Accountability in Canada* (Canadian Judicial Council, 1995) at 234.

365 Sir Hector-Louis Langevin, in *Parliamentary Debates on the Subject of the Confederation of the British North American Provinces*, 8th Prov. Parl. of Canada, 3d Sess., (16 Feb. 1865) at 387–88, as cited in Friedland, *A Place Apart* at 234.

366 Hogg, *Constitutional Law of Canada* at 9-26.2 and n74; Department of Justice, *A New Judicial Appointments Process* (1988) at 1; Privy Council minute, P.C. 3374 (25 Oct. 1935).

section 101 superior court judges are appointed pursuant to the statutes creating their courts. Thus, the Governor-in-Council appoints Supreme Court justices, and Federal and Tax Court judges.[367] The laws creating each of these courts — and for section 96 judges, the *Judges Act* — establish basement-floor requirements for judicial appointments. These are set out in Table 4.8.

Table 4.8   Requirements for Judicial Appointments

Court	Experience Requirements	Regional Requirements
Supreme Court[368]	Any person may be appointed a judge who is or has been a judge of a superior court of a province or a barrister or advocate of at least ten years standing at the bar of a province.	At least three judges must be appointed from the judges of the Court of Appeal or the Superior Court of the Province of Quebec or from among the advocates of that Province.
Section 96 Courts[369]	A judicial appointee must be a barrister or advocate of at least ten years standing at the bar of any province, or for an aggregate of at least ten years, been a barrister or advocate at the bar of any province, and exercised powers and performed duties and functions of a judicial nature on a full-time basis in Canada.	
Federal Courts[370]	A person may be appointed a judge of the Federal Court of Appeal or the Federal Court if the person: (a) is or has been a judge of a superior, county or district court in Canada; (b) is or has been a barrister or advocate of at least ten years standing at the bar of any province; or (c) has, for at least ten years, been a barrister or advocate at the bar of any province, and has exercised powers and performed duties and functions of a judicial nature on a full-time basis in Canada.	At least four of the judges of the Federal Court of Appeal and at least six of the judges of the Federal Court must be persons who have been judges of the Court of Appeal or of the Superior Court of the Province of Quebec, or have been members of the bar of that Province.
Tax Court[371]	Same as Federal Courts.	Either the Chief Justice or the Associate Chief Justice shall be a person who is or was a member of the bar of the Province of Quebec.

---

367 *Supreme Court Act*, R.S.C. 1985, c. S-26, s. 4; *Federal Courts Act*, R.S.C. 1985, c. F-7, s. 5.2; *Tax Court of Canada Act*, R.S.C. 1985, c. T-2, s. 4.

368 *Supreme Court Act*, ss. 5 and 6.

369 *Judges Act*, s. 3.

370 *Federal Courts Act*, ss. 5.3 and 5.4.

371 *Tax Court of Canada Act*, s. 4.

These minor strictures constitute the only formal, legal constraints on Cabinet's discretion to select judges. Coupled with a convention that three Supreme Court judges are appointed from Ontario, two from the West and one from Atlantic Canada,[372] these requirements foster some regional representation and a bare-bones minimum of experience, but say nothing about any other quality judges might be expected to possess.

a) Non–Supreme Court Federal Appointments

Overview

Notwithstanding the views expressed by the framers of the 1867 Act, the federal appointment process was notoriously partisan until relatively recently. In 1932, Prime Minister R.B. Bennett acknowledged that "there has been too much political patronage concerned in the appointments to the Bench. The result has been that the test whether a man is entitled to a seat on the Bench has seemed to be whether he has run an election and lost it."[373] Prior to the Second World War, most appointees to section 96 courts held or ran for political office before their elevation to the bench. Appointments followed party lines in the vast majority of cases.[374]

Only in 1967 did then-Minister of Justice Pierre Trudeau move to open up and depoliticize the Governor-in-Council appointment process. In that year, the government began consulting the judiciary committee of the Canadian Bar Association (CBA) on most federal judicial appointments. This body would review names submitted by the minister, and issue an opinion that the candidate was "very well- qualified," "well-qualified," "qualified" or "not qualified" for the position in question.[375]

Notoriously, however, this review process proved inadequate in 1984, with the selection of six Liberal politicians for judicial positions upon Pierre Trudeau's retirement. One of these 1984 judicial appointments circumvented the CBA committee review process entirely, a first since 1967.[376]

---

372 See the Commons Standing Committee on Justice, Human Rights, Public Safety and Emergency Preparedness, *Improving the Supreme Court of Canada Appointments Process* (May 2004) at 3. Also of interest, see Cabinet document, Privy Council Office, Series A-5-a, vol. 6193 (1962/10/30) at 5, in which Cabinet was unprepared to endorse a requirement that British Columbia have a permanent representation on the Court.

373 *House of Commons Debates*, 17 May 1932 at 2999, as cited in Friedland, *A Place Apart* at 236.

374 Peter Russell, *The Judiciary in Canada: The Third Branch of Government* (Scarborough, ON: McGraw-Hill Ryerson, 1987) at 114–15. See also Ted Morton, *Law, Politics and the Judicial Process in Canada*, 3d ed. (Calgary: University of Calgary Press, 2002) at 121.

375 Friedland, *A Place Apart* at 236.

376 *Ibid.* at 238.

The record of these and other alleged patronage appointments subsequently prompted the clearest "knock-out" blow in Canadian electoral history. During the 1984 leader's debate, Prime Minister Turner pleaded that he had no choice but to make the appointments earmarked by Trudeau. In response, Conservative contender Brian Mulroney famously countered, "You had an option, sir. You could have said 'I am not going to do it. This is wrong for Canada.' This is a confession of non-leadership and this country needs leadership. You had an option. You could have done better."

Subsequently, the CBA concluded in a 1985 study that patronage remained a concern in federal judicial appointments. While it found that "political favouritisim" was not a factor in Supreme Court selections, it was egregious at the Federal Court of Canada. There, "political favouritism has been a dominant, though not sole consideration; many appointees have been active supporters of the party in power."[377]

The record in relation to section 96 courts was more mixed, with political favouritism significant in Alberta, Manitoba, Newfoundland and some Ontario court appointments, and dominant in the Maritime Provinces and Saskatchewan.[378] After interviews with present and former justice ministers, the CBA reported that

> it was admitted that the political affiliation of a candidate plays some part in considering candidates for the bench. One former minister described it as a "background consideration." Another said "politics is politics." Still another said he would select a supporter if candidates had equal qualifications. Yet another said, "Names were usually received through political channels." This indicates that, even in those provinces where political patronage has little or no influence, a person's political affiliation is always given some consideration.[379]

Subsequently, reviewing the Mulroney government's first term, Professors Russell and Ziegel concluded that political favouritism "continued to have a major influence." Almost half of the appointments to the bench during this period "had a known political association with the Conservative Party."[380]

---

377 Canadian Bar Association Committee Report, *The Appointment of Judges in Canada* (1985) at 57.

378 *Ibid.*

379 *Ibid.*

380 Peter Russell and Jacob Ziegel, "Federal Judicial Appointments: An Appraisal of the First Mulroney Government's Appointments and the New Judicial Advisory Committees" (1991) 41 U.T.L.J. 4 at 33.

Following repeated promises to reform the process, the Mulroney government introduced in 1988 a new selection process for federally appointed judges other than those of the Supreme Court.[381] At that time, Minister of Justice Ray Hnatyshyn urged that "by putting in place a modern appointments system dedicated to seeking out candidates of merit from all branches of the legal professions, a system in which broad consultation and community involvement are essential elements, we hope to succeed in reinforcing public confidence in the judiciary and the judicial system."[382]

In introducing the new system, the government announced several principles guiding its operation: first, responsibility for appointments remained the prerogative of the executive branch; second, the appointments system would respect and preserve the independence of the judiciary; third, the principal qualification for candidates was to be merit; fourth, the judiciary would reflect a broad cross-section of Canadian society; and, fifth, suitable candidates would be identified via a broad consultation with provincial attorneys general, the bar, the bench and other interested groups.[383]

Vetting System

Under the 1988 system, as amended, lawyers interested in non–Supreme Court federal judicial appointments either apply — or are nominated — to the Office of the Commissioner of Federal Judicial Affairs.[384] The commissioner then elicits personal information from the candidate, screening out those who do not meet the minimum statutory requirements described in the table above. The commissioner refers the remaining applications to "independent judicial advisory committees."

These vetting committees exist in every province, with three regional committees in Ontario and two in Quebec. Committees are composed of seven members, drawn from the bar, bench and general public. Committees are staffed as follows: a nominee of the provincial or territorial law society; a nominee of the provincial or territorial branch of the CBA; a judge nominated by the chief justice or senior judge of the province or territory; a nominee of the provincial attorney general or territorial minister of justice; and three nominees of the federal minister of justice. The minister of justice makes the final selection of committee members based on a list submitted by each nominating body or official, and bases his or her

---

381   Office of the Commissioner of Federal Judicial Affairs, *Federal Judicial Appointments Process: Guide for Candidates.* See also Andre S. Millar, "The 'New' Federal Judicial Appointments Process: The First Ten Years," (2000) 38 Alta. L. Rev. 616.

382   Department of Justice, *A New Judicial Appointments Process* (1988) at iii.

383   *Ibid.* at 5.

384   Unless otherwise noted, the description in this section is summarized from the Office of the Commissioner of Federal Judicial Affairs, *Federal Judicial Appointments Process.*

selection on "factors appropriate to the jurisdiction, including geography, gender, language and multiculturalism."

Committees are charged with evaluating judicial candidates, according to a series of assessment criteria. These variables include indicia of professional competence and experience, personal qualities and potential impediments to appointment, as set out in Table 4.9.

Table 4.9   Assessment Criteria for Judicial Candidates

Category	Criteria
Professional competence and experience	General proficiency in the law, intellectual ability, analytical skills, ability to listen, ability to maintain an open mind while hearing all sides of an argument, ability to make decisions, capacity to exercise sound judgment, reputation among professional peers and in the general community, area(s) of professional specialization, specialized experience or special skills, ability to manage time and workload without supervision, capacity to handle heavy workload, capacity to handle stress and pressures of the isolation of the judicial role, interpersonal skills — with peers and the general public, awareness of racial and gender issues, bilingual ability
Personal qualities	Sense of ethics, patience, courtesy, honesty, common sense, tact, integrity, humility, punctuality, fairness, reliability, tolerance, sense of responsibility, consideration for others
Potential impediments to appointment	Any debilitating physical or mental medical condition, including drug or alcohol dependency, that would be likely to impair the candidate's ability to perform the duties of a judge; any past or current disciplinary actions or matters against the candidate; any current or past civil or criminal actions involving the candidate; financial difficulties including bankruptcy, tax arrears or arrears of child support payments

Committees are expected to consult widely in reviewing the suitability of the candidate, and "are encouraged to respect diversity and to give due consideration to all legal experience, including that outside a mainstream legal practice." The actual vetting process is conducted on a confidential basis. Once the reviews are complete, candidates are informed of the date of their assessment, but are not notified of the outcome. This secretive quality to the process has sparked controversy. In 1998, the Liberal chair of the House of Commons justice committee complained that the vetting committees respond to bar politics and acted as gatekeepers to the "club."[385] Academic critics have gone further, calling the vetting process "assessment by gossip."[386]

---

385   Cristin Schmitz, "Judge Selection Process Slammed–Liberal MP Levels Charges That Federal Judicial Selection Process Rampant with Leaks, Politics and Unaccountability," *The Lawyers Weekly*, 12 June 1998.

386   F.C. DeCoste, "Political Corruption, Judicial Selection, and the Rule of Law," (2000) 38 Alta. L. Rev. 654 at 675.

Relevance of the Vetting Process to Appointments

Vetting committees place the lawyer candidate in one of three categories: "recommended," "highly recommended" or "unable to recommend" for appointment. This evaluation is certified by the commissioner of judicial affairs, or by his or her delegate, the judicial appointments secretary. It is then supplied to the minister of justice. The minister of justice, meanwhile, may also conduct his or her own consultation with members of the bar, bench and public.[387]

Notably, the recommendations of the vetting committees are not binding on the government. There is no legal obligation that the successful candidate ultimately appointed by the Governor General or Governor-in-Council be approved by the vetting committee.

In 1994, then-Justice Minister Allan Rock committed to appointing only persons receiving a "recommended" or "highly recommended" evaluation from the vetting committees.[388] However, Opposition parties critiqued this practice as an inadequate guard against political patronage in the appointments process.[389] In particular, the federal government has resisted introducing a two-year "cooling-off" period for Members of Parliament and senators prior to any judicial appointment, a measure recommended by the CBA.[390]

Moreover, where a vetting committee declines to recommend a candidate, the minister may ask it to reconsider, raising concerns about political arm-twisting. In fact, then-Justice Minister Anne McLellan requested a reconsideration in 1998 when the Nova Scotia vetting committee accorded

---

387 The process is somewhat different for existing judges being considered for elevation either from a provincial to a superior court or to a higher superior court. With provincial judges, candidates are not assessed by the advisory committees. However, their files are submitted to the appropriate committee for comments. These comments are then provided to the minister of justice, who will also consult with the candidate's current chief judge as well as with the chief justice of the court for which the candidate is being considered (Office of the Commissioner of Federal Judicial Affairs, *Federal Judicial Appointments Process*). Current superior court judges do not apply, and are not reviewed by committees. Instead, their elevation is considered by the minister, after private consultations. Richard Devlin, A. Wayne MacKay and Natasha Kim, "Reducing the Democratic Deficit: Representation, Diversity and the Canadian Judiciary, or Towards a 'Triple P' Judiciary," (2000) 38 Alta. L. Rev. 734, 766.

388 Cristin Schmitz, "Federal Judicial Appointment Reforms Won't Preclude Political Patronage," *The Lawyers Weekly*, 22 April 1994.

389 *Ibid.*; Cristin Schmitz, "Rock Defends Proposals for Judicial Appt. Reforms," *The Lawyers Weekly*, 13 May 1994.

390 Cristin Schmitz, "CBA-NS Suggests 'Cooling-Off' Period for Judicial Candidates," *The Lawyers Weekly*, 21 Aug. 1998.

a prominent Liberal an "unable to recommend" assessment. The candidate was apparently re-evaluated and recommended by the committee. Indeed, some sources said (but the minister denied) that this recommendation was secured only after a second rejection and a third assessment request.[391]

This process sparked an angry letter from the CBA. "I have been advised by the executive of the Nova Scotia Branch of the CBA," wrote the CBA president, "that it is extremely concerned that the process for federal judicial appointments in the province may be undermined by political interference." The letter urged that "at no time, and particularly now, should the process for the selection of the judiciary be compromised by political pressures." "To select individuals who have not been acceptable to the committee," it continued, "or to attempt to manipulate the committee to achieve a desired political outcome, must not be permitted." Minister McLellan's staff and the Office of the Commissioner for Federal Judicial Affairs denied that political interference had any bearing on the committee's work. However, soon after the nominee was approved, the Nova Scotia Court of Appeal judge on the committee resigned her committee position, prompting unconfirmed speculation that her resignation was made to protest the affair.[392]

Political Favouritism
The question of political favouritism in judicial appointments remains a live one. Opposition parties continue to make accusations of political patronage from time to time.[393] Journalistic reports claim that, by the end of the Chrétien years, "federally appointed chief justices in three provinces have been linked to the Liberal party."[394] However, anecdotes aside, no com-

---

391 Cristin Schmitz, "CBA Denounces Political Pressure in Screening Applicants for Bench: Justice Minister Defends Integrity of Judicial Vetting Process," *The Lawyers Weekly*, 21 Aug. 1998.

392 *Ibid.*

393 See, e.g., discussion re: the appointment of Justice Bastarache to the Supreme Court of Canada below and Mr. Peter Mancini (Sydney–Victoria, NDP), *Hansard*, 36th Parl, 1st Sess. (11 June 1998) ("I could go through the annals and point to the members of the judiciary who have been appointed not because they were the best lawyers or because they had the best minds, but because they collected enough money for the right political party at the time. That is a historical reality we have to correct.").

394 Janice Tibbets, "A New Order in the Court," *Vancouver Sun*, 22 Nov. 2003 at ch. 3, reporting: "Newfoundland Chief Justice Clyde Wells, appointed in 1999, is the former Liberal premier of that province; Michel Robert, former president of the Liberal Party of Canada, became Quebec's chief justice last year; and Heather Smith, wife of Senator David Smith, who ran Chrétien's election campaigns, was promoted last year to chief justice of Ontario's Superior Court. ... While the three judges are well respected and qualified, they have been cited as examples of how it pays to have connections.").

prehensive, empirical analysis of the Liberal government's appointment practices since 1993 appears to exist in the academic literature.

Correlating appointments with political affiliation is a complex undertaking, not least because of the difficulty in measuring the latter variable. In their vital study of the first Mulroney government, Professors Russell and Ziegel depended largely on a network of academics, lawyers and journalists to identify the past political involvement of judicial appointees.[395] The outcome of this study is noted earlier in this chapter.

We are not in a position to replicate the Russell/Ziegel procedure. We can, however, offer up a crude alternative, correlating the names of judicial appointees with those of past Members of Parliament or the provincial legislatures and with publicly available political donation information.

By our count, the Liberal government appointed, elevated or promoted 542 non-Supreme Court of Canada judges between 1995 — the year after Minister Rock pledged to appoint only candidates recommended by the advisory committee — and 2003.[396] Of these judges, only nine (or 1.6 percent) were identified as former Members of Parliament or of a provincial legislature in the official biographies accompanying the announcement of their appointment. Of these nine, seven (1.3 percent) were Liberal Party members.

Political office is the most transparent indicator of political affiliation. It may understate, however, the political ties of appointees. Accordingly, we turned to political donation records. We chose to focus on appointments for a single year, 2003, a period in which the transition between Jean Chrétien and Paul Martin took place. Patronage practices might be expected to be more common during transitions — even ones within parties. However, referring to these appointments, journalists reported that "Chrétien has resisted a blatant patronage bonanza in his final months in power."[397] We wished to test empirically this view, to the extent possible.

Donation records from 1997 — an election year — through to 2003 were cross-referenced with the names of the fifty-two new appointees for 2003. Using these donation figures, we divided appointees into four categories, mimicking our study of GIC appointees discussed above: "probable supporters" of the Liberal Party; "possible supporters" of the Liberal Party; or "probable" or "possible" supporters of opposition parties.

395 See Russell and Ziegel, "Federal Judicial Appointments."
396 Data compiled by tabulating the names listed in the Department of Justice judicial appointment press releases between 1995 and 2003. Available at www.justice.gc.ca/en/news/press_releases/judicial.html.
397 Tibbets, "A New Order in the Court."

"Probable supporters" were appointees whose name correlated closely with those of donors. "Close correlation" meant, first, that the appointee's name matched exactly that in the donor base. Second, it also meant that name was unusual or that the name was reported down to the middle initial. Here, we concluded that the overlap between the appointee and the donor's name warranted a conclusion that the two names referred to the same person. We also included in this probable category several appointees with known past political affiliations,[398] based on press or other reports.

In comparison, "possible supporters" were persons whose name was both common and reported in the Elections Canada database without a middle initial. In those circumstances, we had much lower confidence that the appointee and the donor were one and the same.

Finally, one appointee had a very common name correlated with several different donation entries in the Elections Canada database, each to different parties. Given a choice between excluding this appointee and double-counting him (that is, putting him in the "possible" column for both the Liberal and opposition party), we chose to remove him from the pool. This reduced the total sample size to fifty-one.

We acknowledge readily that this study is based on an imperfect methodology, given the lack of absolute certainty that the appointee and donor are one and the same. However, as we urged in our study of GIC appointees, without access to party membership lists and the full *curriculum vitae* of appointees, it was the best methodology available to us. The results of our analysis follow in Table 4.10.

Table 4.10   Judicial Patronage Appointments, 2003

	Number	% (of 51)
"Probable supporter" of the Liberal Party of Canada	21	41
"Possible supporter" of the Liberal Party of Canada	6	12
"Possible supporter" of an opposition party	0	0
"Probable supporter" of an opposition party	2	4
Total	29	57

398   Mr. Justice Alphonsus Faour of the Supreme Court of Newfoundland, a nondonor, was placed in the "probable" column, in this instance for the opposition. Mr. Justice Faour is a former Member of Parliament for the New Democratic Party. Likewise, Madame Justice Georgette Sheridan was a former parliamentarian (and reportedly a donor) for the Liberal Party. Mr. Justice Paul Bedard joined Madame Justice Sheridan on the Tax Court, and was identified in the press as a "veteran Liberal and friend of [Justice Minister] Mr. Cauchon." See Robert Fife, "Chrétien Cabinet Approves 50 Patronage Jobs," *National Post*, 17 Sept. 2003 at A7. Both were therefore listed as probable supporters of the Liberal Party.

In reviewing these data, we wish to emphasize strongly that we do not imply cause and effect between donation and appointment. There is no plausible argument that donations had anything to do with appointee selection. Individual donations ranged from just over a hundred dollars to just under $2,000. These are modest figures in the grand scheme of things.

As a second caveat, we do not imply in any way that the appointees were somehow disqualified or suspect because of partisan leanings. Indeed, we believe that commitment to public service — partisan or not — is an asset in a judge. We are aware of no meaningful critique of the quality and professional quality of the 2003 appointments.

For us, political donations are simply a proxy for active political affiliation.[399] Thus, while we measure political affiliation differently than did Professors Russell and Ziegel in their more extensive and detailed 1991 study of appointments during the Mulroney years, our results are broadly similar: up to half of appointees were affiliated with the governing party.

From this finding, we conclude that if you wished to be a federally appointed judge in the last year of the Chrétien government, being an active supporter of the Liberal Party was a strong asset. Perhaps more concerning, our data also suggest that appointees with certain political affiliations are preferred over others of different political persuasions. There was a striking paucity of appointments in 2003 of persons who had given money to, or otherwise had clear affiliations with, opposition parties. From this we conclude that it did not pay to be in the wrong camp.

Thus, the vetting committee reviewing process introduced in 1988 apparently has not removed political affiliation as an important consideration in appointment decision-making. Indeed, in October 2004, Justice Minister Irwin Cotler acknowledged this problem, noting that "I myself have concerns that we may not have the best process in place" and that

---

399 In this respect, we believe these donation data represent a fairly strong indicator of political preference. The Liberal Party averaged approximately 11,000 donations from individuals in 2000–2003, years for which data are readily available from Elections Canada (average compiled from Elections Canada, *Party-financing data; contributions to registered political parties, by donor category*, for fiscal year 2001, 2002, and 2003). This means that an average of roughly 0.05 percent of registered voters made donations to that party in an average year (number of persons on the electoral list for 2000 drawn from Statistics Canada, *Federal general elections, by electors, ballots cast and voter participation*). In comparison 41 percent — and possibly as many as 53 percent — of the appointees named to the bench in 2003 made donations to the Liberal Party at least once in the period 1997–2003. We acknowledge that comparing the two figures is something of an apple and orange comparison. It is, however, broadly suggestive of a deeper political involvement by appointees than typical members of the electorate.

"[p]eople shouldn't be excluded because somebody doesn't like their ideological persuasion or whatever." The minister promised a rethinking of the lower court appointment process, including improving the quality of persons selected to sit on the appointment vetting committees.[400]

Reforms of these sorts would be a start. However, even more valuable would be a more open selection process, involving public, parliamentary vetting of selection criteria (though probably not the candidate him or herself). We turn to this idea in relation to appointments to the Supreme Court of Canada.

b) Supreme Court Appointments

Overview

Commentary on the Supreme Court appointments process has become a virtual cottage industry,[401] particularly since Prime Minister Martin began mooting the prospect of reform in 2004. This attention — much of it critical — reflects both the prominence of the Supreme Court in Canadian governance, post-*Charter*, and the remarkably opaque, traditional system of appointing Supreme Court judges. Supreme Court justices are not vetted by an advisory committee, as are other federally appointed judges. Instead, they are selected via a closed-door and, until recently, mysterious process. It was only in March 2004 that the Commons justice committee asked the minister of justice to appear before it and "describe publicly for the first time the current process for selecting Supreme Court Justices."[402]

As explained by Justice Minister Cotler, the traditional selection process depends on "a comprehensive consultation process" comprising two steps. First, the minister identifies potential candidates, either through his or her own devices or via nomination. The minister consults with the chief justice of the Supreme Court, and occasionally that court's other judges. He or she also singles out key individuals from the province or region associated with the empty spot on the court: at least one senior member of the CBA and law society, and the attorney(s) general, and chief justice(s) of the courts of the provinces concerned. Typically, the candidates

---

400 Kirk Makin, "Cotler Aims to Revamp System for Appointing Judges," *Globe and Mail*, 11 Oct. 2004, A1.

401 Many excellent articles have been written on this issue, including Lorraine Weinrib, "Appointing Judges to the Supreme Court of Canada in the *Charter* Era: A Study of Institutional Function and Design," in Ontario Law Reform Commission, *Appointing Judges: Philosophy, Politics and Practice* (1991).

402 Commons Standing Committee on Justice, Human Rights, Public Safety And Emergency Preparedness, *Improving the Supreme Court of Canada Appointments Process* at 3.

identified via this processes are current judges of the country's Courts of Appeal, although they may also be senior members of the bar or academia.

Second, the minister assesses the candidate, according to three broad criteria: professional capacity;[403] personal characteristics;[404] and, diversity.[405] The minister's assessment of professional ability is assisted by "jurisprudential profiles" compiled by the Department of Justice, reviewing the candidate's judicial writings as assessed by their "precedent-setting value" and the outcome of any appeals of their decisions.

The minister discusses the candidates with the prime minister. A candidate is selected and the prime minister recommends this person to the Cabinet.[406] Notably, law mandates none of this process, and indeed Minister Cotler could not promise the Commons justice committee that it was followed to the letter in every instance.[407] As a small indicator of variability in the process, the dated Cabinet records declassified by the National Archives provide examples of instances in which Supreme Court recommendations to Cabinet were actually made by the justice minister, and not the prime minister.[408]

---

403 This is defined as proficiency in the law, superior analytical and writing skills, the ability to listen and maintain an open mind, decisiveness and soundness of judgment, the capacity to manage and share a heavy workload in a collaborative context, the capacity to manage stress and the pressures of the isolation of the judicial role, an awareness of social context, bilingual capacity, and the specific legal expertise that may be required for the Supreme Court.

404 Specifically, the minister looks for impeccable personal and professional ethics, honesty, integrity and forthrightness, respect and regard for others, patience, courtesy, tact, humility, impartiality, tolerance, personal sense of responsibility, common sense, punctuality, and reliability.

405 The minister takes the view that the composition of the Court should reflect that of Canadian society as a whole.

406 Commons Standing Committee on Justice, Human Rights, Public Safety and Emergency Preparedness, *Improving the Supreme Court of Canada* at 3-4. See also, e.g., prime minister's recommendation to Cabinet on the appointment of Supreme Court justices Abott and Kerwin in 1954, in Privy Council Office, Series A-5-a, vol. 2655, reel T-2369 (1954/07/01) at 5.

407 Standing Committee on Justice, Human Rights, Public Safety and Emergency Preparedness, *Evidence*, 37th Parl., 3d Sess. (30 March 2004) ("I cannot claim, nor would I, that this consultative process or protocol has always been followed in every particular. I can only undertake to follow it as the protocol by which I will be governed as Minister of Justice. I might add that this is the first time that this protocol or appointments protocol is being released").

408 See, e.g., Privy Council Office, Series A-5-a, vol. 1893, 1958/02/05 at 9 and 1958/02/05 at 6, concerning the appointment of Justice Judson, and Privy Council Office, Series A-5-a, vol. 2744, 1959/05/05 at 13, concerning the appointment of Justice Ritchie.

The only clear legal requirement in the entire appointment process is found in the *Supreme Court Act*: it is the Governor-in-Council that makes the ultimate appointment. Indeed, it is arguable that this Governor-in-Council power is constitutionalized, a position seemingly endorsed by Justice Minister Cotler in his March 2004 presentation to the justice committee.[409]

It is worth reviewing briefly this contention, since constitutionalization of the present system would clearly constrain the quick fixes available for reforming the appointments process. If the Act is constitutionalized, it would be subject to change only via the amendment process in the *Constitution Act, 1982*.

The *Supreme Court Act* is a statute of Parliament, not listed as part of the Constitution of Canada in the *Constitution Act, 1982*. However, section 41 of the 1982 Act specifies (rather ambiguously) that amendments to the "composition" of the Supreme Court of Canada "may be made by proclamation issued by the Governor General under the Great Seal of Canada only where authorized by resolutions of the Senate and House of Commons and of the legislative assembly of each province." Meanwhile, under section 42, amendments to "the Supreme Court of Canada," other than to its composition, require a proclamation by the Governor-in-Council authorized by resolutions of both houses of Parliament and the legislatures of two-thirds of the provinces possessing at least 50 percent of the total provincial population.

One way of reading these provisions is to view them as governing the procedure by which section 101 of the *Constitution Act, 1867*, authorizing a court of appeal for Canada, may be amended. They also govern any *future* constitutionalization of the Supreme Court. More than that, however, some observers have interpreted these two references to the Supreme Court in the 1982 Act as constitutionalizing the status quo and the present version of the *Supreme Court Act*.[410]

This is a claim impossible to dispute fully, without a decision from the Supreme Court itself. However, these status quo arguments may in part be

---

409 See Standing Committee on Justice, Human Rights, Public Safety and Emergency Preparedness, *Evidence*, 37th Parl., 3d Sess. (30 March 2004) ("[T]he *Supreme Court Act* vests the constitutional authority for the appointment of Supreme Court judges with the executive branch of government — or the cabinet — by way of order in council appointment, and the executive remains responsible and accountable for the exercise of this important power.").

410 See discussion in NDP dissenting report, Commons Standing Committee on Justice, Human Rights, Public Safety and Emergency Preparedness, *Improving the Supreme Court of Canada*.

belayed by actual practice since 1982. In 1987, Parliament enacted legislation amending the *Supreme Court Act*, and introducing new procedures for
appeals to the Court.[411] No issue arose as to the constitutionality of these
changes. This 1987 amendment has led Professor Hogg, for one, to conclude in his landmark work on the Constitution that the *Supreme Court Act*
may be amended "by the ordinary legislative process."[412]

As a final point on this issue, even if the current Act is constitutionalized, it specifies only that the appointment must ultimately be made by the
Governor-in-Council. There would be no constitutional infirmity in any
process — mandated by law or otherwise — requiring that certain procedures be followed *prior* to that GIC appointment — for instance, a vetting
committee or even a parliamentary confirmation of the candidate.

With all this in mind, we turn to the issue of reforming the appointments process.

Reforming the Appointment Process

The Supreme Court was once pasturage for former politicians. Up until
1949, twenty-two of forty Supreme Court justices had been politicians. In
1949 itself, four of the Court's seven justices had "extensive political ties to
the Liberal party."[413] Things have changed on the high court. Writing in
1988, *Globe and Mail* columnist Jeffrey Simpson noted that the Supreme
Court is "now completely devoid of patronage, or even the tinge of partisan
appointments."[414] While there have been more recent grumblings about
partisanship and complaints that the government has appointed three justices with reported Liberal ties,[415] few credible observers query the overall
quality of Supreme Court appointments under the Liberals.

411 S.C. 1987, c. 42.
412 Hogg, *Constitutional Law of Canada* at 4-13.
413 Jeffrey Simpson, *The Spoils of Power: The Politics of Patronage* (Toronto: Collins, 1988)
     at 300.
414 *Ibid.*
415 Janice Tibbetts, *CanWest News*, 27 Sept. 2002 ("Three jobs went to people with Liberal
     ties: Deschamps, Justice Louis LeBel and Justice Michel Bastarache. Deschamps' hus-
     band, Paul Gobeil, was a provincial Liberal cabinet minister in Quebec. LeBel was a
     member of the Quebec and federal Liberal parties in the 1970s and helped author the
     provincial Liberal's response to Quebec sovereignty before the 1980 referendum. Bas-
     tarache was a former law firm associate, an avowed federalist who was the national
     chairman of the Yes side in the failed 1992 Charlottetown accord, and an informal
     Liberal party adviser. He also worked in the same law firm as Chrétien in the late
     1980s and he has attended Liberal Party policy meetings. Chrétien also named Michel
     Robert, former president of the Liberal Party of Canada, as chief justice of the Quebec
     Court of Appeal in July."). Professor Morton has implied that Justice Bastarache's
     1998 appointment was "unduly influenced" by the Chrétien government's interest in

Repeated objections have been raised, however, to the inscrutable nature of the appointments process, and the potential for abuse it creates. As the Commons justice committee puts it, the secretive process of selecting Supreme Court judges "could lead to the perception that appointments may be based upon improper criteria."[416]

Depending on your political leanings, this perception may prove well-founded. Indeed, in the 2004 federal election, Minister Cotler himself reportedly claimed that the Conservatives would politicize the Supreme Court by choosing judges on ideological, not purely professional, grounds.[417] These comments followed remarks made months earlier by then-Alliance leader Stephen Harper, reportedly accusing the Liberals of stacking the bench with "pro-gay" judges.[418]

Harper's comments suggest that at least one side in the "culture wars" — that represented by the Conservative Party and its academic brain trust — perceives the judiciary as already tainted by political bias, and thus a legitimate target. As the gay rights issue suggests, these critiques are often motivated by judicial decisions viewed as ideologically undesirable by critics.[419] In other instances, the complaints are predicated on more universal principles, not least democratic accountability.[420] Even this latter, laudable principle simplifies, however, the complex issues at stake.

---

the outcome of the then pending *Quebec Secession Reference.* Morton, *Law, Politics and the Judicial Process in Canada* at 129. See also William Thorsell, "What to Look For, and Guard Against in a Supreme Court Judge," *Globe and Mail,* 20 Dec. 1997, D6 (Justice Bastarache is "a good man, no doubt, but heavy with political baggage").

416 Commons Standing Committee on Justice, Human Rights, Public Safety and Emergency Preparedness, *Improving the Supreme Court of Canada* at 4.

417 Cristin Schmitz, "Cotler, Arbour Differ on Risk Tory Government Would Politicize Supreme Court," *The Lawyers' Weekly,* 18 June 2004.

418 Tonda MacCharles, "Liberals Rigged Same-Sex Rulings, Harper Charges," *Toronto Star,* 5 Sept. 2003.

419 See also the discussion in ch. 2 of this book.

420 See, e.g., Mr. Reed Elley (Nanaimo–Cowichan, Ref.), *Hansard,* 36th Parl, 1st Sess. (1 April 1998) ("Judges are civil servants. What other recourse do the people of Canada have to hold the judiciary accountable except through their elected representatives? If we in this House do not have the freedom to be able to criticize the judiciary of this country, then who does?"); Ted Morton, *Reforming the Judicial Appointment Process for the Supreme Court of Canada,* Presentation to the Commons Standing Committee on Justice and Human Rights (April 2004) ("But when a national court of appeal is given the function of constitutional review, of supervising the laws passed by Parliament, it is no longer simply enforcing laws; it is also making law. In a 21st century democracy, law-making institutions are expected to be accountable and representative, not independent.").

As Professor Ed Ratushny has noted, pure democratic accountability is inconsistent with the very attribute elemental to a functioning judicial system — judicial independence:

> [i]t is incompatible with the judicial role for judges to view themselves as representatives of particular "constituencies." That is a political rather than judicial function. Judges may act "politically," in the broad sense of that term, when their decisions involve policy choices. But those choices are made on different criteria by judges than by politicians. ... The Supreme Court of Canada is not a "democratic" institution even though it is an essential institution within our democratic system under the rule of law. Its role is not to be democratic, but to be judicial. It is not elected by the public and it is not accountable to the public for the content of its decisions.[421]

Professor Lorraine Weinrib has made similar comments.[422]

There is, however, another way of examining the appointments issue through the prism of judicial independence. Professor Martin Friedland, in his influential study on judicial independence, notes several connections between a credible appointments process and judicial independence. First, the better the quality of judge, the less likely subsequent disciplinary action will be required, with its concomitant stresses on independence. Second, weak appointments diminish the status of the judiciary in the public mind, fostering a climate potentially receptive to interference with judicial functions. Last, politically motivated appointments may prompt legitimate questions about a judge's actual independence and impartiality.[423]

As is discussed elsewhere, the test for judicial independence hinges, in part, on whether bias is reasonably apprehended (or not) by an objective observer. The opaque Supreme Court selection process described by Min-

---

421   Ed Ratushny, "Confirmation Hearings for Supreme Court of Canada Appointments: *Not* a Good Idea!" in Pierre Thibault *et al.*, eds., *Essays in Honour of Gérald-A. Beaudoin: The Challenges of Constitutionalism* (Cowansville, PQ: Editions Y. Blais, 2002).

422   Standing Committee on Justice, Human Rights, Public Safety and Emergency Preparedness, *Evidence* (23 March 2004) ("It is regrettable, I think, that we have entered into this process of thinking about the appointing authority as an offshoot from the new government's concern with the democratic deficit. The democratic deficit is primarily focused on the interplay between the legislature and the executive and properly concerns a number of appointments that are made that could benefit by further engagement by parliamentarians. However, the Supreme Court — and the other courts as well, but in particular the Supreme Court — is a very particular type of institution. We have to have concern that we not analyze the appointing power only or even primarily in the context of the democratic deficit question.").

423   Friedland, *A Place Apart* at 233.

ister Cotler to the Commons justice committee has allowed dubious selections in the more distant past and might do so again in the future. To that extent, it potentially imperils judicial independence, measured on a reasonable apprehension standard. The fact that Court appointments may not have been (in fact) tainted by partisan or truly ideologically driven selections since at least the 1980s does not diffuse fully these concerns. In the words of Professor Jacob Ziegel: "If major controversies have been avoided over the appointment of Supreme Court judges since the adoption of the *Charter* ... this is largely because successive Prime Ministers — Trudeau, Mulroney, Chrétien — have shared similar constitutional philosophies and because the full impact of the *Charter* has not yet sunk in."[424]

Echoing Minister Cotler's election-time reproof, Professor Ziegel also predicted consequences were parties not sharing this classic consensus to take office: "Without the restraining force of an independent nomination procedure or confirmation process appointments would become more polarized, as the appointees would be selected on the basis of their ... political and social philosophies."[425]

We share these concerns. While we join others in acknowledging the general excellence of recent Supreme Court appointments, we agree that the increased power of the judiciary under the *Charter* requires an urgent rethink of the appointments process. In this respect, we are discomforted by a system that depends exclusively on the good faith of the executive branch in selecting meritorious candidates. Like Professor Ziegel, we believe that if Canada has been blessed with excellent Supreme Court justices, this is the fortunate byproduct of an honourable, and once widely shared, political culture opposed to politicizing Court appointments. It is not the result of robust checks and balances in the appointments process minimizing the likelihood of such politicization. We fear that this shared political culture is now evaporating. Accordingly, preserving the calibre of an independent judiciary — and insuring that it remains (or becomes, in the view of critics) depoliticized — will require a rethinking of our antiquated and traditional appointment process.

Reform Proposals

Professor Ziegel has described "a near unanimous chorus of opinion among scholars reinforced by many publicly-sponsored reports that the

---

424 Institute for Research on Public Policy (IRPP), "Merit Selection and Democratization of Appointments to the Supreme Court of Canada," by Jacob Ziegel, *Choices* (June 1999) at 10.

425 *Ibid.*

existing system of appointments is incompatible with a modern federal democratic constitution governed by the rule of law and incorporating one of the most powerful bills of rights in the Western hemisphere."[426] Professor Peter Russell, another leading critic of the current system, has noted that Canada is the sole constitutional democracy "in which the leader of government has an unfettered discretion to decide who will sit on the country's highest court."[427] Professor Ted Morton, an admittedly partisan observer, has pointed to the "one-party domination" of Canada's highest constitutional court, noting that by 2006 and the mandatory retirement of Justice Major, the Liberals (assuming they remain in government) will have appointed 100 percent of the Supreme Court's judges.[428] Professor Peter McCormick objects to an appointment system that is "so unilateral, so arbitrary, so clandestine."[429]

Modest reforms to the appointments process were proposed in, and then jettisoned with, the Meech Lake and Charlottetown accords. These agreements would have incorporated the basic appointment requirements found currently in the *Supreme Court Act* into the *Constitution Act, 1867*, and also empowered provinces to nominate Supreme Court candidates for selection by the Governor-in-Council.[430] Since the failure of these initiatives, a large number of reform initiatives have emerged,[431] most of then less clearly focused on enhanced provincial input.

---

426 *Ibid.* at 19.

427 Peter Russell, *A Parliamentary Approach to Reforming the Process of Filling Vacancies on the Supreme Court of Canada* (brief to the Standing Committee on Justice, Human Rights, Public Safety and Emergency Preparedness, 23 March 2004 at 1); Standing Committee on Justice, Human Rights, Public Safety and Emergency Preparedness, *Evidence* (23 March 2004).

428 Ted Morton, *Reforming the Judicial Appointment Process for the Supreme Court of Canada*, Presentation to the Commons Standing Committee on Justice and Human Rights (April 2004).

429 Institute for Research on Public Policy, Peter McCornick, "Could We, Should We, Reform the Senate and the Supreme Court?" (Jan.–Feb. 2000) *Policy Options* at 10.

430 See 1987 Constitutional (Meech Lake) Accord, Proposed Constitutional Amendment, 1987, s. 6; Consensus Report on the Constitution, Charlottetown August 28, 1992, Part II(B).

431 See, e.g., Friedland, *A Place Apart* at 256; Ziegel, "Merit Selection and Democratization"; Weinrib, "Appointing Judges to the Supreme Court of Canada in the *Charter* Era," at 131 *et seq*; Canadian Bar Association, *Supreme Court of Canada Appointment Process* (March 2004).

Categorized simply, these recent reform suggestions may be divided into three camps: those proposing a more formalized and diversified consultation process and the inclusion of a committee system analogous to that employed for other federally appointed judges; those favouring (in addition or instead) some sort of parliamentary confirmation procedure; and those proposing other measures enhancing accountability that do not depend exclusively on a more transparent appointment system.

Table 4.11 distills several proposals covering the first two areas, proposed by presenters before the Commons justice committee in March and April 2004, along with a few others devised in the last decade. The third sort of reform — broader accountability mechanisms — is discussed later in this section.

Table 4.11   Proposals for Reforming the Judicial Appointment Process

Proponent	Judicial Selection Criteria	Consultation/Vetting Process		Parliamentary Confirmation Process
		Committee Role	Committee Structure	
Academics				
Friedland[432]		Committee would prepare a short list of candidates.	Committee includes two nominees of the province or provinces particularly concerned with the appointment; three lawyers selected by the law societies, the CBA and the Canadian Association of Law Teachers; and four representatives selected by the federal government.	Yes, in the form of a joint committee of the Commons and senate if the government did not select a candidate from the committee's short list. Questioning during this process could not elicit responses to questions on how the candidate would decide specific issues.
Manfredi[433]				Prime minister's nominee would be presented to a standing committee on federal judicial appointments. The committee could examine and report on the nominee's suitability for the position. Public hearings might be possible, but are likely unnecessary. The committee would make a recommendation to the House, which would then vote to ratify the nominee or not.

432 Friedland, *A Place Apart* at 256.
433 Standing Committee on Justice, Human Rights, Public Safety and Emergency Preparedness, *Evidence* (March 30, 2004).

	Consultation/Vetting Process		
Proponent	Judicial Selection Criteria	Committee Role	Committee Structure	Parliamentary Confirmation Process
Monahan and Hogg[434]	Selection criteria include personal qualities such as the highest level of proficiency in the law, superior analytical and written skills, proven ability to listen, open-mindedness and soundness of judgment, as well as other considerations relating to diversity.	Committee should meet with prime minister/justice minister's nominee (*after* this person is identified), and question the candidate to measure and assess the way in which publicly announced selection criteria, have been applied. Questioning will be restricted by a protocol precluding questions on how candidates would decide particular issues.	Committee made up of Members of Parliament and other experts or knowledgeable individuals, including nominees of the Canadian Judicial Council, the law societies and the CBA; and representatives of the provincial attorneys general.	Because the committee does not nominate a candidate — instead reviewing their candidacy after nomination — the proposal resembles a sort of confirmation process.
McCormack[435]		Committee would nominate a short list, through super-majority voting. Prime minister would select a candidate from the short list produced by the committee.	Committee includes five judges (other than sitting Supreme Court justices) selected by and from the Canadian Judicial Council; five premiers selected by and from the premiers conference; five members from the Commons justice committee representing the major official parties.	Possibly, the newly minted Supreme Court justice would have a public, post-appointment meeting with the Commons justice committee.

434 *Ibid.* (April 27, 2004); Patrick Monahan and Peter Hogg, "We Need an Open Parliamentary Review of Court Appointments," *National Post*, 24 April 2004, A19.

435 Standing Committee on Justice, Human Rights, Public Safety and Emergency Preparedness, *Evidence* (1 April 2004).

		Consultation/Vetting Process		
Proponent	**Judicial Selection Criteria**	**Committee Role**	**Committee Structure**	**Parliamentary Confirmation Process**
Morton[436]				Parliamentary hearings reviewing the prime minister's nominee, coupled with other accountability mechanisms (discussed below).
Ratushny[437]		None. Instead, the present system would be formalized, requiring the justice minister to publicly elicit recommendations. The minister would develop the shortlist from these recommendations and internal consultations. This list would be published, and the minister would then consult essentially the people he/she consults at present. A final recommendation would be made to Cabinet, for action by that body.		None. Opposed to this process.
Russell[438]		Committee would make recommendations to Cabinet, possibly after a public interview with the candidate. Cabinet retains the appointment power, but the	Not specifically set out, but suggests a Judicial Services Committee (possibly selected by Parliament), which includes parliamentarians.	

436   *Ibid.*
437   Ratushny, "Confirmation Hearings."
438   Standing Committee on Justice, Human Rights, Public Safety and Emergency Preparedness, *Evidence* (1 April 2004).

Proponent	Judicial Selection Criteria	Consultation/Vetting Process		Parliamentary Confirmation Process
		Committee Role	Committee Structure	
		government is required to give reasons for the rejection of candidates recommended by the selection committee and would then be obliged to consider further recommendations.		
Ziegel[437]	Complete personal integrity; robust health; industriousness and good work habits; sense of collegiality; excellent intellect and writing skills; deep understanding of the Constitution and the role of law; and, ability to "project the consequences of a judgement on a broader canvass."	Committee elicits suggested nominations from the legal community, including through advertising. The committee interviews potential candidates. The government would be required to appoint a justice from the committee's short list or give reasons for failing to do so.	Committee includes a nominee of the justice minister; two nominees of provincial governments; two CBA and law society nominees; one First Nations nominee; two members of the public appointed by the Governor General; one chair, also appointed by the Governor General.	Yes, especially if the government insists that it may go outside the shortlist proposed by the committee.
Professional Organizations				
Canadian Bar Association[440]	High moral character; human qualities, such as sympathy, generosity, charity and patience; experience in the law; intellectual and judgmental ability; good health and work habits;	Committee would make recommendations to the prime minister.	Committee composed of nominees of the justice minister, and the attorney general, chief justice and law society of the jurisdiction(s) from which the candidate would be selected; the	None. CBA opposes such a process.

439 Ziegel, "Merit Selection and Democratization" at 10 *et seq.*
440 CBA, *Supreme Court of Canada Appointment Process.*

Proponent	Judicial Selection Criteria	Consultation/Vetting Process		Parliamentary Confirmation Process
		Committee Role	Committee Structure	
	bilingualism, as required. The Court should be representative of the regions and legal systems of Canada and affirmative-action policies for women and minorities are favoured.		president of the CBA; and four parliamentarians elected from the membership of the Commons justice committee.	
Other				
Justice L'Heureux-Dubé[441]		Committee would receive applications, examine candidates and undertake any necessary research.	Committee would include Members of Parliament (e.g., the Speaker of the House and the chair of the justice committee); the president of the CBA, the president of the Bar Association in the province in which the candidate has been working in, the chief justice of that province and the the Supreme Court chief justice.	

441   Standing Committee on Justice, Human Rights, Public Safety and Emergency Preparedness, *Evidence* (23 March 2004).

In its final May 2004 report on the selection process, the Liberal majority on the Commons justice committee proposed modest reform of the appointments process. Specifically, it recommended that the government extend the federally appointed judge-committee vetting process to Supreme Court nominees. This committee would be staffed by representatives from each official party in the Commons, from the provinces, and from the judiciary, bar and public. Following extensive, and confidential, discussions incorporating at least the present level of consultation undertaken by the minister, the committee would be charged with preparing a shortlist of candidates that would be supplied to the minister of justice. Cabinet would then select the best candidate from this confidential list, or could request that the committee prepare another shortlist.

Once the appointment was made, the chair of the advisory body and/or the minister of justice would appear before the Commons justice committee in a public session designed to "make Canadians more aware of the appointments process and constitute an appropriate forum for parliamentary scrutiny."[442]

These proposals fell far short of reforms demanded by opposition parties. The most modest critique — that of the NDP — called for the minister to appear before the parliamentary committee prior to the appointment of the new justice. More radically, the Conservatives urged "substantive input from all the provinces and territories" in the compilation of a list of suitable candidates, a proposal endorsed in even more robust form by the Bloc Québécois.[443] Further, the Conservatives called for a public review of the short list before a parliamentary committee, and parliamentary ratification of a chosen nominee.[444]

The 2004 Appointments

In 2004, the Martin government was surprised by two resignations from the high court, prompting rapid thinking on reform of the appointment process. The result was an *ad hoc* system in which the Governor-in-Council announced the selections of Justices Charon and Abella, the justice minister appeared before a pseudo-parliamentary committee to discuss these candidates, and the Governor-in-General subsequently finalized the appointments.

---

442 Commons Standing Committee on Justice, Human Rights, Public Safety and Emergency Preparedness, *Improving the Supreme Court of Canada* at 6–7.

443 *Ibid.* at 15–16 and 19–20.

444 *Ibid.* at 15–16.

The parliamentary committee's members were three Liberal Members of Parliament, two Conservative members and one member each from the Bloc and the New Democrats. The committee also included a representative of the Canadian Judicial Council and from the Law Society of Upper Canada, Ontario's bar regulator. This body was provided with succinct biographical information on the two candidates the day before Minister Cotler's appearance. Subsequently,

> [i]n his presentation to the Committee, the Minister described the scope and nature of the process used to select the nominees, with particular emphasis upon the consultations he undertook in selecting the two nominees. The Minister also elaborated on the nominees' professional capacity and their personal characteristics that made them suitable candidates for the Supreme Court of Canada. This included highlighting some of their decisions as members of the Ontario Court of Appeal. The Minister was then questioned by the members of the Committee. Following this public session, the Committee then proceeded to discuss its report in an *in camera* meeting.[445]

The committee endorsed the government's candidates. It complained, however, that the process followed was wholly inadequate. It was given little time to review the biographical information on the candidates. This information was scanty. A longer short list allowing comparisons between candidates was not produced.[446] The appointment process was, in other words, an improvement over the old system, but only a way-stop on the path to a more meaningful vetting process.

Another Proposal
The appointment system employed in August 2004 was expressly intended by the government as a temporary measure, pending development of a more permanent process. How, then, to decide among the various reform options provided above? We offer our thoughts.

Guiding Principles
On the whole we find persuasive two complaints about the various proposed solutions: first, we dislike the idea of a committee comprising members of the bar and bench playing a role in reviewing candidates. As Professor Monahan has noted, these jurists and judges are themselves

---

445 Interim *Ad Hoc* Committee on the Appointment of Supreme Court Judges, *Report* (August 2004).
446 *Ibid.*

unaccountable and unelected.[447] Moreover, as our empirical discussion of federally appointed judges in 2003 set out in the preceding section suggests, committee vetting of this sort does little to make appointments less partisan. Even if it did, at best, this model — designed to sidestep politicization from the participation of politicians — simply replaces public politics with the insidious and much less transparent professional politics of the legal profession. In our view, it would be far better to enlist in any vetting process politicians from various perspectives with publicly stated party positions.

As a variant on this issue, it would also be troubling to have members of the profession evaluating candidates, most of whom would be sitting judges. Such a procedure is fraught with potential conflicts of interest and personal imperatives, and risks being very unattractive to potential candidates. Indeed, the committee system employed since 1988 for other federally-appointed judges does not apply to elevations of existing judges to or within the federal bench, probably for these very reasons.

Finally, undue reliance on "experts" to the exclusion of politicians does little to foster deeper parliamentary and public education on the role and function of the Supreme Court, something that public nomination procedures would at least require.[448] That said, we agree that expert, independent opinion is valuable somewhere in the appointment process.

As for "lay" representation on a committee, while public involvement is attractive in principle, it seems dubious in practice. Laypeople must be selected. Without a random, jury-pool procedure, the selection of the layperson would either require the government to name its preferred member or instead would depend on assorted interest groups putting forward a name. In the former circumstance, the layperson is effectively a government representative. In the latter circumstance, questions arise as to which interest groups would have the power to name the representative. In any event, lay representation seems most important where democratically elected parliamentarians are excluded from the process. If elected legislators are included, the process has a democratic legitimacy that is not further enhanced by the presence of a token member of the public.

In relation to a second common complaint, we echo concerns that a full-fledged, American-style parliamentary "confirmation" process would

---

447 Monahan, in Standing Committee on Justice, Human Rights, Public Safety and Emergency Preparedness, *Evidence* (27 April 2004).

448 See C.P. Manfredi, *Judicial Power and the Charter: Canada and the Paradox of Liberal Constitutionalism* (Toronto: McClelland & Stewart, 1993) at 174.

produce little more than embarrassing political theatre,[449] such as that associated with the painful Bork and Thomas confirmation proceedings before the U.S. senate. Such a process would layer explicit partisanship onto the appointment system and open the door to political grandstanding. Quality candidates would likely be deterred by such a peril. Moreover, we share some of Professor Sujit Choudhry's concerns about an open-ended nomination process:[450] any confirmation process in which candidates are pressed to articulate positions on issues raised by interrogating politicians raises the spectre of prejudgment.

In subsequent litigation relating to those same issues, only the most inattentive lawyers would fail to query the judicial independence of a Court comprising justices who had run this inquisitorial gauntlet.

We are not, however, prepared to give up on Parliament. The Commons is ultimately the most vital branch of democratic governance, and should — by any measure of legitimacy — have some role in the appointment process.

Building on the August 2004 Experience

We offer up, therefore, yet another model for reforming the appointments process, building on the *ad hoc* system employed in August 2004. First, when a vacancy arises, the minister of justice should strike a committee of experts nominated by all the likely suspects: the CBA, the Canadian Judicial Council, the Canadian Association of Law Teachers, and lawyers nominated by provincial attorneys general.

The committee of experts would be charged with drafting selection criteria for use by the government, along with explanatory and justifying commentary. Obviously, in their core content, these criteria should vary only modestly from appointment to appointment. However, they would also reflect considerations that will change as the composition of the Court evolves. These variable topics might include regional, ethnic and gender representation issues, adjusting the balance between established judges and senior members of the bar, and changing requirements for specialized legal expertise. All told, this first step in the process would satisfy the requirement for independent, expert participation in the system without asking members of the profession actually to evaluate their peers, colleagues and sometimes competitors.

---

449 See Ratushny, "Confirmation Hearings"; CBA, *Supreme Court of Canada Appointment Process* at 8.

450 Sujit Choudhry, "Judging Supreme Court Judges: Finding a New Way to Pick Them That's Legal Might Not Be Easy," *Montreal Gazette*, 25 April 2004, D8.

The committee of experts' selection criteria would be supplied to the minister of justice, who would then table them publicly before the Commons justice committee. The latter could publicly debate the criteria and propose changes. The minister would then either accept or reject the criteria proposed by the committee of experts, as amended by the justice committee, providing reasons for his or her decision and making public the finalized criteria accepted by the government.

Thus, while the committee of experts and the justice committee could not compel the minister to follow their guidelines, the requirement that the minister provide reasons for his or her rejection of individual criterion, and then release the final set of guidelines, would make the government's thinking transparent. Capricious rejection of criteria established by a committee of experts and the Commons justice committee would obviously raise questions about the government's *bona fides*, a development with political consequences. This political deterrent would likely reduce the risk that guidelines would be rejected or selected by the government for partisan or self-serving reasons.

The minister would then engage in a broad consultation process *per* the current practice, but now with the purpose of identifying candidates meeting the public criteria. The Governor-in-Council would appoint the successful candidate. Subsequently, the minister would appear publicly before the Commons justice committee and provide reasons explaining how the successful candidate met each of the criteria set out in the public guidelines. The justice committee would then report on the extent to which it agreed with the minister's assessment. Obviously, a majority representation on the justice committee could be mobilized to quash a negative report. However, since the media and members of the public would have in hand both the guidelines and the minister's justification, such a move would not necessarily forestall criticism of the government.

While a Commons committee report (or public commentary) condemning the government's choice would likely be embarrassing to the new Supreme Court judge, the focus on contrasting that person's qualifications against already much-vetted public guidelines would likely constrain the debate. With any reasonable appointment, more discussion would likely centre on how the government justified its selection, weighing criteria off one another, than on the personal qualities of the judge, thus sidestepping U.S. confirmation-style antics and personal attacks. Put another way, the judge risks suffering collateral damage in criticisms of the government, rather than confronting a frontal assault. This is not too much of a burden for a judicial appointee to weather. Such collateral condemnations exist even under the present system.[451] In any event, the prospect of embarrassment and political controversy is a net positive. Faced with such scrutiny, the political balance of incentives favours clean, easily defended appointments.

While it would be preferable to codify this reformed procedure in law, all of these changes could be introduced simply as a matter of government practice and policy, held together by the check of public scrutiny. For the reasons enunciated above, we are extremely skeptical that this process would transgress any constitutional principle, as the Governor-in-Council would retain the appointment authority mandated by (even a constitutionalized) *Supreme Court Act*.

"Back End" Accountability Mechanisms

Front-end quality control is only the first step in judicial reform. For instance, Professor Morton proposes supplemental accountability mechanisms in the form of term limits for justices, a proposal echoing the one made in 1990 by Professor David Beatty.[452] This concept draws on the European analogy: several European constitutional courts cap the duration of constitutional court appointments.

We agree that this proposal makes sense for Supreme Court of Canada appointments for several reasons. First, term limits — capped at, say, ten years — mean that a prime minister's legacy endures no more than a decade after his or her departure. Court-packing, even if it were to occur, would have a shelf life. The limited duration of appointments may also reduce the stakes associated with any one appointment, potentially making it easier for governments to maintain a depoliticized selection process.

---

451   See *Hansard*, 36th Parl., 1st Sess. (10 Oct. 1997) ("Mr. Michel Bellehumeur [Berthier–Montcalm, PQ]: "The Prime Minister has just appointed Michel Bastarache to the Supreme Court of Canada, not long after this same Liberal government had appointed him to the New Brunswick Court of Appeal. Does the Prime Minister not find it indecent to appoint to the highest court in the country a former colleague, someone very close to him, someone close to the Liberal Party of Canada, someone who co-chaired the national committee for the yes side during the referendum on the Charlottetown accord? ... Hon. Anne McLellan [Minister of Justice and Attorney General of Canada, Lib.]: Mr. Speaker, if the hon. member is referring to the fact that the hon. Mr. Justice Bastarache worked for three years at the distinguished Canadian law firm of Lang Michener where the Prime Minister also served for some period of time, we do not deny that. Why would we? I am deeply offended that anyone would suggest that Mr. Justice Bastarache's service at that law firm would in some way disqualify this distinguished individual from his appointment.").

452   David Beatty, *Talking Heads and the Supremes: The Canadian Production of Constitutional Review* (Toronto: Carswell, 1990) at 271.

Second, increased judicial turnover also increases the prospect that various constituencies will see at least one appointment during their lifetimes. Visible minority, aboriginal, gender and regional representation, as measured across time, could easily be increased without forever quashing the aspirations of equally qualified candidates who do not fall within these categories.

Third, turnover likely means younger and potentially more productive judges, a not unhelpful quality for a busy court. At present, judges are entitled to remain on the Court from appointment until age seventy-five, ten years beyond the mandatory retirement age imposed on much of Canada's working population.

Last, circulating judges through the Supreme Court and then back to the lower courts on the expiry of the term limitation would diffuse high court expertise, and might also foster understanding and collegiality in what is otherwise an extremely hierarchical system.

Unfortunately, implementing such a proposal requires more careful legal probing than would the selection process described above. First, the *Supreme Court Act* would have to be amended to specify that judges cease to hold office upon expiry of their maximum term. This amendment again raises the question noted above as to whether this Act is constitutionalized.

Second, questions of judicial independence arise any time judicial tenures are limited. There is good reason to believe that single, non-renewable term limits are consistent with judicial independence, in the form of security of tenure.[453] However, a definitive answer to this question would require the Supreme Court itself to rule on the constitutionality of a measure limiting the tenure of its judges.

Implementing term limits, in other words, will require due deliberation. For this reason, reform of the appointments process and term limits should be pursued as separate projects.

---

453 See *Valente v. The Queen* [1985] 2 S.C.R. 673 at 698 ("The essence of security of tenure for purposes of s. 11(d) is a tenure, whether until an age of retirement, *for a fixed term*, or for a specific adjudicative task, that is secure against interference by the Executive or other appointing authority in a discretionary or arbitrary manner") (emphasis added); *Ell v. Alberta*, [2003] 1 S.C.R. 857 at para. 32 (citing this passage with approval). Fixed terms have not violated independence standards in the administrative tribunal context. Indeed, in *Re Remuneration of Judges* itself, the Court viewed fixed-term appointments as indicators of independence on the part of commissions reviewing judicial compensation. *Re Remuneration of Judges*, [1997] 3 S.C.R. 3 at para. 171.

2. Financial and Administrative Independence

Once judges are appointed, they enjoy all the trappings of judicial independence. In chapter 2, we discussed the constitutional prerequisites of this independence: security of tenure and financial and administrative independence. Here, we elaborate somewhat on the details.

As noted in chapter 2, financial independence has both an "individual" and "institutional" dimension. Individually, financial independence means that judges' salaries must be set by law. Institutionally, it means that judges' salaries generally may not be reduced, increased or frozen without recourse to an independent, effective and objective salary commission. For federally appointed judges, both of these requirements are addressed in the *Judges Act*. First, this statute specifies the exact pay of various classes of federally appointed judges, thus satisfying the first dimension of financial independence.[454]

Second, the Act creates the Judicial Compensation and Benefits Commission "to inquire into the adequacy of the salaries and other amounts payable under this Act and into the adequacy of judges' benefits generally."[455] The commission comprises three members appointed by the Governor-in-Council. The judiciary and the minister of justice nominate one member each, and then these two nominees nominate a chair. The commissioners enjoy some security of tenure, being appointed to four-year terms and subject to dismissal by the Governor-in-Council only for cause.[456]

For its part, administrative independence requires that courts themselves have control over the administrative decisions "that bear directly and immediately on the exercise of the judicial function," such as "assignment of judges, sittings of the court, and court lists — as well as the related matters of allocation of court rooms and direction of the administrative staff engaged in carrying out these functions."[457] This requirement is met generally in the statutes creating the various courts, which assign to judges themselves these administrative roles.[458]

---

454 *Judges Act*, s. 9 *et seq.*
455 *Ibid.*, s. 26.
456 *Ibid.*, s. 26.1.
457 *Re Remuneration of Judges*, [1997] 3 S.C.R. 3 at para. 117.
458 See, e.g., *Supreme Court Act*, s. 97, but see also s. 32, fixing the three sessions of the court in the calendar year, but allowing the Governor-in-Council, as well as the Court, to vary these dates. See also *Federal Courts Act*, ss. 15 and 16.

3. Removing Judges: Security of Tenure and Judicial Independence

The hard core of judicial independence is security of tenure. As discussed in chapter 2, constitutionally protected security of tenure has both an individual and an institutional dimension. Individual security of tenure means that the executive may not dismiss judges before the age of retirement — seventy-five — except for misconduct or disability, following a judicial inquiry. Thus, a judge may only be removed from office for a reason relating to his or her capacity to perform his or her judicial duties. Arbitrary removal is prohibited.[459]

a) Canadian Judicial Council

Institutionally, before a judge may be removed for cause, "there must be a judicial inquiry to establish that such cause exists, at which the judge affected must be afforded an opportunity to be heard."[460] In practice, this procedure is governed by the *Judges Act*, and undertaken by the Canadian Judicial Council (CJC) created by this statute.[461] The council — composed of the chief justices of the country's superior courts — is empowered to conduct inquiries into judicial misconduct, on request by the minister of justice or provincial attorneys general.[462] Its writ extends to all superior court judges, defined in the *Interpretation Act* as the judges of the provincial superior courts and the Supreme, Federal and Tax Courts.[463]

On completion of its inquiry — during which the judge subject to investigation is entitled to make submissions — the council reports its findings to the minister. The council may recommend that the judge be removed from office. It does so where it concludes that the judge in question has become incapacitated or disabled from the due execution of his or her office by reason of age or infirmity, has been guilty of misconduct, has failed in the due execution of that office, or has been placed, by his or her conduct or otherwise, in a position incompatible with the due execution of that office.[464]

In deciding this question, past council inquiry committees have asked whether the conduct alleged is "so manifestly and profoundly destructive

---

459 *Mackin v. New Brunswick (Minister of Finance)*, [2002] 1 S.C.R. 405 at paras. 42 and 43.
460 *Re Therrien*, [2001] 2 S.C.R. 3 at para. 39.
461 *Judges Act*, s. 59.
462 *Ibid.*, s. 63.
463 *Interpretation Act*, s. 35.
464 *Judges Act*, s. 65.

of the concept of impartiality and independence of the judicial role that public confidence would be sufficiently undermined to render the judge incapable of executing the judicial office."[465] The Supreme Court has endorsed this test. In its words, set out in a case involving an inferior provincial court judge, "before making a recommendation that a judge be removed, the question to be asked is whether the conduct for which he or she is blamed is so manifestly and totally contrary to the impartiality, integrity and independence of the judiciary that the confidence of individuals appearing before the judge, or of the public in its justice system, would be undermined, rendering the judge incapable of performing the duties of his office."[466]

This is a fairly forgiving threshold. Since its creation in 1971, the CJC has recommended the dismissal of a judge only once, in its 1996 Bienvenue Inquiry.[467] In that case, Mr. Justice Bienvenue made remarks during a criminal trial recounting his views on the capacity of women to do evil. The council viewed these comments as undermining "public confidence in him and strongly contributed to destroying public confidence in the judicial system." The council concluded "that Mr. Justice Bienvenue has breached the duty of good behaviour under section 99 of the *Constitution Act, 1867* and has become incapacitated or disabled from the due execution of the office of judge" and recommended his dismissal.[468] Mr. Bienvenue resigned soon thereafter, removing the need for the government and Parliament to respond to the council's recommendation.[469]

b)   Address of Parliament

If Justice Bienvenue had not resigned, his dismissal process would not have ended with the Canadian Judicial Council. A recommendation by the Canadian Judicial Council is just that — a recommendation. It does not circumvent other constitutionally or statutorily prescribed requirements for the dismissal of a superior court judge.[470]

---

465   See *Report of the Boilard Inquiry Committee to the Canadian Judicial Council* (August 2003) at para. 112.

466   *Re Therrien,* [2001] 2 S.C.R. 3 at para. 147.

467   *Report of the Boilard Inquiry Committee* at para. 110.

468   *Report of the Canadian Judicial Council to the Minister of Justice under ss. 63(1) of the Judges Act concerning the conduct of Mr. Justice Jean Bienvenue of the Superior Court of Quebec in R. v. T. Théberge* (October 1996).

469   See Department of Justice, "Judge Bienvenue Resigns," press release, 24 Sept. 1996.

470   See, e.g., *Judges Act,* s. 71, specifying that an inquiry does not affect "any power, right or duty of the House of Commons, the Senate or the Governor in Council in relation to the removal from office of a judge or any other person in relation to whom an

Section 99 of the *Constitution Act, 1867* adds an additional layer of procedure onto dismissals of "superior" court judges: judges "shall hold office during good behaviour, but shall be removable by the Governor General on Address of the Senate and House of Commons." As noted above, an "address" is "a resolution expressing the wish or request of Parliament."[471] Exactly how this address would work is uncertain, since it has never been employed since Confederation.[472] Nevertheless, an address of Parliament may, as the Supreme Court has speculated, make "removal of a judge more difficult in practice because of the solemn, cumbersome and publicly visible nature of the process."[473] In the Supreme Court's words, this extra level of tenure protection for judges "reflects the historical and modern position of superior courts as the core of Canada's judicial structure and as the central guardians of the rule of law."[474]

Two somewhat obscure legal issues have been raised concerning section 99. First, is the reference to "superior" courts in section 99 restricted to section 96 provincial superior courts only, or does it also encompasses other, section 101 courts? As noted above, the federal *Interpretation Act* labels as "superior" courts the section 101 Supreme, Federal and Tax Courts of Canada. It seems unlikely that Parliament may, using the *Interpretation Act*, legislate the scope of section 99 of the 1867 Act. Yet, at least one Federal Court decision has held that section 99 "provides for the tenure of judges of the superior courts in general. It applies generically to all superior court judges no matter whether the judge has been appointed to a superior court of a province or to a superior court created under section 101." Thus, the Supreme Court of Canada and the Federal Court of Canada are "superior courts" within the meaning of section 99 of the 1867 Act and "the judges of both such courts are and have been since the establishment

---

inquiry may be conducted"; *Gratton v. Canada (Judicial Council)*, [1994] 2 F.C. 769 at 802–3 (T.D.) ("It is for the Canadian Judicial Council to recommend removal, but Parliament has the ultimate responsibility to decide whether to use the only constitutional device for removal, namely the joint address. There is nothing in the *Judges Act* which precludes Parliament considering the removal of a judge without any recommendation from the Council"). Yet, whether the Supreme Court would view as constitutional a dismissal of a judge following a CJC exoneration remains an open question. See *Re Therrien*, [2001] 2 S.C.R. 3 at para. 72 *et seq.*, suggesting, without deciding, that a failure by the executive to abide by a judicial inquiry recommendation concerning a provincially-appointed judge might be unconstitutional.

471 *Roberts* (2002), 45 Admin. L.R. (3d) 45 at para. 81.

472 See Friedland, *A Place Apart* at 77.

473 *Valente*, [1985] 2 S.C.R. 673 at 697.

474 *Ell*, [2003] 1 S.C.R. 857 at para. 31.

of such courts superior court judges."[475] In practice, whether the section 99 procedure is constitutionally required for section 101 courts is largely an incidental question. The address of Parliament dismissal requirement is formally extended to Supreme, Federal and Tax Court judges by virtue of the statutes governing each of these courts.[476]

Second, as discussed with officers of Parliament above, questions have been raised as to whether section 99 contemplates one or two procedures for removal: one for bad behaviour by the Governor-in-Council, and the other by joint address of Parliament for any reason. As noted above, it seems unlikely that any process of removal of superior court judges lacking a joint address would satisfy judicial independence. Thus, the Gratton Inquiry committee of the Canadian Judicial Council concluded in 1994 that, by reason of judicial independence, superior judges could not be removed without a joint address of Parliament.[477] This view also reflects the Supreme Court's sense of how the removal process must operate.[478]

On the further issue of whether Parliament is constrained in the justifications it may invoke in issuing this address, the Gratton Inquiry committee suggested that Parliament was not confined to acting in response to bad behaviour by the judge.[479] The Federal Court rejected this latter view on judicial review. Principles of judicial independence, concluded the court, negate the capacity of Parliament to dismiss judges for other than bad behaviour.[480]

D. CONCLUSION

As this chapter suggests, unelected officials conduct most of Canadian governance. Exactly how this tendency stacks up when measured against the objective of democratic legitimacy is a tricky question. Democratic account-

---

475   *Addy v. R.*, [1985] 2 F.C. 452 at 462–3 (T.D.).

476   *Supreme Court Act*, s. 9; *Federal Courts Act*, s. 8; *Tax Court of Canada Act*, s. 7.

477   Canadian Judicial Council, *Decision of the Gratton Inquiry Committee re Constitutional Questions with respect to the jurisdiction of the Canadian Judicial Council and the Inquiry Committee* (Feb. 1994) at 31.

478   *Re Therrien*, [2001] 2 S.C.R. 3 at para. 63, suggesting that "removal of a [superior court] judge must follow the joint address procedure set out in s. 99(1)"; *Ell*, [2003] 1 S.C.R. 857 at para. 31 ("Superior court judges are removable only by a joint address of the House of Commons and the Senate, as stipulated by s. 99 of the *Constitution Act, 1867*").

479   *Ibid.*

480   *Gratton*, [1994] 2 F.C. 769 at 791–92.

ability, as we have defined it, means that unelected officials should be directly or indirectly accountable to the citizenry.

To this end, *full* democratic control over the selection and dismissal process seems warranted for at least some of Canada's unelected officials. For instance, lying at the apex of the executive branch, the ministry is usually selected from the ranks of elected parliamentarians. The tenure of these people should be (and by virtue of the confidence convention, is) vulnerable to the plenary of Canada's elected officials, sitting as the Commons. On the other hand, the senate is a legislative body for whom democratic accountability should mean *direct* citizen involvement in appointments and dismissals, exercised via elections. At present, the senate is an institution whose members are democratically accountable to no one, although possessed of substantial legislative powers.

This chapter has also suggested, however, that full democratic control over selection and dismissal is *undesirable* for certain other unelected officials. Indeed, there are instances where this sort of control would impair other vital objectives. The two key countervailing objectives canvassed in this chapter are merit — measured as raw competence — and independence from elected officials.

Merit-based considerations should prevail in the executive branch proper. Thus, the ministry has substantial appointment and dismissal power over Governor-in-Council appointees. Superficially, this control is consistent with the view that unelected officials should be accountable, at least indirectly, to those who are elected. However, "control" may mean partisanship. In the vast universe of GIC appointments, partisan selections may grate with other objectives, not least competence. Here, Cabinet discretion in appointments should be tempered by mechanisms ensuring selections based on relevant (and not partisan) criteria. Such a move would build on existing standards for the public service. Public servants are largely shielded from politically motivated selections and dismissals, preserving a merit philosophy in public service staffing.

Security of tenure is an important consideration for other unelected officials as well. Officers of Parliament, for instance, also have substantial security of tenure. Here, however, protected status is motivated by independence concerns: a desire to ensure that these key "agents" of Parliament are insulated from manipulation by the executive branch.

Judges too are insulated from arbitrary dismissals, to the point of being largely invulnerable to political branch machinations. Judicial independence secures from the political branches those who police limited government in our system of government. Nevertheless, while it limits dismissals, this judicial independence has not yet translated into a judicial selection process free of partisan (or at least political) impulses, or the perception thereof. The appointments systems await refinement. The challenge will be to craft a greater role for Parliament that accommodates the legitimate interest of that branch in a meritorious judiciary without rendering appointments a political football.

Roughly analogous independence imperatives may also justify a parliamentary interest in the appointment of the Governor General. At present, that official is appointed by the Queen, at the behest of the prime minister. The Governor General is a mostly ceremonial figure. Nonetheless, he or she might some day be asked to exercise important reserve powers protecting the prerogatives of Parliament. Given this prospect, the Governor General should be selected in consultation with Parliament itself.

In sum, the law on the appointment and dismissal of Canada's unelected officials reflects a grab bag of competing concerns and motivations. In many instances, Canadian democracy has not yet found the soft-spot in relation to the principles that should govern appointment and dismissal of each class of unelected official.

5

Parliament, Democracy and the Legislative Process

In our first several chapters, we have focused on the means by which officials in our democratic government are selected. Beginning with this chapter, we shift focus, examining rules and procedures ensuring that, once selected, these officials govern democratically.

When many Canadians think of democratic governance, they imagine first the role of elected legislatures in passing Acts of Parliament. Indeed, the legislative process lies at the heart of what Parliament does, and is therefore a principal (though far from the exclusive) responsibility of Canada's elected Members of Parliament. Yet, a substantial amount of law is enacted, not by the legislature, but by the executive in the form of "delegated legislation," usually regulations. Legislating is, in other words, a joint executive/legislative branch enterprise.

In this chapter, we explore the parliamentary legislative function, highlighting the institutional and legal context in which it operates. We then turn our attention to executive branch law-making, an area much richer in truly legal considerations. Running through this chapter is one of our key themes: the relationship/tension between the executive and legislative branches of government.

A. THE PARLIAMENTARY LEGISLATIVE ENTERPRISE

In this work, we cannot canvass the complex and lengthy rules of procedure that govern the minutiae of parliamentary law-making. There are
already many comprehensive, technical resources in this area.[1] Instead, we
do two things. First, we provide an overview of the Parliament of Canada,
discussing its workings and some of its key actors. These sections inform
not only the law-making roles of Parliament, but also its other functions,
discussed in chapter 6.

Second, we provide a very succinct overview of the legislative process.
Our focus throughout this discussion is on the House of Commons,
though we raise issues related to the senate from time to time.

1.   Overview of the Parliament of Canada

By the express terms of the *Constitution Act, 1867*, the "Parliament of Canada" consists "of the Queen, an Upper House styled the Senate, and the
House of Commons."[2]

The most important — and democratically legitimate — of these actors
is the Commons, composed of elected Members of Parliament. As material in Appendix 2 demonstrates, the vast majority of parliamentary legislation originates in the Commons.[3]

a)   Summoning, Prorogation and Dissolution of Parliament

The Constitution anticipates the existence of, and extends certain guarantees to, the House of Commons. The *Constitution Act, 1867* empowers the
Governor General "from Time to Time, in the Queen's Name, by Instrument under the Great Seal of Canada, [to] summon and call together the

---

1   See, e.g., Robert Marleau and Camille Montpetit, *House of Commons Procedure and
    Practice* (Ottawa: House of Commons, 2000); Canada, House of Commons, *Beauch-
    esne's Rules and Forms of the House of Commons of Canada*, 6th ed. (Toronto: Carswell,
    1989); Canada, House of Commons, *Précis of Procedure* (2003), available at
    www.parl.gc.ca/information/about/process/house/precis/Précis-e.pdf; Library of Par-
    liament, *The Legislative Process*, BP-151E (1989).
2   *Constitution Act, 1867*, s. 17.
3   Indeed, over time the senate is becoming less and less important as a source of legis-
    lation. The senate is not, however, an inert legislative body. In recent Parliaments, the
    senate has amended a modest, but increasing proportion of bills, as measured as a
    percentage of all bills in each Parliament receiving royal assent. For an overview (and
    strong defence) of the senate's role in Canadian governance, see Serge Joyal, ed., *Pro-
    tecting Canadian Democracy: The Senate You Never Knew* (Kingston, ON: McGill-
    Queen's University Press, 2003).

House of Commons."[4] This power is greatly constrained by convention, and now the *Charter*.

Summoning and Prorogation of Parliament

By convention, the Governor General exercises his or her authority to call Parliament to session on the advice of the prime minister.[5] Indeed, this convention is codified in the Writ of Election, enacted in the *Canada Elections Act*. This writ empowers the monarch (and thus the Governor General) to set the date for a new Parliament "by and with the advice" of the prime minister.[6]

Once summoned, a given Parliament is generally divided into several sessions, separated by a prorogation. A prorogation is again the prerogative of the Governor General, acting on the advice of the prime minister.[7] A prorogation (or a dissolution of Parliament, pending an election) may not endure indefinitely, however. The *Canadian Charter of Rights and Freedoms* specifies that Parliament must sit at least once every twelve months.[8]

Dissolution of Parliament

Subject to an exception in times of emergency discussed in chapter 10,[9] a House of Commons may endure no longer than five years.[10] In a reversal of traditional United Kingdom practice, Parliament is not dissolved as a matter of course by the death of a reigning monarch.[11] Thus, unless terminated automatically on expiry of its maximum, five-year life, the Governor General dissolves Parliament.

In dissolving Parliament, the Governor General acts almost always at a time of the prime minister's choosing.[12] Indeed, the timing of a dissolution is generally considered the personal prerogative of the prime minister,[13] to the point of being a constitutional convention.

Dissolution prompts a new electoral cycle, governed by the *Canada Elections Act* and discussed in chapter 3. In the federal Parliament, there are no fixed election dates. This fact usually guarantees the prime minister substantial discretion to determine the timing of dissolution within the

---

4   *Constitution Act, 1867*, s. 38.
5   *Précis of Procedure* at 6.
6   *Canada Elections Act*, Schedule 1.
7   *Précis of Procedure* at 90.
8   *Charter*, s. 5.
9   See ch. 10.
10 See *Charter*, s. 4; *Constitution Act, 1867*, s. 50.
11 *Parliament of Canada Act*, s. 2.
12 *Précis of Procedure* at 91.
13 Privy Council minute, P.C. 3374 (25 Oct. 1935).

five-year life of a Parliament, a matter of some advantage to incumbent governments. It is critical to recognize, however, that the prime minister is only "generally" free to decide the timing of an election.

Requiring a Dissolution

First, there are instances where a prime minister might be *forced* by constitutional convention to seek a dissolution from the Governor General at a time not of his or her choosing. As discussed in chapters 4 and 6, constitutional convention requires a prime minister to resign his or her government or seek parliamentary dissolution in the wake of a no confidence vote by the House. Indeed, the Governor General is constitutionally obliged to dismiss the prime minister who refuses to either resign or seek dissolution after losing the support of the Commons.[14] We discuss the exact content of a no confidence vote in chapter 6.

When the prime minister requests dissolution after a no confidence vote, the Governor General will generally grant the requested dissolution, subject to the discussion below. This convention extends to the Commons a substantial power to determine its own longevity, especially in minority situations where the prime minister's hold on the confidence of the Commons is shaky.

Absent this no confidence vote in the House, it seems unlikely that the Governor General can dissolve Parliament in the face of opposition from the prime minister. Governor General Edward Schreyer speculated publicly in the early 1980s that he might have acted on his own motion and dissolved Parliament had the Trudeau government not abandoned its project of unilaterally repatriating the Constitution. His power to do so — even to allow fundamental constitutional change to be vetted by the electorate — was heatedly contested.[15]

Refusing a Dissolution

Second, there are instances where the Governor General might *refuse* a dissolution requested by the prime minister. As Professor Dawson notes: "the governor general should in the *vast majority* of cases allow the prime minister to exercise the power of dissolution without interference."[16] There will, however, be some instances where dissolution is not warranted.

---

14   See ch. 4 and *Reference re Resolution to Amend the Constitution*, [1981] 1 S.C.R. 753 at 882.

15   Andrew Heard, *Canadian Constitutional Conventions* (Toronto: Oxford University Press, 1991) at 32–33. See also discussion in David Smith, *The Invisible Crown* (Toronto: University of Toronto Press, 1995) at 58.

16   Norman Ward, *Dawson's The Government of Canada*, 6th ed. (Toronto: University of Toronto Press, 1987) at 109 [emphasis added].

Famously, in 1926, Governor General Byng called upon Conservative leader Arthur Meighen to form a government when Prime Minister Mackenzie King resigned after being refused dissolution. Notably, King had sought this dissolution to pre-empt a lost confidence vote for his minority Liberal government, held together in a precarious coalition with the Progressives in an eleven-month-old Parliament. When Meighen's government quickly collapsed and Parliament was dissolved, King campaigned on Lord Byng's failure to respond to his original dissolution request, soundly defeating the Conservative.[17]

While King's denunciation of the Governor General made for good politics, it was bad constitutional discourse. The precise meaning of the so-called King-Byng matter has been debated for generations. It seems almost certain, however, that Byng acted in keeping with constitutional convention: a Governor General may refuse a dissolution in the wake of the resignation of (at least a minority) government, where another prime minister-apparent is able to command the confidence of the Commons,[18] whether this person comes from the Opposition or from within the governing party.[19] Indeed, the Governor General may have a constitutional duty to exercise this power of refusal.[20]

Writing in 1985, parliamentary scholar Eugene Forsey labelled this prerogative of the Governor General "a power held in reserve, for use only when it provides the sole protection for the House of Commons and the people against the divine right of the Prime Minister."[21] It is, in other words, a last check on a prime ministerial abuse of authority. It de-links the fate of a viable Commons from that of a sitting prime minister incapable of commanding its support, perhaps for good reason. In Senator Forsey's words:

> Our constitutional system was never intended to be a plebiscitary democracy, in which Parliament exists, debates and votes only on sufferance

---

17 Robert Bothwell, Ian Drummond and John English, *Canada 1900–1945* (Toronto: University of Toronto Press, 1987) at 207.

18 See discussion in Heard, *Canadian Constitutional Conventions* at 23–24; Eugene A. Forsey and G.C. Eglington, *The Question of Confidence in Responsible Government* (Ottawa: Special Committee on the Reform of the House of Commons, 1985) at 152 *et seq.*

19 Forsey and Eglington, *The Question of Confidence* at 138.

20 See Ward, *Dawson's The Government of Canada* at 190, noting a 1985 Ontario case in which the Conservatives were defeated by the Liberals and NDP acting jointly in agreeing to support a Liberal premier, and arguing that, had the Conservative leader sought a dissolution "when an alternative government was clearly available, the governor would have had a constitutional duty to refuse."

21 Forsey and Eglington, *The Question of Confidence* at 160.

under threat of dissolution at any moment by the Government in office, whether or not that Government has a majority in the House of Commons. A system of that sort has no right to be called parliamentary governance.[22]

Senator Forsey urged that the exercise of this reserve power is likely most legitimate where a government seeks a dissolution soon after an election.[23] In these circumstances, the Governor General reacts to the fresh electoral mandate of a Parliament by forestalling dissolution until Parliament first is given a chance to throw up a leader able to command its confidence. In comparison, recourse to the reserve power to refuse dissolution is less appropriate if exercised several years into a Parliament, at a time near its natural expiry.[24] In those circumstances, the conundrum of government leadership is best decided by taking the matter to the people.

This question of the Governor General's reserve powers is a live issue with every minority government. Interestingly, just before the commencement of the Martin minority, thirty-eighth Parliament in 2004, the three opposition parties wrote to the Governor General:

> As leaders of the opposition parties, we are well aware that, given the Liberal minority government, you could be asked by the Prime Minister to dissolve the 38th Parliament at any time should the House of Commons fail to support some part of the government's program. ... We respectfully point out that the opposition parties, who together constitute a majority in the House, have been in close consultation. We believe that, should a request for dissolution arise this should give you cause, as constitutional practice has determined, to consult the opposition leaders and consider all of your options before exercising your constitutional authority.

The Liberals reportedly pooh-poohed this approach and the related effort on the part of the opposition to predefine confidence votes. The Liberal deputy House leader urged, "[Y]ou can't have your cake and eat it, too. You can't defeat the government and not expect to have to go to the people."[25]

This may be true politically, as the King-Byng case suggests. However, if the opposition parties in the thirty-eighth Parliament were, in coalition,

---

22   *Ibid* at 161.

23   *Ibid* at 159. See also Ward, *Dawson's The Government of Canada* at 189 ("if a prime minister, having obtained a dissolution, was returned with a majority of members and promptly demanded another dissolution, the governor general would have no real alternative but to refuse the advice and force the resignation of the cabinet").

24   Forsey and Eglington, *The Question of Confidence* at 169.

25   Jane Taber, "Tories, NDP and Bloc Unite to Demand More Clout," *Globe and Mail*, 10 Sept. 2004, citing Liberal deputy House leader Mauril Belanger.

to name a leader able to command their approval, they would enjoy a majority support in the Commons. In these circumstances, the weight of scholarly opinion suggests that the Governor General would act constitutionally in first asking that leader to form a government prior to dissolving a young Parliament. We discussed the Governor General's role in selecting the prime minister further in chapter 4.

b) The Sources of Parliamentary Procedure

While in session, parliamentary activities are governed by a comprehensive procedural code. Parliamentary rules of procedure are designed, in the words of the classic Canadian authority, to "protect a minority and restrain the improvidence or tyranny of a majority; to secure the transaction of public business in an orderly manner; to enable every Member to express opinions within the limits necessary to preserve decorum and prevent an unnecessary waste of time; to give abundant opportunity for the consideration of every measure; and to prevent any legislative action from being taken upon sudden impulse."[26]

The specific rules governing parliamentary activity stem from different sources, not least the incorporation of British parliamentary traditions via the preamble to the *Constitution Act, 1867.* As discussed at length in chapter 2, this Act endows Canada with "a Constitution similar in Principle to that of the United Kingdom." The 1867 Act also speaks of Parliament possessing parliamentary "privileges," as does the *Parliament of Canada Act.*

As discussed as well in chapter 2, parliamentary privileges are those rights "necessary to ensure that legislatures can perform their functions, free from interference by the Crown and the courts."[27] "Privilege," in this context, often means "the legal exemption from some duty, burden, attendance or liability to which others are subject."[28] Parliamentary privilege also extends, however, to Parliament's power "to establish rules of procedure for itself and to enforce them."[29]

Parliament has exercised this internal governance right, and each chamber has promulgated its own rules of procedure.[30] Because of our

---

26 Sir John Bourinot, *Parliamentary Procedure and Practice in the Dominion of Canada,* 4th ed. (Toronto: Canada Law Book Company, 1916) at 200–1.

27 *Re Remuneration of Judges,* [1997] 3 S.C.R. 3 at para. 10.

28 *New Brunswick Broadcasting Co. v. Nova Scotia,* [1993] 1 S.C.R. 319 at para. 117, *per* L'Heureux-Dubé, Gonthier, McLachlin and Iacobucci JJ.

29 *Beauchesne's Rules* at 14.

30 House of Commons, *Standing Orders,* available at www.parl.gc.ca/information/about/ process/house/standingorders/toc-e.htm; Senate of Canada, *Rules of the Senate,* available at www.parl.gc.ca/information/about/process/senate/rules-e/SenRules_00-e.htm.

focus on the Commons, we highlight the Standing Orders of the House of Commons. Broadly speaking, these Commons rules are replicated in the senate's own procedural code.

The Standing Orders are rules of procedure adopted by at least a simple majority vote of the members of the Commons.[31] They constitute a reasonably comprehensive code of Commons operations, including in relation to Commons law-making. The Orders, however, do not anticipate every eventuality, and their meaning often requires elucidation. To this end, the Orders themselves provide that where they are silent, "procedural questions shall be decided by the Speaker or Chair, whose decisions shall be based on the usages, forms, customs and precedents of the House of Commons of Canada and on parliamentary tradition in Canada and other jurisdictions, so far as they may be applicable to the House."[32]

Thus, "parliamentary law" — the rules determining parliamentary procedure — flows from an array of sources: the Constitution, assorted statutes such as the *Parliament of Canada Act*, the Standing Orders, and assorted usages, customs and precedents, as assessed by the Speaker.[33] In the sections that follow, we highlight some of this parliamentary law.

c)   Key Parliamentary Actors

Speaker

Selection
At the opening of a Parliament, the members of the Commons elect a "Speaker." Indeed, the *Constitution Act, 1867* itself specifies that the "House of Commons on its first assembling after a General Election shall proceed with all practicable Speed to elect One of its Members to be Speaker."[34]

Pursuant to the Commons Standing Orders, the election of the Speaker is by secret ballot, in a process overseen by the member with the longest unbroken tenure in the Commons and who is not a minister or office holder in the House. All members are eligible to stand for Speaker, less any who have signified no interest in the position, party leaders and ministers. Members insert the name of their chosen candidate on the ballot, and voting continues until one member receives a majority of votes.[35] While the

---

31   *Beauchesne's Rules* at 5; Marleau and Montpetit, *House of Commons Procedure and Practice* at 215.
32   Commons *Standing Orders*, Order 1.
33   See discussion in *Beauchesne's Rules* at ch. 1.
34   *Constitution Act, 1867*, s. 44.
35   *Précis of Procedure* at 4. Commons *Standing Orders*, Orders 4 and 5.

current Commons Standing Orders are otherwise silent on circumstances constituting a no confidence vote in the government, they are clear that the election of a Speaker may not constitute such a vote.[36]

Once elected, a Speaker serves for an entire Parliament, subject to removal from office through death, resignation or a resolution of the House to that effect.[37] In practice, the Speaker is a member of the party with a majority representation in the House of Commons, should one exist.[38] Indeed, the selection of Speaker James Jerome to his second term as Speaker in 1979 was the first time a member of the opposition was called upon to serve in that capacity.[39]

Role

Supreme Court Chief Justice Beverly McLachlin likens the role of the Speaker to that of a judge:

> Speakers, like judges, spend most of their time doing something most people avoid at all costs — making decisions. Like judges, they rule on points of order and make a myriad of decisions on questions of process. Like judges, they are required to render objective and impartial decisions on issues that can prove controversial and complex. Like judges, they must be above the fray and free from bias. Like judges, they are required to abandon partisan politics and must be independent and free from political influence. Like judges — speakers are human beings. But like judges, they must strive to set aside personal preferences and opinions and rule as objectively as humanly possible. And like judges, speakers doubtless sometimes feel a little lonely.[40]

The Speaker "represents the Commons in all its powers, proceedings and dignity."[41] Generally, he or she has three sorts of roles: ceremonial, quasi-judicial and administrative.[42] In terms of ceremony, the Speaker serves as the House's spokesperson in dealings with the Crown, the senate and nonparlia-

---

36 Commons *Standing Orders*, Order 6.

37 *Beauchesne's Rules* at 52.

38 See Library of Parliament, *Speakers of the Canadian House of Parliament*.

39 See Library of Parliament, *James Alexander Jerome — Biography*. This selection arose during a minority government, likely in part because the governing party was unwilling to see one of its members serve as the impartial and, generally, nonvoting Speaker.

40 B. McLachlin, "Address to the 17th Commonwealth Speakers and Presiding Officers Conference," Montebello, Quebec, 9 Jan. 2004.

41 *Précis of Procedure* at 1.

42 Library of Parliament, *Speakers of the Canadian House of Commons — Historical Roles of the Speaker of the House of Commons* (1996).

mentary authorities. Thus, the Speaker "reads messages from the Governor-General, presents bills for Royal Assent, announces the result of any vote in the House and brings to the attention of the House all matters affecting the rights and privileges of members."[43] At the opening of Parliament, the Speaker leads the House to the senate to notify the Governor General of the Speaker's election. During the session itself, the traditional royal assent procedure — now employed less frequently by virtue of the *Royal Assent Act* — requires the Speaker to again lead the Commons to the senate.[44]

As specified in the *Constitution Act, 1867*, the "Speaker shall preside at all Meetings of the House of Commons."[45] This provision is clearly tempered in practice by the delegation of some such responsibilities to deputies. The Speaker is, however, the central "presiding officer" in the House, interpreting rules of order and conduct. In this fashion, he or she plays a quasi-judicial role. As noted above, the Speaker's rulings on procedural matters form a body of precedent that help elucidate the sometimes vague Standing Orders. The Standing Orders specify that the Speaker shall "[p]reserve order and decorum, and shall decide questions of order. In deciding a point of order or practice, the Speaker shall state the Standing Order or other authority applicable to the case. No debate shall be permitted on any such decision, and no such decision shall be subject to an appeal to the House."[46]

This function is combined with an enforcement role. In enforcing the Commons rules, the Speaker may "name" the offending member, requesting his or her compliance with the Speaker's determination. Should the member resist, the Speaker may order his or her expulsion for that day's sitting of the House.[47] Alternatively, the House itself may take disciplinary action, by voting a motion to suspend the member.[48]

Last, the Speaker undertakes various administrative tasks connected to the House, including chairing the Common's Board of Internal Economy.[49] As discussed later, this body is tasked with preparing the budget for House operations.

The Speaker is expected to be impartial in his or her activities. That means, for instance, that the Speaker is not permitted to cast a vote during

---

43   *Ibid.*
44   *Précis of Procedure* at 1.
45   *Constitution Act*, s. 46.
46   Commons *Standing Orders*, Order 10.
47   Commons *Standing Orders*, Order 11.
48   *Précis of Procedure* at 2.
49   Library of Parliament, *Speakers of the Canadian House of Commons*. See *Parliament of Canada Act*, s. 50.

House proceedings. Only in the event of a tie may the Speaker take a position.[50] Even then, however, the Speaker traditionally votes in a manner that reflects the impartiality of the office. Thus, the Speaker generally votes to preserve the status quo; that is, in a fashion permitting the House to consider the matter further.[51]

Other Presiding Officers

At the commencement of a Parliament, the Commons typically also elects a Deputy Speaker and Chair of the "Committee of the Whole." After consultation with the leaders of each of the officially recognized parties, the Speaker identifies a member he or she considers to be "qualified" for the position. This selection is deemed a motion and is voted upon by the Commons without debate.[52]

The Deputy Speaker performs the role of the Speaker in the latter's absence. The *Parliament of Canada Act* expressly validates the legal authority of the Deputy Speaker, specifying that "[e]very act done ... by a Deputy Speaker ... that relates to any proceedings of the House of Commons or that, under any statute, would be done ... by the Speaker ... has the same effect and validity as if it had been done ... by the Speaker."[53]

The Deputy Speaker also presides over the Committee of the Whole, serving as its chair. The Committee of the Whole is the entire membership of the House sitting as a committee. In this way, the Commons is convened on a less formal basis than during its regular sittings to examine appropriation bills or sometimes to expedite the passage of particular bills.[54] The chair is obliged to maintain order during Committee of the Whole proceedings, subject to his or her rulings being appealed to the Speaker.[55]

Parliamentary Committees

Role

Parliamentary committees are subsets of Parliament tasked with the detail work in Parliament. In the Commons, their terms of reference are established by the Standing Orders and by Special Orders. There are six standard sorts of committees, as set out in Table 5.1.[56]

---

50 *Constitution Act, 1867*, s. 49.
51 *Précis of Procedure* at 37.
52 Commons, *Standing Orders*, Order 7. See also House of Commons, *Journals*, no. 2, 38th Parl., 1st Sess. (5 Oct. 2004).
53 *Parliament of Canada Act*, s. 44.
54 *Précis of Procedure* at 72.
55 *Beauchesne's Rules* at 251.
56 Unless otherwise noted, this material summarizes that found in *Précis of Procedure* at 72–73.

Table 5.1   Parliamentary Committees

Type	Description	Powers
Committee of the Whole	This committee comprises the entire membership of the Commons.	The committee is tasked with examining appropriations bills, and is often constituted to expedite passage of a regular bill.
Standing Committees	While their memberships may change, these committees are appointed for the life of the Parliament to deal with matters of persistent concern to the Commons. There are twenty such committees at the time of this writing.	Standing Committees are usually the committee to which bills are sent for detailed review. They also scrutinize the performance of government departments lying in their mandate, as discussed in chapter 6. Finally, the Commons may task them with special responsibilities from time to time, and committees may also choose to take up issues suggested to them by ministers.
Legislative Committees	These committees are created on an *ad hoc* basis to review specific legislation that, for one reason or another, is not sent to a Standing Committee.	Legislative Committees are to examine and inquire into a bill referred to it by the House and to report the bill to the Commons, with or without amendments.
Special Committees	Also sometimes called "task forces," Special Committees are created on an *ad hoc* basis to study specific matters.	Special Committees have the powers assigned to them by the Commons.
Joint Committees	Joint Committees comprise parliamentarians from both the Commons and the senate. There are Standing Joint Committees, created by the Standing Orders of each House, and Special Joint Committees, created by special resolutions of the two Houses.	Joint Committees have the special responsibilities assigned to them by Parliament.
Subcommittees	Subcommittees may be created by Standing Committees to perform some aspect of the latter's mandate. Subcommittees may not, however, be empowered to report directly to the House. Special Committees may create subcommittees if the Commons so permits. Legislative Committees may, however, only form a subcommittee on agenda, known as a steering committee.	Subcommittees have the powers assigned to them by Committees.

Standing Committees are the most important vessel for committee work in the Commons. Pursuant to the Commons Standing Orders, these Standing Committees are "empowered to study and report on all matters relating to the mandate, management and operation of the department or departments of government which are assigned to them from time to time by the House." In particular, they are charged with reviewing:

(a) the statute law relating to the department assigned to them;

(b) the program and policy objectives of the department and its effective-
     ness in the implementation of these laws;

(c) the immediate-, medium- and long-term expenditure plans and the
     effectiveness of implementation of these plans by the department;

(d) an analysis of the relative success of the department, as measured by
     the results obtained as compared with its stated objectives; and

(e) other matters, relating to the mandate, management, organization or
     operation of the department, as the committee deems fit.[57]

These provisions give Standing Committees a relatively free hand in examining issues within their mandate, as they see fit. Often, the House or senate will refer bills or other matters to committees, but nearly as often, the committee will embark on its own study of an issue.

Standing Committees are considered an extension of the chamber, and the rules of the respective chambers apply, with limited exceptions, to Standing Committees. Standing Committees have expansive powers in carrying out their inquiries. Thus, they have the authority "to send for persons, papers and records,"[58] a matter further discussed later. As noted by Davidson, "[W]hat these grants of power mean, of course, is that, provided a committee's inquiry is related to a subject-matter within Parliament's competence and is also within the committee's own orders of reference, Committees have virtually unlimited powers to compel the attendance of witnesses and to order the production of documents."[59]

Membership

The Procedure and House Affairs Committee officially prepares the list of committee membership for Commons committees and this is then presented for approval by the Commons.[60] The actual choice of members is,

---

57 Commons *Standing Orders*, Order 108.

58 *Ibid.*

59 D. Davidson, "The Powers of Parliamentary Committees" (1994) 18 Canadian Parlia-
    mentary Review no. 1.

60 Commons, *Standing Orders*, Order 104.

however, delegated to party Whips, who are designated as a "striking" committee by motion. In this manner, the party leadership determines each party's committee membership.

In the Liberal Party, each backbench Member of Parliament is reportedly asked to rank his or her three top priorities for committee membership. Foreign Affairs and International Trade, Finance, and Health are said to be among the most sought-after committees. Generally, the House leader and other members of the government leadership then confer and determine who will sit on which committees. Overall membership on committees is roughly proportional to a party's standing in the Commons, giving majority parties in that chamber a majority membership on parliamentary committees.

Within ten days of the House adopting the list of committee members, each committee sits, and the first order of business is to elect a chair and two vice-chairs,[61] a matter now decided by secret ballot.[62] Typically, the chair is from the governing party, as is one of the vice-chairs, while the other vice-chair is from an opposition party. Exceptions to this rule in the thirty-seventh Parliament included the Committee on Public Accounts, which had an opposition chair and two government vice-chairs, and the Standing Joint Committee on Scrutiny of Regulations, whose House joint chair was from the opposition and two vice-chairs from the governing party.[63]

New rules adopted in the minority thirty-eighth Parliament extend this exception. In that Parliament, a member of the official opposition is the chair of the Standing Committees on Public Accounts, on Access to Information, Privacy and Ethics, and on Government Operations and Estimates. On each of these committees, a first vice-chair is a member of the government party and a second vice-chair is a member of another opposition party other than the official opposition.[64]

In keeping with the key role of committees in the legislative project and in overseeing the executive, ministers are not members of committees. Yet parliamentary secretaries generally are. We discuss parliamentary secretaries in greater detail later. In relation to Commons committees, parliamentary secretaries are, in the words of the Privy Council Office, "essential resources and play a key role by representing their Ministers before com-

---

61   Commons, *Standing Orders*, Order 106.

62   Commons, *Standing Orders*, Order 106(3).

63   Commons, *Standing Orders*, Order 106(2).

64   Standing Committee on Procedure and House Affairs, *Eight Report* (adopted by the Commons on 8 Oct. 2004).

mittees. Ministers should ask their Parliamentary Secretaries to address partisan issues raised during departmental appearances, and to act as a liaison between the committee and the Minister and the department."[65]

The 1985 McGrath Report on parliamentary reform recommended an end to the practice of parliamentary secretaries sitting on those parliamentary committees focusing on their minister's portfolios.[66] The presence of these officials was characterized as executive interference in the legislative oversight function of Parliament, and a mechanism used by the prime minister to maintain control over individual Members of Parliament.

The recommendation was briefly accepted in Brian Mulroney's first term in office, but with a diminished majority in 1988, the government reverted to the previous system. With the enhanced profile of parliamentary secretaries in the Martin government — their membership in the Privy Council, their occasional presence at Cabinet meetings and their obligation to observe Cabinet solidarity and confidences — new questions concerning the propriety of these officials serving on committees arise. As one opposition member has put it,

> I am concerned about the enhanced role of parliamentary secretaries on parliamentary committees. I want committees to be independent. A parliamentary secretary is going to those committees with an enhanced role, reporting back to the government, and this runs the risk of the PMO [Prime Minister's Office] having yet more control of committees than it has today. That is something we will have to watch because the goal is going in the opposite direction to what members of Parliament want to have happen.[67]

Whether this is a real concern or not remains to be seen. If parliamentary secretaries were removed from committees, it would fall on some other governing party member to pursue the prime minister's agenda. In addition, the government Whip's assistants would still be in the committee room during key votes, and could still stage manage that vote when necessary. As a result, the presence of parliamentary secretaries on committees grants the prime minister only marginally more control over the proceedings than would otherwise exist. This discussion leads naturally to another issue concerning parliamentary structure: the party apparatuses in Parliament.

---

65   Privy Council Office, *Governing Responsibly: A Guide for Ministers and Ministers of State* (2004).
66   Special Committee on the Reform of the House of Commons, *Report*, 18 June 1985 at 18.

How Parties Organize Themselves in Parliament

The governing party machinery in Parliament is designed to convert government policy, set by Cabinet, into parliamentary action in pursuit of that policy. For opposition parties, their party apparatuses ensure coordinated responses to these policies. We discuss the imperatives of Canadian law encouraging party-based decision-making later. Here, we discuss the key party players in Parliament.

Party Status

The political affiliation of a given parliamentarian is obviously a matter of politics, not law. There is no requirement that a parliamentarian be a member of a party, or that a party have a certain number of members. That said, so-called official party status is reserved with parties possessing a minimum number of members in the Commons.

The magic number for recognized party status in parliamentary practice is twelve Commons members. Once a party claims the allegiance of these twelve members, certain benefits flow to parties outside of the chamber of the Commons. These include membership on the Commons Board of Internal Economy and additional allowances for the party leader, Whip, and House Leader sitting in the Commons.[68] Further, under the board's by-laws, recognized parties are able to tap into caucus research funds authorized by that board.[69]

In Commons proceedings themselves, the same minimum party membership of twelve MPs has come to be standard for recognized party status, although this threshold is not spelled out in the Standing Orders. Once the twelve-MP threshold is reached, party members are then entitled to sit together, have their party affiliation noted with their name in the official records and on television broadcasts of proceedings[70] and are allowed a larger number of questions during Question Period.[71]

House Leaders

The leader of the Government in the Commons is a Cabinet member charged with "translating the Cabinet's policy decisions into bills to be

---

67   Hon. Lorne Nystrom (Regina–Qu'Appelle, NDP), *Hansard*, no. 003, 37th Parl., 3d Sess. (4 Feb. 2004).

68   *Parliament of Canada Act*, ss. 50 and 62.

69   See Marleau and Montpetit, *House of Commons Procedure and Practice* at 30–31, citing Board of Internal Economy, By-Law 302.

70   Marleau and Montpetit, *House of Commons Procedure and Practice* at 33, n186.

71   *Ibid* at 423.

placed before the House of Commons,"[72] a potentially arduous task in a minority government. The House leader scrutinizes draft bills prior to their approval by Cabinet. He or she also determines the priorities for consideration of these government bills, in keeping with Cabinet's approved legislative program.[73]

In the senate, the government leader oversees the government's legislative program in that chamber, as well as responding to questions directed at the government during the senate's Question Period.[74] The existence of senate and Commons House leaders, and their deputies, is acknowledged in law by the *Parliament of Canada Act* provisions on annual allowances.[75]

Opposition parties also have House leaders who serve as the Government House leader's opposition interlocutors on House proceedings.

Parliamentary Secretaries

Although their job description is somewhat fluid, the conventional function of parliamentary secretaries is to ease the workload of ministers. McMenemy defines the role as: "[g]overnment members of parliament appointed by the prime minister for short terms and without statutory powers, to assist cabinet ministers in their work."[76]

In recent practice, a parliamentary secretary's tasks have included representing the minister's interests on parliamentary committees, speaking on behalf of an absent minister when a question is directed at the minister in the House of Commons, and tabling material in the House on behalf of the minister.[77] Informally, a parliamentary secretary acts as a liaison between the minister and caucus, providing feedback and allowing consultation on government initiatives.

It is the minister that directs the parliamentary secretary's work,[78] and quite often, the latter is handed his or her speaking notes from staff of the

---

72 Privy Council Office, *Governing Responsibly: A Guide for Ministers and Ministers of State* (2004).

73 *Ibid.*

74 Office of the Leader of the Government in the senate website at www.pco-bcp.gc.ca/lgs/default.asp?Language=E&Page=Home.

75 *Parliament of Canada Act*, s. 62.

76 J. McMenemy, *The Language of Canadian Politics: A Guide to Important Terms and Concepts* (Waterloo: Wilfrid Laurier University Press, 2001) at 212–13.

77 Under Commons, *Standing Orders*, Order 32(2), a parliamentary secretary may "state that he or she proposes to lay upon the Table of the House, any report or other paper dealing with a matter coming within the administrative responsibilities of the government, and, thereupon, the same shall be deemed for all purposes to have been laid before the House."

78 *Parliament of Canada Act*, s. 47.

minister or the department. As noted previously, the parliamentary secretary also represents the government's views on Commons committees. This may include performing a quasi-Whip function, ensuring that other committee members from the governing party make statements and ask questions that cast the government in a favourable light and vote with the government's direction.

The parliamentary secretary position has often been used to provide a regional or linguistic counterbalance to the minister.[79] In the past, the parliamentary secretary position has been a potential stepping-stone to the ministry. The Chrétien government, however, did not generally follow this pattern. According to one observer, "[r]ather than providing a training ground for the next cabinet ministers, the position has become a tool to reward the loyal, silence the rebellious, and to keep the otherwise unoccupied busy."[80] McMenemy has noted "[w]hile parliamentary secretaries might see themselves as putative cabinet ministers, the practice of Liberal Prime Minister Jean Chrétien was to rotate the positions regularly."[81]

Parliamentarians themselves have viewed the office as debased. Frequent turnover in parliamentary secretaries, as well as other parliamentary offices, "make it difficult, if not impossible, to develop an appropriate level of expertise, and have led to a lack of motivation for many Parliamentarians to invest in learning."[82]

In December 2003, the Martin government announced a re-thinking of the parliamentary secretary role, stating:

> Secretaries will now play a more active role in ensuring meaningful relations between Ministers and Parliamentarians. In Committees, they will support productive dialogue by sharing departmental information and acting as the Minister's representative to address political issues during appearances by departmental officials. In turn, they will also play a greater

---

79 For example, in the late 1990s, Anne McLellan, a unilingual anglophone minister of justice, was assigned Eleni Bakopanos, a bilingual allophone, as her parliamentary secretary. Similarly, Stéphane Dion, an intergovernmental affairs minister from Quebec, was assigned a Westerner, Reg Alcock, as his parliamentary secretary. D.G. Hutchison, "Parliamentary Secretaries in the 36th Parliament" (2000) 23 Canadian Parliamentary Review no. 1.

80 *Ibid.*

81 McMenemy, *The Language of Canadian Politics* at 213.

82 Library of Parliament, *The Parliament We Want: Parliamentarians' Views on Parliamentary Reform* (2003). For a valuable review of the parliamentary secretary turnover and its impact on parliamentary committees, see Peter Dobell, "Reforming Parliamentary Practice: The Views of MPs," 1 *Policy Matters* no. 9 (Dec. 2000).

role in presenting the concerns of Parliamentarians to the Minister and within government more broadly.

Further, the prime minister assigned parliamentary secretaries "specific policy responsibilities in support of the Ministers they are appointed to assist." Meanwhile, "automatic rotation of Parliamentary Secretaries after a two-year term will be ended so that policy continuity and a successful partnership between Ministers and their Parliamentary Secretaries can be maintained."[83]

Perhaps most notably, parliamentary secretaries are now sworn into the Privy Council, allowing them to attend Cabinet "when a policy matter for which they have specific duties is to be discussed" and enjoy Cabinet confidences on an as-needed basis.[84] This change raises new question as to whether parliamentary secretaries are simply elevated legislators, or also formal members of the executive branch.

Status in Government of Parliamentary Secretaries

It could be that the recent elevation of parliamentary secretaries harkens back to the role of "sub-ministers" established by John A. Macdonald "to go in and sit, but not to be members of the Cabinet."[85] Even in their new, Martin-era manifestation, parliamentary secretaries still lack a key quality of ministers. Under the *Parliament of Canada Act*, a parliamentary secretary, "on ceasing to be a member of the House of Commons, ceases to hold the office of Parliamentary Secretary."[86] This is in direct contrast to members of the ministry, who maintain their posts as ministers even when the writ is dropped and Parliament is dissolved.

Nevertheless, since 1994, there has been a clear drift towards treating parliamentary secretaries as executive branch officials. Thus, parliamentary secretaries, like ministers, are required to adhere to the *Conflict of Interest and Post-Employment Code for Public Officials*, an instrument governing ethics among senior members of the executive branch discussed at length in chapter 7. Further, parliamentary secretaries, like ministers, refrain from asking questions of the government in the Commons.[87] In declining to pose these questions, in then responding to questions asked

---

83   Prime Minister's Office, *New Role of Parliamentary Secretaries* (2003).
84   *Ibid.*
85   J.E. Glenn, "Parliamentary Assistant: Patronage or Apprenticeship?" *Fleming's Canadian Legislatures* (Toronto: University of Toronto Press, 1997) at 49.
86   *Parliament of Canada Act*, subs. 46(3).
87   House of Commons, *Fact Sheet: Question Period and Written Questions*.

of their minister[88] and in tabling documents on behalf of a minister,[89] parliamentary secretaries serve essentially as agents of their respective ministers, and therefore of the Cabinet.

Alone, these developments did not render parliamentary secretaries executive officials, given their traditional absence from the Privy Council. As noted by Hutchison in 2000:

> In defining the constitutional status of the Parliamentary Secretary, one must first and foremost keep in mind that Parliamentary Secretaries are not sworn into the Queen's Privy Council and, as such, may not subsequently be sworn into office as a Minister of the Crown and be a part of the Ministry. In Canada, the Ministry and the Cabinet have usually been considered as the same body. As a result, Parliamentary Secretaries are, in a certain sense, backbenchers who are connected to Cabinet vicariously through the Minister.[90]

The Martin government's reforms have now removed this barrier to executive status. Because they are now both agents of the Privy Council in Parliament and sworn members of the Privy Council, parliamentary secretaries may be best viewed as part of the executive branch. In this fashion, the Martin government increased the size of the executive overnight. Indeed, when the Martin government's twenty-eight parliamentary secretaries are combined with thirty-nine ministers, half of the original 135 Liberal members of the thirty-eighth Parliament were members of the executive.[91]

However, whether in fact parliamentary secretaries are formally members of the executive may be immaterial. Either way, their tenure depends on the goodwill of the prime minister and their loyalties lie with Cabinet and their minister. By drawing down the pool of legislators without executive (or at least quasi-executive) office and enhancing their government role, the elevation of parliamentary secretaries leaves fewer Members of Parliament to hold the government accountable.

Caucus and the Whip

Caucus — a term reportedly derived from an Algonquin word for "advisor" — is a plenary of parliamentarians from the same party. In classic, idealized parliamentary tradition, parliamentarians in caucus "make the views

---

88   Commons *Standing Orders*, Order 38

89   Commons *Standing Orders*, Order 32.

90   Hutchison, "Parliamentary Secretaries in the 36th Parliament."

91   After the expulsion of Carolyn Parrish from the Liberal caucus, the figure rose to over 50 percent.

of their constituents known, set parliamentary strategy and decide party policy. It is also here — away from television cameras, reporters and partisan opponents — that members can relax 'the party line,' disagreeing with their colleagues and questioning their actions."[92]

Debate in caucus may be vociferous.[93] However, the precise impact of the governing party's parliamentary caucus on government policy may be quite circumscribed. As recorded by Professor Donald Savoie, governing party members report that "caucus is not a very effective policy vehicle" and caucus has "limited influence on the government."[94] Whether or not this observation captures aptly the role of caucus or not is difficult to gauge looking in from the outside. Faced with policy calls from caucus and conflicting advice from the public service, ministers reportedly favour positions taken by their bureaucratic advisors. At the same time, the anecdotal experience of parliamentary insiders suggests that a determined caucus can occasionally sway outcomes.

In classic, parliamentary tradition, the members of a caucus are expected to vote in House proceedings along party lines, maintaining party "discipline." Within governing parties, party discipline plays a particularly vital role, given the constitutional convention requiring a prime minister to maintain the confidence of the Commons; that is, the votes of a majority of its members. We discuss party discipline and free votes later.

The official charged with rallying the party members, and insuring their presence to vote is known as the Whip. The term originates in a British hunting phrase "whipper-in," an expression referring to "a huntsman's assistant who keeps the hounds from straying by driving them back into the pack with a whip."[95] Party Whips appeared in Britain at the turn of the nineteenth century, reflecting the emergence of political parties as the dominant players in the British Parliament. In Canada, Whips — and their deputies — have some statutory recognition, as reflected in annual allowances accorded these people under the *Parliament of Canada Act*.[96]

Traditionally, the chief government Whip does not maintain a policy portfolio and is not a member of Cabinet, unlike in the United Kingdom.[97]

---

92   Library of Parliament, *Inside Canada's Parliament* (2002) at 28.

93   Heard, *Canadian Constitutional Conventions* at 83.

94   Savoie, *Breaking the Bargain* at 91 and 92. See also Robert Jackson and Doreen Jackson, *Canadian Government in Transition* (1999) at 168 ("[i]n the governing party, caucus is often consulted only after policies have been decided by cabinet, and members are expected to support those decisions").

95   M.W. Westmacott, "Whips and Party Cohesion" (1983) 6 Canadian Parliamentary Review no 3.

96   *Parliament of Canada Act*, s. 62.

The Martin government briefly changed that practice. In 2003, the government's Chief Whip joined Cabinet as the deputy leader of the Government in the House of Commons, in an effort "to ensure better representation of parliamentary concerns within Cabinet."[98] In the thirty-eighth Parliament, however, the Whip's position is once again disaggregated from that of the deputy leader, and the former is not listed as part of the Martin ministry.

Often assisted by one or two deputies, the Whip is charged with reining in the Members of Parliament to ensure adequate support for party positions. The disciplinary function of the Whips has been summarized as follows: "The role of whip is to contain dissent and to promote cohesion, to serve as a 'sounding board' for the concerns of backbenchers and to determine whether accommodation can be reached when the party position and that of an individual member come into conflict."[99]

What power the Whip actually wields is somewhat unclear, even to many MPs. There is clearly some leeway for members to vote against their party, especially on matters of conscience. The Whip and party leadership generally expect, however, that such cases will be rare, and that an effort will be made to communicate with the Whip on the matter beforehand. The Whip may urge the MP to absent him or herself from the vote to avoid the spectacle of a member voting against his or her party.

Faced with dissent, the Whip may recommend that the party leader deny to rebellious members such perks as preferred office space and staff, membership on parliamentary committees, participation in debates, or travel on parliamentary delegations. For the governing party in particular, also hanging over the head of each member is the prospect of party leader disapproval. Damage to Cabinet or committee chair prospects may give pause to insubordinate members of the governing party. The nuclear threat, of course, is that a party leader will exercise his or her power under the *Canada Elections Act* to refuse to endorse the member as a party candidate in the next election.

In practice, the Whip relies primarily on moral suasion in "whipping" Members of Parliament into line,[100] appealing to the party solidarity of members. Nevertheless, despite the Whip's best efforts — and potentially threats — dissent does occur, and dissenting members are occasionally

---

97 Westmacott, "Whips and Party Cohesion."
98 Privy Council Office, *Ethics, Responsibility, Accountability: An Action Plan for Democratic Reform* (4 Feb. 2004).
99 Westmacott, "Whips and Party Cohesion."
100 Heard, *Canadian Constitutional Conventions* at 82.

punished by the party leader, to the point of sometimes being expelled from the party caucus.[101]

d) Rules of Debate and Decision-Making in the Commons

Overview

The precise procedural rules governing parliamentary decision-making are complex and sometimes appear arcane. In this book, we canvass them only briefly.

The Commons makes decisions through the device of motions; basically a question put to the House by the Speaker, in response to a proposition made by a member.[102] There are several different species of motion, each governed by their own procedural niceties. Eventually, however, all motions are debated, amended, superseded, adopted, negatived or withdrawn.[103]

Debate in the House of Commons is governed by its own rules. The Standing Orders list sixteen different sorts of debatable motions, including motions brought in relation to several of the stages in the legislative process.[104] Members catching the "Speaker's eye" are entitled to speak during debate, though there are important constraints on what they may say. For example, to avoid wasting the limited time of the House, members are not to engage in irrelevant or repetitious debate.[105]

Other sometimes sensible and sometimes bizarre conventions also exist. By virtue of the unwritten *sub judice* convention, members are generally not to refer to matters before the courts or a judicial inquiry. The convention is premised on respect for the integrity of the judicial process. Its precise scope is, however, uncertain and depends more on the good judgment of the member than enforcement by the Speaker. The convention has significant traction in criminal matters, where Speakers have stepped in to preserve the rights of citizens undergoing prosecution.[106] The convention

---

101 See discussion in *ibid* at 83. See also Library of Parliament, *Members of the House of Commons who were Suspended from their Caucus or who Quit their Caucus: 1867 to date*; See Lorne Gunter, "Chrétien Browbeats Backbencher," *Calgary Herald*, 24 March 2003, A19, for a discussions of Jean Chrétien's reported threat of expulsions to whip members on an unpopular vote.

102 *Beauchesne's Rules* at 171.

103 *Précis of Procedure* at 33. A "superceded" motion is one replaced by another motion.

104 Commons, *Standing Orders*, Order 67.

105 *Précis of Procedure* at 53.

106 See Marleau and Montpetit, *House of Commons Procedure and Practice* at 428; *Beauchesene's Rules* at 153.

in relation to civil matters is less clear.[107] The *sub judice* convention has a defined outer limit: it should never "stand in the way of consideration of a matter vital to the public interest or to the effective operation of the House."[108] Thus, the *sub judice* custom does not extend to debate during the legislative process.[109] There, its application might impinge on the core competency and responsibility of Parliament: law-making.[110]

There are other rules of parliamentary procedure meant to depersonalize debate and maintain the "decorum" of the House. Debating members may not refer to other members by name or by their characteristics, personalities or motives. Because of this depersonalization of Commons debates, they address the Speaker, not each other. Nor may members use "unparliamentary language," including speaking with a manner disrespectful of the monarch or her family, the Governor General, the judiciary or the powers of either House of Parliament.[111] Members are also expected to speak extemporaneously, and not to read a prepared speech, in order to maintain the cadence of a debate.

Closure and Time Allocation

The Standing Orders specify the duration of debate on some motions. They also enable the government to truncate debate through use of closure and time allocation. Time allocation limits the rights of Members of Parliament to speak to a bill, thereby allowing the Commons to put a bill to a vote more quickly. The procedure for time allocation, originally devised in 1969, is contained in the following Standing Orders:

- Standing Order 78(1), when "there is agreement among the representatives of all parties" on how time shall be allocated;
- Standing Order 78(2), when "a majority of the representatives of the several parties have come to an agreement" on how time shall be allocated; and
- Standing Order 78(3), when there is no agreement obtained under 78(1) or (2).

Under Order 78(3), a minister may simply propose a motion allocating time, which is then voted upon by the Commons.

---

107 *Ibid.* at 153.
108 *Ibid.* at 154.
109 *Précis of Procedure* at 55–56.
110 *Ibid.* at 55.
111 *Ibid.* at 51.

At the inception of these rules opposition parties agreed with procedures (1) and (2). However, procedure (3) was very controversial, as it meant the government could ignore the will of the other parties in the House and force bills through, taking the spotlight off controversial measures that the opposition might wish to exploit.

Initially justified as a system that would be invoked rarely, Order 78(3) has been used by every government since. By the end of the 2003, governments had used the order a total of 157 times. In contrast Order 78(1) (by agreement of all parties) had been used only nine times, and 78(2) (by agreement of a majority of parties) only eleven times.[112]

While time allocation applies only to debate on bills at various stages, "closure" can apply to any motion facing the House. Closure requires the Commons to approve a motion of closure,[113] a possibility usually open to a majority government.

Party-Based Decision-Making, Party Discipline and Free Votes

The Legal Impetus

Political parties are, of course, motivated by a number of considerations, not least the prospect of marshalling collective resources to contest elections. Parties are also, however, the partial product of two *legal* aspects of parliamentary governance.

First, under the *Constitution Act, 1867*, decision-making in Parliament is dependent on swaying a majority of votes in each chamber.[114] This rule places a primacy on commanding the loyalty of that majority, something best accomplished by holding the majority captive to a hierarchical party machine.

Second, since by constitutional convention, the individual commanding the confidence of the House (that is, its majority) is appointed prime minister, party control of a majority of the House brings with it the cornucopia that is executive power. We discuss this issue in greater detail in chapter 6. Suffice to say here that this second consideration makes a Westminster parliamentary system very different from a republican form of government in which control of the executive is determined directly by the electorate rather than the legislature.

---

112   Library of Parliament, personal communication. See also Yves Yvon J. Pelletier, *"Time Allocation" in the House of Commons: Silencing Parliamentary Democracy or Effective Time Management?* (Institute on Governance, Nov. 2000).

113   *Précis of Procedure* at 54.

114   *Constitution Act*, ss. 36 and 49.

Both of these legal considerations ensure that Westminster systems are preoccupied, even obsessed, with maintaining "party discipline" — the *en bloc* votes of party members (or at least a coalition of different party members) sufficient to constitute a majority.

As Professor Heard has argued, "[o]nly through political parties does the election of hundreds of people across the country translate into the election of a cohesive government."[115] Parties are the "channel through which the government can ensure the enactment of its policies."[116] Indeed, party backbench Members of Parliament often serve as little more than voting machines. Prime Minister Trudeau famously observed that Members of Parliament were "nobodies" fifty yards from the Commons. Other commentators have referred to backbenchers in the governing party as "trained seals."[117]

So pervasive is the party system in Parliament that members in the Commons often "pair" votes: if a member of one party cannot be present for a vote, an opposition member will sometimes also absent themselves from the vote. A form of parliamentary decorum and not an affirmative obligation, this practice acknowledges the fact that members of all parties may not always be able to attend Commons proceedings, and permits these absences without changing the relative parity of party support in the Commons.[118]

The Political Impetus

At the *political* root of party discipline is the power balance between party leadership (in the case of the governing party, the prime minister and Cabinet) and caucus. While Cabinet ministers aim to move legislation through Parliament, they realize that they cannot do so without the support of the caucus. Similarly, opposition party leaders and critics must maintain the support of their caucuses, or lose the ability to effectively criticize the government.

---

115   Heard, *Canadian Constitutional Conventions* at 79.

116   *Ibid.*

117   Editorial, "MPs No Longer Trained Seals," *Halifax Daily News*, 14 Oct. 2002, 11; Charles Gordon, "At Last, Backbench Liberals Who Don't Want to Be Trained Seals," *Ottawa Citizen*, 1 March 2003, B6.

118   See definition in House of Commons, *Glossary of Parliamentary Procedure*, 3d ed. (Jan. 2001). The practice is acknowledged in the Standing Orders. Commons, *Standing Orders*, Order 44.1, authorizing a "Register of Paired Members, in which any Member of the government party and any Member of an Opposition party may have their names entered together by their respective Whips." Its performance is, however, a private, moral obligation, stopping short of true parliamentary law or constitutional convention. Heard, *Canadian Constitutional Conventions* at 79. See also Marleau and Montpetit, *House of Commons Procedure and Practice* at 492–93.

In theory, a roused backbench has the strength of numbers to maintain significant influence within their parties. The backbench lacks, however, solidarity, as Members of Parliament are tempted by individual ambitions. Party leaders are the gatekeepers when it comes to opportunities for advancement within the party. The prime minister controls the appointment of ministers, parliamentary secretaries, and various other posts. Opposition leaders control the appointment of critics, who enjoy more public exposure and involvement in policy issues. And if the opposition party becomes the government, the leader first looks to the critics when putting together his or her Cabinet. In these circumstances, party leaders have substantial leverage over their caucus members.

Interpersonal dynamics — the sense of team identity — likely play an even more important role in motivating party discipline. As former MP John Reid, arguing the benefits of party discipline, notes, "you cannot have all the benefits of Party when you want and need them and not pay the price. You cannot vote in response to your own drummer and expect the members of your caucus, who must pick up the extra burden you have placed on them, to look on kindly and applaud your action. The psychological reaction to letting down the team is a powerful one. And the other members of your team will judge your vote and take action accordingly."[119] "Team spirit" party discipline abates only where the individual members see virtue in distancing themselves from the party, and its image, in the eyes of their constituents.

Mixed with all these variables is the question of resources: there is a tremendous imbalance in the resources that the party leadership maintains in terms of research and communications staff as compared to individual members. Most MPs have only one legislative staff person, who must provide a range of functions relating to committee, House, extraparliamentary and often even constituency duties. Members do have additional support from party researchers and various parliamentary offices, including the Library of Parliament. Nevertheless, a resource skew exists between parliamentarians and the ministry, which has access to the central agencies and departments of government. Absent entitlement to greater resources, charting an individual and coherent policy course is difficult for backbench members.

Easing Party Discipline

Recently, commentators and parliamentarians have focused on the question of "free votes": matters on which members vote their conscience, and

---

119   J. Reid, "The Case for Party Discipline" (1993) 16 *Canadian Parliamentary Review* no. 3.

not necessarily along party lines. It seems certain that Canadians have no legal rights to a free-voting Parliament.[120] Nevertheless, opposition parties often champion free votes, mostly as a means of peeling away government support.

Quite understandably, free votes are less popular with members of the Cabinet, the body that almost always introduces government bills in Parliament. After all, the erosion of governing party discipline and an increase of free votes could seriously derail the executive's legislative program and, given the no confidence convention, potentially its very survival as a government.

Assembled in 2003, parliamentarians reviewing the question of parliamentary reform complained that

> the House of Commons and the Senate are no longer places in which meaningful debate occurs. The impetus to get the government's business through and the strongly enforced party discipline have combined to limit the number of voices heard in Parliament. In most matters of public debate, Canadians have many different points of view, while only a limited number of views are expressed within the walls of Parliament — largely as a result of party discipline. Parliament must put the richness of opinion that exists in the Canadian public to the service of the Canadian public by allowing for those multiple voices to be heard in Parliament.[121]

Put another way, Parliament has become a place for ramming through government policy, not querying its merits.

As part of its democratic reform initiative in 2004, the Martin government announced a loosening of the Liberal Party voting procedure, introducing the so-called three-line voting system. This policy partitions votes into three classes:

> On one-line free votes, all government MPs, including Ministers, will be free to vote as they see fit. ... Two-line free votes are votes on which the government will take a position and recommend a preferred outcome to its caucus. Ministers are bound to support the government's position on a Two-line vote, as are Parliamentary Secretaries of Ministers affected by it, but other Members are free to vote as they wish. ... A Three-line vote will be for votes of confidence and for a limited number of matters of fun-

120 McKinney v. Liberal Party of Canada (1987), 43 D.L.R. (4th) 706 at 710–11 (Ont. H.C.J.) ("The exercise of party discipline is not a governmental act but only the act of an unincorporated private association and cannot be regulated by the Charter").

121 Library of Parliament, The Parliament We Want: Parliamentarians' Views on Parliamentary Reform (2003).

damental importance to the government. Government Members will be expected to support the government.[122]

Obviously, the mere classification of votes does not mean that more of them will be free. The government has promised, however, that "[m]ost votes will be either two-line or one-line free votes, and Ministers will be unable to take approval for granted."[123] By December 2004, it remained to be seen how this system would operate in practice in the splintered, thirty-eighth Parliament.

Ultimately, whether this initiative will prove meaningful will depend on Members of Parliament themselves, particularly those from the governing party. As the discussion on party discipline suggests, what stands in the way of greater member independence is not so much the rules of Parliament, but member acquiescence to a collective "party think" and the perceived and real power of their leader's office. True, new rules or a signal from the prime minister would encourage government MPs to act more independently. But the fact remains that the influence — and indeed the very concept of parliamentary sovereignty and responsible government — depends on backbench MPs collectively *choosing* to exercise powers already at their disposal. The executive's notorious indifference to Parliament may reflect its conviction — derived from long experience — that parliamentarians will not flex their muscles.

2. Parliament's Legislative Function

With that institutional background, we turn now to a discussion of Parliament's law-making function.

a) Parliament's Legislative Jurisdiction

As discussed in chapter 2, Parliament is a sovereign body. In its classic manifestation, parliamentary supremacy means that Parliament is the source of all power and Parliament has the jurisdiction "to make or unmake any law whatever."[124]

In Canada, this absolute parliamentary supremacy gives way to other constraints in the Constitution, including certain constitutionalized aspects of the separation of powers, the division of powers between the fed-

---

122 Privy Council Office, *Ethics, Responsibility, Accountability: An Action Plan for Democratic Reform* (4 Feb. 2004).
123 *Ibid.*
124 Albert Venn Dicey, *Introduction to the Study of the Law of the Constitution*, 10th ed. (London: Macmillan, 1964) at 39.

eral and provincial governments and constitutionally protected individual rights and liberties. Constitutional constraints, however, merely demarcate the outer limits of parliamentary jurisdiction to legislate on a substantive matter. So long as it falls within these constitutional bounds, Parliament may make any law on any topic it wishes, as an exercise of its parliamentary supremacy.[125]

This parliamentary supremacy also means that Parliament is free to pass careless, unwise or ill-motivated statutes,[126] so long as these flaws do not also constitute constitutional violations. Indeed, even when it is alleged that an ill-intentioned ministry tricked Parliament into enacting legislation, the courts will not probe the impetus for that statute's promulgation.[127]

The role of courts in reviewing the *process* by which Parliament makes its laws is even more limited. The Constitution is largely silent on how legislation is to be enacted. The *Constitution Act, 1867* specifies only five requirements for the legislative process: matters are to be decided in both the senate and the Commons by a majority of votes;[128] the quorum of the senate is fifteen senators, including the Speaker, and of the Commons, twenty members;[129] money bills must originate in the Commons;[130] bills must be in French and English;[131] and, all bills require royal assent.[132] So long as these prerequisites are met, courts have no role in querying the procedure Parliament selects in passing that law.[133]

---

125 See discussion in *Babcock v. Canada*, [2002] 3 S.C.R. 3 at para. 57.

126 *Wells v. Newfoundland*, [1999] 3 S.C.R. 199 at para. 59, holding that "legislative decision making is not subject to any known duty of fairness" and thus could not be challenged on bad faith grounds; *Bacon v. Saskatchewan Crop Insurance Corp.*, (1999) 180 Sask. R. 20 at para. 36 (C.A.) refusing to strike down legislation said to be "arbitrary," and holding that "the public's protection from the arbitrary use of power by the elected legislators is the ballot box." See also, *PSAC v. Canada* (2000), 192 F.T.R. 23 at para. 17 (T.D.) ("insofar as negligence ... [is] in issue, Parliament is not subject to judicial scrutiny").

127 *Turner v. Canada*, [1992] 3 F.C. 458 at 462 (C.A.) (an "action against Her Majesty based on allegations that Parliament has been induced to enact legislation by the tortious acts and omissions of Ministers of the Crown is not justiciable").

128 *Constitution Act, 1867*, ss. 36 and 49.

129 *Ibid.*, ss. 35 and 48.

130 *Ibid.*, s. 53.

131 *Ibid.*, s. 133; See also *Quebec (Attorney General) v. Collier*, [1990] 1 S.C.R. 260.

132 *Constitution Act, 1867*, s. 55.

133 For an example of where the basic 1867 Act requirements were not met, see *Re Manitoba Language Rights*, [1985] 1 S.C.R. 721 at 777, in a case involving the Manitoba legislature, holding that royal assent is constitutionally required and that any effort to circumvent this procedure in enacting statutes is an unconstitutional interference with the powers of the provincial Lieutenant Governor.

Indeed, as discussed in chapter 2, courts have specifically held that Parliament has the power to administer that part of the statute law relating to its internal procedure,[134] as well as to determine the content of such things as Standing Orders on Procedure,[135] without any intervention from the courts. This internal procedure includes the manner in which Parliament passes Acts. In the British parliamentary tradition, it is for "Parliament to lay down the procedures which are to be followed before a Bill can become an Act."[136] These are all matters of parliamentary privilege.

Certainly, the Supreme Court has implied that "three readings in the Senate and House of Commons" is a procedure due any citizen of Canada" by "[l]ong-standing parliamentary tradition."[137] However, nothing constitutionalizes this practice. Canadians are not entitled to any sort of due process or procedural fairness in the law-making process.[138] If Parliament were, therefore, to dispense with the existing requirements that allow proposed legislation to be publicly debated and vetted, it likely could do so without any real prospect of successful judicial review.

b) Enacting Parliamentary Legislation

As a matter of current parliamentary law, parliamentary bills come in two forms: private bills and public bills. Public bills relate to matters of general public policy and are introduced by either the government (government bills) or private members (private members' bills). Private bills — not to be confused with *public* private members' bills — generally exempt specific individuals from the application of the law or endow them with special powers and are generally sponsored by individual parliamentarians. In the discussion that follows, we look quickly at private bills and then turn to a more detailed discussion of public bills.

---

134 *Carter v. Alberta* (2002), 222 D.L.R. (4th) 40 at 48 (Alta. C.A.), citing Maingot, *Parliamentary Privilege in Canada* at 183–87.

135 *Ontario (Speaker of the Legislative Assembly) v .Ontario Human Rights Commission* (2001), 54 O.R. (3d) 595 at para. 48 (C.A.).

136 Lord Morris of Borth-y-Gest in *Pickin v. British Rys. Board*, [1974] A.C. 765 at 790 (H.L.), cited with approval in *Martin v. Ontario*, [2004] O.J. No. 2247 at para. 21 (S.C.J.).

137 *Authorson v. Canada (Attorney General)*, [2003] 2 S.C.R. 40 at para. 37.

138 See *Wells*, [1999] 3 S.C.R. 199 at para. 59 ("legislative decision making is not subject to any known duty of fairness. Legislatures are subject to constitutional requirements for valid law-making, but within their constitutional boundaries, they can do as they see fit"); *P.H.L.F. Family Holdings Ltd. v. Canada*, [1994] T.C.J. No. 445 (invocation of closure of debate on a bill is a matter of privilege).

Private Bills

Nonparliamentarians have no right to address Parliament in person. However, citizens possess an ancient right to petition Parliament.[139] Private bills are law projects introduced by means of petition from the interested party. In the era before family law reform, many private bills were petitions for divorce. In more recent practice, these law projects are usually petitions from a corporation incorporated by separate and special statute of Parliament for amendments to these charters.

Given the limited number of such entities, private bills have become increasingly uncommon. In the thirty-seventh Parliament, only six private bills were introduced. These bills dealt with such things as amendments to parliamentary Acts incorporating specific religious institutions,[140] financial institutions and organizations,[141] and the Boy Scouts of Canada.[142] In that same Parliament there were 941 *public* private members' bills, more than 157 times the number of private bills. This is the highest ratio — and thus the largest disproportion — between private and public bills sponsored by individual parliamentarians since the Second World War. Yet, while they are uncommon, private bills (unlike *public* private members' bills) usually receive royal assent.[143]

Private bills are more common in the senate, perhaps because they are easier to move onto the less crowded legislative agenda. All six private bills in the thirty-seventh Parliament originated in the Upper Chamber. Under the senate rules, notice of the application for a private bill must be published in the *Canada Gazette*. In several instances, this notice must also be given in "a leading news publication with substantial circulation in the area concerned and in the official gazette of the province concerned."[144] These notices must appear in these publications at least once a week for four weeks.

When the senate receives the petition, the examiner of petitions for private bills reviews it for defects. If the petition is sound, the examiner refers the matter to the senate, which then proceeds to consider a private bill following essentially the same process as with public bills. When a private bill

---

139 See *Beauchesne's Rules* at 277.

140 Bill S-15, 37th Parl., 3d Sess., 52–53 Elizabeth II, 2004; Bill S-25, 37th Parl., 1st Sess., 49–50 Elizabeth II, 2001.

141 Bill S-21, 37th Parl., 2d Sess., 51–52 Elizabeth II, 2002–03; Bill S-27, 37th Parl., 1st Sess., 49–50 Elizabeth II, 2001; Bill S-28, 37th Parl., 1st Sess., 49–50 Elizabeth II, 2001.

142 Bill S-19, 37th Parl., 2d Sess., 51–52 Elizabeth II, 2002–03.

143 Data compiled from Library of Parliament, *Table of legislation introduced and passed by session*.

144 See Senate of Canada, *Rules of the Senate*, Part XI.

is referred to the Commons upon completing the requisite three readings in the senate, it is there deemed to have passed first reading and is referred directly to second reading.[145] We discuss these "readings" processes later in our section on public bills.

Public Bills

Public bills are by far the most important form of parliamentary legislation. As noted, public bills may themselves be divided into government bills or private members' bills.[146] Government bills, of course, are law projects introduced into Parliament by the ministry. Private members' bills, on the other hand, are the initiatives of individual legislators, usually acting without the backing of the ministry.

In the discussion that follows, we discuss briefly the process by which a public bill becomes law. Subsequently, we examine a pressing question of parliamentary governance: the extent to which government bills reflect policies set in Parliament itself. We then look at the particular difficulties private members' bills confront in the parliamentary process. Finally, we look at trends over time in terms of the enactment of bills into statutes.

Process

Table 5.2 outlines the "classic" procedure followed for regular public bills (that is, all government and private members' public bills) originating in the Commons.

Table 5.2   Processing a Bill Through the House

Stage	Description
Commons Introduction	Member gives forty-eight hours' written notice and then obtains leave by motion to introduce a bill. This motion is adopted automatically. Private members usually make a brief speech setting out the purpose of their bills. Ministers may also speak to their law project in "Statements by Minister," a session following the period allocated to introduction of government bills in the Commons schedule. In practice, the minister usually reserves his or her comments until debate on second reading. As a variation on the classic process, amendments to the Commons Standing Orders allow a minister or member to move that a committee be charged with preparing a bill.
Commons First reading	A motion for first reading follows immediately upon introduction of the bill, and is also automatically adopted without debate. A number is assigned to the bill. Government bills are labelled C-1 to C-200. Private members' bills are labelled C-201 to C-1000.

---

145 Commons *Standing Orders*, Order 135.
146 Except as noted, this section summarizes the discussion found in *Précis of Procedure* (2003), ch. 11; House of Commons, *A Practical Guide to Private Members' Business* (Jan. 2001).

Stage	Description
Commons Second reading	On second reading, the principle and object of the bill are debated, and by motion the bill in its entirety is accepted or rejected. Amendments to bills on second reading are limited to three sorts: first, the "six months hoist" (essentially shelving the bill for the remainder of the session of Parliament); a "reasoned amendment" (articulating specific reasons for opposing second reading); and, an amendment referring the bill to a parliamentary committee prior to second reading and the approval of the principles of the bill. (Occasionally, the entire Commons, sitting as the Committee of the Whole, will take up the matter). Where a parliamentary committee is, in fact, asked to take up a bill prior to second reading, the principle and object of the bill have not been approved by the House, empowering the committee to contemplate a broader range of amendments than is the case under the classic process.
Commons Committee stage	Bills are referred to standing, special or legislative committees of the Commons by motion, generally after second reading. This body then reviews the bill on a clause-by-clause basis and considers amendments to the bill's text. Except if the committee is reviewing the bill before second reading, amendments must be consistent with the principle and object of the bill, as approved on second reading in the House. The sponsoring minister or member will generally appear prior to clause-by-clause review, as may other witnesses.
Commons Report stage	Here, members who were not on the reviewing committee may propose amendments to the bill, on giving sufficient notice. Generally, the House will not consider amendments already rejected at committee stage. Once debate on amendments is concluded, a motion on the bill is put to a vote without debate.
Commons Third reading	At third reading, the Commons may consider the amendments analogous to those available on second reading: the six month hoist, the reasoned amendment and a referral back to committee for its further consideration.
Senate	Once a bill passes through the Commons procedure, and a motion on third reading is passed, a message is sent to the senate requesting that body's consideration of the measure. The stages of review employed by the senate are largely identical to those in the Commons. If the senate makes amendments to the bill, the matter is returned to the House, where that body debates acceptance of the senate changes. If the House rejects the senate amendments, the senate decides whether it will accept this rejection. If it insists on the change, the House then again decides whether to accept or reject the senate amendments. In the event of a deadlock, the bill may be referred to a joint conference. A conference is an extremely rare event. Indeed, between 1958 and 2004, the senate proposed amendment of ninety-nine Commons bills. Royal assent was ultimately obtained for ninety of those bills. In seventy-five instances, the Commons agreed to the amendments when the matter was first returned to it. In the other instances in which the bill ultimately received royal assent, there was a back and forth between the Commons and the senate. In no instance was a joint conference held.[147] Indeed, the last joint conference was apparently held in 1947.

147 See Library of Parliament, *Bills Introduced in the House of Commons and Amended by the Senate, 1960 to Date.*

Stage	Description
Royal Assent	A bill becomes law only when given royal assent by the monarch, or his or her representative (i.e., the Governor General). By constitutional convention, this royal assent may not be refused.[148] Once conducted through an intricate formal ceremony, the royal assent process was streamlined for most bills in 2002, and may now be undertaken in most instances on paper.[149]

Two caveats must be raised in relation to the bill process. First, an important subdivision of public bills concern appropriations of public revenue or the raising of these funds through taxation. Parliament's role in relation to money bills is a vital component of responsible government. Therefore, the unique procedure by which these laws are promulgated is discussed in chapter 6. For our purposes here, it suffices to note that a bill appropriating any part of the public revenue or imposing any tax must be preceded by a "Royal Recommendation" from the Governor General.[150] In practice, this gives the government a monopoly on the introduction of these bills.

Second, parliamentary rules impose an additional requirement of "Royal Consent" prior to the passage of bills concerning Crown prerogatives, hereditary revenues, or personal property or interests.[151] In practice, royal consent is likely triggered by measures that impinge on the royal prerogative, those residual monarchial prerogative powers exercised by the executive.[152]

Given the paucity of these remaining prerogative powers, this requirement does not arise frequently.[153] In practice, a minister generally conveys

---

148 *Hogan v. Newfoundland (Attorney General)* (1998), 156 D.L.R. (4th) 139 at para. 30 (Nfld. S.C.) citing Hogg, *Constitutional Law of Canada*: "the imperial conference of 1930 resolved that the powers of reservation and disallowance must never be exercised. This conference and the full acceptance of responsible government have established a convention that the Governor General must always give the royal assent to a bill which has passed both Houses of Parliament. There is no circumstance which would justify a refusal of assent, or a reservation, or a British disallowance." See also Heard, *Canadian Constitutional Conventions* at 36 ("The Governor General's legal power to reserve bills on his or her own initiative for the monarch's pleasure ... has been negated by convention since an Imperial Conference in 1887 agreed that the practice should be ended.").

149 *Royal Assent Act*, S.C. 2002, c. 15.

150 *Constitution Act, 1867*, s. 54; Commons *Standing Orders*, Order 79.

151 *Beauchesne's Rules* at 213. Royal consent is not to be confused with the always necessary "Royal Assent."

152 For examples of royal consent in the context of a statute affecting the royal prerogative, see Senate Speaker's Ruling, Senate *Journals*, Issue 63 (25 Oct. 2001); Senate Speaker's Ruling, *Point of Order raised May 2, 2002 Bill S-20*.

153 Since 1867, royal consent has been given twenty-eight times. See Library of Parliament, *Crown Consent to Bills, 1867 to Date*.

this royal consent, usually by verbal statement in the House.[154] Presumably, this ministerial statement is made as a matter of course for government bills. On the other hand, obtaining royal consent could constitute an awkward extra procedural hurdle for a private member's bill, especially a law project actively opposed by the ministry.

Parliament, Bills and Government Policy

The legislative process described above obviously gives parliamentarians an opportunity to debate and scrutinize bills. It does not necessarily mean, however, that parliamentarians — even those from the governing party — are the source of the policies reflected in government bills.

A government bill is the legislative embodiment of government policy. The prime minister and Cabinet set this policy, sometimes on their own initiative and sometimes in response to proposals from the public service. In either instance, policy is generally formulated with minimal input from non-Cabinet elected members, even those from the governing party. Indeed, the Privy Council Office's *Cabinet Directive on Law-making* anticipates a role for Parliament only once government policy has been determined and the resulting bill has been agreed upon by the executive, vetted and approved by Cabinet and tabled in Parliament.[155] As Senator Forsey observed in 1985, "Parliament never was and still is not a policy-making body. Our system is not governed by Parliament. Government is the business of the Crown."[156]

One relatively new mechanism used by the government to elicit the views of Members of Parliament in the Commons is the "take note" debate.[157] This proceeding is initiated by a minister via motion that "the House 'take note' of" some element of government policy. As described by the Special Committee on the Modernization and Improvement of the Procedures of the House of Commons in 2001, "These debates allow Members to participate in the development of government policy, making their views known before the government makes a decision; they allow the Government to canvass the views of Members. By the same token, Members are enabled to put their comments on the record in a relatively less formal and partisan setting."[158]

154 *Beauchesne's Rules* at 213.
155 Privy Council Office, *Cabinet Directive on Law-Making* (2003).
156 Forsey and Eglington, *The Question of Confidence* at 45.
157 Commons *Standing Orders*, Order 53.1.
158 Special Committee on the Modernization and Improvement of the Procedures of the House of Commons, *Report* (June 2001).

A second policy-input mechanism is government party caucus meetings discussed above. There, the prime minister and Cabinet consult (at least in theory) with their parliamentary party members in caucus on a reasonably regular basis.

Despite these processes, parliamentarians have repeatedly bemoaned their lack of influence in setting the policy direction of government. As described by the Library of Parliament, following a 2003 consultation with parliamentarians:

> By and large, Parliamentarians do not feel their work as legislators has a significant impact on public policy decisions in Canada. By the time issues and ideas are brought to either chamber, positions have by and large been set, partisan lines drawn, and the outcomes determined. What is more, Parliamentarians feel they have little, if anything, to show for those occasions when they have come together on issues, be it a committee recommendation or motion passed in the chamber. Put simply, decisions are made elsewhere.[159]

Reform Initiatives

As part of its 2004 democratic reform initiative, the Martin government promised to enhance the role of Parliament, particularly by promoting the importance of parliamentary committees.[160] Among other things, the government undertook, first, to refer bills subject to its so-called two-line and one-line free votes to committees prior to second reading. In theory, because the principle and object of a bill has not been entrenched prior to second reading, this early referral will provide committees with greater latitude to amend and shape bills. By late 2004, fully thirteen of the government's bills in the first session of the thirty-eighth Parliament — around half the bills that had passed first reading — had been referred directly to committees prior to second reading.

The Martin policy also specified that "Ministers should achieve parliamentary consent through persuasion and coalition building. Ministers are therefore expected to engage Committees early in the policy development process and meet with Committees regularly on priorities and issues to obtain input on legislative initiatives." Government responses to committee reports are to be "comprehensive and substantive."

---

159 Library of Parliament, *The Parliament We Want: Parliamentarians' Views on Parliamentary Reform.*

160 Privy Council Office, *Ethics, Responsibility, Accountability: An Action Plan for Democratic Reform* (4 Feb. 2004). See also similar admonishments in Privy Council Office, *Governing Responsibly: A Guide for Ministers and Ministers of State* (2004).

Critically, the Martin package responds to the problem of committee resources, a bottleneck in enhancing the policy capacity of parliamentarians. In its 2003 parliamentary consultation report, the Library of Parliament reported repeated complaints about resource pressures on parliamentarians. In modern governance, several hundred elected members are not in a position to query policy directions developed by, and for, many thousands of unelected officials. The Library report concluded, "[I]f Parliamentarians are to become knowledge brokers, they will require significantly more resources for independent policy analysis."[161]

Among other things, the 2004 Martin initiative promised "more resources to Committees to conduct independent studies in areas of concern with the right to commission such work, subject to an allocated yearly budget." It also spoke of "[i]ncreasing resources for the House Law Clerk and Parliamentary Counsel Office to provide legislative counsel services."

Securing resources to fulfill its responsibilities lies well within the prerogatives of Parliament. If introduced by the Commons, these changes could well enhance the importance of parliamentarians in setting government policy at the outset and, if not there, then in tempering and amending it through the legislative process.

Distinction Between Government and Private Members' Bills

Parliamentarians discontented with their role in formulating government policy and bills may turn to the private member's bill process. In practice, however, private members' bills are often an unsatisfying venture. It is no shock that the rules of parliamentary procedure shaped by a disciplined and whipped majority party straddling both the legislative and executive branch are strongly sympathetic to government law projects.

Indeed, parliamentary law gives government bills a clear procedural primacy over those of private members. As a result, private members' bills are rarely passed by Parliament. One study of private member's bills shows that less than 2 percent end up being enacted into law.[162] This figure has been in decline in recent Parliaments, as the data in Appendix 2 suggest.

The chief difference between procedures employed for a government bill versus a private member's bill relates to the allocation of scarce legislative time. In the Commons, government bills may be considered each day in which the Commons sits, during the "Government Orders" period. By

---

161 Library of Parliament, *The Parliament We Want: Parliamentarians' Views on Parliamentary Reform.*

162 R.R. Walsh, "By the Numbers: A Statistical Survey of Private members' Bills" (2002), 25 Canadian Parliamentary Review no. 1.

comparison, once introduced and automatically adopted on first reading, further scrutiny of private members' bills is relegated to Private Members' Business, a session limited to one hour per day. Notably, the time in this hour is split between not only the permitted roster of private members' bills, but private members' motions as well.

For this and other reasons, parliamentary law makes further progress on the bill during this Private Members' Business hour a tricky proposition. The precise order in which bills are processed during Private Members' Business is determined by draw, establishing an order of precedence for a regularly replenished pool of some thirty items of private members' business, including both bills and motions.[163]

Merely arriving on this list is not, however, sufficient. Under the conventional rules, the Standing Committee on Procedure and House Affairs designates no more than ten of the items on this list "votable," meaning that the bill will come to a vote eventually. The committee selects the bills that receive this status with an eye to several criteria, including the public interest served by the bill and the evident constitutionality of the law project.[164] Bills not accorded this status are dropped after brief debate.[165]

Provisional rules in place until June 2005[166] have relaxed this approach to nonvotable matters.[167] Thus, under the provisional process, no cap is imposed on votable measures, and the bill is deemed votable subject to the Standing Committee deciding otherwise.[168]

Subsequently, votable bills under both the standard and provisional rules are cycled through Private Members' Business hour. Debate on bills during this period is carefully limited. Under the standard rules, members may speak to a bill for ten minutes each, with the exception of the member moving the bill forward, who may speak for twenty minutes.[169] The provisional rules shorten these time periods.[170]

If debate on the bill has not concluded upon the expiry of the Private Members' Business hour, that bill is listed at the back end of items on the order of precedence. It is only taken up again after the other items on that

---

163 Commons *Standing Orders*, Order 87.
164 *Précis of Procedure* at 85.
165 *Précis of Procedure* at 84. Commons *Standing Orders*, Order 92.
166 See Standing Committee on Procedure and House Affairs, *12th Report* (adopted by the Commons on October 29, 2004).
167 Commons *Standing Orders*, Appendix 1. See also House of Commons, *Fact Sheet: Private Members' Business — The New Procedures at a Glance* (2004).
168 Commons *Standing Orders*, Appendix 1, Order 91.1.
169 Commons *Standing Orders*, Order 95.
170 Commons *Standing Orders*, Appendix 1, Order 95.

list have either been dealt with or have been themselves interrupted by the expiry of the Private Members' Business hour. Debate on the motion related to this bill will continue to cycle in this fashion until the expiry of set periods of time determined by the bill's stage of the legislative process, at which point the motion must be put to a vote.[171] The real timing bottleneck appears to be at second reading. At the report and third reading stage of the bill process members may, by motion, agree to add a modest amount of additional parliamentary time to consider the bill,[172] partially freeing the law project from the full strictures of Private Members' Business hour.

The private members' process — whether under the regular or provisional procedure — is more accommodating of private members' bills than was once the case. It remains the case, however, that close rationing of Commons time allocated to private members' bills greatly reduces their chances of success. About the only rule truly favouring private members' bills in parliamentary law is the Standing Order allowing the bill to be bootstrapped to the same stage in the legislative process it was at when Parliament was prorogued between sessions.[173]

Statistical Trends in Law-Making

In Appendix 2, we examine how parliamentary legislative procedures discussed in this chapter have translated into legislative results. There, we compute trends in the law-making process as reflected in statistics concerning the proportion of bills becoming law over time.

Read together, these data suggest that parliamentary legislative performance has been remarkably regular, as measured by days of parliamentary session time ("session days") per bill introduced. Over time, however, governments have introduced fewer bills per parliamentary session day. Further, the ratio of parliamentary session days to promulgated statutes has increased steadily and markedly. Read together, these figures suggest that modern federal Parliaments are characterized by vigorous private-members'-bill introduction, steadily abating "productivity" in relation to numbers of government bills, and much lower "productivity" in numbers of statutes.

The statistics are silent, however, on why these changes have occurred, and whether these are positive developments or not. Looked at from one

---

171   *Précis of Procedure* at 85; Commons *Standing Orders*, Order 93.

172   Commons *Standing Orders*, Order 98.

173   Commons, *Standing Orders*, Order 86.1. Under the provisional rules, this same rule also apparently applies to motions. See Commons *Standing Orders*, Appendix 1, Order 86.1, speaking of "items" and not just "bills."

optic, a decrease in the number of statutes introduced per day of parliamentary time may signify more careful scrutiny of these measures by parliamentarians. It may also reflect changes in the nature of the instruments coming before Parliament. Law-making and governance may well be more complex today than half a century ago. Massive omnibus bills, like the *Antiterrorism Act* (2001) and the *Public Safety Act* (2004) in the thirty-seventh Parliament, amended or introduced dozens of laws, many of them convoluted and controversial. For these reasons, modern parliamentarians may be — and probably are — just as consumed with law-making as their predecessors. The laws they make, however, require more time to vet carefully.

Another possible explanation for the statistics is that parliamentarians may now be busier with functions other than law-making than were their predecessors. As discussed in chapter 6, the executive tables reports in Parliament in overwhelming numbers. Three hundred and eight Members of Parliament police a government comprising many thousands of unelected officials. This is a very different (and time-consuming) reality than existed in prior generations.

A final, more disquieting, explanation for the figures might be a shift in the nature of governance, one that involves administration through exercise of existing executive powers rather than through parliamentary statute-making. Cabinet may simply not need to turn to Parliament as frequently, relying instead on its own law-making powers. Indeed, complicated legislation and the pressure on parliamentary time likely accelerate the breadth of parliamentary grants of these law-making powers to the executive. In the words of Professor Donald Savoie, "Issues today are far more complex and interwoven than they were forty years ago. For this reason, and because parliamentary time has become a precious commodity in Ottawa, the government has abandoned detailed legislation in favour of very broadly stated laws. ... A good part of the legislative power that once belonged to Parliament is pushed down to the government, which makes detailed regulations."[174] It is to this third issue, executive law-making, that we now turn our attention.

B. EXECUTIVE LAW-MAKING

Like Parliament, Cabinet is a law-making body. Although by constitutional convention, Cabinet exercises the monarch's limited royal prerogative or *Constitution Act, 1867* powers, Cabinet's formal law-making powers stem

---

174 Savoie, *Breaking the Bargain* at 231–32.

from parliamentary grants, usually in the form of provisions permitting the Governor-in-Council to promulgate regulations under a given Act for certain enumerated purposes.

As discussed in chapter 2, Parliament's powers to delegate legislative powers is vast, constrained only by a few, relatively minor constitutional principles. In practice, Parliament has accorded the executive substantial legislative authority. As of December 31, 2003, the *Canada Gazette II* list of regulations issued by executive branch bodies pursuant to parliamentary statutes was fully forty-eight pages long, constituting a vast web of law. Indeed, one Parliamentarian claimed recently that "20% of the law in the country stems from legislation debated and passed in the legislature, and in this case in Parliament. The remaining 80% of the law is made up of regulations."[175] In this section, we discuss this delegated legislation, deferring a discussion of Cabinet's structure, procedure and other functions until chapter 6.

1.   Types of Executive Laws

Executive branch laws are known as "statutory instruments," a term defined in a rather opaque way by the *Statutory Instruments Act*.[176] Put simply, under this Act, there are two sorts of statutory instruments: those that fall within a subset of statutory instrument known as a "regulation" and those that do not.

a)   Definition of a Statutory Instrument

Subject to certain minor exceptions, a statutory instrument is generally any instrument made or established "in the execution of a power conferred *by or under* an Act of Parliament, by or under which that instrument is expressly authorized to be issued" or "by or under the authority of the Governor-in-Council, otherwise than in the execution of a power conferred *by or under* an Act of Parliament."[177] It is, in other words, a very broad concept, one expansive enough to capture both legislative powers delegated to the executive by parliamentary statute, and also orders issued pursuant to the royal prerogative[178] or under the Constitution or constitutional convention.

---

175   Mr. Gurmant Grewal (Surrey Central, Canadian Alliance), *Hansard*, no. 50, 37th Parl., 2d Sess. (31 Jan. 2003).

176   See *Statutory Instruments Act*, R.S.C. 1985, c. S-22, s. 2.

177   *Ibid.*, s. 2 [emphasis added].

178   Department of Justice, *A Guide to the Making of Federal Acts and Regulations* (Ottawa: Public Works and Government Services Canada, 1996).

b) Definition of a Regulation

A regulation is a particular subspecies of statutory instrument, defined as a statutory instrument "made in the exercise of a *legislative power* conferred by or under an Act of Parliament, or ... for the contravention of which a penalty, fine or imprisonment is prescribed by or under an Act of Parliament."[179]

The meaning of this first (and most common) sort of regulation — one constituting an exercise of "legislative powers" — requires some explanation. The Department of Justice interprets the reference to a legislative power in the *Statutory Instruments Act* as signifying a "power to make rules of conduct having the force of law for an undetermined number of persons." This authority is juxtaposed with an "administrative" power: "the power to create norms that apply only to a particular person or situation."[180] As discussed further later, these definitions follow conventional administrative law understandings of legislative powers.

The precise demarcation point between a legislative and an administrative power is obviously a rather uncertain one. There is, therefore, a large margin of subjectivity into the definition of a regulation. Indeed, the *Statutory Instruments Act* recognizes this fact, by empowering the Department of Justice to make the final call on whether an instrument is a regulation or not.[181]

Generally, however, where a statutory instrument makes rules of conduct pursuant to an Act of Parliament for an undetermined number of persons, it should be regarded as a regulation. Alternatively, even if it does make rules for this broad class of persons, but it is *not* issued pursuant to an Act (but instead pursuant to the royal prerogative or the Constitution), it is not a regulation. Meanwhile, if it makes rules of conduct for a *limited* number of people, it is not a regulation, unless it falls into the second category of regulations by imposing a penalty anticipated by an Act.

This distinction between a regulation and a mere statutory instrument is important. As discussed in the section that follows, the promulgation of a regulation is governed both by (relatively rudimentary) statutory requirements[182] and by more detailed government policy.[183] Conversely, fewer formal requirements exist for nonregulatory statutory instruments.

---

179 *Statutory Instruments Act*, s. 2 [emphasis added].

180 Department of Justice, *A Guide*.

181 *Statutory Instruments Act*, s. 4.

182 See *Statutory Instruments Act*, and its own regulations.

183 See Privy Council Office, *Regulatory Process Guide: Developing a Regulatory Proposal and Seeking its Approval* (last updated 07/2004).

2. Executive Branch Regulation-Making

a) Process

Current Government of Canada regulatory policies, approved by Cabinet in 1999, identify several principles guiding regulation-making. These include requirements that: "Canadians are consulted, and that they have an opportunity to participate in developing or modifying regulations and regulatory programs"; a problem that justifies regulation exists; the benefits of the regulation outweigh its cost; adverse impacts on the economy are minimized; international and intergovernmental agreements are observed; resources exist to manage the regulations effectively, in terms of compliance and enforcement; and that other directives and procedures related to regulation-making are followed.[184]

Many — if not most — regulations are "made" by the Governor-in-Council, the Governor General acting on the advice of Cabinet. The Privy Council Office divides the actual process to be followed for Governor-in-Council regulations into ten steps, as detailed in Table 5.3.[185]

Table 5.3   The Process for Governor-in-Council Regulations

Step	Process
Conception and development of a regulation	Government departments contemplating devising a regulation conduct an assessment of whether this instrument is necessary, focusing on such things as environmental, health and safety impacts, and costs and benefits. If the department decides to proceed with its regulatory proposal, it is encouraged to give "early notice," either through its annual report to Parliament on plans and priorities (see chapter 6), a similar list on its webpage or via the *Canada Gazette*. In this fashion, the department may gather important technical and public input on its proposal.
Department drafting	The department works with legal staff to draft the instrument and assorted other required documents. It must also prepare a "regulatory impact analysis assessment" (RIAS) dealing with the principles raised in the 1999 regulatory policy statement.
Review by the Department of Justice and the Privy Council Office	Under the express terms of the *Statutory Instruments Act*,[186] the clerk of the Privy Council, in consultation with the deputy minister of justice, must review draft regulations. This analysis must establish that the regulation is "authorized by the statute pursuant to which it is to be made; ... does not constitute an unusual or unexpected use of the authority pursuant to which it is to be made; ... does not trespass unduly on existing rights and freedoms and is not, in any case, inconsistent with the purposes and

184 Privy Council Office, *Government of Canada Regulatory Policy* (1999).
185 The table summarizes information from Privy Council Office, *Regulatory Process Guide: Developing a Regulatory Proposal and Seeking its Approval* unless otherwise noted.
186 *Statutory Instruments Act*, s. 3.

Step	Process
	provisions of the *Canadian Charter of Rights and Freedoms* and the *Canadian Bill of Rights*; and ... the form and draftsmanship of the proposed regulation are in accordance with established standards."
Ministerial permission for pre-publication	The minister approves the draft regulation for pre-publication.
Pre-publication review by the Privy Council Office and the Treasury Board	Privy Council and Cabinet's Treasury Board review the draft regulation and determine whether to approve it for pre-publication. Under the Martin government, Treasury Board's regulation review jurisdiction has been considerably expanded to include more than simply review of regulations with financial implications.
Pre-publication in the *Canada Gazette*, Part I and Comment Period	Pre-publication in the *Canada Gazette* is intended to provide "various interested groups and individuals, and Canadians in general, a final opportunity to review and comment on a regulatory proposal at the last stages of the regulation-making process" and to assess whether "the final draft proposal is in keeping with previous consultation drafts." The accompanying notice period is usually thirty days, though it may vary. Treasury Board may exempt some regulations from pre-publication.
Departmental preparation of final draft	The department prepares another draft of the regulations, with an updated RIAS that "reflects information relating to the comments received during the pre-publication period, any actions taken to address those comments and the rationale for the department's response." If amendments were made, the revised draft regulations may be referred back to the Justice Department and the Privy Council Office for re-review.
Final review by the Privy Council Office and the Treasury Board	The Privy Council Office reviews the final draft one last time, and Treasury Board decides whether to proceed with the regulation.
Making, registering, publishing in *Canada Gazette*, Part II, and distributing regulations	A regulation is "made" when approved by the Governor-in-Council through an Order-in-Council. An Order-in-Council is an "instrument by which the Governor General, acting on the advice of the Queen's Privy Council for Canada, expresses decisions."[187] The regulation is subsequently "registered" when the Clerk of the Privy Council "records the title of the regulation, the title of the regulation-making authority, the source of the power to make the regulation, the date of making and the date of registration, and assigns it a number, preceded by SOR (Statutory Orders and Regulations)." Pursuant to the *Statutory Instruments Act*, a regulation generally comes into force when registered.[188] That Act also provides, however, that a person may not usually be punished for contravening a regulation until it is also published in the *Canada Gazette*, Part II.[189]

187　Privy Council Office, *Governor in Council Process Guide: Developing a Proposal Seeking the Approval of an Order by the Governor in Council* (July 2004).

188　*Statutory Instruments Act*, s. 9.

189　*Ibid.*, s. 11.

Executive branch bodies other than the Governor-in-Council — such as quasi-judicial tribunals and specialized agencies or commissions — may also have delegated legislative powers. In many instances, instruments introduced by these institutions also fall within the definition of regulation under the *Statutory Instruments Act*. In these circumstances, the basic requirements of the *Statutory Instruments Act* identified in the chart above remain the same, but the policy-based vetting and development process will obviously be different from that discussed above. Cabinet may not be involved in the approval of the regulation.

b) Parliamentary Role

Parliament has traditionally had a minimal role in reviewing executive branch statutory instrument-making. Under the *Statutory Instruments Act*, statutory instruments are referred to Parliament for review.[190] In practice, this referral is to the Standing Joint Committee on Scrutiny of Regulations. This body, however, is overwhelmed. In the words of its co-chair in 2003, "[t]he committee works meticulously and, with the complex nature of its undertaking, work proceeds at a slow pace. The inevitable result, especially considering the large volume of regulations introduced each year, is a huge backlog of work in progress. Staff and resources allotted to the committee are nowhere near adequate."[191] These time and resource limitations make Parliament a much more minor player in the review of statutory instruments than would ideally be the case.

Nevertheless, Parliament has authorized itself to challenge at least those statutory instruments that are also regulations. Beginning in 1986, the Commons Standing Orders included a "disallowance" procedure, empowering the committee to "make a report to the House containing only a resolution which, if the report is concurred in, would be an Order of this House to the Ministry to revoke a statutory instrument, or a portion thereof, which the Governor in Council or a Minister of the Crown has the authority to revoke."[192]

This procedure was criticized as flawed for several reasons. First, it applied to statutory instruments produced by Cabinet, not to other agencies and tribunals with their own regulatory powers. Second, at best it produced an Order of the Commons, calling upon the Governor-in-Council to

---

190 *Ibid.*, s. 19.
191 Mr. Gurmant Grewal (Surrey Central, Canadian Alliance), *Hansard*, no. 50, 37th Parl., 2d Sess. (31 Jan. 2003).
192 Commons, *Standing Orders*, Order 123 (1997 version).

revoke the measure. Such an Order is not a binding legislative directive.[193] If the Governor-in-Council chose to ignore it, the Commons likely could resort only to its contempt powers (discussed later) or to the legislative process itself.

The perceived inadequacies of this limited power prompted Bill C-205, a successful 2003 private member's bill enacting a statutory disallowance power as an amendment to the *Statutory Instruments Act*. Pursuant to these amendments, the Joint Committee may "make a report to the senate and the House of Commons containing only a resolution that all or any portion of a *regulation* that stands permanently referred to the committee be revoked."[194] This resolution is deemed adopted unless within fifteen sitting days "a Minister files with the Speaker of that House a motion to the effect that the resolution not be adopted." If such a motion is introduced, the matter is then debated, and if Parliament adopts a resolution that "all or any portion of a regulation be revoked, the authority authorized to make the regulation shall revoke the regulation or portion of the regulation no later than 30 days, or any longer period that may be specified in the resolution."[195]

This amendment cures the compliance problem associated with the Standing Orders. It also extends the revocation power beyond regulations introduced by Cabinet or its ministers. It is notable, however, that the statute creates a revocation power in relation to regulations only. As noted earlier, regulations are a subset of "statutory instruments." The new law is, therefore, narrower in terms of the instruments to which it applies than was the original Standing Orders the law was designed to replace. We return to this issue later.

Exactly how active a time-strapped Parliament will be in exercising this new power to disallow regulations remains to be seen. The Joint Committee's effectiveness may well have more to do with whether new resources are made available to it than with the actual revocation process.

3. Nonregulatory Orders-in-Council

The Governor-in-Council may act pursuant to statutory authority, but the instrument it issues is not a regulation because it does not impose penalties and is not issued pursuant to a legislative power; that is, a power to make rules of conduct having the force of law for an undetermined num-

---

193 See Mr. Gurmant Grewal (Surrey Central, Canadian Alliance), *Hansard*, no. 50, 37th Parl., 2d Sess. (31 Jan. 2003) discussing these shortcomings.

194 *Statutory Instruments Act*, s. 19.1 [emphasis added].

195 *Ibid.*

ber of persons. In these circumstances, and with instruments issued pursuant to a nonstatutory authority, the resulting law is a nonregulatory Order-in-Council.

a) Less Transparent Procedure

In practice, the process of introducing and developing nonregulatory Orders-in-Council is much less regimented (and transparent) than is the case for regulations.[196] Government policy does not appear to require consultation and pre-publication for nonregulations.[197] The final product is generally available, either in published form in the *Canada Gazette*[198] or more recently, on the Privy Council website.[199] However, these instruments need not comport with the *Statutory Instruments Act* provisions on regulations, not least that statute's procedure for parliamentary revocation of a regulation.

b) No Parliamentary Revocation Powers

The exclusion of these nonregulations from the latter process apparently was no oversight. The original version of Bill C-205 — the private member's law project introducing the revocation process — anticipated a disallowance power in relation to all statutory instruments.[200] Nevertheless, the final version of the law restricted this procedure to regulations, for reasons that are not readily apparent in *Hansard* or the Committee proceedings.

As noted above, the original Standing Orders that were supposedly enhanced by the legislated amendments to the *Statutory Instruments Act* referred to statutory instruments. This terminology has now been discarded in the current Standing Orders. At present, the Standing Orders in operation for the thirty-eighth Parliament mimic the amended *Statutory Instruments Act* in referring to regulations.[201] Apparently, this change was made so that "the procedure would be the same in the legislation and in the Standing Orders and would allow the Speaker to rule on procedures involving delegated legislation, because they would be under the Standing

---

196 For an overview of the internal process, see Privy Council Office, *Governor in Council Process Guide: Developing a Proposal Seeking the Approval of an Order by the Governor in Council* (July 2004).

197 See Privy Council Office, *Guide to Making Federal Acts and Regulations* ("The pre-publication requirement does not apply to documents that are not regulations, unless the enabling Act says so.").

198 See C. Gaz. Part II. See also *Statutory Instrument Act*, s. 6; *Statutory Instruments Regulations*, C.R.C., c. 1509 ss. 11 and 14.

199 See Privy Council Office, Orders-in-Council division, www.pco-bcp.gc.ca/oic-ddc/oic-ddc.asp?lang=EN.

200 Bill C-205, 37th Parl., 2d Sess., 51 Elizabeth II, 2002.

201 *Standing Orders*, Order 123 (2004 version).

Orders. The Speaker cannot interpret or apply law as found in Bill C-205. This would avoid the inconsistencies."[202] No discussion was apparently had in Parliament on whether the Commons should forfeit its reviewing power in relation to nonregulatory statutory instruments.

As a direct result, Parliament has decided (perhaps unwittingly) that it will no longer have an affirmative role in the review of those statutory instruments that are not regulations; typically, those directed at a handful of people, rather than an indefinite number of people. Its authority to call for revocation of these instruments, once in the Standing Orders, has been abandoned. It is left to legislate a revocation or, like other Canadians, Parliamentarians may turn to the courts to strike down instruments that are *ultra vires* the authority possessed by the executive,[203] a matter discussed later. Both of these responses are obviously quite involved, and unlikely to occur.

It remains to be seen whether parliamentary contemplation of the substance of some of these nonregulatory orders will be partially restored by other democratic reforms proposed by the Martin government — such as parliamentary review of Governor-in-Council appointments made by these nonregulatory statutory instruments.

4. Executive Law-Making Jurisdiction and the Role of the Courts

We conclude this section on delegated legislation by considering the role of another branch of government — the courts — in reviewing delegated legislation. As noted above, courts have virtually no place in reviewing the process of enacting parliamentary statutes or in second-guessing the motivational impetus behind the law. By comparison, courts are much more probing in reviewing the executive law-making function. As discussed at length in chapter 2, this more aggressive stance is driven by constitutional imperatives, not the least of which are the separation of powers and the doctrine of parliamentary supremacy.

a) Ensuring That Delegated Legislation Is Authorized by Parliamentary Grant or Some Other Source

First, and most obviously, the executive must possess the power to issue a statutory instrument. Like Parliament itself, its jurisdiction to introduce lawful rules is constrained by the *Charter* and the division of powers

---

202 Mr. James Robertson, committee researcher, Standing Committee on Procedure and House Affairs, *Evidence*, 37th Parl., 2d Sess. (4 Nov. 2003).

203 See, e.g., *Waddell v. Canada (Governor-in-Council)*, (1981) 126 D.L.R. (3d) 431 (B.C.S.C.) holding that it had jurisdiction to entertain a case on the propriety of certain Orders-in-Council brought by a Member of Parliament.

between the provincial and federal levels of government set out in the *Constitution Act, 1867.*

Unlike Parliament, the executive's jurisdiction is also usually limited by the parliamentary grant of power authorizing the measure. As we have already noted, in a Westminster system, parliamentary supremacy, interacting with the separation of powers, means that "there is a hierarchical relationship between the executive and the legislature, whereby the executive must execute and implement the policies which have been enacted by the legislature in statutory form."[204] Official actions undertaken by the executive branch usually must flow from "statutory authority clearly granted and properly exercised."[205] Alternatively, the power may be found to reside in the royal prerogative, itself subject to being trumped by Parliament, or be listed among the constitutional powers possessed by the executive.

A statutory instrument straying outside the confines of one of these sources of executive branch authority is said to be *ultra vires* (beyond the jurisdiction of), and is subject to being reviewed by the courts. In most such court cases, the alleged power is said by the government to flow from an Act of Parliament. In those circumstances, the court will construe the Act allegedly delegating the regulatory jurisdiction to the executive,[206] and discern its overall purpose and the purpose for the delegation of regulatory authority.[207] Where the statutory instrument is inconsistent with this Act of Parliament and its purpose, a court will declare it inoperative and strike it down.[208] Acting in this fashion, courts preserve parliamentary supremacy and the generally subordinate role of the executive branch in law-making.

Courts will also step in not simply where the statutory instrument does not line up with the grant of jurisdiction, but possibly also where the delegated legislative power was exercised in bad faith or for purposes inconsistent with the delegating Act.[209] The exact circumstances in which a court will intervene for these "abuses of discretion" are now governed by the Supreme Court's increasingly opaque "standard of review" test, an issue discussed in chapter 2. Setting out this analysis in full goes beyond the scope of this section.

---

204 *Re Remuneration of Judges,* [1997] 3 S.C.R. 3 at para. 139.

205 *Babcock,* [2002] 3 S.C.R. 3 at para. 20.

206 *Canada v. St. Lawrence Cruise Lines Inc.,* [1997] 3 F.C. 899 at 912 (C.A.).

207 *Société des alcools du Québec v. Canada,* 2002 FCA 69 at para. 33.

208 See, e.g., *ibid.*

209 See, e.g., *Canada (Attorney General) v. National Anti-Poverty Organization,* [1989] 3 F.C. 684 (C.A.) for a court reviewing the exercise of a legislative power on bad faith grounds.

Suffice it to say, however, that while a court cannot probe the motivations of a legislature in enacting law, it may review the impulses that prompted the executive to introduce delegated legislation. Where this legislation is provoked by improper motivations, the court may intervene. Although not often articulated as such, the underlying theory is that Parliament could not have intended that power delegated by it to the executive be exercised in an ill-intentioned manner, without express permission to do so.

b) Due Process and Delegated Legislation

The second, and more difficult, issue in terms of court review of statutory instruments is the extent to which due process rights should attach to the making of statutory instruments. As noted in chapter 2, common law "procedural fairness" is a due process standard imposed on members of the executive branch exercising powers granted to them by Act of Parliament (or the royal prerogative).[210] At base, procedural fairness requires that persons affected by a particular decision be notified prior to that decision and be heard on the issue. The precise scope and content of this notice and comment requirement varies depending on the power being exercised and the implications of the decision for the interested party. In practice, the due process requirement ranges from a very rudimentary notice and comment opportunity to a full-blown, court-like hearing procedure.

No Procedural Fairness where Executive Exercising Legislative Power
Notably, these common law procedural rights do not extend to the legislative process undertaken by Parliament. As discussed above, parliamentary law-making procedure is protected by parliamentary privilege, and is not subject to any standard of due process or procedural fairness. As noted in Chapter 2, the courts have extrapolated from this parliamentary status and concluded that where the executive exercises delegated "legislative" powers, procedural fairness also does not attach. Referring specifically to Cabinet, the Supreme Court has held that "[l]egislative powers so delegated by the Legislature to a constitutional body which is part of itself must be viewed as an extension of the legislative power of the Legislature."[211]

---

210 *Mercier-Neron v. Canada (Minister of National Health and Welfare)* (1995), 98 F.T.R. 36 at para. 14 (T.D.) ("The duty to act fairly must be complied with even when the government ... derives its enabling power from the royal prerogative.").

211 *Quebec (Attorney General) v. Blaikie,* [1981] 1 S.C.R. 312 at 320. See also *Cardinal v. Director of Kent Institution,* [1985] 2 S.C.R. 643 at 653 (there is a "duty of procedural fairness lying on every public authority making an administrative decision which is not of a legislative nature and which affects the rights, privileges or interests of an individual").

This approach depends on an analogy between the legislature and executive law-making that is flawed for at least two reasons. First, exactly what constitutes a "legislative" power is a matter fraught with ambiguity. As noted above, perhaps the best effort to define the term stresses that legislative measures are those with general application, and not directed a particular person. They are also marked by "a broad policy orientation in that the decision creates norms rather than decides on their application to particular situations."[212] Measuring whether government action is legislative or not is obviously a strongly subjective assessment, one with large swaths of gray. Indeed, courts have defined as legislative some delegated powers that look an awful lot like straight adjudication of claims.[213]

Second, this (ambiguous) category of procedurally immune legislative powers ignores the reality of how legislatures make law. Certainly, courts do not mandate its procedures, but in practice, Parliament follows fully *three* public readings in two Houses, supplemented by generally public committee proceedings in these two Houses at which interested parties often appear. In other words, there is substantial notice and comment incorporated into parliamentary law-making. By exempting "legislative" decisions of the executive from common law due process standards, courts empower the executive to follow a much less transparent process in enacting often potent regulations.

Implications

In fact, the divide between these "legislative" and nonlegislative powers exercised by the executive produces paradoxical consequences. As noted above, where a power is legislative and is conferred by or under an Act of Parliament, the resulting instrument is a regulation, subject to the minimal procedural vetting and publication requirements of the *Statutory Instruments Act* and, more importantly, to its parliamentary revocation provisions.

However, this *Statutory Instruments Act* does not mandate the notice and comment, pre-publication *policy* usually (but not always) followed by government in introducing regulations. This oversight is not corrected by the common law: because most regulations reflect the exercise of legislative powers, they need not meet common law procedural standards. As a conse-

---

212 *Potter v. Halifax Regional School Board*, 215 D.L.R. (4th) 441 at para. 40 (N.S.C.A.), relying on D. Brown and J. Evans, *Judicial Review of Administrative Action in Canada* (1998), vol. 2 at 7:2330.

213 See, e.g., *Attorney General of Canada v. Inuit Tapirisat of Canada*, [1980] 2 S.C.R. 735, holding that Cabinet's decision issued in response to an appeal of a CRTC decision was a "legislative" decision, not subject to procedural fairness.

quence, unless the statute under which a regulation is issued itself requires pre-publication followed by a comment period, a regulation is perfectly legal if it were to appear suddenly, with no notice and no public comment.

In comparison, where an Order-in-Council is issued pursuant to power that is not legislative, it is likely not a regulation and thus is immune from even the limited procedural requirements of the *Statutory Instruments Act* and that statute's parliamentary revocation process. Yet, it is subject to common law procedural fairness exactly because it is not a legislative decision. If these instruments were to appear without procedural fairness requirements being met, they could be reviewed successfully in court.

In sum, the net result is that courts are more demanding of the sort of delegated legislation over which the *Statutory Instruments Act* permits Parliament the least oversight. Meanwhile, courts are least demanding of the instruments — regulations — in relation to which the Act anticipates the greatest parliamentary review.

At first blush, the common law and the *Statutory Instruments Act* cancel out each other's procedural shortcomings: courts are most aggressive where the parliamentary role is least pronounced, and vice versa. Yet, in practice, the most important delegated instruments — regulations — escape any formal, legal due process requirements. Notice and comment in relation to regulations depends entirely on potentially mutable Cabinet policy requiring such notice and comment. As a consequence, we believe it sensible that Cabinet's current pre-publication and comment policy for regulations be incorporated into the *Statutory Instruments Act*, rendering these processes mandatory.

C. CONCLUSION

Legally, Parliament's legislative jurisdiction is vast. Evaluated on this basis, it is by far the most important political branch of government, a status constitutionalized by the concept of parliamentary supremacy. Much political nuance is, however, layered onto this simple legal hierarchy. Not least among the political attributes of parliamentary primacy is the predominance of political parties. This party apparatus piggy-backs onto constitutional convention, allowing one party to control both the legislative and the executive branches.

In this dual role, the party wields significant political control over Canadian governance. It produces, however, a political reality entirely at odds with the legal hierarchy between Parliament and the executive. A party leader commanding enough votes in the Commons to constitute a majority of that House is also elevated to the Prime Minister's Office and inherits the executive powers of government. With the party leader at the helm of the executive branch, the priorities of the executive branch become the legislative priorities of the parliamentary majority.

Among these priorities is the implementation of parliamentary rules of procedure favouring efficient dispatch of executive branch law projects in Parliament. This point should not be overstated. Leading parliamentary experts Marleau and Montpetit report that "[m]ore often than not ... procedural changes are the result of a broad consensus among Members of all parties and are readily adopted without debate."[214] Nevertheless, there are instances — such as the rules on closure of debate — where rule changes were contested, and carried only by the majority.[215] At the end of the day, it is indisputable that parliamentary law gives special primacy to government initiatives, especially government law projects.

Thus, the Standing Orders draw a clear distinction between government bills and private members' bills. Government bills are handed down from the ministry, traditionally backed by party discipline, and promulgated via a parliamentary process very generous in the priority it gives these law projects. Private members' bills, on the other hand, are law initiatives not derived from the ministry that generally do not the benefit from disciplined party voting and which are relegated by parliamentary procedure to a handful of hours of parliamentary time.

From one perspective, therefore, Parliament is simply the formal arena in which executive projects requiring statutory sanction in our system of law and governance are given the requisite legal stamp of authority. It is not — at least not often — a place where elected representatives set a legislative policy direction different from that desired by the ministry and its vast government apparatus.

And even then, that executive government has capitalized on its *de facto* control of Parliament to legislate expansions of the powers it may exercise in our system of law and governance without returning to Parliament. These powers come, of course, from the web of delegated legislative authority Parliament has parcelled out to the executive branch. The resulting regulations and other statutory instruments are vulnerable in variable degrees to parliamentary — or at least court — scrutiny. In reality, however, their numbers make effective parliamentary review extremely difficult,

---

214 Marleau and Montpetit, *House of Commons Procedure and Practice* at 216.
215 *Ibid.*

even where — as with regulations — Parliament has not abandoned a reviewing function.

At the time of this writing, there is hope in the air that a better-resourced Parliament with a new tradition of free votes may be rendered more relevant as a deliberative, legislative body. At present, however, it is clear that in its traditional jurisdictional role as legislature, Parliament is much less than might be presumed from its strict legal status as the only truly sovereign body in our system of government.

The question we ask in the next chapter is whether this same supremacy really means much at the institutional level, under the conventions of responsible government supposedly rendering the ministry (and through it, the unelected officials it commands) accountable to Parliament.

6

Parliament, Cabinet, Democracy and Responsible Government

As discussed in chapter 2, "responsible" government is the means by which the executive is held structurally accountable to the legislature. In practice, responsible government hinges on two concepts: first, the ministry is usually expected to exert "command and control" authority over unelected officials. In the words of Governor General Earl Grey: "[A]ll holders of permanent offices must be subordinate to some minister responsible to parliament."[1] Thus, as discussed at various points in this book, the Governor General generally acts only on the advice of the prime minister or Cabinet. Meanwhile, as is explored in greater detail below, departments and agencies of the public administration of Canada report to ministers. Second, these same ministers are accountable to Parliament, both individually and collectively as members of Cabinet. In this fashion, parliamentarians have ultimate responsibility for the governance of the country, through the proxy of ministers. In this chapter, we explore both of these aspects of responsible government. We begin by examining Cabinet's role in executive governance. We then highlight Parliament's function in overseeing that executive.

---

1   Cited in Donald Savoie, *Breaking the Bargain* (Toronto: University of Toronto Press, 2003) at 32.

A. CABINET'S ROLE IN EXECUTIVE GOVERNANCE

Cabinet plays a central role in Canadian governance, exercising hierarchical and structural control over the public administration of Canada. Canadian law includes potent measures ensuring that this public administration remains accountable to Cabinet.

1. Cabinet Procedure and Structure

a) Cabinet Purpose and Organization

In the words of the Privy Council Office, Cabinet's functions include:

> securing agreement among Ministers on government priorities; securing agreement on parliamentary actions by the government; providing a forum for ministerial debate on issues of general interest; providing adequate information to Ministers relative to decisions for which they will be held collectively responsible and which may impact on their individual responsibilities; and providing adequate information to the Prime Minister to carry out his/her responsibilities and his/her leadership role.[2]

Exactly how Cabinet is structured to do all of this, and how it proceeds, is mostly the domain of administration and politics, not law. Prime ministers are entitled to organize their Cabinets mostly as they wish, using any number of different committee structures and delegating various degrees of decision-making autonomy to these committees.[3] As Professor Donald Savoie has detailed, these structures and the way in which Cabinet decisions are made, reflect the personalities and priorities of individual prime ministers.[4] At the time of this writing, the Martin Cabinet employs eight committees, as detailed in Table 6.1.[5]

Table 6.1   Cabinet Committees in the Martin Government

Committee	Responsibility
Operations	Provides the day-to-day coordination of the implementation of the government's agenda, including policy, House planning, urgent issues and communications.
Treasury Board	Manages the government's financial, personnel and administrative responsibilities, as well as approving regulations and most Orders-in-Council.

---

2   Privy Council Office, *Information Resources: About Cabinet.*
3   See discussion in Donald Savoie, *Governing from the Centre* (Toronto: University of Toronto Press, 1999) at 265.
4   *Ibid.*
5   Privy Council Office, *Cabinet Committee Mandates and Membership.*

Committee	Responsibility
Treasury Board	Note that the *Financial Administration Act* legislates some of Treasury Board's responsibilities, and thus the prime minister does not set all of this committee's mandate.[6] Ministers in this committee are appointed by Order-in-Council issued pursuant to the Act.[7]
Expenditure Review Sub-Committee of the Treasury Board	Reviews all programs and areas of cross-cutting interest and makes recommendations to Treasury Board on funding decisions and re-allocations.
Domestic Affairs	Considers, in an integrated manner, social, economic and environmental policy issues.
Global Affairs	Ensures an integrated approach to foreign affairs, defence, international development, international trade and other related issues.
Security, Public Health & Emergencies	Manages national security and intelligence issues and activities, and ensures coordination of the federal response to all emergencies, including natural disasters, public health, and security.
Canada-U.S.	Ensures an integrated, government-wide approach to Canada-U.S. relations.
Aboriginal Affairs	Supports a renewed emphasis on Aboriginal issues.

b) Cabinet Solidarity and Confidence

Cabinet's operations are not entirely the whim of the prime minister. At least one principle is enduring: ministers in Cabinet must act in solidarity. Indeed, this Cabinet solidarity has been described as an unwritten constitutional convention.[8] It "allows ministers to be frank in private but requires them to support the government in public."[9] Thus, a minister must loyally support and defend any Cabinet decision, and not suggest that he or she differed with the prevailing view.[10]

Further, ministers "may speak about government's policy only after it has been agreed to in private by their colleagues."[11] A minister may not publicly initiate new policy, absent this prior Cabinet consent. For this same reason, a minister must not make public statements or speeches that appear to implicate the government.[12] To these attributes is added the

---

6   *Financial Administration Act*, s. 5 *et seq.*

7   See, e.g., Order-in-Council, 2004-0848 (2004-07-20).

8   See, e.g., Privy Council Office, *Governing Responsibly: A Guide for Ministers and Ministers of State* (2004).

9   Privy Council Office, *Information Resources: About Cabinet.*

10   Eugene A. Forsey and G.C. Eglington, *The Question of Confidence in Responsible Government* (Ottawa: Special Committee on the Reform of the House of Commons, 1985) at 84.

11   Privy Council Office, *Information Resources: About Cabinet.*

12   Forsey and Eglington, *The Question of Confidence* at 84.

requirement that advice given to the Governor General must be unanimous, and not reflect unsettled disputes within Cabinet.[13]

This Cabinet solidarity permits collective decision-making, and preserves a government from the erosion of parliamentary (and public) support that might follow open feuding and dissent between ministers. Indeed, an openly fractious Cabinet might invite a no confidence vote in Parliament, precipitating the fall of the government.

Cabinet solidarity predicated on full and frank discussion is built on two other principles. First, Cabinet members are expected, even obliged, to declare their point of view in Cabinet discussions. Indeed, they promise to do exactly this in their Privy Councillor's Oath of Office:

> I, _____ , do solemnly and sincerely swear (declare) that I shall be a true and faithful servant to Her Majesty Queen Elizabeth the Second, as a member of Her Majesty's Privy Council for Canada. I will in all things to be treated, debated and resolved in Privy Council, faithfully, honestly and truly declare my mind and my opinion. I shall keep secret all matters committed and revealed to me in this capacity, or that shall be secretly treated of in Council. Generally, in all things I shall do as a faithful and true servant ought to do for Her Majesty.[14]

A related obligation, highlighted in the third sentence of the oath, goes to Cabinet confidentiality. The Privy Council Office, in its briefing note to ministers, repeatedly warns Cabinet members against breaching Cabinet confidentiality, or releasing Cabinet confidences. "Confidentiality," it admonishes, "ensures that Ministers can frankly express their views before a final decision is made."[15] The exact scope of Cabinet "confidences" is a matter we discuss in chapter 9. For our purposes here, these confidences are the official papers and discussions of Cabinet.

2. Structure of Executive Government

a) Structural Hierarchy

The structure of the federal executive government approaches the Byzantine. At base, however, the executive branch — officially known as the public administration of Canada — shares a common, although sometimes attenuated, fealty to the ministry.

---

13   Andrew Heard, *Canadian Constitutional Conventions* (Toronto: Oxford University Press, 1991) at 63; Forsey and Eglington, *The Question of Confidence* at 84.

14   See Office of Governor General, *Fact Sheet: Oaths.*

15   Privy Council Office, *Governing Responsibly: A Guide for Ministers and Ministers of State.*

As discussed in chapter 4 and set out in Appendix 1 at the end of this book, the heart of the public administration of Canada is the public service; that is, the departments, organizations and agencies of government listed in certain portions of the *Financial Administration Act*.[16] This definition includes the regular, "line" government departments and many of their specialized agencies and organizations, each of which is assigned a responsible minister by various Acts of Parliament. As the Privy Council Office notes, these departmental laws "set out the powers, duties, and functions for which the minister will be responsible, and give him or her the management and direction (control and supervision) of the financial and public service resources deployed in the department."[17]

The "public service" excludes Crown corporations and certain other agencies, such as Canada Customs and Revenue Agency (now simply known as the Canada Revenue Agency).[18] At some level, ministers and/or Cabinet are involved, however, with even these nonpublic service bodies. Thus, even if ministers do not preside formally over portions of the public administration of Canada, a minister is usually named as "responsible" for the entity, by statute or otherwise,[19] and the agency will likely be expected to report to Parliament through this minister. Moreover, the Governor-in-Council often maintains some authority over the body through such functions as appointing (and in some instances, dismissing) its senior officials, a procedure discussed in chapter 4.

These entities must also often comply with the *Financial Administration Act* which provides, for instance, that "[e]ach Crown corporation is ultimately accountable, through the appropriate Minister, to Parliament for the conduct of its affairs."[20] It also specifies that "[t]he Governor in Council may, on the recommendation of the appropriate Minister, give a directive to any parent Crown corporation, if the Governor in Council is of the opin-

16   See *Public Service Employment Act*, s. 2; *Public Service Labour Relations Act*, s. 2; *Financial Administration Act*, s. 11 defining public service for the purposes of human resources management as "(a) the departments named in Schedule I; (b) the other portions of the federal public administration named in Schedule IV; (c) the separate agencies named in Schedule V; and (d) any other portion of the federal public administration that may be designated by the Governor in Council for the purpose of this paragraph." These Acts or portions of Acts enacted by the *Public Service Modernization Act* were not in force at the time of this writing, but were expected to come into force beginning in 2005.

17   Privy Council Office, *Responsibility in the Constitution* (1993).

18   See *Financial Administration Act*, Schedules II and III.

19   See Library of Parliament, *The Ministry and its Responsibilities*.

20   *Financial Administration Act*, s. 88.

ion that it is in the public interest to do so" and that the Crown corporation must then "ensure that the directive is implemented in a prompt and efficient manner."[21] To greater or lesser degrees, therefore, the apex of accountability for the entire public administration of Canada is the ministry.

b) Cabinet Control over Structure

The ministry also has substantial "structural" control over the executive. Most — if not all — government departments, commissions, agencies and boards are created by Acts of Parliament, at some level. More generally, however, the *Public Service Rearrangement and Transfer of Duties Act* allows the Governor-in-Council to tinker with the departmental structure.

Thus, pursuant to the Act, the Governor-in-Council may "transfer any powers, duties or functions or the control or supervision of any portion of the federal public administration from one minister to another, or from one department in, or portion of, the federal public administration to another" or "amalgamate and combine any two or more departments under one minister and under one deputy minister."[22] Further, in the course of this transfer, the Governor-in-Council may substitute the responsibilities of a former departmental minister for a new departmental minister.[23]

This Act has served as the key tool in the most recent government restructurings. Thus, when the Martin government created the new "Public Safety and Emergency Preparedness" portfolio in December 2003, headed by Anne McLellan, it did so by using the Act to peel the Office of Critical Infrastructure Protection and Emergency Preparedness away from the Department of National Defence, and place it into Department of the Solicitor General.[24] Likewise, it transferred supervision over the Canada Border Services Agency from the minister of citizenship and immigration to the Solicitor General, now styled the minister of public safety and emergency preparedness,[25] and then transferred assorted other security and border organizations into the Canada Border Services Agency.[26]

This sort of reallocation of responsibilities between existing departments is exactly what the Act seems to anticipate. However, more than fusing agencies into new departments, the Act has apparently also been used

---

21   *Ibid.*, ss. 89 and 89.1.
22   *Public Service Rearrangement and Transfer of Services Act*, R.S.C. 1985, c. P-34, s. 2, as amended by the *Public Service Modernization Act*.
23   *Public Service Rearrangement and Transfer of Services Act*, ibid., s. 2.
24   Order-in-Council, P.C. 2003-2086 (2003-12-12).
25   Order-in-Council, P.C. 2003-2061 (2003-12-12).
26   See, e.g., Order-in-Council, P.C. 2003-2063 to 2065 (2003-12-12).

to fission existing ministries into separate departments, at least on a *de facto* basis. The Act was employed in December 2003 to partition the Department of Foreign Affairs and International Trade (DFAIT) into the separate Foreign Affairs Canada and International Trade Canada. The trade components of DFAIT were first elevated to a new departmental status, styled the Department of International Trade.[27] Then, the *Public Service Rearrangement and Transfer of Duties Act* was employed to transfer "from the Minister of Foreign Affairs to the Minister of International Trade ... the control and supervision of that portion of the public service known as the Department of International Trade."[28]

This restructuring was accomplished despite the (unamended) *Department of Foreign Affairs and International Trade Act*, which anticipates a single department, albeit one with two ministers.[29] By December 2004, therefore, there remained a formal legal entity known as the Department of Foreign Affairs and International Trade that no longer housed any trade component.[30]

None of these changes triggered parliamentary oversight. There is, in fact, a *Ministries and Ministers of State Act* that is more demanding of the executive but which has a very limited ambit. This Act grants the Governor-in-Council substantial discretion to organize the public administration of Canada into "Ministries of State," where "it appears to the Governor in Council that the requirements for formulating and developing new and comprehensive policies in relation to any matter or matters coming within the responsibility of the Government of Canada warrant."[31] Pursuant to the Act, each ministry of state is "presided over by a minister charged with

---

27   See, e.g., Order-in-Council, P.C. 2003-2046 (2003-12-12) ("Order Amending Schedule I.1 to the *Financial Administration Act* by adding the Department of International Trade"); Order-in-Council, P.C. 2003-2051 (2003-12-12) ("Order Amending Schedule I to the *Public Service Staff Relations Act* by the addition of the Department of International Trade, effective December 12, 2003"); P.C. 2003-2052 (2003-12-12) (Order designating the Department of International Trade as a Department under the *Public Service Employment Act*).

28   Order-in-Council, P.C. 2003-2047 (2003-12-12).

29   *Department of Foreign Affairs and International Trade Act*, R.S.C. 1985, c. E-22.

30   In late 2004, a year after the actual bureaucratic re-organization, the government introduced two bills — C-31 and C-32 — amending the *Department of Foreign Affairs and International Trade Act* and giving legislative authorization to the Department of International Trade. As this book went to press in early 2005, it looked like these law projects — introduced by the minority Martin government — would be defeated by the opposition in the Commons.

31   *Ministries and Ministers of State Act*, s. 2.

responsibility for the formulation and development" of their policies.[32] This minister has those duties in relation to the ministry that is assigned to him or her by the Proclamation creating the body, or by statutes of Parliament.[33]

Critically, under the Act, Parliament is supposed to play an oversight role in the creation and change in name of ministries of state. Thus, the introduction or change in name of such a ministry is conducted by Proclamation of the Governor-in-Council, but must be preceded by the laying of the Order-in-Council authorizing that Proclamation before the Commons and a resolution from that House approving the measure.[34] Read expansively, this requirement implies a reasonable parliamentary oversight of structural change in the public administration of Canada.

However, the government's lawyers interpret the ambit of this Act very narrowly. They emphasize that the ministries of state regulated by the Act are those government bodies dealing strictly with policy development. They find support for this conclusion in the Act's reference to a ministry of state "for formulating and developing new and comprehensive policies." Thus, a new department — such as International Trade — engaged in management or policy *implementation*, as opposed to strict policy development, is not captured by this designation. Given this restrictive scope, it is not surprising that the Act has only been employed a handful of times in the course of its existence.[35]

In sum, Cabinet possesses enormous authority to alter in a real way the structure of executive government. The minor parliamentary oversight role in creating new government structures anticipated by the *Ministries and Minister of State Act* is restricted to a tiny subset of agencies. Meanwhile, massive reorganizations may be made by Order-in-Council through use of the *Public Service Rearrangement and Transfer of Duties Act*.

3. Executive Branch Accountability Mechanisms

"Responsible government" in its conventional sense means an executive branch accountable to Parliament. In practice, of course, Parliament's oversight role is supplemented — at times eclipsed — by the executive's own accountability mechanisms. The ways in which the executive polices itself

32   *Ibid.*, s. 2.
33   *Ibid.*, s. 9.
34   *Ibid.*, ss. 2–6.
35   See Gordon Osbaldeston, *Organizing to Govern*, vol. 1 (Toronto: McGraw-Hill Ryerson, 1992) at 13, indicating that as of 1992 only four "Ministries of State" had been created: urban affairs, science and technology, economic development, social development.

are manifold, ranging from simple employer-employee disciplinary mechanisms through to full-blown public inquiries. The command-control function of public service employment law is discussed in part in chapter 4. Here, we focus on two other devices employed by government to ensure compliance with proper standards of behaviour: institutional control, in the form of central agency management of public policy; and special measures, in the form of public and departmental inquiries.

a) Institutional Control: The Role of the Central Agencies

The so-called central agencies lie at the heart of the Government of Canada. The classic central agencies are the Privy Council Office, the Treasury Board Secretariat and the Department of Finance. Each plays an important role in making government departments and agencies toe to the line. In this book, we do not discuss in detail the public administration function these bodies play, simply noting their role in linking Cabinet governance to the sprawling public administration of Canada.

The Privy Council Office (PCO) "serves as the Prime Minister's public service department and secretariat to the Cabinet and its committees," under the guidance of the Clerk of the Privy Council. The PCO plays a key role in coordinating government policy; indeed, it has sometimes been called the "nerve centre of government."[36] Thus, PCO works closely "with line departments, as well as with the Prime Minister's Office, the Treasury Board Secretariat and the Department of Finance to ensure that new proposals are consistent with the Government's overall objectives and policies, and that all affected interests have been consulted. Once a decision is reached by Cabinet, the Privy Council Office ensures that it is communicated to the affected departments and oversees its effective implementation."[37] Further, PCO provides advice "on such matters as the broad organization of government, the appointment of individuals to key positions and the mandates of these senior office holders."[38]

For its part, Treasury Board is a legislatively prescribed Cabinet committee with a bureaucratic secretariat. Its chief responsibilities are review of government spending and overseeing government personnel management.[39] Thus, with the assistance of its secretariat, Treasury Board assesses departmental money requests, as well as setting public service salary and employment policies. Obviously, control of these two dimensions of

---

36   Savoie, *Governing from the Centre* at 109.
37   Privy Council Office, *Decision-Making Processes and Central Agencies in Canada* (1998).
38   *Ibid.*
39   *Financial Administration Act*, s. 7.

government places Treasury Board and its secretariat in a position of substantial influence in the public administration of Canada.

The Department of Finance is a line department headed by the minister of finance that oversees the government's macroeconomic policy.[40] As such, it focuses on such things as taxation policy, government financing and fiscal policy. Its preeminence on these economic matters and the overarching nature of its mandate gives it a special prominence among government departments, thus placing it in the camp of central agencies.

Government management of the federal treasury is backstopped by another executive branch official. In the wake of the sponsorship scandal in 2004, the Martin government re-invented the Office of the Comptroller General, tasked with "oversee[ing] all government spending ... provid[ing] leadership across the public service financial management community, and ... ensur[ing] standards are set and adhered to."[41] This official will also oversee the appointment of department-specific comptrollers.

The Comptroller General position required no special authorization from Parliament. The office was already anticipated in the *Financial Administration Act*, which provides that "[t]he Governor in Council may appoint an officer called the Comptroller General of Canada to hold office during pleasure and to perform such duties and functions as may be assigned to him by the Treasury Board, and the Comptroller General of Canada shall rank as and have all the powers of a deputy head of a department."[42]

b) Public and Departmental Inquiries

Cabinet's — and particularly the prime minister's — "structural" control over government ensures a large measure of influence over the conduct of executive governance. If all else fails, as discussed in chapter 4, those who do not heed Cabinet and the central agencies' policy dictates are subject to

---

40   *Ibid.*, ss. 14–15. The minister of finance "has the management and direction of the Department, the management of the Consolidated Revenue Fund and the supervision, control and direction of all matters relating to the financial affairs of Canada not by law assigned to the Treasury Board or to any other minister."

41   Treasury Board of Canada, *The New Comptroller General and Accreditation Standards* (March 2004).

42   *Financial Administration Act*, s. 6. Amendments to this Act under the *Public Service Modernization Act*, not in force at the time of this writing, preserve this office, and further specify that "Treasury Board may delegate ... to the Comptroller General of Canada ... any of the powers or functions it is authorized to exercise under any Act of Parliament or by any order made by the Governor in Council. It may make the delegation subject to any terms and conditions that it considers appropriate." See S.C. 2003, c. 22, ss. 3 to 11.

dismissal, either for cause (as with public servants and certain Governor-in-Council appointees), or at the pleasure of the Governor-in-Council.

Nevertheless, there are instances where the regular command-control apparatus of government is so compromised (or the chain of events prompting some public scandal so uncertain) that Cabinet may call for intervention from outside in the form of public inquiries. Recent examples include the 2004 Gomery inquiry into the "sponsorship program and advertising activities of the Government of Canada"[43] and the 2004 O'Connor inquiry "on the actions of Canadian officials in relation to Maher Arar."[44] Also of recent vintage are the 1995 inquiry into "certain matters pertaining to the deployment of Canadian Forces to Somalia,"[45] the 1995 Arbour inquiry into "incidents that occurred at the Prison for Women in Kingston, Ontario"[46] and the 1993 Krever inquiry into "the mandate, organization, management, operations, financing and regulation of all activities of the blood systems in Canada."[47]

Motivations Behind Public Inquiries

Inquiries are motivated by a number of concerns. Thus, there are laudatory goals prompting inquiries. For instance, the "potential for vindication in the face of allegations of governmental wrongdoing ... creates an incentive to establish a commission of inquiry."[48] More cynically, governments may call inquiries to expel controversies from the political arena to a comparatively bloodless quasi-judicial forum. Ministers, once hard pressed on scandals during Question Period in the Commons, may invoke an ongoing inquiry (and the *sub judice* convention in the Commons) to sidestep difficult questions, on apparently principled grounds.[49] Thus, as Centa and

---

43   See Order-in-Council, P.C. 2004-0110 (2004-02-19).
44   See Order-in-Council, P.C. 2004-0048 (2004-02-05).
45   See Order-in-Council, P.C. 1995-0042 (1995-05-20).
46   See Order-in-Council, P.C. 1995-0608 (1995-04-10).
47   See Order-in-Council, P.C. 1993-1879 (1993-10-04).
48   Robert Centa and Patrick Macklem, "Securing Accountability Through Commissions of Inquiry: A Role for the Law Commission of Canada" (2001) 39 Osgoode Hall L.J. 117.
49   See, e.g., Mr. John Richardson (parliamentary secretary to minister of national defence and minister of veterans affairs, Lib.), on the Somalia inquiry: "Mr. Speaker, the minister has covered this issue a number of times. The fact that I will not comment on any evidence to be presented to the commission of inquiry is firm. The commission was established to examine all aspects of the deployment to Somalia. Let the commission take its course," *Hansard*, 35th Parl., 2d Sess. (20 June 1996); Hon. David M. Collenette (minister of national defence and minister of veterans affairs, Lib.), on the Somalia inquiry: "Mr. Speaker, the hon. member knows I cannot comment on any matter before the inquiry," *Hansard*, 35th Parl., 2d Sess. (19 Sept. 1996).

Macklem observe, "[a] government will be under an incentive to establish a commission of inquiry where to do so results in the removal of an unpleasant controversy from the political agenda or focuses on incidents that occurred during the tenure of a previous government."[50]

On the other hand, a gun-shy government also has strong disincentives to calling an inquiry. Inquiries enjoy relative independence from government and can stray in unexpected directions. As the Supreme Court has noted, "[a]s ad hoc bodies, commissions of inquiry are free of many of the institutional impediments which at times constrain the operation of the various branches of government."[51]

Concerns about unpredictable political fallout from an independent and aggressive inquiry — especially one headed by credible commissioners — render inquiries a rare phenomenon, especially in relation to controversies arising on the appointing government's watch. They were clearly anathema to the Chrétien government, which truncated the Somalia inquiry and stonewalled calls for other inquiries into alleged government malfeasance.

Where they are struck, inquiries can be quite vivid in the attention they draw to government wrongdoing. As the Supreme Court of Canada puts it, "Commissions of inquiry have a long history in Canada, and have become a significant and useful part of our tradition. They have frequently played a key role in the investigation of tragedies and made a great many helpful recommendations aimed at rectifying dangerous situations."[52] Indeed, their very notoriety attracts substantial legal scrutiny, as we discuss below.

Initiating Inquiries

Inquiries come in two flavours: public inquiries and departmental inquiries. Both are initiated and governed by the *Public Inquiries Act*.

Thus, in relation to public inquiries, the "Governor in Council may, whenever the Governor in Council deems it expedient, cause inquiry to be made into and concerning any matter connected with the good government of Canada or the conduct of any part of the public business thereof."[53] The scope of the resulting inquiry may be very expansive, although under

---

50 Centa and Macklem, "Securing Accountability Through Commissions of Inquiry" at 134. For an excellent review of policy and law in relation to public inquiries, see Allan Manson and David Mullan, *Commissions of Inquiry: Praise or Reappraise?* (Toronto: Irwin Law, 2003).

51 *Phillips v. Nova Scotia (Commission of Inquiry into the Westray Mine Tragedy)*, [1995] 2 S.C.R. 97 at para. 60.

52 *Canada (Attorney General) v. Royal Commission of Inquiry on the Blood System in Canada*, [1997] 3 S.C.R. 440 at para. 29.

53 *Inquiries Act*, R.S.C. 1985 c. I-11, s. 2.

the Act it must clearly touch on the government of Canada. Further, those selected to head up the inquiry possess significant powers. Thus, the Governor-in-Council generally appoints public inquiry "commissioners,"[54] who then possess powers to summon witnesses and compel the production of documents tantamount to those of a court in a civil case.[55] The Governor-in-Council may also bestow this same public inquiry authority on an international commission or tribunal, should it so desire.[56]

In comparison, a minister presiding over a department of the federal public administration may trigger departmental inquiries. Acting under the "authority of the Governor in Council," that minister may appoint "a commissioner or commissioners to investigate and report on the state and management of the business, or any part of the business, of the department ... and the conduct of any person in that service, so far as the same relates to the official duties of the person."[57] Those commissioners are then accorded substantial investigative powers, including the right to enter into public premises, summon witnesses and compel production of documents.[58]

With public inquiries, commissioners tend to be judges, or at least include a judge among their members. Thus, the two inquiries appointed by the Martin government in 2004 into, first, the role of Canadian officials in the deportation of Maher Arar from the United States to Syria and, second, the government's sponsorship program were both headed by judges, Justices O'Connor and Gomery respectively. Justice Krever headed the inquiry into tainted blood. A judge — Justice Letourneau — chaired the Somalia inquiry. This judicial participation in inquiries is expressly authorized by the *Judges Act*, which bars extrajudicial functions by a judge except where the "judge is by an Act of Parliament expressly authorized so to act or the judge is thereunto appointed or so authorized by the Governor in Council."[59]

A judge serving as a commissioner acts, essentially, as an agent of the executive branch in investigating government malfeasance. This peculiar status does no apparent violence to the concept of judicial independence. The Supreme Court of Canada has blessed much more profound involvement of judges in direct oversight of executive branch activities.[60]

---

54   *Ibid.*, s. 3.
55   *Ibid.*, ss. 4–5.
56   *Ibid.*, s. 14.
57   *Ibid.*, s. 6.
58   *Ibid.*, ss. 7–10.
59   *Judges Act*, s. 56.
60   See, e.g., *Re Application under s. 83.28 of the Criminal Code*, 2004 SCC 42, holding that a judicial investigative hearing for examination pursuant to s. 83.28 of the *Criminal Code* meets judicial independence requirements.

In fact, where inquiries are headed by judges these inquiries enjoy a sort of "derivative" judicial independence: inquiries may be terminated, and commissioners dismissed, but judges need not fear that their activities at the head of an inquiry will cost them their full-time job, given the security of tenure protections extended by judicial independence. Other commissioners, possibly looking over their shoulder in anticipation of the next government appointment once the inquiry ends, may arguably enjoy substantially less autonomy.

Conduct of Inquiries

The *Inquiries Act* is a succinct statute that permits inquiries with substantial powers, but lays down few specifics on how these inquiries are to be conducted. The Act does extend certain procedural rights to persons whose conduct is being investigated. Thus, the inquiry may permit persons being investigated to be represented by counsel. Indeed, it must allow this representation where any charge is made against that individual in the course of the inquiry.[61] Further, "[n]o report shall be made against any person until reasonable notice has been given to the person of the charge of misconduct alleged against him and the person has been allowed full opportunity to be heard in person or by counsel."[62] A "charge of misconduct" is a "potential finding" of misconduct, defined as "improper or unprofessional behaviour" or "bad management."[63]

These statutory provisions are generally enhanced by the inquiry terms of reference issued by the Governor-in-Council when an inquiry is called.[64] They are also informed by conventional administrative and (possibly) constitutional law principles.

Administrative Law Principles

In terms of administrative law, an inquiry, like any other executive decision-maker, is subject to judicial review by a court, both for substantive errors in its conclusions and for procedural errors in its proceedings. Substantively, an inquiry that strays beyond its mandate set out in the Order-in-Council establishing it likely acts without jurisdiction, and can be reined in by the courts. Likewise, where the inquiry renders findings motivated by bad faith or improper considerations, it is vulnerable to review. Factual con-

---

61 *Inquiries Act*, s. 12.

62 *Ibid.*, s. 13.

63 *Royal Commission of Inquiry on the Blood System in Canada*, [1997] 3 S.C.R. 440 at para. 40, citing the *Oxford English Dictionary*.

64 See, e.g., Order-in-Council, P.C. 2004-0048 (2004-02-05) setting out in some detail the terms of reference for the conduct of the Arar inquiry by Mr. Justice O'Connor.

clusions by an inquiry may also be reviewed, but only on a deferential basis.[65]

Procedurally, the *Inquiries Act* notice and comment provision is enhanced by common law procedural fairness requirements.[66] These common law obligations impose essentially the same right to notice and to be heard already found in the Act, and not much more.[67] That said, procedural fairness also requires that a commissioner not be so biased as to create "a reasonable apprehension that the commissioner would reach a conclusion on a basis other than the evidence."[68]

Constitutional Law Principles

A more thorny issue implicating constitutional principles is whether an inquiry must enjoy formal, structural independence from the government, analogous to judicial independence.[69] The case law to date suggests that inquiries need not enjoy this structural independence from the government.[70] An inquiry is not to be equated with court proceedings. The Supreme Court has emphasized:

> [a] commission of inquiry ... cannot establish either criminal culpability or civil responsibility for damages. Rather, an inquiry is an investigation into an issue, event or series of events. The findings of a commissioner relating to that investigation are simply findings of fact and statements of opinion reached by the commissioner at the end of the inquiry. They are unconnected to normal legal criteria. ... There are no legal consequences

65 *Morneault v. Canada (Attorney General)*, [2001] 1 F.C. 30 at paras. 46 and 47 (C.A.): inquiry factual conclusions are to be reviewed "on a standard of whether they are supported by some evidence in the record of the inquiry ... [E]ven if the evidence may not appear to be wholly consistent for, in the final analysis, it was for the Commission to weigh and assess the evidence of the various witnesses in coming to its findings of fact."

66 *Royal Commission of Inquiry on the Blood System in Canada*, [1997] 3 S.C.R. 440 at para. 57 ("a commissioner must ensure that there is procedural fairness in the conduct of the inquiry").

67 *Boyle v. Canada (Commission of Inquiry into the Deployment of Canadian Forces to Somalia)* (1997), 131 F.T.R. 135 (T.D.); *Beno v. Canada (Attorney General)*, [2002] 3 F.C. 499 at para. 116 (C.A.) ("The standards of procedural fairness comprised the applicant's right to be represented by counsel, to receive reasonable notice of the charge of misconduct alleged against him and to have the opportunity to be heard.").

68 *Beno v. Canada (Commission of Inquiry into the Deployment of Canadian Forces in Somalia — Létourneau Commission)*, [1997] 2 F.C. 527 at para. 27 (C.A.) at para. 27.

69 For a full discussion of the independence issue in relation to public inquiries, see Tamar Witelson, "Declaration of Independence: Examining the Independene of Federal Public Inquiries," in Manson and Mullan, *Commissions of Inquiry* at 301.

70 *Dixon v. Canada* (1997), 149 D.L.R. (4th) 269 (F.C.A.).

attached to the determinations of a commissioner. They are not enforce-able and do not bind courts considering the same subject matter.[71]

As an inquiry does not involve the adjudication of criminal charges, the judicial independence requirements flowing from section 11(d) of the *Charter* clearly do not apply, except, perhaps, where an inquiry is imposing penalties for contempt. That may not, however, be the end of the story. Section 7 of the *Charter* requires "fundamental justice" where life, liberty or security of the person is at stake. The Supreme Court has held that section 7 is a source of independence requirements.[72]

While at first blush an inquiry does not directly put a person's life, liberty or security of a person at risk, a finding of misconduct obviously jeopardizes a person's reputation. This possibility raises a question as to whether reputation is a "security of the person" interest protected by section 7. The simple answer is "almost always no."[73] Nevertheless, rare circumstances exist where a psychological harm inflicted by government proceedings could attract section 7 protections.[74]

In that situation, a structural independence obligation could possibly attach to the conduct of the inquiry. If so, then the government would be greatly impeded in its authority to regulate the conduct of the inquiry, including possibly truncating its proceedings. We return to this last issue later in this chapter.

Likewise, the *Canadian Bill of Rights* — a 1960 statute of Parliament that purports to trump all inconsistent federal laws — guarantees in section 2(e) that no law may "deprive a person of the right to a fair hearing in accordance with the principles of fundamental justice for the determination of his rights and obligations."[75] The Supreme Court has recognized

---

71   *Royal Commission of Inquiry on the Blood System in Canada*, [1997] 3 S.C.R. 440 at para. 34.

72   *Re Application under s. 83.28 of the Criminal Code*, 2004 SCC 42 at para. 81. See also
      Ocean Port Hotel Ltd. v. British Columbia (Liquor Control and Licensing Branch), [2001]
      2 S.C.R. 781 at para. 24 acknowledging that, rarely, "tribunals may sometimes attract
      Charter requirements of independence."

73   *Blencoe v. British Columbia*, [2000] 2 S.C.R. 307 at para. 81 ("In order for security of
      the person to be triggered in [cases involving alleged psychological harm], the
      impugned state action must have had a serious and profound effect on the respon-
      dent's psychological integrity. ... There must be state interference with an individual
      interest of fundamental importance.").

74   Thus, an inquiry that might have a bearing on an individual interest of fundamental
      importance analogous to a "woman's choice to terminate her pregnancy, an individ-
      ual's decision to terminate his or her life, the right to raise one's children, and the
      ability of sexual assault victims to seek therapy without fear of their private records
      being disclosed" would likely trigger s. 7. See discussion in *Blencoe, ibid.*, at para. 86.

75   *Canadian Bill of Rights*, S.C. 1960 c.44, subs. 2(e).

that where these provisions apply, a high measure of independence may be required.[76]

It is unclear whether section 2(e) is triggered by the fact an inquiry might come to a damning conclusion concerning the misconduct of an individual. In a decision affirmed on other grounds by the Supreme Court, the Federal Court has held that an inquiry does not determine "rights and obligations," and thus does not trigger section 2(e).[77]

The expression "rights and obligations" may have, however, a broader meaning than that given it by Federal Court;[78] one sufficient to incorporate a right to good reputation. The right to reputation is regularly recognized in Canadian law.[79] It is entirely plausible, therefore, that the *Canadian Bill of Rights* might compel a strong measure of independence on the part of inquiries "determining" reputational matters.

Terminating Inquiries

Governments control the longevity of inquiries in two manners. First, the funds allocated to the inquiry may set a natural limit on its duration. Turning off the financial tap will end an investigation.

Second, the terms of reference creating the inquiry may specify the time by which the inquiry must complete its work. The Somalia inquiry was time-limited in this fashion. Originally slated to report by December 1995, the inquiry was extended twice,[80] until the Chrétien government pulled the plug in March 1997.[81] This decision provoked accusations from

---

76   *Bell Canada v. Communications, Energy and Paperworkers Union of Canada*, [2003] 1 S.C.R. 884 at para. 31.

77   *Canada (Attorney General) v. Canada (Commissioner of the Inquiry on the Blood System)* [1996] 3 F.C. 259 at para. 133, aff'd, [1997] 2 F.C. 36, aff'd [1997] 3 S.C.R. 440.

78   See, e.g., *Air Canada v. Canada (Attorney General)* (2003), 222 D.L.R. (4th) 385 at para. 49 (Que. C.A.) ("To be entitled to the protection of s. 2(e), a party is not required to allege infringement of a fundamental right. Once it is established that the complainant's rights or obligations are affected in the broadest sense, he or she is entitled to a fair hearing of his or her case"), leave to appeal allowed, [2003] 2 S.C.R. x.

79   See, e.g., Quebec *Charter of Human Rights and Freedoms*, R.S.Q., c. C-12, s. 4 ("Every person has a right to the safeguard of his dignity, honour and reputation"); *Gilles E. Neron Communication Marketing Inc. v. Chambre des notaires du Quebec*, 2004 SCC 53 at para. 52 ("reputation, as an aspect of personality, is equally worthy of protection in a democratic society concerned about respect for the individual"); *Hill v. Church of Scientology of Toronto*, [1995] 2 S.C.R. 1130 at para. 108 ("A democratic society, therefore, has an interest in ensuring that its members can enjoy and protect their good reputation so long as it is merited.").

80   See Order-in-Council, P.C. 1995-1273 (1995-07-26); Order-in-Council, P.C. 1996-0959 (1996-06-20).

81   See Order-in-Council, P.C. 1997-0174 (1997-02-04).

media critics that the Chrétien Cabinet was moving expeditiously to pre-serve its own government from criticism as it headed into a federal elec-tion.[82] It also triggered litigation concerning the capacity of the Governor-in-Council to call an end to an ongoing public inquiry.

In this last respect, in *Dixon v. Canada*, the Federal Court of Appeal held that the government decision to terminate the Somalia inquiry was a proper exercise of its powers. As a creature of the Governor-in-Council, the inquiry did not possess some self-standing independence, analogous to judicial independence. As such, the decision to terminate the inquiry was a political decision, not justiciable in court. In the Court of Appeal's words:

> It may well be that the refusal of the Governor in Council to extend the life of the Commission for the entire period requested by the Commis-sioners was motivated by political expediency, but that is simply not the business of the Court. It is a well-established principle of law and a fun-damental tenet of our system of government, in which Parliament and not the Judiciary is supreme, that the courts have no power to review the policy considerations which motivate Cabinet decisions. Absent a jurisdic-tional error or a challenge under the *Canadian Charter of Rights and Free-doms* ... where Cabinet acts pursuant to a valid delegation of authority from Parliament, it is accountable only to Parliament and, through Parlia-ment, to the Canadian public, for its decisions.[83]

We query whether this conclusion must always be the case. As dis-cussed earlier, in certain circumstances, an inquiry might well trigger *Canadian Bill of Rights* protections and, more rarely, *Charter* section 7 pro-tections. In these circumstances, a decision to terminate an inquiry that prejudices the ability of an interested party to preserve their reputational right could well be challenged successfully in court. Likewise, a govern-ment decision to choke an inquiry by starving it of funding might, in cer-tain circumstances, also impair the independence requirement flowing from the application of the *Canadian Bill of Rights* or the *Charter*.

4. Conclusion

In sum, the public administration of Canada is structured in a hierarchical manner. At the apex is the ministry charged with overseeing the operations of executive government. The ministry exercises this authority in a multi-

---

82 See, e.g., Andrew Coyne, "Duplicity Will Come Back to Haunt Liberals," *Ottawa Citi-zen*, 1 April 1997, A14.

83 [1997] 149 D.L.R. (4th) 269 at 279–80 (F.C.A.).

tude of ways, not least through the formal employer relationship between government officials and the Treasury Board. Its dictates are communicated through the central agencies to the other facets of the public administration of Canada. Where all else fails, Cabinet may strike potent ad hoc public inquiries to probe malfeasance and wrongdoing in the executive branch.

B. RESPONSIBILITY TO PARLIAMENT

Ensuring probity in government is not, however, the sole prerogative of the executive. In classic parliamentary governance, Parliament itself has a vital — and indeed, the theoretically pre-eminent — role. The constitutional cornerstones of parliamentary governance are the conventions giving rise to responsible government. We have listed conventions assigning the monarch's power to ministers or Cabinet in chapter 2.

Another prong of responsible government, taken up in greater detail here, is the accountability of this ministry to the Commons. In classic parliamentary governance, the Commons "does control the cabinet — rarely by defeating it, often by criticizing it, still more often by the cabinet anticipating criticism before subjecting itself and its acts to the House, and always by the latent capacity of the House to revolt against its leaders."[84]

Put another way, the ministry is supposedly held to account by Parliament. This ministerial responsibility to Parliament comes in two guises: collective ministerial responsibility and individual ministerial responsibility. We examine both of these conventions, highlighting how they constitute a theoretical check on Cabinet government and noting how, in practice, they are sometimes nominal.

1. The Collective Responsibility of Cabinet

a) Resignation of the Government
Cabinet as a whole is "responsible" to Parliament, and particularly to the House of Commons. As Sir Robert Walpole, the first real British prime minister, observed in 1739, "when I speak here [in this House] as a minister, I speak as possessing my powers from His Majesty, but as being answerable to this House for the exercise of those powers."[85] This collective responsibility to the Commons is manifested in the constitutional convention that a ministry may persist only so long as it possesses the "confi-

---

84   Robert Ward, *Dawson's The Government of Canada* (Toronto: University of Toronto Press, 1987) at 138.
85   Cited in Forsey and Eglington, *The Question of Confidence* at 1.

dence" of the House. A government losing the confidence of the Commons has occurred only a handful of times in the Canadian Parliament.[86]

In fact, the precise circumstances in which such a loss of confidence arises is a matter of some uncertainty in modern Parliaments. Summarizing Commonwealth practice in 1985,[87] Senator Forsey noted several confidence conventions, which we categorize as follows: First, a government must either resign or ask for dissolution of Parliament if defeated on a motion of censure or on a vote that it declares constitutes a test of confidence.

Second, the opposition may itself move a motion of censure or no confidence, especially after the defeat of a measure the Opposition believes should have been treated as a confidence vote. A government defeated on an express no confidence motion must resign or seek dissolution.

Third, when the government is defeated on any other measure, it may treat that defeat as a vote of no confidence triggering resignation or a request for dissolution, or it may itself bring a confidence motion.

Last, while defeat on a money measure is not automatically a no confidence vote (contrary to popular wisdom), a government that does not prevail in carrying the Address in Reply to the Speech from the Throne without amendment must either resign or ask for a dissolution.

For its part, the 1985 McGrath Committee on Commons reform identified three species of confidence vote:

> First, there are explicitly worded votes of confidence. These state expressly that the House has or has not confidence in the government. Next are motions made votes of confidence by a declaration of the government. The government may declare that if defeated on a particular motion before the House, even one that is not an explicitly worded vote of confidence, it will resign or seek a dissolution. Then there are implicit votes of confidence. Traditionally, certain matters have been deemed to involve confidence, even though not declared to be so by the prior statement of the government.[88]

Lost votes on money measures (that is, approval of government expenditures) constitute the classic example of an implicit confidence vote. Like

---

86   Ward, *Dawson's The Government of Canada* at 88 (listing these five instances as: 1873 (Macdonald), 1926 (King), 1926 (Meighen), 1963 (Diefenbaker) and 1979 (Clark)). Note, however, that King resigned prior to a no confidence vote. Bothwell, Drummond and English, *Canada 1900–1945* at 206.

87   Forsey and Eglington, *The Question of Confidence* at 144 *et seq.*

88   Special Committee on the Reform of the House of Commons, *Report* (18 June 1985) at 8.

Senator Forsey, the committee noted in 1985, "[T]his is largely a category that has fallen into disuse."[89]

Commons procedural rules also once anticipated circumstances constituting a vote of no confidence.[90] However, the McGrath Committee favoured increasing free votes in the Parliament. To this end, it proposed a rethinking of confidence votes by eliminating reference to such motions in the Commons Standing Orders. In its words: "In keeping with the desire to make the House more relevant to Members and to the public, your Committee believes that matters of confidence in the government should at all times be clearly subject to political determination. Motions of no-confidence should not be prescribed in the rules but should be explicitly so worded in the text of the motion itself by the Member presenting such a motion."[91] The House followed this recommendation by removing most reference to confidence votes from the Standing Orders.[92]

The result is some murkiness as to when a confidence matter arises. Certainly, confidence motions exist where they are declared to be such either by the government itself, or when introduced as such by the opposition.[93] The government also likely retains the right to treat a lost vote on a matter it views as important as a no confidence vote.[94] Other than in these circumstances (and with the arguable exception of an amendment to the Address in Reply to the Speech from the Throne discussed later), no vote should be considered, as a matter of automatic practice, a confidence measure.[95] Instead, any uncertainty on this question should precipitate an

---

89   *Ibid.* Prime Minister Pearson, e.g., lost on third reading of a budgetary bill in 1968. In response, the Liberal government brought an express confidence motion confirming that the loss did not constitute a vote of no confidence in the government. See Ward, *Dawson's The Government of Canada* at 145.

90   See Canada, House of Commons, *Beauchesne's Rules and Forms of the House of Commons of Canada*, 6th ed. (Toronto: Carswell, 1989) at 49 and 5th ed. (Toronto: Carswell, 1978) at 168; during opposition "allotted" days, votable motions were votes of confidence.

91   Special Committee on the Reform of the House of Commons, *Report* at 106.

92   *Beauchesne's Rules*, 6th ed. at 49.

93   See discussion in Heard, *Canadian Constitutional Conventions* at 69–70.

94   *Ibid.* at 70.

95   See discussion in C.E.S. Franks, "Free Votes in the Commons: A Problematic Reform," *IRRP Policy Options* (Nov. 1997) at 35, noting that "[t]hough majority governments like to claim otherwise, nothing in the conventions of confidence prevents governments from losing votes on many items of the business before Parliament without the defeat being considered a loss of confidence. ... When minority governments have resigned after being defeated in the House — in 1963, 1974 and 1979 — the decisive motion clearly stated that it was a matter of confidence."

express confidence motion by either the government or the Opposition, clarifying the situation. Put another way, the implicit vote of no confidence is likely extinct.[96]

In 2004, opposition parties in the thirty-eighth Parliament were apparently concerned that the minority Martin government would use ambiguity surrounding confidence votes to provoke a call for dissolution blamed on the Opposition. They therefore proposed that Members of Parliament devise a firm understanding of what constitutes a no confidence vote. Just prior to the opening of Parliament in October 2004, the opposition party leaders collectively suggested that "only the final vote on the Speech from the Throne, the final vote on the Budget, global votes on the Main Estimates and votes explicitly identified as questions of confidence be considered as such."[97]

Meanwhile, as discussed in chapter 5, the Martin government proposed relaxing party discipline in Parliament, permitting more free and pseudo-free votes — its "one-line" and "two-line" votes. However, as must be the case for any government interested in self-preservation, its "three-line" vote preserves party discipline for matters of confidence: "Three-line vote will be for votes of confidence and for a limited number of matters of fundamental importance to the government. Government Members will be expected to support the government."[98] How these tendencies — free votes and not-so-free votes and ambiguity over confidence measures — will play out in the Parliaments to come will likely prove an interesting issue.

b) Cabinet's Responsibility to Parliament for Overall Government Policy

Speech from the Throne
Cabinet's collective responsibility to Parliament comes in several other flavours beyond a straight confidence vote, not least in the convention that the government's policy agenda be announced to Parliament in a Speech from the Throne.

The Throne Speech — articulating a government's policy priorities — is given at beginning of each session of Parliament, and delivered by the Queen or, more typically, the Governor General. The Privy Council Office

---

96 For a discussion in *Hansard* on this point, see Mr. Preston Manning (leader of the Opposition, Ref.), *Hansard*, no. 89, 36th Parl., 1st Sess. (21 April 1998).

97 "Harper, Duceppe and Layton Propose Changes to the Standing Orders of the House," press release (from all the opposition parties), 9 Sept. 2004; see also the discussion in Bill Curry, "Opposition Works to Limit PM's Powe," *Ottawa Citizen*, 1 Sept. 2004, A10.

98 Privy Council Office, *About Cabinet*.

describes the preparation of the Speech of the Throne as a prime ministe-rial power.[99] Some prime ministers do, however, carefully consult Cabinet on the Speech's content.[100] For this reason, and because it sets the govern-ment-wide agenda for the session that follows, the Speech from the Throne can be characterized as the parliamentary début of Cabinet's collective gov-ernment project.

The Speech from the Throne does not, of course, bind the government to the course of action it lays out. It is, however, an important form of Cab-inet collective responsibility to Parliament. First, debates following the Speech from the Throne provide Members of Parliament with one of the few opportunities in the parliamentary calendar to debate policy issues broadly.[101] In this regard, the Throne Speech is followed by debate on a motion for an "Address in Reply to the Speech from the Throne."

This Address is essentially a *pro forma* thanks to the Queen or Gover-nor General. However, amendments and sub-amendments to the Address made by the opposition parties may be introduced and debated. Thus, in the third session of the thirty-seventh Parliament, the Opposition Conser-vative Party offered an amendment reading: "And this House regrets that the Speech from the Throne is an advance copy of the Liberal election plat-form filled with empty rhetoric and promises that does nothing to address the very real problems facing Canadians."[102] The Bloc Québécois proposed a sub-amendment: "and that this House finds that the Speech from the Throne denies the existence of the nation and values of Quebec and that it reiterates the federal government's desire to increase its intrusions into the jurisdictions of Quebec and the provinces."[103] Wide-ranging debate sur-rounded the introduction of these amendments, prior to their predictable defeat.

Second, more than simply informing Parliament of (and allowing debate on) the breadth of government policy, the Address process has been perceived as a key reflection of the government's support in the Commons. As noted above, Senator Forsey viewed a government loss on an amend-ment to the Address to be a vote of no confidence, a belief echoed in the

---

99 Privy Council Office, *Governing Responsibly: A Guide for Ministers and Ministers of State*, Annex A.

100 See, e.g., the following Cabinet documents: "Speech from the Throne," RG2, Privy Council Office, Series A-5-a, vol. 6359, 1970/10/01; "Throne Speech," RG2, Privy Council Office, Series A-5-a, vol. 6340, 1969/10/21.

101 *Beauchesne's Rules*, 6th ed. at 82.

102 See *Hansard*, no. 2, 37th Parl., 3d Sess. (3 Feb. 2004).

103 *Ibid.*

House of Commons *Précis of Procedure*. The latter document notes that opposition amendments to the Address constitute "direct questions of confidence in the Government."[104] Thus, a failure by the government to carry an unamended Address in Reply may well remain a confidence matter.

Events early in the thirty-eighth Parliament reaffirm this view. As usual, the Address in Reply to the Speech from the Throne proposed by the government party was a largely ceremonial boilerplate.[105] However, opposition parties proposed an unusually substantive amendment and subsequent sub-amendment.[106] Given the Liberal minority, there was a good prospect that these changes would pass the Commons. Speculation was rife that this would constitute a vote of no confidence, precipitating a trip by the prime minister to the Governor General's residence. The governing party reinforced this view by affirming that amendments would be regarded as a confidence measure.[107]

In the end, Members in the Commons cobbled together compromise changes to the Address in Reply, carried as unanimous amendments not raising questions of confidence.[108]

Emergency Debates

Members of Parliament may also press the government in special and urgent debates. Pursuant to the Commons Standing Orders, members may trigger an "emergency debate" in relation "to a genuine emergency, calling for immediate and urgent consideration."[109]

However, the debate will only ensue if the Speaker decides to give leave. In deciding this matter, the Orders provide that he or she consider the extent to which the proposed debate "concerns the administrative responsibilities of the government or could come within the scope of ministerial action and the Speaker also shall have regard to the probability of the matter being brought before the House within reasonable time by other means."[110] In practice, the Speaker also contemplates a number of other issues, including

---

104 *Précis of Procedure* at 8.
105 See House of Commons, *Journals*, no. 2 (5 Oct. 2004) ("We, Her Majesty's most loyal and dutiful subjects, the House of Commons of Canada, in Parliament assembled, beg leave to offer our humble thanks to Your Excellency for the gracious Speech which Your Excellency has addressed to both Houses of Parliament.").
106 See *ibid.*
107 Brian Laghi, "Commons Sense Will Prevail," *Globe and Mail*, 9 Oct. 2004, A4; Bill Curry, "Don't Block Throne Speech, Liberals Warn," *Ottawa Citizen*, 2 Oct. 2004, A4.
108 See, e.g., House of Commons, *Journals*, no. 4, 7 Oct. 2004.
109 Commons, *Standing Orders*, Order 52.
110 *Ibid.*

whether the debate is simply being used as a vehicle to propound positions of persons not "answerable to or responsible" to the Commons.[111]

In 2001, the Special Committee on the Modernization and Improvement of the Procedures of the House of Commons reported that "[a]lthough Members frequently seek leave to make such motions, few applications are in fact granted."[112] Presumably, many of these rejected requests were frivolous. Nevertheless, the committee's observation raises questions as to how effective emergency debates are as a means to hold Cabinet accountable to Parliament.

c) The Government's Responsibility on Financial Matters

The Commons control of the government's purse strings provides a parliamentary check on Cabinet's agenda that is more nuanced than an outright confidence vote and more meaningful than debates on the Address in Reply or emergency debates. Referring to one aspect of Parliament's financial role, the Auditor General has noted that "[t]he House of Commons has the right and the obligation to review and approve all spending from the public purse. It can hold the government to account because the government must retain the confidence of the House of Commons in order to continue to govern."[113]

Parliament's control over the federal fisc comes in two flavours: control over the process of raising revenues (ways and means proceedings) and the power to authorize government expenditures (the business of supply). As even a cursory review of British parliamentary history reveals, control over revenue and expenditure lies at the heart of the seventeenth- and eighteenth-century struggles between Parliament and the Crown. It is fitting, therefore, that fiscal accountability remains one of the Canadian Parliament's — and particularly the Canadian Commons' — key responsibilities. As discussed later, however, it was until recently a responsibility largely sidelined by Parliament's focus on its legislative function.

Constitutional Basis

Three principles articulated in the *Constitution Act, 1867* constitute the starting point for a discussion of Parliament's fiscal responsibility role. First, the 1867 Act creates a "consolidated revenue fund,"[114] "appropriated by the Par-

111   Marleau and Montpetit, *House of Commons Procedure and Practice* (Ottawa: House of Commons, 2000) at 588.
112   Special Committee on the Modernization and Improvement of the Procedures of the House of Commons, *Report* (June 2001).
113   Auditor General of Canada, *Parliamentary Committee Review of the Estimates Documents* (March 2003).
114   *Constitution Act, 1867*, s. 102.

liament of Canada for the Public Service."[115] Second, it stipulates that "Bills for appropriating any Part of the Public Revenue, or for imposing any Tax or Impost, shall originate in the House of Commons."[116] However, third, the House of Commons may not enact such a bill for "any Purpose that has not been first recommended to that House by Message of the Governor General" in the parliamentary session in question.[117] This request from the Governor General is known as the "Royal Recommendation." These last two constitutional provisions are replicated in the Commons Standing Orders.[118]

Taken together, these three provisions create the architecture for parliamentary management of the public revenue predicated on three notions: first, that the Commons is the pre-eminent house in financial matters; second, that taxation and spending must be authorized by the Commons and ultimately enacted by Parliament; and, third, that the initiative for seeking taxing and spending authorization lies exclusively with the government, not with private members and certainly not with the Opposition, by reason of the royal recommendation.

Supply

Table 6.2 sets out the content and a rough timeline for the Supply process, during the government fiscal year of April 1 to March 31. The structure of the business of supply reflects the fundamental requirement that government expenditures be authorized by Parliament, ultimately in the form of an appropriations bill. The process leading up to this (largely *pro forma*) bill is intended to permit the Commons — particularly its Standing Committees — to vet carefully government spending plans, and reduce or eliminate expenditure items where it chooses.

Table 6.2   Supply Process[119]

Period	Supply
Variable	*Speech from the Throne*: Members of the Commons are advised that they will be asked to appropriate funds required to provide services and payments authorized by Parliament. When business recommences after the Speech, the minister serving as Treasury Board Secretary proposes a motion that supply be considered the next sitting of the House. Nondebated and traditionally adopted

115 *Ibid.*, s. 106.

116 *Ibid.*, s. 53.

117 *Ibid.*, s. 54.

118 Commons, *Standing Orders*, Orders 79 and 80.

119 Except as noted, information contained in this chart summarizes material from House of Commons, *Précis of Procedure* and Marleau and Montpetit, *House of Commons Procedure and Practice*.

Period	Supply
Variable	without dissent, the motion puts the Business of Supply on the *Order Paper* for the remainder of the parliamentary session.
	Supplementary Estimates: The Main Estimates may not always accurately predict the government's financial needs for a fiscal year. Accordingly, Supplementary Estimates meet unforeseen needs, either new supply requests or seeking authorization for "dollar items" (basically, transfers of existing funds between items). The process for Supplementary Estimates follows the same general pattern set out below for Main Estimates.
By end of March	*Tabling of Government Estimates*: The government's expenditure projections for the next fiscal year are set out in the "Estimates," tabled in the Commons along with the royal recommendation on or before March 1 of the prior fiscal year. The Estimates comprise two parts: the Government Expenditure Plan (providing an overview of the government's sum expenditures) and the Main Estimates (setting out the budgetary and statutory expenditures for government ministries and agencies). "Statutory" expenditures are payments already mandated by legislation, and thus already authorized by Parliament. Budgetary expenditures are those for which separate parliamentary approval will be required.
	Tabling of Report on Plans and Priorities: The Report on Plans and Priorities describes a given department or agency's mandate and objectives and results and performance strategies and is tabled before March 31. In the words of the Auditor General, "[r]eports on plans and priorities and departmental performance reports help Parliament hold the government to account because they provide information about departmental priorities, plans, and achievements. These documents enable comparisons because they provide annual information about what a department plans to do, as well as what it has done."[120]
	Interim Supply: Because the concurrence and appropriations period for Main Estimates for the next fiscal year begins by the end of March and ends in June, the government will require financing for this three month period. For this reason, a request for an advance of funds from the Main Estimates is made at the end of March. This Interim Supply — usually a quarter of the amount sought by the Main Estimates — may be granted by the Commons, but this approval does not amount to Commons approval of the programs funded.
April–June	*Legislative Process*: From the tabling of the Main Estimates to a period culminating no later than June 23, government expenditure plans are reviewed and approved by Parliament, as follows:
	Committee Consideration: The Main Estimates are referred to the Standing Committees and each committee may (and most do) undertake a review of the Estimate relevant to the departments or agencies lying within its mandate. The committee reviews each of the budgetary expenditures (but not statutory expenditures) on an individual basis. The committee focuses on "Votes" — the maximum amount the government proposes be spent for a given item in the Estimates. Each Vote is a separate motion which a committee may either agree on (authorizing the expenditure), amend (reducing the expenditure) or negative (rejecting the expenditure). Committees are not free to increase expenditures, a

---

120 Auditor General of Canada, *Parliamentary Committee Review of the Estimates Documents*.

Period	Supply
April–June	prerogative that lies with the Crown. During this process, committees may invite witnesses to appear before them, including the responsible minister.
	Committees report the Estimate back to the Commons by May 31 (after which time committees failing to report are generally deemed to have reported). Committees may not include comments on the Estimate themselves. However, they report on the future departmental or agency expenditure plans and priorities, in response to the Report on Plans and Priorities, by the last sitting day of June.
	The Committee on Government Operations and Estimates has a broader role, reviewing the Estimates as a whole. It has some capacity to amend votes referred to other Committees in co-ordination with the latter.
	In addition, the Standing Orders include procedures by which the leader of the Opposition, in consultation with the opposition parties, may move a motion to refer consideration of the Main Estimate for no more than two departments to the Committee of the Whole (the Commons sitting *en banc*). As the Auditor General puts it, "review of Estimates by the Committee of the Whole House allows for ... a more thorough review of the Estimates of two departments, ministerial presence during the review, all Members of Parliament to review a specific department, and greater visibility of the Estimates review process."[121]
	Commons Concurrence: Once committee reports are tabled, the Commons votes on motions for concurrence. The government may seek to have items reduced or negatived by committees restored and members may oppose items in the Estimates. Motions for concurrence and opposition are debated for a limited time, and the matters are put to a vote.
	Appropriations Bill: Immediately after the Main Estimates receive concurrence, an appropriations bill is given first reading. It them follows the usual steps of the legislative process with a few notable exceptions. First, after second reading, it is referred to the Committee of the Whole. Second, the bill is dealt with expeditiously on the same day, and thus is usually passed without debate or amendment. The bill is then sent to the senate, where it receives three readings, and (in a departure from the practice for nonmoney bills) is returned the Commons for delivery to the Governor General for royal assent.
	Supply Debate: Self-standing debate on government supply is permitted during the annual supply cycle. During 21 "allotted days," distributed through the year, the Commons debates opposition motions on supply.
November	*Tabling of Departmental Performance Reports*: These documents are agency or department-specific assessments of departmental or agency achievements, as contrasted with the planned performance expectations set out in the Report on Plans and Priorities.
December	*Tabling of Public Accounts of Canada: The Financial Administration Act* requires that the Public Accounts of Canada — essentially a statement of the financial transactions of the fiscal year, the expenditures and revenues of Canada for the fiscal year and the government's assets and liabilities — must be tabled in the House of Commons by the December 31 following the end of the fiscal year.[122]

---

121 *Ibid.*

122 *Financial Administration Act*, s. 64.

Shortcomings in the Process

In principle, this process enables Members of Parliament to exercise substantial control over the government's expenditures. In the words of the Auditor General, parliamentary review of the government spending plans — the estimates — may improve public policy by enhancing parliamentary understanding of departmental issues, prompt discussion about government program accomplishments and improved performance, influence government priorities by drawing attention to resource allocation issues and refine the department planning and performance reporting process.[123] Further,

> Committee hearings with officials enable parliamentarians to influence departmental actions. These hearings are public meetings, and the proceedings can be followed by those most affected by government decisions and the media. Officials speak on the record and can be held to account for what they say. By questioning officials, especially when lines of questioning are followed up, parliamentarians can influence departments and agencies by focussing attention on their actions. Committees can report on the management and operation of departments and agencies and their long-term expenditure plans and priorities.[124]

In practice, however, parliamentary oversight is only modest. Indeed, Members of Parliament themselves have questioned the effectiveness of the Commons in policing spending. Since the late 1990s, parliamentary committees have issued a series of comprehensive and learned reports critical of the performance of parliamentarians in reviewing government spending.[125]

Despite several notable reforms flowing from these initiatives, the Standing Committee on Government Operations and Estimates reported in 2003 that Commons Standing Committees "continue to provide relatively cursory attention to the main spending estimates and explanatory reports provided by government departments each year."[126] In fact, government estimates are almost never changed by Parliament, although by the

---

123   Auditor General of Canada, *Parliamentary Committee Review of the Estimates Documents.*
124   *Ibid.*
125   See Standing Committee on Procedure and House Affairs, Report, *The Business of Supply: Completing the Circle of Control* (Dec. 1998); Standing Committee on Procedure and House Affairs, Report, *Improved Reporting to Parliament Project — Phase 2: Moving Forward* (June 2000); House of Commons, Special Committee on the Modernization and Improvement of the Procedures of the House of Commons, *Report* (June 2001).
126   Standing Committee on Government Operations and Estimates, *Meaningful Scrutiny: Practical Improvements To The Estimates Process* (Sept. 2003).

end of 2004, the minority thirty-eighth Parliament had reduced appropriations for the Privy Council Office and the Governor General.[127]

Indeed, there are shades of *Yes, Minister* in the estimates process. In the words of Professor Savoie, "Inexperienced MPs with limited access to expert staff face long-serving officials who are well versed in the ways of government and who have ready access to expertise and the elaborate interdepartmental consultative process."[128] Members of Parliament are themselves partially to blame for their insignificance in this area. Parliamentarians are more preoccupied with political gain than the technical management of government. For these politicians, argues Savoie, "Cartloads of information on program evaluation and performance are beside the point."[129]

To its credit, the Committee on Government Operations and Estimates proposed a number of sensible changes to the supply process in its 2003 report, ones that might give parliamentarians a more meaningful role. All of these quick fixes could be completed easily by committees. For instance, the committee recommended that, given resource constraints, standing-committee review of estimates focus on a single government program or agency, preferably one that has been scurtinized by the Auditor General.

Further, rather than "cold question" public servants appearing before them, the Committee proposed that Standing Committees hold pre-hearing planning meetings laying the groundwork for careful questioning, and also invite other groups with an interest in the agency or program under review to appear before them. Research staff could also be marshalled to review and draft technical questions, and the Commons was asked to consider allocating more resources to support standing-committee estimates work.

In its 2004 response, the government agreed with most of the committee's proposal, although it noted (correctly) that many lay within the House of Commons' purview to implement.[130] It remains to be seen how this issue will develop in the future.

---

127 See Standing Committee on Government Operations and Estimates, *First Report* (26 Nov. 2004). The financial rollback of the Privy Council appropriations reportedly was to compensate for alleged partisan polling expenditures made by that office. The cut in the Goveinor General's budget was designed to clip that official's wings, following controversy over an expensive diplomatic tour undertaken by the Governor General in 2003. Joe Paraskevas and Bill Curry, "MPs' Panel Takes Axe to Clarkson Budget," *Ottawa Citizen*, 26 Nov. 2004, A4. The full Commons endorsed the cuts, despite a government motion to restore full funding. House of Commons, *Journals*, no. 4, 38th Parl., 1st Sess. (9 Dec. 2004).

128 Savoie, *Breaking the Bargain* at 234–35.

129 *Ibid.*

130 Treasury Board, *Government Response to 6th Report of the Standing Committee on Government Operations and Estimates* (Feb. 2004).

New Rules on Borrowing Authority

One possible "hole" in parliamentary control of finances could conceivably flow from executive branch power to raise funds on the credit of the Government of Canada. By law, however, Parliament cannot be excluded from the appropriations process in this manner. Borrowing requires statutory authority of some sort.

Thus, the *Financial Administration Act* provides that "[n]otwithstanding any statement in any other Act of Parliament to the effect that this Act or any portion or provision of it does not apply, no money shall be borrowed by or on behalf of Her Majesty in right of Canada except as provided by or under ... (*a*) this Act; ... (*b*) any other Act of Parliament that expressly authorizes the borrowing of money; or ... (*c*) any other Act of Parliament that provides for the borrowing of money from Her Majesty in right of Canada or of a province."[131]

This language replaced a more general requirement existing in the Act prior to 2001 specifying, simply, that authorization for borrowed money be obtained from Parliament. The new provision reportedly "reinforces the Finance Minister's role in controlling the level of government indebtedness. This amendment circumvents potential borrowings by departments whose own legislation has statements declaring that the *Financial Administration Act* does not apply."[132]

Governor General's Special Warrants

On the other hand, the *Financial Administration Act* expressly allows the government to circumvent parliamentary review of the expenditure process in certain limited circumstances. Thus, the Governor-in-Council may issue Special Warrants permitting a charge on the Consolidated Revenue Fund even absent an appropriations bill.

Up until 1997, the Governor-in-Council Special Warrant power was expansive. The Act provided that where "a payment is urgently required for the public good when Parliament is not in session and there is no other appropriation pursuant to which the payment may be made, the Governor in Council ... may, by order, direct the preparation of a special warrant to be signed by the Governor General authorizing the payment to be made out of the Consolidated Revenue Fund."[133]

---

131   *Financial Administration Act*, s. 43.
132   Library of Parliament, *Bill C-17: An Act to Amend the Budget Implementation Act, 1997 and the Financial Administration Act* (March 2001).
133   *Financial Administration Act*, R.S.C. 1985 c. F-11, s. 30 (unamended).

Parliament was not "in session" when it "is under adjournment *sine die* or to a day more than two weeks after the day the Governor in Council made the order directing the preparation of the special warrant."[134] Put another way, so long as Parliament was adjourned, prorogued or dissolved for more than two weeks, the Governor-in-Council might appropriate funds unilaterally where it believed "payment is urgently required for the public good."

This was a remarkable power. An unprincipled government might well be sorely tempted to govern without parliamentary oversight of its expenditures simply by proroguing Parliament as much as possible and relying on Special Warrants. Senator Forsey, for one, complained vociferously of this power in his 1985 treatise on responsible government, urging amendment of the *Financial Administration Act* to "make it impossible for the Executive Government to drive a coach-and-four through the most fundamental rights and power of the House of Commons, its ultimate control over the expenditure of public money."[135] Remarkably, the Act was only amended in 1997, and then by a private member's and not a government bill.[136]

The *Financial Administration Act* now provides that the Governor-in-Council may only resort to Special Warrants "where a payment is urgently required for the public good" while Parliament is dissolved and for sixty days after an election and there is no other appropriation pursuant to which the payment may be made. The Act expressly bars Special Warrants where Parliament is merely prorogued. It obliges Special Warrants to be published in the *Canada Gazette* within thirty days and laid before the Commons within fifteen days of that body next being called to session.[137]

This approach is much more tempered than its predecessor. Even the most cynical government would be unwilling to dissolve Parliament (and thereby precipitate elections), simply to appropriate funds by Special Warrant.

Ways and Means
The ways and means system asserts the Commons' control over the process of raising government revenues. In practice, it centres on the Budget, the document broadcasting the government's fiscal, economic and social agenda. Traditionally, budgets have been introduced in February, although there is no requirement that this be the case. By convention, the

---

134 *Ibid.*

135 Forsey and Eglington, *The Question of Confidence* at 183. In fact, the Mulroney government resorted to an "unprecedented" use of Special Warrants in 1988–89 to "meet everyday payday requirements" of the sort usually covered by the estimates. Smith, *The Invisible Crown* (Toronto: University of Toronto Press, 1995) at 83.

136 S.C. 1997, c. 5.

137 *Financial Administration Act*, R.S.C. 1985 c. F-11, s. 30 (amended).

Budget is introduced in the Commons chamber. If Parliament were to change this procedure, however, this decision would be protected by privilege and unassailable in the courts.[138]

The budget process in the Commons commences when the minister of finance moves a motion of ways and means, seeking approval of the government's general budgetary framework.[139] The minister makes his or her budget speech. The budget motion is then debated in the Commons for up to four days.

Tax measures required to implement tax changes in the Budget are adopted via legislation. Uniquely, where new taxes or charges on the people are proposed, a ways and means motion approved by the Commons must precede the tax bill. These motions determine the parameters of the subsequent tax bill, constraining its tax rates and their applicability to those set out in the motion.

Over time, the Commons has become more than a reactive institution on ways and means. Since 1994, the Standing Committee on Finance has been authorized to hold pre-budget consultations, beginning in September, with reports by December.[140] This new role has prompted the Standing Committee to undertake extensive consultations on budgetary priorities with interested citizens and to issue detailed policy studies.[141]

2. The Individual Responsibility of Ministers

As well as being collectively responsible to Parliament through the mechanism of confidence votes and the assorted means of policing government *en masse*, ministers are individually responsible to Parliament. Individual ministerial responsibility, in the words of the Privy Council Office, "normally includes responsibility for a department. Ministers receive confidential advice from the public service, make important decisions and are held accountable for these decisions in Parliament and the country."[142] It is, as the Privy Council also states, "a fundamental principle of the constitution."[143]

---

138   *Martin v. Ontario*, [2004] O.J. No. 2247 (S.C.J.), holding that the location of the Ontario budget speech was a matter of parliamentary procedure, protected by privilege, and not reviewable in court.

139   Except as noted, information contained in this section summarizes material from *Précis of Procedure* and Marleau and Montpetit, *House of Commons Procedure and Practice*.

140   Commons *Standing Orders*, Order 83.1.

141   See, e.g., Standing Committee on Finance, *Canada: People, Places and Priorities* (Nov. 2002).

142   Privy Council Office, *Notes on the Responsibilities of Public Servants in Relation to Parliamentary Committees* (Dec. 1990).

143   Privy Council Office, *Responsibility in the Constitution*.

In fact, individual ministerial responsibility is the "clasp" or "buckle" connecting Parliament to the public administration of Canada. In its classic manifestation, ministers are directly accountable to Parliament, but public servants are not. These latter individuals are accountable only to their ministers. As the Privy Council Office puts it, the duty of the public service is "to give loyal, professional and non-partisan support to the Government of the day. It is the responsibility of individual public servants to provide advice and information to Ministers, to carry out faithfully the directions given by Ministers, and in so doing to serve the people of Canada."[144]

Public servants must act in a fashion that permits ministers to maintain "full confidence in the loyalty and trustworthiness of those who serve them."

> The preservation of this relationship of trust and confidence is essential to the conduct of good government. If public servants violate the trust bestowed on them by Ministers they undermine effective (and democratic) government. If they violate that trust on the grounds that they have a higher obligation to Parliament, then they undermine *the fundamental principle of responsible government, namely that it is Ministers and not public servants who are accountable to the House of Commons for what is done by the Government.*[145]

These ministers are "responsible to the House for everything that is done under their authority." They decide policy and they defend that policy before the House "and ultimately before the people of Canada."[146]

These assertions represent the conventional wisdom about ministerial responsibility. This classic division of labour between politician and public servant is, however, largely a myth, a contention we test by examining the manifold fashions in which individual ministers are held to account by Parliament.

a) Legal and Political Culpability for Wrongdoing by Department Officials

In its classic expression, individual ministerial responsibility means that a minister is accountable both in law and to Parliament for wrongdoings in his or her department. This aspect of responsibility might be phrased the "buck stops here" element of a minister's job. In practice, however, responsibility of this sort is nominally, rather than actually, observed.

Legal Culpability

In terms of legal culpability, it is common for legal applications brought against individual government departments to name the "minister" as the

---

144 Privy Council Office, *Notes on the Responsibilities of Public Servants.*
145 *Ibid.* [emphasis in original].
146 *Ibid.*

defendant or respondent. This is most acutely the case in applications for judicial review — typically, administrative law proceedings challenging whether the government acted lawfully and had jurisdiction to make a given decision. In almost every instance, the minister him- or herself did not personally make the impugned decision, but as the head of the department he or she is the nominal party. Being named in the style of cause of these legal applications is, in other words, a formality.

Meanwhile, the Crown as a whole is vicariously responsible for torts committed by its servants. Thus, the *Crown Liability and Proceedings Act* provides that "[t]he Crown is liable for the damages for which, if it were a person, it would be liable ... in respect to ... a tort committed by a servant of the Crown."[147] These claims are made in the name of the Attorney General of Canada,[148] not other ministers or officials.

In the past, it was sometimes argued that ministers' positions as heads of government departments rendered them liable for civil wrongs committed by their officials.[149] Vicarious liability is not, however, recognized in modern law, and ministers named in such actions are regularly struck out as defendants.[150]

Thus, it is true that ministers are generally liable for their own personal actions,[151] like any other person. However, if ministers are to be culpable

---

147 *Crown Liability and Proceedings Act*, R.S.C. 1985, c. C-50, s. 3.
148 *Ibid.*, s. 23.
149 Heard, *Canadian Constitutional Conventions* at 54.
150 *National Harbours Board v. Langelier*, [1969] S.C.R. 60 at 72 ("a servant of the Crown cannot be made liable vicariously for a tort committed by a subordinate"); *Deep v. Ontario*, [2004] O.J. No. 2734 at para. 83 (S.C.J.) ("Ministers are Crown servants for whom the Crown may be held vicariously liable. However, Ministers are not masters to other Crown servants, including their direct subordinates. Consequently, Ministers may not be held vicariously liable for the tortuous conduct of other Crown servants. A minister of the Crown is not vicariously liable for the torts of Crown servants since ministers are themselves servants of the Crown."); *Aristocrat Restaurants Ltd. (c.o.b. Tony's East) v. Ontario*, [2003] O.J. No. 5331 at para. 69 (S.C.J.) (same); *Shubenacadie Indian Band v. Canada (Attorney General)*, 2001 FCT 699 at para. 4 (T.D.) ("While the Minister may be personally responsible for his own actions, including orders which he has personally given, [and there are allegations to that effect] he cannot, as a servant of the Crown, be held responsible for the acts of other Crown servants."). See discussion in Hogg, *Constitutional Law of Canada* at 9-11 n30 ("[t]here is no personal legal responsibility on the part of a minister for torts or crimes committed by civil servants within a minister's department").
151 *National Harbours Board*, [1969] S.C.R. 60 at 72 ("a servant of the Crown, who commits a wrong, is personally liable to the person injured. Furthermore, if the wrongful act is committed by a subordinate, at his behest, he is equally liable, not because the subordinate is his servant, but because the subordinate's act, in such a case, is his

for the actions of their subordinates, it is through the device of ministerial responsibility to Parliament, not the courts of law.

Political Culpability

This raises the question of whether the political form of vicarious responsibility operates effectively. Do ministers resign when pressed by Parliament on the infractions of their subordinates? The simple answer to this question is "no." It is rare to the point of unknown for ministers to resign in response to wrongdoings committed by their subordinates,[152] at least officially.

Table 6.3 shows ministerial resignations, classified by reason for the resignation identified by the Library of Parliament, since the St. Laurent ministry. These reasons are drawn from a variety of media and official documents, and represent the public (and perhaps not always the true) reason for resignation. Yet, even with that caveat, it is still notable that in every instance, ministerial resignations, when they came, were said to be prompted by personal ethical or political failings or personal reasons, never in response to departmental mismanagement or the wrongdoings of departmental officials.[153]

Table 6.3   Ministerial Resignations since St. Laurent, 1950–2004

	Ethics	Policy Difference	Personal Reason	Alternative Appointment	Total
St. Laurent	0	0	1	7	8
Diefenbaker	0	1	2	3	6
Pearson	3	2	4	6	15
Trudeau	3	4	7	4	18
Mulroney	10	2	5	2	19
Chrétien	4	2	5	2	13

Senator Forsey came to similar conclusions in his 1985 review of resignations: "None of the resignations related to issues of maladministration,

---

own act"). The most famous case of a minister being held civilly liable for abusing his or her office is *Roncarelli v. Duplessis*, [1959] S.C.R. 121 (Premier Duplessis of Quebec found liable for exercising his office in a bad faith attempt to harass Mr. Roncarelli for his support of Jehovah's Witnesses). The precise scope of personal liability and the means it interacts with the *Crown Liability and Proceedings Act* is a vast subject stretching beyond the mandate of this book. As an excellent resource, see Peter Hogg, *Liability of the Crown* (Toronto: Carswell, 1989).

152   See discussion in Heard, *Canadian Constitutional Conventions* at 54–59.

153   Library of Parliament, *Ministerial Resignations — 1867 to date.*

pursuit of stupid policies, harsh or improper exercise of administrative discretion, or the taking of improper decisions within Departments."[154]

This record suggests that vicarious political ministerial responsibility for the actions of the public servants in their departments is almost certainly a comforting myth, and not a serious tool of accountability. As Senator Forsey observed, "Governmental bungling is, perhaps, accepted as part of the unchanging order of things."[155]

The nominal "buck stops here" quality of ministerial responsibility is debased further by ministerial preparedness to point fingers at public servants for dubious government behaviour. As early as 1985, Senator Forsey wrote that "there has been a growing tendency to name and blame civil servants, even to hold them personally accountable for policies put forward by their Ministers."[156] Such events have been portrayed by Professor Donald Savoie and others as a "breaking of the bargain" between the civil service and their political masters.[157] In Professor Savoie words, "the traditional bargain between politicians and public servants is coming unglued, and the space that was once established to determine who is responsible for what is no longer clear."[158]

Responses to the Nominal Nature of Ministerial Culpability

One response to the nominal quality of ministerial responsibility — as measured by its indifferent impact on ministerial tenure in office — is to accept the *status quo*. The Privy Council Office has argued that ministerial responsibility functions adequately without the sanction of ministerial dismissal. In its words:

> The fact that ministers will probably not lose office as the result of the exposure of a particular instance of mismanagement, or even the misuse of authority by officials, does not detract from their constitutional responsibility or their obligation to ensure that such instances do not occur. Indeed, this responsibility is honed by the ever-present possibility that in particular circumstances ministers may be embarrassed, suffer loss of prestige weakening themselves and the government, jeopardize their standing with their colleagues and hence their political future, or even be forced to submit to public enquiry possibly resulting in censure and loss

---

154   Forsey and Eglington, *The Question of Confidence* at 22. See also Jackson and Jackson, *Canadian Government in Transition* at 185 ("resignation is extremely unlikely unless political expediency interferes").

155   Forsey and Eglington, *The Question of Confidence* at 23.

156   *Ibid.* at 29.

157   Donald Savoie, *Breaking the Bargain*.

158   *Ibid.* at 5.

of office as a result of the way in which their power has been used. These possibilities underpin the constitutional responsibility of ministers, which forms the basis for accountability throughout the system.[159]

We wonder, however, if public shaming will suffice in a system in which — to quote the 1985 McGrath report on reform of the Commons — many believe it is "no longer reasonable that a minister be accountable or responsible when, through no fault of the minister, senior officials misuse or abuse their powers."[160] If the bar of ministerial expectations is set so low, poor departmental performance likely produces little loss of face for ministers. One wonders, also, if ministers are not at least responsible for managing their senior officials exactly what real role departmental ministers play in Canadian democracy at all.

Deputy Ministers as Accountability Officers

A partial response to the eroded nature of ministerial responsibility is to call for greater accountability of public servants to Parliament. In the United Kingdom, senior officials or "accounting officers" are accountable to Parliament for the financial operations of their departments.[161]

Making deputy ministers directly accountable to Parliament in relation at least to administrative and financial matters within their department seems, superficially, an attractive proposition. In Professor Savoie's view, appointing these officials as parliamentary "accounting officers" would "introduce a personal responsibility for the propriety and regularity of public finances. That officer would be given a specific space from which he or she could take action if the minister should propose a course of action counter to propriety, regularity, and even economy, efficiency, and effectiveness in public spending."[162]

Deputies are, after all, powerful figures. In law, they may exercise most of the statutory powers of ministers. The *Interpretation Act* provides, for instance, that "[w]ords directing or empowering a minister of the Crown to do an act or thing, regardless of whether the act or thing is administrative, legislative or judicial, or otherwise applying to that minister as the holder of the office, include" his or her "deputy," except the power to make regulations.[163]

---

159 Privy Council Office, *Responsibility in the Constitution*.

160 Special Committee on the Reform of the House of Commons, *Report* (18 June 1985) at 20–21.

161 See discussion in Savoie, *Breaking the Bargain* at 53–54.

162 *Ibid.* at 259. See also the Special Committee on the Reform of the House of Commons, *Report* (18 June 1985) at 21, calling for more frequent appearances of deputy ministers before parliamentary committees.

163 *Interpretation Act*, R.S.C. 1985, c. I-21, s. 23.

We echo Savoie, however, in cautioning that "accountability officers" must not supplant ministerial responsibility as the core focus of parliamentary accountability, for both principled and practical reasons. First, this approach abandons even the pretence of responsible government; that those who direct the executive branch are themselves part of the legislative branch and subject to scrutiny both by their fellow parliamentarians, and ultimately by the electorate. Ministers fit these requirements. Public servants do not. In the words of the Privy Council Office, "officials are disqualified from membership in the House of Commons and accordingly may not be held constitutionally responsible by the House."[164] For this reason, only elected ministers should and can be responsible to their elected peers for the bunglings of their departments.

Second, any abandonment of even nominal, "vicarious" ministerial responsibility will create a moral hazard problem. As Senator Forsey wrote in 1985, "[i]t is only if Ministers are accountable and responsible that Parliament, and through it the electorate, can hope to exercise any power or control over the bureaucracy. Without personal accountability and responsibility, ministers will have little incentive to put aside the path of least resistance and to impose political, and hence democratic, control on their departments."[165]

Indeed, absent at least political vicarious responsibility for the machinations of their unelected subordinates, ministers might adopt a policy of willful blindness to departmental wrongdoing. If ministers are not presumed responsible for their departments, they are politically vulnerable only when they have actual knowledge of, or participate in, departmental malfeasance. In these circumstances, a policy of "plausible deniability" may be preferred to hands-on management, thus providing ministers with political cover. This would produce a preposterous manner of governing, one that would do little to ignite the admiration of Canadians. The second aspect of democratic accountability addressed in our introductory chapter — holding unelected officials accountable by leaning on the elected officials charged with their management — would be gravely weakened.

Strengthening Ministerial Responsibility

We are, therefore, sympathetic to approaches that would strengthen rather than further weaken or abandon ministerial responsibility. Certainly, ministers should not be required to resign for every mishap in their department. But major scandals that cast doubt on the integrity of government should precipitate resignations, not obfuscation.

---

164 Privy Council Office, *Responsibility in the Constitution.*
165 Forsey and Eglington, *The Question of Confidence* at 29.

At present, culpability in the system of ministerial responsibility is decided by the prime minister, charged with advising (and in fact commanding) the Governor General on the appointment and dismissal of ministers. Some prime ministers, including, famously, Jean Chrétien, see virtue in steadfast support of besieged ministers, not resignations. However, it is no great leap to say that in a system of responsible government, whether a departmental misfortune constitutes a scandal warranting removal of a minister is rightfully a matter to be decided by Parliament. As Prime Minister Martin's Privy Council Office has underscored, "Parliament confers the powers of the state on Ministers on the condition that they, and through them the officials under their management and direction, be accountable to Parliament for their actions." The question of "[w]hether a Minister has used the powers appropriately is a matter of political judgment by Parliament."[166]

Yet, Parliament is hobbled by the absence of a true mechanism to enforce its displeasure against a minister of the Crown. As Professor Hogg has observed, "if the government does not want a minister to resign, then no matter how clearly the facts would seem to warrant the minister's resignation, there is no way the opposition can force it to happen."[167] A no-confidence vote precipitating resignation of the ministry *en masse* or a new election is a nuclear approach, unlikely to garner governing party support. The use of Parliament's contempt powers may be excessively punitive, and thus also unlikely to attract support. On the other hand, more surgical intervention, permitting the dismissal of single ministers without bringing down the government might appeal even to governing party backbenchers prepared to offer up a minister to appease their constituents in the wake of true scandals.

Responsible government would benefit, in other words, not from a rejection of ministerial responsibility, but by mechanisms permitting the Commons to vote a motion of censure for a minister and thus oblige his or her dismissal by the Governor General. Exactly how such a practice could be initiated is a difficult legal question. U.K. precedent suggests that the Commons has the power to vote censure of a minister.[168] Such motions do not, however, apparently compel the resignation of the minister.[169]

---

166 Privy Council Office, *Governing Responsibly: A Guide for Ministers and Ministers of State*.

167 Hogg, *Constitutional Law of Canada* at 9-12.

168 See Derek Lee, *The Power of Parliamentary Houses to Send for Persons, Papers and Records* (Toronto: University of Toronto Press, 1999) at 213.

169 *Ibid.* at 215.

Still, it is possible to imagine a means by which a creative Commons might couple its traditional parliamentary privileges with constitutional convention to prompt a more or less compulsory resignation by a minister. First, the Commons has the power to suspend and expel its members.[170] A minister so expelled would no longer have a seat in Parliament. Since by constitutional convention, ministers are expected (eventually) to be parliamentarians,[171] a Commons expulsion could greatly increase the pressure on the minister to resign.

Of course, the prime minister might stand by his or her disgraced colleague, treating the matter as a confidence vote, engineering a by-election or appointing the minister to the senate. Each of these responses would do an end-run around the Commons and permit the minister to remain in executive office. Each of these actions would, however, likely carry a political price, both in terms of the prime minister's relations with the House and the perception these events would prompt in the public mind.

In 2004, the Martin government announced a "review of accountabilities and responsibilities of Ministers and senior public servants." Assisted by Professor Savoie and former clerk and deputy clerk of the House of Commons, Robert Marleau and Camille Montpetit, all experts in the subject, the review was charged with examining: "Who is accountable for what and to whom? How well are accountabilities and responsibilities understood by Ministers, political staff and senior public servants? What changes are needed to strengthen the accountability of Ministers and/or public servants?"[172] The report, anticipated for fall 2004, was shelved in early 2005 by the Martin government pending the outcome of the Gomery inquiry into the sponsorship scandal.[173]

b)   Ministerial Responsibility to Inform Parliament

If individual ministerial responsibility does not currently mean that a minister's job is on the line, at least it imposes important obligations on ministers to keep Parliament informed. Thus, a very practical aspect of ministerial responsibility revolves around Parliament's ability to extract information on the government and its activities from ministers.

---

170   *Beauchesne's Rules*, 6th ed. at 16 ("[t]here is no question that the House has the right to expel a Member for such reasons as it deems fit"); Maingot, *Parliamentary Privilege in Canada* at 181 and 189. Note, however, that such suspensions have historically been for serious infractions. See discussion in ch. 3.

171   See discussion in ch. 4. See also Heard, *Canadian Constitutional Conventions* at 49.

172   See Treasury Board, *Strengthening Public Sector Management* (March 2004).

173   See Paco Francoli, "Alcock Ices Ministerial Accountability Report," *The Hill Times* (7 Feb. 2005).

Broadly speaking, ministers provide information to Parliament in two ways: first, through formal reports from government departments and agencies, tabled by ministers in Parliament; and second, in responding to questions from parliamentarians. We discuss each of these information-sharing mechanisms in turn.

Formal Reporting Requirements

Statutory Requirements

As the Commons *Précis of Procedure* notes, the "presentation of reports and returns is one method by which the House obtains information," and can play a key role in the review of a minister's department.[174]

A minister's precise parliamentary information obligations in relation to a given branch of executive government may be specified by statute. A vast array of department or agency-specific statutes and the *Financial Administration Act* impose formal government and ministerial parliamentary reporting obligations.

Pursuant to the Commons Standing Orders, the clerk of the House compiles a list of "reports or other periodical statements which it is the duty of any officer or department of the government, or any bank or other corporate body to make to the House."[175] As of 2002, that list was fully 105 pages long,[176] and in most cases comprised annual reports of one form or another. In practice, it seems unlikely that parliamentarians have the resources or time to digest fully all of this information. Statutory reporting obligations may produce paper in such volumes that key issues upon which parliamentarians should properly focus are buried in reporting minutiae.

Motions for the Production of Papers

One supplemental and very modest means for the Commons to induce government reporting is worth noting: motions for the production of papers. These motions are brought as part of the Commons "routine business."

Should the government fail to produce the requested document, the MP (or the minister) may request that the motion be debated. The motion is debated and adopted, if at all, during Private Members Business, that scarce one hour a day of parliamentary time. This means that only private members with a spot on the order of precedence, established by lottery, may propose these motions. Further, as with private members' bills, if

---

174 *Précis of Procedure* at 26.

175 Commons, *Standing Orders*, Order 153.

176 House of Commons, *List of Reports and Returns to be Made to the House of Commons* (2002).

debate on the motion is not completed during the Private Members Business hour, the matter is cycled to the back of the order of precedence and revisited only after other matters on that list have also been dealt with or themselves run out of time and been circulated to the end of the list.

Under the Standing Orders, the motions for the production of papers must be put to a vote after no more than a cumulative total of one hour and thirty minutes of debate.[177] If adopted, they result in an order for return — an order requiring the government to table certain documents in the House pertaining to federal departments. Alternatively, they take the form of an "address to the Governor General," seeking "inter-governmental correspondence, orders in council or documents pertaining to the administration of justice, the work of magistrates and the exercise of prerogatives of the Crown."[178]

These instruments sound more impressive than they are. They are not themselves legislative requirements. Should a minister refuse to comply with these measures, the Commons is left to employ its contempt powers (discussed later in this chapter) to punish the minister, or suspend or expel that person from the House — all unlikely scenarios.[179]

In 1973, the government of the day articulated its view on what papers could be sought via the motion for the production of papers. While not codified in parliamentary law, these principles have been followed since that time.[180] These guidelines describe the motion as enabling Members of Parliament to "secure factual information about the operations of government" in order to carry out their parliamentary duties. They then carve out specific and at times sweeping exceptions precluding government production of papers, as categorized in Table 6.4.

Questioning of Ministers

As noted above, statutes creating the entities that collectively comprise the public administration of Canada usually anticipate the existence of a "responsible Minister" for each body. Alternatively, the prime minister may assign a minister such responsibility.[181]

Parliamentarians preoccupied with a particular agency (for example, opposition critics) are able to turn to this responsible minister, seeking

---

177   Commons, *Standing Orders*, Order 97.
178   House of Commons, *A Practical Guide to Private Members Business* (2001).
179   Lee, *The Power of Parliamentary Houses* at 138.
180   Marleau and Montpetit, *House of Commons Procedure and Practice* at 402.
181   For a list of ministerial responsibilities, see Library of Parliament, *The Ministry and its Responsibilities*.

Table 6.4   Exceptions in Motions for the Production of Paper

Category	Exemption
Legal	Legal opinion or advice for the use of government.
	Papers that are excluded from disclosure by statute.
	Papers relating to negotiations leading up to a contract until the contract has been executed or the negotiations have been concluded.
	Any proceedings before a court of justice or a judicial inquiry of any sort.
National security or international relations	Papers, the release of which would be detrimental to the security of the state.
	Papers dealing with international relations, the release of which might be detrimental to the future conduct of Canada's foreign relations.
Federal/Provincial relations	Papers, the release of which might be detrimental to the future conduct of federal-provincial relations or provinces *inter se*.
Embarrassing materials	Papers reflecting on the personal competence or character of an individual.
	Papers, the release of which would be personally embarrassing to Her Majesty or the Royal Family or official representatives of Her Majesty.
Senate	Papers relating to the business of the senate.
Cost	Papers of a voluminous character or which would require an inordinate cost or length of time to prepare.
Personal gain	Papers containing information, the release of which could allow or result in direct personal financial gain or loss by a person or group of persons.
Cabinet and government	Cabinet documents and those documents which include a Privy Council confidence.
	Internal government memoranda.
	Certain consultants' studies.
Private	Papers that are private or confidential and not of a public or official character.
	Papers requested, submitted and received in confidence by the government from sources outside the government.

answers to questions. Thus, Prime Minister Martin's Privy Council Office has underscored that "Ministers must be present in Parliament to respond to questions on the use of [their] powers, as well as to accept responsibility and account for that use. ... Ministers are also required to *answer to Parliament* by providing information to Parliament on the use of powers by bodies that report to Parliament through them." "It is of paramount importance for Ministers," the Privy Council Office continues, "to give accurate and truthful information to Parliament, and to correct any error at the earliest opportunity."[182]

Ministers are not equally accountable for everything for which they are named responsible minister. In some instances, the responsible minister's *de facto* authority over an agency is constrained. As the Privy Council Office notes, "[t]he statutes governing many non-departmental bodies such as regulatory commissions or tribunals may assign only limited ministerial responsibility for internal management and operations."[183] Even then, however, ministers have parliamentary responsibilities: "Where Ministers do not have direct responsibility for addressing issues raised by Parliament, they must nevertheless ensure that the non-departmental body concerned does address those issues."[184]

Questioning in the Commons

Question Period

The most famous form of parliamentary interrogation of ministers comes in Question Period, a daily forty-five-minute session that often makes for colourful press copy. The (at least nominal) objective of Question Period is to seek information from ministers and call the government to account for its actions.[185] For this reason, ministers and parliamentary secretaries are barred from asking questions, and most time in the session is devoted to opposition party queries of government ministers.[186]

Despite the drama it sometimes engineers, Question Period is an inefficient information-seeking device. A question presented during Question Period must *not* be many things. For instance, Commons practice requires that a question not be a statement, expression of opinion or argument, not be hypothetical or seek an opinion, not seek information protected by rules of secrecy, such as a Cabinet confidences, and not reflect on the character or conduct of parliamentarians or members of the judiciary.[187] The Speaker will refer oral questions that are too long or technical to the Order Paper, where they may be distilled as written questions to the minister.

More significantly, a member may only question a minister about his or her current portfolio, not a past ministry. A judicious shuffling of Cabi-

---

182 Privy Council Office, *Governing Responsibly: A Guide for Ministers and Ministers of State.*
183 *Ibid.*
184 *Ibid.*
185 *Précis of Procedure* at 15.
186 House of Commons, *Fact Sheet: Question Period and Written Questions* (2004).
187 *Ibid.*; Marleau and Montpetit, *House of Commons Procedure and Practice* at 426–27.

net means that the person to whom questions are directed may not be the person at the top of a department hierarchy at the time of some scandal or another.[188]

These conventions greatly limit the effectiveness of Question Period. The *coup de grâce*, however, are rules governing responses. A minister confronting a question is not in the same position as a witness in a court proceeding. He or she may easily duck the matter. A minister may therefore choose to answer, defer an answer, take notice of the question, explain why they cannot answer or simply say nothing.[189] For what it is worth, members dissatisfied with a response may seek to have the matter raised again during debate on adjournment of the Commons sitting.[190] There, at the so-called late show, they can press their question again, subject to strict time limits on both the questioning and any response.[191]

The bottom line is, however, that a member may ask a question in Question Period but is not entitled to an answer. Indeed, "insistence on an answer is out of order, with no debate being allowed."[192] As Speaker James Jerome noted in 1978, "the Chair cannot compel an answer — it is public opinion which compels an answer."[193]

Why this should be is unclear. Certainly a minister asked to disclose Cabinet confidences could decline to answer, citing that very reason. But non-responsiveness in other circumstances is simple obstructionism that does little credit to either the government or Parliament. As a consequence of all these rules, Question Period is often characterized by short, leading questions selected for sound-bite appeal and dripping with innuendo, followed by cute, irrelevant and sometimes inane answers. As Professor Savoie puts it, Question Period is now "both contrived and overly confrontational."[194]

Question Period is not an entirely fruitless exercise. It does prompt a certain level of government accountability, unearthing and driving home the occasional mega-scandal. Question Period is, however, largely theatre rather than a meaningful, searching parliamentary review of government

---

188 See, e.g., Jack Aubry, "Pettigrew Could Still Testify About Fiasco," *Ottawa Citizen*, 8 Feb. 2000, A3, about Minister Pettigrew declining to testify on the Human Resources Development Canada scandal after he is shuffled from that portfolio.

189 Marleau and Montpetit, *House of Commons Procedure and Practice* at 432.

190 *Précis of Procedure* at 15.

191 Commons, *Standing Orders*, Order 38.

192 *Beauchesne's Rules*, 6th ed. at 123.

193 *Hansard*, 6 Feb. 1978 at 2567. See also House of Commons, *Selected Decisions of Speaker James Jerome 1974–1979* at 12.

194 Savoie, *Breaking the Bargain* at 229.

actions. This may be the irreversible consequence of the electronic age, in which sound bites sometimes determine the fate of one partisan cause or another. The Commons would, however, take an enormous step forward as a credible forum for debate were it at least to reverse its rules permitting ministerial nonresponses.

Written Questions

The Standing Orders also allow members to address written questions to ministers "relating to public affairs." The member may request a response within forty-five days, although, as noted by the Special Committee on the Modernization and Improvement of the Procedures of the House of Commons, "[t]here is considerable frustration on the part of Members that many questions are not answered within this time frame."[195]

Should an answer not be received within this period, the matter is referred to the "appropriate" Standing Committee, which will then meet on the issue within five days. Alternatively, the member whose question remains unanswered may ask that the matter be transferred to the adjournment phase of Commons proceedings, where the issue may then be raised again.[196] As noted above, this is only a modest remedy. Ironically, the Special Committee observed in 2001 that transferring an unanswered question to adjournment proceedings "has the effect of removing it from the *Order Paper*, thereby absolving the government of tabling a written response."[197]

Written questions are, in other words, a process of ministerial interrogation that demands little immediate response and, as with oral questions, does not necessarily guarantee an answer.

Questioning in Committees

Ministers who duck questions in Question Period are not through with Parliament. More meaningful questioning of ministers may take place in parliamentary committees. The Privy Council Office provides guidelines on ministerial appearances before parliamentary committees. Ministers are expected to appear before these House and senate committees as "an essential part of informing Parliament, enabling parliamentarians to represent the views of their constituents in the development of policy and leg-

---

195 Special Committee on the Modernization and Improvement of the Procedures of the House of Commons, *Report* (June 2001).
196 Commons, *Standing Orders*, Order 39.
197 Special Committee on The Modernization and Improvement of the Procedures of the House of Commons, *Report* (June 2001).

islation, and to hold the government to account for its management and policies."[198] Ministerial accountability means that "Ministers are responsible for providing answers to Parliament on questions regarding the government's policies, programs and activities, and for providing as much information as possible about the use of powers assigned to them or delegated by them to others."[199] Uniquely before committees, ministers will share the stage with their officials, raising tricky questions about Parliament's jurisdiction over public servants.

Respective Duties of Ministers and Public Servants

Specifically, in responding to Committee queries, ministers must assess which questions they should address personally, and which should be directed to departmental officials also in attendance. Public servants attending committee hearings often have a more detailed understanding of departmental plans and performance than does the minister. Accordingly, the Privy Council Office asserts that "[o]fficials can assist Ministers by factually answering questions at parliamentary committees, but they are to explain rather than defend or debate policies. When appearing before a parliamentary committee, officials maintain the traditional impartiality of the Public Service. The authoritative political presence of either the Minister or his or her political representative is required if politically controversial matters are likely to arise."[200]

As noted above, the doctrine of ministerial responsibility means that technically, the public servant is responsible to the minister, and not to Parliament. Two important implications flow from this doctrine. First, public servants are not to appear before parliamentary committees, without "clear guidance" from their minister.[201]

Second, public servants "also have a duty and specific legal responsibility to hold in confidence information that may have come into their possession in the course of their duties."[202] Thus, "[i]n the context of a committee hearing, information that is not in the public domain can only be made available on the specific authorization of the minister, and within the context of statutory obligations."[203]

---

198 Privy Council Office, *Governing Responsibly: A Guide for Ministers and Ministers of State.*
199 *Ibid.*
200 *Ibid.*
201 *Ibid.*
202 *Ibid.*
203 *Ibid.*

Committees and Parliament's Oversight Powers in Relation to Public Servants

In fact, the legal powers of Parliament in relation to public servants are much greater than the Privy Council Office distillation above suggests. Parliament has powers to summon and even compel the appearance of officials,[204] including ministers.[205] Likewise, under the Common's Standing Orders, Standing Committees may "send for persons, papers and records."[206] Parliament and its committees may also administer oaths requiring truthful responses.[207] There is, therefore, a potential contradiction between Parliament's powers and the classic expression of ministerial responsibility — public servants accountable only to ministers and ministers accountable to Parliament.

As a partial response to this tension, Parliament and its committees rarely summon officials, leaving it to ministers to select the appropriate representative to speak for them or their department. Further, public servants have traditionally not been sworn during their appearances before committees. The Privy Council Office urges that such a practice would place public servants in a potentially impossible conflict:

> public servants who are asked to be sworn may be placed in a position of
> *prima facie* conflict between an oath to testify and their duty of confidentiality to their Minister or, more generally, their oath of secrecy. In practice, officials would of course be expected to testify within the constitutionally fundamental context of ministerial responsibility to Parliament. In this context, officials (and deputy ministers in particular) have a fundamental duty to advise their Ministers frankly on any matters relevant to their departmental and policy responsibilities. Only Ministers can properly decide when and to what degree any matters that are confidential can and should be disclosed. Testimony under oath could force an official to assume a power of decision in these respects that he or she cannot properly exercise.[208]

---

204 See discussion in Lee, *The Power of Parliamentary Houses; Telezone Inc. v. Canada (Attorney General)* (2004), 235 D.L.R. (4th) 719 at 726 (Ont. C.A.); *Canada (Attorney General) v. Prince Edward Island (Legislative Assembly)* (2003), 46 Admin. L.R. (3d) 171 (P.E.I.S.C.).

205 Lee, *The Power of Parliamentary Houses* at 129 ("[u]nder the law, Ministers of the Crown enjoy no special status or privilege before the House or a committee").

206 Commons *Standing Orders*, Order 108(1).

207 See *Parliament of Canada Act*, ss. 10–13.

208 Privy Council Office, *Notes on the Responsibilities of Public Servants.*

Indeed, placing a public servant under oath "may raise a question as to whether the Minister could also be asked to take an oath. If so, this would touch directly on Ministers privileges as Members, their oath as Privy Councillors and their fundamental relationship of (truthful) accountability to Parliament."[209]

Both of these fears are unpersuasive. The administration of an oath compels a truthful answer. It does not preclude the public servant (or the minister) from declining to respond where a response would violate their respective confidentiality obligations. Only if Parliament or a committee were to subsequently exercise its contempt powers in response to such a demurral would a conflict arise. As discussed in the following section, that contempt power could be exercised whether or not a refusal to respond was given under oath.

Committees and Parliament's Contempt Powers

Parliament's contempt powers are part of its parliamentary privilege. As described by Joseph Maingot, this means that "[a]ny act or omission that obstructs or impedes either House of Parliament in the performance of its functions, or that obstructs or impedes any Member or officer of such House in the discharge of his duty, or that has a tendency, directly or indirectly, to produce such results may be treated as contempt even though there is no precedent of the offence."[210]

The issue of oaths and the scope of parliamentary contempt powers in relation to testimony before committees were raised squarely by the "Radwanski affair" in 2003. Then-Privacy Commissioner Radwanski and several other members of the Privacy Commissioner's Office were called to testify before a special subcommittee of the Commons Standing Committee on Government Operations and Estimates. There, they made statements concerning the operations of Privacy Office characterized by the subcommittee as "deliberately misleading" or "less than forthcoming."[211]

The committee subsequently considered whether these individuals should be held in contempt. Contempt offences, in its view, "directly threaten the effectiveness of Parliament itself, by undermining its performance of central roles in considering legislation and holding governments accountable for their actions." In so doing, they "represent an assault upon the dem-

---

209 *Ibid.*

210 Maingot, *Parliamentary Privilege in Canada* at 193.

211 Standing Committee on Government Operations and Estimates, *Matters Related to the Review of the Office of the Privacy Commissioner* (Nov. 2003).

ocratic process itself, and when they occur in Canada they directly threaten the interests of every Canadian citizen or resident of this country."[212]

After a review of behaviours constituting contempt, the committee recommended that "[s]anctions applied in response to the conduct described in this report, should it be found to constitute a contempt of Parliament, need to fully reflect the gravity of the offence." These sanctions, it concluded, could include reprimand or admonishment before the assembled House, imprisonment or fines.[213]

The committee also noted that witnesses appearing before it in the Privacy Office probe had been "uniformly advised, and accepted, that their testimony before the committee had the same status as testimony under oath, acknowledged that they were testifying as if under oath and acknowledged that they had a duty to speak the truth."

Since this admonishment apparently had not guaranteed truthful responses, the committee proposed that parliamentary committees "consider formally placing witnesses under oath more often, when circumstances warrant."[214] Such a move "would communicate the importance of the obligations to which witnesses are subject more effectively than, for example, simply informing them that their testimony will have the status of testimony given under oath. More obviously, it has clear advantages over merely assuming that witnesses are aware of their duty to speak the whole truth."[215]

It remains to be seen whether any of the committee's proposals will be acted upon. However, in late 2004, parliamentarians raised similar concerns about truthful testimony on the part of a key witness in the sponsorship scandal. At least one Member of Parliament speculated that Parliament might consider exercising its contempt powers.[216]

Committees and the Constitutional Implications of Parliamentary Contempt Powers

An interesting question not addressed by the Standing Committee in its Radwanski report, is the extent to which the parliamentary contempt powers — all stemming from parliamentary privilege — could escape the due process requirements of the *Charter*. As noted elsewhere in this book, *Charter* section 7 requires fundamental justice where life, liberty or securi-

---

212   *Ibid.* at para. 1.5.
213   Whether Parliament has the ability to levy fines as part of its privilege is a contested issue. See discussion in Lee, *The Power of Parliamentary Houses* at 205 *et seq.*
214   Standing Committee on Government Operations and Estimates, *Matters Related to the Review of the Office of the Privacy Commissioner*, Recommendation 1.
215   *Ibid.* at para. 2.24.
216   Canadian Press, "Guité Could Be Jailed if He Lied: MP," *Toronto Star*, 15 Nov. 2004.

ty of the person is at issue. Where these interests are at stake, it may require that the venue in which these matters are decided be sufficiently independent.[217] Section 11, meanwhile, provides certain guarantees to persons charged with an offence, including a "a fair and public hearing by an independent and impartial tribunal."

It seems impossible that Parliament could satisfy these judicial independence-like requirements in sections 7 and 11. By definition, it is not a body insulated from the political branches of government.[218] This raises the question of whether a court would intervene in parliamentary contempt proceedings on *Charter* grounds.

In chapter 2, we noted that courts are loath to review the exercise of a parliamentary privilege once they determine such a privilege exists. This reluctance exists even where *Charter* provisions are in play. Thus, in *New Brunswick Broadcasting Corporation v. Nova Scotia*, at issue was whether a ban by the Nova Scotia legislature on television cameras in the legislative assembly violated the freedom of the press provision in sub-section 2(b) of the *Charter*. A majority of the Supreme Court concluded that the *Charter* did not apply, as the Nova Scotia House of Assembly was exercising its constitutional parliamentary privileges. This majority fissioned into two camps, each applying different reasoning.

Justice McLachlin, writing for a plurality of the Court, noted that "one part of the Constitution cannot be abrogated or diminished by another part of the Constitution."[219] The plurality then held that "if the privilege to expel strangers from the legislative assembly is constitutional, it cannot be abrogated by the *Charter*, even if the *Charter* otherwise applies to the body making the ruling."[220]

Justice Lamer, concurring in the result, arrived at the some result via a different path. He held that a legislature exercising its inherent parliamentary privileges was simply not part of government within the meaning of the section 32 of the *Charter*, and thus was not subject to that instrument's dictates.[221] When the judges supporting either McLachlin or Lamer JJ. were

---

217 *Re Application under S. 83.28 of the Criminal Code*, 2004 SCC 42 at para. 81. See also *Ocean Port Hotel Ltd.*, [2001] 2 S.C.R. 781, acknowledging that, rarely, "tribunals may sometimes attract *Charter* requirements of independence."

218 For a discussion of contempt and the *Charter* rights that might attach to an exercise of this power, see Donald Munn, "Parliamentary Privilege and the *Charter*" (LL.M. thesis, University of Ottawa, 1992).

219 *New Brunswick Broadcasting*, [1993] 1 S.C.R. 319 at 105, *per* L'Heureux-Dubé, Gonthier, McLachlin and Iacobucci JJ.

220 *Ibid.*

221 *Ibid.* at 364–65.

cumulated, a majority of the Court agreed that the exercise of an acknowledged parliamentary privilege was insulated from *Charter* review by the courts.

Whether the Supreme Court would decide the same way were a matter of contempt adjudicated is uncertain. It is hard to imagine that parliamentary privileges — an entirely unwritten and amorphous constitutional principle — are so robust as to render Parliament a *Charter*-free zone when it comes to imposing serious sanctions on individuals, especially given the potential consequences of a contempt ruling.

This concern animated Justice Cory's dissenting views in *New Brunswick Broadcasting*. There, His Lordship speculated that there should be no "question that the *Charter* would apply if, in exercising its jurisdiction with regard to punishment of a member for contempt, the legislative assembly were to sentence that member to life imprisonment without eligibility for parole."[222] In this respect, Justice Cory echoed the reasoning of the Nova Scotia Supreme Court in that same case[223] and of earlier commentary on the relationship between privilege and the *Charter*.[224] As those commentators urge, persuasively, "[i]t would be incongruous if the Houses of Parliament could ignore the *Charter* in circumstances where their non-legislative actions violate fundamental values protected by the *Charter*."[225]

3. Officers of Parliament

As the discussion in this chapter suggests, ministerial responsibility to Parliament comes in all shapes and sizes, from the blunt instrument of confidence votes to the sweeping reporting requirements of government departments and agencies. What also appears clear is that Parliament is hard-pressed to police effectively the activities of a vast public administration. As Professor Savoie has argued, "Parliament is no match for the gov-

---

222 *Ibid.* at 401. In fact, it seems unlikely Parliament has the power to commit someone to jail for life via its contempt powers. See Maingot, *Parliamentary Privilege in Canada* at 208, noting that committal to imprisonment will last the duration of a session of Parliament, subject to being renewed, and that someone incarcerated after a dissolution or prorogation of Parliament could seek a writ of *habeas corpus* from the courts.

223 (1991) 80 D.L.R. (4th) 11 at 19, noting that the *Charter* "would apply, for example, to the penal sanctions which may be imposed on a person found guilty of contempt of Parliament."

224 R. Tasse, "Application of the *Canadian Charter of Rights and Freedoms*," in Beaudoin and Ratushny, eds., *The Canadian Charter of Rights and Freedoms*, 2d ed. (Toronto: Carswell, 1989) at 71–72 ("[the *Charter*] would apply, for example, to the penal sanctions which may be imposed on a person found guilty of contempt of Parliament").

225 *Ibid.*

ernment."[226] With all the goodwill in the world, a handful of parliamentarians, charged with a busy legislative task, cannot possibly monitor the minutiae of government administration.

A partial solution is to empower agents — or officers — of Parliament to do just that: probe the inner secrets of the public administration of Canada. As discussed in chapter 4, Parliament has created seven officer of Parliament positions. These officers are essentially executive arms of the legislative branch. A shared and unique attribute of officers is their obligation to report directly to Parliament, rather than to a minister.

a) Parliamentary Reporting Function

Parliamentarians have singled out this reporting function as an important mechanism for rendering the executive accountable to Parliament. Three officers perform a reporting function closely tied in whole or in part to the workings of the legislative branch itself: the ethics commissioner, the senate ethics officer and the chief electoral officer. The reporting powers of these officers are outlined in chapters 3 and 7. The other four officers — the Auditor General, the information commissioner, the privy commissioner and the official languages commissioner — focus their attention on the executive branch. Their parliamentary reporting obligations are detailed in Table 6.5.

Table 6.5   Reporting Functions for Officers of Parliament

Officer	Reporting Function
Auditor General[227]	• The Auditor General submits an annual report (and up to three other reports on the functioning of his or her office) to the Speaker of the House of Commons which is then laid before the Commons; • The Auditor General may make special reports to the House of Commons on, for instance, any matter of pressing importance or urgency that, in the opinion of the Auditor General, should not be deferred until the presentation of the next annual report.
Information Commissioner[228]	• Within three months after the termination of each financial year, the information commissioner submits an annual report to Parliament on the activities of the office during that financial year; • The information commissioner may, at any time, make a special report to Parliament referring to and commenting on any matter within the scope of the powers, duties and functions of the commissioner where, in the opinion of the commissioner, the matter is of such urgency or importance that a report thereon should not be deferred until the time provided for transmission of the next annual report of the commissioner;

226 Savoie, *Breaking the Bargain* at 232.
227 *Auditor General Act*, R.S.C. 1985, c. A-17, ss. 7 and 8.
228 *Access to Information Act*, R.S.C. 1985, c.A-1, s. 54.

Officer	Reporting Function
	• In both instances, reports are transmitted to the Speakers of the senate and Commons, and from there to the respective houses of Parliament.
Privacy Commissioner[229]	• Same reporting functions as the information commissioner
Official Languages Commissioner[230]	• Within such time as is reasonably practicable after the termination of each year, the commissioner prepares and submits to Parliament a report relating to the conduct of his or her office and the discharge of her or his duties under this Act during the preceding year including his or her recommendations, if any, for proposed changes to the Act that the commissioner deems necessary or desirable; • The commissioner may, at any time, make a special report to Parliament referring to and commenting on any matter within the scope of the powers, duties and functions of the commissioner where, in the opinion of the commissioner, the matter is of such urgency or importance that a report thereon should not be deferred until the next annual report; • In both instances, reports are transmitted to the Speakers of the senate and Commons, and from there to the respective houses of Parliament; • The commissioner may also lodge a report with Parliament where the Governor-in-Council fails to respond in a reasonable time to a report on an investigation conducted by the commissioner.

b) Office of the Auditor General

The specific functions of the information and privacy commissioners are discussed in chapter 9. Here, we examine the role of the Auditor General in enhancing Parliament's capacity to hold the executive accountable on financial matters.

Functions of the Auditor General

Pursuant to the *Auditor General Act*, the Auditor General is "the auditor of the accounts of Canada, including those relating to the Consolidated Revenue Fund."[231] The Auditor General is also charged with reviewing the financial statements in the Public Accounts of Parliament, the government's annual financial statement.[232] The Auditor General also appoints an official known as the commissioner of sustainable development to "to provide sustainable development monitoring and reporting on the progress"

229　*Privacy Act*, R.S.C. 1985, c.P-21, ss. 38–40.
230　*Official Languages Act*, R.S.C. 1985, c. 31 (4th Supp.), ss. 65, 67–69.
231　*Auditor General Act*, s. 5.
232　*Ibid.*, s. 6.

of certain sorts of government departments "towards sustainable development" and report annually to Parliament on these matters.[233]

For his or her part, the Auditor General tables an annual report in Parliament, which is then taken up by the Standing Committee on Public Accounts in the Commons.[234] The annual reports are to include reference to any case the Auditor General observes in which

(a) accounts have not been faithfully and properly maintained or public money has not been fully accounted for or paid, where so required by law, into the Consolidated Revenue Fund;

(b) essential records have not been maintained or the rules and procedures applied have been insufficient to safeguard and control public property, to secure an effective check on the assessment, collection and proper allocation of the revenue and to ensure that expenditures have been made only as authorized;

(c) money has been expended other than for purposes for which it was appropriated by Parliament;

(d) money has been expended without due regard to economy or efficiency;

(e) satisfactory procedures have not been established to measure and report the effectiveness of programs, where such procedures could appropriately and reasonably be implemented; or

(f) money has been expended without due regard to the environmental effects of those expenditures in the context of sustainable development.[235]

The Auditor General also apparently contacts other parliamentary Standing Committees where portions of her report touch on their mandates, and these committees then may examine relevant portions of the report and invite officials of the Auditor General's office to appear before them.

Beyond annual reports, since 1994, the Auditor General may table additional reports "on any matter of pressing importance or urgency that, in the opinion of the Auditor General, should not be deferred until the presentation" of the next annual report.[236] He or she may also make up to three reports per year on the work of his or her office and on whether, in

---

233 *Ibid*, ss. 5.1, 21.1 and 23.
234 Commons *Standing Orders*, Order 108.
235 *Auditor General Act*, s. 7.
236 *Ibid.*, s. 8.

carrying on the work of this office, he or she received all the information and explanations from the government required.[237]

On this last issue, the *Auditor General Act* indicates that the "Auditor General is entitled to free access at all convenient times to information that relates to the fulfillment" of his or her responsibilities and he or she "is also entitled to require and receive from members of the public service of Canada such information, reports and explanations as he deems necessary for that purpose," except where this authority is expressly excluded in another statute.[238] However, where the government refuses the Auditor General access to this information, he or she has no recourse to the courts. Instead, the Supreme Court has held that his or her only remedy is to bring the matter to the attention of Parliament.[239]

The Auditor General as an Arm of Parliament

The Supreme Court's reasoning reflects the fact that the "Auditor General is the political servant of Parliament who carries out Parliament's function on its behalf."[240] In the Court's words: the "Auditor General is acting on Parliament's behalf carrying out a quintessentially parliamentary function, namely, oversight of executive spending pursuant to parliamentary appropriations. Where the exercise of this auditing function involves the Auditor General in a dispute with the Crown, this is in essence a dispute between the legislative and executive branches of the federal government."[241] In these circumstances, the sole remedy anticipated by the Act is a report to Parliament. The political dispute is simply not justiciable in court.

This reasoning clearly envisages the Auditor General as a creature of Parliament. This vision is reflected in the Act itself, which makes clear that the Auditor General's first loyalty is to his or her reporting functions to Parliament. The Governor-in-Council may ask the Auditor General to "inquire into and report on any matter relating to the financial affairs of Canada or to public property or inquire into and report on any person or organization that has received financial aid from the Government of Canada or in respect of which financial aid from the Government of Canada is sought."

237   *Ibid.*, s. 7.
238   *Ibid.*, s. 13. This language is modified slightly by the *Public Service Modernization Act, 2003*, c. 22, s. 90 (not in force at the time of this writing), which replaces "public service of Canada" with "federal public administration."
239   *Canada (Auditor General) v. Canada (Minister of Energy, Mines and Resources)*, [1989] 2 S.C.R. 49.
240   *Ibid.* at 89.
241   *Ibid.* at 103.

However, the Auditor General may undertake this inquiry only if in her or his opinion "such an assignment does not interfere" with his or her "primary responsibilities."[242]

C. CONCLUSION

In sum, Parliament has a central (theoretical) role in holding the ministry accountable, and through the ministry, the broader public administration of Canada. In practice, however, the only truly potent legal powers Parliament possesses to drive home ministerial accountability are no confidence motions (bringing down a government) or Parliament's contempt powers (punishing officials for recalcitrance in responding to Parliament at the possible cost of attracting *Charter* scrutiny). Both of these are expensive and unwieldy devices, used in a vanishingly small number of cases.

Alternatively, Parliament may legislate some responsibility standards, thus potentially placing some enforcement powers in the hand of the courts or broaden its reach by creating statutory "officers" empowered to probe the workings of executive government and report directly to it.

Certainly, Parliament's control over purse strings is real. Because they must ultimately result in legislation, the ways and means and supply processes financing the executive branch are vulnerable to parliamentary oversight. However, in practice, a much over-stretched Commons has been less vigorous in policing the federal treasury than might be hoped. Indeed, Parliament's resource constraints are a constant hobble on its responsible government function, writ large.

Meanwhile, the much ballyhooed concept of "individual" ministerial responsibility is a largely nominal phenomenon, at least as measured by ministerial resignations for ineptitude. Likewise, parliamentarians have a broad capacity to ask ministers for information, and a limited ability to insist on receiving it. Again, only where they impose reporting requirements by statute or are prepared to exercise their contempt powers does Parliament possess a legal "big stick."

All told, therefore, responsible government exists, but it is only enforceable through no confidence, contempt powers and Parliament's legislative prerogatives — blunt instruments all. Responsible government is not truly a phenomenon guaranteed by the everyday, workaday rules of Parliament.

---

242 *Auditor General Act*, s. 11.

7

Democracy, Ethics and Governance in the Public Interest

So far, this book has focused largely on the "procedural" aspects of democratic accountability: mechanisms for rendering elected and unelected officials democratically accountable, ultimately to an electorate. In this chapter, we shift our focus. The Canadian system accepts that good governance in a modern democracy depends not only on procedure, but also on adherence to certain substantive standards of behaviour, falling under the umbrella of "ethics." If electoral politics and responsible government are the process by which officials are held democratically accountable in a democracy, ethical rules answer the question "democratically accountable for what?" The answer is honesty and integrity, producing governance in the public (rather than private) interest.

Ethics standards for Canadian public officials are contained in a perplexing variety of sources, including the *Parliament of Canada Act,* the *Criminal Code,* a *Conflict of Interest and Post-Employment Code for Public Office Holders,* the Standing Orders of the House of Commons and senate, the *Values and Ethics Code for the Public Service,* Administrative Orders and Directives of National Defence Canada, the Canadian Judicial Council's *Ethical Principles for Judges,* and common law sources. Each of these sources of ethics rules, and their interplay, is discussed in this chapter.

A. CORE PRINCIPLES OF CANADIAN ETHICS RULES

1. Regulating the Private Interest

Impartiality is a key principle featured in ethics rules; that is, acting in the public interest, without a predisposition coloured by personal interests. Reconciling the notion of impartiality with a political system that is explicitly partisan can be difficult. However, in the Canadian system, it is accepted (for at least political actors) that allowing party policy to influence a decision is not alone a conflict of interest. Instead, ethics rules are designed to guard against the manipulation of public powers in pursuit of the private interest of the decision-maker.

Ethics rules take an expansive view of the "private" interest. A common thread running through these rules is that public officials must act not only to avoid real conflicts of interest, but also *apparent* or *potential* conflicts of interest.

In the late 1980s, a judicial inquiry was appointed by the Governor-in-Council to investigate allegations of conflict of interest in relation to Cabinet Minister Sinclair Stevens. The 1987 inquiry report defined a *real* conflict of interest as a "situation in which a minister of the Crown has knowledge of a private economic interest that is sufficient to influence the exercise of his or her public duties and responsibilities." A *potential* conflict of interest was defined as "a situation in which the existence of some private economic interest could influence the exercise of his or her public duties or responsibilities ... provided that he or she has not yet exercised such duty or responsibility." Finally, an *apparent* conflict of interest "exists when there is a *reasonable apprehension*, which reasonably well-informed persons could properly have, that a conflict of interest exists." This situation remains an apparent conflict of interest even if there is, in fact, neither a potential nor real conflict.[1]

The Stevens inquiry dealt with a minister's potential economic interests. However, private interests giving rise to a real, potential or apparent conflict of interest may extend beyond economic interest in other instances. Noneconomic private interests that might constitute a conflict

---

[1]   *Commission of Inquiry into the Facts of Allegations of Conflict of Interest Concerning the Honourable Sinclair M. Stevens* (1987) [emphasis added]. In December 2004, the Federal Court held that the Stevens inquiry, in fact, stepped outside its jurisdiction in concocting these definitions of real and apparent conflict of interest. It also held that the absence of an existing definition of conflict of interest in the various ethics codes governing Stevens constituted a failure of notice as to the standard of behaviour to be met, violating procedural fairness. Given these holdings, the government should move promptly to adopt explicitly a definition of conflict of interest in the ethics codes discussed in this chapter. *Stevens v. Canada (Attorney General)* 2004 FC 1746.

include acceptance of an award or honour from a person with a vested interest in some power exercised by the public official, an action by an entity that benefits the official's family member, or, in certain cases, opportunities provided by an entity to the official that allow him or her to gain visibility with his or her constituents.

As a final introductory point, it should be noted that Canada's ethics rules distinguish between matters that are of general (although arguably still "private") interest to a public official, versus those that constitute a more specific interest. Ethics rules generally permit an official to gain from a change in government policy in a general way. For instance, the official, like other Canadians, may be affected by a tax change that benefits the official as a homeowner. Ethics rules are much more preoccupied with circumstances in which the official acts out of his or her *specific* interest; for example, the awarding of a contract to a company that he or she owns.

2. Ethics and the Allure of Public Service

Some observers suggest that stringent ethics rules may discourage people of merit from seeking public office.[2] Underlying this argument is an implicit assumption that "merit" is defined primarily in terms of success in business, since it is most often private business interests that are at the centre of public official conflict of interest issues. Yet merit to hold public office comes in many different flavours, not just in the form of material achievements in the business world.

Further, there is no empirical basis for the complaint that ethics rules actually deter business candidates. Those from the senior ranks of business are already greatly overrepresented in Parliament, and this proportion has been steadily rising over the past several decades.[3] Moreover, there is

---

2   In 2003, responding to demands that he divest from his shipping company Canada Steamship Lines, Paul Martin declared, "I do not think it is advisable to discourage entrepreneurs from making a contribution to public life." This sentiment was echoed by a number of commentators, as well as the then-ethics counsellor. Newspaper columnists warned that if Martin was forced to divest "only those who have failed to make it in the real world need apply for the top political job in the land." John Ibbitson, "Martin Should Stick to His Guns — and Ships," *Globe and Mail*, 27 Feb. 2003, A3. See discussion in A. Freeman, "Don't Become Rt. Hon. Member from CSL," *The Hill Times*, 10 March 2003.

3   In the 37th Parliament, fully one-quarter of MPs were from the senior ranks of business, more than from any other occupation, and nearly twice that number came from the legal profession. This number has been steadily increasing: in the 1950s, just 4 percent came from senior management; in the 1970s, it was 16 percent; in the 1980s, it was 22 percent. See A. Freeman, "Don't Become Rt. Hon. Member from CSL."

simply no evidence that stringent ethics requirements dissuade such people from entering politics. The United States, for instance, has the strictest ethics standards for senior officials, but still has a large portion of the executive drawn from the business sector.[4]

That being said, one body where a *lack* of ethics rules has not deterred membership is the senate. Legislation to establish a senate ethics officer passed in early 2004, but even a year later, had not come into force. Strangely, in late February 2005, the senate had appointed an officer, but the ethics code he was to enforce had still not been passed. A draft code, one of many over the past three decades, had been working its way through the senate for nearly two years, but despite repeated promises and deadlines, it had not been finalized. As we note later, the potential for conflicts of interest is significant among senators, many of whom sit on corporate boards of directors.[5]

B. LEGAL STANDARDS

Basic ethical standards for public officials and politicians are incorporated into Canada's criminal and civil law.

1. *Criminal Code* Provisions

The most potent ethics rules for public officials are found in criminal law. For instance, the *Criminal Code* prohibits the actual or attempted bribing of "members of Parliament" or judges, imposing penalties of up to fourteen years imprisonment upon conviction for both the briber and the recipient.[6]

Other provisions apply to "officials," a term defined broadly to include all those who hold a government office or who are appointed to "discharge a public duty."[7] The *Criminal Code* makes fraud or "breach of trust" commit-

---

4   For example, forty-one members of the George W. Bush Administration had ties to the oil industry before entering government, including the president himself, Vice-President Dick Cheney and National Security Advisor Condoleezza Rice, who is a former Chevron director. See A. Freeman, "Don't Become Rt. Hon. Member from CSL."

5   Polls show Canadians are offended by senators having these directorships. A study published in 1998 showed that 55 percent of Canadians felt it was totally or somewhat unacceptable for senators to sit on corporate boards. Only 7 percent found it totally acceptable. The positions of both senator and director, the study found, are "tainted by suspicion that they offer big money for little actual work." A. Freeman, "Welcome to the Chrétien Senate," *The Hill Times*, 22 April 2002.

6   *Criminal Code*, R.S.C. 1985, c. C-46, s. 119. Interestingly, the reference to "members of Parliament" suggests that this section does not apply to senators.

7   *Ibid.*, s. 118.

ted in connection with an official's duties a crime with a maximum punishment of five years imprisonment.[8] Likewise, the selling or purchasing of government offices is punishable by imprisonment for up to five years.[9]

The *Criminal Code* also makes so-called influence peddling by public officials a crime attracting a penalty of up to five years imprisonment. Put simply, influence peddling is the selling, or offering to sell influence with the government for a fee. The *Criminal Code* provision applies to anyone who makes (and any official who accepts) an offer to sell influence, whether or not the official actually has the power to influence a government decision.[10]

Senator Michel Cogger was convicted under this section in 1998. Between 1986 and 1988, Senator Cogger allegedly accepted $212,000 in payments from a Montreal businessman in exchange for attempting to obtain $45 million in government subsidies. Mr. Cogger was later discharged of the offence in sentencing by the Quebec Court of Appeal, which ruled that the accused's reputation had been sullied out of all proportion to the moral turpitude of the offence.[11] This discharge followed a prolonged legal battle, including a bout at the Supreme Court of Canada.

The Supreme Court, in dealing with the case, stated that the purpose of the influence peddling section of the *Criminal Code* "is to prevent government officials from taking benefits from a third party in exchange for conducting some form of business on that party's behalf with government." It does not matter "whether in conducting this business the official purports to act in another capacity."[12] Moreover, a "corrupt" state of mind is not a required element of the crime. As the Court explained,

> [w]hat is required is that the accused intentionally commit the prohibited act with a knowledge of the circumstances which are necessary elements of the offence. Thus, to be guilty of an offence under this section, the accused must know that he or she is an official; he or she must intentionally demand or accept a loan, reward, advantage or benefit of any kind for himself, herself or another person; and the accused must know that the reward is in consideration for cooperation, assistance or exercise of influence in connection with the transaction of business with or relating to the government.[13]

---

8   *Ibid.*, s. 122.
9   *Ibid.*, ss. 124 and 125.
10   *Ibid.*, s. 121.
11   *R. v. Cogger*, [2001] J.Q. no 2262 (C.A.).
12   *R. v. Cogger*, [1997] 2 S.C.R. 845 at para. 22.
13   *Ibid.* at para. 24.

It was irrelevant to the adjudication of guilt under the influence peddling provision whether the business had been conducted clandestinely or not.[14]

2. *Parliament of Canada Act* Provisions

The *Parliament of Canada Act* also has criminal provisions applying to both senators and MPs. These measures prohibit senators and MPs receiving, or agreeing to receive, any payment to influence proceedings of Parliament.[15] Penalties for violating these sections include fines and, for MPs, disqualification from the House of Commons or from the public service for five years.[16] The penalty of disqualification does not exist for senators, who may only be fined for violations.[17] It may be, however, that conviction for a criminal offence of this nature would mandate a vacancy under section 31 of the *Constitution Act, 1867*, a matter discussed in chapter 4. Persons who seek to influence parliamentarians in violation of the Act also commit a criminal office, triggering relatively modest penalties upon conviction.[18]

The Act contains other basic conflict of interest prohibitions. For example, a senator may not "directly or indirectly, knowingly and wilfully be a party to or be concerned in any contract under which the public money of Canada is to be paid." Indeed, any citizen can sue a senator who is a party to a contract paid for through government funds. If the senator is found guilty, a modest fine can be extracted from the senator and awarded to the citizen who launched the suit.[19] This section has been used very rarely.[20]

Certain exceptions are carved out of this conflict rule. For instance, the senator may be a "shareholder in any corporation having a contract or agreement with the Government of Canada, except any company that undertakes a contract for the building of any public work."[21] This may provide a loophole that allows senators to incorporate a separate entity to engage in a nonpublic works contract.

---

14 *Ibid.* at para. 31.

15 *Parliament of Canada Act*, R.S.C. 1985, c. P-1, ss. 16 and 41.

16 *Ibid.*, s. 41. The *Canada Elections Act* S.C. 2000, c. 9, s. 502, also imposes a disqualification penalty to persons who engage in electoral fraud.

17 *Parliament of Canada Act*, s. 16 provides for fines of between $1,000 and $4,000 for those guilty of this offence.

18 *Ibid.*, ss. 16 and 41; a person found guilty of attempting to influence the parliamentarian is "liable to imprisonment for a term not exceeding one year and to a fine of not less than five hundred dollars and not more than two thousand dollars."

19 *Ibid.*, s. 14.

20 Research for this book did not reveal any instance of a successful conviction under this section, although there have been attempts by citizens to obtain a guilty ruling: *Kelly v. O'Brien*, [1943] 1 D.L.R. 725 (Ont. C.A.).

A person is not eligible to be an MP, meanwhile, who accepts or holds any paid office in the Government of Canada, or is any "sheriff, registrar of deeds, clerk of the peace or county crown attorney in any of the provinces."[22] Exceptions to this rule are made for members of the armed forces and, of course, privy councillors (and thus, ministers) and parliamentary secretaries.[23]

In addition, MPs may not enjoy or engage in contracts with the government.[24] Indeed, an MP's seat is declared vacant and his or her election annulled if they take up a post, contract or commercial transaction barred by the Act.[25] If they continue sitting as an MP, they are subject to a daily fine, one that can be recovered by any citizen from the MP in court.[26]

As with senators, among the exceptions to these provision is a section allowing MPs to be "a shareholder of a company doing business with the government, except for companies undertaking a public works project.[27] Again, this may allow MPs to incorporate a separate entity to engage in a nonpublic works contract, although in the case of MPs this move would likely run afoul of the MP Ethics Code (see later in this chapter).

3. Civil Law Standards

Often overlooked in discussions of ethics and public officials are common law standards for behaviour, not least a tort resuscitated recently by the Supreme Court of Canada in *Odhavji Estate v. Woodhouse*:[28] malfeasance of public office.

Under this common law cause of action, a public official will be civilly liable where he or she, first, "engaged in deliberate and unlawful conduct in his or her capacity as a public officer" and, second, was "aware both that

21   *Parliament of Canada Act*, subs. 14(4).

22   *Ibid.*, s. 32.

23   *Ibid.*, s. 33.

24   *Ibid.*, s. 34.

25   *Ibid.*, s. 35.

26   *Ibid.*, s. 36.

27   These other exceptions include: cases where completion of a contract falls to the MP by reason of circumstances such as marriage or executor (this exception only covers the first year after the contract devolved to the MP); acting as a contractor for the loan of money or securities to the government after public competition; and acting as a contractor purchasing "public stock or debentures of Canada, e.g., Canada Savings Bonds, on terms common to all persons." *Parliament of Canada Act*, s. 40. It should be noted that in certain cases involving these exemptions, the MP may still be found in violation of the MP Code.

28   [2003] 3 S.C.R. 263.

his or her conduct was unlawful and that it was likely to harm the plaintiff."[29] In addition, "the plaintiff must prove that the tortious conduct was the legal cause of his or her injuries, and that the injuries suffered are compensable in tort law."[30] In the Supreme Court's words, "the underlying purpose of the tort is to protect each citizen's reasonable expectation that a public officer will not intentionally injure a member of the public through deliberate and unlawful conduct in the exercise of public functions."[31]

C. ETHICAL CODES OF CONDUCT FOR THE MINISTRY AND PARLIAMENTARIANS

Beyond these basic criminal and civil law standards, most of the ethical standards applied to Canada's federal officials stem from ethical codes of conduct anticipated by law and in parliamentary procedure, but not formally found in Canada's statute books. The key officials charged with overseeing these codes are the ethics commissioner and the senate ethics officer. In the section that follows we outline the role of these officials and then look in detail at the provisions contained in ethical codes of conduct applicable to both elected and senior unelected officials.

1.   Ethics Commissioner and Senate Ethics Officer

a) General Functions
Bill C-4, amending the *Parliament of Canada Act*, established the new posts of ethics commissioner and senate ethics officer in 2004.[32] The ethics commissioner replaced the "ethics counsellor" post. The latter office had been widely derided for its lack of independence from the prime minister, who appointed and directed the work of the ethics counsellor in overseeing the *Conflict of Interest and Post-Employment Code for Public Office Holders* (Public Office Holders Code). As discussed in greater detail later, this code covers ministers and their political staff, parliamentary secretaries, and many Governor-in-Council appointees. Under the new Act, the ethics commissioner's authority includes oversight of this Public Office Holders Code. However, he or she also has responsibilities under the *Conflict of Interest Code for Members of the House of Commons* (MP Code), a code that applies to

---

29   *Ibid.* at paras. 23 and 32.
30   *Ibid.* at para. 32.
31   *Ibid.* at para. 30.
32   *An Act to amend the Parliament of Canada Act (Ethics Commissioner and Senate Ethics Officer) and other Acts in consequence*, S.C. 2004, c. 7.

all Members of Parliament.[33] Finally, the ethics commissioner is also responsible for providing confidential advice to "public office holders" on the application of ethical rules, principles and obligations, and for advising the prime minister on these rules, and ethics issues in general.[34]

For his or her part, the senate ethics officer will administer the not-yet-established senate ethics code.[35] In the absence of this code, fewer ethics rules exist for senators than for MPs. Under the rules of the senate, a senator may not sit on a committee dealing with an issue in which he or she has a pecuniary interest "not held in common with the rest of the Canadian subjects of the Crown."[36] A senate committee "may order its members to disclose the existence of their private financial interests, whether held directly or indirectly" on a particular matter being dealt with by that committee,[37] but this power is purely discretionary and such orders are rare.

b)   Independence

Several provisions in the *Parliament of Canada Act* ensure that both the House and senate ethics positions enjoy stature and independence. As discussed in chapter 4, the senate ethics officer is appointed by the Governor-in-Council, after consultation with the leaders of each recognized party in the senate and a majority vote in that chamber.[38] The renewable term of the position is seven years, and the Governor-in-Council may remove the officer only for cause on address of the senate.[39]

The ethics commissioner, for his or her part, is appointed by the Governor-in-Council, after consultation with the leaders of each recognized party in the House and a majority Commons vote, for a renewable term of five years. The Governor-in-Council may remove the commissioner only for cause on address of the House of Commons.[40]

Meanwhile, like other officers of Parliament, the posts maintain the rank of a deputy minister,[41] and remuneration and expenses are provided for by statute.[42] Each also enjoys the privileges and immunities of Parliament in carrying out their (at least parliamentary) duties.[43] For all of these

---

33   House of Commons, *Standing Orders*, Appendix 2.
34   *Parliament of Canada Act*, s. 72.07.
35   *Ibid.*, s. 20.5 (not in force by early 2005).
36   *Rules of the Senate*, Rule 94(1) (Feb. 2004).
37   *Rules of the Senate*, Rule 94(3).
38   *Parliament of Canada Act*, s. 20.1 (not in force).
39   *Ibid.*, s. 20.2 (not in force).
40   *Ibid.*, subs. 72.02(1).
41   *Ibid.*, ss. 20.4 (not in force) and 72.04(1).
42   *Ibid.*, ss. 20.3, 20.4 (not in force), 72.03 and 72.04.
43   *Ibid.*, ss. 20.5 (not in force) and 72.05.

reasons, the new ethics commissioner and senate ethics officer are undoubtedly more independent and secure than was the ethics counsellor, although they could be significantly more so.[44]

That the House and senate positions are separate raises the possibility that there will be conflicting rulings on similar subjects. However, having separate ethics positions was likely a political compromise to placate senators, who wanted the right to be consulted on their ethics officer. In fact, during debate over the bill establishing the ethics officer, senators also wanted the full right to dismiss this official, a discretionary power that would have seriously undermined the position's independence.[45]

Critics maintain the prime weakness in these new posts is the inability of the officers to levy penalties for breaches of ethics rules.[46] Thus, neither the House nor senate ethics officer has any power to sanction those found guilty of ethics violations. Since the Act expressly preserves parliamentary privileges, penalties for violations of either the MP or senate codes likely remain the sole purview of each respective chamber.[47] Sanctions under at least the conflict of interest provisions of the Public Office Holders Code, meanwhile, are the domain of the prime minister.[48]

c) The Ethics Commissioner's Bifurcated Responsibilities

Although both the MP Code and the Public Office Holders Code are overseen by the ethics commissioner, he or she has somewhat different powers depending on which code is being administered.

For instance, the two codes spell out different investigative powers and procedures for the commissioner. First, while only MPs may file a request for an inquiry under the MP Code,[49] under the Public Office Holders Code, either MPs or senators may do so.[50]

---

44 For instance, the advocacy organization Democracy Watch urges: requiring that the ethics post appointments be explicitly approved by opposition parties; giving the officers the power to levy penalties for ethics violations; providing a public right to complain to the officers; and providing the power to protect whistleblowers who complain to the officers. *Democracy Watch*, "Democracy Watch Calls on Senate, and PM, to Strengthen Bill C-4 and Other Measures to Ensure Effective Ethics/Spending Enforcement," press release, 17 Feb. 2004.

45 A. Freeman, "Ethics Bill Bogged Down in Senate," *The Hill Times*, 3 Nov. 2003.

46 See Democracy Watch, "Democracy Watch Calls on Senate, and PM."

47 *Parliament of Canada Act*, subss. 20.5(5) (not in force), and 72.05(5). See also Commons *Standing Orders*, Appendix 2 (the MP Code), s. 28, which anticipates reports of the ethics commissioner being dealt with by the Commons.

48 Public Office Holders Code, s. 23.

49 Commons *Standing Orders*, Appendix 2, s. 27.

50 *Parliament of Canada Act*, s. 72.08.

Second, the ethics commissioner may dismiss a complaint under the MP Code if he or she considers it to be "frivolous or vexatious or ... not made in good faith," or if there are "insufficient grounds to warrant an inquiry."[51] Under the Public Office Holders Code, the commissioner may dismiss a complaint "having regard to all the circumstances of the case."[52] This latter language appears to provide the commissioner with broader discretion to decline to pursue an ethics matter under the Public Office Holders Code.

The ethics commissioner also has considerable powers of subpoena under the Public Office Holders Code that are not available to him or her under the MP Code. This includes an ability to summon witnesses and require them to give oral or written evidence,[53] and other subpoena powers that a judge would have.[54]

In part, differences between the two codes may be justifiable given the differences in the persons covered by the codes themselves. Public office holders, who include ministers and the prime minister, wield far more power and influence than backbench or opposition MPs. More influence translates into greater potential for conflicts of interest, and as a result, many of the provisions in the Public Office Holders Code are more stringent than those in the MP Code. Post-employment provisions, for example, apply to public office holders but not to other MPs.[55]

Although the commissioner has more authority under the Public Office Holders Code than under the MP Code, the practical consequences of a negative ethics finding under the two codes may vary. As overseer of the MP Code, the commissioner reports to the House of Commons. Given the partisan nature of the Commons, it is almost certain that at least some members will use the parliamentary forum to call attention to any infraction reported by the commissioner.

But as overseer of the Public Office Holders Code, the commissioner's significance is less certain. While the 2004 version of this code does not place the commissioner under the "general direction of the Clerk of the Privy Council" as did earlier editions, the commissioner is subordinated to the prime minister, at least with respect to applying penalties. As noted

---

51   Commons *Standing Orders*, Appendix 2, s. 27.

52   *Parliament of Canada Act*, subs. 72.08(3).

53   *Ibid.*, para. 72.1(1)(a).

54   *Ibid.*, subs. 72.1(2).

55   It is worth noting, however, that public servants are also guided by post-employment rules in their code, as discussed below.

above, it is the prime minister who decides whether to respond to an ethical infraction, when advised of its existence by the commissioner.[56] In part, this approach reflects the fact that in the executive branch, the buck stops with the prime minister. However, in order to preclude a scandal tainting the government as a whole, the prime minister may have a strong interest in ignoring a breach identified by the commissioner. Certainly, this was the concern in the previous ethics regime, overseen by the ethics counsellor. This problem may be mitigated somewhat by a *Parliament of Canada Act* provision requiring the commissioner to report annually to Parliament on his or her activities in relation to the Public Office Holders Code.[57] A solid annual report might reveal ethics investigations in which the prime minister failed to act.

We turn now to a detailed examination of the two codes.

2. MP Code

The *Conflict of Interest Code for Members of the House of Commons* came into effect in October 2004 as part of the Commons Standing Orders.[58] As noted, the ethics commissioner oversees the code and reports to Parliament. Meanwhile, the Procedure and House Affairs Committee is responsible for receiving and considering proposed rules for administering the code, although the House must concur with any new rules in order for them to come into effect.[59]

a) General Principles

The code contains both general principles and specific rules to which MPs must adhere. The "principles" section is worth citing in full:

> 2. Given that service in Parliament is a public trust, the House of Commons recognizes and declares that Members are expected
> a.   to serve the public interest and represent constituents to the best of their abilities;
> b.   to fulfill their public duties with honesty and uphold the highest standards so as to avoid real or apparent conflicts of interests, and maintain and enhance public confidence and trust in the integrity of each Member and in the House of Commons;

---

56   Public Office Holders Code, s. 23.
57   *Parliament of Canada Act*, s. 72.13.
58   Commons *Standing Orders*, Appendix 2.
59   *Ibid.*, s. 30.

    c.   to perform their official duties and functions and arrange their private affairs in a manner that bears the closest public scrutiny, an obligation that may not be fully discharged by simply acting within the law;

    d.   to arrange their private affairs so that foreseeable real or apparent conflicts of interest may be prevented from arising, but if such a conflict does arise, to resolve it in a way that protects the public interest; and

    e.   not to accept any gift or benefit connected with their position that might reasonably be seen to compromise their personal judgment or integrity except in accordance with the provisions of this Code.

These principles set a high standard for MPs, one that is also reflected in other ethics codes for public officials. Most notably, it is not sufficient merely to avoid conflicts of interests. Subsections (b), (d) and (e) make it clear that even the *appearance* of a conflict of interest must be avoided. Subsection (c) adds that it is no excuse for an MP to argue that he or she acted within the law. A significantly higher standard of ethics is applied.

b)   Specific Provisions

Roughly speaking, the MP Code rules may be divided into several categories: rules prohibiting the exercise of public powers in response to private interests; rules barring efforts to influence the MP's conduct of public business; rules on the disclosure of MP assets; and rules on enforcement.

Rules Removing Private Interests from the Conduct of Public Business
The code states emphatically that "[w]hen performing parliamentary duties and functions, a Member shall not act in any way to further his or her private interests or those of a member of the Member's family, or to improperly further another person's private interests."[60] Likewise, an MP is not to use his or her position, or information obtained in that position, to further improperly any person's private interests.[61]

Meanwhile, an MP is obliged to disclose publicly any private interest that the MP or his or her family may have in a matter being considered by the MP during House proceedings.[62] Further, he or she must recuse him or herself from debates or votes on such private interests.[63]

According to the code, a "Member is considered to further a person's private interests, including his or her own private interests, when the Member's actions result, directly or indirectly, in any of the following:

60   *Ibid.*, s. 8.
61   *Ibid.*, ss. 9 and 10.
62   *Ibid.*, s. 12.
63   *Ibid.*, s. 13.

(a) an increase in, or the preservation of, the value of the person's assets;

(b) the extinguishment, or reduction in the amount, of the person's liabilities;

(c) the acquisition of a financial interest by the person;

(d) an increase in the person's income from an employer, contract or business;

(e) the person becoming a director or officer in a corporation, association or trade union; or

(f) the person becoming a partner in a partnership.

On the other hand, an MP is not advancing a private interest "if the matter in question (a) is of general application; (b) affects the Member or the other person as one of a broad class of the public; or (c) concerns the remuneration or benefits of the Member as provided under an Act of Parliament."[64]

Rules Barring Efforts to Introduce Private Influences into the Conduct of Public Business
An MP may receive no gift related to his or her position, except compensation authorized by law.[65] There is an additional exception for gifts received "as a normal expression of courtesy or protocol, or within the customary standards of hospitality that normally accompany the Member's position." However, if the value of any such gift from a single source exceeds $500 in value in a twelve-month period, the MP must disclose the nature of the gifts, the source and the circumstances under which they were given.

When an MP receives a gift in the form of travel costs, he or she must publicly disclose the details of the trip, including the destination, sponsor, purpose and value of the trip. Travel costs paid for by the federal government, a parliamentary association, political parties, or by the MP personally do not need to be disclosed.[66]

An MP may own securities in public corporations, "unless the holdings are so significant that the Ethics Commissioner is of the opinion that they are likely to affect the Member's obligations under the Code."[67] In such a case, the member may comply with the code by placing the securities in an arm's-length trust.[68]

---

64 *Ibid.*, s. 3.
65 *Ibid.*, s. 14.
66 *Ibid.*, s. 15.
67 *Ibid.*, s. 17.
68 *Ibid.*, ss. 17 and 19.

Similarly, an MP is prohibited from being a party benefiting from federal government contracts or having an interest in a party to such a contract,[69] unless the contract existed before the MP's election.[70]

Rules on Disclosure of Assets

The code establishes a public registry of MPs' private interests, including those of family members.[71] For both an MP and his or her family members, the "interests" statement identifies assets and liabilities, income, benefits received from government contracts, directorships and partnerships, and "any other information that the ethics commissioner may require."[72]

A summary of the statement that includes "the source and nature, but not the value" of the assets listed is made publicly available.[73] The summary does not include certain expressly excluded assets or liabilities or other asset or liability deemed by the ethics commissioner to be irrelevant to the purposes of the code or otherwise justifiable to exclude.[74]

One of the more controversial aspects of the code is its inclusion of spouses and common law partners under many of the rules, including the registry provision. This inclusion was resisted by MPs during debate over the code in 2003, but largely due to public and media pressure, the Commons recognized that leaving spouses outside of the ethics regime would allow for too large a loophole.

Investigation and Enforcement

The ethics commissioner has the authority to conduct an investigation into an MP's compliance with the code on his or her own initiative.[75] Otherwise, only an MP (or the Commons as a whole) has the right to request that the ethics commissioner conduct an inquiry into the activities of another member.[76] This is an important limitation that excludes citizens and organizations from the accountability regime. As a practical matter, in many cases citizens or organizations will likely seek to convince MPs to file a complaint against fellow members.

69　*Ibid.*, ss. 16 and 18.

70　*Ibid.*, s. 19.

71　*Ibid.*, s. 20.

72　*Ibid.*, s. 21.

73　*Ibid.*, ss. 23 and 24.

74　*Ibid.*, s. 24. These include such things as assets of less than $10,000, real property used as a principal residence or for recreational purposes, "cash on hand" with a financial institution, fixed-value securities, RRSPs that are not self-directed, interests in pension plans or insurance policies, and open-ended mutual funds.

75　Commons *Standing Orders*, Appendix 2, subs. 27(4).

76　*Ibid.*, subss. 27(1) and (3).

As already noted, the ethics commissioner may dismiss a request if he or she considers it to be "frivolous or vexatious or ... not made in good faith," or if there are "insufficient grounds to warrant an inquiry."[77] It is also notable that there is a point at which the commissioner's authority to deal with ethical infractions is exceeded. Specifically, inquiries are put on hold if there are reasonable grounds to believe that the MP has committed an offence under another Act of Parliament, including the *Criminal Code*, in which case the ethics commissioner must refer the matter to the proper authorities.[78]

At least theoretically, the commissioner cannot stymie complaints by simply sitting on them, a common practice of the commissioner's predecessor, the Chrétien-era ethics counsellor. The Federal Court concluded in *Democracy Watch v. Canada (Attorney-General)* that the pre-code ethics counsellor (and thus likely, the new ethics commissioner) must respond to petitions in a reasonably timely fashion, to protect against claims that he or she is biased.[79] That said, as discussed later, recalcitrance (or indeed any act or omission) by the ethics commissioner under the MP Code is likely immune from court review, making enforcement of this principle next to impossible.

During the course of an investigation, the code includes a sort of *sub judice* rule: "Once a request for an inquiry has been made to the Ethics Commissioner, *Members should* respect the process established by this Code and permit it to take place without commenting further on the matter."[80] This approach is consistent with parliamentary conventions governing commentary on judicial or judicial-like proceedings in the chamber of the Commons, matters discussed in chapter 5. The pluralization of "Members" in the code makes it clear that all MPs, even those who did not file a request for an inquiry, are expected to cease commenting on the alleged violation while the investigation takes place.

Like the *sub judice* convention itself, this rule may not be rigidly observed, given the use of the word "should" instead of "shall." However, if

---

77   *Ibid.*, subs. 27(6).

78   *Ibid.*, s. 29.

79   In the judgment, Gibson J. noted, "The pattern of outcomes on petitions or complaints filed with the Ethics Counsellor by Democracy Watch *and the time taken to respond* to those petitions or complaints are, I am satisfied, both relevant to the issue of specific bias" [emphasis added]. It was these considerations that led the judge to conclude, albeit "reluctantly," that "there existed grounds for a reasonable apprehension of bias": *Democracy Watch v. Canada (Attorney-General)*, 2004 FC 969 at paras. 46–48.

80   Commons *Standing Orders*, Appendix 2, subs. 27(5) [emphasis added].

enforced rigorously, this sort of "gag rule" would seem out of place in our adversarial political system in which MPs can be expected to be preoccupied with the ethics of their colleagues. The rule may deprive opposition parties of a forum for holding the government accountable, allowing the government to more effectively dissipate scandals concerning alleged ethics violations as soon as an ethical issue is steered from the chamber of the Commons into the hands of the ethics commissioner. In effect, this provision codifies the government's typical response to scandal: launch an inquiry of one sort or another and subsequently declare that it is inappropriate to comment on pending investigations. For this reason, we are likely to witness governing party members themselves asking the Ethics Commissioner to investigate alleged abuses among that party's own ranks.

Once the inquiry is completed, the ethics commissioner files a public report containing his or her findings with Parliament, and the MP who is the subject of the report has a right to respond to the report in the House of Commons.[81]

3. Public Office Holders Code

First introduced by Brian Mulroney in 1985, the *Conflict of Interest and Post-Employment Code for Public Office Holders* applies to parliamentary secretaries, ministers and their political staff,[82] and some, but not all, Governor-in-Council appointees.[83] Public servants, even those seconded to ministers' staff, are not included under the Public Office Holders Code, but are covered by the Public Service Code (see later in this chapter).

Notably, the Public Office Holders Code rules are subject to change between ministries, as noted by the *Parliament of Canada Act*: "The ethical principles, rules and obligations for public office holders shall be laid

---

81   *Ibid.*, s. 28.

82   Ministerial staff subject to the post-employment measures must be "designated" by their minister before these post-employment dictates will apply. Public Office Holders Code, s. 24.

83   Governor-in-Council appointees not included under the code include: a lieutenant-governor; officers and staff of the senate, House of Commons and Library of Parliament; a person appointed or employed under the *Public Service Employment Act* who is a head of mission within the meaning of subsection 13(1) of the *Department of Foreign Affairs and International Trade Act*; a judge who receives a salary under the *Judges Act*; a military judge within the meaning of subs. 2(1) of the *National Defence Act*; and an officer of the Royal Canadian Mounted Police, not including the commissioner. Public Office Holders Code, s. 4(1). See also *Parliament of Canada Act*, s. 72.06. See note in "Judges Code" later regarding the application of ethics rules to federally appointed judges.

before each House of Parliament within 30 sitting days after the Prime Minister assumes office."[84] The rules outlined below are those in the version of the code introduced in October 2004 and in effect for the thirty-eighth Parliament.

a) Principles

The Public Office Holders Code contains eleven principles, worth reproducing in full:

1. *Ethical Standards*: Public office holders shall act with honesty and uphold the highest ethical standards so that public confidence and trust in the integrity, objectivity and impartiality of government are conserved and enhanced.

2. *Public Scrutiny*: Public office holders have an obligation to perform their official duties and arrange their private affairs in a manner that will bear the closest public scrutiny, an obligation that is not fully discharged by simply acting within the law.

3. *Decision-Making*: Public office holders, in fulfilling their official duties and responsibilities, shall make decisions in the public interest and with regard to the merits of each case.

4. *Private Interests*: Public office holders shall not have private interests, other than those permitted pursuant to the Code, that would be affected particularly or significantly by government actions in which they participate.

5. *Public Interest*: On appointment to office, and thereafter, public office holders shall arrange their private affairs in a manner that will prevent real, potential or apparent conflicts of interest from arising but if such a conflict does arise between the private interests of a public office holder and the official duties and responsibilities of that public office holder, the conflict shall be resolved in favour of the public interest.

6. *Gifts and Benefits*: Public office holders shall not solicit or accept transfers of economic benefit, other than incidental gifts, customary hospitality, or other benefits of nominal value, unless the transfer is pursuant to an enforceable contract or property right of the public office holder.

7. *Preferential Treatment*: Public office holders shall not step out of their official roles to assist private entities or persons in their dealings with the government where this would result in preferential treatment to any person.

---

84   *Parliament of Canada Act*, s. 72.062.

8. *Insider Information*: Public office holders shall not knowingly take advantage of, or benefit from, information that is obtained in the course of their official duties and responsibilities and that is not generally available to the public.

9. *Government Property*: Public office holders shall not directly or indirectly use, or allow the use of, government property of any kind, including property leased to the government, for anything other than officially approved activities.

10. *Post-employment*: Public office holders shall not act, after they leave public office, in such a manner as to take improper advantage of their previous office.

11. *Fundraising*: Public office holders are not personally to solicit funds from any person, group, organization or corporation where such fundraising could place public office holders in a position of obligation incompatible with their public duties.[85]

The eleventh principle is new as of 2004, and is in line with political fundraising rules brought into effect at the beginning of that year (see chapter 3).

b)   Compliance Measures

The principles are elaborated on in a series of "compliance measures." These provisions deal with such things as disclosure, divestment, gifts, preferential treatment and post-employment. The code indicates specifically that a public office holder must not take any actions in an attempt to circumvent the compliance rules.[86]

Disclosure or Divestment

Disclosure, and associated divestment rules, are summarized in Table 7.1. Disclosure requirements in the Public Office Holders Code come in two forms: a confidential disclosure and a public disclosure.

Confidential Disclosure of Assets and Potential Conflicts

Each public office holder must make a Confidential Report to the ethics commissioner of all assets, liabilities and actual and anticipated income for a twenty-four-month period beginning twelve months before the appointment.[87] Ministers and parliamentary secretaries must also disclose similar

---

85   Public Office Holders Code, s. 3.
86   *Ibid.*, subs. 7(8).
87   *Ibid.*, s. 9.

information with regard to their families,[88] although information on family members "is to be used by the Ethics Commissioner for the sole purpose of advising the ministers, ministers of state and parliamentary secretaries on their own compliance measures."[89]

The code also requires office holders to disclose confidentially "outside activities" — which include "all involvements in activities of a philanthropic, charitable or non-commercial character and involvements as trustee, executor or under power of attorney" — from two years before they became public office holders. For elected public office holders (that is, ministers or parliamentary secretaries), the outside activities of spouses and dependant children must also be disclosed.[90]

Finally, ministers and parliamentary secretaries must notify the commissioner of all benefits they or their family are entitled to receive in the course of a twelve-month period from a contract with the federal government.[91]

Public Disclosure or Divestment Requirements

As part of his or her public disclosure requirements, the public office holder must certify a summary statement that includes "a list of the matters which the Ethics Commissioner has determined could, as a result of the public office holder's private interests or other reasons the Ethics Commissioner considers relevant, create a conflict of interest." When such matters are at issue in the office holder's duties, he or she must recuse him- or herself (that is, avoid any participation in the matter).[92] A schedule to the code provides some guidance on recusal, although each instance is dealt with on a case-by-case basis.

Meanwhile, public office holders must either divest or publicly disclose in a declaration certain "declarable" assets,[93] listed in Table 7.1. For certain "controlled assets" public disclosure does not suffice. These assets must be divested. Controlled assets are "assets that could be directly or indirectly affected as to value by Government decisions or policy."[94] Divestment can be completed via an arm's-length sale of the asset, making the asset subject to a blind trust or blind management trust arrangement, or through a

---

88   Defined as spouse or common-law partner and dependent children. Public Office Holders Code, subs. 4(1).

89   *Ibid.*, subs. 9(2).

90   *Ibid.*, s. 9.

91   *Ibid.*, subs. 9(2).

92   *Ibid.*, para. 7(2)(b). The ethics commissioner has replaced the ethics counsellor pursuant to note 1 of s. 5 of the code.

93   *Ibid.*, s. 11.

recusal method approved by the ethics commissioner.[95] Finally, certain assets and interests "for the private use of public office holders and their families and assets that are not of a commercial character" are exempt from both public disclosure and divestment requirements.[96]

Table 7.1   Disclosure Provisions of the Public Office Holders Code

Class	Asset
Confidential Disclosure	• All income, assets and liabilities of office holder; elected officials must include similar information on family members; • "Outside activities" from two years before they became an office holder; elected officials must include outside activities of family members.[97]
Public Disclosure (Declarable Assets)	Assets that are not controlled assets, including: • Interests in businesses that do not contract with the government, and do not own or control publicly traded securities, other than incidentally, and whose stocks and shares are not traded publicly (interests in businesses that do contract with the government would require divestment); • Farms under commercial operations; • Real property that is not an exempt asset as described below; • Assets that are beneficially owned, that are not exempt assets as described below, and that are administered at arm's length; • Rental property; • Investments in limited partnerships; • Personal loans, greater than or equal to $10,000 receivable from persons other than the public office holder's relatives; and • Money owed under a mortgage greater than or equal to $10,000.[98]
Mandatory Divestment (Controlled Assets)	Assets that "could be directly or indirectly affected as to value by Government decisions or policy," including • publicly traded securities of corporations and foreign governments, whether held individually or in an investment portfolio account [including stocks bonds, etc.] ...; • self-administered Registered Retirement Savings Plans, self-administered Registered Education Savings Plans, and Registered Retirement Income Funds, except when exclusively composed of exempt assets as described below;

94   Ibid., s. 12.
95   Ibid., at subs. 13(1). Some guidance with regard to recusal and blind trust and blind management arrangements is provided in the remainder of s. 13, as well as in the schedule of the code.
96   Ibid., s. 10.
97   Ibid., s. 9.
98   Ibid., s. 11.

Class	Asset
	• commodities, futures and foreign currencies held or traded for speculative purposes; and • stock options, warrants, rights and similar instruments.[99] Declarable assets not publicly declared.[100]
Exempt Assets and Interests	Assets and interests for the private use of public office holders and their families and assets that are not of a commercial character, including: • Residences, recreational property and farms used or intended for use by public office holders or their families; • Household goods and personal effects; • Works of art, antiques and collectibles; • Automobiles and other personal means of transportation; • Cash and deposits; • Canada savings bonds and other similar investments issued or guaranteed by any level of government in Canada or agencies of those governments; • Registered retirement savings plans and registered education savings plans that are not self-administered or self-directed; • Investments in open-ended mutual funds; • Guaranteed investment certificates and similar financial instruments; • Public sector debt financing not guaranteed by a level of government, such as university and hospital debt financing; • Annuities and life insurance policies; • Pension rights; • Money owed by a previous employer, client or partnership; or • Personal loans receivable from the members of the public office holder's relatives, and personal loans of less than $10,000 receivable from other persons where the public office holder has loaned the moneys receivable; and • Money owed under a mortgage of less than $10,000.[101]

Many of the Public Office Holders Code's disclosure and divestment provisions are comparable to U.S. rules governing the executive branch. However, enforcement of the U.S. rules is perceived as far more rigorous, and interpretations of divestment requirements are far more stringent.

Prohibited Activities

The code also lists activities in which public office holders must not engage. Specifically, a public office holder must not:

---

99 *Ibid.*, s. 12.
100 *Ibid.*, subs. 11(3).
101 *Ibid.*, s. 10.

(a)   engage in employment or the practice of a profession;

(b)   actively manage or operate a business or commercial activity;

(c)   retain or accept directorships or offices in a corporation;

(d)   hold office in a union or professional association;

(e)   serve as a paid consultant;

(f)   be an active partner in a partnership or

(g)   personally solicit funds except for participation in fundraising campaigns sponsored by the federal government and participation in discussions of a strategic nature for other charitable campaigns.[102]

Exceptions may apply to this rule in certain limited circumstances,[103] but are subject to public disclosure.[104]

Gifts

Gift Ban

The code contains a blanket rule for receiving gifts as a public office holder: "Gifts, hospitality or other benefits, including those [allowed and discussed below], that could influence public office holders in their judgment and in the performance of official duties and responsibilities shall be declined."[105]

This rule makes it clear that any gift that *could* influence the public office holder must be declined. A later clause carves out an even more specific requirement: "In the case of ministers of the Crown, ministers of state and parliamentary secretaries, travel on noncommercial chartered or private aircraft for any purpose shall be prohibited other than in exceptional circumstances and may only be accepted with the prior approval of the Ethics Commissioner."[106] This paragraph on air travel seems redundant, given the broader, blanket rule on gifts. Prime Minister Paul Martin originally added the air travel section in December 2003 following revelations that several ministers (including Prime Minister Martin himself) had taken free trips on private aircraft owned by prominent, wealthy Canadians with significant interests in federal government policies.[107] The timing of this change was suspicious in that it implied the correction of an oversight in the existing ethics rules. By adding the specific bar on noncommercial

---

102   *Ibid.*, s. 16.

103   *Ibid.*, s. 17.

104   *Ibid.*, s. 18.

105   *Ibid.*, s. 19.

106   *Ibid.*, subs. 20(2).

107   J. Brown, "Few Simple Answers in Furore over Liberal Cabinet Ties to Irving Family," *Canadian Press*, 1 Nov. 2003.

air travel, the prime minister could make it appear as though no breach of the code had taken place earlier. Put another way, in "clarifying" the rule, the prime minister implicitly suggested that the rule was ambiguous in its prior manifestation; at least not clear enough to tell whether ministers who took the free trips were running afoul of it.

Exceptions

Provided they do not breach the gift rule and its reference to influence over the judgment and performance of public duties, gifts may be accepted if they are:

- within the normal bounds of propriety, a normal expression of courtesy or protocol or within the normal standards of hospitality;
- are not such as to bring suspicion on the public office holder's objectivity and impartiality; and
- would not compromise the integrity of the government.[108]

Invitations to attend events, including sporting events and performing arts, may be accepted if, in addition to the above criteria:

- attendance serves a legitimate business purpose;
- the person or a representative of the organization extending the invitation is in attendance; and
- the value is reasonable and the invitations are not frequent.[109]

Finally, gifts may be accepted if they are received from relatives and close friends, or if they are of reasonable value and received from a government or in connection with an official or public event.[110]

Nonetheless, gifts of a value more than $200, except those from family members or close friends, must still be disclosed in the public registry.[111] If the gift arises out of a government function, and its value is more than $1,000, the gift is placed in the government inventory rather than the official's personal possession.[112]

Avoidance of Preferential Treatment

The code specifies: "A public office holder shall take care to avoid being placed or the appearance of being placed under an obligation to any person

---

108 Public Office Holders Code, para. 20(1)(a).
109 *Ibid.*, para. 20(1)(b).
110 *Ibid.*, subs. 20(3).
111 *Ibid.*, s. 21.
112 *Ibid.*, subs. 20(4). In such a case, the gift would remain in the possession of the department or agency overseeing or employing the public office holder.

or organization that might profit from special consideration on the part of the office holder."[113]

It further provides that preferential treatment shall not be given to people based on the identity of their employers[114] or to relatives or friends.[115] Moreover, "A public office holder shall not use information obtained in his or her position as a public office holder that is not generally available to the public to further his or her private interests or those of his or her relatives or friends, or to improperly further another person's private interests."[116] A public office holder is also prohibited by the code from hiring immediate family members, or permitting the departments or agencies they are responsible for from doing so.[117] In addition, ministers "should not hire or contract with their families, non-dependent children, siblings or parents [and] not permit departments or agencies for which they are responsible, or to which they are assigned to hire or contract with their families, non-dependent children, siblings or parents."[118]

Ministers also should not hire the family members of another minister or "party colleague in Parliament" except through "an impartial administrative process in which the minister ... plays no part."[119] Use of the word "should" instead of "shall" (the word used in most other directive sections of the code) in the ministerial preferential hiring sections suggests the code may take a slightly more lenient approach to these practices than with others it expressly bars.

The preferential treatment rules are perhaps the broadest ranging of the sections contained in the Public Office Holders Code, as they affect many of the day-to-day operations of a minister. The current Ethics Commissioner, and the ethics counsellor who preceded him, have developed elaborations of the code's rules for different scenarios, including for how ministers may interact with Crown corporations.[120]

The ethics counsellor also developed rules governing recusal in the specific case of Prime Minister Paul Martin, who owned the major ship-

---

113 *Ibid.*, subs. 22(1).
114 *Ibid.*, subs. 22(2).
115 *Ibid.*, subs. 22(3).
116 *Ibid.*, subs. 22(4).
117 *Ibid.*, subs. 22(5).
118 *Ibid.*, subs. 22(6).
119 *Ibid.*, subs. 22(7). There is an exception to this rule for appointments to ministerial exempt staff.
120 "Guidelines for Ministers Interacting with Crown Corporations," in *The Ministry and Crown Corporations,* produced by the Ethics Councillor's Office (2002), available at http://strategis.ic.gc.ca/epic/internet/inoec-bce.nsf/en/oe01177e.html.

ping company Canada Steamship Lines before transferring it to his sons. The rules require the prime minister to recuse himself only "where the matter under consideration has a specific and direct link to Canada Steamship Lines." The ethics counsellor clarified that "matters of general impact on Canada Steamship Lines, that is, those which impact a broad base of businesses across the economy, would not necessitate recusal," and gave specific areas requiring recusal, including "shipbuilding; marine transportation policy issues; and fees for the St. Lawrence Seaway."[121]

Despite these determinations, it is unclear whether a true recusal can ever take place when it comes to the prime minister. The guidelines note that the prime minister "may need to refer issues to the Deputy prime minister for consideration from time to time," but the deputy prime minister, as with all governing party MPs, would know all too well who his or her boss is. This matter also raises questions on the issue of divestment, as it is unclear whether the sale of Canada Steamship Lines to the prime minister's sons constituted a sufficiently arm's-length transaction as is required by code.

While the ethics counsellor developed the recusal guidelines, and the divestment was approved by the same official, this predecessor office to the ethics commissioner was found to be institutionally biased by the Federal Court in *Democracy Watch* because of its lack of independence from the prime minister.[122] It remains to be seen whether the new (and more independent) ethics commissioner will revisit the recusal issue.

Post-employment

Sometimes known as "revolving door" provisions, post-employment rules deal with activities undertaken after a public office holder leaves office. They apply to all public office holders, except ministerial staff.[123]

The code's general rule states:

> Public office holders shall not act, after they leave public office, in such a manner as to take improper advantage of their previous public office. Observance of this Part will minimize the possibilities of:
>
> (a) allowing prospects of outside employment to create a real, potential or apparent conflict of interest for public office holders while in public office;

---

121 Office of the Ethics Commissioner, "Recusal Process for the Prime Minister" (12 Dec. 2003), available at http://strategis.ic.gc.ca/epic/internet/inoec-bce.nsf/en/oeo1418e.html.

122 *Democracy Watch*, 2004 F.C. 969 at para. 55.

123 Public Office Holders Code, s. 24. Ministerial staff are exempt unless the minister designates that this part of the code applies.

(b) obtaining preferential treatment or privileged access to government after leaving public office;

(c) taking personal advantage of information obtained in the course of official duties and responsibilities until it has become generally available to the public; and

(d) using public office to unfair advantage in obtaining opportunities for outside employment.[124]

On the issue of steps to be taken prior to departure from office, the code provides that "[p]ublic office holders should not allow themselves to be influenced in the pursuit of their official duties and responsibilities by plans for or offers of outside employment."[125] If, while in office, an office holder accepts an offer of employment, he or she "shall immediately disclose in writing to the Ethics Commissioner as well as to his or her superior, the acceptance of the offer. In such an event, where it is determined by the Ethics Commissioner that the public office holder is engaged in significant official dealings with the future employer, the public office holder shall be assigned to other duties and responsibilities as soon as possible."[126]

Meanwhile, all *"firm offers* of outside employment that could place the public office holder in a position of conflict of interest" must be disclosed to the ethics commissioner.[127] However, the term "firm offers" allows considerable wiggle room for public office holders negotiating a career move to escape this provision.

It is common for public office holders to become lobbyists after leaving office. The code regulates this transformation, as follows:

(1) At no time shall a former public office holder switch sides by acting for or on behalf of any person, commercial entity, association, or union in connection with any specific ongoing proceeding, transaction, negotiation or case to which the Government is a party and where the former public office holder acted for or advised the Government.

(2) Nor shall former public office holders give advice to their clients using information that is *not available to the public* concerning the programs or policies of the departments with which they were employed, or with which they had a direct and substantial relationship during the period of one year immediately prior to the termination of their service in public office.[128]

124 *Ibid.*, s. 25.
125 *Ibid.*, subs. 26(1).
126 *Ibid.*, subs. 26(3).
127 *Ibid.*, subs. 26(2) [emphasis added].
128 *Ibid.*, s. 27 [emphasis added].

Arguably, most information relevant to those seeking to influence government is "available" to the public, but knowing how to access this information is often the purview of a limited number of people outside government. For instance, the code's rules may still allow the lobbyist to assist a client by providing strategies on which people in government the client should approach and how best to approach them. In many instances, advising who in government might be in a position to assist the client is likely information "available to the public," at least in theory.

There is also a limitation period, commonly referred to as a cooling-off period, for certain post-employment activities. For ministers, this period is two years after leaving office. For other public office holders, it is one year. During the cooling-off period, public office holders shall not

> accept services contracts, appointment to a board of directors of, or employment with, an entity with which they had direct and significant official dealings during the period of one year immediately prior to the termination of their service in public office;[129] or

> make representations whether for remuneration or not, for or on behalf of any other person or entity to any department, organization, board, commission or tribunal with which they had direct and significant official dealings during the period of one year immediately prior to the termination of their service in public office.[130]

A former minister is not allowed to make representations to any minister in Cabinet who had been a member of Cabinet with the former minister. In the case of ministers who become backbench MPs, there is an exception allowing for activities that constituents normally ask MPs to carry out.[131] The public office holder may apply to the ethics commissioner to reduce the cooling-off period.[132]

4. When the Public Office Holders Code and the MP Code Apply

Ministers and parliamentary secretaries are public office holders under the Public Office Holders Code. Usually, they are also Members of Parliament. They are subject, therefore, to two ethics regimes, creating a potential juris-

---

129 *Ibid.*, subs. 28(1).
130 *Ibid.*, para. 28(2)(a).
131 *Ibid.*, para. 28(2)(b).
132 *Ibid.*, s. 29. A list of factors relevant in consideration of a reduction in the limitation period is provided in this section.

dictional conundrum: a person may be subject to different ethical regimes depending on the capacity in which they are acting in relation to a given matter.

In this section we ask whether a minister or parliamentary secretary is subject to the MP Code when acting in their ministerial or parliamentary secretary capacity. We then ask whether these officials are subject to the Public Office Holder Code when acting as a parliamentarian.

a) Application of MP Code

By its own terms, the MP Code applies to ministers and parliamentary secretaries.[133] However, the MP Code provides that its provisions apply to MPs "when carrying out the duties and functions of their office as Members of the House."[134] This statement suggests that the MP Code applies only to a minister or a parliamentary secretary acting in the capacity of *parliamentarian.*

This approach greatly limits the reach of the MP Code to ministers and parliamentary secretaries. For instance, when a minister is taking part in a Cabinet discussion, he or she is acting strictly in a nonparliamentary capacity and thus is subject only to the Public Office Holders Code. When voting on the same measure in the Commons, however, the MP Code's provisions would attach.

In practice, this "situational" application of ethics rules may make little difference, given the overlap in content between the provisions in both codes. There are, however, subtle differences in the obligations found in each instrument. For instance, the MP Code deals more directly with how an MP must carry out his or her day-to-day functions. It provides a far-reaching provision, for example, that "a Member shall not act in any way to further his or her private interests or those of a member of the Member's family, or to improperly further another person's private interests."[135] While similar provisions exist in the Public Office Holders Code, they are mostly contained in the "Object" and "Principles" sections, in far more general language.[136] The Public Office Holders Code does contain a section on

---

133 Commons *Standing Orders*, Appendix 2, s. 4 ("The provisions of this Code apply to conflicts of interest of all Members of the House of Commons when carrying out the duties and functions of their office as Members of the House, including Members who are ministers of the Crown or parliamentary secretaries.").

134 *Ibid.*, s. 4.

135 *Ibid.*, s. 8.

136 See, e.g., *ibid.*, subs. 3(3), which requires officials to "make decisions in the public interest and with regard to the merits of each case" or subs. 3(7), which states that officials "shall not use their positions of office to assist private entities or persons where this would result in preferential treatment."

"avoidance of preferential treatment," discussed earlier. It does not include, however, an overarching ban on officials acting to further their private interests, instead containing more specific admonishments. For instance, to serve his or her private interest, a public official may not "*influence* a decision of *another person*" (as opposed simply to exercising his or her own power directly to achieve that private interest).

b) Application of Public Office Holders Code

The inverse issue is whether the Public Office Holders Code applies to ministers acting in their parliamentary capacity as Members of Parliament. There are many instances in which a minister is arguably acting solely in his or her MP role; for example, during votes in the House of Commons, or in pursuing matters on behalf of constituents.

In the days before the MP Code, this question on the reach of the Public Office Holders Code was more than a theoretical issue. In 2000, it came to light that Prime Minister Chrétien had phoned one of his appointees, the president of the Business Development Bank (BDC), regarding a loan application. The loan was reportedly to benefit a Liberal member and close friend of Chrétien's. Chrétien asserted that the Public Office Holders Code did not apply to this situation because he was acting in his role as an MP rather than as a minister.[137]

In fact, there is language in the Public Office Holders Code that could be read as precluding its application to ministers in their parliamentary role: "Ministers of the Crown, ministers of state and parliamentary secretaries are subject to the provisions of this Code *when carrying out the duties and functions of their office* as ministers of the Crown, ministers of state or parliamentary secretaries."[138]

If this provision does narrow the scope of the code, its approach differs markedly from provincial practice. As the Library of Parliament notes, at the provincial level, provincial Ethics Commissioners have repeatedly ruled that ministers "always wear the cloak of ministerial responsibility,"[139] and are therefore always be covered by provincial ministers' ethics rules. These comparative findings carry limited weight at the federal level, at least as a purely legal matter. The only court case interpreting federal ethics rules has held that an inconsistency between federal and provincial rulings on ethics

---

137 S. McCarthy, "Day Accuses Chrétien of Breaking the Law," *Globe and Mail*, 19 Nov. 2000.

138 Public Office Holders Code, subs. 4(2) [emphasis added].

139 Library of Parliament, *Bill C-4: An Act to amend the Parliament of Canada Act (Ethics Commissioner and Senate Ethics Officer) and other Acts in consequence* (Feb. 2004) at 5.

matters is, "in and of itself, insufficient" to warrant a finding of reviewable error where the provincial approach is not followed.[140]

The provincial approach is, however, the only logical solution. As the preceding discussion suggests, it may be that an MP is not a parliamentarian when acting as a minister. This is a conclusion consistent with the view that a minister is a Crown servant. It is not true, however, that when a minister acts in his or her parliamentary role, he or she stops being a minister or performing the "duties and functions of their office." As is clear from our discussion in chapter 6 on ministerial responsibility, a minister's role in "carrying out the duties and functions of their office" includes most (if not all) of his or her parliamentary functions. Even when carrying out activities in the Commons, a minister is repeatedly treated as such in the Standing Orders, which sets out special rules governing ministerial participation in such things as private member's business. For this reason, we believe that the Public Office Holders Code's writ does not stop at the doors of Parliament.

A more difficult question is whether a minister carries out "the duties and functions of their office" while furthering the interests of a constituent. In practical terms, a minister will be treated as a minister when intervening with a government office on behalf of a constituent. When the prime minister phones the president of the BDC, that official will respond differently than if it were a backbench MP calling. Further, from the president's perspective, it is irrelevant whether the call is prompted by the prime minister's constituency case work or by the executive portion of his or her psyche.

At some level, the Martin government appears to recognize this fact. In his December 2003 instructions to ministers, the prime minister provided fairly detailed rules for ministers asked to pursue matters for constituents. First, ministers and their staff are not "to intervene, on behalf of anyone, including constituents, with the *judiciary* concerning any matter before the courts." Likewise, "Ministers and their staff are also expected not to intervene, or appear to intervene, on behalf of anyone, including constituents, with *federal quasi-judicial tribunals* on any matter before them that requires a decision in their quasi-judicial capacity, unless otherwise authorized by law."

Second, when ministers contact "agencies within their own portfolios," they are admonished that "governing statutes give some bodies such as Crown corporations a degree of independence from ministerial direction. ... Ministers need to know both the details of their responsibilities and the limits of their powers for these organizations. They must also understand and respect their arm's length relationship with them."

---

140 *Democracy Watch*, 2004 F.C. 969 at para. 86.

Third, "Cabinet convention precludes a Minister from speaking about or otherwise becoming involved in a colleague's portfolio without first gaining the colleague's approval."[141]

The scenario that the prime ministerial guidelines do not seem to deal with is a minister pursuing a constituency matter within a regular, line department in his or her own cabinet portfolio. In this circumstance, we believe that the minister must be regarded as performing the "duties and functions" of his or her office, and the Public Office Holders Code should apply. The minister's very *entrée* with his or her department (or anyone under his or her ministerial authority), after all, will generally stem from the minister's executive office. For these reasons, we believe a minister performing this sort of constituency function must comport with both the MP Code and the Public Office Holders Code.

This dual application is not precluded by Bill C-4's amendments to the *Parliament of Canada Act*. In its discussion of Bill C-4, enacting amendments to the *Parliament of Canada Act* and creating the ethics commissioner's office, the Library of Parliament suggested that the "role of the Ethics Commissioner is to administer one code or the other, but not both at the same time." On this issue, it is not clear that the Library's conclusions are correct. In partial support of its view, the Library cited a new *Parliament of Canada Act* provision indicating that the Commons may not empower the Ethics Commissioner to administer the Public Office Holders Code.[142] This *Parliament of Canada Act* provision can be read, however, as simply consistent with the view that it is the prime minister, and not the Commons, who assigns the ethics commissioner duties and functions under the Public Office Holders Code. It does not preclude the simultaneous *application* of both the MP Code and the Public Office Holders Code to ministers and parliamentary secretaries.

As noted earlier, it is questionable whether this duplicate application would make a real difference in terms of the substantive ethics rules that will be applied. Whether the Public Office Holders Code applies to ministers in their parliamentary role may, however, have significant consequences in terms of independent oversight. As we discuss next, the Ethics Commissioner is likely not amenable to judicial review for his or her actions (or omissions) in relation to the MP Code. He or she is, however,

---

141 Privy Council Office, *Governing Responsibly: A Guide for Ministers and Ministers of State* (Dec. 2003).

142 Library of Parliament, *Bill C-4: An Act to amend the Parliament of Canada Act* at 6, referring to *Parliament of Canada Act*, subs. 72.05(4).

likely reviewable in terms of action or inaction under the Public Office Holders Code.

5. Standard of Judicial Review for Ethics Matters: MPs, Senators and Public Office Holders

The exact legal weight of the MP and Public Office Holder ethics codes, and many other issues relating to their interpretation, remain unclear. In this section, we address two such issues: first, to what extent are decisions taken by the ethics commissioner (or his or her senate counterpart) amenable to judicial review? Second, are the codes themselves justiciable in court?

a) Judicial Review of Ethics Commissioner Decisions

As the discussion above makes clear, the ethics commissioner wears two hats. He or she has an oversight responsibility in relation to the MP Code. He or she also administers the Public Office Holders Code. The question this section deals with is the extent to which the Ethics Commissioner's decisions in performing these roles are reviewable in court. The answer to this question is likely "not at all" with respect to the MP Code and "likely" in relation to the Public Office Holders Code, although not in Federal Court.

MP Code

Bill C-4's amendments to the *Parliament of Canada Act* creating the ethics commissioner aggressively sought to limit judicial review. First, the Bill amended the *Federal Courts Act*, circumscribing the definition of "federal board, commission or other tribunal" in that statute to exclude expressly "the Senate Ethics Officer or the Ethics Commissioner."[143] Since Federal Court judicial review authority extends only to a "federal board, commission or other tribunal,"[144] this amendment precludes any Federal Court judicial review jurisdiction in relation to these ethics officers.

The natural response of any litigant seeking judicial review of a decision of one of these officials would be to turn to the section 96 provincial superior courts. As discussed in chapter 2, these provincial superior courts likely retain a competence, based on the concept of inherent jurisdiction, to hear reviews of federal officials exercising statutory and at least some

---

143 *Federal Courts Act*, R.S.C. 1985, c. F-7, s. 2.
144 *Ibid.*, s. 18.

prerogative powers.[145] However, progress in this venue in a judicial review of at least the MP (or the anticipated senate) Code would be constrained by a second attribute of Bill C-4.

Specifically, the new *Parliament of Canada Act* veils the ethics commissioner (and his or her senate counterpart) in parliamentary privilege.[146] Thus, in relation to the MP Code, "[t]he duties and functions of the Ethics Commissioner are carried out within the institution of the House of Commons. The Ethics Commissioner enjoys the privileges and immunities of the House of Commons and its members when carrying out those duties and functions."[147] As discussed in chapter 2, where parliamentary privilege exists, the courts have no judicial review role.[148] At best, therefore, court review of the ethics commissioner would focus on whether a decision by the commissioner falls within the ambit of his or her parliamentary responsibilities. If it did, the court would have no further review function.

Public Office Holders Code

Whether a court would review the ethics commissioner's activities in relation the Public Office Holders Code is a muddier question. In the recent *Democracy Watch v. Canada* case, the Federal Court treated the old ethics counsellor as a reviewable federal board, commission or other tribunal.[149] The current ethics commissioner has a largely similar role in relation to the Public Office Holders Code to that of his or her predecessor. However, the ethics commissioner enjoys substantial more protection from judicial review in his or her code functions. As already noted, the ethics commissioner is fully exempted from the definition of a federal board, commission

---

145 See, e.g., *Canada (Human Rights Commission) v. Canadian Liberty Net*, [1998] 1 S.C.R. 626 at 658 ("the doctrine of inherent jurisdiction operates to ensure that, having once analysed the various statutory grants of jurisdiction, there will always be a court which has the power to vindicate a legal right independent of any statutory grant. The court which benefits from the inherent jurisdiction is the court of general jurisdiction, namely, the provincial superior court"); *Black v. Canada (Prime Minister)* (2001), 54 O.R. (3d) 215 at para. 76 (C.A.) ("if Parliament has left a 'gap' in its grant of statutory jurisdiction to the Federal Court, the institutional and constitutional position of provincial superior courts warrants granting them this residual jurisdiction over federal matters").

146 *Parliament of Canada Act*, ss. 20.5 and 72.05(2).

147 *Ibid.*, s. 72.05.

148 See, by analogy, *Tafler v. British Columbia (Commissioner of Conflict of Interest)* (1998), 161 D.L.R. (4th) 511 (B.C.C.A.) where the B.C. commissioner was held to be protected from court review by privilege in circumstances, even where this privilege had not been emphatically extended to the commissioner.

149 *Democracy Watch*, 2004 F.C. 969 at para. 21.

or other tribunal, precluding a repeat of the *Democracy Watch* case in the Federal Court. Further, even if this matter were taken up in the provincial superior courts the scope of the ethics commissioner's parliamentary privileges would be a live issue.

We believe, however, that a court considering this question would confine the ethics commissioner's privileges to instances where he or she is performing his or her MP Code functions. Logically, *parliamentary* privilege cannot extend to the Commissioner's role in overseeing the *executive branch* Public Office Holders Code. Indeed, a close reading of the *Parliament of Canada Act* supports this view. The Act provides that the "[t]he Ethics Commissioner shall perform the duties and functions assigned by the House of Commons for governing the conduct of its members when carrying out the duties and functions of their office as members of that House." It then indicates that the "duties and functions of the Ethics Commissioner are carried out within the institution of the House of Commons" and that privilege attaches when "carrying out those duties and functions."[150] In other words, privilege applies while the commissioner performs his or her MP ethics supervision role. The Commissioner's Public Office Holders Code responsibilities, meanwhile, are detailed in a completely different sequence of sections, in which parliamentary privilege is not invoked.[151]

b)   Legal Status of the Codes

A second legal issue relating to the key government ethics codes is whether they are themselves legal standards justiciable in court, creating a legal duty on Parliament, the government or the ethics commissioner to enforce their dictates.

MP Code

The answer in relation to the MP Code is almost surely "no." The MP Code is no more law than is any other provision in the Standing Orders of the House of Commons. Indeed it is annexed to these Standing Orders, and is defined as part of them.[152] It is, in other words, part of the procedural law of Parliament and thus an expression of parliamentary privilege. The fact that the ethics code is anticipated (albeit obliquely) in the *Parliament of Canada Act* does not somehow convert it into statutory law, not encompassed by privilege. The Act specifically provides that the section anticipat-

---

150   *Parliament of Canada Act*, subs. 72.05(2) [emphasis added].
151   *Ibid.*, s. 72.07 *et seq.*
152   Commons *Standing Orders*, Appendix 2, s. 34.

ing the MP code "shall not be interpreted as limiting in any way the powers, privileges, rights and immunities of the House of Commons or its members."[153] For these reasons, the application (or nonapplication) of the MP Code is likely not justiciable in court.

Public Office Holders Code

The legal status of the Public Office Holders Code is less certain. Several cases have referred to the Public Office Holders Code, and specific provisions that are contained within it, and there has arguably been a judicial trend toward applying a duty of adherence to standards contained in the code. Exploring this point requires an examination of common law "conflict of interest" rules.

Common Law Backdrop

As noted repeatedly in this book, officials exercising power pursuant to a statute or the royal prerogative are subject to judicial review by the courts. Among other things, courts have imposed common law administrative law standards on such persons obliging them to meet basic standards of due process. This "procedural fairness" requires that persons affected by the official's decisions be accorded notice of that decision and an opportunity to be heard. More crucially for this section, procedural fairness also requires an unbiased decision maker.

The test for bias in administrative law is a situational one, depending in large measure on the precise nature of the official's role and the nature of the bias alleged. Where the bias is said to stem from prejudgment — the official has already made up his or her mind — the common law anticipates a variable test. Thus, the more the official acts in a "quasi-judicial" function, the stricter the bias requirements imposed on that person. At this end of the spectrum, the official is expected to act without "reasonable apprehension of bias." This test requires the court to ask: "What would an informed person, viewing the matter realistically and practically — and having thought the matter through — conclude. Would he think that it is more likely than not that [the decision-maker], whether consciously or unconsciously, would not decide fairly."[154]

At the other end of the spectrum, inhabited by officials who perform a more "executive," policy oriented or even political function, the test of bias is more forgiving. Here, a court will only discern impermissible bias where the official has a closed mind, unsusceptible to persuasion.

---

153   *Parliament of Canada Act*, subs. 72.05(5).
154   *Wewaykum Indian Band v. Canada*, [2003] 2 S.C.R. 259 at para. 60.

This approach was exemplified in *Democracy Watch*, in relation to the old ethics counsellor. There, the government had argued that the ethics counsellor "was 'closer to the executive end of the spectrum' [rather than the judicial end], its purpose being to develop and supervise the implementation of particular government policies." As such, the government argued, "the appropriate test for determining bias on the part of the Ethics Counsellor was whether or not he approached the petitions or complaints of Democracy Watch with an open mind rather than whether he demonstrated a reasonable apprehension of bias in arriving at the rulings or decisions under review."[155] However, the Court rejected this approach, instead favouring, "the test for determination of bias, whether specific or institutional, urged on behalf of Democracy Watch given the critical role of the Ethics Commissioner [*sic*] in [among other things] enhancing ... public confidence in the integrity of public office holders and the decision making process in government." The court then applied the reasonable apprehension of bias test.[156]

Where the bias is said to flow, not from prejudgment, but from some *personal interest* on the part of the decision-maker in the subject matter of the decision, the concept of a variable test for bias falls away. Here, the courts are very demanding, irrespective of the function of the official. Where, in the words of the Supreme Court, "such [a personal] interest is found, both at common law and by statute," the official is "disqualified if the interest is so related to the exercise of public duty that a reasonably well-informed person would conclude that the interest might influence the exercise of that duty. This is commonly referred to as a conflict of interest."[157]

Particular note should be taken of the Court's reference to conflict of interest standards existing in both statutes and at common law. Statutory standards are obviously those detailed provisions governing public officials and enacted by a legislative body. The common law standard is more opaque, but has been defined as a circumstances in which "an informed person, viewing the matter realistically and practically and having thought the matter through, [would] think it more likely than not that the public servant, whether consciously or unconsciously, will be influenced in the performance of his official duties by considerations having to do with his private interests."[158]

---

155 *Democracy Watch*, 2004 F.C. 969 at para. 38.
156 *Ibid* at para. 39 and 40.
157 *Old St. Boniface Residents Association Inc. v. Winnipeg (City)*, [1990] 3 S.C.R. 1170 at 1196.
158 *Community Before Cars Coalition v. National Capital Commission*, [1997] F.C.J. No. 1060 at para. 65 (T.D.), citing *Threader v. Canada (Treasury Board)*, [1987] 1 F.C. 41 at 56 (C.A.).

From this discussion, it follows that administrative law imposes a common law "conflict of interest" standard applicable to office holders, irrespective of any separate code of conduct. Failure to comply with this standard may vitiate the decision taken by the official. This conclusion is subject to one caveat, noted in chapter 5: common law procedural fairness has no place where the decision taken by the official is said to be "legislative" in nature.

The question we turn to next, given this backdrop, is how have the courts approached the Public Office Holders Code.

Incidental Application of the Public Office Holders Code

A handful of cases have raised the Public Office Holders Code as an incidental consideration in adjudicating other, more squarely legal issues. In *Drummond v. Canada (Minister of Citizenship and Immigration)*,[159] the Public Office Holders Code was used as a grounds for excluding evidence; specifically an affidavit sworn by an official who had been a member of the Immigration Appeal Division (IAD) two months earlier. The IAD held that, in swearing the affidavit, its former member was in violation of the one-year cooling-off period for former public officials, barring representations to the department with which they previously had had dealings. For this reason, the IAD rejected the affidavit on the grounds of reasonable apprehension of bias and non-compliance with the Public Office Holders Code, even though the general rule was for such a tribunal not to exclude evidence. These grounds for rejecting the evidence were subsequently upheld by the Federal Court.

Another case has approved of the use of the Public Office Holders Code (including its Principles section) as an enforceable term of a contract.[160] Here, the judge held that "[d]ecisions under the conflict of interest provisions for former public office holders are amenable to judicial review,"[161] suggesting that at least the post-employment provisions of the code might be enforceable by a court. However, this position was arguably limited to the context of the case, which dealt specifically with whether a contract could be rescinded on the basis of a breach of the post-employment provisions of the code.

---

159 *Drummond v. Canada (Minister of Citizenship and Immigration)*, [1996] F.C.J. No. 477 (T.D.) .

160 See *LGS Group Inc. v. Canada (Attorney General)*, [1995] F.C.J. No. 1128 at paras. 45–46 (T.D.).

161 *Ibid.* at para. 12.

Direct Application of the Public Office Holders Code

In fact, while it is clear from this case law that the courts may accord some legal significance to the Public Office Holders Code, the issue of whether the provisions themselves (that is, absent their inclusion in a contract) are *enforceable* by a court has yet to be squarely determined. This uncertain status may not matter, in practice.

First, language employed by the Supreme Court suggests that courts should treat the Public Office Holders Code as a vital and necessary element of governance. In *R. v. Hinchey*,[162] the Court interpreted section 121 of the *Criminal Code*, which deals with frauds on the government. In so doing, the Court noted the existence of the Public Office Holders Code and observed that "given the heavy trust and responsibility taken on by the holding of a public office or employ, it is appropriate that government officials are correspondingly held to codes of conduct which, for an ordinary person, would be quite severe."[163]

Second, the procedure followed by the government in employing the code is likely justiciable in court. In *Peet v. Canada*, a public servant brought an application for judicial review to the Federal Court, challenging the fairness of findings by his superior that he was in non-compliance with the public service ethics code as it existed in the early 1990s.[164] The government sought to have the matter dismissed, urging that the code was an internal, administrative guideline and not a law amenable to review by a court. The court disagreed, concluding that the public servant should be allowed to at least litigate the fairness of the procedure by which he had been found in violation of the code. This is a reasonable, even banal conclusion, given classic administrative law doctrines of procedural fairness, one that likely applies equally to decisions taken under the Public Office Holders Code.

Last, compliance with the Public Office Holders Code has been taken by the courts to connote compliance with the common law bias standards for conflict of interest discussed above. In *Community Before Cars Coalition v. National Capital Commission*,[165] the Federal Court concluded that while the code was not truly a statutory instrument, compliance with it constituted adherence to a "statutory" standard on conflict of interest. This conclusion bolstered the court's ultimate holding that the official whose decision was being contested in the case was not in violation of common law bias standards.

---

162 *R. v. Hinchey*, [1996] 3 S.C.R. 1128.
163 *Ibid.* at para. 18.
164 (1994), 78 F.T.R. 44 (F.C.T.D.).
165 *Community Before Cars Coalition*, [1997] F.C.J. No. 1060 at para. 64 (T.D.).

Community has important implications. If *compliance* with the code can be equated with compliance with the common law bias standard, the mirror image might also be true: *failure* to comply with the code might be equated with failure to comply with the common law standard. If so, then a decision rendered by an official while in noncompliance with the code may be vitiated on judicial review or declared a violation of the law on a common law procedural fairness theory.

All told, this case law suggests that the code is viewed by the courts as an important component of governance, that its use may be judicially reviewed (at least on procedural grounds) and that adherence (and presumably nonadherence) to its dictates is legally cognizable as evidence of compliance with the self-standing common law bias test. From this, we conclude that the code should be viewed as an instrument with legal significance, notwithstanding its nonstatutory status.

This conclusion is bolstered by the change in the code's relevance, given amendments to the *Parliament of Canada Act*. This statute now anticipates, and indeed mandates, that the prime minister establish ethical principles for ministers, parliamentary secretaries and certain Governor-in-Council appointees.[166] Under these circumstances, the resulting code looks more like a regulation, required by statute, than a simple exercise of prime ministerial prerogative. The *Parliament of Canada Act*, in other words, gives the code a new legal status that should enhance its justiciability in court.

6. Professional Responsibility Obligations

As a final point on codes of conduct applicable to ministers and Parliamentarians, lawyers who maintain posts as senators, MPs and other public officials are also subject to special rules of certain law societies in Canada. In Ontario, for example, the Law Society of Upper Canada's *Rules of Professional Conduct* state that "[a] lawyer who holds public office shall not allow professional or personal interests to conflict with the proper discharge of official duties."[167] The commentary for this rule adds, "the lawyer holding office who sees that there is a possibility of a conflict of interest should declare the possible conflict at the earliest opportunity, and not take part in any consideration, discussion or vote concerning the matter in question."[168]

---

166 *Parliament of Canada Act*, s. 72.061.
167 Law Society of Upper Canada, *Rules of Professional Conduct* (22 June 2000, consolidated with amendments 2004), Rule 6.05(2).
168 *Ibid.*

This requirement may, for example, affect public officials who sit on corporate boards.[169]

D. PUBLIC SERVANTS CODE

The *Values and Ethics Code for the Public Service* (Public Servants Code) that came into effect in September 2003 covers regular public servants. The Public Servants Code applies to anyone employed by the Treasury Board, except for Deputy ministers or associate deputy ministers (who are covered by the Public Office Holders Code).

Those serving in the Canadian Forces are guided by similar rules to the Public Servants Code, but contained in a series of administrative orders and directives issued by the deputy minister of defence and the chief of defence staff (Military Code).[170] Civilian employees of the Department of National Defence (DND) must comply with this Military Code, in addition to the Public Servants Code.

1. Values and General Principles

Many of the Public Servants Code provisions mirror those in other codes, especially the Public Office Holders Code. The Public Servants Code outlines four "families of values" that public servants must observe. These include democratic values ("helping Ministers, under law, to serve the public interest"), professional values ("serving with competence, excellence, efficiency, objectivity and impartiality") and "people" values ("demonstrating respect, fairness and courtesy in their dealings with both citizens and public servants"). Most critically for this chapter, the code also outlines "ethical values," as follows:

> **Ethical Values:** *Acting at all times in such a way as to uphold the public trust.*
> – Public servants shall perform their duties and arrange their private affairs so that public confidence and trust in the integrity, objectivity and impartiality of government are conserved and enhanced.

---

169 See Democracy Watch, "Democracy Watch Calls for Investigations of Senators in Possible Conflicts of Interest, and for Stronger, Fully Enforced Ethics Rules for All Parliamentarians," press release, 23 May 2002.

170 National Defence Canada, DOAD 7021-1 (7 July 2000, modified 1 Sept. 2003), DOAD 7021-2 (7 July 2000, modified 16 Sept. 2003), DOAD 7021-2 (17 Apr. 2000, modified 1 Sept. 2003) and DOAD 7021-4 (8 Aug. 2000).

- Public servants shall act at all times in a manner that will bear the closest public scrutiny; an obligation that is not fully discharged by simply acting within the law.
- Public servants, in fulfilling their official duties and responsibilities, shall make decisions in the public interest.
- If a conflict should arise between the private interests and the official duties of a public servant, the conflict shall be resolved in favour of the public interest.[171]

The code makes it clear that public servants must go beyond simply complying with statutes that relate to their work, such as the *Access to Information Act*, the *Official Languages Act*, Treasury Board policies, and so on.[172] The code also outlines a set of "overall responsibilities" that include:

a. In carrying out their official duties, public servants should arrange their private affairs in a manner that will prevent real, apparent or potential conflicts of interest from arising.
b. If a conflict does arise between the private interests and the official duties of a public servant, the conflict should be resolved in favour of the public interest.[173]

This language is similar to that in Public Office Holders Code.

Separate Treasury Board documents provide rules on sponsorships and other collaborations, requiring that they be undertaken in line with the rules and principles contained in the Public Servants Code.[174]

The Public Servants Code places a strong emphasis on resolving potential conflicts under the code — not least, being asked to do something that contravenes the code's provisions — within the existing bureaucratic hierarchy.[175] This creates a serious dilemma for whistleblowers; those public ser-

---

171 Public Servants Code, ch. 1.

172 *Ibid.*

173 *Ibid.*, ch. 2.

174 See Treasury Board Secretariat, *The Federal Government as 'Partner': Six Steps to Successful Collaboration*; Treasury Board Information Notice 14-05-98, *Financial Considerations to be made when receiving Funds through Donations*; and Treasury Board Information Bulletin, *Financing Conferences and Seminars.*

175 Ch. 1 of the Public Servants Code states, "When faced with an ethical dilemma, public servants are encouraged to use the opportunities and mechanisms established by their Deputy Head to raise, discuss and resolve issues of concern related to this code. Public servants who feel they are being asked to act in a way that is inconsistent with the values and ethics set out in Chapter 1 of this code should first attempt to raise the matter using the usual reporting relationship." Similar language appears throughout the code in dealing with other matters. Also see ch. 4: Avenues of Resolution.

vants inclined to reveal government wrongdoing. The code's model assumes that there are, generally, persons within the hierarchy with an interest in resolving conflicts in the public interest. However, in the case of a whistleblower, the source of conflict may be superiors within this hierarchy who are engaged in the alleged wrongdoing. We revisit this issue later.

The code contains special provisions for "deputy heads." These officials must ensure that compliance with the code is raised in the letter of offer for an appointment to the public service. They must also provide a copy of the code to each of their employees, and conduct education on the rules, and ethics in general, on an ongoing basis. The deputy head must provide ethics resolution mechanisms, including "designating a senior official to assist public servants to resolve issues arising from the application of the Code." Other measures going beyond the code may be implemented by the deputy head, who must consult with bargaining agents of the employees' unions in advance of implementing these measures.[176]

The Treasury Board is also required to provide educational and advisory support in implementing the code, and is to monitor implementation.[177]

2. Disclosure

Within the first sixty days of a public service appointment, the employee must file a confidential report with the deputy head of his or her department or agency. The report contains details of "all outside activities, assets, and direct and contingent liabilities that might give rise to a conflict of interest with respect to their official duties."[178] If a new "real, apparent or potential conflict of interest" arises in the course of the employment, a new report must be filed.

3. Specific Duties in the Course of Employment

The Public Servants Code outlines the following "specific duties" for public servants:

   a. They should not have private interests, other than those permitted pursuant to these measures, that would be affected particularly or significantly by government actions in which they participate.

   b. They should not solicit or accept transfers of economic benefit.

176 Public Servants Code, ch. 1.
177 Ibid.
178 Ibid.

   c.   They should not step out of their official roles to assist private entities or persons in their dealings with the government where this
would result in preferential treatment to the entities or persons.

   d.   They should not knowingly take advantage of, or benefit from, information that is obtained in the course of their official duties and that
is not generally available to the public.

   e.   They should not directly or indirectly use, or allow the use of, government property of any kind, including property leased to the government, for anything other than officially approved activities.[179]

In most cases, the code recognizes that the confidential report to the
deputy head will be sufficient to meet these requirements. But in some situations, the public servant may have to withdraw from an activity or situation, or have an asset sold at arms length or placed in a blind trust. Chapter
2 states:

> In such cases, the Deputy Head will make the decision and communicate
> it to the public servant. In determining appropriate action, the Deputy
> Head will try to achieve mutual agreement with the public servant in
> question and will take into account such factors as:
> a.   the public servant's specific responsibilities;
> b.   the value and types of assets and interests involved; and
> c.   the actual costs to be incurred by divesting the assets and interests,
>   as opposed to the potential that the assets and interests represent for
>   a conflict of interest.

As with other codes, the employee "may not sell or transfer assets to family members or others for purposes of circumventing the compliance measures."[180]

The code notes, "Public servants may engage in employment outside
the Public Service and take part in outside activities unless the employment
or activities are likely to give rise to a conflict of interest or in any way
undermine the neutrality of the Public Service."[181]

Like other codes, there are specific provisions on gifts. The Public Servants Code states

---

179 *Ibid.*, ch. 2.
180 *Ibid.*
181 *Ibid.*

The acceptance of gifts, hospitality and other benefits is permissible if they

a.   are infrequent and of minimal value (low-cost promotional objects, simple meals, souvenirs with no cash value);

b.   arise out of activities or events related to the official duties of the public servant concerned;

c.   are within the normal standards of courtesy, hospitality or protocol; and

d.   do not compromise or appear to compromise in any way the integrity of the public servant concerned or his or her organization.[182]

At no time should public servants solicit gifts from those in the private sector who have dealings with the federal government. In this regard, the Public Servants Code cites paragraph 121(1)(c) of the *Criminal Code*, which states: "every one commits an offence who, being an official or employee of the government, demands, accepts, or offers or agrees to accept, from a person who has dealings with the government, a commission, reward, advantage or benefit of any kind directly or indirectly, by himself or through a member of his family or through any one for his benefit, unless he has the consent in writing of the head of the branch of government that employs him or of which he is an official, the proof of which lies on him."

As with other codes, there is also a provision on preferential treatment that states, "[w]hen participating in any decision making related to a staffing process, public servants shall ensure that they do not grant preferential treatment or assistance to family or friends." The code clarifies that "[p]roviding information that is easily accessible to the public to relatives or friends or to entities in which public servants or their family members or friends have interests is not considered preferential treatment."[183]

4. Postemployment

The Public Servants Code's standard on post-employment is as follows: "Without unduly restricting their ability to seek other employment, former public servants should undertake to minimize the possibility of real, apparent or potential conflicts of interest between their new employment and their most recent responsibilities within the federal public service. Before leaving employment, public servants should disclose their intention of future employment and discuss potential conflicts with their Deputy Head."[184]

---

182 *Ibid.*
183 *Ibid.*
184 *Ibid.*, ch. 3.

There are also specific provisions that relate to those at the executive level of the public service, including disclosure of "all firm offers of employment that could place them in a real, apparent or potential conflict of interest situation," and a one-year cooling-off provision on:

- accepting appointments with entities that they had dealing with in their last year in office;
- making representations to their former office on behalf of such an entity; or
- giving advice to clients based on information that is not available to the public about government offices with which they had a direct and substantial relationship.[185]

As with the Public Office Holders Code, a reduction in the cooling-off period is permitted in certain circumstances, with written permission from the deputy head.

5. Enforcement and Oversight

Enforcement of the Public Servants Code differs from that under the codes for public office holders, MPs and senators, in that adherence to the Public Servants Code is a condition of employment. Any breach of the code is therefore considered a breach of the contract of employment, and may prompt discipline.[186] Employment law issues associated with public servants are discussed in greater detail in chapter 4.

As noted above, the Public Servants Code contains repeated and strong language that resolutions of ethics matters must first take place internally within departments and organizations. Thus, "[i]t is expected that most matters arising from the application of this Code can and should be resolved at the organizational level."[187] The code does provide for a Public Service Integrity Officer, charged with receiving, recording and reviewing "disclosures of wrongdoing in the workplace, including breaches to the Code."[188] The shortcomings of this office and the extent to which whistleblowers are truly protected are discussed in chapter 4. For the purposes of this section, we note that only once internal avenues have been completely exhausted can the employee complain to the Public Service Integrity Offi-

---

185 *Ibid.*
186 See discussion of this point under an earlier version of the code in *Threader v. Canada (Treasury Board)*, [1987] 1 F.C. 41 at para. 20.
187 Public Servants Code, ch. 4.
188 *Ibid.*, ch. 1.

cer. Consequences for going to the officer before internal processes are exhausted (or going public) may be severe. The code specifies that "[a] public servant who does not comply with the requirements of this Code is subject to appropriate disciplinary action, up to and including termination of employment."[189]

E. ETHICS RULES FOR JUDGES

A final subject for this chapter is ethics rules applicable to superior court judges. Ethical rules for these judges fall into three categories. First, there are behaviours that constitute judicial misconduct, sufficient to prompt removal of a judge from the bench. The concept of misconduct and the procedure for removal are discussed at length in chapter 4. As noted there, misconduct of this sort is that which is "so manifestly and profoundly destructive of the concept of impartiality and independence of the judicial role that public confidence would be sufficiently undermined to render the judge incapable of executing the judicial office."[190]

Second, there are infractions (including but not necessarily limited to behaviour constituting misconduct) that, if they were to occur, could vitiate decisions rendered by a judge and/or disqualify a judge from hearing a matter. These behaviours fall under the category of bias, and resemble (and indeed are at the origin) of the equivalent concept for public officials discussed above. In *Wewaykum Indian Band v. Canada*, the Supreme Court recently outlined its understanding of judicial bias, reiterating that the standard to be employed is "reasonable apprehension of bias":

> ... the apprehension of bias must be a reasonable one, held by reasonable and right minded persons, applying themselves to the question and obtaining thereon the required information. In the words of the Court of Appeal, that test is what would an informed person, viewing the matter realistically and practically — and having thought the matter through — conclude. Would he think that it is more likely than not that [the decision-maker], whether consciously or unconsciously, would not decide fairly.[191]

---

189 *Ibid.*, ch. 4.

190 See *Report of the Boilard Inquiry Committee to the Canadian Judicial Council* (August 2003) at para. 112.

191 [2003] 2 S.C.R. 259 at para. 60, citing *Committee for Justice and Liberty v. National Energy Board*, [1978] 1 S.C.R. 369 at 394 (*per* de Grandpré J.).

Third, there are behaviours listed in the Canadian Judicial Council's *Ethical Principles for Judges*. The code has sections on judicial independence, impartiality, integrity, diligence and equality. However, the code is expressly not to be used "as a code or a list of prohibited behaviours. They do not set out standards defining judicial misconduct."[192] Nevertheless, the code's provisions are persuasive in determining, for instance, the standards for judicial impartiality, violation of which may give rise to a reasonable apprehension of bias.[193] Further, the code has been used as an interpretative device in deciding whether judicial behaviour constitute misconduct justifying removal.[194]

F. CONCLUSION

As this chapter suggests, ethics rules for both elected and unelected officials are contained in a variety of sources, some statutory, some common law, and some of a species that has yet to be determined. At their core, all of these ethics rules emphasize the need for impartiality among those involved in governance. Without strict adherence to this principle power may not be exercised in the broader public interest, compromising the ultimate objective of a democracy.

---

192 *Ethical Principles for Judges* (Ottawa: Canadian Judicial Council, 1998) at 9.
193 See, e.g., *Wewaykum*, [2003] 2 S.C.R. 259 at para. 59, citing with approval the code's concept of impartiality.
194 See, e.g., *Report of the Flynn Inquiry Committee to the Canadian Judicial Council* (Dec. 2002).

Lobbying, Democracy and Governance in the Public Interest

As suggested in chapter 7, the Canadian system accepts that good government in a modern democracy depends on adherence to certain substantive standards of ethical behaviour among public officials. The instruments obliging ethical behaviour often underscore that public officials are to act in the "public interest." Thus, these ethics rules are designed, principally, to preclude a public official from acting in response to his or her private or self-interest.

But the concept of public interest governance has another dimension, one connected to a utilitarian vision of democracy: in a democracy, a government "of the people for the people" should govern for the greatest good of the greatest number. Put another way, public officials should resist tailoring policy to suit narrow "special" interests seeking a disproportionate benefit from government not in the interest of the broader public.

Guarding against special interest governance is a difficult task. In Canada, we have responded by regulating the activities of those who would influence government in one direction or another, namely lobbyists. In this chapter, we explore these rules, focusing first on the concept of lobbying and then on the manner in which it is regulated. As this discussion will make clear, Canada regulates lobbyists, not by restricting their influence so much as by requiring modest transparency in relation to their activities.

A. LOBBYING: AN OVERVIEW

There is a story most people in the Ottawa lobbying business know. Harvie André, the Commons House leader under Brian Mulroney, once reportedly walked into a party at the lavish home of a well-connected lobbyist in Ottawa's stylish Rockcliffe Park neighbourhood. Peering about at the expensive decor, he wondered aloud, "Why is it worth more to *know* Harvie André than it is to *be* Harvie André?"[1]

The answer, of course, is straightforward. The House leader helps make decisions with serious financial consequences for people with lots of money. Barred or limited by the various rules and laws described in chapter 3 (on election law) and chapter 7 (on ethics) from directly influencing officials through financial contributions, these people expend resources instead on those close to the politician who purport to know his or her mind, or to be in a position to shape his or her views.

The term "lobbyist" was an expression first coined by U.S. President Ulysses S. Grant, the general who defeated the South in the U.S. Civil War. Grant took regular cigar and brandy breaks from his presidential duties, frequenting the bar of the Willard Hotel, just two blocks from the White House. His routine became well-known among those trying to influence government, who would wait for Grant in the hotel lobby. Grant called them "lobbyists," and the name has stuck ever since.

The role of lobbyists, and the role they play in the democratic process, has grown considerably since that time. In Canada, professional lobbyists outnumber MPs by about five to one,[2] and sometimes wield more power. Yet, for all the clout that lobbyists have, the average Canadian has only a foggy sense of what lobbyists do.

"Lobbying" is defined rather literally by the *Oxford English Dictionary*: "[t]o influence (members of a house of legislature) in the exercise of their legislative functions by frequenting the lobby." This definition includes two elements worth flagging. First, it suggests that lobbyists exercise influence. In Canada, while lobbyists often dispute the notion that they can personally influence a governmental decision, it is this perception that is the primary reason for the robustness of their practice. Put simply, lobbyists are

---

1   Legislative Assembly of Ontario, Alex Cullen (Ottawa–West), *Hansard* (13 Oct. 1998).

2   Lobbyists Registry's 2003–2004 *Annual Report* shows that there are 1,598 lobbyists registered federally in Canada, compared to 308 MPs.

often hired for their perceived influence, and without it, lobbying would quickly become a failed industry, something it definitely is not.[3]

Second, the *Oxford* definition focuses on lobbyists' efforts to influence the legislative branch. In fact, in Canada, most lobbyists position themselves nowhere near the lobby of the House of Commons, and instead focus their efforts on bureaucrats — those who shepherd legislative initiatives through drafting and development stages or who award contracts or grants.

There are exceptions to this rule, but the earlier a lobbyist can intervene in the decision-making process, the more likely he or she will be to succeed. Once a proposed law measure arrives in Parliament, many levels of the public service have usually vetted it. In addition, once in Parliament, a legislative initiative's trajectory is a matter of public record, and its progress is more difficult to affect through the exercise of backroom influence.

B. THE LOBBYING INDUSTRY

Lobbying as a formal industry in Canada goes back to 1968, when Bill Lee and Bill Neville, both executive assistants to Liberal Cabinet ministers, left the government to form Executive Consultants Ltd. (ECL).[4]

The process of lobbying predates this, of course. In fact, law firms often billed themselves as "Parliamentary Agents," although this more often referred to the use of lawyers for certain statutory applications such as divorce or corporate charters than to the performance of lobbying roles *per se*. Before ECL, lobbyists were generally party-connected lawyers and "bagmen" who could fix a client's problem with a call to a minister.

ECL filled a new niche, one reflecting the fact that government decision-making processes were changing. Government was becoming more complex, based on more rational, collective processes involving not just ministers, but Cabinet committees and policy bureaucrats. With decision-making diffused through a growing bureaucracy, the business community found it more difficult to track and access the process.

The new industry changed dramatically in the 1980s. Suspicious of a public service that had served successive Liberal governments for most of the previous two decades, Prime Minister Mulroney relied less than his predecessors on the expertise of public servants, and placed his ministers

3   To take one illustration of the industry's success, from 1997 to 2004, according to annual reports of the Lobbyists Registrar, the number of registered lobbyists grew steadily, from 1,129 to 1,598, an increase of 41.5 percent.
4   Chris Cobb and Mark Kennedy, "The Influence Industry: Political Junkies at Work," *Ottawa Citizen*, 18 Feb. 1993, A3.

at the centre of policy-making. The lobbying industry responded accordingly, focusing increased attention on these ministers in their campaigns, and
those with personal contacts with these ministers often sold their services
for a premium. Legislation designed to rein in the power of lobbyists — the
1988 *Lobbyists Registration Act* — was passed under the Progressive Conservatives, largely in response to the excesses of the industry.

Since the Liberal victory in 1993, the industry has witnessed continued
growth. It is clear that lobbyists have become more influential in the
decade of Liberal governance. Commenting on the growth in lobbying, in
its October 1997 issue, *Canadian Lawyer* magazine noted that "lobbyists
are becoming a new kind of power broker, a sort of surreptitious civil service that wields real clout." The growth of the industry has continued since
then. Between 1995 and 2003, the number of "hired-gun" lobbyists —
what Canadian law calls "consultant lobbyists" (see later in this chapter) —
grew from 290 to 980.[5]

Meanwhile, nothing prevents lobbyists from making political contributions — a practice that was restricted in at least seventeen U.S. states by the
early 1990s — and lobbyists can, and quite frequently do, run the election
campaigns (including party leadership campaigns) of high-level elected
officials, a prohibited activity in several U.S. states.[6]

Lobbyists generally take unpaid leave while working on campaigns to
avoid allegations under the *Canada Elections Act* that their labour constitutes a nonmonetary contribution to candidates from lobbying firms. Nevertheless, their principal employment as lobbyists for private interests has
the potential to taint how they advise the candidates for whom they volunteer. Subsequently, their experience on these campaigns can afford lobbyists privileged access once their candidates are elected and/or elevated to
high office.

C. THE LAW OF LOBBYIST REGULATION

The emergence of a potent lobbying industry has prompted modest legal
regulation of lobbying practices. The key instrument at the federal level for
policing lobbyist activity is the *Lobbyists Registration Act (LRA)*.[7] Amend-

---

5 Industry Canada, *Lobbyists Registration Act Annual Report* (1995 and 2003).
6 Democracy Watch, "Spring Cleaning: A Model Lobbying Disclosure and Ethics Pack-
    age for Those Hard to Reach Places in the Federal Government" (May 1994) at 28. In
    most states, this restriction is in the form of "blackout periods." For example, a lobby-
    ist may be banned from making donations while the legislature sits.
7 *Lobbyists Registration Act (LRA)*, R.S.C. 1985, c. 44 (4th Supp.).

ments to this Act were passed in 2003 as Bill C-15, but had not come into force by early 2005.[8] We note in the discussion that follows the important changes this bill makes.

1.   The *Lobbyists Registration Act*

a)   Application
The *LRA* tracks two categories of professional lobbyists. The Act covers only those who are paid to lobby, and does not, therefore, apply to persons who engage in lobbying activities on a strictly volunteer basis.

Consultant Lobbyists
Consultant lobbyists, the first category, are essentially those who are hired by a company or other type of client. Currently, a consultant lobbyist includes "[e]very individual who, for payment, on behalf of any person or organization ... undertakes to ... communicate with a public office holder in *an attempt to influence*" a government decision, including decisions over policy, programs, regulations, legislative acts or bills, grants or other financial benefit or contracts. This definition also covers any undertaking to "arrange a meeting between a public office holder and any other person."[9]

A public office holder is defined broadly in the Act to mean "any officer or employee of Her Majesty in right of Canada," including a senator or MP or their staff, most non-judicial Governor-in-Council appointees, an officer, director or employee of any non-judicial federal body exercising powers conferred by or under an Act of Parliament or pursuant to the royal prerogative, and members of the armed forces and the RCMP.[10]

The reference in the current Act to "attempt to influence" has created significant hurdles in its enforcement. As Industry Canada — charged with administering the Act — puts it:

> The focus on the expression "attempt to influence" entails that in order to successfully obtain a prosecution [for failure to comply with the registration requirements discussed below] one must demonstrate beyond a reasonable doubt that an individual has attempted to influence a public office holder. The criminal nature of the offence requires a very high standard of proof, which is analogous to the standard required to prove the more

---

8   One reason for this delay was an extended consultation period on the regulations to bring the law into force. Lobbyists strongly resisted many of the changes: K. O'Malley, "Proposed Lobby Regs Create Stir," *The Hill Times*, 28 Feb.–6 March 2005, 1.

9   *LRA*, subs. 5(1).

10   *Ibid.*, s. 2, cross-referenced to the *Federal Courts Act*, R.S.C. c. F-7, s. 2.

serious offence of influence peddling under the Criminal Code thereby making it very difficult to secure a conviction under the LRA.[11]

Bill C-15, once in force, attempts to correct this problem. It replaces the "attempt to influence" language with communication "in respect of" the listed government decisions.

In-House Lobbyists
Secondly, the Act regulates in-house lobbyists, divided into "in-house (corporate)" and "in-house (organizations)." These include lobbyists who are *employees* of a corporation or organization that is lobbying. The current in-house (corporate) lobbyist provisions are triggered "[w]here a person employs an individual a significant part of whose duties as an employee is to communicate with public office holders on behalf of the employer [or a subsidiary of the employer] in an attempt to influence" government activities that are — subject to a few exceptions discussed later — similar in scope to those just discussed in relation to consultant lobbyists.[12]

Under the current Act, the definition for in-house lobbyists (organizations) covers "an organization [that] employs one or more individuals any part of whose duties is to communicate with public office holders on behalf of the organization in an attempt to influence" a similar list of activities as in house (corporate) lobbyist. The Act's registration provisions, discussed later, are triggered where the lobbying "constitute[s] a significant part of the duties of one employee or would constitute a significant part of the duties of one employee were those duties to be performed by only one employee."[13]

Unlike a consultant lobbyist, an in-house lobbyist (corporate or organizational) is not lobbying when he or she arranges a meeting between a public office holder and any other person. A second notable difference in the scope of in-house lobbying compared to consultant lobbying is that in-house lobbyists are not regulated if lobbying only for government contracts. The inclusion of contract lobbying in the definition of consultant lobbyist, but not of in-house lobbyists, may have been intended to ensure that not every person or entity doing business with the government should have to deal with the administrative burden of registering, especially if they are lobbying on their own behalf. Imposing the contract requirement for consultant lobbyists may also reflect concern at the time of the Act's pas-

---

11 Industry Canada, *Enforcement of the Lobbyists Registration Act*, available at http://strategis.ic.gc.ca/epic/internet/inlr-el.nsf/en/lr01091e.html.

12 *LRA*, subs. 6(1) [emphasis added].

13 *Ibid.*, subs. 7(1).

sage over "contingency fee" lobbyists — essentially consultant lobbyists who were reportedly making huge sums by obtaining major government contracts for their clients based on their personal contacts in the government. We discuss contingency fees later in this chapter.

Notably, the definition of both in-house (corporate) and in-house (organization) lobbyists depends on the employee of the corporation or the organization engaging in lobbying as a "significant part of their duties." The lobbyists registrar has interpreted this expression, pursuant to his or her power under the Act to issue advisory opinions and interpretation bulletins on the registration portions of the Act.[14] For in-house (corporate) lobbying, the Act's provisions are triggered where the employee expends a "substantial or large amount of time" lobbying, defined as 20 percent of their time. For in-house (organization) lobbying, "[w]hen all the lobbying by all paid employees would amount to 20 percent or more of the employment time of one employee, then the senior officer of the organization must register and list in the form the names of those employees who lobby."[15]

Unfortunately, this definition is likely underinclusive, leaving out most lobbying that occurs in Ottawa. Very few executives and other well-connected people spend this much time lobbying. They are aware that minimal communication from a well-heeled and influential executive may carry far more weight than the efforts of an entire team of full-time lobbyists.

Once in force, Bill C-15 will change substantially the Act's provisions on in-house lobbyists. The new law will fold together in house (corporate) and in house (organizations) lobbyists. It will retain the "significant part of their duties" language, with one important alteration: the new Act will impose a disclosure obligation on each "senior officer" of a corporation "any part of whose duties" is to communicate in respect of the listed government decisions.[16] In other words, senior officers — defined quite broadly in the bill — will be captured by the Act's registration requirements and also the Lobbyists' Code, described later, even if they do not lobby as a "significant part of their duties."

As with consultant lobbyists, the amendments will also remove the reference to "attempt to influence" in the lobbying definition, replacing it with the broader "in respect of."

---

14   *Ibid.*, s. 10.
15   *Lobbyists Registration Act* Interpretation Bulletin, "A Significant Part of the Duties" (1995).
16   This requirement will appear in new *LRA*, para. 7(3)(f.1).

b) Registration

Obligation to Register

The key obligation under the Act is registration of the lobbyist in a public registry[17] managed, in practice, by Industry Canada and made available on the Internet.[18] Thus, a consultant lobbyist must file a form with the Lobbyists Registry within ten days of becoming engaged in a lobbying activity.[19] Under Bill C-15, he or she will also be required to file a return every six months, unless the lobbying activity ceases during this period.

In-house lobbyists must register within two months of engaging in a lobbying activity, and then must continue to file an update every six months in the case of organizations, and once a year for corporate lobbyists.[20] In the case of in-house (organization) lobbyists, this registration must be completed, not by the lobbyist employee, but by the senior officer of the organization.[21] Bill C-15 will standardize this requirement for both sorts of in house lobbyists: the senior paid officer in the organization or corporation will bear the registration obligation within two months of the lobbying commencing and every six months thereafter.

Failure to comply with the Act's registration requirements may result in criminal penalties.[22] Even so, it is common knowledge in the industry that many lobbyists fail to register, even where the Act likely requires it. Some do not wish to taint themselves with a lobbyist label, while others do not consider what they do to be lobbying. Some, for example, consider their work to obtain government contracts to be "sales" rather than lobbying.

Disclosure Requirements in Registration Documents

The original Act took a largely hands-off approach to lobbying, imposing only minimal disclosure requirements when lobbyists registered under the Act. More recent amendments to the Act in 1995 require professional lobbyists to disclose more information about their contact with the government, including the subject matter of lobbying activities, the names of corporations controlling the lobbyists' clients, and the names of members of a coalition sponsoring a lobbying initiative.

---

17 *LRA,* s. 9.

18 The Lobbyists Registry website is at http://strategis.ic.gc.ca/epic/internet/inlr-el.nsf/ en/Home.

19 *LRA,* subs. 5(1).

20 *Ibid.,* subss. 6(2) and 7(2).

21 *Ibid.,* subs. 7(1).

22 *Ibid.,* s. 14.

A full list of information to be included in the lobbyists disclosure form, as spelled out in the Act, appears in Table 8.1. At first blush, the information contained in the registry is expansive. There are, however, several notable omissions.

First, there is no mandatory disclosure of lobbyists' fees or of how much a client is spending on a lobbying campaign. While they are secretive about the fees they charge, many top lobbyists reportedly make annual salaries of more than $250,000 and charge monthly retainer fees of anywhere from $3,000 to $15,000 per client. For those who prefer to pay by the meter, hourly rates are typically $200 to $250, but can be as high as $450. Disclosure of this information by consultant lobbyists and the corporations and organizations employing in-house lobbyists would allow Canadians to assess just how great a stake a client has in a piece of legislation or contract. By the early 1990s, fee and expenditure disclosure was required federally in the United States, as well as in most individual states.[23]

A second striking disclosure omission relates to lobbyist work (volunteer or otherwise) for politicians or political contenders. As noted above, a "revolving door" between lobbyists and advisors and volunteers on political campaigns is a virtual *sine qua non* of the contemporary political environment. In our view, lobbyists should be obliged to file annually a declaration of their political work, allowing any suspect link between political activity and lobbying to be tracked. Bill C-15 goes halfway on this issue: once in force, it will oblige disclosure of any offices held if a lobbyist is a former public office holder. Unfortunately, this requirement will not capture volunteer contributions.

Last, it seems sensible that lobbyist political donations, subject to disclosure under the *Canada Elections Act* in most instances, should be cross-referenced in the lobbyists registrar's database.

---

23   Democracy Watch, "Spring Cleaning" at 26; and Gary Ruskin, Congressional Accountability Project, Washington, D.C., personal communication. Although certain states' provisions require disclosure of retainer fees and compensation, others only require disclosure of expenditures.

Table 8.1   *Disclosure Requirements for Lobbyists*

Lobbyists	Disclosure Requirements
Consultant lobbyist[24]	(a) the name and business address of the individual and the firm where the individual is engaged in business; (b) the name and business address of the client and of any person or organization that, to the knowledge of the individual, controls or directs the activities of the client and has a direct interest in the outcome of the individual's activities on behalf of the client; (c) where the client is a corporation, the name and business address of each subsidiary of the corporation that, to the knowledge of the individual, has a direct interest in the outcome of the individual's activities on behalf of the client; (d) where the client is a corporation that is a subsidiary of any other corporation, the name and business address of that other corporation; (e) where the client is a coalition, the name and business address of each corporation or organization that is a member of the coalition; (e.1) where the client is funded in whole or in part by a government, the name of the government or government agency, as the case may be, and the amount of funding received by the client from that government or government agency; (f) particulars to identify the subject-matter in respect of which the individual has undertaken to communicate with a public office holder or to arrange a meeting, and such other information respecting the subject-matter as is prescribed; (g) where applicable, whether the payment to the individual is in whole or in part contingent on the individual's degree of success in influencing any of the government decisions discussed above; (h) particulars to identify any relevant legislative proposal, Bill, resolution, regulation, policy, program, grant, contribution, financial benefit or contract; (i) the name of any department or other governmental institution in which any public office holder with whom the individual has communicated or expects to communicate, or with whom a meeting is to be or has been arranged, is employed or serves; (j) where the individual has undertaken to communicate with a public office holder in an attempt to influence a government decision described above, the particulars to identify any communication technique, including appeals to members of the public through the mass media or by direct communication that seek to persuade members of the public to communicate directly with a public office holder in an attempt to place pressure on the public office holder to endorse a particular opinion (in the Act referred to as "grass-roots communication"), that the individual has used or expects to use in an attempt to influence that matter; and (k) such other information relating to the identity of the individual, the client, any person or organization referred to in paragraph (b), any subsidiary referred to in paragraph (c), the other corporation referred to in paragraph (d), any member of a coalition referred to in paragraph (e) or any department or institution referred to in paragraph (i) as is prescribed.

24   *LRA*, s. 5.

Lobbyists	Disclosure Requirements
In-house (corporate) lobbyist[25] (current requirements). Note that Bill C-15 will change some of these requirements in relatively minor ways.	(a) the name and business address of the employee; (b) the name and business address of the employer; (c) where the employer is a corporation, the name and business address of each subsidiary of the corporation that, to the knowledge of the employee, has a direct interest in the outcome of the employee's activities on behalf of the employer; (d) where the employer is a corporation that is a subsidiary of any other corporation, the name and business address of that other corporation; (e) if applicable, the financial year of the employer; (f) a description in summary form of the employer's business or activities and such other information to identify the employer's business or activities as is prescribed; (f.1) where the employer is funded in whole or in part by a government, the name of the government or government agency, as the case may be, and the amount of funding received by the employer from that government or government agency; (g) where the employee is attempting to influence any government decision discussed above at the time the return is filed, particulars to identify the relevant subject-matter and such other information respecting the subject-matter as is prescribed; (h) particulars to identify the subject-matter in respect of which the employee has communicated or expects to communicate with the public office holders during the financial year of the employer in which the return is filed or, if the employer does not have a financial year, during the calendar year in which the return is filed, in an attempt to influence the government decision described above, and such other information respecting those subject-matters as is prescribed; (i) particulars to identify any relevant legislative proposal, Bill, resolution, regulation, policy, program, grant, contribution or financial benefit; (j) the name of any department or other governmental institution in which any public office holder with whom the employee has communicated or expects to communicate, in connection with any matter referred to in paragraph (g) or (h), is employed or serves; (k) particulars to identify any communication technique, including grass-roots communication, that the employee has used or expects to use in an attempt to influence any matter referred to in paragraph (g) or (h); and (l) such other information relating to the identity of the employee, the employer, any subsidiary referred to in paragraph (c), the other corporation referred to in paragraph (d) or any department or institution referred to in paragraph (j) as is prescribed.

---

25   *Ibid.*, s. 6.

Lobbyists	Disclosure Requirements

In-house (organization) lobbyist[26] (current requirements). Note that Bill C-15 will change some of these requirements in relatively minor ways.	(a) the name and business address of the senior officer;
	(b) the name and business address of the organization;
	(c) a description in summary form of the organization's business or activities and such other information to identify its business or activities as is prescribed;
	(d) a description of the organization's membership and such other information to identify its membership as is prescribed;
	(e) where the organization is funded in whole or in part by a government, the name of the government or government agency, as the case may be, and the amount of funding received by the organization from that government or government agency;
	(f) the name of each employee of the organization whose duties include lobbying;
	(g) where any such employee is attempting to influence any matter government decision described above at the time the return is filed, particulars to identify the relevant subject-matter and such other information respecting the subject-matter as is prescribed;
	(h) particulars to identify the subject-matters in respect of which any such employee
	  (i) has communicated with public office holders during the period for which the return is filed, and
	  (ii) is expected to communicate with public office holders during the next following six-month period, in an attempt to influence any government decision described above and such other information respecting those subject-matters as is prescribed;
	(i) particulars to identify any relevant legislative proposal, Bill, resolution, regulation, policy, program, grant, contribution or financial benefit;
	(j) the name of any department or other governmental institution in which any public office holder with whom any such employee
	  (i) has communicated during the period for which the return is required to be filed, and
	  (ii) is expected to communicate during the next following six-month period, in connection with any government decision described above, is employed or serves;
	(k) particulars to identify any communication technique, including grass-roots communication, that any such employee
	  (i) has used during the period for which the return is required to be filed, and
	  (ii) is expected to use during the next following six-month period, in an attempt to influence any government decision described above; and
	(l) such other information relating to the identity of the senior officer, the organization, any employee referred to in paragraph (f) or any department or institution referred in paragraph (j) as is prescribed.

---

26   *Ibid.*, s. 7.

c) Exceptions to Registration

The Act carves out several exceptions to its registration requirements. First, the Act does not apply to provincial politicians, employees of the federal, provincial, municipal or international governments and First Nations leaders,[27] among others. Second, the Act also does not apply with respect to individuals or groups making submissions to parliamentary committees, or with respect to communication to an enforcement body for the purposes of enforcing an Act of Parliament or regulation.[28]

Third, the types of activities triggering registration hinge on efforts to influence the outcome of a defined set of government decisions. They do not include efforts by a lobbyist to gather information, even information not easily accessible to the public. Information gathering is, therefore, an important exclusion from the Act's registration requirements, one that will be made more explicit when Bill C-15 comes into force.[29] This type of information gathering is the main activity of most lobbyists.

Fourth, the current Act does not apply to "any oral or written submission made to a public office holder by an individual on behalf of any person or organization in direct response to a written request from a public office holder, for advice or comment in respect" to a government decision that would otherwise trigger registration.[30] This exception marks a loophole, in our view, allowing lobbyists to "launder" their efforts to influence decisions by first seeking a pro forma invitation to submit those views from a public office holder. Happily, Bill C-15, once in force, will eliminate this provision.

d) Lawyers as Lobbyists

Lobbyist registration may have a direct impact on lawyers. As law firms strive to become "full-service," many have created lobbying divisions. Lawyers certainly are not always required to register under the LRA. If lawyers are only interpreting a statute, for example, they need not register. On the other hand, if they are seeking out public officials in the hope of inducing a policy change, they generally must register. Similarly, if lawyers are acting as counsel in a regulatory hearing, registration should not be required. However, if they are also acting in a lobbying capacity on the same or any other issue, they must register.

---

27   *Ibid.*, subs. 4(1).
28   *Ibid.*, paras. 4(2)(a) and (b).
29   Bill C-15 will amend para. 4(2)(c) to preclude the application of the Act where the communication is "restricted to a request for information." This narrows the bill's definition of lobbying, which otherwise includes communication "in respect of" government decisions, as discussed earlier.
30   *LRA*, para. 4(2)(c).

Public disclosure of lawyer lobbying activities raises questions about solicitor-client privilege. As described recently by Justice Deschamps, concurring in the Supreme Court's decision in *Maranda v. Richer*, "The [solicitor-client] privilege performs the social function of preserving the quality, freedom and confidentiality of information exchanged between a client and his or her lawyer in the context of a legal consultation. It enables all individuals to participate in society with the benefit of the information and advice needed in order to exercise their rights. It is closely associated with access to justice."[31]

Lawyers have raised concerns that disclosure of clients' names, information on lobbying activities and the publication of this information in the publicly accessible registry violates the solicitor-client confidentiality requirement. However, these complaints overstate the scope of solicitor-client privilege. As the Supreme Court has observed, "Not all communications between a lawyer and her client are privileged. In order for the communication to be privileged, it must arise from communication between a lawyer and the client where the latter seeks lawful legal advice. ... [O]nly communications made for the legitimate purpose of obtaining lawful professional advice or assistance are privileged."[32]

By any reasonable measure, discussing a strategy for communicating with a public official to influence a government decision is not legal advice. Disclosure of the identity of the client retaining the lawyer's services and information on the nature of this communication therefore violates no privilege.

Moreover, there can be no privilege unless the communication between client and lawyer is intended to be confidential.[33] Logically, where a public law clearly obliges disclosure of lobbying activity, this expectation of confidentiality is negated, and a lawyer should be obliged to disabuse a client of any belief to the contrary. Indeed, the Lobbyists' Code of Conduct discussed in the next section requires this notice.

2. The Lobbyists' Code of Conduct

a) Overview

The *LRA* deals primarily with disclosure. Under amendments introduced in 1995 however, a Lobbyists' Code of Conduct[34] governs certain activities of lobbyists beyond those pertaining to disclosure. The Lobbyists' Code,

---

31 [2003] 3 S.C.R. 193 at para. 40.
32 *R. v. McClure*, [2001] 1 S.C.R. 445 at paras. 36 and 37.
33 *Solosky v. The Queen*, [1980] 1 S.C.R. 821 at 837.
34 The *Lobbyists' Code of Conduct* is available at http://strategis.ic.gc.ca/epic/internet/ inlr-el.nsf/en/lro1044e.html.

anticipated specifically in the Act,[35] sets out three principles for lobbyists: integrity and honesty, openness, and professionalism. Eight rules govern lobbyists conduct. Lobbyists are:

- to provide accurate and factual information to the public official, and "use proper care to avoid [misleading anyone] inadvertently";
- to indicate to their client, employer or organization the lobbyist's obligations under the *Lobbyists Registration Act*, and their obligation to adhere to the *Lobbyists' Code of Conduct*;
- not to disclose confidential information without the consent of their client, unless that disclosure is required by law;
- not to use confidential information obtained in the course of lobbying to the disadvantage of their client, employer or organization;
- to refrain from representing competing interests without the informed consent of those involved;
- to advise public office holders that they have informed their clients (where the lobbyist is a consultant lobbyist) of any actual, potential or apparent conflict of interest, and obtained the informed consent of each client concerned before proceeding or continuing with the undertaking; and
- not to place public office holders in a conflict of interest by proposing or undertaking any action that would constitute an improper influence on a public office holder.

Because the code is a set of general principles, it requires careful interpretation. The lobbyists registrar enforces the code. Originally, this post was filled by the ethics counsellor, the official who was also charged with administering the Public Office Holders Code, discussed in chapter 7. Thus, the counsellor oversaw both lobbying activity under the code and the ethics of those most likely to be lobbied — senior public officials. At the same time, the counsellor was appointed by, and reported to, the prime minister. As a result, the ethics counsellor post was constantly criticized for a lack of independence. In 2004, in response to this criticism, the responsibilities of administering the Public Office Holders Code and the *LRA* and its code were split between the new ethics commissioner and the lobbyists registrar, respectively.

b) Legal Status and Oversight of the Lobbyists' Code

The *LRA* specifies that "[t]he Code is not a statutory instrument for the purposes of the *Statutory Instruments Act*, but the Code shall be published in

---

35   *LRA*, s. 10.2.

the Canada Gazette."[36] At the same time, the *LRA* specifies that both in-house and consultant lobbyists "shall comply" with the code.[37] This latter provision gives the code legal significance.

This interpretation is consistent with the holding in *Democracy Watch v. Canada (Attorney General)*,[38] the only court case in this area. In that case, the Federal Court concluded that while the status of the code "would appear to be somewhat unclear," the code is not "non-law." In partial support of this view, the Court noted the "extensive consultation" undertaken in developing the code, as well as the fact that "it was reviewed by a Standing Committee of the House of Commons and was published in the *Canada Gazette*."[39]

For this reason, and also because the registrar exercises power pursuant to the *LRA* itself when conducting investigations under the Act, the registrar's investigations under the code are reviewable in Federal Court on standard administrative law grounds.[40]

In relation to these investigations, the *LRA* provides that "[w]here the registrar believes on reasonable grounds that a person has breached the Code, the registrar *shall* investigate to determine whether a breach has occurred."[41] Therefore, the Act *requires* the registrar to act where he or she has reasonable grounds to believe a breach has occurred. "Reasonable grounds" to believe is a substantially less exacting standard than that employed in criminal proceedings — the beyond a reasonable doubt threshold. As a consequence, even if the facts establishing a violation have not been established beyond a reasonable doubt in a criminal proceeding in a particular case, the registrar must still consider whether there are reasonable grounds to believe these facts exist[42] (although, as noted below, the registrar may need to wait until after a criminal investigation has been completed before continuing his or her own investigation).

If a complaint or petition is filed with the registrar, the *Democracy Watch* case suggests the registrar is not necessarily required to conduct a "full and detailed investigation" of the matter. Rather, if a "preliminary investigation" does not reveal any information that suggests the code has

---

36   *Ibid.*

37   *Ibid.*, s. 10.3. Under this section, as amended by Bill C-15, senior officers any part of whose duties is to lobby will also have to comply with the code.

38   2004 FC 969.

39   *Ibid.* at para. 23.

40   See discussion in *ibid.* at para. 21.

41   *LRA*, s. 10.4 [emphasis added].

42   *Democracy Watch*, 2004 FC 969 at paras. 73 and 74.

been breached, the registrar may conclude that a full investigation is not needed.[43]

In conducting an investigation, the registrar may employ broad powers, including the capacity to compel oral or written testimony, the production of documents, or to administer oaths. The Act also establishes how the registrar is to conduct an investigation:

- investigations shall be done in private, and evidence in the investigation shall not be used against the alleged violator in another proceeding, except one for perjury relating to statements given to the registrar;
- the registrar shall provide an opportunity to the person subject to the investigation to have his or her views heard;
- the proceedings are to be confidential; and
- the registrar is required to file a report to Parliament following the investigation.[44]

Under Bill C-15, the lobbyists registrar will be obliged to inform a peace officer of any infractions of the Act or any other law he or she believes on reasonable grounds to have been committed. The registrar will also have to suspend an investigation of a breach of the code where this reasonable belief arises or where a police investigation has commenced.

The actual consequences of a registrar investigation finding noncompliance with the code are unclear. While generally, a violation of the LRA is punishable with a fine of up to $25,000 and, in relation to misfiling with the registrar, a much larger fine and a possible prison term of up to two years, these punishments are specifically *precluded* in cases where the lobbyist fails to comply with the code.[45] Further, the Act states that "[s]ection 126 of the *Criminal Code* does not apply in respect of a contravention of" the provision obliging lobbyist adherence to the code.[46] Section 126 deals with general breaches of Acts of Parliament, providing for punishment of up to two years imprisonment unless the Act in question otherwise provides.

Hence, sanctions for a violation of the code generally come only in the form of negative media attention in response to the registrar's report, or via some intervention by Parliament.

---

43   *Ibid.* at paras. 77 and 78.
44   *LRA*, ss. 10.4 and 10.5.
45   *Ibid.*, s. 14.

3. Important Regulatory Issues Not Addressed in the *LRA*

We conclude this chapter by discussing several issues on which the *LRA* is silent.

a) Contingency Fees

The Act requires consultant lobbyists to disclose whether their payment is "in whole or in part contingent on the individual's degree of success in influencing" the government decision.[47] A standard "contingency fee" arrangement would involve the lobbyist taking a cut from the value of a government contract he or she obtained for a client.

Concerns over these arrangements arose in the early 1990s, following reports that substantial fees were paid to well-connected lobbyists involved in the Pearson Airport privatization and the purchase of EH-101 helicopters during the Mulroney era. Contingency fees raise the prospect that, with millions of dollars at stake, a lobbyist might be tempted to overstep the bounds of propriety in using his or her connections with public office holders.

When the Liberals took power in 1993, they sought to limit these arrangements. A ban on contingency fees was apparently abandoned for fear that it would infringe on provincial jurisdiction, which includes laws governing contracts. The government's policy is now instead to bar government contractors from using an outside lobbyist paid on a contingency basis.[48] Thus, according to the Treasury Board Secretariat, "a clause prohibiting payment [of a lobbyist] on a contingency fee basis must be included in the contract documentation between the Crown and the supplier."[49] A sample clause proposed by the secretariat is found in Annex 8.1.

However, despite this change in policy, dozens of lobbyists still charge contingency fees, and some lobbyists carry on lobbying primarily through contingency fee arrangements. Our review of lobbyists registry data reveals that, from January 1996 to June 2004, eighty lobbyists had conducted business under contingency fee arrangements, representing 241 clients. Many

---

46   *Ibid.*, s. 10.3.

47   *Ibid.*, para. 5(2)(g).

48   Treasury Board Secretariat, *Contracting Policy* (2003), Appendix M ("contractors who do business with the government must not retain lobbyist whom they pay on a contingency basis. This means that lobbyists must not be paid a fee or compensation related to the value of the contract. If lobbyists are retained in connection with a proposed or actual contract with the Crown, they should be paid on a fee for services or retainer basis.").

49   *Ibid.*

of these were for contracts, including for property management,[50] land deals with the government,[51] supplying products such as foam materials,[52] branding and communications,[53] "to erect a statue of Louis Riel in Ottawa,"[54] defence,[55] a satellite station,[56] "modular tent systems,"[57] a pilot program for employment insurance recipients,[58] and Internet services.[59]

It is not known whether these lobbyists were successful in their efforts to win contracts, and if so, whether their clients signed the standard provision in government contracts that states that no contingency fee lobbyist was used to obtain the contract. Without fuller disclosure of each lobbyists activities and his or her success, it is difficult to determine if a lobbyist or contract bidder has crossed the line.

Definitional uncertainty compounds this monitoring and enforcement problem. Under the Treasury Board Secretariat policy, the key question with regard to contingency fee arrangements is whether they involve lobbying for a government contract. The government's contingency rules apparently still allow contingency fees to be charged for those applying for policy changes, loans, or even grants from the government, and many lobbyists still lobby for these direct benefits for their clients. The preceding review of data, for example, showed that lobbyists charge contingency fees in many controversial areas, including to obtain softwood lumber quotas, fish quotas, tax credits, "tariff relief," grain subsidies, event sponsorships, immigration permits, privatization of government assets, certification of a mine, grants for First Nations and various loans and granting programs

---

50 See lobbyist registration for Richard Bower, representing Performco Properties Ltd., Doc. #1-1996165-16.

51 See lobbyist registration for John Crosbie, representing Texada Land Corp., Doc. #1-2000357-1.

52 See lobbyist registration for Alfred (Fred) Doucet, representing Kristofoam Industries Inc., Doc. #1-1996072-1.

53 See lobbyist registration for Randal Goodfellow, representing Hewson, Brigde & Smith, Doc. #1-2001176-1.

54 See lobbyist registration for Jerry Kovacs, representing Miguel Joyal, Doc. #1-1998246-1.

55 See lobbyist registration for John Lutes, representing Sagem, Doc. #1-2004009-2.

56 See lobbyist registration for Richard Mann, representing Satlantic Inc., Doc. #1-2000054-13.

57 See lobbyist registration for Ian Murray, representing Hovtec Manufacturing Inc., Doc. #1-2002135-4.

58 See lobbyist registration for Michel A. Verret, representing Webnet, Doc. #1-2001107-4.

59 See lobbyist registration for Michel A. Verret, representing Centre de technologie AIQ, Doc. #1-2001115-4.

such as Technology Partnerships Canada and Western Economic Diversification Canada.

Drawing the line between one of these lobbying objectives and a "Contract" can be tricky. Some lobbyists have worked on behalf of clients to encourage privatization of government assets. In such a case, the lobbyist is not directly lobbying for a contract (that is, the contract to coordinate the selling off of a government asset). Rather, what is being sought is a policy decision to create that contract. However, the client nonetheless benefits when it can subsequently bid on the contract that flows from the new privatization policy.

On the whole, we believe a more sensible solution to the contingency fee issue would be to ban these sort of fees for registered lobbyists entirely, a common rule in the United States. Constitutional excuses for inaction on this issue are unpersuasive. The fact that the provinces generally regulate contracts as part of their powers over property and civil rights in the *Constitution Act, 1867* is not a serious barrier. Constitutionally, the federal government could craft a contingency fee prohibition using its criminal law power in the 1867 Act.

At the very least, the federal government should extend the current rule requiring government contractors to certify that they did not use lobbyists paid under contingency fee arrangement to cover also those seeking government grants or loans under the rules governing those programs. More effective monitoring of the current contract rule would also be advisable, given evidence in the lobbyist registry itself suggesting contingency fees are regularly charged by lobbyists where government contracts are sought.

b) Multitasking Lobbyists

Charging contingency fees is not the only lobbying practice that should be banned. Firms that act both as lobbyists and as government consultancies create difficult conflicts of interest scenarios. Current rules require lobby firms to set up "Chinese walls" partitioning businesses to separate their lobbying operations from other functions, such as conducting government communications work.[60] However, in our view, communications consultants should be obliged to decide whether they wish to be private lobbyists or public service confidantes. A business should not be allowed, through its owners, partners, employees, or subsidiaries, or in partnership with other firms, to act as a consultant providing high-level advice to a public

---

60 Industry Canada, Office of the Lobbyists Registrar, Advice: "The Issue of Chinese Walls" (last updated 27 July 2004).

office while simultaneously being paid to lobby that office. Given the cozy nature of lobbying, it is simply too likely that Chinese walls might "leak," especially when principals in a lobbying firm act on both the communications and lobbying sides of the business.

Some critics, including the democratic reform group Democracy Watch, also advocate that lobbyists should be prohibited from serving in senior positions for political parties or candidates, as was legislated in several U.S. states by the early 1990s.[61]

D. CONCLUSION: AN ALTERNATIVE TO LOBBYING?

Lobbying regulation at the federal level is designed to render lobbying more transparent, while doing very little to govern how lobbying takes place. The expectation here, as in many other areas, is that sunshine will be the best disinfectant, deterring suspect lobbying practices. But whether the disclosure regime instituted under the *LRA* goes far enough is arguable.

As the introduction to this chapter notes, the end objective of lobbyist regulation is to ensure that government decisions reflect a broad public interest, and not a narrow special interest. Regulating special interest lobbying is one way to move toward that objective. A second is to enhance the capacity of decision-makers to understand the broader public interest.

We conclude this chapter with a few comments on this second approach: governments currently conduct consultations with citizens, but these exercises are often frustrating for both citizens and policy-makers. The source of frustration for both sides is a poorly-organized citizenry that is not always given the tools to articulate its desires effectively, and in a language that is useful and understandable for policy-makers.

As a result, most consultation involves the government meeting with representatives of "civil society" organizations, rather than citizens exercising a right to direct input.[62] Even these organizations may be ill-equipped

---

61   Democracy Watch, "Spring Cleaning" at 10.

62   According to Ekos Research, "charitable and non-profit organizations" enjoyed a high level of public confidence from 66 percent of Canadians, versus 46 percent for companies and 28 percent for government. When asked whether these organizations "understand the needs of average citizens more than government," 68 percent agreed whereas only 13 percent disagreed. The study also found that more Canadians felt this charitable sector would be more influential in their lives in ten years' time: *The Voluntary Sector Initiative: Positioning the Voluntary Sector in Canada: What the Elite and the General Public Say* (Toronto: Ekos Research Associates, 2002).

to counter monied lobby interests. Currently, in order to maintain their charitable status, charitable organizations may devote no more than 10 percent of their resources to "advocacy" activities. As a result, despite the expertise that many in this sector have in their areas, it is often difficult for civil society groups to meaningfully engage government when it comes to policy-making. This is often in contrast to well-heeled industry lobbies, which may deduct their lobbying costs as a business expense, a tax provision that should be eliminated.

Consultation with organizations is, in any event, a second-best approach. It seems to us that one of the best ways to level the playing field between business and union lobbyists and ordinary people is to require government departments to resort to "citizen participation" methods of consultation on major issues of public policy — consultation that gives citizens an opportunity to participate in meaningful ways so that their views are heard, and their concerns addressed, to the same extent that the views of better organized and financed lobbyists are heard. There are many models of "deliberative" consultation that more meaningfully engage citizens themselves in a discussion of government policy. Most have mechanisms for ensuring that the group being consulted is representative of the population at large that will be affected by the government policy at issue. Information, often agreed to by various stakeholders, is provided to the citizens in advance of the consultation, and the process is facilitated to ensure a well-informed debate where all may be heard. One of the more interesting deliberative consultation methods is the Citizens Assembly, discussed in chapter 3 and used in British Columbia and Ontario to canvass alternatives to the provinces' first-past-the-post electoral systems.

Such proactive measures, if properly implemented, would counterbalance the influence of lobbyists by ensuring that policy-makers also hear the citizen voice in deciding how to govern in the public interest.

Annex 8.1   Sample Treasury Board Clause Prohibiting Payment of a Lobbyist on a Contingency Fee Basis

(i) The Contractor certifies that it has not directly or indirectly paid or agreed to pay and covenants that it will not directly or indirectly pay a contingency fee for the solicitation, negotiation or obtaining of this Contract to any person other than an employee acting in the normal course of the employee's duties.

(ii) All accounts and records pertaining to payments of fees or other compensation for the solicitation, obtaining or negotiating of the Contract shall be subject to the Accounts and Audit provisions of the Contract.

(iii) If the Contractor certifies falsely under this section or is in default of the obligations contained therein, the Minister may either terminate this Contract for default provisions of the Contract or recover from the Contractor by way of reduction to the Contract Price or otherwise the full amount of the contingency fee.

(iv) In this section:

"contingency fee" means any payment or other compensation that is contingent upon or is calculated upon the basis of a degree of success in soliciting or obtaining a Government Contract or negotiating the whole or any part of its terms.

"employee" means a person with whom the Contractor has an employer/employee relationship;

"person" includes an individual or group of individuals, a corporation, a partnership, an organization an association and, without restricting the generality of the foregoing, includes any individual who is required to file a return with the registrar pursuant to section 5 of the *Lobbyists Registration Act* R.S. 1985 c. 44 (4th Supplement) as the same may be amended from time to time.

(Source: Treasury Board Secretariat, *Contracting Policy*, 2003)

9

Information and the Currency of Democracy

In previous chapters, we have focused on standards of probity imposed on public officials and on efforts to make lobbying transparent. In so doing, we urged that the law of democratic accountability in Canada is about more than checks and balances between branches of government. In this chapter we underscore this point.

This chapter has as its first focus transparency in government; specifically, mechanisms ensuring that what government does is readily ascertainable not only by parliamentarians, but also by the general public. Second, it looks at a related issue: strictures on how much the government may know about the public. Last, we look at an issue of renewed importance for a democracy in the current world climate: the extent to which the national security imperatives of our democratic state affect information access and privacy. Here, we analyze Canada's secrecy laws and statutes limiting privacy rights. In this regard, we query at length whether Canada's new and reinvigorated national security secrecy and intelligence-gathering laws go too far, undermining vital concepts of open government and privacy.

The importance of these issues to democratic accountability should not be underestimated. Access to information contributes significantly to the ability of the citizenry as a whole to hold government answerable, while limitations on government use of personal information are a vital component of limited government in a liberal democracy.

A. INFORMATION DISCLOSURE

1. Information Disclosure and Democracy

Access to information is an essential attribute of democracy. U.S. consumer advocate Ralph Nader has called information the "currency of democracy."[1] Openness and transparency preserve citizens from the malfeasance, incompetence, corruption and self-serving behaviour of incumbent governments. They are, as U.S. Supreme Justice Louis Brandeis once quipped, "the best disinfectant."[2] As one of the founders of the United States, James Madison, noted, "[a] popular government without popular information or the means of acquiring it is but a prologue to a farce or a tragedy, or perhaps both. Knowledge will forever govern ignorance; and the people who mean to be their own Governors, must arm themselves with the power which knowledge gives."[3]

Madison's sentiments were echoed repeatedly in discussions of what would become the U.S. *Freedom of Information Act (FOIA)*,[4] introduced in 1966. In hearings leading up to passage of the law, it was argued that "[f]ree people are, of necessity, informed; uninformed people can never be free."[5] In a 1978 decision under the *FOIA*, the U.S. Supreme Court echoed this observation, noting that "[t]he basic purpose of *FOIA* is to ensure an informed citizenry, vital to the functioning of a democratic society, needed to check against corruption and to hold the governors accountable to the governed."[6]

A relative latecomer to the open government game, Canadians have shared this suspicion of government secrecy. Former Auditor General of Canada Denis Desautels has urged that "[i]nformation is the current that

---

[1]   See, e.g., Ralph Nader interview at www.achievement.org/autodoc/page/nadoint-4.

[2]   Louis Brandeis, *Other People's Money and How the Bankers Use It* (New York: Frederick A. Stokes Company, 1914) at 92.

[3]   James Madison in a letter to W.T. Barry (4 Aug. 1822) in S. Padover, ed., The Complete Madison (New York: Harper, 1953) at 337, as cited in T. Murray Rankin, *Freedom of Information in Canada: Will the Doors Stay Shut?* (Canadian Bar Association, 1979) at 1.

[4]   *Freedom of Information Act of 4 July 1966*, Pub. L. No. 89-487, 80 Stat. 250 (5 U.S.C. § 552).

[5]   Freedom of Information: Hearings on S. 1666 and S. 1663 Before the Subcomm. on Admin. Practice and Procedure of the Senate Comm. on the Judiciary, 88th Cong. 3 (1964) (statement of Sen. Edward Long), cited in Charles J. Wichmann, "Ridding FOIA of those 'Unanticipated Consequences': Repaving a Necessary Road to Freedom," (1998) 47 Duke L.J. 1213 at 1217.

[6]   *NLRB v. Robbins Tire and Rubber Company*, 437 U.S. 214 at 242 (1978).

charges accountability in government."[7] Similar views were expressed in Canada during discussions of federal information access laws. Prime Minister Pierre Trudeau noted in 1975 that "[d]emocratic progress requires the ready availability of true and complete information. In this way people can objectively evaluate the government's policies. To act otherwise is to give way to despotic secrecy."[8] The legislative history of what became the *Access to Information Act* contains similar statements of principle. For example, in introducing the Access bill for second reading in the House of Commons, Minister of Communications Francis Fox urged that "[t]his legislation will, over time, become one of the cornerstones of Canadian democracy. The access legislation will be an important tool of accountability to Parliament and the electorate."[9] During the review of the Act undertaken in the mid-1980s by the Standing Committee on Justice and the Solicitor General, the committee cited with approval the sentiments expressed in some of the statements reproduced above and noted that the *Access Act*, along with the *Canadian Charter of Rights and Freedoms* and the *Privacy Act*, "represent significant limits on bureaucracy and have provided a firm anchor to individual rights."[10]

These views continue to be expressed by the information commissioners appointed pursuant to the Act. Then-Information Commissioner John Grace used colourful language to describe this perspective in his 1998 annual report:

> Any society aspiring to be free, just and civil must depend upon and nurture a wide array of methods for exposing, and imposing sanctions on, ethical failures. ... In one way or another, all the checks and balances designed to limit abuses of government power are dependent upon there being access by outsiders to governments' insider information. ... Yes, webs of intrigue are more easily woven in the dark; greed, misdeeds and honest mistakes are more easily hidden. A public service which holds tight to a culture of secrecy is a public service ripe for abuse.[11]

---

7   Cited in Information Commissioner, *Annual Report 2000–01*, available at www.info-com.gc.ca/reports/2000-2001-e.asp (accessed 3 June 2004).

8   Pierre Elliott Trudeau, quoted by G. Baldwin, M.P. in Standing Joint Committee on Regulations and other Statutory Instruments, *Minutes of Proceedings and Evidence*, 30th Parl., 1st Sess. (1974–85), 22:7, as cited in Rankin, *Freedom of Information*.

9   *Commons Debates* (29 Jan. 1981) at 6689.

10   House of Commons Standing Committee on Justice and Solicitor General, *Open and Shut: Enhancing the right to know and the right to privacy* (March 1987) at 1.

11   Information Commissioner, *Annual Report 1997–98* at 4.

Canadian courts have also recognized the importance of free access to information in a democracy. In his reasons in *Dagg v. Canada*, La Forest J. urged that "[t]he overarching purpose of access to information legislation … is to facilitate democracy. It does so in two related ways. It helps to ensure first, that citizens have the information required to participate meaningfully in the democratic process, and secondly, that politicians and bureaucrats remain accountable to the citizenry."[12] While La Forest J. was writing in dissent, his approach to interpreting the Act was endorsed by the majority in that case and has since been followed by the lower courts.[13] More recently, the Supreme Court has noted that the federal *Access to Information Act* makes information "equally available to each member of the public because it is thought that the availability of such information, as a general matter, is necessary to ensure the accountability of the state and to promote the capacity of the citizenry to participate in decision-making processes."[14]

From this discussion, it should be apparent that open government and ready citizen access to information are cornerstones of democratic accountability, as that term is used in this book. Information enables citizens themselves to assess whether government officials — appointed or elected — are performing to expectations. Only access to information enables citizens to cast their ballots in an informed manner and only information allows parliamentarians and the citizens who elect them to clamour for improved performance on the part of the executive branch.

2. International Context

a) Access to Information as an International Right
Often overlooked in discussions of information law are the international legal principles favouring openness in government. Article 19 of the Universal Declaration of Human Rights (UDHR) provides that "[e]veryone has the right to freedom of opinion and expression; this right includes the right to … *seek and impart information* and ideas through any media and regardless of frontiers."[15] As the UN Special Rapporteur on freedom of expression

---

12   [1997] 2 S.C.R. 403 at para. 60.
13   See, e.g., *Canada (Attorney General) v. Canada (Information Commissioner)*, 2004 FC 431 at para. 22, *Yeager v. Canada (Correctional Service) of Canada*, [2003] 3 F.C. 107 at para. 29 (C.A.); *Rubin v. Canada (Minister of Transport)*, [1998] 2 F.C. 430 at para. 36 (C.A.).
14   *Canada (Information Commissioner) v. Canada (Commissioner of the RCMP)*, [2003] 1 S.C.R. 66 at para. 32.
15   Adopted and proclaimed by General Assembly Resolution 217 A (III) of 10 Dec. 1948.

has noted, this provision creates a right to disclosure of information.[16] Notably, the UDHR arguably has legal force as customary international law,[17] and is therefore part of the common law of Canada.[18]

Article 19 of the International Covenant on Civil and Political Rights (ICCPR), ratified by (and thus directly binding on) Canada,[19] also provides that "[e]veryone shall have the right to freedom of expression; this right shall include freedom to *seek, receive and impart information and ideas of all kinds*, regardless of frontiers, either orally, in writing or in print, in the form of art, or through any other media of his choice."[20] This right is subject *only* to such restrictions "as are provided by law and are necessary, (a) For respect of the rights or reputations of others; (b) For the protection of national security or of public order (ordre public), or of public health or morals."

16   Report of the special rapporteur, *Promotion and Protection of the Right to Freedom of Opinion and Expression*, UN Doc. E/CN.4/2000/63 (18 Jan. 2000) at paras. 42–44 ("the Special Rapporteur wishes to state again that the right to seek, receive and impart information is not merely a corollary of freedom of opinion and expression; it is a right in and of itself. As such, it is one of the rights upon which free and democratic societies depend. It is also a right that gives meaning to the right to participate which has been acknowledged as fundamental to, for example, the realization of the right to development" and noting "[p]ublic bodies have an obligation to disclose information and every member of the public has a corresponding right to receive information; 'information' includes all records held by a public body, regardless of the form in which it is stored").

17   See *Statement 95/1, Notes for an Address by the Honourable Christine Stewart, Secretary of State (Latin America and Africa), at the 10th Annual Consultation Between Non-Governmental Organizations and the Department of Foreign Affairs and International Trade*, Ottawa, 17 Jan. 1995 ("Canada regards the principles of the Universal Declaration of Human Rights as entrenched in customary international law binding on all governments"). See also case law from the United States: *Alvarez-Machain v. United States*, 331 F.3d 604 at 618 (9th Cir. 2003) ("We have recognized that the Universal Declaration, although not binding on states, constitutes 'a powerful and authoritative statement of the customary international law of human rights'."), citing *Siderman de Blake v. Republic of Argentina*, 965 F.2d 699 (9th Cir. 1992).

18   See *José Pereira E. Hijos S. A. v. Canada (Attorney General)*, [1997] 2 F.C. 84 at para. 20 (T.D.) ("The principles concerning the application of international law in our courts are well settled ... One may sum those up in the following terms: accepted principles of customary international law are recognized and are applied in Canadian courts, as part of the domestic law unless, of course, they are in conflict with domestic law. In construing domestic law, whether statutory or common law, the courts will seek to avoid construction or application that would conflict with the accepted principles of international law.").

19   See UN Treaty database, available at http://untreaty.un.org/ENGLISH/bible/englishinternetbible/partI/chapterIV/treaty7.asp.

20   G.A. res. 2200A (XXI), 21 UN GAOR Supp. (No. 16) at 52, UN Doc. A/6316 (1966), 999 U.N.T.S. 171, entered into force 23 March 1976 [emphasis added].

b)   International "Best Practices" for Information Access

There is also a body of comparative law influential in understanding information law and policy. Indeed, as of May 2004, more than fifty countries had introduced freedom of information laws.[21] Building on this rich experience, the international free-expression nongovernmental organization "Article 19" proposes several "best practice" principles that should guide government access to information policies (see Table 9.1).[22] These principles "are based on international and regional law and standards, evolving state practice (as reflected in national laws and judgments of national courts) and the general principles of law recognised by the community of nations."[23]

Table 9.1   Article 19's "Best Practices"

Principle	Description
Maximum Disclosure	To maximize disclosure, the law should be broad in its scope, capturing the full range of government information.[24] The government body refusing disclosure bears the onus of demonstrating the legitimacy of this course of action.[25]
Narrow Exemptions from Access	Exemptions from access "should be clearly and narrowly drawn and subject to strict 'harm' and 'public interest' tests."[26] The legitimacy of an exception should be measured via a three-part test. First, "the information must relate to a legitimate aim listed in the law." Second, "disclosure must threaten to cause substantial harm to that aim." Third, "the harm to the aim must be greater than the public interest in having the information."[27]
Prompt Responses	Information requests should be processed "rapidly and fairly" and refusals to disclose should be subject to an independent review.[28] Specifically, access laws should include clear — and short — deadlines for responses to request. Appeals of refusals should be directed to an independent administrative body, which in turn should have full powers to investigate government information decisions and to issue binding orders.[29]
Reasonable Costs	Costs charged to requestors should not be used to deter information requests.[30]

21   David Banisar, *The Freedominfo.org Global Survey: Freedom of Information and Access to Government Records Around the World* (May 2004).
22   See Toby Mendel, *Freedom of Information: A Comparative Legal Survey* (Paris: UNESCO, 2003).
23   *Ibid.* at 23.
24   *Ibid.*
25   *Ibid.* at 26.
26   *Ibid.*
27   *Ibid.* at 28–29.
28   *Ibid.* at 31.
29   *Ibid.* at 33.
30   *Ibid.*

Principle	Description
Legal Consistency	Laws inconsistent with the notion of maximum disclosure should be amended or repealed.[31] Laws governing government secrecy inconsistent with access laws should be subordinated to these access laws, since the later already include carefully demarcated exceptions that should capture any legitimate secrecy objectives the government might have.
Whistleblower Protection	Persons who expose government wrongdoing should be protected by whistleblower laws.[32]
Public Decision-Making	Meetings of public bodies should be open.[33]
Publication	Governments must publish key information. Put another way, access policies require not simply proper responses to requested information, but pro-active dissemination by the government of its information.[34]
Open Government	A policy of "open government" may require such measures as adequate training of officials and the public, policing by an independent agency and criminal penalties for obstruction of legitimate access. Further, open government requires proper record management and maintenance by government.[35]

3. Canada's Federal "Open Government" Information Laws

a) *Access to Information Act*

Background

An assessment of whether Canada's information laws reflect these international benchmarks requires close scrutiny of the *Access to Information Act* (*Access Act*).[36] This statute was the product of two decades of lobbying, not least from Conservative MP Gerald Baldwin, who introduced access to information private member's bills in 1969 and again in 1974. Baldwin also founded ACCESS, a group that lobbied for access legislation. A second prominent *Access Act* advocate was NDP MP Barry Mather, who introduced his own private member's bill in 1965 and in each parliamentary session between 1968 and his retirement in 1974. None of these bills became law, but they did help put the issue on the political agenda.[37]

---

31 *Ibid.*

32 *Ibid.* at 35.

33 *Ibid.* at 34.

34 *Ibid.*

35 *Ibid.* at 27–28.

36 R.S.C. 1985, c. A-1. For an excellent reference resource on the Act, see Michel Drapeau and Marc-Aurèle Racicot, *Federal Access to Information and Privacy Legislation Annotated, 2004* (Toronto: Carswell, 2003).

37 Information Commissioner, *The Access to Information Act: 10 Years* (Ottawa: Minister of Public Works and Government Services Canada, 1994) at 5–7.

Through the 1970s, the debate over access laws focused on the relative virtues of disclosure and openness versus the need for privacy in conducting the processes of government. A 1977 government Green Paper on the subject placed a heavy emphasis on withholding policy documents, urging that release of such records would involve a high administrative cost.[38] At issue, the Green Paper suggested, was the neutrality of the civil service and the tradition of ministerial responsibility,[39] as well as the "candour and comprehensiveness of recorded dialogue within the government."[40]

When the Progressive Conservatives were elected in 1979, they introduced Bill C-15, the *Freedom of Information Act*. Balanced more toward disclosure than was the Green Paper, this bill died on the order paper when the government was unseated later that year. However, this aborted effort prompted a subsequent Liberal bill under the new Trudeau government in 1980. Like the Conservative bill, this new legislative proposal anticipated a broad right of access to government records, circumscribed exemptions, and a review process. The bill, with last-minute amendments excluding Cabinet documents, became the *Access Act* in 1983.[41]

Scope

The *Access Act* applies to "government institutions."[42] Notably, the Act does not establish a principled definition of "government institution," instead simply listing the institutions to which the Act applies in Schedule I. Appendix 1 at the end of this book compares this list to the full listing of all current Government of Canada departments, agencies, Crown corporations and special operating agencies. While many of these bodies are included in the *Access Act*, a substantial number are not. Unless these non-listed bodies are organizationally incorporated into a government department that is itself subject to the *Access Act*, they are not obliged to meet the Act's requirements. Put another way, the *Access to Information Act* does not apply to the federal public administration in its entirety. In fact, the Act's scope is much narrower than that of access laws in other jurisdictions.[43]

---

38   The Honourable John Roberts, "Green Paper" (1977), in Drapeau and Racicot, *Federal Access* at 7.

39   *Ibid.* at 13.

40   *Ibid.*

41   Information Commissioner, *The Access to Information Act* at 8–9.

42   *Access Act*, s. 3.

43   Jerry Bartram, *The Scope of the Access to Information Act: Developing Consistent Criteria for Decisions Respecting Institutions*, Report 12 (Access to Information Review Task Force, July 2001).

As a result, two key criticisms have been levelled at the concept of "government institution" in the Act. First, critics have argued against the exclusion of Crown corporations and other government bodies.[44] As early as 1987, a parliamentary review of the *Access Act* recommended extending the law to Crown corporations.[45] More recently, the Information Commissioner has urged that the Act be extended to "all federal government institutions including Special Operating Agencies, Crown corporations and wholly-owned subsidiaries; any institution to which the federal government appoints a majority of governing body members; the senate, House of Commons, Library of Parliament and all officers of Parliament."[46] Indeed, several private members' bills have been proposed in recent years, the express purpose of which is to extend the Act to Crown corporations.[47] By December 2004, none of these proposed laws had been successful. Treasury Board Secretariat pledged, however, in February 2005 to bring several non-commercial Crowns within the ambit of the Act, and to consider the inclusion of the remaining corporations in a wider review of the access law.[48]

Second, observers have noted that Schedule I of the Act has failed to keep pace with changes in the nature of government. In its 2002 report, the government's Access to Information Task Force observed that

> [w]hen the *Access to Information Act* first came into force in 1983, departments and a few Crown corporations carried out most of the work of government. Since then, the Government of Canada has made changes to the public sector in order to reduce costs and improve efficiency. These changes have included the transfer of functions out of government, the creation of alternative service delivery organizations (some with a partial "for profit" mandate), and partnerships with other levels of government and the private sector.[49]

---

44 See, e.g., the Halifax Initiative submissions to the EDC on disclosure, available at www.halifaxinitiative.org/index.php/EDC_Policies_Disclosure/197 (accessed 16 June 2004).

45 House of Commons Standing Committee on Justice and Solicitor General, *Open and Shut: Enhancing the right to know and the right to privacy* (March 1987).

46 Information Commissioner, *Annual Report 1998–99*, Appendix 1: Proposed Amendments, No. 43.

47 See, e.g., Bill C-302, 37th Parl., 2d Sess., 51 Elizabeth II, 2002; Bill C-462, 37th Parl., 2d Sess., 51–52 Elizabeth II, 2002–03.

48 Treasury Board Secretariat, *Review of the Governance Framework for Canada's Crown Corporations — Meeting the Expectations of Canadians* (2005) at 37.

49 Access to Information Review Task Force, *Access to Information: Making It Work for Canadians* (2002) at 21.

These changes raise concerns that, in outsourcing its functions, government may be circumventing citizen access to information.[50]

In response to the absence of any principled definition of "government institution" in the Act, the government's 2002 Access to Information Task Force proposed that the Act's coverage be expanded to include institutions to which the government appoints a majority of board members, provides all of the financing through appropriations, or owns a controlling interest. It also recommended the Act include institutions performing functions in an area of federal jurisdiction in relation to health and safety, the environment or economic security. In each case, application of the *Access Act* could be excluded where coverage would be inconsistent with the organization's structure or mandate. The Task Force proposed the Act be extended to Parliament, albeit limited by parliamentary privilege and excluding political records. Further, the Act should extend to parliamentary officers such as the Auditor General, the Commissioner of Official Languages and the Information and Privacy Commissioners.[51]

For its part, Bill C-462,[52] the 2003 version of then-Liberal MP John Bryden's *Access Act* reform project, would have extended the reach of the Act to capture Crown corporations and "any incorporated not-for-profit organization which receives at least two-thirds of its financing through federal government appropriations."[53] Receiving substantial all-party support, Mr. Bryden's bill was referred to the Commons justice committee after Second Reading in April 2004, before dying on the order paper at the 2004 election call.

NDP MP Pat Martin introduced a similar bill in the thirty-eighth Parliament, but reportedly withdrew his law project when he received a verbal promise from Liberal Justice Minister Irwin Cotler in November 2004 that substantial reforms to the *Access Act* would be made.[54]

Purpose

The *Access Act* creates a broad principle of access in its first dozen or so sections and then spends a sizeable portion of its remaining sections creating exceptions and caveats to this principle. It articulates a purpose broadly consistent with Article 19's information law "best practices" described earlier. Specifically, the express purpose of the Act is

---

50   See, e.g., Alasdair Roberts, "Structural Pluralism and the Right to Information" (2001) 51 U.T.L.J. 243.

51   Access to Information Review Task Force, *Access to Information* at 24, 30.

52   37th Parl., 2d Sess., 51–52 Elizabeth II, 2002–03.

53   *Ibid.*, subclause 3(1).

54   Paco Francoli, "Marriage Debate Back at Top of Agenda," *The Hill Times*, 15 Nov. 2004.

to extend the present laws of Canada to provide a right of access to information in records under the control of a government institution in accordance with the principles that government information should be available to the public, that necessary exceptions to the right of access should be limited and specific and that decisions on the disclosure of government information should be reviewed independently of government.[55]

The courts have referred repeatedly to this section 2 purpose clause in interpreting the Act.[56] In *Canada (Information Commissioner) v. Canada (Prime Minister)*,[57] Rothstein J., denied that section 2 was merely descriptive and without substantive effect, stating, "[s]tatutes are to be interpreted with a view to carrying out their objects and purposes. When Parliament has been explicit in setting forth the purpose of an enactment and principles to be applied in construing it, I am of the opinion that such purpose and principles must form the foundation on which to interpret the operative provisions of the Act."

In fact, in applying the purpose clause, the Federal Court has concluded that "public access to information ought not be frustrated by the courts except in the clearest of circumstances and the burden of persuasion in this regard rests upon the party resisting disclosure."[58] As noted later in this chapter, this approach informs the court's approach to exceptions from the Act's right to access.

The Right to Access
Section 4 is the single-most important of the Act's operative provisions. It provides that every Canadian citizen and permanent resident "has a right to and shall, on request, be given access to any record under the control of a government institution," subject to other sections in the Act. By extension order, this right is extended to all individuals and corporations present in Canada.[59] Notably, the *Access Act* "does not confer on the heads of government institutions the power to take into account the identity of the applicant or the purposes underlying a request."[60] Indeed, the identity of an

---

55   *Access Act*, s. 2.

56   *Rubin v. Canada (Clerk of the Privy Council)*, [1993] F.C.J. No. 287 (T.D.).

57   *Canada (Information Commissioner) v. Canada (Prime Minister)*, [1993] 1 F.C. 427 (T.D.).

58   See, e.g., *Maislin Industries Limited v. Canada (Minister for Industry, Trade and Commerce)*, [1984] 1 F.C. 939 at 943; *Wyeth-Ayerst Canada Inc. v. Canada (Attorney General)*, 2002 FCT 133 at para. 38 (F.C.T.D.).

59   *Access to Information Act* Extension Order no. 1, SOR/89-207, authorized by *Access Act*, subs. 4(2).

60   *Canada (Information Commissioner) v. Canada (Commissioner of the RCMP)*, [2003] 1 S.C.R. 66 at para. 32.

individual (as opposed to a corporate) requester is itself protected personal information.[61]

The Federal Court of Appeal has held that courts should give the same "liberal and purposive construction" to the interpretation of this section 4 public right to access as they give to statutory rights to be free from discrimination.[62] Indeed, the Federal Court has since referred to the *Access Act* as "quasi-constitutional" in nature.[63] In part, this status reflects language in subsection 4(1) providing that the right in section 4 applies "notwithstanding any other statute." The Federal Court of Appeal has characterized this provision as a "notwithstanding clause" trumping all other federal laws.[64]

That said, it remains unclear whether the right to access articulated in section 4 also has a truly constitutional counterpart. Lower courts have refused to find a right to information disclosure in section 2(b) of the *Charter* (the constitutional free expression provision),[65] or in the unwritten principles of the Constitution.[66] Yet, in a different context, the Supreme Court has held that "freedom of expression in section 2(b) protects both listeners and readers."[67] It therefore supports open courts: "[o]penness permits pub-

---

61   See, e.g., Treasury Board, *Implementation Report No. 65: Guidelines on Treating the Identity of a Requestor as Personal Information* (1999).

62   *Canada Post Corporation v. Canada (Minister of Public Works)*, [1995] 2 F.C. 110 at 128 (F.C.A.); 3430901 *Canada Inc. v. Canada (Minister of Industry)*, [2002] 1 F.C. 421 at para. 26 (F.C.A.).

63   See *Canada (Attorney General) v. Canada (Information Commissioner)*, [2002] 3 F.C. 630 at para. 20 (F.C.).

64   *Canada Post Corporation*, [1995] 2 F.C. 110 at 129 ("subsection 4(1) contains a 'notwithstanding clause' which gives the Act an overriding status with respect to any other Act of Parliament").

65   See *Criminal Lawyers' Assn. v. Ontario (Ministry of Public Safety and Security)* (2004), 70 O.R. (3d) 332 at para. 42 (Div. Ct.), declining to find s. 2(b) applied where access had been denied under the Ontario law; *Ontario (Attorney General) v. Fineberg* (1994), 19 O.R. (3d) 197 at 202 (Div. Ct.) ("it is not possible to proclaim that s. 2(b) entails a general constitutional right of access to all information under the control of government"); *Yeager v. Canada (Correctional Service)*, 2003 FCA 30 at para. 65 (citing and then stating: "Without endorsing all the reasons for decision given in that case, I am in respectful agreement with the conclusion of the Motions Judge that the respondent's *Charter* right was not contravened here.").

66   *Criminal Lawyers' Assn.* (2004), 70 O.R. (3d) 332 at para. 42, holding that the unwritten "democratic principle ... is more concerned with matters relating to the proper functioning of responsible government, and with the proper election of legislative representatives and the recognition and protection of minority and cultural identities, than it is with promoting access to information in order to facilitate the expressive rights of individuals."

67   *Ruby v. Canada (Solicitor General)*, [2002] 4 S.C.R. 3 at para. 52.

lic access to information about the courts, which in turn permits the public to discuss and put forward opinions and criticisms of court practices and proceedings."[68] It is not a tremendous leap to apply similar reasoning to openness of government generally. Whether the courts will eventually do so or not remains to be seen.

Basic Mechanics of the Access Act

All manner of information, except those listed as exemptions or exclusions to the Act (see later) may be released. Under the Act, each minister must publish a description of the organization and responsibilities of each government institution, a description of all classes of records under the control of the institutions, a description of the manuals used by employees, and the title and address of the responsible *Access Act* official for each institution.[69] This is generally done in a publication called *InfoSource*, published by the Treasury Department.

Two key issues that relate to the operation of the Act are time limits and fees, each explored in the following sections.

Time Limits

Under the Act, requests for information to government institutions must be made in writing, and "shall provide sufficient detail to enable an experienced employee of the institution with a reasonable effort to identify the record."[70] While the government provides easy-to-use forms for requesters, any written request will be accepted. Once a satisfactory request is made, the government must make "all efforts" to locate and identify records relevant to that request.[71] "Record" is a broadly defined term, and includes both paper and machine-readable mediums,[72] including electronic mail.[73]

Most government agencies have Access to Information and Privacy (ATIP) coordinators, whose job it is to oversee access to information requests within their respective government agencies. These coordinators are the cornerstone of the system. For instance, although there is no requirement for this in the Act, departmental guidelines generally require ATIP officers to call requesters to clarify the request and ensure that ATIP staff understands what information the requester is seeking. This proce-

---

68 *Ibid.* at para. 53, citing *Canadian Broadcasting Corp. v. New Brunswick (Attorney General)*, [1996] 3 S.C.R. 480, at para. 23.

69 *Access Act*, s. 5.

70 *Ibid.*, s. 6.

71 *X v. Canada (Minister of National Defence)*, [1992] 1 F.C. 77, 87 (T.D.).

72 *Access Act*, s. 2.

73 Treasury Board, *Manual: Access to Information Policy and Guidelines* at chs. 2–4.

dure reduces the risk that information will be excluded as a result of a mere technical error in the wording of the request. ATIP officers may also facilitate amendment of a request following such a consultation, and some departments even have simple forms that can be faxed back to the ATIP coordinator in such cases.

The Act provides that within thirty days of receipt of the request, the government institution must respond as to whether or not access will be granted.[74] The institution may extend this time limit if the request is for a large amount of information, if it requires a great deal of search time, or if consultations (for example, with third parties) are necessary and cannot be done within the original time limit.[75] That said, the extension power does not provide an automatic end-run around the thirty-day limit. As the Federal Court has held, extensions are only reasonable if the government states cogent, genuine reasons for the extension, and its duration.[76]

The Act contains a "deemed refusal" provision in cases where an institution fails to provide access within the time limits.[77] The Federal Court views this section as signalling Parliament's intent that the Act not be "frustrated by bureaucratic procrastination: foot-dragging equates refusal."[78]

Once the deemed refusal provision is triggered, the requester is free to make a complaint to the information commissioner, who may then conduct an investigation.[79] However, as discussed later, the commissioner him- or herself has no powers to compel disclosure. Instead, court orders requiring a response to the request within a specified time frame have been sought, and have sometimes been received.[80] In practice, however, seeking a remedy from the Federal Court, with all the attendant delays, is an unlikely way of compelling compliance with a thirty-day time limit under the *Access Act*. Court review gives, therefore, little incentive to departments to comply with the *Access Act* time requirements.

Tardy processing of access requests has been a key point of friction in the operation of the Act. A 1999 study by Professor Alasdair Roberts found

---

74   *Access Act*, s. 7.

75   *Ibid.*, s. 9.

76   *Canada (Information Commissioner) v. Minister of External Affairs*, [1990] 3 F.C. 514 at 526 (F.C.).

77   *Access Act*, subs. 10(3).

78   *X v. Canada (Minister of National Defence)* (1990), 41 F.T.R. 16.

79   *Canada (Information Commissioner of Canada) v. Canada (Minister of National Defence)*, (1999), 240 N.R. 244 (F.C.A.).

80   See *Canada (Attorney General) v. Canada (Information Commissioner)*, [1996] F.C.J. No. 1204 (T.D.).

that processing time lengthened over the 1990s. "A small number of federal institutions have cut response times and moved toward increased disclosure over the last five years," he noted, but "[m]ost have not."[81] Whereas in 1993–94, 79 percent of requests were filled within sixty days, that figure dropped to 68.1 percent in 1997–98.[82]

More recently, the chronic problem of delays shows signs of abating. By 2002–03, requests received a response within thirty days in 69 percent of instances, and sixty days in 82 percent of cases.[83] In his 2002–03 *Annual Report*, the information commissioner noted that, since 1998, "there has been a dramatic reduction in the number of complaints of delay received by the commissioner, from a high of 49.5 percent of all complaints to a low, this year, of 16.2 percent." In 2002–03, 38 percent of "resolved" (that is, meritorious) complaints concerned delays or time extensions,[84] down from 65 percent in 1998–99.[85]

Fees

Fees are another point of controversy. Under the Act, a fee must accompany the *Access Act* request.[86] The Act allows an application fee of up to $25. By regulation, however, the application fee is set at $5.[87] Further, the requester may also be charged for the staff time involved in responding to the request, although the requester receives five hours of free search time, and the time taken for ATIP staff to clarify, process, or amend the request does not encroach on this free time.

Beyond the five free hours, reproduction costs may be charged to cover photocopying, although institutions may allow requesters to view the documents in-house so that copies do not have to be made. There may also be costs if the information must be generated from a complex computer database involving CPU time. In addition, there is no requirement for government institutions to organize their information in a particular fashion, so if a department has organized the requested information in a system that

---

81 Alasdair Roberts, *Monitoring Performance by Federal Agencies: A Tool for Enforcement of the Access to Information Act* (Kingston, ON: School of Policy Studies, Queen's University, 1999) at 5.

82 *Ibid.* at 2–6.

83 Calculated from Treasury Board, *InfoSource Bulletin*, no.26 (2003).

84 Calculated from Information Commissioner, *Annual Report 2002–03*, Table 2 "Complaint Findings."

85 Calculated from Information Commissioner, *Annual Report 1998–99*, Table 2 "Complaint Findings."

86 *Access Act*, s. 11.

87 SOR/83-507, s. 7.

is difficult to access, costs may be incurred by the requester, even if similar information from another department that organizes its information differently would not cost this amount.

Between 1983 and 2003, the average government cost per request processed was $948. The average fee collected per request was $13.99.[88] Perhaps reflecting this spread, the government's Access to Information Task Force found that views on fees are "polarized."[89] On the one hand, requesters prefer minimal fees, and are suspicious of fee increases. Indeed, in a review of the first ten years of the *Access Act*, the information commissioner noted the view held by some critics that the government charged well in excess of the administrative costs of gathering information "in order to dissuade potential applicants."[90] Government institutions, on the other hand, told the Task Force that "the current fee structure is out of date and is not providing the right balance."[91]

In its 2002 report, the Task Force recommended that the *Access Act* application fee be increased to $10, in part to deter frivolous requests, and that hourly processing and reproduction rates be set according to whether the request is a "general" or a "commercial" request. For general requests, it proposed a rate of $5 per quarter hour of search, preparation and review, after the first five hours. Reproduction costs would be imposed after the first 100 pages of copying. For cases where the cost of processing is more than $10,000, the government should have the option of charging cost-recovery.[92] Data collected by the Task Force suggest that, typically, seventy-one pages of information are released per request and that the typical search time is less than one hour.[93] If so, using the system proposed by the Task Force would not trigger additional processing or reproduction costs for the average request. On the other hand, using the average request as the benchmark for fees may have the effect of rendering the most important requests — those that truly probe the workings of government and consume substantial government research time — prohibitively expensive for all but well-heeled requesters.

The Act does include a broad discretion for departmental officials to waive processing and reproduction fees, but is silent as to the circumstances

88   Treasury Board, *InfoSource Bulletin*, no. 26 (2003).
89   Access to Information Review Task Force, Report at 77.
90   Information Commissioner, *The Access to Information Act* at 18.
91   Access to Information Review Task Force, *Report* at 78.
92   *Ibid.*
93   Goss Gilroy Inc., *An Analysis of Fees for Access to Information Requests*, Report 24 (Access to Information Review Task Force, 2002) at Tables 5 and 9.

under which this waiver should take place.[94] Treasury Board has issued guidelines indicating that government institutions should consider waiving fees where the amount owing is less than $25. Otherwise, the decision to waive costs should be made on a case-by-case basis and include consideration of whether a "general public benefit is obtained through the release of the information."[95] Despite these guidelines, the information commissioner noted in the late 1990s that "there is no uniformity in fee waiver policies across government. Some institutions have no written policy. And in some, the policy is brutally straightforward: There will be no fee waivers!"[96]

Exemptions under the Access Act

The Act includes a large number of exemptions to access. Where access is explicitly refused, the government must indicate either that the requested record does not exist or that a specific exemption in the Act applies.[97]

Alternatively, where the government institution declines to indicate whether a record exists, it must note the provision on which a refusal "could reasonably be expected to be based if the record existed." There is no requirement that exemptions be linked to specific deletions in material that is released. That said, the Federal Court has encouraged this standard practice, calling it "highly commendable" and "in keeping with the basic purpose" of the Act.[98] The Federal Court of Appeal has suggested that some sort of reasons must be supplied by the government when it relies on discretionary exemptions to refuse disclosure,[99] though more recent lower courts decisions have been unprepared to draw this conclusion.[100]

One thing on which both the Act and the courts are clear: exemptions to access are to be construed narrowly. In the words of the Federal Court of Appeal,

> all exemptions to access must be limited and specific. This means that where there are two interpretations open to the Court, it must, given Parliament's stated intention, choose the one that infringes on the public's right to access the least. It is only in this way that the purpose of the Act

---

94 *Access Act*, subs. 11(6).

95 Treasury Board, *Manual* at ch. 1.

96 Information Commissioner, *Annual Report, Information Commissioner, 1997–98* at 21.

97 *Access Act*, subs. 10(1).

98 *Vienneau v. Canada (Solicitor General)*, [1988] 3 F.C. 336 at 342 (F.C.T.D.).

99 *3430901 Canada Inc. v. Canada (Minister of Industry)*, [2002] 1 F.C. 421 at 465–66.

100 *Canada Post Corp. v. Canada (Minister of Public Works and Government Services)*, 2004 FC 1 at paras. 60 and 61.

101 *Rubin v. Canada (Minister of Transport)*, [1998] 2 F.C. 430 at para. 23 (F.C.A.).

can be achieved. It follows that an interpretation of an exemption that allows the government to withhold information from public scrutiny weakens the stated purpose of the Act.[101]

In another case, the Federal Court of Appeal held that "Parliament intended the exemptions to be interpreted strictly. ... The general rule is disclosure, the exception is exemption and the onus of proving the entitlement to the benefit of the exception rests upon those who claim it."[102]

The one, clear exception to this rule of narrow and strict interpretation of exemptions concerns personal information protected by the *Privacy Act* and also exempted from the *Access Act*.[103] When introducing the two laws, the then-minister of communications noted that "[p]arallel rights of access to information held by the government and parallel rights of review of decisions to refuse access have been created. At the same time, however, the principle that the right to privacy takes precedence over the general right of access has been clearly recognized."[104] Thus, the personal information exemption to the *Access Act* is not to receive "a cramped interpretation" that gives the *Access Act* primacy over privacy protections in the *Privacy Act*.[105]

In practice, the *Access Act*'s exemptions can be categorized based on two sets of criteria. First, some exemptions are "injury-based" while others are merely "class-based." In keeping with the "Article 19" view of best international practices discussed above, injury-based exemptions may only be employed where the government concludes that disclosure will produce the harm enumerated by the Act.[106] In almost every injury-based exemption, the question is whether the government institution could have a reasonable expectation of injury stemming from disclosure. Commenting on

---

102 *Rubin v. Canada (Canada Mortgage and Housing Corp.)*, [1989] 1 F.C. 265 at 274 and 276 (F.C.A.), *per* Mr. Justice Heald J., with whom Urie J.A. and Stone J.A. concurred; see also *Canada Post Corp. v. Canada (Minister of Public Works)*, [1995] 2 F.C. 110 at 128–29.

103 *Access Act*, s. 19.

104 Commons Debates at 18853 (28 June 1982).

105 *Dagg v. Canada (Minister of Finance)*, [1997] 2 S.C.R. 403 at para. 51, *per* LaForest J., dissenting but not on this point; *Canada (Information Commissioner) v. Canada (Commissioner of the RCMP)*, [2003] 1 S.C.R. 66 at para. 21 ("it is clear that the *Privacy Act* and the *Access Act* have to be read jointly and that neither takes precedence over the other").

106 See, e.g., *Rubin v. Canada (Minister of Transport)*, [1998] 2 F.C. 430 at para. 30, citing *Canada Packers Inc. v. Canada (Minister of Agriculture)*, [1989] 1 F.C. 47 at 60 (F.C.A.) ("Subsection 2(1) provides a clear statement that the Act should be interpreted in the light of the principle that government information should be available to the public and that exceptions to the public's right of access should be 'limited and specific.' With such a mandate, I believe one must interpret the exceptions to access in paragraphs [20(1)] (c) and (d) to require a *reasonable expectation of probable harm*") [emphasis added].

identical language in a disclosure exemption under the *Privacy Act* (see later in this chapter), the Supreme Court has held that "'the reasonable expectation of probable harm implies a confident belief.' There must be a clear and direct connection between the disclosure of specific information and the injury that is alleged. The sole objective of non-disclosure must not be to facilitate the work of the body in question; there must be professional experience that justifies non-disclosure."[107]

By comparison, class-based exemptions are triggered as soon as the requested information is found to fall within a certain class of information, as defined by the Act. There need not be any subsequent assessment of whether injury would result from disclosure, creating a substantial number of exceptions that do not meet Article 19's best practices standards.

Second, exemptions to access under the Act are of two sorts: mandatory and discretionary. With mandatory exemptions, the government is obliged to decline disclosure, subject in a few instances to a public interest override that allows disclosure where the public interest in disclosure outweighs the interest in nondisclosure.

In fact, the majority of exceptions in the Act are not mandatory, but rather discretionary, allowing government to choose to withhold a document captured by the exemption. While these discretionary exemptions do not include a public interest override, the recent government Access to Information Review Task Force concluded that such an explicit override "is not necessary" as discretionary exemptions "already imply a balancing of the public interest in protecting the information, and the public interest in disclosure."[108]

The Act's exemptions are set out by category in Table 9.2.[109]

---

107 *Lavigne v. Canada (Office of the Commissioner of Official Languages)*, [2002] 2 S.C.R. 773 at para. 58, citing, in part, *Canada (Information Commissioner) v. Canada (Immigration and Refugee Board)*, (1997), 140 F.T.R. 140 at para. 43 (F.C.T.D.).

108 Access to Information Review Task Force, *Report* at 43. Authority supporting this conclusion exists in the case law. See, e.g., *Rubin v. Canada (Minister of Transport)* (1995), 105 F.T.R. 81 at para. 30 (F.C.T.D.) ("While not every exemption has a subsection 20(6) public interest override clause, each exemption is subject to section 2. Thus, all exemptions must meet an implicit injury test that by its very nature means balancing the harm of release against the injury that comes with non-release. Paragraph 16(1)(c) has a public interest emphasis because it stipulates an explicit injury test"), rev'd, but aff'd on this ground, *Rubin*, [1998] 2 F.C. 430 at para. 40 ("As for the third issue, of whether or not to consider the public interest as an independent step under the test for reasonable expectation of probable injury ... Suffice it to say that I am in general agreement with the method adopted by the Trial Judge.").

109 Adapted from Access to Information Review Task Force, *Access to Information* at 41.

Table 9.2   Access Act *Exemptions*

	Class Test	Injury Test
Mandatory exemptions	1. Section 13 — Information received in confidence from other governments or an international organization. If the body gives disclosure permission (or this body has itself made public the information), the information may be disclosed. 2. Sub-section 16(3) — Information obtained or prepared by the RCMP while performing policing services for a province or municipality. 3. Section 19 — Personal information as defined in the *Privacy Act*. If disclosure permission has been obtained, the information is publicly available, or the information may be disclosed under the *Privacy Act*, the information may be disclosed. 4. Paragraph 20(1)(a) — Trade secrets of a third party. 5. Paragraph 20(1)(b) — Financial, commercial, scientific or technical information that is confidential information supplied to a government institution by a third party, subject to a public interest override. 6. Section 24 — Information protected under other, listed statutes.	1. Paragraph 20(1)(c) — Information that reasonably could be expected to result in material financial loss or gain to, or could reasonably be expected to prejudice the competitive position of, a third party, subject to a public interest override. 2. Paragraph 20(1)(d) — Information that could reasonably be expected to interfere with contractual or other negotiations of a third party, subject to a public interest override.
Discretionary exemptions	1. Paragraph 16(1)(a) — Information obtained or prepared by listed investigative bodies pertaining to crime prevention, law enforcement or threats to the security of Canada, if less than twenty years old. 2. Paragraph 16(1)(b) — Information on techniques or plans for specific lawful investigations. 3. Paragraph 18(a) — Trade secrets or financial, commercial, scientific or technical information that belongs to the Government of Canada or a government institution and has substantial value or is reasonably likely to have substantial value.	1. Section 14 — Information that could reasonably be expected to be injurious to the conduct of federal-provincial affairs, including federal strategy or information on federal-provincial consultations or negotiations. 2. Section 15 — Information that could reasonably be expected to be injurious to the conduct of international affairs or to the defence of Canada or an allied state, or the prevention or suppression of subversive or hostile activities. 3. Paragraph 16(1)(c) — Information that could reasonably be expected

	Class Test	Injury Test
Discretionary exemptions	4. Paragraph 21(1)(a) — Advice or recommendations developed by or for a government institution or a minister. 5. Paragraph 21(1)(b) — An account of consultations or deliberations involving officers or employees of a government institution, a minister or the staff of a minister. 6. Paragraph 21(1)(c) — Positions or plans developed for the purpose of negotiations carried on or to be carried on by or on behalf of the Government of Canada and considerations relating thereto. 7. Paragraph 21(1)(d) — Plans relating to the management of personnel or the administration of a government institution that have not yet been put into operation, if the record came into existence less than twenty years prior to the request. 8. Section 23 — Information that is subject to solicitor-client privilege. 9. Section 26 — Information that will be published by the government within ninety days.	to be injurious to law enforcement or to the conduct of lawful investigations, including information on confidential sources. 4. Paragraph 16(1)(d) — Information that could reasonably be expected to be injurious to the security of penal institutions. 5. Sub-section 16(2) — Information that could reasonably be expected to facilitate the commission of an offence, including information that is technical information relating to weapons or potential weapons; or on the vulnerability of particular buildings or other structures or systems. 6. Section 17 — Information the disclosure of which could reasonably be expected to threaten the safety of individuals. 7. Paragraph 18(b) — Information that could reasonably be expected to prejudice the competitive position of a government institution. 8. Paragraph 18(c) — Scientific or technical information obtained through research by an officer or employee of a government institution, the disclosure of which could reasonably be expected to deprive the officer or employee of priority of publication. 9. Paragraph 18(d) — Information that could reasonably be expected to be materially injurious to the financial interests of the government or its ability to manage the economy or could reasonably be expected to result in an undue benefit to any person. 10. Section 22 — Information relating to testing or auditing procedures or techniques or details of specific tests to be given or audits to be conducted if the disclosure would prejudice the use or results of particular tests or audits.

In 2002–03, the most common exceptions invoked by government were the section 19 personal information exemption (32.6 percent), the section 20 third-party information exemption (18.8 percent), and the section 21 operations of government exemption (16.4 percent).[110] This pattern has remained more or less constant through the life of the Act, although the relative importance of the government operations and personal information provisions as against the third-party information exemption has increased in the last several years.[111]

Enforcement by the Access Commissioner

The Act creates a mechanism for policing government decisions on disclosure, and its use of exemptions. An Office of the Information Commissioner is charged with investigating access complaints brought by requesters.[112] As noted in chapter 4, the information commissioner is one of the few government appointees whose appointment follows a joint resolution of Parliament. He or she has tenure for seven years.[113] The Act mandates that the commissioner ranks as a deputy head of a department.[114] This is a significant inclusion, because when complaints are filed the commissioner can deal with the deputy head of government departments as an equal.

Users who are unsatisfied with the treatment of their requests may file a complaint to the information commissioner. The commissioner will hear complaints from persons who, amongst other things, have been refused access to a record, asked to pay an unreasonable amount for access or suffered unreasonable delays. The commissioner may also initiate a complaint.[115]

The Act outlines the investigations procedure to be followed by the information commissioner.[116] Investigations are conducted in private, and a reasonable opportunity to make representations must be given to the requester, the head of the government office concerned, and any third parties involved. However, none of these parties are entitled, as of right, "to be

---

110   Treasury Board, *InfoSource Bulletin*, no. 26 (2003).

111   In the period 1983–91, 40 percent of the exemptions used involved third party information, 21.3 percent involved personal information and 12.1 percent involved the operations of government. Treasury Board, *InfoSource Bulletin*, no. 14 (1991). In the period 1993–98, 28.4 percent of the exemptions used by government institutions invoked the third-party exception, whereas 26.8 percent relied on the personal information exception and 15 percent cited the government operations provision. Figures calculated from *InfoSource Bulletin*, nos. 16–21 (1993–98).

112   *Access Act*, s. 30.

113   *Ibid.*, s. 54.

114   *Ibid.*, s. 55.

115   *Ibid.*, s. 30.

116   *Ibid.*, ss. 32–37.

present during, to have access to or to comment on representations made to the Commissioner by any other person."[117] Procedurally, other than these requirements, "the Information Commissioner may determine the procedure to be followed in the performance of any duty or function of the Commissioner under this Act."[118]

In conducting investigations, the commissioner has the power to: compel oral or written evidence and produce documents; administer oaths; accept evidence, whether or not such evidence would be admissible in a court of law; enter and carry on interviews with people in government offices, and gather documents or make copies. The commissioner also has the power to compel the requested information, and the record cannot be withheld from the commissioner "on any grounds." However, evidence given by a person to the commissioner is inadmissible as evidence against that person in other proceedings (for example, a criminal proceeding), except perjury.[119]

Despite these rules, up until recently, the information commissioner was powerless when confronted with intentional noncompliance with the Act. Thus, in 1996, when the information commissioner determined that records relating to the so-called tainted blood scandal were destroyed in order to avoid responding to an information request, the commissioner had no authority to punish those involved in the destruction of records.[120] Similarly, the information commissioner was helpless to prevent or punish a variety of tactics used by officials at the Department of National Defence which the Somalia inquiry characterized as "a vulgar scheme to frustrate" information requests relating to the activities of the Canadian Forces in Somalia.[121]

Recent amendments to the Act attempt to stamp out such practices. In 1999, a private member's bill resisted by the Liberal front-bench, but supported by Liberal back-benchers, was enacted, creating section 67.1 of the Act. This section imposes penalties of two years' imprisonment and up to a $10,000 fine on persons who destroy, falsify or conceal records with intent to deny the right of access under the Act. The new provision also penalizes those who "direct, propose, counsel or cause any person in any manner to do" these acts.[122]

---

117 *Ibid.*, para. 35(2)(c).
118 *Ibid.*, s. 34.
119 *Ibid.*, s. 36.
120 Information Commissioner, *Annual Report, Information Commissioner, 1996–97* at 64–74.
121 Canada, Commission of Inquiry into the Deployment of Canadian Forces to Somalia, *Dishonoured Legacy: The Lessons of the Somalia Affair* (1997) at 1236–46.
122 Bill C-208, *An Act to amend the Access to Information Act*, 36th Parl., 1st Sess., 46–47 Elizabeth II, 1997–98.

While these criminal penalties likely deter malfeasance under the Act, they do little to ensure disclosure to the requester him or herself. Under the *Access Act*, the information commissioner cannot compel disclosure to the requestor. If a complaint investigated by the commissioner is well founded, the commissioner files a report containing the findings and recommendations, and a request that the government office lay out a plan to implement the recommendations, or provide reasons why no such action can be taken.[123] However, the commissioner's ruling is not binding, a phenomena out of step with the equivalent powers of information commissioners in Ontario, Alberta and British Columbia.

If the government office persists in refusing to disclose the information, the complainant, or the information commissioner, may apply to the Federal Court for a review of the matter. The process of Federal Court judicial review is discussed in greater detail later.

Government Performance

As well as investigating complaints, the information commissioner also reports on — and critiques — government performance in annual reports. The commissioner's assessment of government responsiveness to the Act has often been scathing. Information Commissioner John Grace had this evaluation in his 1998 annual report:

> A culture of secrecy still flourishes in too many high places even after 15 years of life under the *Access to Information Act*. Too many public officials cling to the old proprietorial notion that they, and not the *Access to Information Act*, should determine what and when information should be dispensed to the unwashed public. ... The commitment, by word and deed, to the principle of accountability through transparency has been too often, faltering and weak-kneed.[124]

In the 1990s, the information commissioner exhaustively documented increasing problems with administration of the Act, as well as the diminishing power of his own office. In the period 1990 to 1998, the office handled a 300-percent increase in the number of complaints filed against the government, while experiencing a simultaneous 60-percent budget cut. As a result, according to the commissioner, "the office is itself becoming a troubling source of delay in the system." The commissioner noted "the office's ability to travel to regional offices of government institutions to

---

123   *Access Act*, s. 37.
124   Information Commissioner, *Annual Report, Information Commissioner, 1997–98* at 3.

inspect original records in original files is virtually non-existent." Moreover, "through court actions against the commissioner, the government drains further the office's resources. No matter that none have been successful, the costs of defending them is significant."[125]

Other observers have echoed the commissioner's concerns. In a review of the Act issued in the late 1990s, Professor Alasdair Roberts concluded, "[t]here is now significant evidence that the administration of the [Act] has deteriorated significantly over the last five years. The time taken to process requests has lengthened; disclosure practices appear to be more restrictive; and the probability that a request will result in a substantiated complaint to the Information Commissioner has almost doubled."[126]

More specifically, Roberts found that the number of complaints upheld by the information commissioner had tripled between 1991 and 1998, a pace of increase far exceeding that in the number of requests. In fiscal year 1997–98, 7.9 percent of all requests resulted in meritorious (that is, resolved) complaints, as opposed to 2.9 percent in 1991–92. It was felt that these figures understated the extent of noncompliance with the Act, as many requesters abandon unfilled requests early in the process. The number of exemptions invoked in the context of requests had also increased, from an average of 2.2 exemptions in 1993–94 to 2.44 in 1997–98.[127]

Since the Roberts report, some performance indicators have improved. Specifically, the number of meritorious (that is, resolved) complaints as a proportion of total requests had fallen to 2.6 percent by 2002–03.[128] Other indicators are, however, more mixed. As Figure 9.1 shows, the proportion of access requests resulting in full disclosure stood at about one-third from 1983 to 1998, spiked at 40.6 percent in the late 1990s and now has dropped to below the historical average, standing at 29.6 percent in 2002–03.

The government's Access to Information Review Task Force found in 2002 that many requestors continue to feel that the Act is applied "inconsistently and in such a way as to contradict the principles of openness,

125 *Ibid.* at 8–9.
126 Alasdair Roberts, "Monitoring Performance by Federal Agencies: A Tool for Enforcement of the *Access to Information Act*" (working paper, School of Policy Studies, Queen's University, Kingston, 1999) at 12.
127 *Ibid.* at 2–6.
128 Calculated from Treasury Board, *InfoSource Bulletin*, no. 26 (2003), statistical tables (total requests) and Information Commissioner, *Annual Report, Information Commissioner, 2002–03* statistical tables ("resolved" column, in "Complaints Finding" table).

Figure 9.1   Percentage of Requests Resulting in Full Disclosure

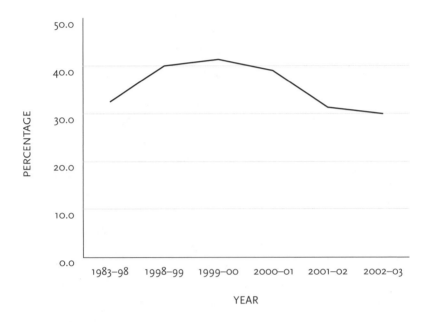

Source: Treasury Board, *InfoSource*, 1998–2003[129]

transparency and accountability that underlie it."[130] In deciding to exercise discretionary exemptions, "heads of government institutions (or their delegates) do not always consider all relevant factors in exercising their discretion, nor do they articulate clear reasons for withholding information."[131] Roberts also flagged this problem in the late 1990s, noting then that government departments and agencies "may try to stretch and test the law in an effort to protect bureaucratic or governmental interests."[132] Officials were said to be adopting broad interpretations of exemptions.[133]

In his 2003–04 report, the information commissioner reviewed the Chrétien legacy in open government, comparing it to Mulroney's tenure. In the commissioner's words: "Nothing undermined the right of access

129   Available at http://infosource.gc.ca/bulletin/bulletin_e.asp (last accessed 05/25/04).
130   Access to Information Review Task Force, *Report* at 3.
131   *Ibid.* at 43.
132   Roberts, "Monitoring Performance" at 1–2.
133   Alasdair Roberts, *Limited Access: Assessing the Health of Canada's Freedom of Information Laws* (Kingston, ON: School of Policy Studies, Queen's University, 1998) at 12.

more, in the past twenty years, than the disdain shown for it by two long-serving Prime Ministers. Their destructive example spread like a cancer through successive PMOs, PCOs and the senior bureaucracy. For twenty years, Canadians seeking information — especially about any subject the government considered "sensitive" — have been met by a wall of obstruction, obfuscation and delay."[134]

Given these conclusions, it is difficult to view government performance under the *Access Act* as fully satisfactory or to describe its support for open government as enthusiastic.

Exclusions under the Access Act

In a jarring break with its emphasis on access, narrowly tailored exemptions and independent review of access decisions, the *Access Act* also includes three exclusions: three classes of information that are excluded entirely from the operation of the Act.

The first exclusion is the least problematic: the Act does not apply to published materials, library or museum material preserved solely for public reference or exhibition purpose, or material placed in the National Archives or other cultural institutions by or on behalf of persons other than government bodies.[135]

Second, and more controversially, in the wake of the government's 2001 anti-terrorism law, the Act does not apply to information certified by the government as national security information under the *Canada Evidence Act*.[136] This exclusion is discussed in greater detail below, in the section on government national security secrecy laws.

Last, the Act does not apply to confidences of the Queen's Privy Council for Canada that are less than twenty years old.[137] These Cabinet confidences are defined in the Act as including the following documents:

- *Memoranda*: Paragraph 69(1)(a) refers to memoranda containing proposals and recommendations to Cabinet. On its face, this category is broad, covering even records or draft records government officials intend to be submitted to Cabinet that may not have been actually submitted.[138] However, Treasury Board policy narrows the category somewhat by stating that materials appended to memoranda, not originally

---

134 Information Commissioner, *Annual Report, Information Commissioner, 2003–04* at 5.
135 *Access Act*, s. 68.
136 *Ibid.*, s. 69.1.
137 *Ibid.*, s. 69.
138 Treasury Board, *Manual* at chs. 2–6.

intended in their creation to comprise advice to Cabinet (for example, newspaper clippings, tables of statistics, reports prepared for use within a department), are not confidences in their original state.[139]

- *Discussion Papers*: This exclusion, under paragraph 69(1)(b), includes documents containing background explanations, analyses of problems or policy options for Cabinet to consider. Notably, paragraph 69(3)(b) carves out an exception to the definition of discussion papers protected by Cabinet confidence. Thus, where four years have passed since the decision that the paper deals with has been made or the decision to which the paper relates has been made public, the discussion paper is subject to the *Access Act*.

The information commissioner has argued that the discussion paper category is largely outdated, since "[t]he discussion paper seems to have been largely abandoned in the Cabinet Paper System in favour of 'Analysis and Background' sections in memoranda to Cabinet," themselves exempt under paragraph 69(1)(a). This change, a report prepared for the information commissioner suggests, "was done, in the main part, to streamline the Cabinet decision-making process. An ancillary objective may have been to prevent these types of records from becoming accessible under the *Access to Information Act*."[140]

However, to a certain extent, this potential end-run around the paragraph 69(3)(b) limit on Cabinet confidences was curtailed by the Federal Court of Appeal in *Canada (Minister of Environment) v. Canada (Information Commissioner)*.[141] Here, the Court of Appeal concluded that paragraph 69(3)(b) applies even where the discussion paper is appended to memoranda to Cabinet protected under 69(1)(a). Thus, where the discussion paper constitutes an "organized body or corpus of words which looked upon its own, comes within the definition" of a discussion paper, it must be severed from the Cabinet confidence to which it is attached, and released to the public once the criteria in paragraph 69(3)(b) are met, subject to any proper exemption under the Act.[142] Notably, this ruling has important implications for any sort of document appended to a Cabinet confidence. It suggests that the simple attach-

---

139   *Ibid.*

140   Information Commissioner, *The Access to Information Act and Cabinet Confidences* (report prepared by RPG Information Services Inc., 1996) at 9–10.

141   (2003), 2 Admin. L.R. (4th) 271 (F.C.A.).

142   "Privy Council Memorandum to Access to Information and Privacy Coordinators (8 April 2003), responding to *Canada (Minister of Environment) v. Canada (Information Commissioner)*" (2003), 2 Admin. L.R. (4th) 271.

ment of such a document to a Cabinet confidence cannot be used to "launder" that document, and exclude it from the scope of the *Access Act*.

- *Agenda and minutes of Cabinet meetings*: Paragraph 69(1)(c) covers meeting agendas of Cabinet, as well as the minutes and records of the decisions made in such meetings. Treasury Board policy draws, however, a distinction between the formal record (which is excluded from the *Access Act*), and a published summary or substance of a Cabinet decision that is made public (which is not excluded).[143]
- *Ministerial correspondence*: Paragraph 69(1)(d) covers correspondence, or records of correspondence, between ministers on matters relating to government decisions or policy. The exclusion only covers matters tied to the formulation of policy, not discussions of current government policy, for example.[144]
- *Briefing notes*: Briefing notes on matters before Cabinet that are prepared for ministers are excluded from the *Access Act* under paragraph 69(1)(e). However, the notes must have been prepared for use by the minister, not for use in departmental or other policy development.[145]
- *Draft legislation*: All draft legislation is excluded from the Act under paragraph 69(1)(f), even after the final version has been passed by Parliament.
- *Records containing information about confidences*: Paragraph 69(1)(g) excludes records relating to the contents of any of the other confidences described under the section. However, if the record contains information that is also found in a Cabinet confidence, it is not automatically excluded. In order to qualify for this exclusion, the record must connect the allegedly excluded information to the decision-making and policy function of the minister or Cabinet as a whole.[146]

In interpreting the Cabinet confidences rule, "Cabinet" includes committees of Cabinet — standing, *ad hoc*, and any other committees of ministers — as well as informal meetings between ministers, provided that the records concern government decisions or the formulation of government policy.

The Cabinet confidence exclusion has been a source of considerable controversy. It exists to preserve Cabinet government. As the Supreme Court has noted

> [c]abinet confidentiality is essential to good government ... Those charged with the heavy responsibility of making government decisions must be

---

143 Treasury Board, *Manual* at chs. 2–6.
144 Information Commissioner, *The Access to Information Act and Cabinet Confidences* at 10.
145 *Ibid.* at 11.
146 Treasury Board, *Manual* at chs. 2-6.

free to discuss all aspects of the problems that come before them and to express all manner of views, without fear that what they read, say or act on will later be subject to public scrutiny ... If Cabinet members' statements were subject to disclosure, Cabinet members might censor their words, consciously or unconsciously. They might shy away from stating unpopular positions, or from making comments that might be considered politically incorrect.[147]

A similar rationale for protecting Cabinet confidences is articulated in the Treasury Board's access to information guidelines:

> The Canadian government is based on a Cabinet system. Thus, responsibility rests not in a single individual, but on a committee of ministers sitting in Cabinet. As a result, the collective decision-making process has traditionally been protected by the rule of confidentiality. This rule protects the principle of the collective responsibility of ministers by enabling them to support government decisions, whatever their personal views. The rule also enables ministers to engage in full and frank discussion necessary for effective functioning of a Cabinet system of government.[148]

Nevertheless, at the time the Act was passed, the Cabinet confidence rule was the most contentious clause. A report prepared for the information commissioner notes that

> the decision to exclude Cabinet confidences from the coverage of the *Access to Information Act* was made at the eleventh hour (June, 1982 as a parliamentary session was closing) by a nervous Trudeau Government which sought to protect the essential processes of Cabinet and parliamentary government while proceeding with access legislation. ... [It] ... served as a lightening rod for criticism which brought the legislation into some disrepute even before it was proclaimed in July, 1983.
>
> Dubbed the "Mack Truck" clause by the Opposition and media alike, the exclusion of Cabinet confidences was immediately fastened on as evidence that the Trudeau Liberals, long in power and with many secrets to keep, had brought forth a secrecy law camouflaged in the language of openness.[149]

The original version of the Act, contained in the Clark government's Bill C-15, *exempted* (rather than excluded) Cabinet confidences. Similarly,

---

147 *Babcock v. Canada (Attorney General)*, [2002] 3 S.C.R. 3 at paras. 15 and 18.
148 Treasury Board, *Manual* at chs. 2–6.
149 Information Commissioner, *The Access to Information Act and Cabinet Confidences* at 2.

Australia, which was considering access to information legislation at the same time as was the Canadian federal government, maintained Cabinet confidences as an exemption, giving users recourse to the ordinary review processes.[150] The more recent legislation of British Columbia[151] and Ontario[152] also grant their information and privacy commissioners the power to review decisions to withhold records under Cabinet confidence. A parliamentary committee reviewing the law in 1987 went so far as to state that the exclusion of Cabinet confidences from the Act undermined the credibility of the access statute, and recommended that decisions to withhold records classified as Cabinet confidences be reviewable by the Associate Chief Justice of the Federal Court.[153]

However, the blanket exclusion remains in the Act, prompting consultants retained by the information commissioner to call the provision "arguably the major gap in the law's coverage."[154] If the government decides that a record is excluded from the Act, there is no recourse to independent review, by either the information commissioner or the Federal Court. Section 69 specifies that "[t]his Act does not apply to confidences." Lest there be any doubt, section 39 of the *Canada Evidence Act* specifies that where a minister or the clerk of the Privy Council specifies in writing that information is a confidence, "disclosure of the information shall be refused without examination or hearing of the information by the court, person or body."

The apparent absence of independent review raises the prickly problem of policing government use of exclusions. This conundrum was resolved in part by two recent cases. In *Babcock v. Canada (Attorney General)*,[155] the Supreme Court concluded that, in certifying a Cabinet confidence under section 39 of the *Canada Evidence Act*, the clerk of the Privy Council must answer two questions. First, is the information a confidence within the meaning of the section; and, second, is it information that the government should protect, given competing interests in disclosure versus confidentiality. Only when these two questions are asked and answered in the affirmative is the certificate valid, and the bar on court review triggered. Thus, if "it can be shown from the evidence or the circumstances that the power of certification was exercised for purposes outside those contemplated by s. 39,

---

150 *Freedom of Information Act*, 1982 (Aust.) s. 34.

151 *Freedom of Information and Protection of Privacy Act*, R.S.B.C. 1996, c.165, para. 12(2)(a).

152 *Freedom of Information and Privacy Act*, R.S.O. 1990, c.F-31, s. 12.

153 House of Commons Standing Committee on Justice and Solicitor General, *Open and Shut* at 33.

154 Information Commissioner, *The Access to Information Act and Cabinet Confidences*.

155 [2002] 3 S.C.R. 3 at para. 22.

the certification may be set aside as an unauthorized exercise of executive power."[156] A certificate may, in other words, be challenged on judicial review, not on its merits, but on the basis that the information "does not on its face fall within s. 39(1), or where it can be shown that the Clerk or minister has improperly exercised the discretion conferred by s. 39(1)."[157]

The Supreme Court's reasoning in Babcock was adopted by the Federal Court of Appeal in relation to section 69 of the *Access Act* in *Canada (Minister of Environment) v. Canada (Information Commissioner).*[158] There, the Court of Appeal upheld a Federal Court decision in which the judge concluded he had jurisdiction to review the application of section 69 of the *Access Act* to a putative Cabinet confidence, and the issuance of a certificate under section 39 of the *Canada Evidence Act*, on the standard of review of "correctness." Together with Babcock, this decision — which the government has decided not to appeal — is an "enormously important catalyst ... for reducing the zone of cabinet secrecy at the federal level."[159]

b) *Privacy Act*

In many respects, the *Privacy Act*[160] is the flipside of the *Access Act*. While the *Access Act* has as its purpose the promotion of disclosure, the *Privacy Act* has both a nondisclosure and a disclosure function. First, the Act is designed to "protect the privacy of individuals" in relation to personal information about those individuals held by government. Second, individuals are to be given a right of access to their personal information in the possession of government.[161] In light of these purposes, the Supreme Court of Canada has agreed that the *Privacy Act* has a "special status," potentially of a "quasi-constitutional" nature.[162]

How the Act addresses its first purpose of protecting privacy is discussed later. This section addresses the Act's second objective — disclosure of personal information.

---

156 *Ibid.* at para. 25.

157 *Ibid.* at para. 39.

158 (2003), 2 Admin. L.R. (4th) 271.

159 Information Commissioner, "Remarks: The Freedom of Information and Protection of Privacy Act 10th Anniversary Conference," Vancouver, B.C., 25 Sept. 2003.

160 R.S.C. 1985, c. P-21.

161 *Privacy Act*, s. 2.

162 *Lavigne v. Canada (Commissioner of Official Languages)*, [2002] 2 S.C.R. 773 at para. 24, citing with approval *Canada (Privacy Commissioner) v. Canada (Labour Relations Board)*, [1996] 3 F.C. 609, 652 (T.D.) ("A purposive approach to the interpretation of the *Privacy Act* is ... justified by the statute's quasi-constitutional legislative roots") and at para. 23, indicating that the Court recognizes the "quasi-constitutional" statute of the *Privacy Act*.

Disclosure of Personal Information

The disclosure provisions of the *Privacy Act* track fairly closely the comparable sections in the *Access Act*. Indeed, the two Acts are considered woven together in a "seamless code."[163]

Every Canadian citizen or permanent resident has a right to access personal information contained in a personal information bank and any other personal information held by a government institution which the requester can describe sufficiently to allow retrieval.[164] By extension order, this right now extends to all persons present in Canada.[165] Coupled with this right of access is a right to request correction of this personal information.[166]

The "government institutions" to which the Act applies are listed in a schedule to the statute, and include government departments and ministries of state, and many boards, tribunals and agencies. The Act also covers a number of Crown corporations not included under the *Access Act*, as Appendix 1 shows.

"Personal information" means "information about an identifiable individual that is recorded in any form,"[167] a definition that is "deliberately broad" and "is entirely consistent with the great pains that have been taken to safeguard individual identity."[168] For this reason, courts should be reluctant to narrow the ambit of personal information, within the meaning of the Act.[169] That said, the statute itself excludes from the definition of personal information data on government employees or officers relating to their positions.[170]

Government "personal information banks" that fall under the *Privacy Act*'s provisions include all personal information controlled by a government institution available for use for an administrative purpose — basically, use in a decision-making process directly affecting the individual — or that

163 *Dagg*, [1997] 2 S.C.R. 403 at para. 45, *per* LaForest J., dissenting but not on this point; *Canada (Information Commissioner) v. Canada (Commissioner of the RCMP)*, [2003] 1 S.C.R. 66 at para. 22 ([t]he *Access Act* and the *Privacy Act* are a seamless code with complementary provisions that can and should be interpreted harmoniously").

164 *Privacy Act*, s .12.

165 *Privacy Act* Extension Order no. 2, SOR/89-206, made pursuant to *Privacy Act*, subs. 12(3).

166 *Privacy Act*, s. 12.

167 *Ibid.*, s. 3.

168 *Lavigne*, [2002] 2 S.C.R. 773 at para. 26, citing with approval *Canada (Information Commissioner) v. Canada (Solicitor General)*, [1988] 3 F.C. 551 at 557 (F.C.T.D.).

169 *Canada (Information Commissioner) v. Canada (Commissioner of the RCMP)*, [2003] 1 S.C.R. 66 at para. 26 ("it is not for this Court to limit the scope" of the s.3 definition of personal information).

170 *Privacy Act*, subs. 3(j).

may be retrieved by a person's name or some other identifying indicator assigned to an individual.[171] Every year, the government is required to produce an index of all personal information banks describing, amongst other things, the bank, the class of individuals to whose personal information the bank relates, the purposes for which the information in the bank was obtained or compiled and a statement of consistent uses for which this information is used or disclosed.[172] The index must also describe classes of personal information not contained in personal information banks in sufficient detail to facilitate the right of access under the Act.[173]

A request for access to personal information must be made in writing.[174] Unlike the *Access Act*, a requester is not obliged to pay an application fee. On receipt of the request, the government must respond within thirty days.[175] Much like with the *Access Act*, the government can extend this time limit should the thirty-day requirement unreasonably interfere with government operations or where consultations that cannot be completed in the thirty-day window are necessary to comply with the request.[176] In 2002–03, over 74 percent of requests were processed within thirty days, and almost 91 percent of requests were completed within sixty days.[177] These figures compare favourably with historical response times since the introduction of the Act in 1983 — 57.1 percent in thirty days and 76.1 percent within sixty days.[178]

The government's response to a personal information access request must indicate whether access will be given.[179] Where it is not, the government must state that the personal information does not exist or list the specific provisions of the Act that would exempt disclosure were the information to exist.[180] As with the *Access Act*, the *Privacy Act* includes a deemed refusal provision, equating a failure to comply with the Act's time limits with a refusal to give access.[181]

A number of exemptions exist under the Act. As with the *Access Act*, exemptions to disclosure under the *Privacy Act* have been interpreted narrow-

---

171   *Ibid.*, s. 10.
172   *Ibid.*, s. 11.
173   *Ibid.*
174   *Ibid.*, s. 13.
175   *Ibid.*, s. 14.
176   *Ibid.*, s. 15.
177   Treasury Board, *InfoSource Bulletin*, no. 26 (2003).
178   *Ibid.*
179   *Ibid.*, s. 14.
180   *Ibid.*, s. 16.
181   *Ibid.*, subs. 16(3).

ly.[182] Again, like the *Access Act*, these exemptions may be classed as mandatory and discretionary, and as class-based and injury-based, *per* Table 9.3.

Table 9.3   *Exemptions to Disclosure under the* Privacy Act

	Class Test	**Injury Test**
Mandatory exemptions	1. Section 19 — Information received in confidence from other governments or an international organization. If the body gives disclosure permission (or this body has itself made public the information), the information may be disclosed. 2. Section 18 — Exempted information banks that consist principally of personal information covered by s. 21 or s. 22 of the Act. Certain personal information banks operated by the RCMP and the Canadian Security Intelligence Service are exempted.[183] 3. Subsection 22(2) — Information obtained by the RCMP while performing policing services for a province or municipality. 4. Section 26 — Personal information about another person where disclosure is prohibited under s. 8 of the Act (discussed below).	
Discretionary exemptions	1. Paragraph 22(1)(a) — Information pertaining to crime prevention, law enforcement or threats to the security of Canada, if less than twenty years old. 2. Section 26 — Personal information about an individual other than the requester, where disclosure is not prohibited by s. 8 of the Act (see below) 3. Section 27 — Information subject to solicitor-client privilege.	1. Section 20 — Injury to the conduct of federal-provincial affairs. 2. Section 21 — Injury to the conduct of international affairs or to the defence of Canada or an allied state, or the prevention or suppression of subversive or hostile activities. 3. Paragraph 22(1)(b) — Injury to law enforcement or to the conduct of lawful investigations, including information on confidential sources. 4. Paragraph 22(1)(c) — Injury to the security of penal institutions.

182 See *Lavigne*, [2002] 2 S.C.R. 773 at para. 30, citing *Canada (Information Commissioner) v. Canada (Immigration and Refugee Board)* (1997), 140 F.T.R. 140 at paras. 34–35 ([t]he *Privacy Act*'s purpose is to provide access to personal information maintained by government. ... The necessary exceptions to the access must be strictly construed").

183 See Exempt Personal Information Bank Order no. 13 (RCMP), SOR/90-149; Exempt Personal Information Bank Order, No. 14 (CSIS), SOR/92-688; Exempt Personal Information Bank Order no. 25 (RCMP), SOR/93-272.

	Class Test	Injury Test
Discretionary exemptions (con't)		5. Section 23 — Information obtained or prepared by an investigative body to determine whether to grant government or foreign government security clearances, if this information could reasonably be expected to reveal the identity of the person furnishing the information to the agency. 6. Paragraph 24(a) — Information collected by Corrections Canada or the National Parole Board while the requester was under sentence if disclosure could reasonably be expected to seriously disrupt the individual's release program. 7. Paragraph 24(b) — Information collected by Corrections Canada or the National Parole Board while the requester was under sentence if disclosure could reasonably be expected to reveal information about the requestor obtained under a promise of confidentiality. 8. Section 25 — Information the disclosure of which could reasonably be expected to threaten the safety of individuals. 9. Section 28 — Information relating to the physical or mental health of the requestor where examination of this information would be contrary to the best interests of the individual.

In 2002–03, the top three exemptions, expressed as a proportion of all exemptions used, were: section 26 (information about another individual — 63 percent); section 22 (law enforcement and investigation — 19 percent); and, section 19 (personal information obtained in confidence — 9.1 percent).[184] On the whole, exemption use under the *Privacy Act* appears to be on the rise. The proportion of requests resulting in full disclosure has declined over time from a long-term average during the period 1983–97 of 62 percent to just over 45 percent in 2002–03.[185]

Enforcement by the Privacy Commissioner

The Office of the Privacy Commissioner polices government use of exceptions under the Act. Like the information commissioner, the privacy commissioner has the rank of deputy head of a department, and is appointed after approval by resolution of the senate and House of Commons.[186]

Individuals refused access to their personal information may complain in writing to the privacy commissioner.[187] Complaints may also be brought where, amongst other things, the government extends the time limit for a

---

184 Treasury Board, *InfoSource Bulletin*, no. 26 (2003).
185 Calculated from Treasury Board, *InfoSource Bulletin*, nos. 20–26 (1997–2003) reports.
186 *Privacy Act*, s. 54.
187 *Ibid.*, ss. 29 and 30.

response to a request in a fashion that the requester considers unreasonable.[188] An investigation may also be requested in the wake of a deemed refusal, stemming from a failure to comply with the Act's time limitations.[189] The commissioner may initiate a complaint him- or herself, where reasonable grounds to investigate a matter under the Act exist. In 2002–03, 43 percent of complaints made to the commissioner concerned allegations that access rights under the *Privacy Act* had been violated, while another 33 percent complained of government delay.[190]

Investigations of complaints by the commissioner are to be conducted in private.[191] During the course of these investigations, the commissioner has the same power as superior court of record to summon and enforce the appearance of persons or compel the production of documents and things. He or she may also administer oaths, and enter any government premise and examine any information within the control of the government, other than a Cabinet confidence.[192] In fact, the commissioner may even review information in "exempt" information banks, such as those held by the RCMP and CSIS to review whether a file is properly included in these exempt banks.[193]

If the commissioner concludes a complaint is well-founded, he or she provides the head of the government institution controlling the personal information with a report outlining the commissioner's findings and, where appropriate, a request that he or she be informed of the government's progress in responding to the recommendations contained in the report.[194] The complainant is also informed of the commissioner's findings. Where the government refuses access despite the commissioner's report, the commissioner notifies the complainant of his or right to apply to the Federal Court for judicial review. The Federal Court's role in reviewing government use of exemptions is discussed later.

Government performance under the *Privacy Act*, on the whole, appears to be better than under the *Access Act*. In 2002–03, the proportion of meritorious complaints to total completed *Privacy Act* personal information

188 *Ibid.*, s. 29.
189 *Cunha v. Minister of National Revenue*, [1999] F.C.J. No. 667 (F.C.T.D.) at para. 9 ("[w]hile there is no specific reference in subsection 29(1) to deemed refusals pursuant to 16(3), I am persuaded that a complaint with respect thereto falls within subparagraph 29(1)(h)(i)", allowing complaints concerning the collection, retention or disposal of personal information by a government institution).
190 Privacy Commissioner, *Annual Report 2002–03*.
191 *Privacy Act*, s. 33.
192 *Ibid.*, s. 34.
193 *Ibid.*, s. 36.
194 *Ibid.*, s. 35.

requests was only 1.63 percent, a figure that compares favourably to the 2 percent proportion averaged over the period 1998–2002.[195]

Exclusions under the Privacy Act

Finally, like the *Access Act*, the *Privacy Act* contains exclusions that mimic in large part the exclusions from the *Access Act*. First, the *Privacy Act* does not apply to library or museum materials preserved for public reference. This exclusion also includes exhibition materials placed in national archives and museums on behalf of those outside government.[196] Second, the Act does not apply to Cabinet confidences, defined in a fashion identical to the *Access Act*.[197] Finally, the Act does not apply where a national security certificate is issued under s. 38.13 of the *Canada Evidence Act*.[198] This last exclusion is discussed further later, under government secrecy law.

c) Judicial Review of Exemption Decisions under the *Access* and *Privacy Acts*

Basic Mechanics

The *Access* and *Privacy Acts* contain very similar judicial review provisions. Both authorize a requester to seek judicial review of government nondisclosure within forty-five days of the completion of an investigation by the information commissioner or the privacy commissioner, as the case may be.[199] Further, each statute enables the relevant commissioner to request such a review, if s/he has the consent of the requester.[200] Under the *Access Act*, third parties may also apply to review decisions to release information that may affect them.[201] Under both the *Access* and *Privacy Acts*, the burden of proof on judicial review rests on the government institution, obliging the government to demonstrate its authorization for refusing to release the information.[202]

---

195 Calculated by dividing the sum of "well-founded," "well-founded/resolved," "resolved" and "settled" complaints regarding access and time limits (as reported by the Privacy Commissioner, *Annual Reports*, 1997–2003, table Completed Investigations by Grounds and Results) by total *Privacy Act* requests completed (reported by Treasury Board, *InfoSource Bulletin*, nos. 20-26 (1997–2003).

196 *Privacy Act*, s. 69.

197 *Ibid.*, s. 70. Application of this section is likely informed by the recent Supreme Court of Canada and Federal Court of Appeal cases discussed earlier in relation to the equivalent *Access Act* exclusion.

198 *Privacy Act*, s. 70.1.

199 *Access Act*, s. 41; *Privacy Act*, s. 41. Section 43 of the *Privacy Act* also allows the privacy commissioner to apply for court review of whether a file should be included or not in an exempt information bank.

200 *Access Act*, s. 42; *Privacy Act*, s. 42.

201 *Ibid.*, s. 44.

Notably, both statutes contain protections against involuntary disclosure of the contested information during judicial review. Thus, both statutes instruct the Federal Court to take "every reasonable precaution" to avoid disclosure of information that the government would be authorized not to disclose under the *Access* or *Privacy Acts*.[203] Reasonable precautions suggested by the statute include receiving representations *ex parte* (that is, privately, from the government, in the absence of the applicant) or conducting hearings *in camera* (that is, behind closed doors).

An even more rigorous nondisclosure system is set in place where the review concerns information the government has declined to disclose because it was received in confidence from foreign governments or international organizations[204] or information reasonably injurious to international affairs or to the defence of Canada or an allied state, or the prevention or suppression of subversive or hostile activities.[205] Here, the case must be heard and determined by the Chief Justice of the Federal Court or a judge designated by the Chief Justice. Further, the hearing must be *in camera* and the government must be given an opportunity to make submissions on an *ex parte* basis, if it so requests.[206] In a recent *Privacy Act* case that likely applies equally to the *Access Act*, the Supreme Court concluded that by reason of the free expression guarantee in section 2(b) of the *Charter*, the mandatory *in camera* hearing requirement applies only to those portions of the hearing in which *ex parte* submissions are heard. In other instances, the court retains the discretion to close the hearing or not.[207]

Where a court concludes that the government institution acted improperly in refusing to disclose a record, it is required to order disclosure of the record, subject to whatever conditions the court views as reasonable.[208] On the other hand, under the *Access Act*, where a court concludes that the government institution is "required to refuse to disclose a record," the court will order the government institution not to disclose the record, or issue whatever other order the court views as proper.[209]

---

202 *Access Act*, s. 48; *Privacy Act*, s. 47.

203 *Access Act*, s. 47; *Privacy Act*, s. 46.

204 *Access Act*, paras. 13(1)(a) or (b); *Privacy Act*, paras. 19(1)(a) or (b).

205 *Access Act*, s. 15; *Privacy Act*, s. 21.

206 *Access Act*, s. 52; *Privacy Act*, s. 51.

207 *Ruby v. Canada (Solicitor General)*, [2002] 4 S.C.R. 3 at para. 60.

208 *Access Act*, ss. 49 and 50; *Privacy Act*, ss. 48 and 49. Under s. 50 of the *Privacy Act*, where the application is made by the privacy commissioner under s. 43, in relation to a file contained in an exempt information bank, the Court assesses the propriety of the inclusion of that file in the bank.

209 *Access Act*, s. 50.

A key question is how demanding the court will be of the government in evaluating the nondisclosure decision under review before it. Specifically, what "standard of review" will the court apply?

The "Not Authorized" or "Reasonable Grounds" Standards of Review

On their faces, the two statutes each create two standards of review, depending on the justification for nondisclosure invoked by the government. In most instances, the Federal Court may order disclosure, subject to any conditions it views appropriate, "if it determines that the head of the institution is *not authorized* to refuse to disclose the record or part thereof."[210]

Conversely, where the government justifies nondisclosure with reference to certain exemptions, the Federal Court will only step in "if it determines that the head of the institution did not have *reasonable* grounds on which to refuse to disclose the record or part thereof."[211] The exemptions evaluated on this reasonable grounds basis are listed in Table 9.4.

Table 9.4   "Reasonable Grounds" Review

Access Act	Privacy Act
1. Section 14 — Information that could reasonably be expected to be injurious to the conduct of federal-provincial affairs, including federal strategy or information on federal-provincial consultations or negotiations 2. Section 15 — Information that could reasonably be expected to be injurious to the conduct of international affairs or to the defence of Canada or an allied state, or the prevention or suppression of subversive or hostile activities 3. Paragraph 16(1)(c) — Information that could reasonably be expected to be injurious to law enforcement or to the conduct of lawful investigations, including information on confidential sources 4. Paragraph 16(1)(d) — Information that could reasonably be expected to be injurious to the security of penal institutions 5. Paragraph 18(d) — Information that could reasonably be expected to be materially injurious to the financial interests of the government or its ability to manage the economy or could reasonably be expected to result in an undue benefit to any person	1. Section 20 — Injury to the conduct of federal-provincial affairs 2. Section 21 — Injury to the conduct of international affairs or to the defence of Canada or an allied state, or the prevention or suppression of subversive or hostile activities 3. Paragraph 22(1)(b) — Injury to law enforcement, including information on confidential sources 4. Paragraph 22(1)(c) — Injury to the security of penal institutions 5. Paragraph 24(a) — Information collected by Corrections Canada or the National Parole Board while the requester was under sentence if the disclosure could reasonably be expected to seriously disrupt the individual's release program

---

210   *Access Act*, s. 49; *Privacy Act*, s. 48.
211   *Access Act*, s. 50 [emphasis added]; *Privacy Act*, s. 49.

Some Federal Court cases have focused on the "not authorized" versus "reasonable grounds" distinction in the *Access* and *Privacy Acts* in deciding the standard of review to be employed in *Access* and *Privacy Act* cases. For instance, in *Hien Do-Ky Vietnamese Refugee Sponsorship Committee v. Canada*,[212] the Federal Court held that where the government refuses to release documents that are reviewed under the "not authorized" provision, "the court looks only at the category or type of document at issue," reviewing whether the government has properly invoked the cited exception in relation to that document.[213] This review has been characterized as *de novo* in nature,[214] allowing the court to supplant the institution's decision with its own.

On the other hand, when reviewing a decision not to disclose under the "reasonable grounds" provision, "what the Court is looking for is support for the honestly held but perhaps subjective opinions of the Government witnesses based on general references to the record."[215] A review under the "reasonable grounds" provision, in other words, is "more limited" than under the "not authorized" section. A court may not intervene where an exemption is reviewable on reasonable grounds simply where the court would have reached a different conclusion than the head of the institution. Rather, the court must conclude that, on the facts before it, no reasonable person could have come to the conclusion that the records in question should be exempted.[216]

This approach has been justified by the fact that each of the exemptions reviewable on the "reasonable grounds" basis is an injury-based exception.[217] Still, many other injury-based exemptions are reviewable under the "not authorized" standard, rendering the not authorized and reasonable grounds distinction quite opaque. In practice, this uncertainty has likely been superseded by more recent developments in administrative law, resulting in a deferential standard of review of all discretionary exemptions, regardless of whether they fall in the not authorized or reasonable grounds category.

---

212 [1997] 2 F.C. 907 at para. 32 (T.D.). See also *Hoogers v. Canada*, [1998] F.C.J. No. 834 (T.D.) treating "authorized" and "reasonable grounds" as standards of review.

213 *Hien Do-Ky Vietnamese Refugee Sponsorship Committee v. Canada*, [1997] 2 F.C. 907 at para. 32.

214 *Dagg*, [1997] 2 S.C.R. 403 at para.107, *per* LaForest J., dissenting but not on this point; ("[i]t is clear that in making this determination [of whether information falls within an exemption], the reviewing court may substitute its opinion for that of the head of the government institution").

215 *Hien Do-Ky*, [1997] 2 F.C. 907 at para. 32.

216 *X v. Canada (Minister of National Defence)* (1992), 58 F.T.R. 93 at 96 (F.C.T.D.).

217 *Hien Do-Ky*, [1997] 2 F.C. 907 at para. 32.

Standard of Review in Practice

Developments in Administrative Law

Over the last several decades, Canadian administrative law has, on the whole, taken on a deferential stance when dealing with decisions made by members of the executive branch. Where the decision made by an administrative decision-maker is viewed as "discretionary," reviewing courts in Canada have traditionally been quite undemanding, requiring an "abuse of discretion" before intervening in the decision. In practice, such an abuse was demonstrated by evidence of bad faith, reliance on improper purposes or discrimination considerations.

As the Supreme Court has recently acknowledged in *Baker v. Canada*,[218] this approach sat uncomfortably with the jurisprudence on deference in relation to so-called errors of law — errors made by decision-makers in interpreting statutes they were obliged to apply. With errors of law, for some time, the Supreme Court has extended deference or not depending on its assessment of a number of variables. These variables, components of what the Court has called the "pragmatic and functional test," historically have been marshalled by the court to decide whether the error of law is best viewed as a matter within the jurisdiction of the administrative decision-maker, in which case a court will intervene in the decision only if "patently unreasonable," or if it is a matter outside the scope of the decision-maker's jurisdiction, in which case the court will intervene in response to any error.[219]

After *Pushpanathan v. Canada*,[220] this traditional justification of locating the error as within or at the margins of the decision-maker's jurisdiction has eroded and the Court engages in the pragmatic and functional test simply to decide how much deference must be extended to a decision-maker making an alleged error of law. As discussed also in chapter 2, this deference is now measured on a three-point spectrum running from the

---

218 [1999] 2 S.C.R. 817 at para. 54.

219 See, e.g., *U.E.S., Local 298 v. Bibeault*, [1988] 2 S.C.R. 1048 at para. 123, setting out the purpose and content of the pragmatic and functional test; *Canadian Broadcasting Corp. v. Canada*, [1995] 1 S.C.R. 157 at para. 30, discussing the role of the pragmatic and functional test in "distinguishing jurisdictional questions from questions of law within a tribunal's jurisdiction."

220 [1998] 1 S.C.R. 982 at para. 28, incorporating a three-spectrum standard of review into judicial review and noting that "it should be understood that a question which 'goes to jurisdiction' is simply an error on an issue with respect to which, according to the outcome of the pragmatic and functional analysis, the tribunal must make a correct interpretation and to which no deference will be shown."

zero deference standard of "correctness," through the intermediate deference "reasonableness *simpliciter*," to the maximum deference standard of "patently unreasonable."

In *Baker*, the Court acknowledged that the distinction between a decision that is discretionary (traditionally reviewable on an abuse of discretion standard) or a decision of law (reviewable on a standard determined by the pragmatic and functional test) is often impossible to make.[221] Accordingly, in *Baker*, the Court extended the pragmatic and functional test to both discretionary decisions and decisions interpreting law.

Application of Administrative Law Principles in Access and Privacy Cases

This spectrum of standards approach appears to be the driver in *Access* and *Privacy Act* reviews, regardless of whether the exemption in question falls within the not authorized or reasonable grounds classes.[222] For instance, the Federal Court has followed La Forest J.'s reasoning in *Dagg v. Canada*[223] in holding that "not authorized" refers "only to the question of whether a document falls within an exemption, and not also to whether the head of the government institution lawfully exercised the discretion to withhold."[224] This second issue — whether discretion has been properly exercised — is fully informed by the Supreme Court's common law jurisprudence.

In practice, therefore, judicial review of discretionary exemptions is a two-step process: "first, a factual determination as to whether the material comes within the description of material potentially subject to being withheld from disclosure; and second, a discretionary decision as to whether that material should nevertheless be disclosed."[225]

---

221 *Baker v. Canada*, [1999] 2 S.C.R. 817 at para. 54. See also *Suresh v. Canada*, [2002] 1 S.C.R. 3 at paras. 35 and 36, noting that *Baker* "confirmed that the pragmatic and functional approach should be applied to all types of administrative decisions in recognition of the fact that a uniform approach to the determination of the proper standard of review is preferable. ... The Court specified in *Baker*, *supra*, that a nuanced approach to determining the appropriate standard of review was necessary given the difficulty in rigidly classifying discretionary and non-discretionary decisions (paras. 54 and 55)."

222 See *H.J. Heinz Co. of Canada Ltd. v. Canada (Attorney General)*, [2003] 4 F.C. 3 at para. 20 (F.C.) listing the discretionary exemptions — including those subject to a "reasonable grounds" review, and then setting out the standard two-prong test without suggesting it would be applied different for exemptions subject to the "authorized" versus "reasonable grounds" standard of review, aff'd [2004] F.C.J. No. 773 (F.C.A.).

223 *Dagg*, [1997] 2 S.C.R. 403 at para. 115, *per* LaForest J., dissenting.

224 *3430901 Canada Inc.*, [2002] 1 F.C. 421, at para. 89 (F.C.A.) summarizing the *Dagg* holding.

225 *Kelly v. Canada (Solicitor General)* (1992), 53 F.T.R. 147 at 149 (F.C.T.D.), aff'd (1993) 13 Admin. L.R. (2d) 304 (F.C.A).

In the oft-cited case *Kelly v. Canada*, the Federal Court concluded that the first, "factual" decision was one that "the Court can review and in respect of which it can substitute its own conclusion," subject "to the need ... for a measure of deference to the decisions of those whose institutional responsibilities put them in a better position to judge the matter."[226] More recently, the Federal Court abandoned references to deference in respect to this first inquiry, arguing that the question of whether the material comes within the class of that which may be withheld is reviewable on a standard of correctness.[227] Likewise, in *3430901 Canada Inc. v. Canada (Minister of Industry)*,[228] the Federal Court of Appeal held that "[i]n reviewing the refusal of a head of a government institution to disclose a record, the Court must determine on a standard of correctness whether the record requested falls within an exemption."

Kelly also suggested that the second, "discretionary" decision would be reviewed where "the discretion appears [not] to have been exercised in good faith and for some reason which is rationally connected to the purpose for which the discretion was granted."[229] In other words, the exercise of discretion associated with a discretionary exemption is reviewable on the classic, conventional administrative grounds for reviewing discretionary decisions.[230]

While *Kelly*'s approach to this second question has been followed in other Federal Court cases as recently as 2003,[231] there is some question whether it remains good law in light of recent Supreme Court jurisprudence on the standard of review in administrative law. As noted above, in *Baker*, the Court extended the pragmatic and functional test for standard of review in relation to errors of law to alleged errors of discretion. This case, and those that followed, suggests that the old abuse of discretion categories of bad faith and improper purposes invoked in *Kelly* have been superseded by a requirement that courts perform a pragmatic and functional analysis and then apply the standard of review produced by this test. There is now,

---

226 *Ibid.*

227 *Thurlow v. Canada (Solicitor General)*, [2003] F.C.J. No. 1802 at para. 28 (F.C.) ("[t]he decision with respect to whether a requested document falls within statutory exemption should be reviewed on a standard of correctness").

228 [2002] 1 F.C. 421, at para. 47 (F.C.A.).

229 *Kelly*, (1992), 53 F.T.R. 147.

230 *Dagg*, [1997] 2 S.C.R. 403 at para. 115, *per* La Forest J., dissenting. The majority in *Dagg* did not find it necessary to decide this issue, but did note "[i]n general, I agree with La Forest J.'s conclusion that a minister's discretionary decision under s. 8(2)(m)(i) is not to be reviewed on a *de novo* standard of review" (at para. 16).

231 *Cemerlic v. Canada (Solicitor General)*, [2003] F.C.J. No. 191 (F.C.) involving a review of, *inter alia*, the "threats to the security of Canada" exemption under the *Privacy Act*.

therefore, some prospect that courts performing the pragmatic and functional test might arrive at less demanding standard of review, one that might motivate court intervention even where no bad faith or improper purpose is demonstrated.

This was exactly the conclusion of the Federal Court of Appeal in *3430901 Canada Inc. v. Canada (Minister of Industry)*,[232] where the court evaluated a ministerial decision to refuse disclosure under the *Access Act* on a discretionary ground. Concluding that the *Access Act*'s objective of enhancing public disclosure tempered any deference owed the minister's discretionary decision, the court applied an intermediate standard of review, reasonableness *simpliciter*.[233] The Supreme Court of Canada has since approved the Federal Court of Appeal's invocation of the purposes of the Act in support of this less deferential standard of review.[234]

B. PROTECTING PRIVACY

1. Privacy and Democracy

Privacy has been defined as "the claim of individuals, groups, or institutions to determine for themselves when, how, and to what extent information about them is communicated to others."[235] In modern democracies, privacy rights exist to "impose limits on the extent of control and direction that the state exercises over the day-to-day conduct of individual lives."[236] Sometimes labelled "a right to be left alone," an erosion of privacy potentially results in innocent people being "identified, tagged and monitored by the state."[237]

---

232 [2002] 1 F.C. 421, at para. 44 (F.C.A.) noting that "in light of *Baker* ... the grounds on which the legality of the minister's discretionary decision not to disclose records is reviewable must be considered to have been expanded from ... bad faith, breach of natural justice and the relevancy of the considerations relied on by the decision-maker."

233 *Ibid.* at para. 45. The Federal Court of Appeal did not spell out what reasonableness *simpliciter* demanded in the circumstances, but it did suggest it meant less than the old nominate categories found in abuse of discretion.

234 See *Canada (Information Commissioner) v. Canada (Commissioner of the Royal Canadian Mounted Police)* \, [2003] 1 S.C.R. 66 at para. 17 noting that a less deferential standard of review is consistent with the information disclosure and independent review of refusals to disclose purpose of the *Access Act* and also that less deference was warranted because "those charged with responding to requests under the federal *Access Act* might be inclined to interpret the exceptions to information disclosure in a liberal manner so as to favour their institution."

235 Alan Westin, *Privacy and Freedom* (New York: Atheneum, 1967) at 7.

236 Jed Rubenfeld, "The Right of Privacy," 102 Harv. L. Rev. 737 at 805 (1989).

237 Privacy Commissioner, *Annual Report 2002–03* at 5.

Measured against the standard of democratic accountability set out in this book, privacy protection reinforces the concept of limited government: the notion that there are areas in which even a democratic government should not go.

Canadian courts have spoken of three "zones" of privacy: "The territorial zone refers to places such as one's home. Personal or corporeal privacy is concerned with the human body (body, images such as photographs, voice or name). Finally, a person can make a claim to informational privacy that shelters intimate details concerning matters such as health, sexual orientation, employment, social views, friendships and associations."[238] Justice La Forest, in *R. v. Dyment*,[239] wrote of this third, informational form of privacy as follows: "In modern society, especially, retention of information about oneself is extremely important. We may, for one reason or another, wish or be compelled to reveal such information, but situations abound where the reasonable expectations of the individual that the information shall remain confidential to the persons to whom, and restricted to the purposes for which it is divulged, must be protected."

In that same case, Justice La Forest vigorously underscored the connection between democracy and privacy: "society has come to realize that privacy is at the heart of liberty in a modern state. ... Grounded in man's physical and moral autonomy, privacy is essential for the well-being of the individual. ... The restraints imposed on government to pry into the lives of the citizen go to the essence of a democratic state."[240]

Subsequently, in *Dagg v. Canada*, La Forest J. held that "[t]he protection of privacy is a fundamental value in modern, democratic states ... An expression of an individual's unique personality or personhood, privacy is grounded on physical and moral autonomy — the freedom to engage in one's own thoughts, actions and decisions."[241] Indeed, privacy interests have a "privileged, foundational position ... in our social and legal culture."[242] Other

---

238 *Ruby v. Canada*, [2000] 3 F.C. 589 at para. 166, varied, [2002] 4 S.C.R. 3. In *Ruby*, the Federal Court of Appeal was following *R. v. Dyment*, [1988] 2 S.C.R. 417 at 428, *per* La Forest J., concurring (speaking of three zones: "those involving territorial or spatial aspects, those related to the person, and those that arise in the information context").

239 [1988] 2 S.C.R. 417 at 429-430, *per* La Forest J., concurring.

240 [1988] 2 S.C.R. 417 at 427, 428, *per* La Forest J., concurring.

241 [1997] 2 S.C.R. 403 at para. 65. See also *Lavigne*, [2002] 2 S.C.R. 773 at para. 25, citing this passage with approval and noting that while La Forest J. dissented, "he spoke for the entire Court on this point".

242 *Dagg*, [1997] 2 S.C.R. 403 at para. 69. See also *Lavigne*, [2002] 2 S.C.R. 773 at para. 25, citing this passage with approval.

Supreme Court justices have since echoed this position. Thus, Justice L'Heureux-Dubé urged in *R. v. O'Connor* that "[r]espect for individual privacy is an essential component of what it means to be 'free.' As a corollary, the infringement of this right undeniably impinges upon an individual's 'liberty' in our free and democratic society."[243]

2. International Standards

Privacy rights are entrenched in international human rights law. Article 12 of the Universal Declaration of Human Rights provides that "[n]o one should be subjected to arbitrary interference with his privacy, family, home or correspondence, nor to attacks on his honour or reputation. Everyone has the right to the protection of the law against such interferences or attacks." The International Covenant on Civil and Political Rights contains identical language.[244]

International "soft law" standards also exist. Notable among these are the Organization for Economic Cooperation and Development's Guidelines Governing the Protection of Privacy and Transborder Data Flows of Personal Data.[245] These guidelines provide that "[t]here should be limits to the collection of personal data and any such data should be obtained by lawful and fair means and, where appropriate, with the knowledge and consent of the data subject."[246] This person should be notified of the use to which this information will be put, and any subsequent disclosure of this information should be consistent with this use.[247] The United Nations General Assembly has also proposed guidelines with similar provisions.[248]

---

243 [1995] 4 S.C.R. 411 at para. 113, speaking for herself, La Forest and Gonthier JJ., with McLachlin J. concurring. See also L'Heureux-Dubé J., *R. v. Osolin*, [1993] 4 S.C.R. 595 at 614, dissenting but not on this point ("[t]he importance of privacy as a fundamental value in our society is underscored by the protection afforded to *everyone* under s. 8 of the *Charter* "to be secure against unreasonable search or seizure". This value finds expression in such legislation as the *Privacy Act* ... which restricts the purposes for which information may be used to those for which it was received"), cited with approval in *Lavigne*, [2002] 2 S.C.R. 773 at para. 25.

244 ICCPR, Article 17. For a discussion of the legal state of the Universal Declaration and the ICCPR, see above.

245 Paris (1981); available at www1.oecd.org/publications/e-book/9302011E.PDF.

246 *Ibid.*, Principle 7.

247 *Ibid.*, Principles 9 and 10.

248 United Nations General Assembly, *Guidelines Concerning Computerized Personal Data Files*, 14 Dec. 1990.

3. Federal Privacy Laws

a) Constitutional Protections

To some extent, privacy has been given constitutional protection in the *Canadian Charter of Rights and Freedoms*. Section 8 of the *Charter* encompasses the privacy right to be free from unreasonable searches and seizures.[249] Supreme Court jurisprudence makes clear that this section creates a "reasonable expectation of privacy."[250] This reasonable expectation of privacy requires an assessment "as to whether in a particular situation the public's interest in being left alone by government must give way to the government's interest in intruding on the individual's privacy in order to advance its goals, notably those of law enforcement."[251]

While typically invoked in the criminal context, section 8 has relevance where government uses personal information collected for one purpose for another objective. The Federal Court of Appeal held recently that a provision of the *Income Tax Act* disclosing to any person the tax return of an applicant appealing a tax ruling constituted an unreasonable seizure.[252] Caution should be exercised, however, in reading too much into section 8 privacy protections outside the criminal context. In many instances involving the sharing of personal information for regulatory (as opposed to criminal) purposes, the state's interests in ensuring compliance seem likely to outweigh the individual's reasonable expectation of privacy.[253]

The *Charter*'s section 7 — protecting against deprivation of life, liberty or security of the persons — may also incorporate privacy protections.[254] Summarizing Supreme Court jurisprudence on section 7, the Federal Court of Appeal has held that it "includes the right to privacy of information in regard to intimate questions as well as the use of personal information."[255] In another case considering the constitutionality of certain provisions of the *Privacy*

---

249 See *Lavigne*, [2002] 2 S.C.R. 773 at para. 25, labelling this a privacy right.

250 *R. v. B.(S.A.)*, 2003 SCC 60 at para. 38.

251 *Ibid.*, citing *Hunter v. Southam Inc.*, [1984] 2 S.C.R. 145 at 159–60.

252 *Gernhart v. Canada*, [2000] 2 F.C. 292 at para. 41 (F.C.A.).

253 *Smith v. Canada (Attorney General)* (2000), 252 N.R. 172 (F.C.A.) aff'd [2001] 3 S.C.R. 902, concluding that applicant could be said to have held a reasonable expectation of privacy in relation to unemployment insurance information disclosed to the government that outweighs the government's interest in enforcing the laws disentitling unemployment insurance claimants from receiving benefits while outside of Canada.

254 *Lavigne*, [2002] 2 S.C.R. 773 at para. 25.

255 *Zarzour v. Canada* (2000), 268 N.R. 235 at para. 68 (F.C.A.), citing *B.(R.) v. Children's Aid Society of Metropolitan Toronto*, [1995] 1 S.C.R. 315 at 368; *R. v. Morgentaler*, [1988] 1 S.C.R. 30; *R. v. Mills*, [1999] 3 S.C.R. 668 at paras. 80 and 81; and *Blencoe v. British Columbia (Human Rights Commission)*, 2000 SCC 44.

Act, the Federal Court of Appeal held that the fact that "the Act provides for the acquisition and accumulation of personal information and its dissemination, in circumstances where the person affected may be unable to test the truth of the information so acquired, may bring into issue the right of privacy ... and the potential application of section 7 of the *Charter*."[256]

While the Supreme Court has yet to definitively announce that section 7 protects privacy rights, such a conclusion seems plausible in light of its jurisprudence to date.[257]

b) Privacy Act

The principal restrictions on government use of personal information are set out in the *Privacy Act*. This Act, in the words of the Supreme Court of Canada, is "a reminder of the extent to which the protection of privacy is necessary to the preservation of a free and democratic society."[258]

Collection and Use of Personal Information

The *Privacy Act* admonishes that no personal information is to be collected by a government institution unless it relates directly to an operating program or activity of the institution.[259] The Act sets out requirements as to how this information must be collected. First, any information that is collected for an administrative purpose — that is, personal information used in a decision-making process directly affecting that individual — should, wherever possible, come directly from the individual concerned.[260] Second, the government institution has a duty to inform the individual as to how the information will be used.

Both of these collection procedure obligations may be ignored if compliance with them would result in the collection of inaccurate information, or if it would defeat the purpose of gathering the information, or prejudice its use.[261]

---

256 *Ruby v. Canada*, [2000] 3 F.C. 589 at para. 170, varied, [2002] 4 S.C.R. 3, at para. 33 ("it is unnecessary to the disposition of this case to decide whether a right to privacy comprising a corollary right of access to personal information triggers the application of s. 7 of the *Charter*").

257 See *M.(A.) v. Ryan*, [1997] 1 S.C.R. 157, *per* L'Heureux-Dubé J., dissenting, concluding that she had spoken for the Court in *R. v. O'Connor*, [1995] 4 S.C.R. 411 on the whether privacy protection was available in that case under s. 7. See discussion in Barbara McIsaac, Rick Shields and Kris Klein, *The Law of Privacy in Canada* (Scarborough, ON: Thomson, 2004) at section 2.2.1.

258 *Lavigne*, [2002] 2 S.C.R. 773 at para. 25.

259 *Privacy Act*, s. 4.

260 This requirement need not be met when the individual concerned authorizes the government to collect it from another source, or where information is disclosed to the institution under other provisions of the Act itself. See, specifically, *Privacy Act*, s. 8.

261 *Privacy Act*, s. 5.

Personal information controlled by a government institution may only be used for purposes consistent with the authorized justification for which it was collected, except with permission from the individual to whom it relates.[262]

Personal information used by a government institution for an administrative purpose must be retained for a standard period of two years, or until the completion of a privacy access request.[263] Government records, including those with personal information, may not be destroyed without the permission of the national archivist of Canada.[264]

Disclosure of Personal Information

Section 8 of the Act bars disclosure of personal information under the control of a government institution absent consent, subject to certain enumerated exceptions. As Table 9.5 suggests, these exceptions — set out in subsection 8(2) — provide that personal information may be disclosed for reasons that may be classed, loosely, under the headings of litigation and law enforcement purposes, government financial purposes, research, historical and statistical purposes, purposes for the benefit of the individual or the public interest, and for other reasons announced in the *Privacy Act* or other statutes or regulations.

Table 9.5   *Section 8 of the* Privacy Act

Class of Purpose	Specific Reasons
Litigation & law enforcement	1. Paragraph 8(2)(c) — for the purpose of complying with a subpoena, warrant or court order 2. Paragraph 8(2)(d) — to the Attorney General of Canada for use in legal proceedings involving the Crown 3. Paragraph 8(2)(e) — to a specified investigative body for the purpose of law enforcement 4. Paragraph 8(2)(f) — under a federal-provincial or international agreement, for the purpose of law enforcement or investigation 5. Paragraph 8(2)(k) — to any aboriginal government, association or band, for the purpose of researching or validating aboriginal claims, disputes or grievances
Government financial	1. Paragraph 8(2)(h) — to a government institution for internal audit purposes 2. Paragraph 8(2)(l) — to a government institution for the purpose of locating an individual in order to collect a debt owing to the government
Research, historical & statistical	1. Paragraph 8(2)(i) — to the National Archives of Canada for archival purposes

262 *Ibid.*, s. 7.
263 *Ibid.*, s. 6; *Privacy Act Regulations*, SOR/83-508, s. 4.
264 *Zarzour* (2000), 268 N.R. 235 at para. 24.

Class of Purpose	Specific Reasons
	2. Paragraph 8(2)(j) — to any person or body for research or statistical purposes if the head of the government institution (i) is satisfied that the purpose for which the information is disclosed cannot reasonably be accomplished unless the information is provided in a form that would identify the individual to whom it relates, and (ii) obtains from the person or body a written undertaking that no subsequent disclosure of the information will be made in a form that could reasonably be expected to identify the individual
Benefit of the individual or the public interest	1. Paragraph 8(2)(g) — to a member of Parliament for the purpose of assisting the individual to whom the information relates in resolving a problem
	2. Paragraph 8(2)(m) — for any purpose where, in the opinion of the head of the institution, (i) the public interest in disclosure clearly outweighs any invasion of privacy that could result from disclosure, or (ii) disclosure would clearly benefit the individual to whom the information relates
Statutory or regulatory reasons	1. Paragraph 8(2)(a) — for the purpose for which the information was collected by the institution
	2. Paragraph 8(2)(b) — for any purpose in accordance with any Act of Parliament or any regulation made thereunder that authorizes disclosure

Unless already included in the annual statement of uses and purposes for government information banks,[265] the government institution must keep a record of the use to which personal information is put, as well as any reason this information is disclosed. This information is deemed part of the personal information to which it relates.[266]

Enforcement by the Privacy Commissioner

Where the government uses or discloses personal information in a fashion inconsistent with the Act, an individual may make a complaint to the privacy commissioner,[267] triggering the same investigative powers described above in relation to complaints concerning failure to give access to personal information. The privacy commissioner may also initiate an investigation on his or her own where he or she concludes that there are reasonable grounds.

Where the commissioner concludes that a government institution has failed to comply with privacy protections, he or she provides the head of that institution with a report setting out findings from the investigation and the commissioner's recommendations.[268] This report may subsequently be included in the privacy commissioner's annual report to Parliament.[269]

---

265 See *Privacy Act*, s. 11.
266 *Ibid.*, s. 9.
267 *Ibid.*, s. 29.
268 *Ibid.*, s. 37.
269 *Ibid.*, ss. 37, 38 and 39.

In 2002–03, the privacy commissioner received a total of 2,616 complaints on government collection, retention, disposal, use and alleged improper disclosure of personal information. A fraction of these complaints, 5.9 percent, were meritorious.[270]

c) *Personal Information Protection and Electronic Documents Act*

Application to Government

In 2001, Parliament enacted the *Personal Information Protection and Electronic Documents Act (PIPEDA)*,[271] the long-awaited extension of privacy protections beyond the public sector. Thus, Part I of this Act is directed at regulating use of personal information by commercial organizations. This part does not apply to government institutions covered by the *Privacy Act*.[272] However, as noted above, many government bodies are not listed as government institutions under the *Privacy Act*. Whether *PIPEDA* extends to these institutions is obviously a matter of interest, lest these agencies fall under neither the *PIPEDA* nor the *Privacy Act*.

The Act explicitly provides that, by regulation, the government may extend application of the Act to "any agent of Her Majesty in right of Canada to which the *Privacy Act* does not apply."[273] To date, the government has issued a regulation expressly obliging three Crown corporations to comply with Part I of the Act: Atomic Energy of Canada Limited; the Canadian Broadcasting Corporation; and the Enterprise Cape Breton Corporation.[274]

Whether the Act should extend to other Crown corporations not listed as "government institutions" under the *Privacy Act* is less clear. It seems sensible, however, that *PIPEDA* should apply to a government body not covered by the *Privacy Act* but which satisfies the threshold requirements in the *PIPEDA* itself: specifically, the government body is an "organization" — defined broadly to include "a person"[275] — that collects, uses or discloses personal information in the course of commercial activities or collects, uses or discloses personal information about an employee in connection with the operation of a federal work, undertaking or business.[276]

---

270 Calculated from Privacy Commissioner, *Annual Report 2002–03*, table titled "Completed Investigations by Grounds and Results," summing complaints held to be well-founded, well-founded/resolved, resolved or settled.

271 S.C. 2000, c. 5.

272 *PIPEDA*, para. 4(2)(a).

273 *Ibid.*, para. 26(2)(a).

274 SOR/2001-8 13 Dec. 2000.

275 *PIPEDA*, s. 2.

276 *Ibid.*, subs. 4(1).

Pursuant to the federal *Interpretation Act*, the reference to "persons" "includes a corporation."[277] The expressions "commercial activities" and "a federal work, undertaking or business" are defined expansively in the *PIPEDA* itself. All told, these definitions are sufficiently broad that they should capture the activities of at least some Crown corporations.[278] This is, in fact, the conclusion that the Canada Industrial Relations Board has reached in relation to Via Rail.[279]

Collection, Use and Disclosure of Personal Information

The purpose of Part I of the *PIPEDA* "is to establish, in an era in which technology increasingly facilitates the circulation and exchange of information, rules to govern the collection, use and disclosure of personal information in a manner that recognizes the right of privacy of individuals with respect to their personal information and the need of organizations to collect, use or disclose personal information for purposes that a reasonable person would consider appropriate in the circumstances."[280]

To this end, Division 1 of the Act incorporates into Canadian law a model Code for the Protection of Personal Information.[281] Amongst other things, this code calls on organizations to identify the purposes for which personal information is collected prior to this collection, and to disclose this purpose to the individuals from whom the information is obtained.[282] Consent of this individual is required for the collection, use and disclosure of the personal information,[283] particularly where subsequent use and disclosure is for a purpose other than that for which the information was collected.[284]

Information may only be collected,[285] used,[286] or disclosed[287] without the knowledge or consent of the person to whom it pertains in limited circumstances. These grounds are set out in Table 9.6.

---

277 *Interpretation Act*, R.S. 1985, c. I-21, s. 35.
278 Under the *Financial Administration Act*, R.S. 1985, c. F-11, s. 83, Crown corporation means "a parent Crown corporation or a wholly-owned subsidiary." Both these sorts of entities are "corporations," defined in the Act as a "company or other body corporate wherever or however incorporated."
279 *VIA Rail Canada Inc. v. National Automobile, Aerospace Transportation and General Workers' Union, National Council 4000* (2003), 116 L.A.C. (4th) 407 at para. 8 (holding that VIA Rail "as a federal work or undertaking, must comply with the Act").
280 *PIPEDA*, s. 3.
281 *Ibid.*, Schedule I.
282 *Ibid.*, Schedule I, Principle 2.
283 *Ibid.*, Schedule I, Principle 3.
284 *Ibid.*, Schedule I, Principle 4.
285 *Ibid.*, subs. 7(1).
286 *Ibid.*, subs. 7(2).
287 *Ibid.*, subs. 7(3).

Table 9.6   *Collection, Use and Disclosure of Personal Information Without Knowledge or Consent*

Grounds	Collected Without Knowledge or Consent	Used Without Knowledge or Consent	Disclosed Without Knowledge or Consent
Interests of the individual	Paragraph 7(1)(a) —Collection is clearly in the interests of the individual and consent cannot be obtained in a timely way.	Paragraph 7(2)(d) — Original collection was clearly in the interests of the individual and consent cannot be obtained in a timely way.	
Enforcement of agreement	Paragraph 7(1)(b) — Collection with the knowledge or consent of the individual could be reasonably expected to compromise the availability or the accuracy of the information and the collection is reasonably related to investigating a breach of an agreement.		Paragraph 7(3)(b) — Disclosed for the purpose of collecting a debt owed by the individual to the organization. Paragraph 7(3)(h.2) — Disclosure made by an investigative body and the disclosure is reasonable for purposes related to investigating a breach of an agreement.
Law enforcement	Paragraph 7(1)(b) — Collection with the knowledge or consent of the individual could be reasonably expected to compromise the availability or the accuracy of the information and the collection is reasonably related to investigating a contravention of the laws of Canada or a province.	Paragraph 7(2)(d) — Original collection with the knowledge or consent of the individual could be reasonably expected to compromise the availability or accuracy of the information and the collection is reasonably related to investigating a contravention of the laws of Canada or a province; or Paragraph 7(2)(a) — Organization has reasonable grounds to believe information could be useful in law enforcement or investigation.	Paragraph 7(3)(c.1) — Disclosure is made to a government institution that has made a request for the information, identified its lawful authority to obtain the information and indicated that: (ii) the disclosure is requested for the purpose of enforcing any law of Canada, a province or a foreign jurisdiction, carrying out an investigation relating to the enforcement of any such law or gathering intelligence for the purpose of enforcing any such law, or (iii) the disclosure is requested for the purpose of administering any law of Canada or a province.

Category	Collection	Use	Disclosure
			Paragraph 7(3)(c.2) — Disclosure made to the Financial Transactions and Reports Analysis Centre of Canada, under the *Proceeds of Crime (Money Laundering) and Terrorist Financing Act* (see discussion below on national security). Sub-Paragraph 7(3)(d)(i) — Disclosure made on the initiative of the organization to an investigative body or government institution, and the organization has reasonable grounds to believe that the information relates to a breach of an agreement or a possible contravention of the laws of Canada, a province or a foreign jurisdiction. Paragraph 7(3)(h.2) — Disclosure made by an investigative body and the disclosure is reasonably for law enforcement.
National security	Paragraph 7(1)(e) — Collection is made for the purposes of making a disclosure under sub-paragraphs 7(3)(c.1)(i) or 7(3)(d)(ii) (see far right column).	Paragraph 7(2)(d) — Information was collected pursuant to Paragraph 7(1)(e) (see left column).	Sub-Paragraph 7(3)(c.1)(i) — Disclosure is made to a government institution that has made a request for the information, identified its lawful authority to obtain the information and indicated that it suspects that the information relates to national security, the defence of Canada or the conduct of international affairs. Sub-Paragraph 7(3)(d)(ii) — Disclosure is made on the initiative of the organization to an investigative body or a government institution and the organization suspects that the information relates to national security, the

Grounds	Collected Without Knowledge or Consent	Used Without Knowledge or Consent	Disclosed Without Knowledge or Consent
Judicial process			defence of Canada or the conduct of international affairs. Paragraph 7(3)(c) — Disclosure required to comply with a subpoena or warrant issued or an order made by a court, person or body with jurisdiction to compel the production of information, or to comply with rules of court relating to the production of records.
Journalistic, artistic or literary purposes	Paragraph 7(1)(c) — Collection is solely for artistic or literary purposes.		
Publicly available and specified by the regulations.[288]	Paragraph 7(1)(d).	Paragraph 7(2)(c.1).	Paragraph 7(3)(h.1).
Emergencies		Paragraph 7(2)(b) — Information used for the purpose of acting in respect of an emergency that threatens the life, health or security of an individual.	Paragraph 7(3)(e) — Disclosure made to a person who needs the information because of an emergency that threatens the life, health or security of an individual and, if the

288 The regulations list as public information: information in a public telephone directory; in a public professional or business directory; listing or notice, in a registry collected under a statutory authority and to which a right of public access is authorized by law; in a public record or document of a judicial or quasi-judicial body; or in a public publication, including a magazine, book or newspaper, in printed or electronic form, that is available to the public, where the individual has provided the information. Some of these public source exceptions are constrained by the requirement that the collection, use and disclosure of the personal information relate directly to the purpose for which the information appears in the public source. SOR/2001-7 13 (Dec. 2000).

			individual whom the information is about is alive, the organization informs that individual in writing without delay.
Research and archival purposes		Paragraph 7(2)(c) — Information used for statistical, or scholarly study or research purposes that cannot be achieved without using the information, the information is used in a manner that will ensure its confidentiality, it is impracticable to obtain consent and the organization informs the privacy commissioner of the use before the information is used.	Paragraph 7(3)(f) — Information used for statistical, or scholarly study or research, purposes that cannot be achieved without using the information, the information is used in a manner that will ensure its confidentiality, it is impracticable to obtain consent, and the organization informs the privacy commissioner of the use before the information is used. Paragraph 7(3)(g) — Disclosure made to an institution whose functions include the conservation of records of historic or archival importance, and the disclosure is made for the purpose of such conservation.
Organization's lawyer			Paragraph 7(3)(a) — Disclosed to, in the Province of Quebec, an advocate or notary or, in any other province, a barrister or solicitor who is representing the organization.
Dated information			Paragraph 7(3)(h) — Disclosure made after the earlier of (i) 100 years after the record containing the information was created, and (ii) twenty years after the death of the individual whom the information is about.
Required by law	Paragraph 7(1)(e).	Paragraph 7(2)(d) — Information was collected pursuant to Paragraph 7(1)(e) (see far left column).	Paragraph 7(3)(i).

Notification of Personal Information

The privacy code also provides that individuals are to be informed "of the existence, use, and disclosure of his or her personal information and shall be given access to that information."[289] An individual makes a request in relation to this information in writing. The organization must then respond with due diligence, and in any event within thirty days. This time limit may be extended by up to thirty days if meeting the original time limit would unreasonably interfere with the activities of the organization, or more time is required to undertake any consultations necessary to respond to the request. A requester must be notified of this extension, and the reasons for it, within the original thirty-day period, and also alerted that he or she may complain to the privacy commissioner. As with the *Privacy Act*, a failure to respond within the time limits constitutes a deemed refusal to disclose.[290]

The *PIPEDA* contains several exceptions to this disclosure requirement, some of which are clearly obligatory and others discretionary, as detailed in Table 9.7.

Where an organization refuses disclosure, it must inform the requester of the reasons for this refusal and notify him or her of remedies under the Act. The organization must retain the information in question for as long as required for these remedies to be pursued.[291]

Enforcement by the Privacy Commissioner and the Federal Court

Under Division 2 of Part I of the Act, individuals may file complaints with the privacy commissioner against an organization believed not to be complying with the Act's provisions on collection, use or disclosure of personal information. Complaints may also be filed regarding refusals to grant access to that personal information, or for not adhering to assorted other "recommendations" contained in the Code for the Protection of Personal Information appended to the Act. The commissioner may then investigate the matter, if he or she is persuaded that there are reasonable grounds to do so.[292] The commissioner's powers to conduct this investigation are analogous to those he or she possesses for an equivalent investigation under the *Privacy Act*.[293]

Unless the complaint is frivolous or it falls under other limited exceptions, the commissioner must prepare a report detailing his or her findings

---

289 *PIPEDA*, Schedule I, Principle 9.
290 *PIPEDA*, s. 8.
291 *Ibid.*, s. 8.
292 *Ibid.*, s. 11.
293 *Ibid.*, s. 12. See discussion on *Privacy Act* above.

Table 9.7   *Exceptions to Access to Personal Information Under the PIPEDA*

Discretionary	Obligatory
Paragraph 9(3)(a) — information is protected by solicitor-client privilege.	Subsection 9(1) — access would likely reveal personal information about a third party, but the information may be released with consent from that party or in circumstances where an individual's life, health or security is threatened.*
Paragraph 9(3)(b) — access would reveal confidential commercial information.*	Subsection 9(2.4) — access to information disclosed or disclosable under paragraph 7(3)(c), subparagraphs 7(3)(c.1)(i) or (ii) or paragraph 7(3)(d) is barred by the government (see chart above). This exception is discussed in greater detail below in the section on national security.
Paragraph 9(3)(c) — access could reasonably be expected to threaten the life or security of another individual.*	
Paragraph 9(3)(c.1) –information was collected without consent or knowledge because it was reasonable to expect that collection with the knowledge or consent of the individual would compromise the availability or the accuracy of the information and the collection is reasonable for purposes related to investigating a breach of an agreement or law enforcement.	
Paragraph 9(3)(d) — information was generated in the course of a formal dispute resolution process.	
* Where this sort of information may be severed from the personal information, it must be so severed.	

and recommendations and any settlement that was reached by the parties. As with the equivalent determination under the *Privacy Act*, the report must also include, where appropriate, a request that the organization describe any action taken or proposed to be taken to implement the recommendations contained in the report or provide reasons why no such action has been taken or is proposed. The report must also note that recourse is available under the Act in the Federal Court.[294]

In this last respect, as with both the *Access* and *Privacy Acts*, the complainant, or the commissioner, may apply to the Federal Court for a binding legal order requiring compliance with the *PIPEDA* by the organization. Unlike under the *Access* or *Privacy Acts*, the court also has the power to award damages to the complainant, including damages for any humiliation that the complainant has suffered.[295]

---

294 *Ibid.*, s. 13.
295 *Ibid.*, ss. 14–16.

As well as investigating complaints, the commissioner also has an auditing function: he or she may audit the personal information management practices of an organization where he or she has reasonable grounds to believe that the organization is contravening the Act or the accompanying privacy code.[296] The commissioner provides the results of this audit to the organization, along with any relevant recommendations.[297] Beyond that, the commissioner's only enforcement power is to include the audit's findings in his or her annual report to Parliament. Any interference with an investigation of a complaint or an audit conducted by the privacy commissioner is an offence.[298]

Notably, the Act includes whistleblower protection for employees who, in good faith, disclose to the commissioner a reasonable belief that the employer or any other person has contravened or intends to contravene Division 1 of the Act. This protection bars the employer from disadvantaging an employee because of their act of disclosure.[299]

C.　THE NATIONAL SECURITY CHALLENGE TO ACCESS AND TO PRIVACY

Since 9/11, the national security imperative has driven a large portion of the public agenda on many issues, including access to information and privacy protection. The key question with which Canadian governments are grappling in the post-9/11 period is how much erosion of access and privacy is consistent with Canada's liberal democracy.

1.　Legitimate National Security Constraints on Access to Information

Few credible observers would deny that there are secrets that states must keep in safeguarding the security of their citizens. On the other hand, national security should not be used to cloak governments from criticism or answerability. To the extent it does so, it runs counter the concept of democratic accountability lying at the heart of our system.

296　*Ibid.*, s. 18.
297　*Ibid.*, ss. 19 and 25.
298　*Ibid.*, s. 28.
299　*Ibid.*, s. 27.1.

a) Openness and National Security

As one critic has noted, national security is an imprecise concept. As a consequence, it is often used "to suppress precisely the kinds of speech that provide protection against government abuse," including damage to the environment, corruption, wasting of public assets, and other forms of wrongdoing by government officials.[300] Even within the realm of *bona fide* national security matters, some argue that transparency *enhances*, rather than prejudices, national security by increasing a flow of information essential in the coordination of national security efforts. Professor Alasdair Roberts has argued that

> [a]n informed public can help policymakers to formulate better policy, monitor the readiness of national security bureaucracies and act independently to preserve security. An information-rich environment is one in which citizens and frontline government employees are better able to make sense of unfolding events and respond appropriately to them. ... In the jargon of the American military, a policy of transparency can be a powerful "force multiplier," which helps to build a state that is resilient as well as respectful of citizen rights.[301]

From this perspective, national security matters should not be excluded, *prima facie*, from open government laws. Openness should remain the default, with the burden on government to show that disclosure truly prejudices national security. However, deciding how best to define legitimate "national security" interests is tremendously difficult.

b) The *Johannesburg Principles on National Security and Information Access*

In partial response to this problem, experts on the topic proposed, in 1995, the *Johannesburg Principles: National Security, Freedom of Expression and Access to Information*. The UN Special Rapporteur on Freedom of Opinion and Expression has since endorsed the Johannesburg principles.[302] They have

---

300 Sandra Coliver, "Commentary on the Johannesburg Principles on National Security, Freedom of Expression and Access to Information," in Sandra Coliver, Paul Hoffman, Joan Fitzpatrick and Stephen Brown, eds., *Secrecy and Liberty: National Security, Freedom of Expression and Access to Information* (The Hague: Martinus Nikhoff Publishers, 1999) at 12–13.

301 Alasdair Roberts, "National Security and Open Government," 9 *The Georgetown Public Policy Review* (Spring 2004) at 82.

302 See Report of the Special Rapporteur, *Promotion and Protection of the Right to Freedom of Opinion and Expression*, UN Doc. E/CN.4/1996/39 (22 March 1996) at para. 145 ("the Special Rapporteur recommends that the Commission on Human Rights

also been invoked by the UN Human Rights Commission in the preamble of many of its resolutions (each time, during years in which Canada was a member).[303] Further, the definition of "legitimate" national security contained in the Principles has also been cited — arguably with approval — by the House of Lords in *Secretary of State for the Home Department v. Rehman*.[304]

In their material parts, the Johannesburg principles underscore that "[e]veryone has the right to freedom of expression, which includes the freedom to seek, receive and impart information and ideas of all kinds." They acknowledge that these rights "may be subject to restrictions on specific grounds, as established in international law, including for the protection of national security." However, any restriction must be "prescribed by law and ... necessary in a democratic society to protect a legitimate national security interest." In practice, this requirement obliges a government to show that "the expression or information at issue poses a serious threat to a legitimate national security interest; ... the restriction imposed is the least restrictive means possible for protecting that interest; and ... the restriction is compatible with democratic principles."[305]

The principles carefully circumscribe what is meant by a "legitimate" national security interest. Principle 2 provides that a restriction justified on the ground of national security "is not legitimate unless its genuine pur-

---

endorse the Johannesburg Principles on National Security, Freedom of Expression and Access to Information, which are contained in the annex to the present report and which the Special Rapporteur considers give useful guidance for protecting adequately the right to freedom of opinion, expression and information").

303 See United Nations Human Rights Commission, *The Right to Freedom of Opinion and Expression*, Resolution 2003/42 ("*Recalling* the Johannesburg Principles on National Security, Freedom of Expression and Access to Information adopted by a group of experts meeting in South Africa on 1 Oct. 1995 (E/CN.4/1996/39, annex)"); UN Human Rights Commission, Resolution 2002/48; UN Human Rights Commission, Resolution 2001/47; UN Human Rights Commission, Resolution 2000/38; UN Human Rights Commission, Resolution 1999/36; UN Human Rights Commission, Resolution 1998/42; UN Human Rights Commission, Resolution 1997/27. These resolutions are available at www.unhchr.ch/huridocda/huridoca.nsf/Documents?OpenFrameset (accessed 7 June 2004).

304 [2003] 1 AC 153 at para. 15, *per* Lord Slynn, referring to the Johannesburg principles and then indicating that "[i]t seems to me that the appellant is entitled to say that 'the interests of national security' cannot be used to justify any reason the Secretary of State has for wishing to deport an individual from the United Kingdom. There must be some possibility of risk or danger to the security or well-being of the nation which the Secretary of State considers makes it desirable for the public good that the individual should be deported."

305 Johannesburg principles, Principle 1.

pose and demonstrable effect is to protect a country's existence or its territorial integrity against the use or threat of force, or its capacity to respond to the use or threat of force, whether from an external source, such as a military threat, or an internal source, such as incitement to violent overthrow of the government." The principles further specify that "a restriction sought to be justified on the ground of national security is not legitimate if its genuine purpose or demonstrable effect is to protect interests unrelated to national security, including, for example, to protect a government from embarrassment or exposure of wrongdoing, or to conceal information about the functioning of its public institutions, or to entrench a particular ideology, or to suppress industrial unrest."

In this manner, the principles set a high threshold of national security legitimacy, with a clear focus on actual or threatened use of physical force. National security would not, therefore, apply where the secret related to some question of economic advantage or policy, say, an anticipated Bank of Canada interest rate change. Nor would it attach to simple diplomatic correspondence, or information about Canada's negotiating position in a trade agreement. Other justifications may exist for restraining access to this information, but these justifications must flow from rationales other than national security.

The principles also contain standards curbing government responses to unauthorized disclosure of secrets. Principle 15 precludes punishment of a person on national security grounds "for disclosure of information if (1) the disclosure does not actually harm and is not likely to harm a legitimate national security interest, or (2) the public interest in knowing the information outweighs the harm from disclosure." Likewise, Principle 16 condemns subjecting a person "to any detriment on national security grounds for disclosing information that he or she learned by virtue of government service if the public interest in knowing the information outweighs the harm from disclosure."

2. Canadian Government Secrecy Laws

The natural question arising from the discussion above is how well Canada's government secrecy laws measure up both against its commitment to open government, articulated in the *Access Act*, and the standards set out in the Johannesburg principles.

Unfortunately, when Canada's secrecy laws are read together, they comprise a poorly integrated body of legal rules that apparently lack the checks and balances proposed by the Johannesburg principles.

a) *Security of Information Act*

Background

The cornerstone of Canada's secrecy law is the *Security of Information Act*.[306] Originally enacted in 1939 as the *Official Secrets Act*,[307] the statute was amended substantially and renamed in December 2001, as part of the government's anti-terrorism omnibus law.[308] The 1939 Act, for its part, was a variant on the 1889 U.K. *Official Secrets Act*, and had two main foci. First, it created an offence of espionage or spying in section 3 and second, it criminalized wrongful dissemination of information, sometimes called "leakage," in section 4.[309]

This statute was roundly condemned, beginning at least in the 1960s, for its breadth and ambiguity. The Royal Commission on Security (Mackenzie Commission) called it "an unwieldy statute, couched in very broad and ambiguous language."[310] In 1986, the Law Reform Commission condemned the statute "as one of the poorest examples of legislative drafting on the statute books."[311] It called the Act and other laws penalizing "crimes against the state" as "out of date, complex, repetitive, vague, inconsistent, lacking in principle and overinclusive," as well as potentially inconsistent with the *Charter*.[312] Criticism of the statute was voiced by the government itself in 1998, when the then-Solicitor General called the Act "badly outdated and overbroad."[313]

Perhaps for these reasons, the Act has rarely been invoked. The Canadian Security Intelligence Agency (CSIS) reports that since 1939 there have been two-dozen prosecutions under the Act, but only six in the past forty years.[314] In one of these cases, Stephen Ratkai pleaded guilty in 1989 under the statute's espionage provisions of spying for the USSR.[315] In sentencing Ratkai to two concurrent terms of nine years, the court commented that the object of the *Official Secrets Act* "is to protect the safety and interests of the

---

306 R.S.C. 1985, c. O-5.

307 R.S.C. 1970, c. O-3. This Act, in turn, is an "adoption of the English statutes as enacted in Great Britain (1911 (U.K.) c. 28, and 1920 (U.K.), c. 75)". *R. v. Toronto Sun Publishing Limited* (1979), 24 O.R. (2d) 621 at 623 (Prov. Ct.).

308 S.C. 2001, c. 41 (known as Bill C-36).

309 See Canadian Security Intelligence Service (CSIS), *Security of Information Act* (2 April 2002).

310 Mackenzie Commission, *Report of the Royal Commission on Security* (1969) at para. 204.

311 Law Reform Commission, *Crimes Against the State* (1986) at 30.

312 *Ibid* at 38–39.

313 The Honourable Andy Scott, Solicitor-General of Canada, *Hansard* no. 96 (30 April 1998).

314 CSIS, *Security of Information Act* (April 2004).

315 *R. v. Ratkai*, [1989] N.J. No. 334 (Nfld. S.C.).

state. Every country has an obligation to protect its citizens and its territory and countries must depend and rely upon its citizens to ensure its safety and security. What is disturbing and despicable about offences of this nature is that a citizen betrays his country which he has a duty to protect and defend."

However, in *R. v. Toronto Sun* — probably the leading case on the *Official Secrets Act* — the court was moved much less by the Act's objectives than by its awkward structure. At issue in this pre-*Charter* case was whether a newspaper and its editors had violated the Act by printing excerpts of a top secret document concerning Soviet intelligence activities in Canada. The court concluded that they had not, as the allegedly secret information had been previously invoked in the public domain. However, the court was also critical of the Act itself. In the court's words,

> [s]ince the *Official Secrets Act* is a restricting statute, and seeks to curb basic freedoms, such as freedom of speech and the press, it should be given strict interpretation. ... The statute must, in clear and unambiguous language, articulate the restriction it intends to impose upon a citizen. A reading of ss. 3 and 4 of the *Official Secrets Act* amply demonstrate its failure to do so; the provisions are ambiguous and unwieldy. ... A complete redrafting of the Canadian *Official Secrets Act* seems appropriate and necessary.[316]

Post-9/11 Amendments
In fact, the *Official Secrets Act* was substantially amended — and renamed — by Bill C-36, the government's 2001 antiterrorism law. The Bill C-36 changes are notable both for what they did and what they failed to do.

New Espionage Offences
First, Bill C-36 replaced with the old section 3 espionage provisions with a new series of offences listed under the heading "Special Operational Information and Persons Permanently Bound to Secrecy." Most notably, under the revamped Act, persons employed at a number of security and intelligence government agencies are deemed permanently bound to secrecy.[317] As Table 9.8 suggests, these persons are criminally liable for the commu-

---

316 *Toronto Sun* (1979), 24 O.R. (2d) 621 at 632.

317 *Security of Information Act*, s. 8 and accompanying schedule. Further, under s. 10, other persons may be designated "a person permanently bound to secrecy" if certain senior government officials believe that "by reason of the person's office, position, duties, contract or arrangement ... the person had, has or will have authorized access to special operational information; and ... it is in the interest of national security to designate the person."

nication of "special operation information" under sections 13 and 14. "Special operational information" is a defined term and basically means military and intelligence-related information that the government seeks to "safeguard,"[318] an undefined expression.

Both sections 13 and 14 are subject to a carefully defined "public interest defence." Thus, "[n]o person is guilty of an offence under section 13 or 14 if the person establishes that he or she acted in the public interest." A person "acts in the public interest" if his or her purpose is to disclose illegal actions performed in the course of some other person's official functions in circumstances where "the public interest in the disclosure outweighs the public interest in non-disclosure."[319]

These provisions supplement sections of the *Canadian Security Intelligence Service Act* which criminalize unauthorized disclosure of information from which the identity of any CSIS informant or operative may be discerned.[320]

Criminalizing Leakage

While the Bill C-36 amendments to the Act introduced in 2001 eliminated the antiquated spying provision in section 3 of the *Official Secrets Act*, they left intact section 4, criminalizing leakage. As past criticisms cited above suggest, the precise scope of section 4 of the *Security of Information Act* is difficult to discern from the drafting of the section itself. In *Keable v. Cana-*

---

318 *Security of Information Act*, s. 8.

319 *Ibid.*, s. 15. In weighing the relative public interests of disclosure versus nondisclosure, subs. 15(4) instructs a court to consider whether the disclosure is narrowly confined to that required to forestall the alleged offence, the seriousness of this alleged offence, whether the whistleblower resorted to other reasonable alternatives prior to disclosure, whether the whistleblower had reasonable grounds to believe that disclosure was in the public interest, the nature of that public interest, the harm or risk created by disclosure and any exigent circumstances justifying disclosure. Except where necessary to avoid grievous bodily harm, the public interest defence only exists where two prerequisites are met. First, prior to disclosure, the whistleblower must have provided all relevant information to his or her deputy head or the deputy Attorney General of Canada and have received no response within a reasonable time. Subsequently, the whistleblower must have also provided the information to the Security Intelligence Review Committee or, where the alleged offence concerns the Communications Security Establishment, the Communications Security Establishment Commissioner, and not received a response within a reasonable time. The Act leaves open the question of what would constitute a "reasonable time". Likewise, it does not address whether the public interest defence would apply were the responses received from these bodies inadequate.

320 *CSIS Act*, s. 18.

Table 9.8   New Espionage Offences

Type of Information	Person to Whom Prohibition Applies	Prohibition in the Offence
"Special operational information"	Persons permanently bound by secrecy	Intentionally and without authority, communicates or confirms information that, if it were true, would be special operational information.[321]
		Intentionally and without authority, communicates or confirms special operational information.[322]
	Every person	Intentionally and without lawful authority, communicates special operational information to a foreign entity or to a terrorist group if the person believes, or is reckless as to whether, the information is special operational information.[323]
Information the government is "taking measures to safeguard"	Every person with a security clearance given by the Government of Canada	Intentionally and without lawful authority, communicates, or agrees to communicate, to a foreign entity or terrorist group any information that is of a type that the Government of Canada is taking measures to safeguard.[324]
	Every person	Without lawful authority, communicates to a foreign entity or terrorist group information while believing (or reckless as to whether) that information is safeguarded and in order to increase the capacity of that foreign entity or terrorist group to do harm to Canadian interests.[325]
		Without lawful authority, communicates to a foreign entity or to a terrorist group information while believing (or reckless as to whether) that information is safeguarded and harm to Canadian interests results.[326]
Trade secret	Every person	At the direction of, for the benefit of or in association with a foreign economic entity, fraudulently and without colour of right, communicates a trade secret to another person or organization or obtains, retains, alters or destroys a trade secret "to the detriment of" Canada's economic interests, international relations or national defence or national security.[327]

---

321 *Security of Information Act*, s. 13.
322 *Ibid.*, s. 14.
323 *Ibid.*, s. 17.
324 *Ibid.*, s. 18.
325 *Ibid.*, s. 16.
326 *Ibid.*
327 The economic espionage offence in s. 19 is constrained in subs. 19(3) by certain defences protecting independent development of trade secrets or reverse engineering.

da (Attorney General),[328] the Supreme Court held that "Section 4 of the Official Secrets Act makes it clear that it is the duty of every person who has in his possession information entrusted in confidence by a government official and subject to the Act, to refrain from communicating it to any unauthorized person." However, the section is much broader in its scope than this interpretation suggests.

With a few exceptions noted in Table 9.9, section 4 protects "any secret official code word, password, sketch, plan, model, article, note, document or information that relates to or is used in a prohibited place or anything in a prohibited place."[329]

An initial interpretation question is whether the adjectives "secret official" extend to all the nouns that follow, or simply to code words and possibly pass words.[330] If the adjectives apply to the full string of nouns in section 4, then the government must prove that the information is both secret and official, and will not secure a conviction where the impugned information is in the public domain or is not classified by the government as secret.[331] While the old English law was apparently interpreted differently,[332] Canadian courts addressing this issue have limited the scope of the Act, holding that the terms "secret" and "official" apply to all the listed sorts of information. Thus, in *R. v. Toronto Sun*,[333] the courts took the view that an accused could not be convicted under the *Official Secrets Act* unless the information at issue was "secret."

---

328 [1979] 1 S.C.R. 218 at 250–51.

329 Under the Act, "prohibited place" means "any work of defence" owned or occupied by the government, including such things as arsenals, ships, factories, dockyards and the like. Further, a "prohibited place" may also include a privately owned establishment used to store, manufacture or repair any "munitions of war." Finally, the government may itself designate prohibited places where information relating to such a place "would be useful to a foreign power."

330 See Mackenzie Commission, *Report of the Royal Commission on Security* at para. 204 ("In fact there is sufficient inconsistency in the Act for there to have arisen in Canada a question as to whether the words 'secret' or 'official' qualify only 'code word,' or 'code word or pass word' or [more importantly] also the words 'sketch, plan, model, article, or note, or other document or information.'").

331 *Ibid.*

332 Law Reform Commission of Canada, *Crimes Against the State* at 34 (noting that the 1972 U.K. Franks Committee "concluded that the English Act has much wider application, with the words 'secret and official' only qualifying 'code word or password,' and not the other items listed").

333 *Toronto Sun* (1979), 24 O.R. (2d) 621 at 632–33.

However, section 4 also includes a number of provisions criminalizing disclosure and receipt of even *nonsecret,* but "official," information. The Act's antileakage provisions are summarized in Table 9.9.

Table 9.9   Leakage Provisions

Type of Information	Person to Whom Prohibition Applies	Prohibition in the Offence
Any secret official code word, password, sketch, plan, model, article, note, document or information that relates to or is used in a prohibited place	Every person in possession	Fails "to take reasonable care of," or endangers the "safety of" the information.[334]
		Communicates the information "to any person, other than a person to whom he is authorized to communicate with, or a person to whom it is in the interest of the State his duty to communicate it"[335] [*sic*]
		Uses the information "for the benefit of any foreign power or in any other manner prejudicial to the safety or interests of the State."[336]
		Retains the information in the absence of a "right to retain it or when it is contrary to [the receiving person's] duty to retain it or [he or she] fails to comply with all directions issued by lawful authority with regard to the return or disposal thereof."[337]
Any secret official code word, password, sketch, plan, model, article, note, document or information	Every person receiving this information	Knows, or has reasonable ground to believe, at the time he or she receives it, that the information is communicated to him or her in contravention of this Act, unless he or she proves that the communication of the information was contrary to his or her desire.[338]
Any sketch, plan, model, article, note, document or information that relates to munitions of war	Every person in possession	Communicates the information to "any foreign power" or "in any other manner prejudicial to the safety or interests of the State."[339]

---

334 *Security of Information Act,* para. 4(1)(d).
335 *Ibid.,* para. 4(1)(a).
336 *Ibid.,* para. 4(1)(b).
337 *Ibid.,* para. 4(1)(c).
338 *Ibid.,* subs. 4(3).
339 *Ibid.,* subs. 4(2).

Type of Information	Person to Whom Prohibition Applies	Prohibition in the Offence
Any official document	Person for whose use the information was issued	Allows any other person to have possession of the document.[340]
	Every person	Has possession "without lawful authority or excuse" of "any official document ... issued for the use of a person other than" him or herself.[341]
		Upon "obtaining possession of any official document by finding or otherwise," fails to "restore it to the person or authority by whom or for whose use it was issued, or to a police constable."[342]
		Retains "for any purpose prejudicial to the safety or interests of the State" an "official document, whether or not completed or issued for use, when he has no right to retain it, or when it is contrary to his duty to retain it" or in contravention of instructions from the government to return or dispose of it.[343]

The breadth of section 4 is staggering. Communication of information is criminalized in a fashion likely to render most public service "whistle-blowing" a crime. As the Law Reform Commission noted in 1986, the then-*Official Secrets Act* "always treats the loquacious public servant and the secret agent alike: both may be charged under the same section (section 4), the punishment is the same, and, more importantly, the terrible stigma of prosecution under the [Act] is identical for both, because the public and the news media are unable to discern whether it is a case of calculated espionage or careless retention of documents."[344]

So broadly crafted is section 4 that is difficult to imagine the government would, for example, fail to secure convictions for the almost daily "leaks" of written government information that fill newspaper pages. More than that, it seems likely that they would secure the conviction of the journalist and newspaper reporting these leaks.

---

340 *Ibid.*, para. 4(4)(b).
341 *Ibid.*
342 *Ibid.*
343 *Ibid.*, para. 4(4)(a).
344 Law Reform Commission, *Crimes Against the State* at 37.

The historical absence of prosecutions brought under section 4 likely reflects a sober appreciation of the political consequences flowing from aggressive uses of secrecy law. The mere presence of the law on the books, however, may have a chill effect on information-sharing.

Moreover, a law of this breadth may be used to either threaten a prosecution or obtain warrants, both tactics that raise civil liberties issues. Most notoriously, in January 2004, the RCMP raided *Ottawa Citizen* reporter Juliet O'Neill's home and office looking for leaked information pertaining to Maher Arar, a Canadian deported by U.S. officials to Jordan and then incarcerated and tortured in Syria. The warrant alleged a violation by Ms. O'Neill of subsections 4(1)(a), 4(3) and 4(4)(b) of the *Security of Information Act*.[345]

That case has sparked a constitutional challenge to section 4.[346] Specifically, Ms. O'Neill and the *Ottawa Citizen* contend that paragraph 4(1)(a), subsection 4(3) and subsection 4(4)(b) violate section 2(b) of the *Charter* by infringing on the freedom of the press to gather and disseminate information of public interest and concern, and violate section 7 of the *Charter* on the basis of vagueness and overbreadth. Further, subsection 4(3) is said to create a reverse onus provision, in violation of the presumption of innocence set out in section 11(d) of the *Charter*, and also criminalizes conduct on the basis of a standard of "reasonable ground to believe," in violation of section 7 fundamental justice.

This case was still proceeding by December 2004. However, to its credit the government has acknowledged the shortcomings of section 4. Liberal MP Andy Scott indicated

> [t]he Government of Canada recognizes that Section 4, which was largely not amended under the new *Security of Information Act*, needs to be reviewed and modernized. ... While there is scope for the courts to interpret section 4 properly, it is appropriate for Parliament to have the opportunity to consider many of the policy issues section 4 raises, such as what information should be protected and in what circumstances should disclosure be justified in the public interest.[347]

---

345 Gowling LaFleur Henderson LLP, "Juliet O'Neill and CanWest Attack Unconstitutional Search and Seizure" (media advisory, 28 Jan. 2004); Notice of Application and Constitutional Issue, filed on behalf of the applicants Juliet O'Neill and the *Ottawa Citizen* on 11 Feb. 2004, at para. 4.

346 *Ibid.*

347 The Honourable Andy Scott, *Topical Issues*, available at www.andyscott.parl.gc.ca/hot-topics/review.htm.

In January 2004, the government announced a review of section 4.[348] By December 2004, a review of Canada's terrorism law — Bill C-36 — had begun, but it was unclear whether this study would capture section 4 of the *Security of Information Act*.

b) National Security Exemptions Under the *Access* and *Privacy Acts* and the *PIPEDA*

The *Security of Information Act* is not the only statute deterring release of national security information. The *CSIS Act*, for example, bars disclosure of information on the performance of the duties and functions of the Service under the Act, subject to certain exceptions.[349]

Most critically, both the *Access to Information Act* and the *Privacy Act* curb releases of national security information through a series of exemptions and exclusions in both statutes. Both laws allow the government to refuse release of records less than twenty years old containing information prepared by the government during the investigation of activities suspected of constituting "threats to the security of Canada" within the meaning of the *Canadian Security Intelligence Service Act*.[350] The *Access Act* contains a number of other potential national security provisions, such as information that could facilitate an offence (including in relation to critical infrastructure) and information the disclosure of which could be injurious to law enforcement.[351]

---

348   Transcript of news conference with Hon. Anne McLellan, deputy prime minister and minister of public safety; Hon. Yvon Charbonneau, parliamentary secretary (28 Jan. 2004).

349   *Canadian Security Intelligence Service (CSIS) Act*, s. 19.

350   *Access Act*, s. 16; *Privacy Act* s. 22. Section 2 of the *CSIS Act*, R.S. 1985, c. C-23, defines threats to the security of Canada as: "(a) espionage or sabotage that is against Canada or is detrimental to the interests of Canada or activities directed toward or in support of such espionage or sabotage, (b) foreign influenced activities within or relating to Canada that are detrimental to the interests of Canada and are clandestine or deceptive or involve a threat to any person, (c) activities within or relating to Canada directed toward or in support of the threat or use of acts of serious violence against persons or property for the purpose of achieving a political, religious or ideological objective within Canada or a foreign state, and (d) activities directed toward undermining by covert unlawful acts, or directed toward or intended ultimately to lead to the destruction or overthrow by violence of, the constitutionally established system of government in Canada". Obviously, each of these categories of national security threat is broad and vague, and thus capable of expansive definition. On the other hand, much like the Johannesburg Principles, this definition constrains the potential for abuse, not least because of a caveat to the definition that expressly excludes "lawful advocacy, protest or dissent, unless carried on in conjunction with any of the activities referred to" earlier.

351   *Access Act*, s. 16. See also the *Privacy Act* s. 22, which echoes some, but not all, of these exemptions.

Meanwhile, in a provision the Supreme Court of Canada has labelled a "national security" exemption,[352] the government may refuse to disclose any record requested under the Acts "that contains information the disclosure of which could reasonably be expected to be injurious to the conduct of international affairs, the defence of Canada or any state allied or associated with Canada or the detection, prevention or suppression of subversive or hostile activities."[353]

Other national security-like exemptions in the statutes include the *Privacy Act* exemptions for certain national security-related personal information banks operated by CSIS and the RCMP and information obtained in preparing security clearances.[354] Both the *Access* and *Privacy Acts* exempt "information the disclosure of which could reasonably be expected to threaten the safety of individuals."[355] Also notable are the exemptions for information (including intelligence information) obtained in confidence from other countries.[356]

Likewise, under the *PIPEDA*, an individual whose personal information has been disclosed to the government by an organization regulated by that Act may be denied access to the information disclosed, or even knowledge of the disclosure, on national security grounds. Specifically, where an organization regulated by the *PIPEDA* receives a request from an individual for personal information relating to national security, the defence of Canada or the conduct of international affairs, the organization must notify the government. The government must then, within thirty days, communicate to the organization any objection it would have to compliance with the individual's request, on national security grounds. If the government does object, the organization must reject the individual's request, decline to disclose the information in question to the individual, and notify the privacy commissioner.[357]

Read together, these provisions provide government with substantial power to shield national security secrets from the effects of information access laws. Indeed, in 2002–03, the section 16 *Access Act* law-enforcement exemption ranked as the fourth most frequently employed exemption under that Act, used in 8.6 percent of all cases in which exemptions were

---

352   *Ruby*, [2002] 4 S.C.R. 3 at para. 5.
353   *Access Act*, s. 15. See also *Privacy Act*, s. 21, incorporating by reference s. 15 of the *Access Act*.
354   *Privacy Act*, ss. 18 and 23.
355   *Access Act*, s. 17; *Privacy Act*, s. 25.
356   *Access Act*, s. 13; *Privacy Act*, s. 19.
357   *PIPEDA*, subss. 9(2.2)-(2.4).

invoked. The section 15 international affairs and defence exception followed as the fifth most common exemption, at 7 percent. The section 13 information obtained in confidence exemption ranked sixth, at 5.1 percent. *Privacy Act* figures show a higher use of the law enforcement and information obtained in confidence exemptions, and less frequent use of the international affairs and defence exception.[358]

No statistics are publicly available assessing the number of *Access* or *Privacy Act* complaints made by exemption, or whether the use of these exemptions was proper. Thus, it is impossible to assess whether these national security exceptions are being employed reasonably. The information commissioner has, however, criticized the performance of national security agencies under the *Access Act*, noting "Canadians continue to complain about excessive secrecy on the part of government institutions which play a role in ensuring public safety."[359] In the commissioner's words:

> The *Access to Information Act* was intended to move us beyond a form of government accountability based solely on trusting the word and good faith of public officials. While trust in our public officials is important, and usually deserved, the *Access Act* allows us to verify that our trust is well-placed. This important role of openness in our society is not given adequate weight by our public officials who are involved in security-related work.[360]

That said, because the data available are limited, it is hard to draw a conclusion that the *Access* and *Privacy Act* exemptions are abused by agencies with national security responsibilities. As noted above, the number of meritorious (that is, resolved) complaints relating to the use of all *Access Act* exemptions as a proportion of total requests was 2.6 percent, government-wide, in 2002–03. The performance of agencies with some national security functions for which data were available was mixed, but generally not far off this average. For example, the number of meritorious complaints filed with the information commissioner as a proportion of total requests was low at Citizenship and Immigration Canada, at 0.75 percent, but high at the Department of Foreign Affairs and International Trade, at 5.67 percent. Other agencies with national security responsibilities for which data are available fell in-between: 4 percent for the RCMP; 3.8 percent at Nation-

---

358 Section 22 law enforcement and investigation, ranked second at 19 percent; s.19 personal information obtained in confidence ranked third at 9.1 percent; s. 21 international affairs and defence ranked fifth at 1.7 percent. See Treasury Board, *InfoSource Bulletin*, no. 26 (2003).

359 Information Commissioner, *Annual Report 2002-03*, at ch. 1, pt. D.

360 *Ibid.*

al Defence; 2.09 percent at the then-Canada Customs and Revenue Agency; and 1.87 percent at Transport Canada.[361]

These statistics may reflect the fact that the security and intelligence community itself apparently has few quibbles with the proper scope of the *Access Act* (and equivalent *Privacy Act*) exemptions. In an August 2001 study prepared for the government's Access to Information Review Taskforce, security and intelligence specialist Wesley Wark reported that "[b]oth the Canadian Security and Intelligence Service and the Communications Security Establishment, the two main collectors of sensitive intelligence in the community, regard the *Access Act* as offering sufficient protection."[362] Indeed, given the breadth of these exemptions, Wark labelled access to contemporary intelligence records under the Act "a fiction" and concludes that "[t]he current Access exemptions provide powerful and sufficient tools" for protecting intelligence information.[363]

c) *Canada Evidence Act* and the National Security Exclusions Under the *Access* and *Privacy Acts*

Canada Evidence Act *Powers*
Notwithstanding the breadth of existing Canadian secrecy law, and exemptions from Canada's access statutes, the government moved to enhance its power to keep information secret in Bill C-36, the government's 2001 antiterrorism law. Specifically, since Bill C-36, the *Canada Evidence Act*[364] now has a central place in government secrecy law.

While primarily a law setting out important evidentiary rules for "proceedings,"[365] the Act contains special rules limiting access to certain sensitive information during these proceedings. The statute defines "potentially injurious information" as "information of a type that, if it were disclosed to the public, could injure international relations or national defence or national security." "Sensitive information," meanwhile, means "informa-

---

361 Calculated from Treasury Board, *InfoSource*, no. 26 (2003), statistical tables (total requests) and Information Commissioner, *Annual Report 2002-03* statistical tables ("resolved" column in table titled "Complaints Finding by Government Institution"). It is not possible to construct similar figures for the *Privacy Act*, as complaint results statistics by department are not disaggregated between access complaints and complaints relating to improper disclosure of personal information.
362 Wesley Wark, *The Access to Information Act and the Security and Intelligence Community in Canada*, Report 20 (Access to Information Review Task Force, Aug. 2001).
363 *Ibid.*
364 R.S.C. 1985, c. C-5.
365 A proceeding means "a proceeding before a court, person or body with jurisdiction to compel the production of information." *Canada Evidence Act*, s. 38.

tion relating to international relations or national defence or national security" that the Government of Canada is "safeguarding." These terms are not defined in greater detail.

Participants in a civil or criminal proceeding must notify the federal Attorney General when they intend (or believe another participant or person intends) to disclose these classes of information. The Attorney General may then authorize disclosure, or alternatively, may deny this authorization, in which case the matter is taken up by the Federal Court. Under section 38.06, the court authorizes disclosure unless persuaded that disclosure would be injurious to international relations or national defence or national security. Even where disclosure would be injurious, the information may still be released if the public interest in disclosure exceeds the injury.[366]

However, section 38.13 of the *Canada Evidence Act* also empowers the Attorney General to issue personally a certificate "in connection with a proceeding for the purpose of protecting information obtained in confidence from, or in relation to, a foreign entity as defined in subsection 2(1) of the *Security of Information Act* or for the purpose of protecting national defence or national security."[367]

The expressions "national defence" and "national security" are not defined. Moreover, there is an important ambiguity in this provision. Should it be read as relating to information obtained from a "foreign entity" in confidence or from that "foreign entity" for the purpose of protecting national defence or security? If so, then the certificate may only issue for information with a foreign origin. Alternatively, should the section cover information obtained in confidence from a foreign entity, *and* information obtained to protect national defence or security, regardless of its origins? At the time the bill was passed, at least some parliamentarians thought that the provision had the latter, broader meaning.[368]

Notably, the Attorney General may only issue the *Canada Evidence Act* certificate in response to an order or decision requiring the disclosure of that information under any federal statute. However, issuance of the certificate has the effect of barring disclosure of the information in a proceeding. In other words, the certificate may reverse an order from the Federal Court authorizing disclosure under section 38.06 of the *Canada Evidence Act*.

---

366 *Ibid.*, s. 38.06
367 *Ibid.*, s. 38.13.
368 See, e.g., Senator Bryden and Senator Joyal describing the provision as having two purposes: first, protection of confidential foreign information; and second, protection of national defence and national security information. The Special Senate Committee on Bill C-36, *Evidence* (6 Dec. 2001).

The New Access and Privacy Acts Exclusions

The Attorney General's certificate may also bar disclosure under the *Access to Information Act* and *Privacy Act*. Indeed, amendments introduced to the *Access to Information Act* in Bill C-36 give certificates clear primacy over the right to access by establishing a new exclusion. A new section 69.1 specifies that the *Access Act* "does not apply" to information covered by a *Canada Evidence Act* certificate issued before an access complaint is filed with the information commissioner and, if issued after a complaint, quashes all proceedings in relation to that complaint.[369] At first blush, this appears to permit the government to stamp information "top secret" using a certificate and remove *ab initio* that information from the carefully tailored balance of access and exceptions (including those already relating to national security) set out in the *Access Act* regime.

This drastic result appears to be ruled out, at least in part, by the requirement in section 38.13 of the *Canada Evidence Act* that the certificate only be issued in response to an order or decision requiring disclosure. In defending C-36, the government argued that since the information commissioner has no power to "order" or make a decision "requiring" disclosure, in theory, a certificate should only issue once a federal court has ordered disclosure on judicial review under the *Access Act*.[370]

However, as correctly noted by the information commissioner, the commissioner does have power under the *Access Act* to order disclosure to the Office of the Information Commissioner itself, in the course of investigating an access complaint.[371] As a result, it is now "open to the Attorney General to issue a secrecy certificate for the purpose of resisting an order made by the Information Commissioner requiring that records be provided to him."[372]

Indeed, this seems to be the exact intent of the Bill C-36 amendment to the *Access Act*. Subsection 69.1(2) of the *Access Act* indicates that a certificate "discontinues ... all proceedings under this Act in respect of the complaint, including an investigation, appeal or judicial review."[373] Since the information commissioner undertakes an "investigation" under the *Access Act*, this section anticipates a certificate being issued to circumscribe the

369 *Access Act*, s. 69.1.

370 Information Commissioner, *Annual Report 2001–02*, "Antiterrorism and Secrecy," citing then-Minister of Justice McClellan ("the certificate could only be issued after the judicial review of an access or privacy request").

371 *Access Act*, s. 36.

372 *Ibid.*

373 *Ibid.*, subs. 69.1(2).

commissioner's powers precisely in the fashion feared. Indeed, the government has tried to bar disclosure of information to the information commissioner using the *Canada Evidence Act* in the past, even before the new certificate process was introduced.[374]

The breadth of subsection 69.1(2) also exceeds that strictly necessary to bring the *Access Act* into conformity with the amended *Canada Evidence Act*. While the *Canada Evidence Act* precludes the specific information covered in a certificate from being disclosed in a proceeding, the new *Access Act* provision discontinues all proceedings in respect to the "complaint." In critiquing this language, the information commissioner noted that access requests typically ask for information on a subject matter, rather than for specific government records. Various exemptions on access may apply to assorted records falling within this subject matter. In response to a complaint concerning nondisclosure, the commissioner reviews the use of each exemption in relation to each record. Under the new subsection 69.1(2), the application of a certificate to a single record covered in an access complaint discontinues "all proceedings" in respect of the *complaint*, not simply proceedings in relation to that single record. As noted by the commissioner, "[t]he federal government has given itself the legal tools to stop in its tracks any independent review of denials of access under the *Access to Information Act*. The interference is not even limited to the information covered by the secrecy certificates,"[375] as it also captures all other information raised in the complaint.

The information commissioner views the new amendments as an unnecessary over-reaction: "the *Access to Information Act* posed no risk of possible disclosure of sensitive intelligence information, ... no such information had ever been disclosed under the Act in the 18 years of its life and ... the *Access to Information Act* régime offered as much or more secrecy to intelligence information as do the laws of our allies."[376] As noted earlier, this conclusion is supported, at least in part, by Professor Wesley Wark's assessment of national security protection under the regular *Access Act* exemptions.

---

374 See, e.g. *Canada (Attorney General) v. Canada (Information Commissioner)*, [2002] 3 F.C. 606 at para. 9 (F.C.T.D.) ("Three of the applications were brought by the Information Commissioner for orders in the nature of *certiorari* quashing Certificates issued pursuant to ss. 37 and 38 of the *Canada Evidence Act*, pursuant to which certain information and documents ... were not provided to the Information Commissioner.").

375 Information Commissioner, *Annual Report, Information Commissioner, 2001–02*.

376 *Ibid*. For an academic critique of the amendments, see Patricia McMahon, "Amending the *Access to Information Act*: Does National Security Require the Proposed Amendments of Bill C-36," 60 U.T. Fac. L. Rev. 89 (2002).

In a mild response to criticisms sparked by its changes, the government introduced in Bill C-36 an appeal mechanism for certificate determinations under the *Canada Evidence Act*. The minister's certificate decision may be challenged before a single judge of the Federal Court of Appeal. The role of this judge is simply to determine whether the information covered by the certificate relates to the permissible grounds for issuing a certificate, in which case the judge must confirm the certificate.[377] The information commissioner, in his review of this appeal mechanism, called it "woefully inadequate." In his words:

> The reviewing judge is not permitted by this amendment to conduct any of the usual types of judicial review of an administrative decision (*de novo*, legality, correctness); rather the reviewing judge's sole authority is to review the information covered by the certificate for the purpose of deciding whether or not it "relates to":
>
> 1. information disclosed in confidence from, or in relation to, a foreign entity;
> 2. national defence; or
> 3. security.
>
> One would be hard pressed to imagine any operational information held by any of our investigative, defence, security, intelligence, immigration or foreign affairs institutions, which would not "relate to" one or more of these three broad categories. ... This form of judicial review is significantly less rigorous than the independent review of secrecy certificates available in our major allied countries. This form of review has been aptly termed "window dressing" because it does not subject the Attorney General to any meaningful accountability for the use of certificates.[378]

To this criticism might be added the observation that the expressions national "defence" and "security" are undefined, rendering it very difficult for a judge to second-guess the executive branch.

The new exclusion under the *Privacy Act* tracks very closely the *Access Act* equivalent. Notably, however, the *Privacy Act* specifies that a *Canada Evidence Act* section 38.13 certificate discontinues "all proceedings" in relation to the certified personal information, not the complaint *per se*.[379] This

---

377 *Canada Evidence Act*, s. 38.131.
378 Information Commissioner, *Annual Report 2001–02*.
379 *Privacy Act*, s. 70.1.

provision likely bars investigations and court reviews only in relation to the *specific* information covered by the certificate, not investigations and court review of a complaint as a whole that may include both certificate information and other information not captured by the certificate.

d) Extraneous National Security-Related Restrictions on Privacy

The flipside to information-limiting invocations of national security are those provisions allowing select, national security-motivated disclosure of information that would otherwise be protected. Since 9/11, this issue has sparked substantial debate in Canada. The most controversial privacy-restricting statute is the *Public Safety Act*, enacted in 2004.[380] The privacy commissioner objected to this legislation's breadth and its creation of "a general, rather than specific, regime for coopting private sector organizations by pressing them into service in support of law enforcement activities,"[381] and not just anti-terrorism efforts.[382] Of particular concern, in the commissioner's view, were the amendments made by the statute to the *Aeronautics Act* and the *PIPEDA*.[383]

Airline Passenger Information

The new *Aeronautics Act* provisions allow the Department of Transport, the RCMP and CSIS to extract personal information from air carriers and related entities in the interest of transportation security.[384]

The amendments empower the government to require any air carrier or operator of an aviation reservation system to disclose information set out in a schedule to the *Public Safety Act* under certain defined circumstances. Information listed in the Act's schedule includes assorted passenger biographical, booking, ticketing, flight, and itinerary information. The circumstances in which disclosure may be made are set out in Table 9.10,

---

380 S.C. 2004, c. 15.

381 Jennifer Stoddart, Privacy Commissioner of Canada, "Public Safety and Privacy: An Inevitable Conflict?" (lecture, Reboot Communications Public Safety Conference Strategies for Public Safety Technology and Counter-Terrorism: Prevention, Protection and Pursuit, Ottawa, 27 April 2004).

382 George Radwanski, Privacy Commissioner of Canada, Privacy Commissioner of Canada's *Appearance before the Subcommittee on National Security of the Standing Committee on Justice and Human Rights*, 10 Feb. 2003.

383 Jennifer Stoddart, Privacy Commissioner of Canada, *Statement to the Senate Standing Committee on Transport and Communications regarding Bill C-7*, 18 March 2004.

384 *Aeronautics Act*, R.S.C. 1985, c. A-2, ss. 4.81 and 4.82. Note that not all the sections discussed in this part are in force at the time of this writing.

and involve primary disclosure by the air carrier to the government. Secondary and tertiary disclosure of this information by the government is controlled by a series of special rules, again outlined in the chart below.

With respect to information disclosed to the Department of Transportation, following primary, secondary or tertiary disclosure, the information must be destroyed within seven days of that disclosure.[385] The information retention regime is slightly different where information is disclosed by the air carrier or reservation system to the RCMP or CSIS. Here, information disclosed directly to these bodies (or presumably obtained as a secondary disclosure from the Department of Transport) need not be destroyed if it is reasonably required for security purposes.[386] Where information is retained, a record setting out the reasons for this retention must be prepared and the RCMP and CSIS must review their retention decisions annually to determine whether the purposes for retaining information persist.[387]

Secondary disclosure by CSIS and the RCMP must also be documented. Secondary disclosure in most instances requires the CSIS or RCMP discloser to keep a record summarizing the information disclosed, the elements of the information listed in the schedule to the *Public Safety Act* disclosed, the reasons for the disclosure and the name of the person or body to whom the information was disclosed.[388]

---

385 *Ibid.*, subs. 4.81(6), (7) and (8). This destruction requirement applies despite any other Act of Parliament. *Ibid.*, subs. 4.8(9).

386 *Ibid.*, subs. 4.82(14) (section not yet in force at the time of this writing).

387 *Ibid.*, subs. 4.82(15). The document destruction and retention rules in subs. 4.82(14) and (15) apply despite any other Act of Parliament. *Ibid.*, subs. 4.82(17).

388 *Ibid.*, subs. 4.82(13).

Table 9.10   *Primary, Secondary and Tertiary Disclosure Rules of Passenger Information under the Aeronautics Act*

Primary Disclosure	Grounds for Primary Disclosure	Secondary Disclosure	Grounds for Secondary Disclosure	Tertiary Disclosure	Grounds for Tertiary Disclosure
Subsection 4.81(1) — To the Minister of Transport or a designated officer of the Department of Transport.	Subsection 4.81(1) — For the purposes of transportation security, a) information in the schedule on the persons on board or expected to be on board an aircraft should the minister or the officer be of the opinion that there is an immediate threat to that flight; b) information in the schedule on a particular person that comes into the air carrier or aviation reservation systems control within thirty days after the information is requested.	Paragraph 4.81(3)(a) — To the Minister of Citizenship and Immigration.	Subsection 4.81(3) — Only for the purposes of transportation security.	Paragraph 4.81(4)(a) — Only to persons in the Department of Citizenship and Immigration.	Subsection 4.81(4) — Only for the purposes of transportation security.
		Paragraph 4.81(3)(b) — To the Minister of National Revenue.	Subsection 4.81(3) — Only for the purposes of transportation security.	Paragraph 4.81(4)(b) — Only to persons in the Department of National Revenue.	Subsection 4.81(4) — Only for the purposes of transportation security.
		Paragraph 4.81(3)(c) — To the CEO of the Canadian Air Transport Security Authority.	Subsection 4.81(3) — Only for the purposes of transportation security.	Paragraph 4.81(4)(c) — Only to persons in the Canadian Air Transport Security Authority.	Subsection 4.81(4) — Only for the purposes of transportation security.
		Paragraph 4.81(3)(d) — To a person designated by the Commissioner of the RCMP under subs. 4.82(2) (see below).	Subsection 4.81(3) — Only for the purposes of transportation security.	Subsection 4.82(7) — Tertiary disclosure apparently governed by the secondary and tertiary disclosure rules for RCMP and CSIS designates noted below.	
		Paragraph 4.81(3)(e) — To a person designated by the Director of CSIS under subs. 4.82(3) (see below).	Subsection 4.81(3) — Only for the purposes of transportation security.	Subsection 4.82(7) — Tertiary disclosure apparently governed by the secondary and tertiary disclosure rules for RCMP and CSIS designates noted below.	

Subsection 4.82(4) — To a person designated by the Commissioner of the RCMP under s-s.4.82(2).	Subsection 4.82(4) — For the purposes of transportation security, a) information in the schedule on the persons on board or expected to be on board; or b) information in the schedule on a particular person that comes into the air carrier or aviation reservation systems control within thirty-days after the information is requested.	Subsection 4.82(6) — To any other person designated by the Commissioner of the RCMP under subs. 4.82(2)	
		Subsection 4.82(8) — To the Minister of Transport, any peace officer, any employee of CSIS, or to the Canadian Air Transport Security Authority or any air carrier or operator of an aviation facility, along with the Minister of Transport.	Subsection 4.82(8) — Designated person has reason to believe that the information is relevant to transportation security.[389]
		Subsection 4.82(9) — To an Aircraft Protective Officer (an undefined person under the Act).	Subsection 4.82(9) — If the designated person believes that the information may assist this person in performing duties relating to transportation security.

389 Note that it is not entirely clear from the drafting if this purpose is meant to modify simply disclosure to an air carrier or operator of an aviation facility, or to apply also to the other persons who may receive secondary disclosure.

Primary Disclosure	Grounds for Primary Disclosure	Secondary Disclosure	Grounds for Secondary Disclosure	Tertiary Disclosure	Grounds for Tertiary Disclosure
		Subsection 4.82(10) — To the extent necessary to respond to a threat to transportation security or the life, health or safety of a person, to a person in a position to take measures to respond to the threat who needs the information to respond.	Subsection 4.82(10) — Designated person has reason to believe that there is an immediate threat to transportation security or the life, health or safety of a person.		
		Subsection 4.82(11) — To any peace officer.	Subsection 4.82(11) — If designated person has reason to believe that the information would assist in the execution of a warrant.		
		Subsection 4.82(7) — As required by the purpose.	Subsection 4.82(7) — For the purpose of complying with a subpoena or document issued or order made by a court, person or body with jurisdiction to compel the production of information, or the purpose of complying with rules of court relating to the		

	production of information.	
Subsection 4.82(3) — To a person designated by the Director of CSIS under subs. 4.82(3).	Subsection 4.81(5) — For the purposes of transportation security or the investigation of activities relating to violence against persons or property for political, religious or ideological objectives within Canada or a foreign state a) information in the schedule on the persons on board or expected to be on board or b) information in the schedule on a particular person that comes into the air carrier or aviation reservation systems control within thirty-days after the information is requested.	Subsection 4.82(6) — To any other person designated by the Director of CSIS under subs. 4.82(3).
	Subsection 4.82(8) — To the Minister of Transport, any peace officer, any employee of CSIS, or to the Canadian Air Transport Security Authority or any air carrier or operator of an aviation facility, along with the Minister of Transport.	Subsection 4.82(8) — Designated person has reason to believe that the information is relevant to transportation security.[390]
	Subsection 4.82(9) — To an Aircraft Protective Officer (an undefined person under the Act).	Subsection 4.82(9) — If the designated person believes the information may assist this person in performing duties relating to transportation security.
	Subsection 4.82(10) — To the extent necessary to respond to a threat	Subsection 4.82(10) — If the designated person has reason to believe

390 See above note 388.

Primary Disclosure	Grounds for Primary Disclosure	Secondary Disclosure	Grounds for Secondary Disclosure	Tertiary Disclosure	Grounds for Tertiary Disclosure
		to transportation security or the life, health or safety of a person, disclosure may be made to a person in a position to take measures to respond to the threat and who needs the information to respond.	that there is an immediate threat to transportation security or the life, health or safety of a person.		
		Subsection 4.82(11) — To any peace officer.	Subsection 4.82(11) — If the designated person has reason to believe that the information would assist in the execution of a warrant.		
		Subsection 4.82(12) — To an employee of CSIS.	Subsection 4.82(12) — If authorized by a senior designated person, for the purpose of an investigation of activities relating to violence against persons or property for political, religious or ideological objectives within Canada or a foreign state.		

			Subsection 4.83(2) — Only for the purpose of protecting national security or public safety or for the purpose of defence or administering or enforcing any federal statute prohibiting, controlling or regulating the importation or exportation of goods or the movement of people in or out of Canada.
		Subsection 4.82(7) — For the purpose of complying with a subpoena or document issued or order made by a court, person or body with jurisdiction to compel the production of information, or the purpose of complying with rules of court relating to the production of information.	Subsection 4.83(2) — Any further disclosure.
	Subsection 4.82(7) — As required by the purpose.	Subsection 4.83(2) — Information can be collected only for the purpose of protecting national security or public safety or for the purpose of defence or administering or enforcing any federal statute prohibiting, controlling or regulating the importation or exportation of goods or the movement of people in or out of Canada.	
	Subsection 4.83(2) — Information provided to a foreign state may be collected by a government institution (as defined under the *Privacy Act*).		
Subsection 4.83(1) — To a competent authority in a foreign state	Subsection 4.83(1) — Information may be provided in accordance with the laws of the foreign state either where the aircraft is Canadian and flying an international route or where an aircraft is departing from Canada and is scheduled to land in a foreign state.		

Other Information That May be Disclosed

The *Immigration and Refugee Protection Act (IRPA)*[391] supplements the disclosure obligations of transportation companies under the *Aeronautics Act*. Under the *IRPA*, a person who owns or operates a transportation facility must disclose to the government assorted passenger identity and travel information.[392]

Several other statutes also limit privacy on clear national security grounds. For instance, the *Proceeds of Crime (Money Laundering) and Terrorist Financing Act* creates a Financial Transactions and Reports Analysis Centre tasked with reviewing financial data disclosed to it by financial institutions, among other entities, for evidence of money laundering and terrorist financing. Information the Centre believes is relevant to threats to the security of Canada is to be disclosed to CSIS.[393]

Also, as noted above, under the *Personal Information Protection and Electronic Documents Act*,[394] as amended by the *Public Safety Act*, an organization otherwise barred from collecting, using or disclosing personal information without the consent of the person concerned may do so if "made to a government institution or part of a government institution that has made a request for the information, identified its lawful authority to obtain the information and indicated that" it suspects that "the information relates to national security, the defence of Canada or the conduct of international affairs."

Information Interception

Lawful Access Provisions

Finally, in addition to these disclosure laws, the Canadian statute books include legislation allowing "lawful access" by police, security and intelligence agencies to personal information. Lawful access is the "lawful interception of communications and the lawful search and seizure of information, including computer data."[395] The key lawful access provisions are found in the *Criminal Code*[396] and a full discussion of these criminal law investigative provisions lies outside the scope of this book.

---

391 *Immigration and Refugee Protection Act (IRPA)*, S.C. 2001, c. 27.

392 *Ibid.*, ss. 148 and 149.

393 S.C. 2000, c. 17, s. 55.1.

394 S.C. 2000, c. 5, s. 7.

395 *Lawful Access — FAQ*, consultation report prepared for the Department of Justice.

396 See, e.g., Part VI Invasion of Privacy provisions in the *Criminal Code*, R.S. 1985, c. C-46.

Other lawful access provisions motivated by national security impulses are found in the *CSIS Act*[397] and the *National Defence Act*.[398] Since 2001, the *National Defence* Act empowers the Department of National Defence's Communications Security Establishment (CSE) to intercept private communications. A private communication is defined, in keeping with the *Criminal Code*, as "any oral communication, or any telecommunication" originating or intending to be received in Canada that reasonably would not be expected by its originator to be intercepted other than by the intended recipient.[399] Likewise, the *CSIS Act* allows CSIS to engage in intelligence gathering activities involving authorized invasions of privacy.

The CSE's powers in relation to the interception of external (as opposed to internal) private communications are set out in Table 9.11, as are the CSIS privacy-limiting powers.

Oversight of the CSE

Each of these intelligence statutes has its own review and complaints mechanisms. The *National Defence Act* establishes a commissioner of the communications security establishment — a supernumerary or a retired judge of a superior court appointed by the Governor-in-Council. The commissioner is tasked with reviewing the activities of the establishment to ensure that they are in compliance with the law, to undertake any investigation that the commissioner considers necessary in response to a complaint, and to inform the minister of national defence and the Attorney General of Canada of any activity of the establishment that the commissioner believes may not be in compliance with the law.[400] Further, the commissioner is required to review the establishment's activities undertaken in response to an authorization set out in Table 9.11, and report annually to the minister of national defence.[401] The commissioner reports on his or her activities in an annual report tabled in Parliament.[402]

In his 2003 *Annual Report*, the outgoing commissioner summarized his activities since 1996. He noted that none of the 23 classified reports he provided to the minister of national defence over his tenure had identified incidents of unlawfulness or unauthorized activity.[403] Since the commis-

---

397 R.S. 1985, c. C-23.
398 R.S. 1985, c. N-5.
399 R.S. 1985, c. C-46, s. 183.
400 *National Defence Act*, s. 273.63.
401 *Ibid.*, s. 273.66.
402 *Ibid.*, subs. 272.63(3). The commissioner also has responsibilities under the *Security of Information Act*.
403 Communications Security Establishment Commissioner, *Annual Report 2002–03* at 5.

Table 9.11   CSE and CSIS Privacy Limiting Powers

Agency	Type of Infringement of Privacy	Grounds for Infringement	Prerequisites to Infringement
Communications Security Establishment	*National Defence Act* subs. 273.65 (1) — Interception of private communications	Subsection 273.65(1) — For the sole purpose of obtaining foreign intelligence	Subsection 273.65(2) — Authorized by the minister of national defence on the basis that: • the interception will be directed at foreign entities located outside Canada; • the information to be obtained could not reasonably be obtained by other means; • the expected foreign intelligence value of the information that would be derived from the interception justifies it; and • satisfactory measures are in place to protect the privacy of Canadians and to ensure that private communications will only be used or retained if they are essential to international affairs, defence or security.
		Subsection 273.65(3) — For the sole purpose of protecting the computer systems or networks of the Government of Canada from mischief, unauthorized use or interference	Subsection 273.65(4) — Authorized by the minister of national defence on the basis that: • the interception is necessary to identify, isolate or prevent harm to Government of Canada computer systems or networks; • the information to be obtained could not reasonably be obtained by other means; • the consent of persons whose private communications may be intercepted cannot reasonably be obtained; • satisfactory measures are in place to ensure that only information that is essential to identify, isolate or prevent harm to Government of Canada computer systems or networks will be used or retained; and • satisfactory measures are in place to protect the privacy of Canadians in the use or retention of that information.

Agency	Type of Infringement of Privacy	Grounds for Infringement	Prerequisites to Infringement
Canadian Security Intelligence Agency	*CSIS Act* subs. 21(3) — Interception of any communication or obtaining any information, record, document or thing and, for that purpose: • to enter any place or open or obtain access to any thing; • to search for, remove or return, or examine, take extracts from or make copies of or record the information, record, document or thing; or to install, maintain or remove any thing	Subsection 21(3) — Required to enable CSIS to investigate a threat to the security of Canada or to collect information or intelligence relating to the capabilities, intentions or activities of any foreign state or group of foreign states or foreign person, other than a permanent resident.	Subsection 21(3) — By warrant, where a judge is satisfied that the facts justify the belief, on reasonable grounds, that a warrant under this section is required to serve the purpose in the column to the left. The judge must also be satisfied that: • other investigative procedures have been tried and have failed (or why it appears that they are unlikely to succeed); • the urgency of the matter is such that it would be impractical to carry out the investigation using only other investigative procedures; or • without a warrant under the Act it is likely that information respecting the threat to the security of Canada would not be obtained.

sioner's role in addressing complaints was mandated in 2001, the commissioner had received only a single complaint, directed to him by a member of the public in 2001–02. The commissioner reviewed this matter and concluded that no further action was required.[404]

Oversight of CSIS

The *Canadian Security Intelligence Service Act* sets out a multitiered CSIS review mechanism. First, the CSIS director is obliged to prepare reports on the operational activities of CSIS on an annual basis or more frequently on demand of the solicitor general, and to submit these documents to the solicitor general and the CSIS inspector general.[405] This latter official is appointed by the Governor-in-Council and is responsible to the deputy solicitor general. The inspector general monitors compliance by the service with its operational policies and examines its operational activities.[406] To this end, the inspector general is given full access to the service's information, except Cabinet confidences.[407]

The inspector general certifies whether the reports provided by the director are adequate and whether they reveal any action of the service that the inspector general views as an unauthorized or an unreasonable or unnecessary exercise of its powers.[408]

The solicitor general transmits the inspector general's report and certificate to the Security Intelligence Review Committee (SIRC).[409] The members of SIRC are appointed by the Governor-in-Council (after consultation with the leaders of official parties in the Commons) and are tasked with, among other things, reviewing the performance by the Service of its duties and functions, including reviewing reports of the director and certificates of the inspector general.[410] Like the inspector general, SIRC has broad rights to CSIS information.[411]

Any person may make complaints concerning CSIS, directed first to the director. SIRC may investigate nonfrivolous, good faith complaints if the director fails to respond in a period of time the committee views as reasonable, or provides an inadequate response.[412] These investigations are

---

404 Communications Security Establishment Commissioner, *Annual Report 2001–02*.
405 *CSIS Act*, s. 33.
406 *Ibid.*, s. 30.
407 *Ibid.*, s. 31.
408 *Ibid.*, s. 33.
409 *Ibid.*
410 *Ibid.*, s. 38.
411 *Ibid.*, s. 39.
412 *Ibid.*, s. 41.

held in private.[413] The committee has broad powers to subpoena persons and documents.[414] The outcome of this report is conveyed to the solicitor general and the director, along with SIRC's recommendations. The complainant is also notified of the committee's finding,[415] subject to security requirements on disclosure of information.[416]

SIRC also prepares an annual report, tabled by the solicitor general in Parliament,[417] which in practice contains summaries of the committee's investigations.

By December 2004, the sufficiency of these review mechanisms was a matter of debate in public policy circles. A move was afoot to supplement SIRC with a parliamentary national security committee.[418]

D. CONCLUSION

Canadian democracy acknowledges the importance of both open government and privacy. It also accepts limitations on those rights. The secret is to find the fine balance between rights and limitations.

On the whole, the material canvassed in this chapter suggests that government performance under at least the *Access Act* has been unspectacular, and at times poor. Open government is not as open as it ought to be, given the broad right to access anticipated by the *Access Act*. Preserving privacy, meanwhile, is a persistent challenge, as the privacy commissioner's annual reports suggest.[419]

At the same time, an increasingly perplexing "complex" of secrecy and national security provisions temper greatly both access and privacy. Where once there was a general right to access and privacy, constrained by already generous exceptions, now there are even more sweeping and more poorly defined national security exclusions from access and privacy rights.

Specifically, the relative clarity of the original *Access Act* exemptions are not echoed in the *Canada Evidence Act*, amended by the 2001 *Anti-Terrorism Act*. The *Canada Evidence Act* creates classes of secret information far

---

413 *Ibid.*, s. 48.

414 *Ibid.*, s. 50.

415 *Ibid.*, s. 52.

416 *Ibid.*, s. 55.

417 *Ibid.*, s. 53.

418 See discussion in Public Safety and Emergency Preparedness Canada, *A National Security Committee of Parliamentarians* (2004).

419 See, e.g., Privacy Commissioner, *Annual Report 2002–03*, "Overview," detailing new challenges in preserving privacy rights.

broader than the equivalent *Access Act* provisions. Meaningful court scrutiny of these open-ended secrecy claims may be short-circuited by government issuance of a "certificate." Barely reviewable in court, this certificate may also be marshaled to trump the *Access Act* and *Privacy Act* disclosure requirements, negating the careful and balanced approach of these laws.

Meanwhile, lurking in the background is section 4 of the *Security of Information Act*. Under this statute, unauthorized disclosure of even non-secret but "official" government documents brings with it the possibility of criminal prosecutions. Where the document is "secret" within the (undefined) meaning of the Act, the prospect of being found criminally culpable multiplies. Further, since the Act criminalizes receipt as much as disclosure, it makes leaked government information a hot potato. The net effect is a possible chill on the sharing of information, even when a clear public interest in disclosure may exist.

The over-breadth of these laws is deeply troubling. Secrecy, even when motivated by an objective as fundamental as national security, may sometimes create more perils than it forestalls. In 2003, the Standing Senate Committee on Defence and National Security released its report, *The Myth of Security at Canada's Airports*. The study documented deeply inadequate security at Canadian airports, even in the post-9/11 era, and concluded that the "front door of air security ... [is] now being fairly well secured, with the side and back doors wide open."[420]

In the course of preparing its report, the committee was criticized "for calling witnesses that have shared knowledge of these breaches with the Canadian public."[421] It rejected this criticism, observing:

> You can be sure that ships really will sink if they have a lot holes in them. And those holes aren't likely to get patched unless the public applies pressure to get the job done. They certainly aren't patched yet.
>
> The Committee recognizes the need to balance the public's right to know against the interests of national security. But unreasonable secrecy acts against national security. It shields incompetence and inaction, at a time that competence and action are both badly needed.[422]

---

420 Standing Senate Committee on Defence and National Security, *The Myth of Security at Canada's Airports* (2003) at 9.

421 *Ibid.* at 11.

422 *Ibid.* at 12–13. Similar comments have been made by academic observers. See Coliver, "Commentary on the Johannesburg Principles on National Security, Freedom of Expression and Access to Information," at 11–12 ([f]reedom of expression and access to information, by enabling public scrutiny of government action, serve as safeguards

National security, in other words, is not about insulating governments from embarrassment.

Nor can it be a *carte blanche* for government snooping in the private affairs of citizens. New laws compelling the sharing of private information with the government in the interests of security raise clear concerns about where the line should be drawn between a vital civil liberty and state protection.[423]

Over three years into the post-9/11 era, there is a good argument to be made that in the name of protecting the Canadian state and its people, Canada's access (and potentially its privacy-limiting) laws now go too far in undermining rights essential to maintaining accountability in a liberal democracy.

against government abuse and thereby form a crucial component of genuine national security"); Paul H. Chevigny, "Information, the Executive and the Politics of Information," in Shimon Shetreet, ed., *Free Speech and National Security* (Boston: M. Nijhoff Publishers, 1991) at 138 ("[t]he problem with the 'national security state' is not so much that it violates [fundamental] rights, although it sometimes does just that, but that it can lead to the repetition of irrational decisions").

423 For a discussion of government performance on this issue, see Arthur Cockfield, "The State of Privacy Laws and Privacy-Encroaching Technologies after September 11: A Two-Year Report Card on the Canadian Government," U. Ottawa L. & Tech. J. (Spring 2004) at 325–44.

10

Democratic Governance in Times of Emergency

Emergencies present enormous difficulties for democracies. As this book has suggested, democracies are built on a system of checks and balances, conventions and mores, which constrain the exercise of power. Yet, emergencies often, if not usually, require the exercise of power. Moreover, this power must be implemented swiftly and with resolution. While democracy aims to diffuse power, emergencies concentrate it.

In the 1970 October Crisis, the federal Cabinet debated whether to rely on executive powers under the *War Measures Act* to authorize the detention of suspects in Quebec or to enact special legislation.[1] Then-Justice Minister John Turner urged recourse to Parliament, but noted that with letters from the political and police authorities in Quebec the government could proclaim the *War Measures Act*, rendering police raids and detentions legal. The government could then go to Parliament asking it to approve further, more specialized legislation.[2] In other words, the executive branch could exercise powers immediately, leaving the potential delays associated with

---

1　"The FLQ Situation," RG2, Privy Council Office, Series A-5-a, vol. 6359 (15 Oct. 1970; afternoon session) at 5.
2　See discussion *ibid.* at 6.

the parliamentary process to another day.[3] In the end, Cabinet chose to rely on the *War Measures Act*, authorizing extraordinary police powers.

What Canada learned from the October Crisis is that during political emergencies, the executive branch is typically strengthened at the expense of the legislative and judicial branches. Urgency tends to trump sober second thought, and the rule of law may be suspended for a perceived greater good. "Society," argued Prime Minister Pierre Trudeau three days before the *War Measures Act* was invoked, "must take every means at its disposal to defend itself against the emergence of a parallel power which defies the elected power in this country."[4]

Any emergency presents three questions, the answer to which determines its impact on democracy. First, how does one determine when an emergency exists? Second, how should the state respond to the emergency? Third, when does the emergency end? Answering these questions is not straightforward. On one end of the spectrum are "clear" emergencies. In recent history, these are usually natural disasters, such as the Manitoba flood of 1997 or the Central Canadian ice storm of 1998. Other such clear emergencies are unexpected, but noncatastrophic systems failures, like the blackout of 2003 in Central Canada and the Eastern United States.

The course of action to be followed in responding to natural or accidental disaster emergencies is usually straightforward. If a sizeable portion of a region is flooded, flood interdiction, search and rescue, and financial, medical and material assistance are the order of the day. If power supplies are disrupted, restoring electricity and accommodating essential services pending the return of power are the priorities. Further, with these sorts of crises, the duration of the emergency is reasonably certain: floodwaters recede, electrical supplies return. Emergencies like these may require the assistance of the military or that extra policing resources deter civil unrest. Nevertheless, although a truly catastrophic natural or artificial disaster could undermine Canadian democracy, calamities like these historically have not disrupted democratic practices or institutions. Whether this pattern will remain true in the face of global threats of climate change or infectious diseases is a question this book cannot answer.

---

3   In fact, these fears of delays in part explain the government's ultimate decision to invoke the *War Measures Act*. *Ibid.* at 6 for Prime Minister Trudeau explaining that there was no way legislation could be put through all its stages to authorize action before the next morning.

4   Pierre Elliott Trudeau, interview by CBC-TV reporter Tim Ralfe, 13 Oct. 1970, reprinted in J.R. Colombo, *Famous Lasting Words* (Vancouver: Douglas & McIntyre, 2000) at 376.

More problematic to any democracy, historically, are political emergencies: a state of war, an insurrection, a terrorist threat or strike, or the like. Citizens can turn on their televisions or even glance out their windows to have a clear sense of the gravity and immediacy of a flood or ice storm. The scope of political emergencies is more difficult to assess. In this respect, they are less "empirical" than natural or artificial disasters. As Prime Minister Trudeau observed in the course of Cabinet discussions prior to the invocation of the *War Measures Act*, one only knows *after* the fact whether one is facing an insurrection or not.[5] Perhaps most troubling, the uncertainty prompted by this "fog of war" may be motivated by other concerns. Thus, emergencies are most corrosive of democracy where, as writer Michael Ignatieff puts it, they are proclaimed "on grounds that involve bad faith, manipulation of evidence, exaggeration of risk, or the prospect of political advantage."[6]

All told, a government's assessment of the scope of a political emergency, and the propriety of the government response to it, are difficult to second-guess. This uncertainty is particularly problematic where, as is usually the case, political emergencies require that those constituting the threat be interdicted quickly, before they compound the danger. Moreover, deciding whether political emergencies have abated is also tremendously difficult. As Ignatieff has noted, the problem with these sorts of emergencies is that "only the executive has sufficient information to know whether they remain justified. Hence the speedy termination of emergencies remains a recurrent problem. Electorates and legislators are invariably told by their leaders, 'If you only knew what we know ... ,' in justification of the continued suspension of civil liberties."[7] The result may be a prolonged state of emergency, and measures designed to give the executive branch extraordinary and temporary powers may persist.

All told, therefore, emergencies — particularly political emergencies — may constitute a serious threat to democracy. Discussing the current "war on terror," Ignatieff proposes that "[i]n a long twilight war, largely fought by secret means, the key issue is maintaining as much legal and legislative oversight as is compatible with the necessity for decisive action."[8] To this end, an assessment of emergency action obliges three questions:

---

5   "The FLQ Situation," (15 Oct. 1970; morning session) at 8.
6   Michael Ignatieff, *The Lesser Evil: Political Ethics in an Age of Terror* (Toronto: Penguin, 2004) at 37.
7   *Ibid.* at 51.
8   *Ibid.* at 39.

first, is the action authorized by law; second, are the extraordinary measures authorized by this law proportional and adequately linked to reasonable assessments of the threat; and, third, does the law contain provisions for the review and termination of these extraordinary powers.

This chapter takes up the issue of emergencies and Canadian democracy. It examines, first, the concept of emergencies as a constraint on democracy and civil and human rights in international law. It then examines the extent to which Canadian constitutional and statutory law permits a similar abrogation, and evaluates these Canadian provisions against this three-question test of legitimacy.

A. EMERGENCY POWERS AND INTERNATIONAL LAW

The *UN International Covenant on Civil and Political Rights* — a cornerstone of international human rights law — contemplates derogation from some of its rights in times of emergency. Pursuant to Article 4(1), states may take measures abridging most rights in the time of a public emergency that "threatens the life of the nation."

There are safeguards. The derogation may only be what is strictly required by the exigencies of the situation. A state making use of the right of derogation must immediately inform the other states that are parties to the covenant and explain why. Further, the measures introduced must not be inconsistent with a state's other obligations under international law and must not involve discrimination solely on the ground of race, colour, sex, language, religion or social origin. Finally, not all rights are trumped. Article 4(2) asserts that no derogation is permissible from the rights to life, to recognition as a person, and to freedom of thought, conscience and religion. Likewise, an Article 4 emergency may not negate the bans on torture or cruel, inhuman or degrading treatment or punishment, and the prohibition on slavery and servitude, imprisonment for contractual breach, and retroactive criminal law.

Still, Article 4 accords states substantial authority to negate rights unilaterally. It applies to many of the covenant's most important provisions, including most of the legal rights, the freedom of expression and association provisions, the right to privacy, and the democratic rights. Concern with the reach of this Article has prompted the UN Human Rights Committee — the body established by the covenant — to offer narrow interpretations of the provision. In 1981, the committee urged that "measures taken under article 4 are of an exceptional and temporary nature and may only last as long as the life of the nation concerned is threatened and that in times of emergency, the protection of human rights becomes all the more important, particularly those rights from which no derogations can be made."[9]

In a more expansive commentary adopted in 2001, the committee echoed this view, concluding that "[m]easures derogating from the provisions of the Covenant must be of an exceptional and temporary nature."[10] Moreover, because states must abide by their other international law obligations, Article 4 cannot, in fact, authorize derogations from international humanitarian law applicable in armed conflicts and so-called pre-emptory norms of international law. These include the bars on taking hostages, the imposition of collective punishments, arbitrary deprivations of liberty or deviations from fundamental principles of fair trial. Further, with the coming into force of the *Rome Statute of the International Criminal Court* (of which Canada is a party) emergency situations clearly do not relieve perpetrators of culpability for crimes against humanity.[11]

At the end of the day, therefore, international law accommodates public emergencies. However, it would be wrong to view it as extending states a *carte blanche* to respond to these calamities as they will.

B. EMERGENCY POWERS AND THE CONSTITUTION

Unlike the *International Covenant on Civil and Political Rights*, Canadian constitutional and quasi-constitutional law generally does not expressly anticipate abridgment of rights in the event of emergencies. With the exception of section 4(2) of the *Charter*, discussed later in this chapter, both the *Canadian Charter of Rights and Freedoms* and the 1960 *Canadian Bill of Rights* are silent on emergencies. However, both these instruments allow Parliament to circumscribe at least some of the rights they protect, pursuant to "notwithstanding" provisions.

1. *Canadian Bill of Rights*

An Act of Parliament may expressly limit the reach of the *Canadian Bill of Rights*.[12] For example, the *War Measures Act*, prior to its repeal by the *Emer-*

---

9   UN Human Rights Committee, *General Comment 5*, A/36/40 (1981) Annex VII at 110; CCPR/C/21/Rev.1 at 4.
10   UN Human Rights Committee, *General Comment 29*, CCPR/C/21/Rev.1/Add.11 (2001).
11   *Ibid.*
12   S.C. 1960, c. 44, s. 2, noting that the rights described in that section may be negated if it is "expressly declared by an Act of the Parliament of Canada that [a statute] shall operate notwithstanding the *Canadian Bill of Rights.*"

gencies Act in 1988, provided that "[a]ny act or thing done or authorized or any order or regulation made under the authority of this Act, shall be deemed not to be an abrogation, abridgement or infringement of any right or freedom recognized by the *Canadian Bill of Rights.*"[13]

2. *Charter of Rights and Freedoms*

a) Section 33

Likewise, the "notwithstanding" clause in section 33 of the *Charter* allows Parliament or the provincial legislatures to remove a statute from *Charter* scrutiny by explicitly indicating it operates "notwithstanding" the *Charter.* This immunity persists for five years, subject to any renewal.

Critically, this section applies to most, but not all, rights in the *Charter.* It extends to the fundamental freedoms provisions in section 2, the legal rights in sections 7 to 14, and the equality provisions in section 15. It does not, however, authorize Parliament to negate many other *Charter* rights, including the mobility right in section 6 or, notably, the democratic rights in sections 3 to 5. As discussed at various points in this book, these democratic rights affirm the right to vote (section 3), limit the duration of a House of Commons to five years (section 4(1)), and require annual sittings of Parliament (section 5).

As a result, subject to our discussion below of section 4(2) of the *Charter*, were Parliament to rely on section 33 to negate the *Charter*'s civil rights sections in response to an emergency, it could not also rely on section 33 to deny voting rights to citizens, or prolong its existence past the five years anticipated by section 4(1).[14] Also section 5, requiring an annual sitting of Parliament, restricts Parliament's capacity to delegate governance to the executive and retire pending the conclusion of a state of emergency. In any event, a Parliament tempted to delegate indefinitely its full plenary powers, perhaps in response to an emergency, would also run afoul of a long-established, pre-*Charter* constitutional restriction barring complete abdication of Parliament's responsibilities in favour of the executive.[15]

---

13   *War Measures Act*, R.S. 1970, c. 288, s. 6.

14   The importance of s. 4's immunity from s. 33 has been noted by the Supreme Court. See *Reference re Secession of Quebec*, [1998] 2 S.C.R. 217 at para. 65, holding that the democratic principle said to reside in the Canadian Constitution "is affirmed with particular clarity in that s. 4 is not subject to the notwithstanding power contained in s. 33."

15   See *Re Gray* (1918), 57 S.C.R. 150 at 157, holding that the broad delegation of powers under the *War Measures Act, 1914* was *intra vires* Parliament, but also noting "Parliament cannot, indeed, abdicate its functions, but within reasonable limits at any rate it can delegate its powers to the executive government. Such powers must necessarily be

b) Section 1

Even if section 33 were not used, and Parliament's enactment violated the *Charter*, the statute could be saved from a *Charter* challenge by section 1. Section 1 circumscribes all *Charter* rights by "such reasonable limits prescribed by law as can be demonstrably justified in a free and democratic society." What those reasonable limits might be in an emergency would depend on the nature of the crisis. It seems likely, however, that courts would be prepared to endorse some abridgment of rights in a good faith emergency. For instance, in *R. v. Heywood*,[16] the Supreme Court suggested that a violation of the section 7 right to life, liberty and security of the person, though generally difficult to justify on section 1 grounds, could be reasonable "in times of war or national emergencies."

c) Section 4(2)

The discussion thus far suggests that the Canadian Constitution is a flexible instrument, able to accommodate legitimate emergencies. It is not, therefore, akin to the rigid "suicide pact" about which U.S. Supreme Court Justices Jackson[17] and Goldberg[18] both warned in litigation concerning the U.S. Constitution.

At the same time, the discussion to this point suggests that the Canadian Constitution does not extend a *carte blanche* to the government. The section 33 override could insulate a law from court scrutiny in relation to civil rights, but the House of Commons that chooses to invoke section 33 cannot use that same provision to prolong its existence in violation of section 4(1) and stave off the judgment of the electorate. Generally, a failure to comply with the democratic rights in sections 3 to 5 of the *Charter* could only be justified under section 1, again putting courts in the position as ultimate arbiter of whether the constitutional infraction is justified. All told, this system of checks and balances would make it very difficult for a government to remain onside the Constitution while maintaining an unwarranted, permanent state of emergency.

---

subject to determination at any time by Parliament, and needless to say the acts of the executive, under its delegated authority, must fall within the ambit of the legislative pronouncement by which its authority is measured"; *British Columbia Native Women's Society v. Canada*, [2000] 1 F.C. 304 at para. 23, noting that the federal Parliament must not abdicate its legislative functions or efface itself.

16 [1994] 3 S.C.R. 761 at 802. See also *Newfoundland (Treasury Board) v. N.A.P. E.*, 2004 SCC 66 for the Court citing a putative fiscal crisis in upholding a discriminatory law under s. 1.

17 *Terminiello v. City Of Chicago*, 337 U.S. 1 at 37 (1949), *per* Jackson J., dissenting.

18 *Kennedy v. Mendoza-Martinez*, 372 U.S. 144 at 160 (1963).

That said, there is an evident Achilles heel in this effort to preserve constitutional probity in a time of emergency: section 4(2) of the *Charter*. Section 4(2) provides that "[i]n time of real or apprehended war, invasion or insurrection, a House of Commons may be continued by Parliament ... beyond five years if such continuation is not opposed by the votes of more than one-third of the members of the House of Commons." Since "Parliament" consists of the Queen (usually in the person of the Governor General), the senate and the Commons,[19] section 4(2) should be read as authorizing the continuance of the Commons by two-thirds vote of the Commons, a majority vote of the senate, and assent by the Governor General. Once this continuance is obtained, the same House of Commons that employs section 33 to curb civil rights could also insulate itself from electoral pressure for the duration of a "real or apprehended war, invasion or insurrection."

Exactly how Parliamentary reliance on section 4(2) could be policed is unclear. Presumably, the courts could review the existence of a "real or apprehended war, invasion or insurrection." How aggressively a court would query the judgment of the political branches of government on this issue is an open question, especially where the emergency justifying the invocation of section 4(2) is "apprehended" rather than real.

Another, perhaps only academic uncertainty is the relationship between section 4(2) and section 50 of the *Constitution Act, 1867*. The latter provides that "[e]very House of Commons shall continue for Five Years from the Day of the Return of the Writs for choosing the House (subject to be sooner dissolved by the Governor General), and no longer." While the *British North America Act* — as the *Constitution Act, 1867* was called prior to 1982 — contained a provision equivalent to subsection 4(2) of the *Charter*,[20] this section was repealed by the *Constitution Act, 1982*.

The Constitution now contains, therefore, a limit on the duration of the House of Commons in both the *Charter* and the *Constitution Act, 1867*, but an exception to that limit in only the *Charter*. There is an apparent inconsistency, in other words, between two instruments, each of which constitute equal parts of the Constitution of Canada.[21] Since the Supreme Court has declared that the Constitution is to be read as a whole, and not

---

19 *Constitution Act, 1867*, s. 17.
20 *British North America (No. 2) Act, 1949*, 13 Geo. VI, c. 81 (U.K.), subs. 91(1) reading, in part, "a House of Commons may in time of real or apprehended war, invasion or insurrection be continued by the Parliament of Canada if such continuation is not opposed by the votes of more than one-third of the members of such House."
21 See s. 52 of the *Constitution Act, 1982*.

as a set of hermetically sealed obligations,[22] the most sensible interpretation of these two provisions is to view section 4(2) as authorizing derogation from section 50 of the *Constitution Act, 1867* as much as from subsection 4(1) of the *Charter*. Any other reading would render subsection 4(2) a nullity.

As a result of this reading, there is a real possibility that section 4(2) could inhibit efforts to hold the government accountable in times of emergency by rendering the Commons immune to electoral displeasure.

C. EMERGENCY POWERS IN STATUTORY LAW

The constitutional discussion set out above is entirely hypothetical. No emergency attracting the application of section 33 or section 4(2) of the *Charter* has ever been declared. Perhaps of more immediate relevance are those statutes presently on the books designed to deal with anticipated emergencies. In this regard, three laws lie at the heart of Canada's emergency powers law: the *Emergencies Act*, the *Emergency Preparedness Act*, and the *National Defence Act*.[23] Each is discussed in turn later. The recent omnibus *Anti-Terrorism Act*[24] and *Public Safety Act*[25] were sparked by national security imperatives, particularly the "war on terror." The *Anti-Terrorism Act* in particular was passed by Parliament on an expedited basis in the months after 9/11. Each statute enhances greatly the powers of the executive branch in a variety of areas, some of which are discussed in chapter 9. Those aspects of the *Public Safety Act* that enhance executive powers to respond to an emergency are discussed later.

With the exception of the *Emergencies Act*, none of these statutes empowers the government to trump the regular democratic process.[26]

---

22 *Reference re Secession of Quebec*, [1998] 2 S.C.R. 217 at para. 50 ("Our Constitution has an internal architecture, or … a 'basic constitutional structure'. The individual elements of the Constitution are linked to the others, and must be interpreted by reference to the structure of the Constitution as a whole.").

23 Two other more specialized statutes should also be flagged as relevant in emergencies: *Energy Supplies Emergency Act*, R.S. 1985, c. E-9, an Act governing the conservation of supplies of energy within Canada during periods of national emergency caused by shortages or market disturbances affecting the national security and welfare and the economic stability of Canada; and, *Defence Production Act*, R.S. 1985, c. D-1, an Act allowing the government to organize production and procurement for national defence purposes.

24 S.C. 2001, c. 41.

25 S.C. 2004, c. 15.

26 As the Supreme Court noted recently, the *Anti-Terrorism Act* is itself a normal law. *Application under s. 83.28 of the Criminal Code (Re)*, [2004] 2 S.C.R. 248 at para. 39 ("the

1. *Emergencies Act*

The most important of Canada's three principal emergency statutes, the *Emergencies Act*[27] has never been used since its enactment in 1988. In fact, although the statute was passed to replace the *War Measures Act*,[28] it is arguable whether the new law could ever be employed the way the *War Measures Act* was in October 1970, to abridge fundamental civil rights. A post-*Charter* instrument, the *Emergencies Act* rebalances the separation of powers between Parliament and the executive in times of emergency, subject to a series of important safeguards, but leaves intact *Charter* and *Canadian Bill of Rights* provisions and, implicitly, the judicial review authority of the courts.

Indeed, the Act notes in its preamble that "the preservation of the sovereignty, security and territorial integrity" may be seriously threatened by national emergencies, and thus the Governor-in-Council "should be authorized, subject to the supervision of Parliament, to take special temporary measures that may not be appropriate in normal times." It goes on to say, however, that these "special temporary measures" are subject to the *Charter*, the *Canadian Bill of Rights* and "must have regard to the *International Covenant on Civil and Political Rights*, particularly with respect to those fundamental rights that are not to be limited or abridged even in a national emergency."

a) Content

The Act defines a "national emergency" as "an urgent and critical situation of a temporary nature that … seriously endangers the lives, health or safety of Canadians and is of such proportions or nature as to exceed the capacity or authority of a province to deal with it, or … seriously threatens the ability of the Government of Canada to preserve the sovereignty, security and territorial integrity of Canada" and that cannot be dealt with effectively under any other law of Canada.[29]

Nondiscrimination

The statute states emphatically that it does not confer on the government the power to make orders or regulations "providing for the detention,

---

Canadian government opted to enact specific criminal law and procedure legislation and did not make use of exceptional powers, for example under the *Emergencies Act*, R.S.C. 1985, c. 22 (4th Supp.), or invoke the notwithstanding clause at s. 33 of the *Charter*").

27 R.S.C. 1985, c. 22 (4th Supp.).

28 *Emergencies Act*, s. 80.

29 *Ibid.*, s. 3.

imprisonment or internment" of Canadian citizens or permanent residents "on the basis of race, national or ethnic origin, colour, religion, sex, age or mental or physical disability."[30]

This provision is more definitive than the equivalent concept in Article 4 of the *International Covenant on Civil and Political Rights*, which bars discrimination "solely" on one of the enumerated grounds. By the covenant's logic, discrimination motivated by considerations in addition to (for example) religion, could conceivably satisfy its nondiscrimination requirements. A controversial example might be religious profiling of Muslims, based not on religion *per se*, but a perceived correlation of Islamic religious beliefs and terrorism. This result could be allowed, in fact, by the interpretation of the article adopted by the United States in its ratification of the covenant.[31] On its face, the *Emergencies Act* is not so forgiving, barring detention on the basis of enumerated grounds outright.

Types of Emergency

The Act anticipates four categories of emergencies: public welfare emergency, public order emergency, international emergency, and war emergency. Table 10.1 describes how the Act defines each of these concepts, the circumstances in which the emergency can be triggered, the extraordinary government powers it extends and how these states of emergency may be terminated.

b) Parliamentary Oversight

As Table 10.1 suggests, the *Emergencies Act* extends substantial power to the Governor-in-Council to declare public emergencies, and then to employ extraordinary powers. The effect is to rebalance the relative powers of the executive branch and Parliament. Nevertheless, the Act clearly recognizes its impact on the separation of powers and incorporates certain checks and balances designed to subordinate executive action to parliamentary review.

---

30   *Ibid.*, s. 4.

31   See UN Treaty Database, *International Covenant on Civil and Political Rights*, Declarations and Reservations ("The United States understands distinctions based upon race, colour, sex, language, religion, political or other opinion, national or social origin, property, birth or any other status — as those terms are used in article 2, para. 1 and article 26 — to be permitted when such distinctions are, at minimum, rationally related to a legitimate governmental objective. The United States further understands the prohibition in para. 1 of article 4 upon discrimination, in time of public emergency, based 'solely' on the status of race, colour, sex, language, religion or social origin, not to bar distinctions that may have a disproportionate effect upon persons of a particular status"), available at http://untreaty.un.org/ENGLISH/bible/englishinternetbible/partI/chapterIV/treaty6.asp.

Table 10.1   *Four Categories of Emergencies in the* Emergencies Act

Type	Definition	Trigger	Powers	Termination
Public welfare emergency	Section 5 — An emergency caused by a real or imminent fire, flood, drought, storm, earthquake or other natural phenomenon; disease in human beings, animals or plants; or accident or pollution that results or may result in danger to life or property, social disruption or breakdown in the flow of essential goods, services or resources so serious as to be a national emergency.	Section 6 — Upon consultation with the provincial cabinet in the affected provinces, the Governor-in-Council may, if it believes on reasonable grounds that a public welfare emergency exists and necessitates special temporary measures, declare by proclamation such an emergency. This declaration must identify the state of affairs constituting the emergency, the special temporary measures anticipated and the area affected by the emergency. This sort of emergency may not be declared unless, where the emergency is confined to one province, the provincial cabinet indicates that emergency exceeds the capacity of the province to deal with it.	Section 8 — The Governor-in-Council may issue orders or regulations to the extent it believes (on reasonable grounds) necessary for dealing with the emergency in the declared area, covering the following: (a) travel restrictions where necessary for the protection of the health or safety of individuals; (b) evacuation of persons and the removal of personal property from any specified area and the making of arrangements for the adequate care and protection of the persons and property; (c) requisition, use or disposition of property; (d) authorization of or direction to any person to render essential services of a type that that person is competent to provide (with compensation provided for the services); (e) regulating distribution of essential goods, services and resources; (f) authorization and making of emergency payments; (g) establishment of emergency shelters and hospitals; (h) assessment of damage to any works or undertakings and the repair, replacement or restoration thereof; (i) assessment of damage to the environment and the elimination or alleviation of the damage; and (j) imposition of a fine or imprisonment or both, for contravention of any order or regulation made under the section. These powers may not be exercised to impose a settlement in a labour dispute.	Subsection 7(2) — At the end of ninety days unless continued by the Governor-in-Council, after consultation with the implicated provincial cabinet. This, and any subsequent continuation, also expires after ninety days. Under s. 10, Parliament may revoke the declaration of a public welfare emergency.

Type	Definition	Trigger	Powers	Termination
Public order emergency	Section 16 — An emergency that arises from threats to the security of Canada that are so serious as to be a national emergency. Threats to the security of Canada are defined in keeping with the *Canadian Security Intelligence Service Act*.[32]	Section 17 — On consultation with the provincial cabinet in the affected provinces, the Governor-in-Council may, if it believes on reasonable grounds that a public order emergency exists and necessitates special temporary measures, declare by proclamation such an emergency. This declaration must identify the state of affairs constituting the emergency, the special temporary measures anticipated and the area affected by the emergency. This sort of emergency may not be declared unless, where the emergency is confined to one province, the provincial cabinet indicates that emergency exceeds the capacity of the province to deal with it. However, where the effects of the emergency extend beyond one province, the Governor-in-Council need not consult with provincial cabinets prior to issuance of the declaration where consultation would unduly jeopardize the effectives of the proposed action.	Section 19 — The Governor-in-Council may issue orders or regulations to the extent it believes (on reasonable grounds) necessary for dealing with the emergency in the declared area, covering the following: (a) regulation or prohibition of (i) any public assembly that may reasonably be expected to lead to a breach of the peace, (ii) travel to, from or within any specified area, or (iii) the use of specified property; (b) designation and securing of protected places; (c) assumption of the control, and the restoration and maintenance, of public utilities and services; (d) authorization of or direction to any person to render essential services of a type that that person is competent to provide (with compensation provided for the services); and (e) imposition of a fine or imprisonment or both for contravention of any order or regulation made under the section.	Subsection 18(2) — At the end of thirty days unless continued by the Governor-in-Council, after consultation with the implicated provincial cabinet. This, and any subsequent continuation, also expires after thirty days. Under s. 21, Parliament may revoke the declaration of a public order emergency.

---

32   See R.S.C. 1985, c. C-23, s. 2.

	Section 27	Section 28	Section 30	Subsection 29(2)
International emergency	An emergency involving Canada and one or more other countries that arises from acts of intimidation or coercion or the real or imminent use of serious force or violence and that is so serious as to be a national emergency.	After whatever consultation with provincial cabinets that is practicable, the Governor-in-Council may declare by proclamation such an emergency on reasonable grounds. This declaration must identify the state of affairs constituting the emergency, and the special temporary measures anticipated.	The Governor-in-Council may issue orders or regulations to the extent it believes on reasonable grounds necessary for dealing with the emergency, including: (a) control or regulation of any industry or service; (b) appropriation, control, forfeiture, use and disposition of property or services; (c) authorization and conduct of inquiries in relation to defence contracts or defence supplies or to hoarding, overcharging, black marketing or fraudulent operations in respect of scarce commodities; (d) search and seizure authorization for any thing that may be evidence relevant to any matter that is the subject of an inquiry referred to in paragraph (c); (e) authorization of or direction to any person to render essential services of a type that that person is competent to provide (with compensation provided for the services); (f) designation and securing of protected places; (g) travel restrictions outside Canada by Canadian citizens or permanent residents; (h) deportation of persons, other than citizens, permanent residents or otherwise admissible protected persons; (i) control or regulation of international financial activities within Canada; (j) authorization of expenditures for dealing	At the end of sixty days unless continued by the Governor-in-Council, after any practicable consultation with provincial cabinets. Under s. 32, Parliament may revoke the declaration of an international emergency.

Type	Definition	Trigger	Powers	Termination
			with an international emergency in excess of any limit set by an Act of Parliament; (k) authorization of any Cabinet Minister to discharge specified responsibilities of a political, diplomatic or economic nature; and (l) imposition of a fine or imprisonment or both for contravention of any order or regulation made under the section. However, these powers must not be exercised for the purpose of censoring, suppressing or controlling the publication or communication of any information.	
War emergency	Section 37 — A war or other armed conflict, real or imminent, involving Canada or any of its allies that is so serious as to be a national emergency.	Section 38 — After whatever consultation with provincial cabinets that is practicable, the Governor-in-Council may, if it believes on reasonable grounds that an international emergency exists and necessitates special temporary measures, declare by proclamation such an emergency. The declaration must specify the state of affairs constituting the emergency to the extent that the Governor-in-Council believes is possible without jeopardizing any special temporary measures proposed.	Section 40 — The Governor-in-Council may issue orders or regulations to the extent it believes (on reasonable grounds) necessary for dealing with the emergency. These orders may not include conscription into the Canadian Forces. Cabinet may make regulations governing the imposition of a fine or imprisonment or both for contravention of any order or regulation made under the section.	Subsection 39(2) — At the end of 120 days unless continued by the Governor-in-Council, after any practicable consultation with provincial cabinets. Under s. 41, Parliament may revoke the declaration of a war emergency.

First, a motion for confirmation of any declaration of emergency, complete with reasons and a report on any consultation with the provinces, must be tabled in Parliament within seven sitting days after the Governor-in-Council issues the declaration. If Parliament is not sitting, it must be summoned to sit within seven days of the declaration, and if dissolved, it must be summoned to sit at the earliest opportunity. In either case, the motion is to be laid before Parliament on the first sitting day after Parliament is summoned.

The motion must be taken up the day after it is tabled, and is to be debated without interruption and voted on in each chamber of Parliament when it is ready for the question. If either House votes down the motion, the declaration of emergency is revoked.[33] The Act sets out similar provisions for the continuance or amendment of a declaration of emergency, although without the requirement that Parliament be summoned if the continuance or amendment occurs when Parliament is not sitting.[34]

Even when a declaration of emergency is affirmed, Parliament may act subsequently to revoke it. If ten senators or twenty MPs file a motion with the Speaker seeking revocation, this motion is taken up within three sitting days after it is filed. Debate may continue for no more than ten hours, at which point the vote is called. If adopted by the relevant chamber of Parliament, the declaration of emergency is revoked.[35]

Meanwhile, except as discussed later, every order or regulation made by the Governor-in-Council pursuant to its powers under the Act must be tabled in Parliament within two sitting days. A motion may then be brought by no fewer than ten senators or twenty MPs calling for the revocation or amendment of a given order or regulation. This motion must be considered within three sitting days, and debated without interruption until the House is ready for the question. If one House adopts the motion, and if the other House concurs, the order or regulation is revoked or amended.[36]

The Act also provides for a Parliamentary Review Committee, comprising members from each official party in the Commons and at least one counterpart senator. An order or regulation is referred to this committee within two days.[37] The committee may then adopt a motion revoking or amending the order within thirty days.[38] The committee is also charged

---

33   *Emergencies Act*, s. 58.
34   *Ibid.*, s. 60.
35   *Ibid.*, s. 59.
36   *Ibid.*, s. 61.
37   *Ibid.*
38   *Ibid.*, s. 62.

with reviewing "the exercise of powers and the performance of duties and functions pursuant to a declaration of emergency." It is required to report to Parliament on the results of this review at least once every sixty days, and more frequently in specified cases.[39]

As a final accountability mechanism, the Governor-in-Council must call an inquiry into the circumstances resulting in the declaration of emergency with sixty days of its termination. The report of this inquiry must be tabled in Parliament within 360 days after the end of the declaration.[40]

c) Judicial Review of Orders and Regulations under the *Emergencies Act*

The *Emergencies Act* is silent on the role of the courts in relation to an emergency declaration and any subsequent orders or regulations issued by the government. This failure to formally identify a role for the courts was cited as a shortcoming in Parliamentary debate on the Act.[41] However, silence on this issue likely leaves intact conventional court review powers under administrative law and the *Charter*, even during a declared emergency. Indeed, when the law was enacted, the government clearly contemplated judicial review of emergency measures.[42]

Administrative Law

Jurisdiction

As discussed throughout this book, the Federal Courts conduct judicial review of federal executive authority pursuant to the *Federal Courts Act*.[43] One of the key roles of the Federal Courts is to ensure that the executive branch operates within the parameters of the powers delegated to it by Parliament. The *Emergencies Act* does not purport to change this Federal Court role; it does not explicitly authorize the executive to curb access to the courts as part of its extraordinary powers. Thus, under conventional administrative law doctrine, the executive would be acting outside the jurisdiction conferred by the statute were it to issue an order precluding judicial review of its actions.

The one arguable exception to this observation is in relation to war emergencies. The war emergencies provisions bear the closest resem-

---

39   *Ibid.*

40   *Ibid.*, s. 63.

41   See, e.g., Mr. John Parry (Kenora–Rainy River), House of Commons, *Debates*, 33rd Parl., 2d Sess., vol. 9 (1987) at 10890.

42   See Mr. Bud Bradley (parliamentary secretary to minister of national defence), House of Commons, *Debates*, 33rd Parl., 2d Sess. (1987) at 14765.

43   R.S. 1985, c. F-7.

blance to the old *War Measures Act*, extending to the executive virtually unfettered powers once an emergency is declared. Even here, however, it seems unlikely that the government could issue a regulation under its emergency powers precluding judicial review of whether its action comported with the *Emergencies Act*. As discussed in chapter 2, even an express statutory privative clause attempting to supplant the jurisdiction of the courts to review executive decisions likely cannot bar court review on jurisdictional grounds; namely, judicial review scrutinizing whether the executive has the power it purports to exercise.[44] As the Supreme Court noted recently in *Babcock v. Canada*, even "draconian" statutory language meant to usurp a review power by the court "cannot oust the principle that official actions must flow from statutory authority clearly granted and properly exercised."[45] It follows that even a regulation issued in emergency circumstances cannot bar court review by, for instance, purporting to limit Federal Court jurisdiction under the *Federal Courts Act*.[46]

For these reasons, standard judicial review of executive regulation-making under the *Emergencies Act* would persist. This view is supported by Parliamentary debates on the Act. In the Commons, opposition members expressed concern that courts would not probe rigorously a government declaration of emergency. This fear was sparked by language in the original bill authorizing declaration of an emergency where cabinet was "of the opinion" the necessary trigger circumstances existed.[47] In response, the government amended the original bill to indicate that government action would require "reasonable grounds." This amendment was made, in the words of the parliamentary secretary to the minister of national defence, to ensure that "all important decisions by the Governor in Council relating to the invocation and use of emergency powers will be challengeable in the courts."[48]

---

44 See *Crevier v. Québec*, [1981] 2 S.C.R. 220. See also *Blanchard v. Control Data Canada Ltd.*, [1984] 2 S.C.R. 476 at 488 *per* Lamer J., concurring in the result, and interpreting *Crevier* as teaching that a privative clause "can in no way impede judicial review regarding questions of jurisdiction."

45 [2002] 3 S.C.R. 3 at para. 39.

46 See *Friends of Oldman River Society v. Canada*, [1992] 1 S.C.R. 3 at 38 ("[j]ust as subordinate legislation cannot conflict with its parent legislation ... so too it cannot conflict with other Acts of Parliament ... unless a statute so authorizes ... Ordinarily, then, an Act of Parliament must prevail over inconsistent or conflicting subordinate legislation").

47 See Mr. Dan Heap (Spadina), House of Commons, *Debates*, 33rd Parl., 2d Sess. (1987) at 10900.

48 Mr. Bud Bradley (parliamentary secretary to minister of national defence), House of Commons, *Debates*, 33rd Parl., 2d Sess. (1987) at 14765.

Standard of Review

Any administrative law judicial review likely would be conducted on a highly deferential basis, in keeping with the Supreme Court's jurisprudence on
the standard of review to be applied where the executive has a high measure of expertise or disproportionate access to relevant information.

The closest analogy to judicial review of emergency powers is recent
jurisprudence on the review of national security provisions in immigration
law. In *Suresh v. Canada (Minister of Citizenship and Immigration)*,[49] the
Supreme Court of Canada was asked, among other things, to review the
minister of citizenship and immigration's "discretionary" determination
that a refugee, Mr. Suresh, constituted a "danger to the security of Canada,"
as that phrase was used in the then-*Immigration Act*. Applying its standard
"pragmatic and functional" test to determine the measure of deference to be
accorded the minister, the Court pointed to the fact that the minister "has
access to special information and expertise in" matters of national security.[50]

This fact — read together with the limited appeal mechanism in the
Act, the difficult balancing of the competing humanitarian purposes of the
Act and the extremely fact-intensive and contextual nature of the national
security determination — prompted the Court to extend a large measure of
judicial deference to the minister. The minister's decision would only be
disturbed if "patently unreasonable" which, in the Court's mind, meant a
decision "made arbitrarily or in bad faith, [un]supported on the evidence,
or [where] the Minister failed to consider the appropriate factors."[51]

All told, a government order or regulation under the *Emergencies Act*
would also reflect these same considerations invoked in *Suresh*. Normal,
statutory appeal rights do not exist in the *Emergencies Act*. The Act will likely be viewed as requiring the balancing of competing, legitimate objectives.
Any emergency declaration or resulting decision to issue regulations will
be fact-intensive and highly contextual. Finally, the government will likely
have access to special information and expertise in rendering its decisions.
On this basis, it seems improbable a court would review a government
decision connected to the *Emergencies Act* on anything other than a highly
deferential standard of review, the reference to "reasonable grounds" in the
Act's provisions notwithstanding.

Judicial review is likely to be undemanding even in an area where
courts have traditionally extended little deference to governments — proce-

---

49   [2002] 1 S.C.R. 3.
50   *Ibid.* at paras. 31 and 33.
51   *Ibid.* at para. 29.

dural fairness. As noted at various points in this book, this common law due process standard requires that notice of a pending decision be given to affected persons, that these persons be given an opportunity to comment, and that decisions be rendered by an unbiased decision-maker. The precise content of these obligations — how much notice, how much opportunity to comment and how unbiased a decision-maker — is decided by the courts on a contextual basis, and is often affected by the gravity of the decision to the affected persons.

Yet, as discussed in chapters 2 and 5, courts have carved out an exception to procedural fairness in circumstances where the decision taken by the executive is characterized as "legislative" rather than "administrative." The distinction between these concepts is opaque in Supreme Court jurisprudence. Suffice it to say that a legislative decision is one that is general, rather than directed at a single person or class of persons, and is based on broad policy considerations. Delegated law-making by the executive — the making of regulations or orders pursuant to a power set out in an Act of Parliament — is almost invariably viewed as a legislative decision, and a court would likely place the orders and regulations issued under the *Emergencies Act* in this category. Where the executive exercises these "legislative" powers, the courts will not impose procedural fairness requirements.

Moreover, even if courts did conclude procedural fairness obligations attached to such regulations or orders, the very context in which these instruments are introduced — in response to an emergency — likely limits the due process requirements courts would impose. Procedural fairness requirements where executive decisions are made in the face of an emergency are minimal.[52]

Constitutional Review

Judicial review of measures introduced under the *Emergencies Act* on constitutional grounds may be more demanding than review on administrative law bases. As its own preamble indicates, the *Emergencies Act* and any orders or regulations issued under its authority are subordinate to the *Charter* and the *Canadian Bill of Rights*. As noted above, an Act of Parlia-

---

52   See, e.g., *Walpole Island First Nation v. Ontario (Ministry of Environment and Energy)* (1996), 31 O.R. (3d) 607 at 617 (Gen. Div.) holding that emergency character of an order authorizing discharge of waste water from an industrial holding pond after heavy precipitation "clearly takes it out of the reach of the doctrine" of procedural fairness. But see *Ross v. Mohawk of Kanesatake*, 2003 FCT 531 at para. 79 ("the right to procedural fairness may be suspended in an emergency situation. It is not eliminated. It is respected by the provision of an opportunity to be heard, after the emergency situation has been relieved").

ment may abridge, in part, these two instruments, should certain requirements be met. However, the key trigger here is "an Act of Parliament," certainly not an executive regulation or order, issued under the *Emergencies Act*
or any other statute.

For these reasons, executive orders or regulations made pursuant to
the *Emergencies Act* cannot trump constitutional rights, including the fundamental freedoms and legal rights found in sections 2 and 7 to 14 of the
Charter and the equivalent provisions of the *Canadian Bill of Rights*.

In fact, if the government were to exercise its full powers under the
Act, it is difficult to imagine it would remain fully onside in relation to
Charter rights, not least the free association rights in section 2(c) and (d),
the section 6 mobility right and the section 8 search and seizure right. As
a consequence, a government relying on the full range of authority issued
to it under the *Emergencies Act* would either have to seek an additional parliamentary statute authorizing its action under section 33, or rely instead
on a section 1 justification in any litigation over the government measures.

For all these reasons, the *Emergencies Act* can be read as leaving intact
constitutional civil liberties, and the role of the courts in protecting these
rights.

2. *National Defence Act*

A second statute conveying extraordinary powers on the executive branch in
the event of an emergency is the *National Defence Act*. Principally the law
governing the Canadian Forces, the Act authorizes the Governor-in-Council
to put the Canadian Forces on duty anywhere in or beyond Canada at any
time when it appears advisable to do so by reason, among other things, of
an emergency or for the defence of Canada.[53] An emergency is an "insurrection, riot, invasion, armed conflict or war, whether real or apprehended."[54]

Further, the Act permits the deployment of military units in response
to a requisition from a provincial attorney general in aid to civil power.
Specifically, a "call out" of the Forces may be made in response to an actual or anticipated riot or disturbance of the peace, beyond the powers of the
civil authorities to suppress, prevent or deal with.[55]

For its part, the Governor-in-Council (or minister of national defence)
may also deploy the Canadian Forces to perform "public service" duties.
Similarly, the Governor-in-Council, or the minister of national defence

53   *National Defence Act*, s. 31.
54   *Ibid.*, s. 2.
55   *Ibid.*, ss. 274–85.

responding to a request from the Solicitor General or any other minister, may authorize military assistance in law enforcement, so long as such assistance is required to deal effectively with the matter and it is in the national interest.[56]

Notably, in listing the circumstances in which the Canadian Forces may be put on an operational footing or deployed for civil assistance, the Act does not purport to trump the application of other laws. As a result, Canadian Forces operations would presumably be subject to the full panoply of statutory and constitutional civil and political rights, and the mere presence of the military acting pursuant to the *National Defence Act* does not authorize the imposition of martial law.

This situation would have been changed somewhat had Parliament enacted the original *Public Safety Act*, introduced as Bill C-42 in November 2001. In Bill C-42, and several successive bills, the government proposed amendments to the *National Defence Act* permitting the creation of something called, ominously, "Military Security Zones."[57] These zones were to be created at the discretion of the minister of national defence if, in the opinion of the minister, necessary for the protection of international relations or national defence or security, all terms left undefined by the bill. Among other things, the zone could be declared over material or property under control of the government, or, even more ambiguously, any other place that the Canadian Forces were directed to protect in order to fulfill a duty required by law. The Canadian Forces would then control entry into this zone, with unauthorized persons subject to forcible removal.[58] In fact, persons violating regulations respecting access to, or exclusion from, military security zones, faced criminal prosecution, and possibly twelve months in prison.[59] While the bill proposed compensating any person who suffered loss, damage or injury by reason of the zone, government liability for harm suffered by reason of the designation or implementation of the zone would have been precluded.[60]

Civil society groups reacted fiercely to the proposal, and similar provisions in later iterations of the bill. The Canadian Bar Association, for instance, worried that the zone provisions would be used to subdue and control democratic dissent. Indeed, media reports suggested that military

---

56   *Ibid.*, s. 273.6.
57   See Bill C-42, 37th Parl., 1st Sess., 49–50 Elizabeth II, 2001, House of Commons, at Clause 84.
58   *Ibid.*
59   *Ibid.* at Clause 90.
60   *Ibid.* at Clause 84.

security zones would be declared around international meeting places, in an effort to control regular civil society protests at such events.[61]

When passed in 2004, the *Public Safety Act* no longer included provisions relating to a military security zone. However, in December 2002, the federal Cabinet issued an Order-in-Council creating "controlled access zones" in Halifax, Esquimalt and Nanoose Harbours, all key naval facilities.[62] These measures were issued, not pursuant to statutory authority, but under royal prerogative.[63] It seems unlikely to us that any equivalent royal prerogative authority exists that could be employed to create controlled-access zones in other, *nonmilitary* facilities.

3. *Emergency Preparedness Act*

The most banal, and yet the most frequently employed, of the emergency laws discussed in this chapter is the *Emergency Preparedness Act*,[64] enacted in 1988. This statute instructs a minister — designated the minister of public safety[65] — to advance "civil preparedness in Canada for emergencies of all types, including war and other armed conflict" by coordinating the development and implementation of civil emergency plans.[66] In relation to these plans, the minister is tasked with, among other things, establishing arrangements for "the continuity of constitutional government during an emergency."[67] Other ministers are charged with developing plans within their own department for civil emergencies or for war or other armed conflicts.[68]

Last, the Act allows the Governor-in-Council to make orders or regulations pertaining, among other things, to the use of federal civil resources in response to civil emergencies and the provision of assistance to a province where a civil emergency has been declared a concern to the federal government, and the province has requested assistance.[69] Since 1992, the federal government has issued approximately forty-five orders under

---

61 Canadian Bar Association, *Submissions on Bill C-42* (Feb. 2002) at 11.

62 PC 2002-2190, SI/2003-0002.

63 See Parliamentary Research Branch, *Bill C-7: The Public Safety Act, 2002*, LSE-463-E.

64 R.S.C. 1985, c. 6 (4th Supp.).

65 *Order Designating the Deputy Prime Minister and Minister of Public Safety and Emergency Preparedness as Minister for Purposes of the Act*, SI/2004-106.

66 *Emergency Preparedness Act*, s. 4.

67 *Ibid.*, para. 5(1)(f).

68 *Ibid.*, s. 7.

69 *Ibid.*, s. 9.

the Act declaring floods to be a concern to the federal government and authorizing federal financial assistance. Another eight such orders concerned hurricanes, tornadoes or other severe storms; three involved forest fires; three involved the 1998 ice storm — and in fact authorized "other" assistance beyond financial aid — and one involved a disease outbreak.[70]

Notably, like the provisions of the *National Defence Act* discussed earlier, the *Emergency Preparedness Act* does not purport to trump the application of other laws, or authorize regulations abridging these laws. Again, therefore, the law does not interfere with statutory or constitutional civil or political rights.

4. *Public Safety Act*

For its part, the omnibus *Public Safety Act*, enacted in 2004, enhanced the powers of several ministers to respond to emergencies, under assorted statutes. For instance, the transportation minister may impose special emergency measures under the *Aeronautics Act* in response to threats to aviation security. Responsible ministers may also issue "interim orders" under the *Canadian Environmental Protection Act*, the *Department of Health Act*, the *Food and Drug Act*, the *Hazardous Products Act*, the *Navigable Waters Protection Act*, the *Pest Control Products Act*, the *Quarantine Act*, the *Radiation Emitting Devices Act*, and the *Canada Shipping Act*. While the language in each statute varies, ministers are to issue these orders largely in response to "significant" dangers to the environment or to human life or health. In each case, the order is exempted from some of the regular regulation-making procedures under the *Statutory Instruments Act*,[71] but must be published within twenty-three days in the *Canada Gazette* and tabled in each House of Parliament within fifteen days.[72]

D. CONCLUSION

On balance, Canada's emergency laws are consistent with the criteria for evaluating such measures set out in the introduction to this chapter.

---

70   Data collected from the Orders-in-Council database, available at www.pco-bcp.gc.ca/oic-ddc/oic-ddc.asp?lang=EN.

71   R.S.C. c. S-22. Most notably, the interim order need not be reviewed by the Department of Justice for its legality prior to being made, something generally required by s. 3 of the *Statutory Instruments Act*.

72   See *Public Safety Act*, Parts 1, 3, 6, 9, 10, 15, 18, 20, 21 and 22.

First, the key statute — the *Emergencies Act* — contemplates that actions taken by the government in the event of an emergency will be authorized by law, not arbitrary or *ad hoc*.

Second, this statute is not so open-ended as to permit the invocation of an emergency in every circumstance. The thresholds for the declaration of an emergency are spelled out in the Act, albeit in broad terms likely to attract only the most deferential of judicial review. Further, the measures authorized by this declaration are limited to those believed necessary on reasonable grounds to deal with the situation. Some effort is made, in other words, to ensure that the measures authorized by this Act are proportional and adequately linked to reasonable assessments of the threat.

Third, the *Emergencies Act* contemplates fairly substantial review and involvement by Parliament, requires a proactive continuance of an emergency declaration to circumvent automatic sunsetting provisions, and preserves the administrative and constitutional law judicial review powers of the courts. In this last regard, the Act expressly leaves intact the *Charter of Rights and Freedoms* and the *Canadian Bill of Rights*.

The other laws on the statute books designed to accommodate government responses to emergencies also do not purport to trump rights and fundamental freedoms, or even (in most instances) suspend the regular statutory law of the land.

For its part, the Constitution — with its notwithstanding clause and section 1 justification — does permit some derogation from civil and political rights. However, by confining use of section 33 to an Act of Parliament, the constitution removes the possibility of executive branch unilateralism in suspending civil rights. Further, by limiting the effect of a section 33 override to five years, excluding democratic rights from section 33's ambit, and then including among these democratic rights a requirement that each Commons persist no more than five years, the *Charter* ensures that, in the normal course, a Parliament resorting to section 33 will be tested by the electorate.

The one shortcoming to this constitutional scheme is section 4(2), permitting Parliament to persist without going to the polls in times of "real or apprehended war, invasion or insurrection." A Parliament combining action under section 33 with action under section 4(2) would be a remarkably unaccountable body. Were these circumstances ever to arise, the preservation of democracy in Canada would depend largely on the good faith of this country's political class.

Democratic Accountability in a Globalized Confederation

This book has described in detail the many rules designed to render federal governance in Canada "democratically accountable." As we have defined it, democratic accountability at the federal level depends on the fair election of representatives, the primacy of these representatives over unelected officials, judicial review and oversight of both unelected and elected officials, and a series of detailed rules concerning government ethics, lobbying and transparency.

Canada's federal government does not, however, operate in splendid isolation. Accordingly, this chapter focuses on the implications of a changing national and international environment for democratic accountability. Specifically, as policy-making influence and power is globalized in international venues and at the same time decentralized in Canada's increasingly diffuse federation, what are the consequences for democratic governance in Canada?

A. THE INTERNATIONALIZATION OF PUBLIC POLICY

Modern international policy-making involves an alphabet soup of international institutions. By the end of the last century, there were around 250 intergovernmental organizations, almost double the number that existed in the immediate post–World War II period.[1] In this environment, a growing proportion of Canadian public policy is influenced by international developments. Indeed, Canada is a signatory of scores of treaties, many of which oblige this country to adopt or modify its laws. It is also a member of the key multilateral "clubs" — the United Nations, the G8, the WTO, the Organization for Economic Cooperation and Development, the Commonwealth, the Organization of American States and many others.

We obviously cannot, in this book, discuss the specific implications of Canada's participation in each of these international conventions and organizations. Rather, our focus in this section is on a more general question: what consequences does Canada's active engagement in the world have for the concept of democratic accountability introduced in our introductory chapter? At first blush, this seems a peculiar question. While we have pointed to international law and practice from time to time in this work in discussing some attributes of the law of democracy in Canada, international policy-making does not appear to impede or really even affect the workings of Canadian parliamentary democracy.

From a procedural perspective, this supposition is probably true. What the internationalization of policy does do, however, is affect the balance of power in Canadian democracy. For the most part, the checks and balances discussed in this book existing at the national level do not exist — or are at best rudimentary — at the international level, among international institutions. The resulting "democratic deficit" in international organizations has two common attributes.

1. The Democratic Deficit and Intergovernmental Organizations

First, the very manner in which intergovernmental organizations function raises concerns about democratic accountability. Specifically, these institutions typically conduct their activities insulated from meaningful scrutiny by a broader public. In international lawyer Eric Stein's words, intergovernmental organizations "themselves are considered 'undemocratic' since they operate with little transparency or public and parliamentary scrutiny. They are seen as being governed by an elite group of national officials who are instructed by their respective executives, and by international secretariats whose staffs at times act independently of the top [intergovernmental organization] management."[2]

---

1   Eric Stein, "International Integration and Democracy: No Love at First Sight" (2001) 95 Am. J. Int'l L. 489 at 489.
2   *Ibid.* at 490.

For instance, World Trade Organization panels and the Appellate Body adjudicate trade disputes between state members of the WTO. Conducting these proceedings in a quasi-judicial manner, these bodies nevertheless hear arguments *in camera* and pleadings are confidential, a practice deeply inconsistent with domestic judicial proceedings in Canada and other developed democracies. Notably, the writ of Canada's *Access to Information Act* likely would not extent to this — or any other — intergovernmental organization.[3]

Likewise, except in the rarest of circumstances — such as the negotiations of the treaties governing the International Criminal Court or the ban on landmines — international treaty-making is an obscure process. Negotiations are *in camera*, and treaties are concluded by the negotiating states without any public hearing or vetting process. Subsequently, in Canada, there are no real automatic or formal means for public input prior to Canadian acceptance of a treaty text and its subsequent ratification. Here again, the *Access to Information Act* is of little use in unearthing factual information concerning government positions during these treaty negotiations.[4]

2. The Democratic Deficit and the Separation of Powers

Second, in international policy-making, the executive branches of state governments are enhanced at the expense of the other branches. By way of example, the United Nations Security Council's powers in the *United Nations Charter* are expansive, and subject to broad interpretation. Its resolutions, issued pursuant to Chapter VII of the *UN Charter* by the Security Council's handful of members, are the most legally potent determinations of any international decision-making body. Yet, despite these broad powers, the Security Council is not subject to judicial oversight.[5]

Legislative bodies also exercise little control over international policy-making. As Stein has observed: "A new level of normative activity superimposed on national democratic systems makes citizen participation more

---

3   The *Access to Information Act*, R.S.C. 1985, c. A-1, includes exemptions to disclosure in ss. 13 and 15 that could both be used to bar release of information on international negotiations.

4   See *ibid.*

5   While this issue is not yet fully resolved, the International Court of Justice expressed reluctance to perform a judicial review function in *Aerial Incident over Lockerbie Case*, [1992] ICJ Rep. 3. Note that in principle, domestic courts could (indirectly) review Security Council resolutions. Thus, in Canada, the Governor-in-Council may implement the Security Council's sanctions resolutions by regulation, pursuant to the *United Nations Act*, R.S.C. 1985, c. U-2. These regulations are Canadian legal instruments, and thus justiciable in a Canadian court. Were the regulations to violate Canadian constitutional or administrative law principles, a Canadian court might rule them illegitimate.

remote, and parliamentary control over the executive, notoriously loose in foreign affairs matters, becomes even less effective."[6]

The impact of this short-circuiting of the democratic process is most apparent where international obligations, once entered into by the executive, compel states to embark on policies that would otherwise be carefully scrutinized by Parliaments, courts or citizens. The WTO and other free trade agreements, for instance, are frequently criticized for constraining the "sovereignty" of their members — the freedom to choose a given policy path. In their denunciations of international organizations such as the World Trade Organization, critics complain that these bodies are nontransparent, unaccountable places where domestic law-making is thwarted by a parochial trade perspective.[7] In the words of one Canadian member of Parliament:

> International trade policy is increasingly intersecting with domestic social and economic policy. While individual nations used to have complete sovereignty over policies related to intellectual property, services and telecommunications, for example, international agreements are setting new boundaries for those nations that sign trade agreements. Legislators and voters are frequently frustrated when options for solutions to domestic challenges are met with lawsuits based on these international agreements. This is especially so in cases where they feel they have had little input or choice in developing the international agreement.[8]

As a practical matter, Canadian law guards poorly against what Stein calls the "de-parliamentization" of the international political processes, a point illustrated by the rules on the incorporation of international treaties into Canadian law. As a matter of international law, international treaties

---

6　Stein, "International Integration and Democracy" at 490.

7　See Joseph E. Stiglitz, *Globalization and Its Discontents* (New York: W.W. Norton & Co., 2002), and Ralph Nader and Lori Wallach, "GATT, NAFTA and the Subversion of the Democratic Process," in Jerry Mander and Edward Goldsmith, *The Case Against the Global Economy and for a Turn Toward the Local* (San Francisco: Sierra Club Books, 1996) at 92–107. It should be noted that, at the libertarian end of the ideological spectrum, advocates of the global trade regime argue that insofar as they encourage a free trade agenda, the WTO and other international agencies promote democracy by opening societies to new technologies and ideas and creating an economically affluent and more politically aware middle class. This analysis, however, is generally applied to less industrialized countries and repressive regimes. Daniel Griswold, "Trading Tyranny for Freedom: How Open Markets Till the Soil for Democracy," Cato Institute for Trade Policy Studies, Trade Policy Analysis no. 26 (6 Jan. 2004). Also see Milton Friedman, *Capitalism and Freedom* (Chicago: University of Chicago Press, 1962).

8　Paddy Tornsey, "The World Trade Organization and Parliamentarians" (2003) 26 Canadian Parliamentary Review no. 3.

bind a state once it has signified consent to be bound.[9] How this consent is indicated varies, but usually takes the form of a simple signature by an accredited representative or, more frequently with multilateral treaties, signature followed by ratification.[10] International law does not dictate the procedure to be followed in completing this ratification. Instead, each state's domestic law governs this process.

In Canada, signifying consent to be bound is the prerogative of the executive branch, operating pursuant to royal prerogative. As a result, the executive may choose to sign and ratify an international treaty, binding Canada as a matter of international law, without any recourse to Parliament.[11]

If these international legal obligations entered into by the executive were of immediate and direct effect as the laws of Canada, this prerogative power could, in theory, enable the executive to do an end-run around Parliament's federal law-making monopoly. By signing an international treaty requiring, for instance, extended patent protection, the executive would essentially legislate a matter otherwise governed by an Act of Parliament, in this case the *Patent Act*. In this way, the executive would short-circuit Parliament supremacy. Where the treaty dealt with matters in provincial jurisdiction, the federal executive could also dance around the division of powers in the *Constitution Act, 1867* by employing its treaty-signing powers effectively to legislate in provincial areas.

Largely to avoid these problems, the Canadian common law provides that international treaties have no legal effect as the law of Canada, unless first incorporated into that law by an Act of Parliament (or where the treaty deals with provincial matters, the provincial legislatures).[12] To some extent, the Supreme Court of Canada has eroded this classic approach. On several occasions, that court has imposed international treaty obligations on Canadian public officials, even where those treaties remain unimplemented by a statute.[13] Nevertheless, it remains true that the better part of substantive

---

9 See *Vienna Convention on the Law of Treaties*, Articles 2 and 26.

10 *Vienna Convention*, Article 11.

11 Hugh Kindred *et al.*, *International Law Chiefly as Practiced in Canada*, 6th ed. (Toronto: Emond Montgomery, 2000) at 103. In practice, the government has sought parliamentary approval on some key treaties, not least those involving large expenditures of public funds.

12 See discussion in John Currie, *Public International Law* (Toronto: Irwin Law, 2001) at 205 *et seq.*

13 See, e.g., *Baker v. Canada*, [1999] 2 S.C.R. 817 at para. 70 in relation to the *UN Convention on the Rights of the Child*, holding that "the values reflected in international human rights law may help inform the contextual approach to statutory interpretation and judicial review"; *Suresh v. Canada*, [2002] 1 S.C.R. 3 at paras. 60 and 76 in rela-

international treaty obligations do not exist as Canadian law unless Parliament has enacted them.

This "incorporation" approach is a modest response to a federal state with a separation of powers between executive and legislative branches. It is also true that this back-end strategy to preserving parliamentary supremacy — barring the domestic application of properly concluded international law until Parliament acts — is ill-conceived.

First, by precluding the application of treaty law without action by Parliament, Canada follows a "dualist" approach, conceiving of the international domestic legal regimes as separate and distinct. Where Parliament fails to incorporate treaty law into domestic law — something that is surprisingly common, at least with human rights law — the result is an unfortunate legal schizophrenia: Canada is bound by the treaty as a matter of international law, and yet its policy-makers need not abide by the treaty under the terms of domestic law. It is exactly this unfortunate tendency that the Supreme Court seems preoccupied with in its recent attempts to apply these international legal principles in evaluating the conduct of Canadian decision-makers.[14]

Second, where legislators are sensitive to allegations of noncompliance with Canada's international obligations, they will obviously be inclined to enact legislation incorporating Canada's treaty obligations into domestic law. These parliamentarians preoccupied with Canada's good name in the international community must curb their discretion and toe the line on an agreement ratified only by the executive branch. Little practical room remains for a parliamentarian intent on observing Canada's international obligations to tinker with and amend a government bill incorporating an international treaty with precise dictates. Put another way, a parliamentarian inclined to bring Canadian law into compliance with international law is conceding the practical primacy of the executive over Parliament. In enacting international treaties, Parliament is little more than a rubber stamp.

In sum, where the executive exercises its prerogative power to conclude an international treaty, Parliament confronts a dilemma. It may choose to disregard that international obligation, preserving its supremacy at the potential cost of Canada's adherence to an international rule of law. Alternatively, it

---

tion to the *Convention against Torture and other Cruel, Inhuman or Degrading Treatment or Punishment*, holding that "The Canadian rejection of torture is reflected in the international conventions to which Canada is a party. The Canadian and international perspectives in turn inform our constitutional norms," even where the international convention is not incorporated directly into Canadian law.

14   *Ibid.*

may act to incorporate these international requirements into domestic law, conceding the power to shape the content of that law to the executive.

As international policy-making — conducted increasingly through so-called law harmonization treaties — increases, this dilemma will become progressively more acute.

3. Responses

These two trends — the "de-parliamentization" of the international political processes and the lack of transparency in intergovernmental organizations and negotiations — do little to enhance the careful balance of democratic accountability discussed elsewhere in this book.

An obvious solution to the democratic deficit problem in international agencies is to correct the transparency problem, as well as to give Parliament a more prominent role in the international policy mix. On the first issue, we echo several of Stein's proposals for more democratic intergovernmental organizations:

- most decision-making sessions of intergovernmental institutions should be public, and documents, including draft proposals, should be freely available on the Internet;
- decision-making powers should not be the reserve of major powers acting in a "clublike setting" but rather the broader membership should have an opportunity for genuine participation;
- the public should have adequate and fair access to the institutions for exchange of data and consultation; and
- an ombudsperson should be appointed for intergovernmental organizations to receive complaints from citizens concerning maladministration.[15]

We have no illusions that at least some of these proposals will quickly run aground on the *realpolitik* of international power politics. Nevertheless, the simpler and less-contentious quick fixes — not least greater transparency — would go a long way in alleviating concerns about international policy-making. Recent Canadian government efforts to open up NAFTA and WTO trade proceedings are an excellent step in this direction.[16]

In terms of a parliamentary role in intergovernmental organizations, we note proposals from the Inter-Parliamentary Union, among others, propos-

---

15   Stein, "International Integration and Democracy" at 533.

16   See, e.g., Notes of Interpretation of Certain Chapter 11 Provisions (NAFTA Free Trade Commission, 31 July 2001); Department of International Trade, *Canada and the WTO: WTO Transparency*, available at www.dfait-maeci.gc.ca/tna-nac/WTO-Trans-en.asp.

ing that parliamentarians from member states form a standing "consulta-tive body" at intergovernmental organizations, and in particular the WTO.[17]

Meanwhile, Canada itself could grapple with the "de-parliamentization" issue by limiting the executive's discretion to bind Canada as a matter of inter-national law. As discussed in chapter 2, royal prerogative powers exist at the sufferance of the federal Parliament. The executive's primacy in foreign affairs is no different.[18] It is not "constitutionalized." Even if it were, a consti-tutionalized executive foreign affairs power would be a matter concerning (exclusively) the "executive government of Canada," and thus could be amend-ed by an Act of Parliament.[19] One way or another, therefore, the foreign affairs power may be constrained and regulated by Parliament with relative ease.

Some parliamentarians have recognized this fact. Bill C-315, a private member's bill introduced in 2001 before dying on the order paper, pro-posed a parliamentary vetting prior to Canadian ratification of at least some treaties.[20] Treaties whose implementation, for instance, would require a new Act of Parliament, or which expanded the powers of the executive or involved the imposition of a new tax could not be ratified without a resolu-tion from Parliament. This resolution itself would follow a review by a par-liamentary committee in which public hearings were held.

This approach would be a welcome advance for several reasons. First, it would obviously give Parliament a say before Canada bound itself as a matter of international law. Because this parliamentary confirmation could reduce the executive's capacity to make firm promises to other states in international negotiations, it might also drive the government to consult more broadly with parliamentarians prior to launching these talks, in an effort to secure a uniform position.

Second, having had this opportunity to approve a treaty obligation, Par-liament might be encouraged to subsequently incorporate that treaty into the domestic law of Canada with reasonable dispatch.

---

17   See, e.g., Inter-Parliamentary Union, Declaration, Cancun Session of the Parliamen-tary Conference on the WTO, Cancun (Mexico), 9 and 12 Sept. 2003, available at www.ipu.org/english/strcture/splzdocs/cancun/declaration.htm. See also Inter-Parlia-mentary Union, "The Role of Parliaments in Developing Public Policy in an Era of Globalisation, Multilateral Institutions and International Trade Agreements, *Resolu-tion adopted by consensus by the 107th Conference* (Marrakech, 22 March 2002), avail-able at www.ipu.org/conf-e/107-1.htm.

18   See discussions in Anne Marie Jacomy-Millette, *Treaty Law in Canada* (Ottawa: University of Ottawa Press, 1975) and A.E. Gotlieb, *Canadian Treaty-Making* (Toronto: Butterworths, 1968) referring to the treaty-making power as a form of royal prerogative, and describing this prerogative as the residue of the Crown's historical powers not revoked by Parliament.

19   See *Constitution Act, 1982*, s. 44.

20   Bill C-315, 37th Parl., 1st Sess., 49–50 Elizabeth II, 2001.

B. OTHER LEVELS OF GOVERNMENT WITHIN CANADA

The inverse of internationalization of public policy is the diffusion of governance within Canada. This diffusion is obviously anticipated in a federal system of government, in which power is divided between a federal and provincial level. It is further facilitated by provincial delegations of power to municipalities and federal agreements on self-government with First Nations.

While we have not focused on either provinces or municipalities in this book, these other levels of government in Canada practise democracy according to laws and legal principles largely similar to those we have described at the federal level. In some instances, these sub-federal governments have become laboratories for innovative approaches to democratic governance. Meanwhile, self-government agreements with First Nations also incorporate democratic accountability mechanisms. Rather than conduct a full analysis of these sub-federal laws, we simply provide a sense of their scope and flavour, and how they accord with the principles outlined in other parts of this book.

1. Law and Democracy at the Provincial and Municipal Level

Provincial governments are legislative bodies governed by the principles of Westminster-style government. For this reason, the legislative process, the concepts of parliamentary privilege and the conventions of responsible government generally mirror those at the federal level. Further, the provinces have their own electoral laws providing for the democratic election of legislators. Many provinces have also introduced laws regarding access to information and privacy, government ethics and lobbying.

In some areas, the provinces have gone further than the federal government. As noted in chapter 3, several provinces have referendum laws with a broader scope than their federal equivalents.[21] At the time of this writing, one province has enacted fixed election dates,[22] and several provinces are also contemplating this reform. Also on electoral reform, several provinces are considering a move from the first-past-the-post candidate selection process toward some system of proportional representation.[23]

In ethics, too, several provinces have gone beyond the federal approach — built largely on codes with uncertain legal effect — and legislated expansive ethical obligations for elected public officials, overseen by independent

---

21 See, e.g., British Columbia, *Recall and Initiative Act*, R.S.B.C. 1996 c. 398.

22 British Columbia, *Constitution Act*, R.S.B.C. 1996, c. 66, s. 23.

23 These provinces are British Columbia, Ontario, New Brunswick, Prince Edward Island and Quebec. See Brian Laghi, "Ottawa May Open Debate on Electoral Reforms," *Globe and Mail*, 15 Nov. 2004, A1.

ethics officers.[24] Some provinces have also introduced ombudspersons, charged with investigating complaints by the public concerning the conduct of government.[25] In the privacy and access to information area, several provincial laws extend robust and binding powers to information and privacy commissioners, a striking improvement over the federal system.[26] A few provinces have introduced statutes designed to make the government's budgetary process more transparent.[27]

Municipalities, for their part, are not legislatures, and are instead creatures of the province. They exercise only those powers delegated to them by these legislatures. Thus, the rules governing their conduct are determined either by the general laws on municipalities[28] or by the individual municipal charters enacted by provincial legislatures.[29] The practices introduced by these provincial laws — or those adopted by municipalities themselves — reflect several of the principles discussed in this book. Municipal councils are democratically elected, according to procedures outlined in provincial laws. In at least some provinces, municipalities are subject to access to information and privacy laws,[30] and electoral finance restrictions. Some cities, meanwhile, have lobbying disclosure rules.[31]

2. Law and Democracy in Canada's First Nations

Self-government by Canada's First Nations raises a series of complex issues, very few of which can be addressed in this book. We confine our remarks to a review of government policy in relation to democratic accountability and self-government.

---

24   See, e.g., Alberta, *Conflict of Interest Act*, R.S.A. 2000, c. C-23.

25   See, e.g., Alberta, *Ombudsman Act*, R.S.A. 2000, c. O-2; British Columbia, *Ombudsman Act*, R.S.B.C. 1996, c. 340.

26   See, e.g., Alberta, *Freedom of Information and Protection of Privacy Act*, R.S.A. 2000, c. F-25; British Columbia, *Freedom of Information and Protection of Privacy Act*, R.S.B.C. 1996, c. 165.

27   See, e.g., British Columbia, *Balanced Budget and Ministerial Accountability Act*, S.B.C. 2001, c. 28.

28   See, e.g., Alberta, *Municipal Governance Act*, R.S.A. 2000, c. M-26; British Columbia, *Local Government Act*, R.S.B.C. 1996, c. 323; British Columbia, *Members' Conflict of Interest Act*, R.S.B.C. 1996, c. 287.

29   See, e.g., British Columbia, *Vancouver Charter*, S.B.C. 1953, c. 55; Ontario, *City of Toronto Act*, S.O. 1997, c. 2.

30   See, e.g., Ontario *Municipal Freedom of Information and Protection of Privacy Act*, R.S.O. 1990, c. M.56.

31   See, e.g., City of Toronto, Lobbying Disclosure Rules, adopted by Council at its meeting held on March 1, 2 and 3, 2004, Report No. 2, Clause 16 of the Administration Committee.

Once a controversial idea, self-government is now official government policy. In its 1995 policy statement on self-government, the federal government endorsed self-government as a constitutional principle:

> The Government of Canada recognizes the inherent right of self-government as an existing Aboriginal right under section 35 of the *Constitution Act, 1982*. It recognizes, as well, that the inherent right may find expression in treaties, and in the context of the Crown's relationship with treaty First Nations. Recognition of the inherent right is based on the view that the Aboriginal peoples of Canada have the right to govern themselves in relation to matters that are internal to their communities, integral to their unique cultures, identities, traditions, languages and institutions, and with respect to their special relationship to their land and their resources.[32]

The policy statement emphasized that self-government is also to be *accountable* government. In the government's words, "[m]echanisms to ensure political and financial accountability should be comparable to those in place for other governments and institutions of similar size, although they need not be identical in all respects." First Nations groups must establish internal constitutions containing "[m]echanisms to ensure political accountability."

The specific accountability measures selected should reflect the "particular functions of Aboriginal governments and institutions, such as the exercise of jurisdiction, the delivery of programs and services, and/or the administration and enforcement of regulations." However, First Nations governments

exercising law-making authority must establish:
- clear and open processes of law-making;
- transparent processes for proclaiming a law in effect;
- procedures for the notification and publication of laws; and
- procedures for the appeal of laws or other decisions.[33]

Further, First Nations institutions exercising authority must:
- ensure that the decision-making processes central to the core functions of those institutions are open and transparent;

---

32   Government of Canada, *Aboriginal Self-Government: The Government of Canada's Approach to Implementation of the Inherent Right and the Negotiation of Aboriginal Self-Government* (1995).

33   *Ibid.*

- ensure that information on administrative policies and standards is readily obtainable by clients; and
- establish procedures, where appropriate, for administrative review, including appeal mechanisms.[34]

Specific principles of financial accountability are articulated in the policy statement. For instance,

[a]boriginal governments and institutions must develop rules with respect to conflict of interest for both elected and appointed officials. In particular, conflict-of-interest rules must ensure that services that provide an opportunity for financial gain operate at arm's length from elected and appointed officials.

Also,

[a]boriginal governments and institutions must ... be accountable to Parliament for funding provided by the federal government as a result of self-government agreements. Specifically, financing agreements must provide for a mechanism enabling Parliament to assess the extent to which public funds have contributed to the objectives for which they were voted.[35]

At present, there are a vast number of specific self-government agreements between First Nations and the federal government, and land claims and land governance accords or settlements that include governance mechanisms.[36]

By way of example, the most recent of these at the time of this writing — the Westbank First Nation Self-Government Agreement — provides that the Westbank First Nation is to develop a Constitution governing, among other things, "democratic elections of Council by Members, rules for the composition of Council, tenure of Council members and provision for the removal of Council members," "conflict of interest rules," "procedures for the passage and amendment of laws for Westbank First Nation," "appeal mechanisms," and "referendum procedures."[37]

Accordingly, the Westbank First Nations Constitution includes specific rules on these matters. For instance, the Westbank First Nations Council is

---

34   *Ibid.*
35   *Ibid.*
36   See the list provided by the Department of Indian and Northern Affairs, at www.ainc-inac.gc.ca/pr/agr/index_e.html.
37   Westbank First Nation — Self-Government Agreement, s. 43, available at www.ainc-inac.gc.ca/nr/prs/s-d2003/wfn06_e.html#part6.

to be democratically elected, accountable to the membership and to conduct its affairs in an "open and transparent" manner.[38] The Constitution
includes very detailed rules on the conduct of elections. These elections are
by secret ballot,[39] and the chief and councillors serve terms of three years.[40]
Council members may be removed from office for violating the Westbank
Constitution or their oaths of office.[41] The latter oath obliges councillors to,
among other things, "carry out their duties faithfully, honestly, impartially
and to the best of their abilities."[42]

The Constitution prescribes a transparent system of law-enactment by
the council, one giving First Nation members notice and an opportunity to
comment and in the case of taxing measures, an opportunity to vote.[43] The
voting procedure on this and other questions (such as amendment of the
Constitution itself) is set out in detailed rules concerning referendums.[44]

The Constitution also includes conflict-of-interest provisions for council members, including rules on the receipt of gifts.[45] In addition, it establishes detailed financial accountability strictures.[46]

How First Nations self-government will evolve in the future remains to
be seen. The discussion in this brief section suggests, however, that democratic accountability considerations have figured in government policy on
self-government and in First Nations articulation of self-government rules.

3. The Challenges of Diffuse Government

More than ever in the Canadian federation, the federal government and the
provinces do not govern according to a hermetically sealed division of powers. While the *Constitution Act, 1867* does partition jurisdiction between levels of government — and those powers are jealously guarded by the
respective governments — governance in a modern state requires substantial cooperation vertically between the provincial, federal and increasingly
First Nations levels, and horizontally among provinces. The result is a form
of contractual governance, with assorted federal-provincial agreements,
federal, provincial and First Nations agreements, and interprovincial agree-

---

38   Westbank First Nation Constitution, s. 15.
39   *Ibid.*, s. 21.
40   *Ibid.*, s. 23.
41   *Ibid.*, s. 42.
42   *Ibid.*, s. 40.
43   *Ibid.*, s. 60.
44   *Ibid.*, s. 121.
45   *Ibid.*, ss. 70 and 71.
46   *Ibid.*, s. 72 *et seq.*

ments on a dizzying array of issues. The Privy Council Office, for instance, lists fourteen "sectors" as implicating intergovernmental relations.[47] These expansive sectors, in turn, include a complicated series of bilateral and multilateral federal-provincial agreements.

This contractual federalism does not imperil democratic accountability *per se*. As discussed above, the levels of government that conduct this process are themselves each subject to mechanisms of democratically accountable. Plausible arguments may be made, however, that contractual federalism raises milder versions of the same complaints voiced in relation to international policy-making.

First, contractual federalism is the product of intractable negotiations between the executive branches of federal and provincial governments. The legislature is not, of course, cut out of the picture. Parliament and its provincial equivalents are, however, presented with a completed understanding, accord or agreement, not one that was vetted by Parliamentarians during its development. Presented with a *fait accompli* agreed to by Confederation's partners, only a determined legislator would seek to bar the agreement's progress, as did Manitoba MLA Elijah Harper in relation to the *Meech Lake accord*. We hypothesize, therefore, that the net effect of contractual federalism is to strengthen the executive branches of provincial and federal governments and their capacity to determine outcomes when matters eventually reach Parliament.

Second, with a few exceptions, contractual federalism is practised in an opaque manner. For instance, despite a promise by Prime Minister Paul Martin to conduct the 2004 federal-provincial health care summit in an open, televised forum, the substantive negotiations were quickly moved behind closed doors, consistent with other similar meetings.

Meanwhile, the public ability to extract information on these proceedings is curtailed sharply in access to information laws. The federal law, for instance, exempts from disclosure information obtained in confidence from "the government of a province or an institution thereof"[48] and information, disclosure of which could "reasonably be expected to be injurious

---

47   The sectors are Aboriginal Affairs, Immigration and Citizenship, Communications, Culture, Parks and Sport, Infrastructure, Domestic Economy, International, Environment, Justice, Public Security and Civil Emergency Preparedness, Finance and Revenue, Natural Resources, Health and Social Programs, Official Languages, Human Resources, and Technological Innovation. See Privy Council Office, Intergovernmental relations by sector, www.pco-bcp.gc.ca/aia/default.asp?Language=E&Page=relations.

48   *Access Act*, s. 13.

to the conduct by the Government of Canada of federal-provincial affairs, including ... (*a*) on federal-provincial consultations or deliberations; or (*b*) on strategy or tactics adopted or to be adopted by the Government of Canada relating to the conduct of federal-provincial affairs."[49] A similar exemption exists for information from First Nations governments.[50] Meanwhile, most provinces have mirror federal-provincial provisions.[51] The more public policy conducted through contractual federalism, the more information likely to be swept up in these exceptions.

There are instances where making progress in Canada's complicated federation does require strong executive leadership exercised *in camera*. The challenge is, and will remain, ensuring this practice goes no further than is absolutely necessary for transparent and accountable governance.

C. CONCLUSION

In conclusion, the diffusion and globalization of public policy raise roughly similar issues. A system of democratic accountability built on responsible government depends on legislative safeguards exercised over executive government. To the extent that governance is exercised through Canada's foreign missions or via contractual federalism, elected Parliamentarians and legislators may be even more ill-placed than at present to scrutinize fully the activities of the executive branch.

---

49 *Ibid.*, s. 14.
50 *Ibid.*, s. 13.
51 For a comparison of federal/provincial laws, see Michel Drapeau and Marc-Aurèle Racicot, *Federal Access to Information and Privacy Legislation Annotated 2004* (Toronto: Carswell, 2003) at 1669.

Concluding Thoughts on the Law of Canadian Democracy

How best to evaluate Canadian democracy? The answer to this question depends on which criteria are used, and which democratic principles one chooses to emphasize.

In keeping with the structure laid out in this book, in this concluding chapter we examine the performance of Canadian democracy by focusing first on the democratic selection of representatives and second on the relationship between these individuals and their unelected counterparts. We then conclude with a few thoughts on the relationship between law and democracy.

A. THE DEMOCRATIC SELECTION OF OFFICIALS

Canadian electoral law is, in significant ways, the envy of many nations around the world. Compared to other countries, we have reasonably clean elections and a stable system of governance. Recent changes to political fundraising rules limit the influence of wealthy interests in elections and improve disclosure of electoral finance, although gaps remain in several areas, including trust funds and leadership races.

On the other hand, our level of civic engagement — including our voter participation rate — is lower than that of many other nations. As chapter 3 notes, our first-past-the-post electoral system routinely renders many votes meaningless, and produces results that are often inconsistent with voter preferences. In the future, Canada's traditional first-past-the-post system in Commons elections may be tempered with the introduction of some sort of proportional representation. Such a reform — permitting a closer correspondence between votes cast and representation — could have important spinoff benefits, including a correction in the gender and ethnic imbalance in Canada's current Commons.

B. THE ACCOUNTABILITY OF UNELECTED OFFICIALS

1. Selection, Dismissal and Ethics

Perhaps the most indefensible aspect of Canadian democracy is the anachronistic senate. As noted in chapter 4, the senate is a legislative body for whom democratic accountability should mean *direct* citizen involvement in appointments and dismissals, exercised via elections. At present, the senate is democratically accountable to no one, although possessing substantial legislative powers. There are constitutional hurdles to senate reform, and sadly there is currently no serious movement afoot to democratize this chamber.

In recent years, various government scandals have pointed to the need for better transparency and accountability in the activities of public officials. Adherence to well-enforced ethics rules, for public officials as well as lobbyists, is essential to maintain good governance. However, as we argue in chapter 4, full democratic control over selection and dismissal is undesirable for some public officials. There are instances where this sort of control would impair other vital objectives, including merit and independence from elected officials.

Canadian practice has not yet achieved a full balance between democratic control, on the one hand, and merit and independence, on the other, particularly in relation to two broad classes of unelected officials: judicial and nonjudicial Governor-in-Council appointments. In both instances, recent developments suggest that Cabinet's appointment discretion will be constrained by mechanisms ensuring selections based on relevant (and not partisan) criteria. The key reform challenge will lie in crafting a greater role for Parliament that accommodates the legitimate interest of that branch in meritorious executive and judicial appointments without rendering the selection process a partisan circus.

2. Parliamentary Oversight

Legally, Parliament's legislative jurisdiction is vast. Evaluated on this basis, it is by far the most important political branch of government, a status constitutionalized by the concept of parliamentary supremacy. Parliamentary supremacy is, however, limited both by law and practice.

In its relationship with the executive, Parliament's legal supremacy is constrained by the practical reality of party politics. As outlined in chapter 5, constitutional convention allows one party to control both the legislative and the executive branches. A party leader commanding enough votes in the Commons to constitute a majority of that House is also elevated to the prime minister's office and inherits the executive powers of government. With the party leader at the helm of the executive branch, the priorities of the executive branch become the legislative priorities of the parliamentary majority. A majority Parliament is not a venue in which elected representatives often set a legislative policy direction different from that desired by the ministry and its vast government apparatus. The key reform question in the air at the time of this writing is whether a better resourced Parliament with a new tradition of free votes will become more relevant as a deliberative, legislative body.

Similar issues are raised by Parliament's role in maintaining responsible government. As discussed in chapter 6, Parliament has a central role, at least in theory, in holding the ministry accountable, and through the ministry, the broader public administration of Canada. In practice, responsible government exists, but it is only enforceable through no confidence votes, contempt powers and Parliament's legislative prerogatives — blunt instruments all. Further, in its workaday oversight role, Parliament's resource constraints are a constant hobble. Stirrings in the minority thirty-eighth Parliament at the time of this writing suggest that Parliament may be a more aggressive overseer. The key reform challenge will lie, however, in maintaining this position in future, majority Parliaments.

3. Transparency

Finally, democratic accountability depends to a large degree on the public's right of access to government information. Chapter 9 suggests that government performance under the *Access to Information Act* has been weak. Meanwhile, an increasingly perplexing "complex" of secrecy and national security provisions risk even further restricting information access. The key reform challenge in the post-9/11 era will be to preserve and improve transparency in a government now inclined to circle the wagons in the name of security.

C. HOW MUCH LAW IS ENOUGH?

With the exception of our comments on senate reform, the critiques we raise above and throughout the book are legal reforms that arguably only tinker at the margins of Canadian democracy. While some readers will disagree with these proposals, and urge that we go too far, still others may argue that we have been insufficiently ambitious. Why not insist upon more law? Should we not "legalize" the basic mechanics of Canadian democracy, concepts that the framers of our Constitution left unarticulated? As a close read of this book suggests, the place in which there is the least "hard" law in modern Canadian democracy is in relation to unwritten constitutional principles and conventions governing, among other things, responsible government and the relationship between the branches of government.

Clarifying Canada's democratic practices in relation to responsible government through legislation has been tried before. In 1978, the Trudeau government introduced Bill C-60. Among other things, this law project would have entrenched in the Constitution the Governor General's powers, and would have codified the existence of Cabinet, underscored the responsibility of this body to the Commons and set out the consequences should the government lose the confidence of the Commons. This initiative failed. It is worth pondering, however, whether introducing new written law of this sort would mean more democratic government.

There is room to differ on this question. On the one hand, reliance on flexible, uncodified constitutional conventions or uncertain unwritten constitutional rules like parliamentary privilege makes Canada's democracy a pliable, flexible system, one capable of accommodating measured change. Because constitutional conventions are just that — conventions — their observance is a matter determined principally by the political branches of government, not by the courts. Similarly, while courts do have a role in ascertaining the existence of parliamentary privileges, they do not purport to regulate their exercise. This is probably as it should be.

On the other hand, the conventions of responsible government and the unwritten norms of the Constitution are often opaque and uncertain. There is merit in a democracy to having clear rules establishing readily ascertained powers and relationships. Otherwise important questions of democratic accountability are left to be decided only by the initiated, examining the entrails of uncertain precedent and practice to discern answers to such questions as "What exactly are the reserve powers of the Governor General?" or "how far do the privileges of Parliament extend?"

Where one comes down on the issue of codification versus constructive opacity may depend on the answer one gives to the following question: is it rules themselves that make and uphold a democracy or is a democracy ultimately more dependent on political culture? The United States Constitution — with its robust checks and balances between branches of government — envisages law as the guardian of democracy. Canada's Westminster system relies more heavily on an honourable political culture.

This latter, less legalistic approach has its benefits, at least to a point. We need not codify definitively every dimension of democratic accountability if we build a legal infrastructure, not to regulate the minutiae of responsible and democratic government, but designed instead to preserve the integrity of our political culture. Areas that benefit from having clear lines in this regard include those we have discussed throughout this book: elections and election financing, appointment and dismissal rules, ethics, lobbying and transparency. Strong laws here prop up good government and allow Canadian democracy to "muddle through." Once rigorous rules of these sorts are created, the benefits of reaching further, and codifying and refining many of the conventions and unwritten rules that have their origins in parliamentary tradition — or at the very least, that harm of not doing so — is less apparent.

Our reform focus, therefore should probably not be on a grand attempt to legislate the foundations of Canadian democracy in statutes and written constitutions, but instead on efforts to buttress and sustain its surrounding, legal scaffolding. While this approach may seem far less dramatic, it is consistent with a mature democracy, and a suitably Canadian contribution to the globe's accelerating democratic tradition.

a1

Appendix 1: The Public Administration of Canada

The following tables include all the federal public administration bodies listed in the Treasury Board *Population Affiliation Report*, posted as of June 2004.[1] They indicate whether that body is expressly listed as a "government institution" under the *Access* and *Privacy Acts* or noted in the *Personal Information Protection and Electronic Documents Act* (*PIPEDA*) or is expressly governed by the *Public Service Employment Act*, S.C. 2003, c. 22, or its predecessor. Note that in some instances, bodies in the *Population Affiliation Report* not expressly mentioned in these statutes may still be covered by virtue of their position in the organizational structure of a body that is listed in the laws.

---

1   Available at www.tbs-sct.gc.ca/pubs_pol/hrpubs/PopAffRep/Intro_e.asp. For the most part, these tables do not take into account reorganizations under consideration in Parliament during the 38th Parliament at the time of this writing in late 2004.

Table A1.1   Public Service Bodies

Department or Agency Name	Access Act	Privacy Act	PIPEDA	PSEA
Atlantic Canada Opportunities Agency	✓	✓		✓
Canada Border Services Agency	✓	✓		✓
Canada Revenue Agency	✓	✓		✓
Canada Industrial Relations Board	✓	✓		✓
Canada Investment and Savings				✓
Canada School of Public Service	✓	✓		✓
Canadian Artists and Producers Professional Relations Tribunal	✓	✓		✓
Canadian Dairy Commission	✓	✓		✓
Canadian Environmental Assessment Agency	✓	✓		✓
Canada Firearms Centre	✓	✓		2
Canadian Food Inspection Agency	✓	✓		✓
Canadian Forces Grievance Board	✓	✓		✓
Canadian Forces Non-Public Funds				✓
Canadian Grain Commission	✓	✓		✓
Canadian Human Rights Commission	✓	✓		✓
Canadian Human Rights Tribunal	✓	✓		✓
Canadian Institutes of Health Research	✓	✓		✓
Canadian Intergovernmental Conference Secretariat				✓
Canadian International Development Agency	✓	✓		✓
Canadian International Trade Tribunal	✓	✓		✓
Canadian Nuclear Safety Commission	✓	✓		✓
Canadian Polar Commission	✓	✓		✓
Canadian Radio-television and Telecommunications Commission	✓	✓		✓
Canadian Security Intelligence Service	✓	✓		✓
Canadian Space Agency	✓	✓		✓
Canadian Transportation Accident Investigation and Safety Board	✓	✓		✓
Canadian Transportation Agency	✓	✓		✓
Communication Canada	✓	✓		✓
Communications Security Establishment				✓
Copyright Board	✓	✓		✓
Correctional Service of Canada	✓	✓		✓

2   This body, although part of the public service pursuant to the old *PSEA*, is not listed as part of the public service in the 2003 *PSEA*.

Department or Agency Name	Access Act	Privacy Act	PIPEDA	PSEA
Courts Administration Service				✓
Department of Agriculture and Agri-Food	✓	✓		✓
Department of Canadian Heritage	✓	✓		✓
Department of Citizenship and Immigration	✓	✓		✓
Department of Finance	✓	✓		✓
Department of Fisheries and Oceans	✓	✓		✓
Department of Foreign Affairs and International Trade	✓	✓		✓
Department of Health	✓	✓		✓
Department of Human Resources Development	✓	✓		✓
Department of Indian Affairs and Northern Development	✓	✓		✓
Department of Industry	✓	✓		✓
Department of International Trade	✓	✓		✓
Department of Justice	✓	✓		✓
Department of National Defence	✓	✓		✓
Department of Natural Resources	✓	✓		✓
Department of Public Works and Government Services	✓	✓		✓
Department of the Environment	✓	✓		✓
Department of the Solicitor General	✓	✓		✓
Department of Transport	✓	✓		✓
Department of Veterans Affairs	✓	✓		✓
Department of Western Economic Diversification	✓	✓		✓
Economic Development Agency of Canada for the Regions of Quebec	✓	✓		✓
Energy Supplies Allocation Board	✓	✓		✓
Financial Consumer Agency of Canada	✓	✓		✓
Financial Transactions and Reports Analysis Centre of Canada	✓	✓		✓
Hazardous Materials Information Review Commission	✓	✓		✓
Immigration and Refugee Board	✓	✓		✓
Indian Oil and Gas Canada				✓
International Joint Commission				✓
Law Commission of Canada	✓	✓		✓
Military Police Complaints Commission	✓	✓		✓
NAFTA Secretariat — Canadian Section				✓

Department or Agency Name	Access Act	Privacy Act	PIPEDA	PSEA
National Archives of Canada	✓	✓		✓
National Capital Commission	✓	✓		✓
National Energy Board	✓	✓		✓
National Farm Products Council	✓	✓		✓
National Film Board	✓	✓		✓
National Library of Canada	✓	✓		✓
National Parole Board	✓	✓		✓
National Research Council of Canada	✓	✓		✓
National Round Table on the Environment and the Economy	✓	✓		✓
National Search and Rescue Secretariat				3
Natural Sciences and Engineering Research Council	✓	✓		✓
Northern Pipeline Agency	✓	✓		✓
Office of Indian Residential Schools Resolution of Canada	✓	✓		✓
Office of Infrastructure of Canada	✓	✓		✓
Office of the Auditor General of Canada		✓		✓
Office of the Chief Electoral Officer		✓		✓
Office of the Commissioner for Federal Judicial Affairs				✓
Office of the Commissioner of Official Languages		✓		✓
Office of the Co-ordinator, Status of Women	✓	✓		4
Office of the Correctional Investigator	✓	✓		✓
Office of the Director of Veterans' Land Act	✓	✓		✓
Office of the Governor General's Secretary				✓
Office of the Registrar of the Supreme Court of Canada				✓
Office of the Superintendent of Bankruptcy				✓
Office of the Superintendent of Financial Institutions	✓	✓		✓
Offices of the Information and Privacy Commissioners				✓

---

3   See above note 2.

4   See above note 2.

Department or Agency Name	Access Act	Privacy Act	PIPEDA	PSEA
Organizing Committee for International Summits				5
Parks Canada Agency	✓	✓		✓
Patented Medicine Prices Review Board	✓	✓		✓
Prairie Farm Rehabilitation Administration	✓	✓		✓
Privy Council Office	✓	✓		✓
Public Service Commission	✓	✓		✓
Public Service Human Resources Management Agency of Canada	✓	✓		6
Public Service Labour Relations Board	✓	✓		✓
Public Service Staffing Tribunal	✓	✓		✓
Registry of the Competition Tribunal				✓
Royal Canadian Mounted Police (Civilian Staff)	✓	✓		✓
Royal Canadian Mounted Police External Review Committee	✓	✓		✓
Royal Canadian Mounted Police Public Complaints Commission	✓	✓		✓
Security Intelligence Review Committee	✓	✓		✓
Social Sciences and Humanities Research Council	✓	✓		✓
Statistical Survey Operations				✓
Statistics Canada	✓	✓		✓
Transportation Appeal Tribunal of Canada				7
Treasury Board (Secretariat)	✓	✓		✓
Veterans Review and Appeal Board	✓	✓		✓

---

5   See above note 2.
6   See above note 2.
7   See above note 2.

Table A1.2   Crown Corporations and Other Canadian Government Corporate Interests

Organization Name	Access Act	Privacy Act	PIPEDA[8]	PSEA[9]
Asia-Pacific Foundation of Canada				
Atlantic Pilotage Authority	✓	✓		
Atomic Energy of Canada Limited			✓	✓
Bank of Canada	✓	✓		
Blue Water Bridge Authority	✓	✓		
Buffalo and Fort Erie Public Bridge Authority				
Business Development Bank of Canada	✓	✓		
Canada Council for the Arts	✓	✓		✓
Canada Deposit Insurance Corporation	✓	✓		
Canada Development Investment Corporation				
Canada Foundation for Innovation				
Canada Foundation for Sustainable Development Technology				
Canada Lands Company Limited	✓	✓		
Canada Millennium Scholarship Foundation				
Canada Mortgage and Housing Corporation	✓	✓		
Canada Pension Plan Investment Board				
Canada Post Corporation		✓		
Canadian Air Transport Security Authority	✓	✓		
Canadian Broadcasting Corporation			✓	
Canadian Centre on Substance Abuse				
Canadian Commercial Corporation	✓	✓		✓
Canadian Dairy Commission Corporation				
Canadian International Grains Institute				
Canadian Livestock Records Corporation				
Canadian Museum of Civilization	✓	✓		

---

8   Many of these corporate interest are likely captured by the *PIPEDA*'s requirements. See discussion in chapter 9. This table shows which Crown corporations the government has expressly declared bound by *PIPEDA*.

9   Where the *PSEA* applies, it usually does so by virtue of a designation by the Governor-in-Council by virtue of s. 37(2) of the old *PSEA*, R.S.C. 1985, c. P-33.

Organization Name	Access Act	Privacy Act	PIPEDA	PSEA
Canadian Museum of Nature	✓	✓		
Canadian Race Relations Foundation				
Canadian Tourism Commission	✓	✓		✓
Canadian Wheat Board		✓		
Cape Breton Development Corporation				
Cape Breton Growth Fund Corporation				
Defence Construction (1951) Limited	✓	✓		✓
Enterprise Cape Breton Corporation			✓	
Export Development Canada		✓		✓
Farm Credit Canada	✓	✓		✓
Fraser River Port Authority	✓	✓		
Freshwater Fish Marketing Corporation	✓	✓		
Great Lakes Pilotage Authority	✓	✓		
Halifax Port Authority	✓	✓		
Hamilton Port Authority	✓	✓		
International Boundary Commission				
International Centre for Human Rights and Democratic Development	✓	✓		
International Development Research Centre	✓	✓		
International Monetary Fund				
Laurentian Pilotage Authority	✓	✓		
Lower Churchill Development Corporation				
Marine Atlantic Inc.				
Montreal Port Authority	✓	✓		
Multilateral Investment Guarantee Agency				
Nanaimo Port Authority	✓	✓		
National Arts Centre Corporation		✓		✓
National Capital Commission Corporation	✓	✓		
National Gallery of Canada	✓	✓		
National Museum of Science and Technology	✓	✓		
NAV CANADA				
North Fraser Port Authority	✓	✓		
North Portage Development Corporation and The Forks Renewal Corporation				
Old Port of Montreal Corporation Inc. (Canada Lands Company)	✓	✓		

Organization Name	Access Act	Privacy Act	PIPEDA	PSEA
Pacific Pilotage Authority	✓	✓		
Petro-Canada				
Port Alberni Port Authority	✓	✓		
Prince Rupert Port Authority	✓	✓		
Public Sector Pension Investment Board				
Quebec Port Authority	✓	✓		
Queens Quay West Land Corporation				
Ridley Terminals Inc.				
Roosevelt Campobello International Park Commission				
Royal Canadian Mint	✓	✓		✓
Saguenay Port Authority	✓	✓		
Saint John Harbour Bridge Authority				
Saint John Port Authority	✓	✓		
Seaway International Bridge Corporation Limited	✓	✓		✓
Sept-Îles Port Authority	✓	✓		
St. John's Port Authority	✓	✓		
Standards Council of Canada	✓	✓		
Telefilm Canada	✓	✓		
The Federal Bridge Corporation Limited	✓	✓		
The Jacques-Cartier and Champlain Bridges Incorporated	✓	✓		
Thunder Bay Port Authority	✓	✓		
Toronto Port Authority	✓	✓		
Trois Rivières Port Authority	✓	✓		
Vancouver Port Authority	✓	✓		
Vanier Institute of the Family				
VIA Rail Canada Inc.				
Windsor Port Authority	✓	✓		

Table A1.3   Miscellaneous Organizations

Organization Name	Access Act	Privacy Act	PIPEDA	PSEA[10]
Advisory Committee on Retirement Compensation Arrangement				
Advisory Council on Adjustment				
Advisory Council on Public Safety in the Transportation of Dangerous Goods				
AIDS Advisory Committee				
Alberta-British Colombia Boundary Commission				
Alberta-Northwest Territories Boundary Commission				
Arctic Waters Advisory Committee				
Atlantic Advisory Council				
Atlantic Canada Opportunities Agency Advisory Board				
Atlantic Canada Opportunities Board				
Board of Arbitration and Review Tribunal				
Board of Internal Economy of the House of Commons				
Boards of Referees				
British Colombia-Yukon-Northwest Territories Boundary Commission				
Canada Employment and Insurance Commission	✓	✓		
Canada Pension Appeals Board	✓	✓		
Canada Pension Plan Advisory Board				
Canada Pension Plan Review Tribunals				
Canada Petroleum Resources Act Advisory Bodies				
Canada-Newfoundland Offshore Petroleum Board	✓	✓		
Canada-Nova Scotia Offshore Petroleum Board	✓	✓		
Canadian Centre for Occupational Health and Safety	✓	✓		
Canadian Centre for Occupational Health and Safety Council				
Canadian Citizenship Court				

---

10   Where the *PSEA* applies, it usually does so by virtue of a designation by the Governor-in-Council by virtue of s. 37(2) of the old *PSEA*, R.S.C. 1985, c. P-33.

Organization Name	Access Act	Privacy Act	PIPEDA	PSEA
Canadian Council of Ministers of the Environment				✓
Canadian Council on Social Development				
Canadian Council on the Status of the Artist				
Canadian Cultural Centre in Paris				
Canadian Cultural Property Export Review Board	✓	✓		
Canadian Dairy Commission Consultative Committee				
Canadian Environmental Advisory Council				
Canadian Environmental Protection Act, 1999 Board of Review				
Canadian Environmental Protection Act, 1999 National Advisory Committee				
Canadian Food Inspection Agency Advisory Board				
Canadian Forces (military personnel)	✓	✓		
Canadian Forces Pension Advisory Committee				
Canadian Heritage Languages Institute				
Canadian Judicial Council				
Canadian Multiculturalism Advisory Committee				
Canadian Penitentiary Services Disciplinary Courts				
Canadian Permanent Committee on Geographical Names				
Canadian Polar Commission Advisory Committee				
Canadian Race Relations Foundation Advisory Committee				
Canadian Race Relations Foundation Investment Committee				
Canadian Transportation Accident Investigation and Safety Board Act Review Commission				
Canadian Wheat Board Advisory Committee				
CANMET National Advisory Council				
Cape Breton Advisory Council				
Coal Mining Safety Commission				
Columbia River Treaty Permanent Engineering Board				

Organization Name	Access Act	Privacy Act	PIPEDA	PSEA
Commission of Inquiry into Certain Events at the Prison for Women in Kingston				
Commission of Inquiry into a National Integrated Inter-city Passenger Transportation System				
Commission of Inquiry into the Actions of Canadian Officials in Relation to Maher Arar				
Commission of Inquiry into the Sponsorship Program and Advertising Activities				
Commission to Review Allowances of Members of Parliament				
Cree-Naskapi Commission				
Dangerous Offender Consultation Committee				
Eastern-Western Grain Standards Committee				
Education Statistics National Advisory Committee				
Electoral Boundaries Commission				
Enterprise Cape Breton Board				
Environmental Assessment Review Panel				
Environmental Impact Review Board				
Environmental Impact Screening Committee				
Environmental Studies Management Board				
Executive Compensation Advisory Group				
Fair Play Commission				
Farm Credit Appeal Boards				
Farm Credit Corporation Advisory Committee				
Farm Products Promotion and Research Agencies (various)				
Federal Court of Canada				
Financial Institutions Advisory Committee				
Firearms National Advisory Council				
Fisheries and Oceans Research Advisory Council				
Fisheries Joint Management Committee				

Organization Name	Access Act	Privacy Act	PIPEDA	PSEA
Fitness and Amateur Sport National Advisory Council				
Foreign Claims Commission				
Forestry Advisory Committee				
Free Trade Commission				
Freshwater Fish Marketing Corporation Advisory Committee				
Government House (Employees)				
Government of Nunavut				✓
Government of the Northwest Territories				✓
Government of Yukon				✓
Grain Appeal Tribunal				
Grain Transportation Senior Committee				
Great Lakes Fishery Commission				
Great Lakes Science Advisory Board				
Great Lakes Water Quality Board				
Gwich'in Land and Water Board	✓	✓		
Gwich'in Land Use Planning Board	✓	✓		
Hazardous Materials Information Review Commission Appeal Board				
Hazardous Materials Information Review Commission Board of Review				
Heritage Canada				
Historic Sites and Monuments Board of Canada	✓	✓		
House of Commons (Employees)				
House of Commons Standing Committees				
Indian Commission of Ontario				
Indian Specific Claims Commission				
Industrial Regional Development Board				
Industrial Technical Liaison Committee on Industrial Research and Development				
Industry Advisory Committee				
Industry, Science and Technology Advisory Committees				
Intellectual Property Advisory Committee				
Intercolonial and Prince Edward Island Railways Employees Provident Fund Board				
International Atomic Energy Agency				
International Commission on the Conservation of Atlantic Tuna				

Organization Name	Access Act	Privacy Act	PIPEDA	PSEA
International North Pacific Fisheries Commission				
International Pacific Halibut Commission				
International Pacific Salmon Fisheries Commission				
International Tin Council				
International Trade Advisory Committee				
International Trade Sectorial Advisory Groups				
Judicial Compensation and Benefits Commission				
Labour Adjustment Review Board				
Labour Statistics Advisory Committee				
Lake of the Woods Control Board				
Law Commission of Canada Advisory Council				
Library of Parliament				
Machinery and Equipment Advisory Board				
Mackenzie Valley Environmental Impact Review Board	✓	✓		
Mackenzie Valley Land and Water Board	✓	✓		
Management of Severe Pain Advisory Committee of Experts				
Marine Training National Advisory Council				
Medical Advisors Group				
Merchant Seaman Compensation Board	✓	✓		
Minister for International Cooperation				
National Advisory Council on Aging				
National Battlefields Commission	✓	✓		✓
National Biotechnology Advisory Committee				
National Capital Commission Arts, Design and Real Property Advisory Committees				
National Council of Welfare				
National Energy Board Act Arbitration Committee				
National Innovations Advisory Committee				
National Research Council Associate Committees				
National Transportation Act Review Commission				
Native Economic Development Board				

Organization Name	Access Act	Privacy Act	PIPEDA	PSEA
Networks of Centres of Excellence Advisory Committee				
North Atlantic Salmon Conservation Organization Council				
Northern Ontario Development Advisory Board				
Northwest Territories Water Board	✓	✓		
Nuclear Safety Advisory Committee				
Nunavut Surface Rights Tribunal	✓	✓		
Nunavut Water Board	✓	✓		
Office of the Administrator of the Ship-Source Oil Pollution Fund				
Office of the Commissioner of Nunavut				✓
Office of the Communications Security Establishment Commissioner				
Office of the Custodian of Enemy Property				✓
Office of the Deputy Prime Minister (Employees)				
Office of the Ethics Commissioner				✓
Office of the Government House Leader (Employees)				
Office of the Inspector General Canadian Security Intelligence Service Review Committee	✓	✓		
Office of the Leader of the Government in the Senate (Employees)				
Office of the Leader of the Opposition in the House of Commons (Employees)				
Office of the Leader of the Opposition in the Senate (Employees)				
Office of the Prime Minister (Employees)				
Office of the Senate Ethics Officer				✓
Office of the Umpire Unemployment Insurance Act				
Offices of Members of the House of Commons (Employees)				
Offices of Ministers (Employees)				
Official Languages Advisory Council				
Offshore Oil and Gas Training Standards Advisory Board				
Oil and Gas Administration Advisory Council				

Organization Name	Access Act	Privacy Act	PIPEDA	PSEA
Pacific Advisory Council				
Patented Medicine Prices Review Board Advisory Panel				
Petroleum Industry Advisory Committee				
Pipeline Arbitration Committee				
Plant Breeders' Rights Advisory Committee				
Plant Breeders' Rights Office				
Prairie Farm Rehabilitation Advisory Committee				
Priority Substance Advisory Panel				
Provincial Advisory Board				
Provincial-Territorial Advisory Committee				
Public Service Superannuation Act Advisory Committee				
Radiological Protection Advisory Committee				
Railway Safety Consultative Committee				
Regional Development Incentives Board	✓	✓		
Remote Sensing Canadian Advisory Committee				
Royal Canadian Mounted Police (Force members)	✓	✓		
Royal Canadian Mounted Police Pension Advisory Committee				
Sahtu Land and Water Board	✓	✓		
Sahtu Land Use Planning Board	✓	✓		
Science and Technology National Advisory Board				
Security Advisory Committee				
Senate (Employees)				
Small Business Consultative Committee				
Space Advisory Board				
Standards Council of Canada Advisory Committees				
Standards Development Organizations Advisory Committee.				
Statute Revision Commission	✓	✓		
Steering Group on Prosperity				
Superintendent of Financial Institutions Committee				
Supreme Court of Canada				

Organization Name	Access Act	Privacy Act	PIPEDA	PSEA
System of National Accounts Advisory Committee				
Tax Court of Canada (Judges)				
Trade Test Boards				
Transportation of Dangerous Goods General Policy Advisory Council				
Travellers Advisory Committee				
Western Arctic Claims Settlement Act Arbitration Board				
Western Grain Stabilization Administration Advisory Committee				
Wildlife Advisory Board — Wood Buffalo National Park				
World Energy Conference Canadian National Committee				
Yukon Environmental and Socio-Economic Assessment Board	✓	✓		

Table A1.4   Special Operating Agencies

Agency Name	Access Act Privacy Act PIPEDA	PSEA
Canada Investment and Savings	None of these special operating agencies are expressly listed in these statutes. Their status and functions are governed by agreements with line government departments. The Treasury Board Secretariat reports that "these special operating agencies are, in most cases, subject to the same acts and regulations as their home department."[11] This includes *Access* and *Privacy Act* requirements.[12]	✓
Canadian Conservation Institute		✓
Canadian Forces Housing Agency		✓
Canadian Heritage Information Network		✓
Canadian Intellectual Property Office		✓
Canadian Pari-Mutuel Agency		✓
Consulting and Audit Canada		✓
CORCAN		✓
Defence Research and Development Canada		✓
Indian Oil and Gas Canada		✓
Measurement Canada		✓
Passport Office		✓
Physical Resources Bureau		✓
Superintendent of Bankruptcy		✓
Technology Partnerships Canada		✓
Training and Development Canada		✓
Translation Bureau		✓

11   *Ibid.*

12   Personal communication, Jocelyne Chabot, Treasury Board Secretariat, 15 May 2004.

Appendix 2: Statistical Trends in Law-Making

This section outlines long-term statistical trends in parliamentary legislative activity.

1. General Observations

As Table A2.1 indicates, the proportion of all bills receiving royal assent by Parliament since the Second World War is erratic, but in overall decline. Thus, in stark contrast to the early postwar era, most bills now introduced in Parliament never receive royal assent and become a statute. Some are rejected, but most "die on the order paper" when Parliament is either prorogued or dissolved.

Most of this trend is attributable to increases in the number of private member bills. The rate of success for nongovernmental bills has been paltry for decades, except in the senate where the reasonable success rate for private (as opposed to public private members') bills has pulled up the overall success rate on nongovernment bills. Indeed, in the thirty-seventh Parliament, a total of only eleven substantive private members' bills (i.e., those other than simply constituency change-of-name bills) received royal assent.[1]

---

[1] Library of Parliament, "Private Member's Bills Passed by Parliament," available at www.parl.gc.ca/information/about/process/info/pmb.asp?lang=E&param=Y&parl=N.

In comparison, government bills receive royal assent on a relatively regular basis, albeit not as often in recent Parliaments as during the immediate postwar period. As the numbers of (almost always) unsuccessful private members' bills increase, relative to government bills, the proportion of all bills introduced receiving royal assent has been driven lower.

Table A2.1   Statistics on Bills[2]

Parliament	Bills Introduced Receiving Royal Assent (%)	Government Bills Receiving Royal Assent (%)	Nongovernment Public Bills Receiving Royal Assent (%)	All Commons Bills Receiving Royal Assent (%)	Commons Government Bills Receiving Royal Assent (%)	Commons Nongovernmental Bills Receiving Royal Assent (%)	All Senate Bills Receiving Royal Assent (%)	Government Senate Bills Receiving Royal Assent (%)	Nongovernment Senate Bills Receiving Royal Assent (%)
37th	11	65	1	10	62	1	29	94	10
36th	13	74	1	12	73	1	30	78	6
35th	26	71	2	26	70	2	28	100	16
34th	31	85	5	30	85	5	56	83	30
33d	47	81	3	47	82	3	44	67	22
32d	29	78	4	25	78	4	81	71	36
31st	2	18	0	2	21	0	10	10	0
30th	18	63	3	16	64	3	56	56	15
29th	14	61	2	14	64	2	18	0	15
28th	23	78	3	18	77	3	71	81	20
27th	29	86	1	22	94	2	63	65	22
26th	35	86	1	23	88	1	76	79	35
25th	18	50	0	15	52	0	30	0	16
24th	58	95	2	47	94	2	95	97	41
23d	66	88	0	57	90	0	93	75	42
22d	78	96	3	71	97	3	93	90	39
21st	83	95	8	78	96	8	93	92	32
20th	82	93	17	79	96	2	88	82	37

2   Data compiled from Library of Parliament, "Table of Legislation Introduced and Passed by Session," available at www.parl.gc.ca/information/about/process/info/Parl-Bills.asp?lang=E.

2. Senate versus House of Commons

The majority of both government and private members' bills originate in the Commons. Over time, this trend has accelerated, although recent senates have been more willing to amend Commons bills, as shown in Table A2.2.

Table A2.2   Percentage of Bills Originating in the Senate[3]

Parliament	Government Bills Originating in Senate (%)	All Bills Originating in Senate (%)	Commons Bills Amended by the Senate as Percent of all Commons Bills Receiving Royal Assent
37th	9	7	11.02
36th	12	7	8.06
35th	1	4	8.28
34th	3	5	3.25
33d	2	5	7.14
32d	7	6	0.42
31st	26	3	0.00
30th	13	4	3.72
29th	4	2	1.47
28th	19	8	4.98
27th	28	15	2.94
26th	18	22	1.64
25th	3	17	0.00
24th	13	23	1.21
23d	12	24	No data
22d	18	33	No data
21st	23	33	No data
20th	19	33	No data

3. Overall Parliamentary Legislative "Productivity"

The proportional figures in Table A2.1 say little about how "productive" Parliament is in its law-making role. Productivity is generally measured as quantity of output *per* unit of input. Figures provided by the Library of Par-

---

3   Data compiled from Library of Parliament, "Table of Legislation Introduced and Passed by Session, 1909.11.11 to Date" and Library of Parliament, "Bills Introduced in the House of Commons and Amended by the Senate — 1960 to Date."

liament make it possible to measure legislative productivity, defined as legislative activity *per* unit of the key parliamentary input, time.

Table A2.3 and the graph that follow attempt to apply the variable of parliamentary time in an effort to measure parliamentary legislative productivity from 1945 through to the close of the thirty-seventh Parliament in 2004. We measure performance in two ways: first, in introducing bills and, second, in enacting laws.

Productivity in Introducing Bills

All Bills (Combined Private Members and Government Bills)

One indicator of how vigorous Parliament is in legislating may be derived by dividing the number of bills introduced during a Parliament by the number days that each Parliament was in session ("parliamentary session days").[4] Remarkably, this figure has remained relatively stable since the Second World War, deviating in most instances by mere fractions of a day.

Ranked against other Parliaments, the thirty-seventh Parliament between 2001 and 2004 was the most vigorous legislature since the Second World War, excepting the hyperactive, but ultimately short-lived, Clark minority government of the thirty-first Parliament. During the thirty-seventh Parliament, 1119 bills were introduced over three sessions of Parliament lasting a total of 1117 Parliamentary session days, producing a ratio of roughly one bill *per* day. The vast majority of these bills were private members' projects, some of which were reintroduced after the previous prorogation of Parliament.

Government Bills Only

Not surprisingly, this measure of legislative "productivity" produces different results when private members' bills are eliminated from the equation. Since there are many fewer government than private members' bills, figures for Parliamentary session days *per government* bill introduced are universally higher for all Parliaments than the equivalent figure for "all bills" cited above.[5] Unlike with the equivalent "all bills" statistic, there is also a substantial variation in the number of Parliamentary session days *per* government bill *between* Parliaments.

---

4   Measured in the table and chart by the statistic: Number of Days of Parliamentary Session/Bill Introduced (All Bills). Note that days of Parliament are not necessarily the sum of calendar days during which that Parliament was in existence. Rather, parliamentary days are the sum of days in which Parliament was actually in session (i.e., not prorogued or dissolved).

5   Measured in the table and chart by the statistic: Number of Days of Parliamentary Session/Bill Introduced (Government Bills).

Here, the Clark government, during the thirty-first Parliament, proved most productive, introducing a large number of government bills during its short period in office. Overall, however, our figures show that governments since 1945 are less "productive" in introducing government law projects. There has been a reasonably steady increase over the decades in the number of Parliamentary session days *per* government bill.

Productivity in Enacting Laws

All Statutes (Combined Private Members and Government Bills)
This same trend is reflected in a more meaningful measure of legislative performance: the number of parliamentary session days *per* bill receiving royal assent.[6] As Table A2.3 and the accompanying graph suggest, measured against this statistic, the twentieth Parliament (1945–49) was significantly more "productive" than any Parliament since, producing a statute every two days.

In comparison, the most recent thirty-seventh and thirty-sixth Parliaments have been significantly less prolific, producing a statute only every nine parliamentary session days. This level of productivity is not much better than the truncated Clark government, and is significantly worse than the historical pattern since the Second World War. The latter, long-term trend shows a marked increase in the number of parliamentary session days *per* bill receiving royal assent.

Government Statutes Only
When Parliamentary productivity is measured only with respect to Parliamentary session days *per government* bills receiving royal assent, it is even lower.[7] Many fewer government bills are receiving royal assent *per* parliamentary session day in recent Parliaments than in their predecessors, reflecting a steady, long-term increase in parliamentary time *per* government-sponsored statute.

To control for changes between Parliaments in the proportion of *calendar* days in which Parliament was in session, we wished to test this last result against one final statistic. Accordingly, we measured productivity in terms of output of government bills receiving royal assent against the total number of "calendar days" in a Parliament.

---

6   Measured in the table and chart by the statistic: Number of Days of Parliamentary Session/Royal Assent received (All Bills).

7   Measured in the table and chart by the statistic: Number of Days of Parliamentary Session/Royal Assent received (Government Bills).

Calendar days were computed for each Parliament by adding the number of days during which Parliament was in session to the number of days it was prorogued or dissolved.[8] As Table A2.3 suggests, the proportion of days in which Parliament was in session as against total calendar days have increased markedly from the Second World War to the present, again excepting the Clark government. Nevertheless, parliamentary productivity in promulgation of government bills has still diminished appreciably during this same period.

Table A2.3   Days of Parliamentary Sessions per Bill and Statutes[9]

Parliament	Number of Days of Parliamentary Session/Bill Introduced (All Bills)	Number of Days of Parliamentary Session/Royal Assent Received (All Bills)	Number of Days of Parliamentary Session/Bill Introduced (Government Bills)	Number of Days of Parliamentary Session/Royal Assent received (Gov't Bills)	Proportion of Days in Session to Sum of Days in Session and Days not In Session ("Calendar Days")	Calendar Days per Government Bill Receiving Royal Assent
37th	1.00	8.80	6.49	10.06	92	9.55
36th	1.19	8.90	7.35	9.94	90	9.87
35th	1.79	6.94	5.38	7.62	87	7.96
34th	2.14	6.91	7.08	8.29	91	7.58
33rd	2.61	5.54	4.79	5.89	93	5.95
32nd	1.85	6.45	6.29	8.12	92	6.98
31st	0.20	9.57	1.76	9.57	35	27.00
30th	1.21	6.78	5.17	8.24	89	7.60
29th	1.02	7.22	5.28	8.61	77	9.35
28th	1.36	6.02	5.78	7.44	92	6.55
27th	1.39	4.87	5.34	6.23	85	5.71
26th	1.50	4.31	6.06	7.04	80	5.36
25th	1.00	5.54	3.91	7.82	57	9.67
24th	1.62	2.79	3.72	3.92	57	4.85
23rd	1.79	2.71	3.26	3.70	53	5.15
22nd	2.47	3.16	4.17	4.34	65	4.85
21st	2.46	2.97	3.54	3.73	76	3.92
20th	1.67	2.04	2.49	2.67	51	4.03

8   Data compiled from Library of Parliament, "Table of Legislation Introduced and Passed by Session," available at www.parl.gc.ca/information/about/process/info/Parl-Bills.asp?lang=E and Library of Parliament, "Period Between Prorogations and Openings of Ensuant Parliaments," available at www.parl.gc.ca/information/about/process/info/Parliament.asp?lang=E&Hist=Y&param=PRO.

9   Data compiled from Library of Parliament, "Table of Legislation Introduced and Passed by Session," available at www.parl.gc.ca/information/about/process/info/Parl-

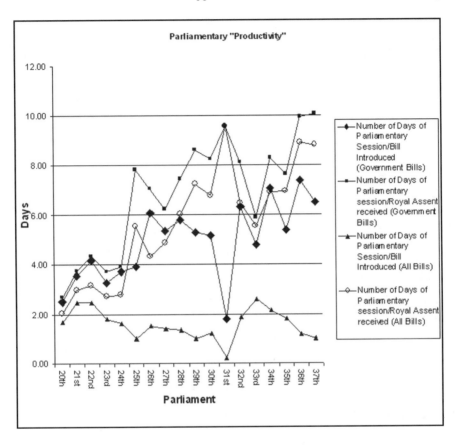

Bills.asp?lang=E and Library of Parliament, "Parliaments — Durations of Sessions," available at www.parl.gc.ca/information/about/process/info/Parliament.asp?lang= E&Hist=Y&param=D.

Glossary

Address of Parliament: a parliamentary resolution expressing the wish or request of Parliament.

Alternative vote: a voting system in which candidates are ranked by voters; if no single candidate wins 50 percent of the first choices, the candidate with the least number of votes is excluded and the preferences recalculated until a majority candidate emerges.

Auditor General: the officer of Parliament who serves as the auditor of the accounts of Canada.

Cabinet: the collective decision-making body of the ministry.

Cabinet confidence: a Cabinet document, as defined in the *Access to Information Act*, which is excluded from the application of that Act.

Cabinet solidarity: the convention requiring Cabinet ministers to support Cabinet decisions in public.

Caucus: a plenary of parliamentarians from the same party that meets, typically *in camera*, to discuss party issues.

Chief Electoral Officer (CEO): an officer of Parliament charged with overseeing the administration of federal elections.

Commissioner of Canada Elections: an independent official, appointed by the chief electoral officer, charged with receiving and investigating complaints about infringements of the *Canada Elections Act*.

Common law: the centuries-old, evolving body of judge-made precedent that governs a large part of legal relations in the Anglo-Saxon tradition and lies at the core of the law in nine of the ten provinces.

Confidence vote: a vote of the Commons triggering the convention that a ministry losing the confidence of the Commons must itself resign, or alternatively the prime minister must obtain a dissolution of Parliament, prompting new elections.

Constitution of Canada: the written Constitution includes three categories of instruments: 1) the *Canada Act 1982*, which contains the *Constitution Act, 1982* (which in turn includes the *Canadian Charter of Rights and Freedoms*); 2) thirty imperial or Canadian statutes and orders (such as the *Constitution Act, 1867*) set out by schedule to the *Constitution Act, 1982*; and 3) amendments to any of these instruments (of which there are presently eight).

Constitutional conventions: constitutionalized practices based on precedents established by the political institutions of government themselves, not court jurisprudence, and which are not enforced by the courts.

Constitutional "principle": when used with reference to unwritten constitutional norms, constitutional concepts that are, in the words of the Supreme Court of Canada, "invested with a powerful normative force, and are binding upon both courts and governments."

Consultant lobbyist: a lobbyist hired by a company or other type of client.

Contingency fee (lobbyist): an arrangement in which a payment to a lobbyist is in whole or in part contingent on the individual's degree of success in influencing a government decision.

Contribution: political donations used for a candidate or party electoral campaign; may also include the commercial value of a service, other than volunteer labour, or of property or of the use of property or money to the extent that they are provided without charge or at less than their commercial value.

Dissolution: the dissolving of Parliament for the purposes of an election.

Division of powers: the constitutional partition of legislative powers between the federal and provincial levels of government.

"During pleasure" appointments: appointees who, in theory, may be replaced or removed at the discretion of the appointing body.

Election advertising: the transmission to the public by any means during an election period of an advertising message that promotes or opposes a registered party or the election of a candidate, including one that takes a position on an issue with which a registered party or candidate is associated; the definition excludes groups communicating with their members, employees or shareholders (through newsletters, for example), publications of books that would have been published regardless of the election call, transmission to the public of an editorial, a debate, a speech, an interview, a column, a letter, a commentary or news item, and generally, transmissions made over the Internet.

Election expense: costs incurred and nonmonetary contributions received by a registered party or candidate and used to directly promote or oppose a registered party, its leader or a candidate during an election period.

Electoral district: a place or territorial area that is represented by a member in the House of Commons; also widely referred to as a "riding."

Electoral district association: an association of members of a political party in an electoral district; the local organizational unit of the party that operates at the riding level.

Ethics Commissioner: the officer of Parliament who advises public office holders on the application of ethical rules, oversees the Public Office Holders Code, and also has responsibilities under the *Conflict of Interest Code for Members of the House of Commons.*

"Good behaviour" appointments: appointees who may only be removed "for cause" by the appointing authority.

Governor-in-Council (GIC): the Governor General acting on the advice of Cabinet.

Information Commissioner: the officer of Parliament who receives complaints concerning government responses to *Access to Information Act* requests and who reports regularly to Parliament on government performance under the Act.

In-house lobbyist: a lobbyist who is an employee of a corporation or organization.

Judicial independence: the constitutional rule that the judiciary is to be insulated from manipulation and the perception of manipulation from the other branches of government.

Lobbyists registrar: a public official who oversees the *Lobbyists Registration Act* and the Lobbyists' Code of Conduct.

Minister of state: a junior minister, appointed to assist a minister under the *Ministries and Ministers of State Act.*

Ministerial responsibility: the doctrine that ministers are accountable to Parliament for the actions of their departments.

Ministry: a body comprising the ministers and the prime minister of a given government.

Motion: a question put to a House of Parliament by the Speaker, in response to a proposition made by a parliamentarian.

Officers of Parliament: positions created by statute for the purpose of providing Parliament with information, advice and other services needed in holding governments accountable. The existing officers are: the Chief Electoral Officer, the Auditor General, the Information Commissioner, the Privacy Commissioner, the Official Languages Commissioner, the Ethics Commissioner and the Senate Ethics Officer.

Order-in-Council: a statutory instrument by which the Governor General, acting on the advice of the Queen's Privy Council for Canada (in practice, Cabinet), expresses decisions.

Parliament of Canada: the federal legislative branch that, by the terms of the *Constitution Act, 1867,* consists "of the Queen, an Upper House styled the Senate, and the House of Commons."

Parliamentary law: the rules determining parliamentary procedure, flowing from an array of sources: the Constitution, assorted statutes such as the *Parliament of Canada Act,* the Standing Orders, and assorted usages, customs and precedents, as assessed by the Speaker.

Parliamentary privileges: the immunities and privileges extended by unwritten constitutional law to parliamentarians to better enable them to carry out their functions.

Parliamentary secretaries: Members of Parliament appointed by the prime minister from the backbenches of the governing party to assist Cabinet ministers in their parliamentary activities.

Parliamentary supremacy: a doctrine that, in its pure form, means that Parliament is the source of all governing power.

Personal expense: costs reasonably incurred in relation to an electoral campaign, including such items as travel and living expenses and childcare expenses, among other things.

Political party: an organization in which a fundamental purpose is to participate in public affairs by endorsing one or more of its members as candidates and supporting their election.

Privacy Commissioner: the officer of Parliament who receives complaints concerning government responses to *Privacy Act* requests and performance and who reports regularly to Parliament on government performance under the Act.

Private bills: a law project introduced into Parliament by means of petition from an interested, private party.

Private member's bill: a public bill introduced in Parliament by an individual legislator, usually acting without the backing of the ministry.

Privy Council Office (PCO): the central government agency that serves as the prime minister's public service branch and the secretariat to the Cabinet and its committees, under the guidance of the Clerk of the Privy Council.

Procedural fairness: a common law administrative law doctrine that requires a person exercising statutory (or potentially royal prerogative) power to give some form of notice of a pending decision to a person owed the fairness; an opportunity for that person to comment; and the requirement that the official making the decision be sufficiently unbiased.

Proportional representation (PR): a voting system that allots the number of seats per party according to the proportion of the popular vote received by that party.

Prorogation: the recessing of Parliament between sessions within a given Parliament.

Public bills: law projects that relate to matters of general public policy and are introduced by either the government (government bills) or private members (private members' bills).

Queen's Privy Council for Canada: a body named in the *Constitution Act, 1867* to "aid and advise in the Government of Canada" whose powers are, in practice, exercised by Cabinet.

Recall: a means for citizens to remove their representatives midterm by way of a petitioning process.

Referendum: a method of referring a question or set of questions to the people directly, rather than allowing them to be settled by the people's representatives in the legislature; the term is often used interchangeably with "plebiscite," although as a technical matter, the latter is nonbinding, whereas "referendum" is a binding process.

Regulation: a particular subspecies of statutory instrument, defined as a statutory instrument made in the exercise of a legislative power conferred by an Act of Parliament, or for the contravention of which a penalty, fine or imprisonment is prescribed by an Act of Parliament.

Reserve powers: powers that the Governor General exercises independently of any request from the prime minister or Cabinet.

Responsible government: the means by which the executive is held accountable to the legislature and usually associated with the notion that those who run the executive must sit also in Parliament.

Returning officer: a person appointed to administer a federal election at the electoral-district level.

Royal assent: the final stage in the enactment of a law in which the monarch or the Governor General authorizes a bill to become a statute.

Royal consent: the requirement that permission be obtained, usually from a minister, prior to the passage of bills impinging on the Crown's royal prerogatives, hereditary revenues or personal property or interests.

Royal prerogative: the residue of royal power once exercised directly by the Crown, and now, by constitutional convention, exercised either directly by Cabinet or the prime minister, or by the Crown at the behest of the prime minister or Cabinet.

Royal recommendation: a procedure involving the Governor General that precedes the appropriation of any part of the public revenue or the imposition of any tax.

Senate Ethics Officer: an appointed officer of Parliament who administers the senate ethics code.

Separation of powers: the partition of legal powers between branches of government, most often categorized as the legislature, the executive and the judiciary.

Single transferable vote (STV): a voting system in which voters rank the various candidates on the ballot in multimember constituencies; at the counting of the first-choice votes, once a candidate receives a winning threshold of votes, the remaining voters who ranked his or her as their first choice will have their votes transferred to their second choice until another candidate reaches the winning threshold, a step that may be repeated until the required number of candidates is elected.

Speaker: the central presiding officer in a House of Parliament, interpreting rules of order and conduct.

Standard of review: a measure of the amount of deference that a court will extend on judicial review to an administrative decision-maker.

Standing Committees: committees of parliamentarians that are, in the case of the Commons, empowered to study and report on all matters relating to the mandate, management and operation of the department or departments of government that are assigned to them from time to time by the Commons.

Standing Orders: the procedural orders governing proceedings in the Commons or the senate, as the case may be.

Statutory instrument: generally any instrument made or established in the execution of a power conferred by an Act of Parliament or by the authority of the Governor-in-Council.

***Sub judice* convention:** the practice that in parliamentary discussions, parliamentarians are generally not to refer to matters before the courts or a judicial inquiry.

Third-party spending: election advertising expense by a group other than a party, candidate or electoral district association.

Treasury Board: a legislatively prescribed Cabinet committee with a bureaucratic secretariat whose chief responsibilities are reviewing government spending and overseeing government personnel management.

Whip: the parliamentarian charged with rallying his or her party members, and insuring their presence at a vote.

Writ: a legal order.

Table of Cases

3430901 Canada Inc. v. Canada (Minister of Industry) (2001), 2001
    FCA 254, [2002] 1 F.C. 421, [2001] F.C.J. No. 1327......492, 497, 523, 524, 525

Addy v. R., [1985] 2 F.C. 452, 22 D.L.R. (4th) 52, 8 C.C.E.L. 13 (T.D.)................294
Ainsworth Lumber Co. v. Canada (Attorney General), 2003 BCCA 239,
    226 D.L.R. (4th) 93, [2003] B.C.J. No. 901 ....70, 71
Air Canada v. Canada (Attorney General), [2003] R.J.Q. 322, 222 D.L.R.
    (4th) 385, [2003] J.Q. no 21 (C.A.), leave to appeal allowed, [2003]
    2 S.C.R. x, [2003] C.S.C.R. no 111..368
Alvarez-Machain v. United States, 331 F.3d 604 (9th Cir. 2003).........................485
Angus v. Canada, [1990] 3 F.C. 410, 72 D.L.R. (4th) 672, [1990] F.C.J.
    No. 610 (C.A.) 34, 203
Aristocrat Restaurants Ltd. (c.o.b. Tony's East) v. Ontario, [2003] O.J.
    No. 5331 (S.C.J.) 386
Attorney General of Canada v. Inuit Tapirisat of Canada, [1980] 2 S.C.R. 735,
    115 D.L.R. (3d) 1, 33 N.R. 304..348
Attorney General of Quebec v. Blaikie, [1981] 1 S.C.R. 312, 123 D.L.R.
    (3d) 15, 36 N.R. 120..21
Authorson v. Canada (Attorney General), 2003 SCC 39, [2003] 2 S.C.R. 40,
    [2003] S.C.J. No. 40 ....73, 327

B.(R.) v. Children's Aid Society of Metropolitan Toronto, [1995] 1 S.C.R. 315,
    153 C.C.C. (3d) 284, [1994] S.C.J. No. 24 528

Babcock v. Canada (Attorney General), 2002 SCC 57, [2002] 3 S.C.R. 3,
    [2002] S.C.J. No. 58 ....18, 20, 22, 23, 326, 346, 510, 511–12, 593
Bacon v. Saskatchewan Crop Insurance Corp., [1999] 11 W.W.R. 51,
    180 Sask. R. 20, [1999] S.J. No. 302 (C.A.) 326
Baker v. Canada, [1999] 2 S.C.R. 817, 174 D.L.R. (4th) 193, [1999]
    S.C.J. No. 39 ....522, 523, 605
Beaumier v. Brampton (City), [1998] O.J. No. 1303, 59 O.T.C. 157,
    46 M.P.L.R. (2d) 32 (S.C.J.), aff'd [1999] O.J. No. 4407 (C.A.) 119
Beauregard v. Canada, [1986] 2 S.C.R. 56, 30 D.L.R. (4th) 481,
    [1986] S.C.J. No. 50..62, 65
Bell Canada v. Canadian Telephone Employees Association, 2001 FCA 161,
    [2001] 3 F.C. 481, [2001] F.C.J. No. 776, aff'd 2003 SCC 36, [2003]
    1 S.C.R. 884, [2003] S.C.J. No. 36..238
Bell Canada v. Communications, Energy and Paperworkers Union of
    Canada, 2003 SCC 36, [2003] 1 S.C.R. 884, [2003] S.C.J. No. 36 ......204, 368
Beno v. Canada (Attorney General), 2002 FCT 142, [2002] 3 F.C. 499,
    [2002] F.C.J. No. 192 (T.D.) 366
Beno v. Canada (Commission of Inquiry into the Deployment of Canadian
    Forces in Somalia — Létourneau Commission), [1997] 2 F.C. 527,
    146 D.L.R. (4th) 708, [1997] F.C.J. No. 509 (C.A.).......................................366
Black v. Canada (Prime Minister), 54 O.R. (3d) 215, 199 D.L.R. (4th) 228,
    [2001] O.J. No. 1853 (C.A.) 10, 29, 30, 57, 443
Blanchard v. Control Data Canada Ltd., [1984] 2 S.C.R. 476, 14 D.L.R.
    (4th) 289, 55 N.R. 194 593
Blencoe v. British Columbia (Human Rights Commission), 2000 SCC 44,
    [2000] 2 S.C.R. 307, [2000] S.C.J. No. 43 ....367, 528
Bowman v. United Kingdom (1998), 26 E.H.R.R. 1 (E.Ct.H.R.) 102
Boyle v. Canada (Commission of Inquiry into the Deployment of Canadian
    Forces to Somalia), [1997] F.C.J. No. 942, 131 F.T.R. 135 (T.D.) 366
British Columbia Native Women's Society v. Canada (1999), [2000]
    1 F.C. 304, [1999] F.C.J. No. 1296, [2000] 3 C.N.L.R. 4 (T.D.) 25, 582
Brown v. Alberta, 1999 ABCA 256, 244 A.R. 86, 177 D.L.R. (4th) 349 ....18, 185
Buckley et al. v. Valeo, 424 U.S. 1 (1976) 101

Cameron v. Boyle, [1994] O.J. No. 782 (Gen. Div.) 95, 206
Campbell v. Canada (Attorney General), 49 D.L.R. (4th) 321, [1988]
    4 W.W.R. 441, [1988] B.C.J. No. 442 (C.A.) 83, 84
Canada (Attorney General) v. Canada (Commissioner of the Inquiry on the
    Blood System), [1996] 3 F.C. 259, [1996] F.C.J. No. 864, 115 F.T.R. 81
    (T.D.), aff'd [1997] 2 F.C. 36, 142 D.L.R. (4th) 237, [1997] F.C.J. No. 17
    (C.A.), aff'd [1997] 3 S.C.R. 440, 151 D.L.R. (4th) 1, [1997]
    S.C.J. No. 83 ....363, 365, 366, 367, 368
Canada (Attorney General) v. Canada (Information Commissioner), [1996]
    F.C.J. No. 1204, 119 F.T.R. 77 (T.D.) 494

Canada (Attorney General) v. Canada (Information Commissioner),
2004 FC 431, [2004] 4 F.C.R. 181, [2004] F.C.J. No. 524 484

Canada (Attorney General) v. Canada (Information Commissioner),
2002 FCT 128, [2002] 3 F.C. 630, [2002] F.C.J. No. 225 492

Canada (Attorney General) v. Canada (Information Commissioner),
2002 FCT 129, [2002] 3 F.C. 606, [2002] F.C.J. No. 224 558

Canada (Attorney General) v. National Anti-Poverty Organization, [1989]
3 F.C. 684, 60 D.L.R. (4th) 712, [1989] F.C.J. No. 433 (C.A.) 346

Canada (Attorney General) v. Prince Edward Island (Legislative Assembly),
2003 PESCTD 6, 221 Nfld. & P.E.I.R. 164, 46 Admin. L.R. (3d) 171 ......70, 400

Canada (Attorney General) v. Public Service Alliance of Canada, [1993]
1 S.C.R. 941, 101 D.L.R. (4th) 673, [1993] S.C.J. No. 35 59

Canada (Auditor General) v. Canada (Minister of Energy, Mines &
Resources), [1989] 2 S.C.R. 49, 61 D.L.R. (4th) 604, [1989]
S.C.J. No. 80...37, 71, 408

Canada (Director of Investigation and Research) v. Southam Inc., [1997]
1 S.C.R. 748, 144 D.L.R. (4th) 1, [1996] S.C.J. No. 116 59

Canada (House of Commons) v. Vaid (2002), 2002 FCA 473, [2003]
1 F.C. 602, [2002] F.C.J. No. 1663, leave to appeal to S.C.C. granted,
[2003] 2 S.C.R. vii, [2003] S.C.C.A. No. 24 ....57, 69, 71, 73

Canada (Human Rights Commission) v. Canadian Liberty Net, [1998]
1 S.C.R. 626, 157 D.L.R. (4th) 385, [1998] S.C.J. No. 31 ....57, 257, 443

Canada (Information Commissioner of Canada) v. Canada (Minister of
National Defence), 240 N.R. 244, [1999] F.C.J. No. 522 (C.A.) 494

Canada (Information Commissioner) v. Canada (Commissioner of
the RCMP), 2003 SCC 8, [2003] 1 S.C.R. 66, [2003]
S.C.J. No. 7..484, 491, 498, 513, 525

Canada (Information Commissioner) v. Canada (Immigration and
Refugee Board), [1997] F.C.J. No. 1812, 140 F.T.R. 140,
4 Admin. L.R. (3d) 96 (T.D.) 499, 515

Canada (Information Commissioner) v. Canada (Prime Minister) (1992),
[1993] 1 F.C. 427, [1992] F.C.J. No. 1054, 57 F.T.R. 180 (T.D.)......................491

Canada (Information Commissioner) v. Canada (Solicitor General),
[1988] 3 F.C. 551, [1988] F.C.J. No. 408, 20 F.T.R. 314 (T.D.) 513

Canada (Information Commissioner) v. Minister of External Affairs,
[1990] 3 F.C. 514, [1990] F.C.J. No. 721, 3 T.C.T. 5297 (T.D.) 494

Canada (Minister of Environment) v. Canada (Information Commissioner),
2003 FCA 68, [2003] F.C.J. No. 197, 2 Admin. L.R. (4th) 271..............508, 512

Canada (Privacy Commissioner) v. Canada (Labour Relations Board), [1996]
3 F.C. 609, [1996] F.C.J. No. 1076, 118 F.T.R. 1 (T.D.) 57, 512

Canada Packers Inc. v. Canada (Minister of Agriculture), [1989] 1 F.C. 47,
53 D.L.R. (4th) 246, [1988] F.C.J. No. 615 (C.A.) 498

Canada Post Corp. v. Canada (Minister of Public Works and Government
   Services), 2004 FC 1, [2004] F.C.J. No. 6, 244 F.T.R. 207 497
Canada Post Corp. v. Canada (Minister of Public Works), [1995] 2 F.C. 110,
   179 N.R. 350, [1995] F.C.J. No. 241 (C.A.) 492, 498
Canada v. St. Lawrence Cruise Lines Inc., [1997] 3 F.C. 899, 148 D.L.R.
   (4th) 480, [1997] F.C.J. No. 866 (C.A.) 346
Canadian Broadcasting Corp. v. Canada, [1995] 1 S.C.R. 157, 121 D.L.R.
   (4th) 385, [1995] S.C.J. No. 4 ....58, 522
Canadian Broadcasting Corp. v. New Brunswick (Attorney General), [1996]
   3 S.C.R. 480, 139 D.L.R. (4th) 385, [1996] S.C.J. No. 38 493
Canadian Imperial Bank of Commerce v. Rifou, [1986] 3 F.C. 486,
   72 N.R. 12, [1986] F.C.J. No. 454 (C.A.) 57
Cardinal v. Director of Kent Institution, [1985] 2 S.C.R. 643, 24 D.L.R.
   (4th) 44, [1985] S.C.J. No. 78...347
Carter v. Alberta, 2002 ABCA 303, 317 A.R. 299, 222 D.L.R. (4th) 40 ....70, 327
Cawley v. Branchflower, 1 B.C.R. (Pt. II) 35, [1884] B.C.J. No. 4 (S.C.) 81
Cemerlic v. Canada (Solicitor General), 2003 FCT 133, [2003] F.C.J. No. 191,
   228 F.T.R. 1...524
Committee for Justice and Liberty v. National Energy Board, [1978]
   1 S.C.R. 369, 68 D.L.R. (3d) 716, 9 N.R. 115 456
Community Before Cars Coalition v. National Capital Commission,
   [1997] F.C.J. No. 1060, 135 F.T.R. 1 (T.D.)..446, 448
Cooper v. Human Rights Commission (Canada), [1996] 3 S.C.R. 854,
   140 D.L.R. (4th) 193, [1996] S.C.J. No. 115 26–28
Crevier v. Quebec (Attorney General), [1981] 2 S.C.R. 220, 127 D.L.R.
   (3d) 1, 38 N.R. 541..27, 593
Criminal Lawyers' Assn. v. Ontario (Ministry of Public Safety and Security),
   70 O.R. (3d) 332, [2004] O.J. No. 1214, 184 O.A.C. 223 (Div. Ct.) 492
Cunha v. Minister of National Revenue, [1999] F.C.J. No. 667,
   164 F.T.R. 74, 99 D.T.C. 5432 (T.D.) 517
Cureatz v. Progressive Conservative Party of Canada, [1997] O.J. No. 2309,
   36 O.T.C. 127 (Gen. Div.) 95

Dagg v. Canada [1997] 2 S.C.R. 403, 148 D.L.R. (4th) 385, [1997]
   S.C.J. No. 63 ....484, 513, 521, 523, 524, 526
Deep v. Ontario, [2004] O.J. No. 2734, [2004] O.T.C. 541 (S.C.J.)........................386
Democracy Watch v. Canada (Attorney General) 2004 FC 969, [2004]
   4 F.C.R. 83, [2004] F.C.J. No. 1195 ....425, 435, 440, 443, 446, 473–74
Dixon v. British Columbia (Attorney General), 59 D.L.R. (4th) 247,
   [1989] 4 W.W.R. 393, [1989] B.C.J. No. 583 (S.C.)......................................77, 79
Dixon v. Canada, [1997] 3 F.C. 169, 149 D.L.R. (4th) 269, [1997]
   F.C.J. No. 985 (C.A.)...366, 369
Doucet-Boudreau v. Nova Scotia (Minister of Education), 2003 SCC 62,
   [2003] 3 S.C.R. 3, [2003] S.C.J. No. 63 20

Drummond v. Canada (Minister of Citizenship and Immigration), [1996]
   F.C.J. No. 477, 112 F.T.R. 33, 33 Imm. L.R. (2d) 258 (T.D.)............................447

Edwards v. Canada (Attorney General) (1929), [1930] A.C. 124, [1930]
   1 D.L.R. 98, [1929] 3 W.W.R. 479 (J.C.P.C.) 183
Ell v. Alberta, 2003 SCC 35, [2003] 1 S.C.R. 857,
   [2003] S.C.J. No. 35 ....62–63, 64, 65, 66, 289, 293, 294
Eurig Estate (Re), [1998] 2 S.C.R. 565, 40 O.R. (3d) 160, [1998] S.C.J. No. 72 25

Federal Election Commission v. National Right to Work Committee,
   459 U.S. 197 (1982) 110
Figueroa v. Canada (Attorney General), 2003 SCC 37, [2003] 1 S.C.R. 912,
   [2003] S.C.J. No. 37......32, 34, 35, 75, 76, 77, 78, 89–91, 93, 148, 166, 203, 213
Fitzgerald (Next friend of) v. Alberta, 2002 ABQB 1086, 331 A.R. 111,
   104 C.R.R. (2d) 170, aff'd 2004 ABCA 184, 348 A.R. 113,
   27 Alta. L.R. (4th) 205, leave to appeal to S.C.C. refused (2005),
   [2004] S.C.C.A. 349 81
Fraser v. Canada (Public Service Staff Relations Board), [1985] 2 S.C.R. 455,
   23 D.L.R. (4th) 122, [1985] S.C.J. No. 71 ....13, 21, 226
Friends of Democracy v. Northwest Territories (Attorney General),
   171 D.L.R. (4th) 551, [1999] N.W.T.J. No. 28 (S.C.) 79
Friends of Oldman River Society v. Canada, [1992] 1 S.C.R. 3, 88 D.L.R.
   (4th) 1, [1992] S.C.J. No. 1 593
Friesen v. Hammell, 1999 BCCA 23, 57 B.C.L.R. (3d) 276, [1999]
   B.C.J. No. 76 69

Gao et al. v. Canada (Minister of Citizenship and Immigration), [2000]
   O.J. No. 2784, [2000] O.T.C. 581, 7 Imm. L.R. (3d) 21 (S.C.J.).....................56
Gernhart v. Canada, [2000] 2 F.C. 292, 181 D.L.R. (4th) 506, [1999]
   F.C.J. No. 1669 (C.A.) 528
Gilles E. Neron Communication Marketing Inc. v. Chambre des notaires
   du Quebec, 2004 SCC 53, [2004] 3 S.C.R. 95, [2004] S.C.J. No. 50............368
Global Television v. CEP, 2004 FCA 78, 318 N.R. 275, [2004] F.C.J. No. 359 57
Gratton v. Canadian Judicial Council, [1994] 2 F.C. 769, [1994]
   F.C.J. No. 710, 78 F.T.R. 214 (T.D.) 250, 293, 294
Groenewegen v. Northwest Territories (Legislative Assembly), [1998]
   N.W.T.J. No. 129, 12 Admin. L.R. (3d) 280, 23 C.P.C. (4th) 314 (S.C.) 69

H.J. Heinz Co. of Canada Ltd. v. Canada (Attorney General), 2003 FCT 250,
   [2003] 4 F.C. 3, [2003] F.C.J. No. 344, aff'd [2004] F.C.J. No. 773
   (C.A.) 523
Haig v. Canada, [1993] 2 S.C.R. 995, 105 D.L.R. (4th) 577, [1993]
   S.C.J. No. 84 ....77, 81

Halpern v. Canada, 60 O.R. (3d) 321, 215 D.L.R. (4th) 223, [2002] O.J.
No. 2714 (Div. Ct.)...17
Harper v. Canada (Attorney General), 2004 SCC 33, [2004] 1 S.C.R. 827,
[2004] S.C.J. No. 28 ....77, 78, 80, 125–26, 127, 129
Harvey v. New Brunswick (Attorney General), [1996] 2 S.C.R. 876,
137 D.L.R. (4th) 142, [1996] S.C.J. No. 82 ....20, 69, 70, 72–73, 77, 80, 136
Haydon v. Canada (2000), [2001] 2 F.C. 82, [2000] F.C.J. No. 1368,
192 F.T.R. 161 (T.D.) 226–27
Haydon v. Canada (Treasury Board), 2004 FC 749, [2004] F.C.J. No. 932,
253 F.T.R. 230..225, 227–28
Hewat v. Ontario, 37 O.R. (3d) 161, 156 D.L.R. (4th) 193, [1998] O.J.
No. 802 (C.A.) 240–41
Hien Do-Ky Vietnamese Refugee Sponsorship Committee v. Canada,
[1997] 2 F.C. 907, 143 D.L.R. (4th) 746, [1997] F.C.J. No. 145 (T.D.)............521
Hill v. Church of Scientology of Toronto, [1995] 2 S.C.R. 1130, 24 O.R.
(3d) 865, [1995] S.C.J. No. 64 368
Hogan v. Newfoundland (Attorney General), 162 Nfld. & P.E.I.R. 132,
156 D.L.R. (4th) 139, [1998] N.J. No. 7 (S.C.), aff'd 2000 NFCA 12,
189 Nfld. & P.E.I.R. 183, 163 D.L.R. (4th) 672 ....33, 331
Hoogers v. Canada, [1998] F.C.J. No. 834, 10 Admin. L.R. (3d) 232,
83 C.P.R. (3d) 380 (T.D.)..521
House of Commons v. Vaid (2002), 2002 FCA 473, [2003] 1 F.C. 602,
[2002] F.C.J. No. 1663, leave to appeal to S.C.C. allowed, [2003]
2 S.C.R. vii, [2003] S.C.C.A. No. 24...200
Hunter v. Southam Inc., [1984] 2 S.C.R. 145, 11 D.L.R. (4th) 641,
55 N.R. 241 528

In Re M. (A.P.) (1993), 154 N.R. 358 (H.L.) 31
In the Matter of a Reference by the Governor in Council concerning the
Proposal for an Act respecting certain aspects of legal capacity for
marriage for civil purposes, as set out in Order in Council P.C.
2003-1055, 2004 SCC 79, 246 D.L.R. (4th) 193, [2004] S.C.J. No. 75 52

José Pereira E. Hijos S. A. v. Canada (Attorney General) (1996), [1997]
2 F.C. 84, [1996] F.C.J. No. 1669, 126 F.T.R. 167 (T.D.) 485

Keable v. Canada (Attorney-General), [1979] 1 S.C.R. 218, 90 D.L.R.
(3d) 161, 24 N.R. 1..548
Kelly v. Canada (Solicitor General), [1992] F.C.J. No. 302, 53 F.T.R. 147,
6 Admin. L.R. (2d) 54 (T.D.), aff'd 154 N.R. 319, [1993]
F.C.J. No. 475, 13 Admin. L.R. (2d) 304 (C.A) 523, 524
Kelly v. O'Brien, [1943] 1 D.L.R. 725 (Ont. C.A.) 415
Kennedy v. Mendoza-Martinez, 372 U.S. 144 (1963) 582

Knight v. Indian Head School Division No. 19, [1990] 1 S.C.R. 653,
  69 D.L.R. (4th) 489, [1990] S.C.J. No. 26 239
Krieger v. Law Society of Alberta, 2002 SCC 65, [2002] 3 S.C.R. 372,
  [2002] S.C.J. No. 45 28

Laidlaw et al. v. Canada (Attorney General), [1999] F.C.J. No. 566,
  166 F.T.R. 217(T.D.) 219
Lakeside Colony of Hutterian Brethren v. Hofer, [1992] 3 S.C.R. 165,
  97 D.L.R. (4th) 17, [1992] S.C.J. No. 87.......................................206
Lavigne v. Canada (Office of the Commissioner of Official Languages),
  2002 SCC 53, [2002] 2 S.C.R. 773,
  [2002] S.C.J. No. 55 ....499, 512, 513, 515, 526, 527, 528, 529
LGS Group Inc. v. Canada (Attorney General), [1995] 3 F.C. 474,
  [1995] F.C.J. No. 1128, 34 Admin. L.R. (2d) 208 (T.D.)..............................447
Libman v. Quebec (Attorney General), [1997] 3 S.C.R. 569,
  151 D.L.R. (4th) 385, [1997] S.C.J. No. 85.....................................78, 162

M.(A.) v. Ryan, [1997] 1 S.C.R. 157, 143 D.L.R. (4th) 1, [1997] S.C.J. No. 13 529
MacKeigan v. Hickman, [1989] 2 S.C.R. 796, 61 D.L.R. (4th) 688,
  [1989] S.C.J. No. 99...65
Mackin v. New Brunswick (Minister of Finance), 2002 SCC 13, [2002]
  1 S.C.R. 405, [2002] S.C.J. No. 13..62, 64–65, 66, 291
MacMillan Bloedel Ltd. v. Simpson, [1995] 4 S.C.R. 725, 130 D.L.R.
  (4th) 385, [1995] S.C.J. No. 101 26
Maislin Industries Limited v. Canada (Minister for Industry, Trade and
  Commerce), [1984] 1 F.C. 939, 10 D.L.R. (4th) 417, 8 Admin. L.R. 305
  (T.D.) 491
Manitoba Language Reference, [1985] 1 S.C.R. 721, 19 D.L.R. (4th) 1,
  [1985] S.C.J. No. 36 13
Maranda v. Richer, 2003 SCC 67, [2003] 3 S.C.R. 193, [2003] S.C.J. No. 69 471
Martin v. Ontario, [2004] O.J. No. 2247 (S.C.J.).....................................70, 327, 384
McConnell v. Federal Election Commission, 540 U.S. 93 (2003) 102, 128
McKinney v. Liberal Party of Canada, 61 O.R. (2d) 680, 43 D.L.R.
  (4th) 706, [1987] O.J. No. 1293 (H.C.J.) 324
Mercier-Neron v. Canada (Minister of National Health and Welfare), [1995]
  F.C.J. No. 1024, 98 F.T.R. 36 (T.D.) 347
Moreau-Berube v. New Brunswick (Judicial Council), 2002 SCC 11, [2002]
  1 S.C.R. 249, [2002] S.C.J. No. 9...60
Morin v. Northwest Territories (Conflict of Interest Commissioner), [1999]
  N.W.T.J. No. 5, 14 Admin. L.R. (3d) 284, 29 C.P.C. (4th) 362 (S.C.)..............69
Morneault v. Canada (Attorney General) (2000), [2001] 1 F.C. 30,
  189 D.L.R. (4th) 96, [2000] F.C.J. No. 705 (C.A.) 366

National Corn Growers Assn. v. Canada, [1990] 2 S.C.R. 1324,
   74 D.L.R. (4th) 449, [1990] S.C.J. No. 110 ....54, 59
National Harbours Board v. Langelier (1968), [1969] S.C.R. 60,
   2 D.L.R. (3d) 81 386
National Party of Canada v. Canadian Broadcasting Corp., 144 A.R. 50,
   106 D.L.R. (4th) 568, [1993] A.J. No. 677 (Q.B.) 141
Natural Law Party of Canada v. Canadian Broadcasting Corp. (1993), [1994]
   1 F.C. 580, [1993] F.C.J. No. 992, 77 F.T.R. 73 (T.D.)..............................141
New Brunswick Broadcasting v. Nova Scotia (Speaker of the House of
   Assembly), [1993] 1 S.C.R. 319, 100 D.L.R. (4th) 212, [1993]
   S.C.J. No. 2, rev'g 102 N.S.R. (2d) 271, 80 D.L.R. (4th) 11,
   [1991] N.S.J. No. 124 (S.C.A.D.) 13, 21, 22, 67, 68, 69, 71, 72, 303, 403–4
Newfoundland (Treasury Board) v. N.A.P.E., 2004 SCC 66,
   244 D.L.R. (4th) 294, [2004] S.C.J. No. 61 582
NLRB v. Robbins Tire and Rubber Company, 437 U.S. 214 (1978)....................482
Nova Scotia (Worker's Compensation Board) v. Martin, 2003 SCC 54,
   [2003] 2 S.C.R. 504, [2003] S.C.J. No. 54..28

O'Donohue v. The Queen, [2003] O.J. No. 2764, [2003] O.T.C. 623,
   109 C.R.R. (2d) 1 (S.C.J) 169, 170
Ocean Port Hotel Ltd. v. British Columbia (Liquor Control and Licensing
   Branch), 2001 SCC 52, [2001] 2 S.C.R. 781, [2001] S.C.J. No. 17 ....240, 367
Odhavji Estate v. Woodhouse, 2003 SCC 69, [2003] 3 S.C.R. 263, [2003]
   S.C.J. No. 74 416–17
Old St. Boniface Residents Association Inc. v. Winnipeg (City), [1990]
   3 S.C.R. 1170, 75 D.L.R. (4th) 385, [1990] S.C.J. No. 137 446
Ontario (Attorney General) v. Fineberg, 19 O.R. (3d) 197, 116 D.L.R.
   (4th) 498, [1994] O.J. No. 1419 (Div. Ct.) 492
Ontario (Speaker of the Legislative Assembly) v. Casselman, [1996]
   O.J. No. 5343 (Gen. Div.) 69
Ontario (Speaker of the Legislative Assembly) v. Ontario Human Rights
   Commission, 54 O.R. (3d) 595, 201 D.L.R. (4th) 698, [2001]
   O.J. No. 2180 (C.A.) 70, 327
Ontario Catholic Teachers' Assn. v. Ontario (Attorney General),
   2001 SCC 15, [2001] 1 S.C.R. 470, [2001] S.C.J. No. 14 ....25, 32
Ontario Hydro v. Ontario (Labour Relations Board), [1993] 3 S.C.R. 327,
   107 D.L.R. (4th) 457, [1993] S.C.J. No. 99 33
Ontario v. Mar-Dive Corp., 141 D.L.R. (4th) 577, [1996] O.J. No. 4471,
   20 O.T.C. 81 (Gen. Div.) 29, 30
OPSEU v. Ontario (Attorney General), [1987] 2 S.C.R. 2, 41 D.L.R. (4th) 1,
   [1987] S.C.J. No. 48 33
Osborne v. Canada (Treasury Board), [1991] 2 S.C.R. 69, 82 D.L.R.
   (4th) 321, [1991] S.C.J. No. 45 ....33, 222, 223

P.(N.I.) v. B.(R.), 2000 BCSC 1563, 193 D.L.R. (4th) 752,
[2000] B.C.J. No. 2254 31
P.E.I. Potato Marketing Board v. H.B. Willis Inc., [1952] 2 S.C.R. 392,
[1952] 4 D.L.R. 146 25
P.H.L.F. Family Holdings Ltd. v. Canada, [1994] T.C.J. No. 445, [1994]
G.S.T.C. 41, 2 G.T.C. 1039 ....73, 327
Peet v. Canada, [1994] 3 F.C. 128, [1994] F.C.J. No. 559, 78 F.T.R. 44 (T.D.)......449
Pezim v. British Columbia (Superintendent of Brokers), [1994] 2 S.C.R. 557,
114 D.L.R. (4th) 385, [1994] S.C.J. No. 58..59
Phillips v. Nova Scotia (Commission of Inquiry into the Westray Mine
Tragedy), [1995] 2 S.C.R. 97, 124 D.L.R. (4th) 129, [1995] S.C.J. No. 36 363
Pickin v. British Railways Board, [1974] A.C. 765 (H.L.)............................71, 73, 327
Potter v. Halifax Regional School Board, 2002 NSCA 88, 215 D.L.R.
(4th) 441, [2002] N.S.J. No. 297 348
PSAC v. Canada, [2000] F.C.J. No. 754, 192 F.T.R. 23 (T.D.)...............................326
Pushpanathan v. Canada, [1998] 1 S.C.R. 982, 160 D.L.R. (4th) 193,
[1998] S.C.J. No. 46 522

Quebec (Attorney General) v. Blaikie, [1981] 1 S.C.R. 312, 123 D.L.R. (3d) 15,
36 N.R. 120 ....203, 347
Quebec (Attorney General) v. Collier, [1990] 1 S.C.R. 260, 66 D.L.R.
(4th) 575, [1990] S.C.J. No. 13 326

R. v. B.(S.A.), 2003 SCC 60, [2003] 2 S.C.R. 678, [2003] S.C.J. No. 61 528
R. v. Berntson, 2001 SCC 9, [2001] 1 S.C.R. 365, [2001] S.C.J. No. 10 188
R. v. Big M Drug Mart, [1985] 1 S.C.R. 295, 18 D.L.R. (4th) 321, [1985]
S.C.J. No. 17 44
R. v. Bryan, 2003 BCSC 1499, 233 D.L.R. (4th) 745, [2003] B.C.J. No. 2479,
leave to appeal granted, 2004 BCCA 140, 236 D.L.R. (4th) 340,
[2004] B.C.J. No. 451..133–34
R. v. Cogger, [1997] 2 S.C.R. 845, 148 D.L.R. (4th) 649, [1997]
S.C.J. No. 73..414–15
R. v. Cogger, [2001] J.Q. no 2262 (C.A.) 188, 414
R. v. Dyment, [1988] 2 S.C.R. 417, 55 D.L.R. (4th) 503, [1988] S.C.J. No. 82 526
R. v. Heywood, [1994] 3 S.C.R. 761, 120 D.L.R. (4th) 348, [1994]
S.C.J. No. 101 582
R. v. Hinchey, [1996] 3 S.C.R. 1128, 142 D.L.R. (4th) 50, [1996]
S.C.J. No. 121 448
R. v. McClure, 2001 SCC 14, [2001] 1 S.C.R. 445, [2001] S.C.J. No. 13 471
R. v. Mills, [1999] 3 S.C.R. 668, 180 D.L.R. (4th) 1, [1999] S.C.J. No. 68 ....45, 528
R. v. Morgentaler, [1988] 1 S.C.R. 30, 44 D.L.R. (4th) 385, [1988] S.C.J. No. 1 528
R. v. O'Connor, [1995] 4 S.C.R. 411, 130 D.L.R. (4th) 235, [1995]
S.C.J. No. 98..527, 529
R. v. Oakes, [1986] 1 S.C.R. 103, 26 D.L.R. (4th) 200, [1986] S.C.J. No. 7 ......15, 48

R. v. Osolin, [1993] 4 S.C.R. 595, 109 D.L.R. (4th) 478, [1993] S.C.J. No. 135 527
R. v. Ratkai, [1989] N.J. No. 334 (S.C.) 544
R. v. Toronto Sun Publishing Limited, (1979) 24 O.R. (2d) 621,
    98 D.L.R. (3d) 524, 47 C.C.C. (2d) 535 (Prov. Ct.) 544, 545, 548
Raîche v. Canada (Attorney General), 2004 FC 679, [2004] F.C.J. No. 839,
    252 F.T.R. 221 85
Ramsden v. Peterborough (City), [1993] 2 S.C.R. 1084, 15 O.R. (3d) 548,
    [1993] S.C.J.No. 87 119
Re Application under s. 83.28 of the Criminal Code, 2004 SCC 42, [2004]
    2 S.C.R. 248, [2004] S.C.J. No. 40 ....63, 64, 364, 367, 403, 584
Re Authority of Parliament in Relation to the Upper House (1979),
    [1980] 1 S.C.R. 54, 102 D.L.R. (3d) 1, 30 N.R. 271................................179, 196
Re Gray (1918), 57 S.C.R. 150, 42 D.L.R. 1, [1918] 3 W.W.R. 111 581
Re Gray, 57 S.C.R. 150, 42 D.L.R. 1, [1918] 3 W.W.R. 111.......................................25
Re Lincoln Election, 2 O.A.R. 316, [1876] O.J. No. 8 (C.A.) 81
Re Manitoba Language Rights, [1985] 1 S.C.R. 721, 19 D.L.R. (4th) 1,
    [1985] S.C.J. No. 36 326
Re Ouellet, [1976] C.S. 503, 67 D.L.R. (3d) 73, 28 C.C.C. (2d) 338, aff'd
    [1976] C.A. 788, 72 D.L.R. (3d) 95, 32 C.C.C. (2d) 149 69
Re Remuneration of Judges, [1997] 3 S.C.R. 3, 150 D.L.R. (4th) 577, [1997]
    S.C.J. No. 75 ....12, 13, 18, 19, 23, 24, 56, 63, 64, 65, 67, 289, 290, 303, 346
Re Residential Tenancies Act, [1981] 1 S.C.R. 714, 123 D.L.R. (3d) 554,
    37 N.R. 158 26
Re Resolution to Amend the Constitution, [1981] 1 S.C.R. 753, 125 D.L.R.
    (3d) 1, 39 N.R. 1..197, 203, 207, 208
Re The Initiative and Referendum Act, [1919] A.C. 935, 48 D.L.R. 18,
    [1919] 3 W.W.R. 1 (J.C.P.C.) 161
Re Therrien, 2001 SCC 35, [2001] 2 S.C.R. 3, [2001] S.C.J. No. 36 ....66, 291, 292,
    293, 294
Re Treasury Board (Health Canada) and Chopra, 2001 PSSRB 23,
    96 L.A.C. (4th) 367, [2001] C.P.S.S.R.B. No. 13 227
Ref. Re Constitutional Question Act (British Columbia), 78 D.L.R. (4th) 245,
    [1991] 4 W.W.R. 97, [1991] B.C.J. No. 244 (C.A.)...34
Reference re Anti- Inflation Act, [1976] 2 S.C.R. 373, 68 D.L.R. (3d) 452,
    9 N.R. 541 30
Reference re Appointment of Senators Pursuant to the Constitution Act,
    1867, s. 26, 78 D.L.R. (4th) 245, [1991] 4 W.W.R. 97, [1991] B.C.J.
    No. 244 (C.A.) 183
Reference re Bill 30, An Act to amend the Education Act (Ont.), [1987]
    1 S.C.R. 1148, 40 D.L.R. (4th) 18, [1987] S.C.J. No. 44 72
Reference Re Canada Assistance Plan, [1991] 2 S.C.R. 525, 83 D.L.R.
    (4th) 297, [1991] S.C.J. No. 60 23

Reference re Effect of Exercise of Royal Prerogative of Mercy Upon
Deportation Proceedings, [1933] S.C.R. 269, [1933] 2 D.L.R. 348,
59 C.C.C. 301 28
Reference Re Objection by Quebec to a Resolution to Amend the
Constitution, [1982] 2 S.C.R. 793, 140 D.L.R. (3d) 385, 45 N.R. 317 32
Reference Re Power of Disallowance and Power of Reservation, [1938]
S.C.R. 71, [1938] 2 D.L.R. 8 33
Reference re Provincial Electoral Boundaries (Sask.), [1991] 2 S.C.R. 158,
81 D.L.R. (4th) 16, [1991] S.C.J. No. 46 ....77, 79, 85
Reference re Resolution to Amend the Constitution, [1981] 1 S.C.R. 753,
125 D.L.R. (3d) 1, 39 N.R. 1 ....12, 22, 32, 34, 55, 300
Reference re Resolution to Amend the Constitution, [1981] 1 S.C.R. 753,
125 D.L.R. (3d) 1, 39 N.R. 1 ....
Reference Re Secession of Quebec, [1998] 2 S.C.R. 217, 161 D.L.R.
(4th) 385, [1998] S.C.J. No. 61....................13, 14, 15–17, 26, 52, 581, 584
Reform Party of Canada v. Canada (Attorney General), 165 A.R. 161,
123 D.L.R. (4th) 366, [1995] A.J. No. 212 (C.A.)....................................120
Reid v. Canada, [1994] F.C.J. No. 99, 73 F.T.R. 290 (T.D.)....................................81
Reza v. Canada, [1994] 2 S.C.R. 394, 116 D.L.R. (4th) 61, [1994] S.C.J. No. 49....56
Roberts v. Northwest Territories (Commissioner), 2002 NWTSC 68,
[2002] N.W.T.J. No. 81, 45 Admin. L.R. (3d) 45 ....249, 293
Roncarelli v. Duplessis, [1959] S.C.R. 121, 16 D.L.R. (2d) 689 ....24, 387
Ross River Dena Council Band v. Canada, 2002 SCC 54, [2002]
2 S.C.R. 816, [2002] S.C.J. No. 54 ....29, 30
Ross v. Mohawk of Kanesatake, 2003 FCT 531, [2003] F.C.J. No. 683,
232 F.T.R. 238 595
Rowat v. Information Commissioner of Canada, [2000] F.C.J. No. 832,
193 F.T.R. 1, 77 C.R.R. (2d) 79 (T.D.) 251, 252
Rubin v. Canada (Canada Mortgage and Housing Corp.) (1988), [1989]
1 F.C. 265, 52 D.L.R. (4th) 671, [1988] F.C.J. No. 610 (C.A.)........................498
Rubin v. Canada (Clerk of the Privy Council), [1993] F.C.J. No. 287,
62 F.T.R. 287, 48 C.P.R. (3d) 337 (T.D.) 491
Rubin v. Canada (Minister of Transport) (1997), [1998] 2 F.C. 430,
154 D.L.R. (4th) 414, [1997] F.C.J. No. 1614 (C.A.), rev'g [1995]
F.C.J. No. 1731, 105 F.T.R. 81, 39 Admin. L.R. (2d) 301 (T.D.) 484, 497, 499
Ruby v. Canada (Solicitor General), 2002 SCC 75, [2002] 4 S.C.R. 3,
[2002] S.C.J. No. 73, var'g [2000] 3 F.C. 589, 187 D.L.R.
(4th) 675, [2000] F.C.J. No. 779 (C.A.) 492–93, 519, 526, 529, 552
Russow & The Green Party of Canada v. Canada (Attorney General),
(1 May 2001), Doc. 01-CV-210088 (Ont. S.C.J.)..148

Samson Indian Nation and Band v. Canada (2003), 2003 FC 975,
[2004] 1 F.C.R. 556, 238 F.T.R. 68 ....70, 71

Samson v. Canada (Attorney General), 165 D.L.R. (4th) 342, [1998]
  F.C.J. No. 1208, 155 F.T.R. 137 (T.D.) 18, 35, 184, 185
Sauvé v. Canada (Attorney General), [1993] 2 S.C.R. 438, 153 N.R. 242,
  [1993] S.C.J. No. 59 77
Sauvé v. Canada (Chief Electoral Officer), 2002 SCC 68, [2002] 3 S.C.R. 519,
  [2002] S.C.J. No. 66..45, 77
Scarborough (City) v. Ontario (Attorney-General), 32 O.R. (3d) 526,
  144 D.L.R. (4th) 130, [1997] O.J. No. 701 (Gen. Div.) 30
Schachter v. Canada, [1992] 2 S.C.R. 679, 93 D.L.R. (4th) 1, [1992]
  S.C.J. No. 68..44
Secretary of State for the Home Department v. Rehman, [2003] 1 AC 153
  (H.L.)..542
Seniuk v. Saskatchewan (Minister of Justice), [1996] 8 W.W.R. 16, [1996]
  S.J. No. 286, 143 Sask. R. 268 (Q.B.) 70
Shubenacadie Indian Band v. Canada (Attorney General), 2001 FCT 699,
  [2001] F.C.J. No. 1028 386
Siderman de Blake v. Republic of Argentina, 965 F.2d 699 (9th Cir. 1992)......485
Singh v. Canada (1991), 3 O.R. (3d) 429, 80 D.L.R. (4th) 641, 47 O.A.C. 391
  (C.A.) 181, 182
Singh v. Canada (Attorney General), [2000] 3 F.C. 185, 183 D.L.R. (4th) 458,
  [2000] F.C.J. No. 4 (C.A.) 22
Smith v. Canada (Attorney General), 252 N.R. 172, [2000] F.C.J. No. 174,
  73 C.R.R. (2d) 196 (C.A.) aff'd 2001 SCC 88, [2001] 3 S.C.R. 902,
  [2001] S.C.J. No. 85 528
Société des alcools du Québec v. Canada, 2002 FCA 69, 300 N.R. 232,
  [2002] F.C.J. No. 255 346
Solosky v. The Queen (1979), [1980] 1 S.C.R. 821, 105 D.L.R. (3d) 745,
  30 N.R. 380...471
Somerville v. Canada (Attorney General), 184 A.R. 241, [1996] 8 W.W.R. 199,
  [1996] A.J. No. 515 (C.A.)..124
Stenhouse v. Canada (Attorney General), 2004 FC 375, [2004] 4 F.C.R. 437,
  [2004] F.C.J. No. 469 228
Stevens v. Canada (Attorney General), 2004 FC 1746, [2004] F.C.J. No. 5116 411
Suresh v. Canada (Minister of Citizenship and Immigration), 2002 SCC 1,
  [2002] 1 S.C.R. 3, [2002] S.C.J. No. 3 ....59, 523, 594, 605
Switzman v. Elbling, [1957] S.C.R. 285, 7 D.L.R. (2d) 337, 117 C.C.C. 129 12

Tafler v. British Columbia (Commissioner of Conflict of Interest), [1995]
  B.C.J. No. 1042, 5 B.C.L.R. (3d) 285, 31 Admin. L.R. (2d) 6 (S.C.),
  aff'd 161 D.L.R. (4th) 511, [1998] B.C.J. No. 1332, 11 Admin. L.R.
  (3d) 228 (C.A.) 69, 443
Telezone Inc. v. Canada (Attorney General), 69 O.R. (3d) 161, 235 D.L.R.
  (4th) 719, [2004] O.J. No. 5 (C.A.)...70, 400
Terminiello v. City Of Chicago, 337 U.S. 1 (1949)..582

Thomson Newspapers Co. v. Canada (Attorney General), [1998]
1 S.C.R. 877, 38 O.R. (3d) 735, [1998] S.C.J. No. 44 ....76, 77, 79, 122
Thomson v. Canada (Deputy Minister of Agriculture), [1992] 1 S.C.R. 385,
89 D.L.R. (4th) 218, [1992] S.C.J. No. 13 216
Threader v. Canada (Treasury Board) (1986), [1987] 1 F.C. 41, 68 N.R. 143,
[1986] F.C.J. No. 411 (C.A.)..446, 455
Thurlow v. Canada (Solicitor General), 2003 FC 1414, [2003] F.C.J.
No. 1802, 242 F.T.R. 214 524
Toronto (City) v. C.U.P.E., Local 79, 2003 SCC 63, [2003] 3 S.C.R. 77,
[2003] S.C.J. No. 64 61
Tucci v. Attorney General of Canada, [1997] F.C.J. No. 159, 126 F.T.R. 147
(T.D.) 219
Tunda v. Canada, 2001 FCA 151, 285 N.R. 386, [2001] F.C.J. No. 835....................37
Turner v. Canada, [1992] 3 F.C. 458, 93 D.L.R. (4th) 628, [1992] F.C.J.
No. 573 (C.A.) 326

U.E.S., Local 298 v. Bibeault, [1988] 2 S.C.R. 1048, 95 N.R. 161, [1988]
S.C.J. No. 101 ....58, 59, 522

Valente v. The Queen, [1985] 2 S.C.R. 673, 24 D.L.R. (4th) 161, [1985]
S.C.J. No. 77...289, 293
VIA Rail Canada Inc. v. National Automobile, Aerospace Transportation
and General Workers' Union, National Council 4000, (2003)
116 L.A.C. (4th) 407 (Weatherill) 533
Vienneau v. Canada (Solicitor General), [1988] 3 F.C. 336, [1988] F.C.J.
No. 211, 24 C.P.R. (3d) 104 (T.D.)..497
Vriend v. Alberta, [1998] 1 S.C.R. 493, 156 D.L.R. (4th) 385, [1998]
S.C.J. No. 29 ....44, 45, 47, 48

Waddell v. Canada (Governor-in-Council), 126 D.L.R. (3d) 431, [1981]
5 W.W.R. 662, [1981] B.C.J. No. 1858 (S.C.) 345
Walpole Island First Nation v. Ontario (Ministry of Environment and
Energy) (1996), 31 O.R. (3d) 607, 146 D.L.R. (4th) 141, [1996]
O.J. No. 4682 (Div. Ct.) 595
Weatherill v. Canada (Attorney General), [1999] 4 F.C. 107, [1999]
F.C.J. No. 787, 168 F.T.R. 161 (T.D.)..239
Wedge v. Canada (Attorney General), [1997] F.C.J. No. 872, 133 F.T.R. 277,
4 Admin. L.R. (3d) 153 (T.D.) 238
Weir v. Canada, 119 N.B.R. (2d) 337, 84 D.L.R. (4th) 39, [1991] N.B.J. No. 820
(C.A.) 182
Wells v. Newfoundland, [1999] 3 S.C.R. 199, 177 D.L.R. (4th) 73, [1999]
S.C.J. No. 50..20, 21, 61, 326
Wewaykum Indian Band v. Canada, 2003 SCC 45, [2003] 2 S.C.R. 259,
[2003] S.C.J. No. 50 ....445, 456, 457

Wyeth-Ayerst Canada Inc. v. Canada (Attorney General), 2002 FCT 133,
[2002] F.C.J. No. 173 491

X v. Canada (Minister of National Defence) (1991), [1992] 1 F.C. 77,
[1991] F.C.J. No. 817, 46 F.T.R. 206 (T.D.) 493
X v. Canada (Minister of National Defence), [1990] F.C.J. No. 540,
41 F.T.R. 16 (T.D.) 494
X v. Canada (Minister of National Defence), [1992] F.C.J. No. 1006,
58 F.T.R. 93 (T.D.)..521
Xwave Solutions Inc. v. Canada (Public Works & Government Services),
2003 FCA 301, 310 N.R. 164, [2003] F.C.J. No. 1089 60

Yeager v. Canada (Correctional Service) of Canada, 2003 FCA 30, [2003]
3 F.C. 107, [2003] F.C.J. No. 73 ....484, 492

Zarzour v. Canada, 268 N.R. 235, [2000] F.C.J. No. 2070, 153 C.C.C.
(3d) 284 (C.A.) 528, 530
Zündel v. Liberal Party of Canada, 46 O.R. (3d) 410, 181 D.L.R. (4th) 463,
[1999] O.J. No. 4244 (C.A.) 69

Index

Access Act, see Access to Information Act

Access to Information Act, 487–512, 513, 514, 517, 518, 543, 573, 603, 618, 621, 645

    Access to Information and Privacy coordinators (ATIP) and, 493, 494, 495

    application of administrative law in review of cases, 523–25

    background of, 487–88

    basic mechanics of, 493–95

    Canada Evidence Act, security exclusions to, 555–56

    developments in administrative law and, 522–23

    enforcement by Access Commissioner, 502–4

    exclusions of information, 507–12

    fees for requests, 495–97

    mandatory and discretionary exemptions under, 497–502

    mechanics of judicial review of exemption, 518–20

    new exclusions to disclosure rules due to national security, 557–60

    purpose of, 490–91

    right to access, 491–93

    scope of, 488–90

    security exemptions to, 552–55

    standards of judicial review in "discretionary" exemptions, 522–25

    standards of judicial review when exemption is "not authorized," 520

    standards of judicial review when exemption is on "reasonable grounds," 520–21

    time limits for information requests, 493–95

Access to information security constraints, 540–43

    Johannesburg principles on national security and information access, 541–43

openness of government and
national security, 541
Accountability, 3–8, 15, 18, 19, 45, 75,
231n, 288–289, 363n, 410
administrative law principles and,
365–66
conduct of inquiries, 365–68
constitutional law principles and,
366–68
deputy ministers and, 389–90
executive branch, 359–69
in globalized confederation, 601–15
institutional control of: role of central agencies (Privy Council
Office (PCO), Treasury Board,
Department of Finance),
360–61
ministerial, 385–92
officers of Parliament and, 405–9
public and departmental inquiries,
361–69
termination of inquiries, 368–69
unelected officials and, 617–19
Act of Settlement, 1701, 169, 170
Address in Reply, 372, 374, 375, 376
Address of Parliament, 248, 249–52,
292–94
definition of, 248, 249, 645
Administrative judicial review of the
executive, 54–62, 222, 445,
592–96
constitutional basis for, 55–57
courts and the executive, 54–57
developments in law, 522–23
implications of, 61–62
jurisdictional error and, 54, 55, 56,
58, 62
overview of, 54–57
pragmatic and functional test,
58–59, 523, 524
procedural fairness and, 60–61
section 96 of the Constitution Act
and, 56–57

spectrum of standards review and,
59–60
Administrative law, 24, 26, 27, 445,
447, 448, 521
Emergencies Act and, 592–95
application of principles in Access to
Information Act and Privacy
Act, 523–25
inquiries and, 365–66
parliamentary supremacy and, 24
Advertising in elections, see Election
Advertising
Aeronautics Act disclosure rules, 560,
562–68
Agency principle, 103
Airline passenger security information, 560–68
Alternate vote (AV) system, 150–51
definition of, 645
Appropriations bill, 377, 379
Attorney General
Canada Evidence Act and the,
556–57
Auditor General
appointment, tenure and dismissal
of, 247
as an arm of Parliament, 408–9
definition of, 645
financial and administrative independence, 254–55
functions of, 406–8
office of, 405–6

Barbeau Commission, 108, 109
"Best practices" for information
access, 486–87
Bill of Rights, 1689, 22
British North America Act, 10, 33n, 44,
186n, 583
Budgets, 383–384
By-elections, 97–100
expulsions and, 98
warrant issuances and, 98

Cabinet
    budgets and, 383–84
    collective responsibilty of, 370–84
    confidence vote and, 370–73, 645
    constitutional basis for financial
        responsibility, 376–77
    definition of, 645
    emergency debates and, 375–76
    executive government and, 353–70
    ministry and, 200–15
    new rules on borrowing authority
        and, 382
    resignation of the government and,
        370–73
    responsibility on financial matters
        and, 376–84
    responsibility to Parliament for
        overall government policy,
        373–76
    solidarity and, 354–55, 645
    Speech from the Throne and,
        373–75
    Supply process and, 377–81
Cabinet ministers
    power of, 36
    selection of, 35
Cabinet's role in executive governance
    control over structure, 357–59
    executive branch accountability
        mechanisms, 359–69
    procedure and structure, 353–55
    purpose and organization, 353–54
    solidarity and confidence, 354–55
    structure of federal executive gov-
        ernment, 355–59
Canada Act, 1982, 9, 11n
Canada Elections Act, 5, 75, 80, 81n, 83,
    86, 87, 88, 89, 90n, 94, 97, 98,
    102n, 103, 106, 111n, 112n, 113,
    114n, 116n, 117, 119, 120n, 122n,
    123, 124, 125, 126, 127n, 131,
    132n, 133, 134, 135, 136n, 249,
    255n, 299, 318, 461, 466

    enforcement of and penalties,
        135–36
    lobbyists and, 461
    right to vote and, 80–85
Canada Evidence Act, 555–60, 573
    Attorney General and, 556–57
    national security exclusions under
        the *Access to Information Act*
        and the *Privacy Act* and,
        555–60
    powers of, 555–56
Canadian Bill of Rights, 580–81, 595,
    596, 600
    nondiscrimination policy in,
        585–86
*Canadian Charter of Rights and Free-
    doms*, 9, 11, 12, 17n, 19n, 27,
        28n, 39, 44, 45, 46n, 47, 48, 49,
        50, 60, 72, 73, 75, 76, 77, 80,
        90, 100, 101n, 119, 120, 169,
        170, 200, 209, 223, 226, 240,
        251, 252, 269, 275, 299, 345,
        367, 369, 402, 403, 404, 483,
        528, 529, 544, 545, 551, 580,
        581–84, 582, 585, 592, 595, 600
    democratic rights and, 42
    equality rights and, 43
    fundamental freedoms and, 42
    judicial review of, 39, 42–43
    language rights and, 43
    legal rights and, 42–43
    minority language educational
        rights and, 43
    mobility rights and, 42
    section 1, 582
    section 4(2), 582
Canadian Judicial Council (CJC), *see*
    Unelected judicial officials
Canadian Security Intelligence Service
    (CSIS), 544, 546, 553, 554, 555,
        560, 561, 568, 569
    oversight of Canadian Security,
        570–71

Canadian Security Intelligence Service Act, 546, 552

Candidates
  independent (unaffiliated), 96
  party-endorsed, 96
  rights of, 97

Caucus
  definition of, 316–17, 645
  the Whip and, 316–19

Central agencies, defined, 360

Chief electoral officer (CEO), 86–87, 404–9
  appointment, tenure and dismissal of, 247
  definition of, 645
  financial and administrative independence, 255

Chief Justice of the Supreme Court, 37

Civil laws and ethics rules, 416–17

CJC, *see* Unelected judicial officials

Code for Protection of Personal Information, 533, 539

Codes of conduct and ethics, *see* Ethics rules

Cogger and Berntson cases, 188–90, 414

Commissioner of Canada Elections, 135
  definition of, 646

Committee of the Whole
  Chair of, 307
  description and powers of, 307, 308, 379

Committees
  constitutional implications of parliamentary contempt powers over, 402–4
  Parliament's contempt powers over and, 401–2
  Parliament's oversight powers over and, 400–1

Common law, defined, 646

Common law procedural fairness, 60–61, 347–49, 445, 446, 594, 595

Communications Security Establishment (CSE), 569, 570–71

Comptroller General
  role of, 361

Compulsory voting, 139

Confidence votes, defined, 646

Conflict of Interest and Post-Employment Code for Public Office Holders, *see* Public Office Holders Code

Conflict of Interest Code for Members of the House of Commons, *see* MP Code

Constitution Act, 1867, 9, 10, 11, 12, 20n, 22, 23, 25, 29, 33, 34, 35, 36n, 37, 40, 64, 66, 71, 73, 74, 83, 146, 148, 149, 168, 170, 173, 178, 179, 180, 183, 185–86, 187, 188, 194, 195, 197, 250, 251, 257, 258, 260, 293, 298, 299, 303, 304, 321, 327, 331n, 337, 346, 376, 478, 583, 584, 605, 613

Constitution Act, 1982, 9, 11, 44, 170, 178, 195n, 198, 271, 583, 608n

Constitution of Canada, 5, 9–74, 89

Constitution, unwritten principles and conventions, 5, 12–20
  the democracy principle and, 12–16
  judicial review of, 39
  legal implications of the democracy principle, 16–18
  overview of, 12–13
  parliamentary supremacy and, 22
  separation of powers and, 20
  troubling provenance and, 18–20

Constitutional basis for Canadian Democracy, 9–74
  democracy in Canada's unwritten constitution, 12–20
  democracy in Canada's written constitution, 10–12

parliamentary supremacy and the
separation of powers, 20–73
Constitutional conventions, 17
definition of, 646
responsible government and, 32–37
Constitutional division of powers
federal vs. provincial governments,
40–41
Constitutional judicial independence
requirements, 66–67
Constitutional judicial review of Parliament, 39–54
cowardly political branches of Parliament and, 51–54
implications of, 46–47
limited government and, 39–46
overview of, 39
the usurping court and, 47–51
Constitutional law principles
inquiries and, 366–68, 646
parliamentary supremacy and,
24–28
Constitutional voting rights, 76–79
effective representation and the
right to a roughly equal
impact on results, 79
effective representation and the
right to participate in, 77–78
Constitutionalism, 15–16, 20, 32n
Consultation/vetting process and the
Supreme Court, 278–82, 287–88
Contingency fee, 646
Contractual governance, 613–15
Contributions, *see* Election donations
Corporate and union contributions,
107–13, 115n
background, 108–10
displaced donations, 112–13
downstream donations, 111–12
splitting donations, 111
Criminal Code and ethics rules, 413–15,
448

Crown corporations and other government corporate interests, 626–29
Culpability, 385–92
legal, 385–87
political, 387–88

Democracy
and accountability, *see* Accountability
in Canada's unwritten constitution,
12–20
in Canada's written constitution,
10–12
constitutional basis for, 9–74
definition of, 1–3
limited government and, 3
principle of, 13–20
Democracy, ethics and governance in
the public interest, 410–57
core principles of Canadian ethics
rules, 411–13
ethical codes of conduct for the
ministry and parliamentarians, 417–50
ethics rules for judges, 456–57
legal standards, 413–17
Public Servants Code, 450–56
Democratic accountability in globalized confederation, 601–15
the diffusion of governance within
Canada, 609–15
international policy-making and,
601–8
Democratic deficit and intergovernmental organizations, 602–3,
607
Democratic deficit and the separation
of powers, 603–7
Democratic governance in times of
emergency, 576–600
emergency powers and international law, 579–80
emergency powers and the Constitution, 580–84

emergency powers in statutory law, 584–99

Department of Finance
role of, 361

Deputy Heads, 218, 219, 223
Deputy Governor General, 37
Deputy ministers as accountability officers, 389–90
Deputy Speaker, 307

Disclosure of information, *see* Information disclosure

Disclosure requirements: Public Office Holders Code
confidential disclosure of assets and potential conflicts, 428–29, 430
public disclosure or divestments, 428, 429–30

Donations, *see* Election donations

Due process rights
procedural fairness and, 347–49
During-pleasure appointees, 239–41

Election Advertising
broadcasting time, 119–21
definition of, 647
facilitating advertising, 119–21
from foreign sources, 123
general rules for, 118–23
government advertising, 131–32
polling restrictions, 122–23
restrictions on polling day, 121–22
signage, 119
third-party spending limits, 124–31
transparency requirements, 121, 125

Election donations, 106–14
corporate and union contributions, 107–13, 115n
displaced, 112–13
downstream donations, 111–12
limits on, 106–14
overview of, 106–7
trust funds, 113–14

unincorporated contributions, 107

Election expenses, 103–6
Agency principle and, 103
definition of, 103–4, 647
leadership contests/races and, 105–6
limits, 104–105

Election law and policy
emerging issues in, 135–62
fixed election dates and, 139–40
leaders' debates and, 140–41
more diverse Parliament, 151–54
proportional representation in electoral system, 141–51
recall, 151–54
voter participation and, 136–39

Elections
administration of, 75, 97–132
advertising in, 118–32, 140
boundaries, 83, 84, 85
by-elections, 97–100
contested results, 134–35
effective representation and the right to a roughly equal impact on results, 79
effective representation and the right to participate in, 77–78
electoral officials, 86–89
enforcement of *Canada Election Act* and penalties, 135–36
finance disclosure and, 116–18
financing of, 75, 96, 100–18, 140
fixed dates for, 76, 139–40
general, 97
judicial recounts, 134
key actors in, 86–97
parties and candidates, 89–97
proportional representation in, 76, 141–51
recounts, 134
regulation of, 76
results reporting, 133–34

right to representation and electoral boundary readjustment, 83–85

the right to vote as *per* the *Canada Elections Act*, 80–85

statutory basis for, 97–100

straddling, 76

triggering of, 97–100

voter's list, 132

writ and, 97, 98, 99

Elections Canada, 87, 95, 99n, 113n, 115n, 116, 117, 124, 125n, 133n, 137n, 237, 267, 268

Electoral districts, 79, 84, 85, 96, 647

associations, 94, 105, 647

Electoral financing, 96, 100–18

agency principle and, 103

competing values: egalitarian vs libertarian, 100–18

donation limits and, 106–14

expenses and, 103–6

fairness and, 100

finance disclosure, 116–18

key areas for reform, 105–6

leadership contests, 105–6

limits and, 100–3

public subsidies and, 114–16, 117

spending levels, 105

Electoral officials, 86–89

chief electoral officer (CEO), 86–87

returning officers, 87–89, 245

Electoral spending caps, 92

Emergencies Act, 584, 585–96

categories of, 586, 587–90

content, 585–86

judicial review on constitutional grounds, 595–96

judicial review standard and, 594–95

jurisdiction of judicial review and, 592–93

parliamentary oversight, 586, 591–92

Emergency debates, 375–76

Emergency powers and the Constitution

Canadian Bill of Rights, 580–81

Canadian Charter of Rights and Freedoms, 581–84

Emergency powers in statutory law

Emergencies Act, 584

Emergency Preparedness Act, 584

National Defence Act, 584

Emergency Preparedness Act, 584, 598–99

EMILY's List, 153, 154n

Ethics commissioner, 246, 417–21, 423, 647

appointment, tenure and dismissal of, 247

financial and administrative independence of, 255

general functions of, 417–18

independence of, 418–19

investigation and enforcement of the MP Code and, 424–26

judicial review of decisions of, 442–49

responsibilities re MP and Public Office Holders Codes, 419–21

Ethics rules, 410, 416–17

the allure of public service and, 412–13

civil law provisions and, 416–17

codes of conduct for ministers and parliamentarians, 417–50

core principles of, 411–13

Criminal Code provisions and, 413–15

ethics commissioner and senate ethics officer, 417–21

impartiality of, 411–12

for judges, 456–57

legal standards for, 413–17

MP Code, *see* MP Code

Parliament of Canada Act provisions and, 415–16

professional responsibility obligations, 449–50

at the provincial level, 609–10
Public Office Holders Code, *see*
    Public Office Holders Code
Public Servants Code, 450–56
regulating the private interest,
    411–12
the senate and, 190, 413
standard of judicial review for,
    442–49
unelected officials and, 617–19
Executive government, 10, 11, 21,
    361–69
accountability mechanisms, 359–69
Cabinet's role in, 353–70
delegated power of, 24–28
institutional control of and the cen-
    tral agencies, 360–61
legislative powers of, 61
prerogative powers of, 28–31
public and departmental inquiries,
    361–69
Executive government vs. Parliament
    powers, 21–37
Parliament's institutional supremacy,
    31–37
Parliament's jurisdictional
    supremacy, 22–31
Executive law-making, 337–49
due process and delegated legisla-
    tion, 347–49
executive branch regulation-mak-
    ing, 340–43
nonregulatory Orders-in-Council,
    343–45
parliamentary grant or other source
    of power and, 345–47
role of the courts in, 345–49
statutory instruments, 338–39
types of executive laws, 338–39
Expense reimbursement, *see* Public
    subsidies
Extraneous security-related restrictions
    on privacy, 560–73

airline passenger security informa-
    tion, 560–61
Canadian Service Intelligence Ser-
    vice powers and oversight
    (CSIS), 569, 570–71
Communications Security Estab-
    lishment (CSA) powers and
    oversight, 569, 570–71
financial institutions and, 568
lawful access provisions and,
    568–569
PIPEDA and, 568
transportation facilities and, 568

Federal courts (Non-Supreme)
appointment to, 259, 260–29
assessment criteria for, 263
patronage appointments and, 260,
    261, 265–69
vetting system, 262–65, 268
Federal public administration bodies
Crown corporations and govern-
    ment corporate interests,
    626–28
miscellaneous organizations,
    629–36
public service administration bodies,
    621–25
special operating agencies, 636
Federal vs. provincial government
division of powers, 40–41
shared powers, 41
Federalism, 14, 16
judicial review of, 39
Financial responsibility of govern-
    ment, 376–84
budgets and, 383–84
constitutional basis for, 376–77
Governor General's Special War-
    rants and, 382–83
new rules on borrowing authority,
    382
shortcomings in process, 380–81
Supply process and, 377–81

First Nations
    law and democracy in, 153, 610–13
First-past-the-post (FPP) systems, 138,
        141–43, 144, 145, 146, 148, 149,
        150, 152, 153, 163, 196
Fixed election dates, 139–40
Flag of convenience parties, 92, 93, 94
FPP systems, *see* First-past-the-post
    systems
Fractious Parliaments, *see* Proportional
    representation (PR) in electoral
    system
Free votes, 323–25

General elections, 97
GIC, *see* Governor-in-Council
Gifts and public office holders, 432–35
Good-behaviour appointees, 238–39,
    248, 249
Government bills, *see* Public bills
Government performance
    report and critique of by informa-
        tion commissioner, 504–7
Governor General
    appointment of, 33, 171–73, 260
    Cabinet ministers and, 35, 36, 200,
        202
    delegation of power and, 37
    dismissal of government and,
        207–9
    dissolution of Parliament and,
        299–300
    judges and, 35, 258–59
    ministry and, 213, 214
    Parliament and, 35
    powers of, 10, 34–36
    prime minister and, 34, 35, 36,
        172–73, 174, 203–9, 211
    reform of, 175–77
    refusal of a dissolution, 300–3
    reserve powers of, 35–36, 650
    royal assent of bills and, 35
    royal prerogative and, 29
    senators and, 35, 183–85

    Special Warrants and, 382–83
    tenure and dismissal of, 173–75
Governor-in-Council
    definition of, 648
    general election and, 97
    prime minister and, 36
    regulations process, 340–41
    returning officers and, 87, 88
Governor-in-Council appointees (non-
    judicial), 233–46
    appointment of, 234–38
    appointment reform, 241–46
    during-pleasure appointees, 239–41
    good-behaviour appointees, 238–39,
        248, 249
    NCC patronage appointments and,
        237
    political favouritism, 236–38, 242,
        243n, 244, 245
    tenure and dismissal of, 238–41

House of Commons
    closure and time allocation for
        debate and decision-making,
        320–21
    debate and decision-making rules
        in, 319–25
    easing party discipline and free
        votes, 323–25
    leaders of, 312–13
    legal impetus of party-based deci-
        sion-making, 321–22
    overview of rules of debate and
        decision-making, 319–20
    political impetus of party-based
        decision-making, 322–23

Information and the Currency of
    Democracy, 481–575
    information disclosure, 482–525
    national security challenge to infor-
        mation access and privacy,
        540–73
    protecting privacy, 525–40

Information commissioner
  appointment, tenure and dismissal
    of, 248
  financial and administrative inde-
    pendence, 256
  investigations procedure, 502–4
  report and critique on government
    performance, 504–7
Information disclosure, 482–525
  Access to Information Act, 487–512
  access to information as an interna-
    tional right, 484–85
  democracy and, 482–84
  federal "open government" infor-
    mation laws, 487–525
  international "best practices" for
    information access, 486–87
  Privacy Act, 512–18
Information laws
  Access to Information Act, 487–512
  Privacy Act, 512–18
Infosource, 493
Inquiries, 361–369
  administrative law principles and,
    365–66
  conduct of, 365–69
  constitutional law principles and,
    366–68
  initiation of departmental, 364
  initiation of public, 363–64
  motivations behind public, 362–63
  termination of, 368–69
Instant run-off system, 150–51
Instrument of Advice, 172
Internal Disclosure Policy, 229–30
International Covenant on Civil and
    Political Rights (ICCPR), 485
International emergency, 586, 589–90
International policy-making
  de-parliamentization of political
    process, 604–5, 607, 608
  democratic accountability and,
    602–3

the separation of powers and,
  603–7
Issue advertising, see Third-party
  spending

Johannesburg principles on national
  security and information access,
  541–43
Joint Committees
  description and powers, 308
Judges
  appointment of, 35
  dismissal of, 250
Judicial activism, 50
Judicial independence, 4, 240n, 250,
    251, 254, 274, 275, 289, 290,
    294, 296, 364, 365
  administrative independence, 65,
    66–67
  assessing, 64
  constitutional basis for, 63–64
  definition of, 647
  elements of, 64–67
  financial security of, 65, 66–67
  individual independence of, 64, 65,
    66–67
  institutional independence of, 65,
    66–67
  judiciary vs. parliamentary powers,
    62–67
  security of tenure, 65, 66–67
  significance of, 62–63
Judicial officials, see Unelected judicial
  officials
Judicial recounts and contested elections, 134–35
Judicial review, 18, 19, 38–62
  application of administrative law
    principles in Access to Infor-
    mation Act and Privacy Act
    cases, 523–25
  Emergencies Act and, 592–96

of exemption decisions under the *Access to Information Act* and the *Privacy Act*, 518–25
pragmatic and functional test and, 522, 523
standard of review, 522–25
Judicial review for ethics matters, 442–49
common law backdrop, 445–49
of ethics commissioner and Public Office Holders Code and, 442, 443–44
MP Code and, 442–43
MP Code legal status, 444–45
Public Office Holders Code direct application, 448–49
Public Office Holders Code incidental application, 447
Public Office Holders Code legal status, 445
Judiciary, 21
Judiciary role in executive law-making, 345–49
Judiciary vs. Parliament powers, 37–73
administrative judicial review and: courts and the executive, 54–62
constitutional judicial review and: courts and Parliament, 38–54
cowardly political branches of Parliament and, 51–54
dialogue between courts and Parliament, 45, 47n, 48n
implications of separation of powers, 46–47
institutional separation of powers, 62–73
judicial creativity and, 38
judicial independence and, 62–67
jurisdictional separation of powers, 38–62
parliamentary privilege and, 67–73
private law and, 38

public law and, 38
the usurping court and, 47–51
Jurisdictional error, 54, 55, 56, 58, 62
Jurisdictional separation of powers, 38–62

Law and democracy at provincial and municipal levels, 609–10
Law and democracy in Canada's First Nations, 610–13
Law Commission of Canada, 142, 143
Law-making
statistical trends in, 637–44
Lawful access provisions, 568–569
Leadership
contests/races, 105–6
conventions, 95
debates, 140–41
Legislative Committees
description and powers, 308
Legislative process
requirements of, 326
Letters Patent (1947), 10, 37
Limited government, 39–45
judicial function in, 44–45
Lobbying, democracy and governance in the public interest, 458–80
the law of lobbyist regulation, 461–79
lobbying: an overview, 459
the lobbying industry, 460–61
at the municipal level, 609, 610
Lobbyists
Canada Elections Act and, 461
code of conduct, 471–74
consultant, 461, 462–63, 464, 467, 646
definition of, 459, 460
disclosure requirements in registration documents, 465–69
exceptions to registration requirements, 470
in-house (corporate/organizations), 463–64, 468, 647
lawyers as, 470–71

Lobbyists' Code of Conduct and,
471–74
obligation to register with Lobbyists
Registry, 465
registrar, 648
Lobbyists' Code of Conduct, 471–74
legal status and oversight of,
472–74
overview of, 471–72
Lobbyists Regulation Act (LRA)
application of, 461–64
contingency fees and, 464, 475–78,
646
disclosure requirements and, 465–69
multitasking lobbyists and, 478–79
registration obligation exceptions,
470
registry obligation, 465
Lortie Commission, 126
LRA, see Lobbyists Regulation Act

Manitoba Language Reference, 13n
Military security zones, 597, 598
Minister of state, 358, 648
Ministerial political staff, 215–16
Ministers
deputy ministers as accountability
officers, 389–90
duties of, 399
formal informing requirements,
393–94
legal culpability for wrongdoing,
385–87
motions for production of papers,
393–94
political culpability for wrongdoing,
387–88
Question Period and, 396–98
questioning in Committees,
398–99
questioning in the House of Commons, 396–98
questioning of, 394–96

resignation of the government,
387–88
responsibility of, 384–404, 648
responsibility to inform Parliament,
392–404
strengthening responsibility of,
390–92
written questions and, 398
Ministers and ministers of state,
212–15
appointment of, 213
dismissal of, 213–15
Ministry and the Cabinet, 200–15
definitions of, 201–3
Mixed-member proportional (MMP)
systems, 146, 147
legal issues with, 148–50
MMP systems, see Mixed-member proportional systems
Monarch, 168–71
Motions for production of papers,
393–94, 395
MP Code, 417, 419, 420
application of, 438–39
barring introduction of private
influences into conduct of
public business rules, 423–24
disclosure of assets rules, 424
the Ethics Commissioner and,
424–26
general principles of, 421–22
judicial review of, 442–43
legal status of, 444–45
removal of private business interests from conduct of public
business rules, 422–23
specific provisions of, 422–26

National Capital Commission (NCC),
236, 237
National Defence Act, 584, 596–98,
599
National emergency
definition of, 585

types of, 586, 587–590
National secrecy laws, 543–73
   Canada Evidence Act and security
      exclusions under the *Access to
      Information Act* and the *Priva-
      cy Act*, 555–60
   extraneous security-related restric-
      tions on privacy, 560–73
   security exemptions under *Access to
      Information Act, Privacy Act*
      and *PIPEDA*, 552–55
   Security of Information Act, 543–52
National security challenge to information access and privacy protection, 540–73
   legitimate constraints on access to
      information, 540–43
   national secrecy laws, 543–73
NCC, *see* National Capital Commission
Non-confidence votes, 207, 208, 209,
   210, 300, 371, 372, 375, 376

Office of the Director of Appointments, 234, 235
Officers of Parliament, 246–57
   Address of Parliament requirement,
      249–52
   appointment of, 247–48
   chief electoral officer (CEO), 88, 89
   definition of, 648
   dismissal of, 248–53
   financial and administrative inde-
      pendence, 254–56
   good-behaviour and, 248, 249
   parliamentary reporting function
      and, 405–6
   recent controversies and, 252–53
   tenure and, 247, 295
Official languages commissioner, 246
   appointment, tenure and dismissal
      of, 248
   financial and administrative inde-
      pendence, 256
Opinion surveys, 122–23

Order-in-Council
   definition of, 648
Order-in-Council, nonregulatory,
   343–45
process for introduction and development of, 344
revocation process and, 344–45

Parliament, Cabinet, democracy and
   responsible government,
   352–409
   Cabinet's role in executive gover-
      nance, 353–70
   responsibility and accountability to
      Parliament, 370–409
Parliament, democracy and the legislative process, 297–351
   executive law-making, 337–49
   parliamentary legislative enterprise,
      298–337

Parliament of Canada
   caucus and the Whip, 316–19
   Chair of the Committee of the
      Whole, 307
   definition of, 648
   Deputy Speaker, 307
   employees and parliamentary politi-
      cal staff, 199–200
   House leaders, 312–13
   key parliamentary actors, 304–19
   legislative function of, 325–37
   nonconfidence vote and dissolution
      of, 300
   organization of parties in, 312–19
   overview of, 298–325
   parliamentary committees, 307–11
   parliamentary privilege, 303
   parliamentary secretaries, 313–16
   party status in, 312
   powers of vs. executive, 21–37
   powers of vs. judiciary, 37–73
   refusing a dissolution, 300–3
   reporting to by ministers, 392–404

reporting to by officers of Parliament, 405–6
rules of debate/decision-making in
the House of Commons,
319–25
sources of parliamentary procedure, 303–4
Speaker, 304–7
summoning, prorogation and dissolution of by Governor General, 35, 298, 299–303
Parliament of Canada Act, 71, 72
and ethics rules, 415–16, 417, 418,
420n, 421, 426, 441, 443,
444, 449
Parliamentary bills, 327–37, 347
government vs. private members'
bills, 334–36
private bills, 327, 328–29
public bills, 327, 329–32
Parliamentary committees, 307–11
Committee of the Whole, 308
Joint Committees, 308, 343
Legislative Committees, 308
membership in, 309–12
role of, 307–9
Special Committees, 308
Standing Committees, 308
Subcommittees, 308
Parliamentary confirmation process
and the Supreme Court, 278–82,
285–86
Parliamentary debate and decision-
making, 319–25
closure and time-allocation, 320–21
easing party discipline, 323–25
legal impetus of decisions, party
discipline and free votes,
321–22
practical impetus of decisions, party
discipline and free votes,
322–23
Parliamentary governance

collective responsibility of Cabinet,
370–84
contempt powers over Committees,
401–4
individual responsibility of ministers, 384–404
legal aspects of, 321
office of the Auditor General and,
406–9
officers of Parliament and, 404–9
oversight powers over Committees,
400–1
Public Servants Code, 450–56
resignation of the government,
370–73
responsibility of financial matters,
376–84
responsibility of Parliament,
370–409
Parliamentary impeachment of prime
minister, 210–11
Parliamentary institutional supremacy
over executive government, 31–37
crown vs. cabinet powers, 31
responsible government and constitutional conventions, 32–37
Parliamentary jurisdictional supremacy
over executive government, 22–31
administrative law and, 24
constitutional law and, 24–28
delegated legislative power and, 25–26
executive prerogative powers and,
28–31
judicial powers and, 26–28
Parliamentary law
definition of, 648
Parliamentary legislative enterprise,
298–337
enacting parliamentary legislation,
327–37
government vs. private members'
bills, 334–36

impact on government policy,
332–33
legislative jurisdiction, 325–27
legislative results and statistical
trends in law-making, 336–37,
637–43
private bills, 327, 328–29
processing a public bill through the
House, 329–31
public bills, 327, 329–32
public government bills, 329
public private members' bills, 329
reform initiatives and, 333–34
requirements of legislative process,
326
role of courts and, 345
Parliamentary privilege, 303
constitutional basis of, 71–72
constitutional implications of parliamentary contempt powers,
402–4
contempt powers over Committees,
401–2
content of, 68–70
definition of, 648
implications of, 72–73
meaning of, 67–68
oversight powers over Committees,
400–1
significance of, 67
Parliamentary secretaries, 310, 311,
313–16, 396
definition of, 648
role of, 313–15
status in government of, 315–16
Parliamentary supremacy and the separation of powers, 20–73
executive vs. Parliament, 21–37
judiciary vs. Parliament, 37–73
Parties and candidates, 89–97
electoral district associations, 94
financing of, 96

nomination contestants and candidates, 95–97
parties, 89–94, 649
party leaders, 94–95, 96
spending caps, 92
Personal information
definition of, 513
*Personal Information Protection and
Electronic Documents Act, see
PIPEDA*
PIPEDA, 532–40, 621, 626
application to government, 532–33
collection, use and disclosure of
personal information without
knowledge or consent, 533–37
enforcement by privacy commissioner and federal court,
539–40
exception to personal information
access, 538–39
individual's access to existence, use
and disclosure of personal
information, 538
security exemptions to, 552–55, 568
Political favouritism, 166–68, 217,
236–38, 242, 243n, 244, 245,
261, 265–69, 272, 433–35
PR systems, 138, 143–51
Pragmatic and functional test, 58–59,
523, 524
Prime minister
appointment of, 203–6
commanding confidence of the
House, 203–6, 207, 208,
209, 210, 212
dismissal of, 34, 36, 207–12
Governor General and, 34, 35, 36,
172–73, 203–9, 211
Governor-in-Council and, 36
the ministry and, 36
parliamentary impeachment of,
210–11
powers of, 36

Queen's Privy Council and, 36
replacement prime ministers and,
205–6
role of political parties and, 205–6
selection of, 34
Privacy Act, 512–18, 529–32, 539, 573, 621
application of administrative law in
review of cases, 523–25
Canada Evidence Act security exclusions to, 555–56
collection and use of personal information, 529–30
developments in administrative law
and, 522–23
disclosure of personal information,
499, 513–18, 530–31
enforcement by privacy commissioner, 516–18, 531–32
exclusions under, 518
exemptions to disclosure, 515–16
mandatory and discretionary
exemptions under, 514–16
mechanics of, 514
mechanics of judicial review of
exemption, 518–20
new exclusions to disclosure rules
due to national security,
557–60
purpose of, 512
reasons for disclosure of personal
information, 530–31
security exemptions to, 552–55
standards of judicial review in "discretionary" exemptions, 522–25
standards of judicial review when
exemption is "not author-
ized," 520
standards of judicial review when
exemption is on "reasonable
grounds," 520–21
Privacy commissioner, 539–40
appointment, tenure and dismissal
of, 248

definition of, 649
enforcement of *Privacy Act* duties,
516–18
financial and administrative independence, 256
Privacy laws, federal, 528–40
constitutional protections, 528–29
*Personal Information Protection and
Electronic Documents Act
(PIPEDA)*, 532–40
Privacy Act, 529–32
Privacy protection, 525–40
federal privacy laws, 528–40
international standards, 527
national security challenge to,
540–73
privacy and democracy, 525–27
Private bills, 327, 328–29
Private members' bills, *see* Public bills
Privative clauses, 54, 55
Privy Council
membership in, 202
role of, 11, 202
Privy Council Office (PCO)
definition of, 649
Procedural fairness, 60–61, 238, 347–49,
366, 445, 446, 447, 594, 595
definition of, 649
Professional public service
appointment of, 216–22
dismissal for disclosure of wrongdoing, 225–32
dismissal for overt political activity,
222–25
dismissal for wrongdoing at common
law, 225–28
integrity officer, 230
Internal Disclosure Policy, 229–30
whistleblowing law and policy, 228–33
Proportional representation (PR),
defined, 649
Proportional representation (PR) in
electoral system, 141–51

alternate vote (AV) system, 150–51, 645

first-past-the-post (FPP) system, 138, 141–43, 144, 145, 146, 148, 149, 150, 152, 153, 163

fractious Parliaments, 144–46

legal issues with MMP systems, 148–50

mixed-member proportional (MMP) systems, 146

prime ministrial power, 147–48

recall, 153, 154–55

referendums, 156–62

single transferable voting (STV), 144, 150, 650

Prorogation of Parliament, 299

PSEA, see Public Service Employment Act

PSIO, *see* Public Service Integrity Office

Public administration of Canada, 621–36

Public bills
government bills definition, 329, 350
private members' bills definition, 327, 328, 329, 350
processing of through the House, 329–31

Public Inquiries Act, 363, 365, 366

"Public interest defence," 546

Public Office Holders Code, 235, 417, 419, 420, 421n, 426–37, 451, 472
application of, 439–42
avoidance of preferential treatment, 433–35
compliance measures and, 428–37
direct application of, 448–49
disclosure or divestment requirements, 428, 429, 430, 431
gifts ban, 432–33
gifts ban exception, 433
incidental application of, 447
judicial review of, 443–44
legal status of, 445

post-employment rules (revolving door provisions), 435–37, 447
principles of, 427–28
prohibited activities, 431–32

Public order emergency, 586, 588

Public Safety Act, 599

Public servants
duties of, 399, 452, 454
Parliament's oversight powers and, 400–1
specific duties for, 452–454

Public Servants Code, 230, 410, 450–56
disclosure of activities, assets and liabilities, 452
enforcement and oversight of, 455–56
post-employment and, 454–55
preferential treatment of public servants and, 454
provisions for gifts to public servants, 453–54
public servants' specific duties in the course of employment, 452–54
values and general principles of, 450–52

Public service administration bodies, 621–25

Public Service Commission (PSC), 217, 219, 220, 221, 222, 224, 232

Public Service Employment Act (PSEA), 217, 218, 219, 222, 223, 245, 255, 256, 622n, 626, 629

Public Service Integrity Commissioner, 232

Public Service Integrity Office (PSIO), 230, 231, 232, 455

Public Service Staffing Tribunal, 221

Public subsidies, 114–16
expense reimbursement, 114
quarterly allowance, 114–15
tax credit, 115–16

Public welfare emergency, 586, 587

Quarterly allowance, *see* Public subsidies
Quebec Secession Reference, 13, 14, 15n, 16, 26n, 49, 53, 184, 581n
Queen, 168–71
   powers of, 10, 12, 33–34
Queen's Privy Council
   definition of, 650
   prime minister and, 36
   role of, 360
Questioning
   in Committees, 398–99
   in the House of Commons, 362, 396–98
   of ministers, 394–96
   Question Period, 312, 313, 396–98
   written questions and, 315, 398

Recall, 76, 153, 154–55
Referendums, 76, 156–62
   ballot initiatives and, 157–58, 160, 162
   definition of, 650
   legal issues of, 159–61
   mechanics of, 161–62
   overview of, 156–58
   plebiscites and, 158, 159, 160, 161
   pros and cons of, 158–59
   third-party spending and, 162
Regulation-making, 340–43
   Governor-in-Council process for, 340–41
   non-Governor-in-Council process for, 342
   parliamentary role in, 342–43
Regulations, 338, 339
   definition of, 339, 650
Resignation of the government, 370–73, 390
Returning officers, 87–89, 97, 650
Revocation process, 344–45
Revolving door provisions, 435–37, 447
Royal assent of bills, 11, 35, 161, 306, 326, 331, 637–42, 650

Royal consent, 332, 650
Royal prerogative, 28–31, 32, 35n, 234, 331, 337, 445, 605, 608n, 650
Royal recommendation, 331, 377, 650
Rule of law, 15, 16, 24, 32n, 54, 577
Run-off system, 151

Section 96 provincial courts
   appointment to, 259
Security Intelligence Review Committee (SIRC), 572
Security of Information Act, 544–52, 574
   background, 544–45
   criminalizing leakage, 546, 548–52
   new espionage offences, 545–46, 547
   post-9/11 amendments, 545–52
Senate
   appointment of, 178–85
   Cogger and Berntson cases, 188–90
   constitutional reform and, 195–99
   dangers of incrementalism in, 193–95
   democracy issues and, 196
   events leading to vacancies in, 185–86
   expansion of, 180–83
   independence issues and, 195–96
   primacy issues and, 197–98
   reform of, 190–99
   regional distribution of, 178–83
   regional representation issues and, 197
   representation by division, 178–80
   selection of individual senators, 183–85
   sober second thoughts and, 198–99
   tenure and dismissal of, 185–90
   Thompson case and, 186–88
   vacancies in, 185–86, 194n
Senate ethics officer, 246, 417–21
   definition of, 651
   general functions of, 417–18
   independence of, 418–19

Senators
appointment of, 34, 35
Separation of powers
and the constitution, 20
definition of, 651
executive ("government") vs. Parliament (legislature), 21–37
judiciary vs. Parliament, 37–73
Single transferable voting (STV), 144,
150, 650
SIRC, *see* Security Intelligence Review
Committee
Speaker, 304–7, 375, 651
role of, 305–7
selection of, 304–5
Special Committees
description and powers of, 308
Special operating agencies, 636
"Special operation information"
definition of, 546
Special Warrants, 382–83
Speech from the Throne, 373–75, 377
Standard of review test, 346, 651
Standing Committees
description and powers of, 308,
309, 651
Standing Orders
definition of, 304, 651
Statistical trends in law-making,
336–37
days of parliamentary sessions *per*
bill and statutes, 642
general observations, 637–38
legislative productivity in enactment government vs. private
members bills, 641–42
legislative productivity in introduction of government vs. private
members bills, 640–41
parliamentary productivity, 643
percentage of bills originating in
senate, 639

royal assent of bills statistics,
637–38
Statutory instruments
definition of, 338, 651
due process and, 347–49
parliamentary role in regulation-making, 342–43
revocation process and, 344–45
role of courts in, 346–49
when statutory instrument is a regulation, 338, 339
Statutory voting rights, 80–85
protection of the right to vote,
81–83
right to representation and electoral
boundary readjustment, 83–85
the right to vote as *per* the *Canada
Elections Act*, 80–85
Subcommittees
description and powers of, 308
Supply process, 377–81
shortcomings of, 380–81
Supreme Court
appointment accountability, 288–89
appointment reform proposals,
275–83
appointment to, 259, 269–89
appointment via consultation/vet-
ting process, 278–82
appointment via parliamentary confirmation process, 278–82,
285–86
assessment criteria of candidates,
270
"back end" accountability mechanisms, 288–89
reforming the appointment
process, 272–75

Tax courts
appointment to, 259
Tax credit, *see* Public subsidies
Third-party spending, 92, 93, 100
advertising limits, 124–31

chronological difficulties with issue
    advertising, 129–31
constitutional issues, 12528
definition of, 651
difficulty defining the issue,
    128–129
issue advertising, 128–31
overview of, 124–25
referendums and, 162
Thompson case, 186–88
Three-line-voting system, 324–25, 373
Treasury Board
    definition of, 651
    role of, 360–61
Trust funds, 113–14
Two-vote system, 151

*UN International Covenant on Civil and
    Political Rights*, 579, 585, 586
Unelected executive officials, 200–57
    ministerial political staff, 215–16
    ministers and ministers of State,
        212–15
    ministry and Cabinet members,
        200–15
    nonjudicial Governor-in-Council
        appointees, 233–46
    officers of Parliament, 246–57
    prime minister, 203–12
    professional public service, 216–33
Unelected judicial officials, 257–94
    appointment of, 258–89
    appointment to non-Supreme Court
        federal courts, 259, 260–69
    appointment to Section 96 courts,
        259
    appointment to Supreme Court,
        259, 269–89
    appointment to tax courts, 259
    assessment criteria for judicial can-
        didates, 263
    Canadian Judicial Council (CJC)
        and, 291–92, 294

dismissal and Address of Parlia-
    ment, 291–94
dismissal of: security of tenure and
    judicial independence,
    262–69, 291–94
financial and administrative inde-
    pendence, 290
judicial reform and, 272–83
political favouritism, 265–69
Unelected legislative officials, 168–200
    Governor General, 168–77
    Parliament employees and parlia-
        mentarian political staff,
        199–200
    senate, 178–99
Unelected officials
    ethics and, 617–19
    executive branch, 200–57
    judicial branch, 257–94
    legislative branch, 168–200
    parliamentary oversight and, 618
    selection, tenure and dismissal of,
        165–296
Universal Declaration of Human
    Rights (UDHR), 484, 527

*Values and Ethics Code for the Public
    Service, see* Public Servants Code
Vetting system, 262–69, 278–82, 327,
    337, 342, 348
Voter participation, 136–39, 141–43,
    616
    compulsory voting and, 139
    first-past-the-post (FPP) systems
        and, 138, 141–43, 144, 145,
        146, 148, 149, 150, 152, 153
    proportional representation (PR)
        and, 138, 143–51
Voting, elections and selection of
    members of parliament, 75–164
    after the vote, 132–36
    constitutional voting rights, 76–79
    emerging issues in Canada's elec-
        tion law and policy, 136–62

how elections are run, 97–132
integrity of voting process, 81, 82, 88
key factors in elections, 86–97
statutory voting rights, 80–85
voter parity, 79
voter's list, 132

War emergency, 586, 590
War Measures Act, 25n, 576, 577, 578,
 580, 581n, 585, 593
Warrant, 98, 99
Westbank First-Nation Self-Govern-
 ment Agreement, 612, 613
Whip
 caucus and, 316–19
 definition, 317, 652
Whistleblowing law and policy,
 228–232
Writ, 97, 98, 99, 132, 299, 315, 652

About the Authors

Craig Forcese teaches administrative law, public international law, and national security law in the Faculty of Law, University of Ottawa. His present research and writing relates to democratic accountability, national security, and international law. Prior to joining the law school faculty, he practiced law with the Washington D.C. office of Hughes Hubbard & Reed LLP, specializing in international trade law. He has law degrees from the University of Ottawa and Yale University, a B.A. from McGill, and an M.A. in international affairs from the Norman Paterson School of International Affairs, Carleton University. He is a member of the bars of Ontario, New York, and the District of Columbia.

Aaron Freeman is a writer and advocate on democratic reform and corporate accountability issues. His regular political column, "Money and Influence," is published in *The Hill Times*, Canada's parliamentary newspaper, and his work often appears in Canada's leading newspapers and publications. He is a former "Nader's Raider" at Ralph Nader's Center for the Study of Responsive Law in Washington, D.C. and was a founding director of Democracy Watch, Canada's leading democratic reform advocacy organization. Mr. Freeman is an Ottawa-based communications and policy consultant to non-profit organizations and part-time faculty member of the University of Ottawa's Faculty of Law. He is a graduate of McGill University and the University of Ottawa's Faculty of Law.

Please visit the authors online at <www.democracylaw.ca>.